SCORPION
DOWN

ALSO BY ED OFFLEY

Pen & Sword:
A Journalist's Guide to Covering the Military

Lifting the Fog of War
(with William A. Owens)

ED OFFLEY

SCORPION DOWN

Sunk by the Soviets, Buried by the Pentagon: The Untold Story of the

USS SCORPION

BASIC
BOOKS

A MEMBER OF THE PERSEUS BOOKS GROUP
NEW YORK

"The Scorpion Departs But Never Returns" lyrics © 1969 Phil Ochs (A&M Records)

Published by Basic Books,
A Member of the Perseus Books Group

Books published by Basic Books are available at special discounts for bulk purchases in the United States by corporations, institutions, and other organizations. For more information, please contact the Special Markets Department at the Perseus Books Group, 11 Cambridge Center, Cambridge MA 02142, or call (617) 252–5298 or (800) 255–1514, or e-mail special.markets@perseusbooks.com.

Interior design by Jeff Williams

Library of Congress Cataloging-in-Publication Data
Offley, Edward.
    Scorpion down : sunk by the Soviets, buried by the Pentagon : the untold story of the USS Scorpion / Ed Offley.
        p. cm.
    Includes bibliographical references.
    ISBN-13: 978-0-465-05185-4 (hc : alk. paper)
    ISBN-10: 0-465-05185-5 (hc : alk. paper) 1. Scorpion (Submarine) 2. Nuclear submarines—United States. I. Title.
    VA65.S394O44 2006
    359.9'3834—dc22
                                                                    2007004729

10 9 8 7 6 5 4 3 2 1

This book is dedicated to the memory of the crew of the nuclear attack submarine *USS Scorpion* (SSN 589), who died in combat in the service of their country on May 22, 1968—and to the families they left behind.

Cmdr. Francis Atwood Slattery, Commanding Officer

Lt. Cmdr. David Bennett Lloyd, Executive Officer

Torpedoman Chief Walter W. Bishop, Chief of the Boat

Lt. Cmdr. Daniel Peter Stephens

Lt. John Patrick Burke

Lt. George Patrick Farrin

Lt. Robert Walter Flesch

Lt. William Clarke Harwi

Lt. Charles Lee Lamberth

Lt. John Charles Sweet

Lt.j.g. James Walter Forrester

Lt.j.g. Michael Anthony Odening

Lt.j.g. Laughton Douglas Smith

FTG2 Keith Alexander Martin Allen

IC2 Thomas Edward Amtower

MM2 George Gile Annable

FN Joseph Anthony Barr Jr.

RM2 Michael Jon Bailey

IC3 Michael Reid Blake

MM1 Robert Harold Blocker

MM2 Kenneth Ray Brocker

MM1 James Kenneth Brueggeman

MMC Robert Eugene Bryan

RMSN Daniel Paul Burns Jr.

IC2 Ronald Lee Byers

MM2 Duglas Leroy Campbell

MM2 Samuel Cardullo

MM2 Francis King Carey II

SN Gary James Carpenter

MM1 Robert Lee Chandler

MM2 Mark Helton Christiansen

SD1 Romeo S. Constantino

MM1 Robert James Cowan

SD1 Joseph Cross

RMC Garlin Ray Denney

FN Michael Edward Dunn

ETR2 Richard Phillip Engelhart

FTGSN William Ralph Fennick

IC3 Vernon Mark Foli

SN Ronald Anthony Frank

CSSN Michael David Gibson

IC2 Steven Dean Gleason

ST2 Michael Edward Henry

SK1 Larry Leroy Hess

ET1 Richard Curtis Hogeland

MM1 John Richard Houge

EM2 Ralph Robert Huber

TM2 Harry David Huckelberry

EM3 John Frank Johnson

RMCS Robert Johnson

IC3 Steven Leroy Johnson
QM2 Julius Johnston III
FN Patrick Charles Kahanek
TM2 Donald Terry Karmasek Sr.
MMCS Richard Allen Kerntke Sr.
ETR3 Rodney Joseph Kipp
MM3 Dennis Charles Knapp
MM1 Max Franklin Lanier
ET1 John Weichert Livingston
ET2 Kenneth Robert Martin
QMCS Frank Patsy Mazzuchi
ET1 Michael Lee McGuire
TM3 Steven Charles Miksad
TM3 Joseph Francis Miller Jr.
MM2 Cecil Frederick Mobley
QM1 Raymond Dale Morrison
EMC Daniel Christopher Petersen
QM3 Dennis Paul Pferrer
EM1 Gerald Stanley Pospisil
IC3 Donald Richard Powell
MM1 Earl Lester Ray
CS1 Jorge Louis Santana
HMC Lynn Thompson Saville
ET2 Richard George Schaffer
SN William Newman Schoonover
SN Phillip Allan Seifert
ETC George Elmer Smith Jr.
MM2 Robert Bernard Smith

ST1 Harold Robert Snapp Jr.
ETN2 Joel Candler Stephens
MM2 David Burton Stone
EM2 John Phillip Sturgill
YN3 Richard Norman Summers
TMSN John Driscoll Sweeney Jr.
ETN2 James Frank Tindol III
CSSN Johnny Gerald Veerhusen
TM3 Robert Paul Violetti
STS3 Ronald James Voss
FTG1 John Michael Wallace
MM1 Joel Kurt Watkins
MMFN Robert Westley Watson
MM2 James Edwin Webb
YNCS Leo William Weinbeck
MMC James Mitchell Wells
SN Ronald Richard Williams
MM3 Robert Alan Willis
IC1 Virgil Alexander Wright III
IC1 Donald Howard Yarbrough
ET2 Clarence Otto Young Jr.

SURVIVORS

SD2 Frederico L. DeGuzman
ST1 Bill G. Elrod
RMC Daniel K. Pettey
IC1 Joseph D. Underwood

The truth was erased,
the erasure was forgotten, the lie became truth.

—GEORGE ORWELL, *1984*

The radio is begging them to come back to the shore,
all will be forgiven, it'll be just like before.
All you've ever wanted will be waiting by your door,
we will forgive you, we will forgive you,
tell me we will forgive you. . . .

But no one gives an answer, not even one goodbye.
Oh, the silence of their sinking is all that they reply.
Some have chosen to decay and others chose to die,
but I'm not dying, no I'm not dying,
tell me I'm not dying. . . .

Captain will not say how long we must remain.
The phantom ship forever sail the sea,
It's all the same.

—PHIL OCHS,
"THE SCORPION DEPARTS BUT NEVER RETURNS," 1969

CONTENTS

Prologue   *xi*

1   "We May Have Lost a Submarine"   1

2   The Old Admiral's Revelation   27

3   The Sports Car of Ships   53

4   The Secret War   83

5   The Russians Are Coming   109

6   Leaving Home   143

7   A Soviet Submarine Vanishes   165

8   The Last Voyage   179

9   A Twisted, Shiny Piece of Metal   211

10 What Were They Trying to Hide?   241

11 Burn Before You Read   281

12 The Fatal Triangle   317

13 With Maximum Punishment   349

    Epilogue   365

Acknowledgments   *377*
Glossary   *383*
USS Scorpion *Search Roster*   *393*
USS Scorpion *Chronology of Events*   *399*
Notes   *411*
Bibliography   *453*
Index   *467*

PROLOGUE

THIS IS THE LAST THING THEY HEARD IN THEIR CLOSED WORLD: the faint *scree-scree-scree* of the incoming torpedo's high-speed propeller. Then, an ear-splitting thunderclap as the torpedo warhead detonated, and its underwater fireball slammed a shock wave into the center of the submarine, ripping a hole through the outer steel plating.*

Close behind—in less than a heartbeat, not nearly long enough for a thought or a regret—the ocean thundered in, shorting out lights and plunging the confined spaces of the submarine into chaos.

The explosion penetrated the submarine amidships on the port side. It was the perfect impact point to destroy the *USS Scorpion* (SSN 589) and kill its ninety-nine officers and enlisted crewmen, because this was the control room—the brain of the attack submarine—where the captain and his maneuvering watch operated the *Scorpion* on her underwater missions.

The first casualties occurred in a millisecond—lives extinguished in less time than it takes to blink an eye. The water column swept away the

* The narrative of the *Scorpion* sinking is based on extensive interviews with former navy officials and scientific experts and a number of declassified navy documents, particularly the *Supplementary Record of Proceedings of a Court of Inquiry Convened by Commander-in-Chief, United States Atlantic Fleet . . . to Inquire into the Loss of* USS Scorpion *(SSN–589)*, vol. 1, released with extensive security deletions on January 28, 1969 and later declassified from top secret with text restorations in October 1993. Interpretation of the events stemmed from interviews with participants in the *Scorpion* search and court of inquiry, particularly Dr. John P. Craven, director of the Deep Submergence Systems Project and chairman of the *Scorpion* Technical Advisory Group, and Dr. Chester L. Buchanan, chief of the Ocean Engineering Branch of the Naval Research Laboratory and on-scene technical adviser when the wreckage of the *Scorpion* was officially discovered in October 1968.

two duty control planesmen from their pedestal seats at the forward end of the control compartment, where they operated the controls that moved the ship's rudder and diving planes. It dashed the captain and the officer of the deck from the raised control station where they supervised the maneuvering watch. The torrent took out the crew manning the ballast control station, torpedo fire-control computers, electronic countermeasure sensors, and navigating gear.

Inside the cylinder, the world of U.S. Navy regulations and procedure—of hot bunks and the late-night meals called midrats, of dreams of liberty ports and loved ones at home, of bureaucratic routines and top-secret operational plans—vanished as the seawater thundered through. The lights blinked out, the instrument panels sparked a final short-circuit and went black, and the screams of the crew went unheard behind the baritone roar of the flood.

But it did not stop there.

The sea hurtled aft, drowning the men in the enclosed sonar shack and radio room. It raced two decks down to destroy the crew's berthing compartment, mess decks, officer's staterooms, and food storage areas. It plunged further down into the belly of the *Scorpion,* surging toward the battery compartment and storage areas at the keel. Aft of the control room, the water raced through the open hatchway and reactor compartment access tunnel into the relatively spacious auxiliary machinery compartment—a thirty-five-foot-long segment of the submarine—and sought out every open space at the center of the hull.

Only seconds had elapsed since the blast, but already more than a third of the *Scorpion's* crew were dead, including the captain, executive officer, navigator, and members of the maneuvering watch, and most off-duty crewmen whose berthing spaces were closest to the explosion's impact.

The immense fist of hydrostatic pressure from the surrounding ocean continued to press on the *Scorpion's* inner space. It squeezed the watertight bulkheads fore and aft with a force far stronger than the steel walls were designed to survive. Within a minute of the torpedo's impact, the circular bulkhead separating the reactor compartment from the rest of the submarine buckled under the pressure.

Only in the rear of the submarine, the place of the reactor, main engines, and maneuvering room where the duty engineers operated the propulsion system, did enough men survive to fight back against the inevitable. They sent the *Scorpion* to high speed. The propeller churned against the water outside, and its control vanes—responding to orders from an emergency control station at the aft end of the engine room—pointed the submarine up to the ocean surface.

But nothing was possible anymore.

The entire center of the 252-foot-long hull filled with water as the *Scorpion* struggled upward. The weight overcame the submarine's residual buoyancy as well as the forward motion directed by the reactor, drive train, and control planes. The nose of the submarine briefly leveled out but then plunged down in a deepening arc that soon reached sixty degrees.

Only ninety-one seconds after the torpedo struck, the *Scorpion* plunged through an invisible barrier 1,300 feet below the surface. Submariners call it "crush depth," a point where the hydrostatic pressure outside simply overpowers the tensile strength of the steel hull. The small group of survivors in the aft end of the submarine had mere seconds to live.

In the large torpedo compartment at the forward end of the ship, about a dozen members of the torpedo gang and a handful of off-duty crewman had been protected from the original blast by the closed, oval watertight hatch that connected the forward compartments with the rest of the submarine. Some might have had time to don survival gear in the hopes of escaping the submarine via the forward escape trunk. But they too were powerless to save themselves.

At the ninety-one-second mark, the bulkhead at Frame 26—the circular steel wall that defined the after end of the torpedo compartment—gave way, and the seawater that had invaded the submarine slammed into the compartment so furiously that the closed and locked circular access hatch leading out of the torpedo compartment to the curved deck plates on the forward hull blew open to the sea.

Four seconds later, in the final assault, the same force crushed the *Scorpion*'s stern. Here, the tapering cylindrical section of the hull gave way and the eighty-foot-long section containing the engine room rammed violently forward into the auxiliary machinery and reactor compartments just forward of the breaking point. The aft third of the submarine in effect became a plunger that eviscerated the two compartments immediately forward of the breaking point as the giant ram collapsed the auxiliary machinery compartment and reactor compartment.

If any of the crewmen were still alive, they would have died at that instant.

The violence of the final implosion ripped the sail superstructure away from the submarine, leaving the *Scorpion*'s hull in two sections barely dangling together by a slender piece of hull plating. It blew the ninety-foot-long propeller shaft and screw off of their mounts and spat them out into the void.

The final sounds from the *Scorpion* were a muted staccato drumbeat as various tanks, pressurized containers, torpedo tubes, and other devices ruptured and imploded as the dead hulk continued its last dive down 11,100 feet to the floor of the Atlantic abyssal plain.

It was Wednesday, May 22, 1968. The U.S. Navy had just suffered a major Cold War disaster: A nuclear submarine and its crew of ninety-nine had just perished in the eastern Atlantic Ocean.

"WE MAY HAVE LOST A SUBMARINE"

IT WAS A MISERABLE DAY FOR A SAILOR'S HOMECOMING.[1]

A late-spring Nor'easter swept in across Chesapeake Bay, lashing Eastern Virginia. Whitecaps surged into the protected naval base at Hampton Roads as the rain blew nearly sideways across the piers and parking lots. The destroyers and other warships nesting at the piers were dim silhouettes in the gloom. Even at noon, it was so dark that the cars splashing through the guarded gates to the Destroyer-Submarine Piers at Norfolk Naval Station kept their headlights on.[2]

But the storm did not keep several dozen *Scorpion* families from coming to meet their men, due home that day. Huddling under umbrellas or peering through their foggy windshields, they could just see, moored to Pier 22, the massive silhouette of the submarine tender *USS Orion* (AS 18), which provided administrative, maintenance, and logistical support to the fifteen submarines and 2,117 officers and enlisted men of Submarine Squadron 6, one of ten such units in the Atlantic Submarine Force.

Hand-drawn signs, bright balloons, and restive children crammed the cars. Occasionally someone would brave the slashing rain to better see if the submarine was in sight. The base was nearly empty, as most of the navy had a rare day off.

It was Monday, May 27, Memorial Day, 1968.

The *USS Scorpion* underway off the coast of Connecticut in 1960. At the time it joined the fleet, the 251-foot-long nuclear attack boat was the fastest submarine in the world.
U.S. Navy Photo

Barbara Foli was one of the wives who went to the Destroyer-Submarine piers to watch for the *Scorpion's* return. Her husband, Vernon, a twenty-year-old Interior Communications Electrician Third Class, had joined the navy in 1965 and entered submarine school at Groton, Connecticut. In 1967, he boarded the *Scorpion,* and for the past three months he and his young family had been enduring their first prolonged separation. Their daughter Holli's first birthday was coming up, and she hadn't seen her father since the *Scorpion* departed that same pier on February 15. Decades later, Barbara Foli Lake, now remarried, remembered the day. "It was a very cold, very dreary morning. The wind was sucking the umbrellas away."

Theresa Bishop and her three children—John, eight, Mary Etta, seven, and Michael, six—waited, too. As chief of the boat, her husband, Torpedoman Chief Walter Bishop, thirty-seven, was the *Scorpion's* senior enlisted man and a father figure to the crew. A submariner for twenty years, he had served on the *Scorpion* since its commissioning in 1960.

Families of the *Scorpion* crew waited for the submarine in a driving storm on May 27, 1968. The submarine tender *USS Orion* and several nuclear attack submarines are shown moored at Pier 22, at left, at the Norfolk Naval Station in late 1968. *U.S. Navy Photo*

In a nearby car Ann Morrison and her sister waited for Ann's husband, Quartermaster First Class Raymond Dale Morrison, thirty-one. A thirteen-year veteran of navy service, Raymond had joined the *Scorpion,* his third submarine, a month before it left Norfolk on February 15.

Julie Sue Smith could not be at Pier 22. She was sitting with her sister ten miles away in a lounge at Portsmouth Naval Hospital, cradling her two-day-old daughter. Julie was expecting her husband, Machinist's Mate Second Class Robert B. Smith, twenty-two, to drive straight from the base to pick them up. "If they had been on schedule, Robert could have been here to see his daughter being born," Julie later recalled. "I was disappointed in that, but excited that he would be there to pick us up."

The week before, several families had received letters from their crewmen saying the *Scorpion* would arrive on Friday, May 24, after its three-month deployment to the Mediterranean and a return crossing of the Atlantic. But when Friday came, Atlantic Submarine Force officials informed them that the arrival was delayed until Memorial Day.

From Miami to Maine, and in towns as far from Hampton Roads as La Puenta, California, Kincaid, Illinois, and Deweyville, Utah, relatives waited for the phone call from a son, a brother, or a husband. In the Philadelphia suburb of Broomall, Salvatore and Luella Violetti waited to hear from their son, Robert, twenty-one, a Torpedoman Third Class.

The ninety-nine *Scorpion* crewmen came from thirty-three states. Three of them had been born overseas, in Italy, the United Kingdom, and the Philippines. The oldest was forty-seven-year-old Steward First Class Joseph Cross, the only African-American crewman, a Louisiana native and decorated World War II submariner who, after twenty-six years in the navy, was nearing retirement. This *Scorpion* deployment was to have been his last, and his wife, Anna, and young son were eagerly awaiting his return. Four of the twelve commissioned officers on the submarine—Lieutenants William Harwi, George Farrin, John Burke, and Charles Lamberth—were nearing the end of their mandatory five years of military service and had submitted letters of resignation from the navy.

For one crewman, this deployment seemed, ironically, a beginning, and not the end that it became. Just out of high school, Ronald Williams, from Glastonbury, Connecticut, had enlisted as a way to eventually get a college education. In September 1967, five months before its deployment, nineteen-year-old Seaman Williams boarded the *Scorpion*.[3]

Several hundred feet away on Pier 21, the *Gearing*-class destroyer *USS William M. Wood* (DD 715) was preparing to get underway for a classified anti-submarine warfare exercise off the Virginia Capes. Adding to the sailors' stress of taking their ship out to sea in such foul weather was the presence on board of two senior officers and their staffs. Rear Admiral Douglas Plate, commander of Cruiser-Destroyer Flotilla Two, was riding the *William M. Wood* as exercise coordinator. In addition, the destroyer's squadron commander, a captain, was onboard with his staff. By 10:02 A.M., the *William M. Wood* had completed all preparations for separating from a mooring nest of two sister ships, the *USS Robert L. Wilson* (DD 847) and *USS Gyatt* (DD 712).[4]

Nearly four decades later, George Williams, who was a lieutenant (junior grade) aboard the *William M. Wood,* recalled the sight of the

Scorpion families: "As we were leaving, we noticed that there were family members milling around on the next DESSUB Pier north of us, milling around under umbrellas in the cold."[5]

ABOARD THE *ORION,* two of the *Scorpion's* crewmen were helping the staff at Submarine Squadron 6 prepare for their ship's arrival. The first was Interior Communication Electrician First Class Joseph D. Underwood. An X-ray had shown a spot on his lung that doctors feared might be tuberculosis, an illness dreaded by submariners because it is highly contagious, so he, along with the second crewman, were taken off the *Scorpion* at Rota, Spain, on May 17.

The second was Bill G. Elrod, a sonarman first class. After four years on the *Scorpion,* Elrod had orders to report for a new assignment aboard the *USS Chivo* (SS 341), a diesel boat in Charleston, South Carolina. He had been training his relief, Sonarman First Class Bob Snapp, throughout the Mediterranean cruise. But Elrod and his wife had suffered a major heartbreak on May 16. Julianne had gone into labor at the Portsmouth Naval Hospital, and their baby son, Gordon Vincent Elrod, died at birth. Elrod was sent home the next day on emergency leave to be with her. Now he was working on the *Orion* helping squadron officials prepare for the submarine's return.

For Elrod, the last ten days passed in a blur. He and Underwood caught a Military Airlift Command transport plane back to the United States, where Elrod rejoined his wife and his four stepchildren from her previous marriage, and buried his infant son at the Babyland section of Norfolk's Maplewood Cemetery. "It was the worst of times and it was the worst of times. I [had been] so elated about coming home on this trip. There was so much good stuff at the conclusion of this trip. My baby was going to be born, I was getting transferred, moving, a new experience coming up."[6]

It was mid-afternoon on Memorial Day. The one P.M. arrival time had come and gone without a sign of his submarine or shipmates. "Somebody from squadron came down on the pier and said that they were

Bill Elrod was on board the *Scorpion* when he received word that his newborn son, Gordon, had died at birth. Given leave to return to be with his wife, Julianne, in Norfolk, he was not on board when the *Scorpion* went down. *Courtesy of Bill G. Elrod*

delayed," Elrod recalled. "They had a bunch of people come up on the tender to get in out of the rain, while some people went to sit in their cars to get out of the rain. I went down hanging around the squadron [offices on the *Orion*]. At some point in the afternoon, it was getting dark, around three to four p.m., somebody said, 'Everybody go home.'"

Elrod drove back to his apartment in the Ocean View section of Norfolk and told Julianne that the family members had been sent home for the day.

"Is the boat in?" she asked.

"No."

"What's going on?"

"I didn't hear a thing," Elrod replied.

But the first signs of trouble had already appeared.

Navy Captain James C. Bellah was beginning to worry. As commanding officer of the *Orion,* the twenty-three-year submarine veteran would normally not have been involved in the *Scorpion*'s homecoming. However, his boss, Submarine Squadron 6 skipper Captain Jared E. Clarke III, had taken several days of leave, so Bellah was standing in as acting squadron commander.

Bellah had come aboard his ship at six in the morning that Memorial Day. Five days earlier, *Scorpion* skipper Commander Francis A. Slattery had announced his arrival date and time in his last encrypted message transmitted to COMSUBLANT headquarters several hours after midnight on May 22. Bellah dropped by the squadron offices to ask if the submarine had established radio communications yet. Normally, a returning submarine would call in on a harbor circuit when it was just off the coast to verify its arrival time and request a navy tug to assist it in mooring. Duty personnel in Submarine Squadron 6 that morning fully expected to hear Slattery's voice at any moment on the radio breaking the *Scorpion's* long communications silence.

"When is *Scorpion* due in?" Bellah asked one of the squadron watchstanders. The sailor's reply was unusual but not yet a matter of concern: "We haven't heard anything from them." For a while, the storm raging outside led Bellah and other COMSUBLANT officials to think the rain, wind, and sea conditions were causing the *Scorpion's* failure to check in. "Up until eleven A.M. we weren't that concerned," the captain recalled. "We got no indication there was a problem with that submarine at all."[7]

At 12:40 P.M., Bellah called COMSUBLANT headquarters a mile away to ask if the submarine had called in on another radio channel. The reply was negative. The headquarters staff now launched what officials later described as an "intense" effort to reach the submarine by radio. When the *Scorpion's* one P.M. arrival time came and went, a few navy officers in the sprawling Atlantic Fleet headquarters complex began to fear that something had happened. Telephones began ringing in the command centers across Hampton Roads as senior officials informally alerted their counterparts that the Memorial Day holiday routine was about to come to an abrupt end.

At the Atlantic Fleet's Anti-Submarine Warfare Force command, known by its acronym, COMASWFORLANT, the telephone rang at 2:15 P.M., and the duty officer received jolting news. His counterpart at

COMSUBLANT headquarters was on the line requesting that the aviation command immediately launch a pair of search flights along the western portion of the submarine's projected track. As Rear Admiral Paul Masterton, the unit's commanding officer, later noted in a memorandum for the record:

> On May 27, approximately one hour before the official *Scorpion* SUBMISS [submarine missing alert], the COMASWFORLANT OPCON [operational control] was informed of the situation and asked to launch two search flights immediately. By telephone, Commander Bermuda ASW [anti-submarine warfare] Group was directed to search from 65° W [longitude] to 71° W along *Scorpion's* projected track; Commander Norfolk ASW Group to search from 71° W to 76° W. Flights were launched at 1713 from Bermuda and at 1745 from Norfolk (all times local).[8]

At 3:15 P.M., the alert became official. A flash message from COMSUBLANT shrieked out over the navy's Fleet Broadcast System to naval bases from Brunswick, Maine to Jacksonville, Florida, and out to Bermuda, the Azores, and the Mediterranean. Its terse technical phrases meant only one thing: The *Scorpion* was missing.

> Executed Event SUBMISS at 271915Z for *USS Scorpion* ETA NORVA 271700Z. . . . All submarine units surface or remain surfaced until this message cancelled. Units in port prepare to get underway on one hour's notice. . . .[9]

The news raced up the navy chain of command to the Pentagon, where at 3:30 P.M. the Navy Department duty captain reported a phone call from his counterpart at Atlantic Fleet headquarters. But the officer hedged his assessment:

> "The CINCLANTFLT [Commander in Chief, U.S. Atlantic Fleet] Duty Officer Commander Weed . . . advised that *Scorpion* has had communication problems recently and that CINCLANTFLT was

not overly concerned at this point. SUBMISS/SUBSUNK procedures are being reviewed for possible execution."

The message was later watered down even more to note that weather
conditions had caused general communications problems throughout
the Virginia Capes area.[10]

Word quickly spread throughout the Pentagon's twenty-two miles of
corridors. Before long, the senior military commanders and civilian military department secretaries had learned that a major crisis was brewing
in Norfolk.

In the White House, President Lyndon B. Johnson was in a late afternoon meeting in the Cabinet Room when a secretary stepped inside
and handed him a note.

Tom Johnson [a presidential aide] just called to advise that Defense
called to advise that we may have lost a submarine with 90 men
aboard going into Norfolk. [National Security Adviser Walt W.] Rostow is checking.

The secretary later entered a notation in the president's daily log: "I
took it to him—no comment."[11]

Meanwhile, in navy ports up and down the Atlantic coast the recall
orders were going out.

The *Scorpion* families knew nothing of this yet. After Captain Bellah's
people told them to go home, most had ended their vigil on Pier 22.

At three P.M. Julie Smith and her sister gave up waiting at the naval
hospital and drove home. She called Jann Christiansen, the wife of Machinist's Mate Second Class Mark Christiansen, who told her the word
was the submarine would now arrive at eight that night. Smith settled in
to feed her newborn.

But shortly after six P.M., the world came crashing down for the
Scorpion families. WTAR Norfolk, the local CBS network affiliate, broke
into its local news show with a bulletin from Washington that the *Scorpion* was overdue and missing.

John Bishop, eight years old, was the first in his family to hear the news. He had returned home from Pier 22 that afternoon with his mother, sister, and brother. Over the years, their father, Walter, had devised a playful family tradition for his return from sea: He would slip into the house and hide in a closet or some other place. Coming home from school or in from play on the appointed day, the children would race through the rooms, opening all the doors until their father leaped out with a shout and a bear hug for them all. John went running from room to room looking for his father, but his mother, instead of joining in, stayed quietly in the kitchen making dinner.

The TV was on in the living room, and young John heard the news. "I remember seeing that first story," he recalled decades later. "I remember hearing them saying it. I knew what the words meant." He went into the kitchen and told his mother.

She was initially doubtful. "But suddenly," John continued, "the house was full of people. It was our neighbors. I was overwhelmed. I was numb for quite awhile." His mother echoed that description when recalling that time. "I went totally numb. Nobody said anything. We just sat around waiting for the telephone to ring."

The news staggered the *Scorpion* families. Joan Cowan, wife of Machinist's Mate First Class Robert James Cowan, was waiting at her Norfolk home when a neighbor pounded on the door. The same thing happened to Barbara Foli.

For one group of *Scorpion* wives, the decision to wait on the *Orion* to get the first confirmation of the *Scorpion's* arrival meant they were among the last to hear. Ann Morrison and her sister, Florence, missed the newscast because they had remained behind in the submarine tender's visitors' lounge with a few other spouses. When Charlice Bledsoe, a close friend of Ann's and herself a navy wife, saw the TV bulletin, she drove to Pier 22, climbed up the gangway onto the ship, and broke the news.[12]

Sitting in his home, still grieving with his wife over their lost infant, Bill Elrod grew even more despondent as he heard the WTAR news anchor announce the *Scorpion* bulletin. "It was over," he remembered saying to himself. "They never, *never* announced anything like that. I don't care if the boat was three days late coming in, they never said anything on television, no one ever said anything about a boat being late, they just kept nudging the [arrival] dates. When they announced it on television, I knew the boat was gone."

Later that evening, a local reporter knocked on the Elrods' front door and asked to speak with him. Bill snarled, "Get the hell away from me," and slammed the door shut.

For two navy officials who would go on to play key roles in the *Scorpion* search, the bad news arrived in completely different ways.

Vice Admiral Arnold F. Schade, a decorated World War II combat veteran and now the Atlantic Submarine Force commander, had left his Norfolk headquarters at dawn that Monday morning for a visit to the submarine base at Groton, Connecticut. He was going to take a check ride aboard his command's newest submarine, the *USS Pargo* (SSN 650). Commissioned on January 5, 1968, the *Pargo* brought to nineteen the number of nuclear-powered attack submarines under Schade's command. Escorted by three staff aides, he flew by navy plane from Norfolk up to Groton. By 9:52 A.M. the *Pargo* was underway down the Thames River for Long Island Sound and the Atlantic. It reached deep water by 1:59 P.M. Its skipper, Commander Steven A. White, ordered the submarine to dive.[13]

Schade later said he first learned the *Scorpion* was overdue at 4:15 P.M. when the *Pargo*, steaming submerged one hundred miles south of Block Island, picked up the 3:45 P.M. COMSUBLANT message formally declaring the *Scorpion* missing. With Event SubMiss underway, Schade directed White to head south at high speed for the transit lanes off the coast of Norfolk.

Dr. John P. Craven heard the news on his car radio. A World War II enlisted sailor, Craven had risen in the postwar navy as a civilian scientist involved with the development of the Polaris missile submarine system and a number of highly classified research and development projects. In May 1968, he was director of the navy's Deep Submergence Systems Project, whose activities included top-secret programs involving development of deep-diving manned submersibles and intelligence operations to find and retrieve objects on the ocean floor.[14]

"I'm driving home from work one day . . . right past the Pentagon with the radio on, and the navy announces that the *Scorpion* has not come into Norfolk," Craven recalled. "All I did was to turn my car around on the highway and went to the Pentagon, to the ops center, and walked in." Craven, whose work in highly classified intelligence operations was known to the navy's top leaders, asked what he could do. They put him to work reviewing all known underwater systems in the Atlantic, including the top-secret Sound Surveillance System (Sosus), that might have recorded the acoustic signals of a submarine in distress.

Craven and a small group of civilian colleagues spent that night phoning various navy sites asking for copies of their acoustic recordings. It was the first step in what would become an ambitious technical search operation employing science and experimental navigational gear to narrow the search area from millions of square miles of ocean to a specific section of the Atlantic where the searchers might hope to find the *Scorpion*.

In Norfolk, night came with no letup in the Nor'easter. Keeping vigil with neighbors in her home on Johnston's Road, Theresa Bishop peered out her front door and saw that a large oak tree at the end of her street had been blown down by the storm.

But then, over the sound of the wind, she heard something else. A muted chorus of sirens, foghorns, and klaxon alarms from the naval station four miles away signaled the confirmation of her nightmare: The U.S. Atlantic Fleet was putting to sea to look for her husband and his submarine.

Except for the 1962 Cuban Missile Crisis, the search for the *Scorpion* was the largest naval operation since World War II. From Newport, Rhode Island to Mayport, Florida, engineering watchstanders threw down their paperback books, acknowledged the emergency orders to get underway, and raced to light the boilers and make steam. Sailors with the day off abandoned their holiday routine and streamed down the piers and up the gangways. By midnight, more than forty surface ships and submarines were at sea or making final plans to get underway.[15]

In Charleston, South Carolina, the *USS Petrel* (ASR 14) was moored at the November Pier at the naval base when the SubMiss alert went off. One of sixteen surface ships under Schade's control that supported the submarine fleet, the *Petrel* had a McCann Rescue Chamber that could retrieve the crew of a submarine stranded several hundred feet down. At 4:05 P.M., Rear Admiral Lawrence G. Bernard, commander of Submarine Flotilla 6, ordered the *Petrel* on thirty-minute emergency standby to get underway. At 5:30 P.M. he bounded up the gangway followed by eleven members of his staff, and the *Petrel* was soon heading out to sea.

Nearly 700 miles to the north, in the *Pargo's* cramped control room, Schade decided that the search for the *Scorpion* would be his operation, and Bernard would become his on-scene commander once the search team had fully gathered.[16]

For the first night, a destroyer admiral from the "black shoe" navy and not a submariner would be in charge. The SubMiss alert had reached out into the Atlantic as well, where at least a dozen navy warships and submarines were on patrol, training missions, or engaged in routine transits to or from the Mediterranean. At sea in the storm-tossed Atlantic about eighty miles east of land, Rear Admiral Douglas Plate on-board the *William M. Wood* received a message from Atlantic Fleet headquarters at 7:30 P.M. canceling the anti-submarine warfare exercise and directing him to serve as initial officer-in-command of the *Scorpion* search effort. On his order, the *William M. Wood* executed a ninety-degree left turn to a heading of due north and went to flank speed. Within minutes the destroyer, followed by two other Norfolk-based destroyers in the exercise group—the destroyers *USS Douglas H. Fox* (DD 779) and *Robert L. Wilson*—were churning through the whitecaps heading for the *Scorpion's* projected course track into Norfolk. Sailors onboard clung to stanchions and vomited onto the tiled decks as their ships labored through the twenty-five-foot-high waves. Not far away, the *USS Shark* (SSN 591), a sister sub of the *Scorpion,* reported that it too was experiencing severe turbulence on the surface.[17]

Even submarines operating far out in the Atlantic were touched by the growing emergency. Hundreds of miles to the east and hundreds of

14

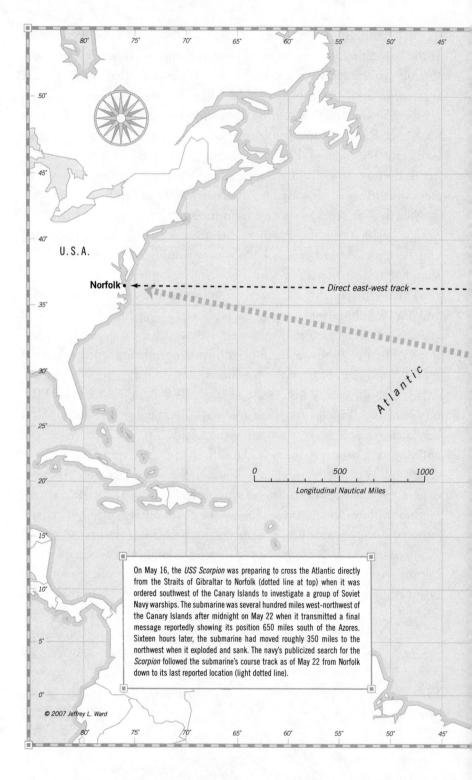

On May 16, the *USS Scorpion* was preparing to cross the Atlantic directly from the Straits of Gibraltar to Norfolk (dotted line at top) when it was ordered southwest of the Canary Islands to investigate a group of Soviet Navy warships. The submarine was several hundred miles west-northwest of the Canary Islands after midnight on May 22 when it transmitted a final message reportedly showing its position 650 miles south of the Azores. Sixteen hours later, the submarine had moved roughly 350 miles to the northwest when it exploded and sank. The navy's publicized search for the *Scorpion* followed the submarine's course track as of May 22 from Norfolk down to its last reported location (light dotted line).

© 2007 Jeffrey L. Ward

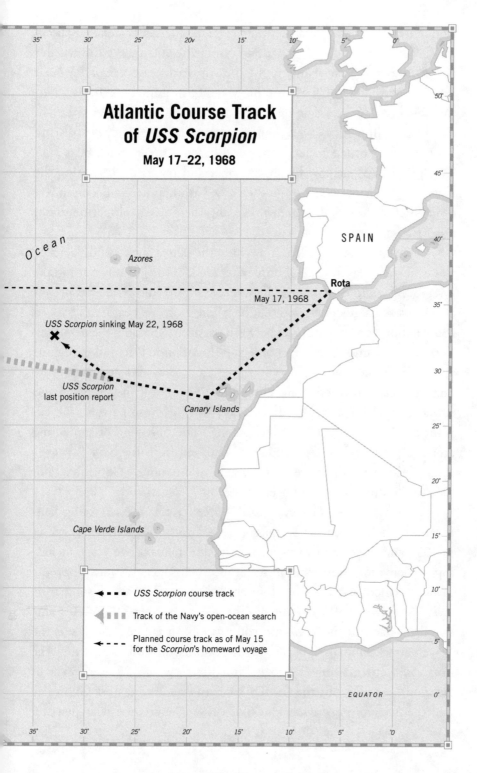

Atlantic Course Track of *USS Scorpion*
May 17–22, 1968

Ocean

Azores

SPAIN

Rota

May 17, 1968

USS Scorpion sinking May 22, 1968

USS Scorpion
last position report

Canary Islands

Cape Verde Islands

EQUATOR

◄ ▬ ▬ ▬   *USS Scorpion* course track

◄ ▮ ▮ ▮   Track of the Navy's open-ocean search

◄ ▬ ▬ ▬   Planned course track as of May 15
for the *Scorpion*'s homeward voyage

feet below the stormy Atlantic, the *Scorpion* emergency derailed an exercise involving two of Schade's submarines. Under Commander Ralph Ghormley, the ballistic missile submarine *USS Sam Rayburn* (SSBN 635) had left Charleston on May 20. It headed north for a routine seventy-day "strategic deterrent patrol," but with a new twist in the plan. Ghormley, who had commanded the *Scorpion* during 1964–66, had orders to let the Groton-based nuclear attack boat *USS Gato* (SSN 615) shadow his missile boat and try to track it using the *Gato*'s BQS-6 sonar system. On the *Gato,* Commander Al Baciocco, Jr., trailed behind the *Sam Rayburn,* keeping the Polaris submarine under quiet surveillance.[18]

"We were a day away [from reaching the patrol "box"] and Baciocco was echo-ranging on us," Ghormley recalled. "Our job was not to take evasion, he could use whatever he wanted. I don't know whether he was able to track us, my guess was that he could probably hear us and take a couple of pings and track us in between passively." Because the *Sam Rayburn* was now under the direct orders of the Atlantic Fleet rather than its submarine force component, Ghormley said, they did not receive the SubMiss order instructing all submarines to break off their mission and surface. "We didn't work for the Navy during those patrols," he explained. "We were in the strategic force." The only sign of something amiss came when the *Gato* suddenly vanished from the *Sam Rayburn*'s sonar. "All of a sudden we didn't hear him anymore," Ghormley said. "We found out later he had been pulled off."

Baciocco, like Ghormley, was a *Scorpion* veteran. As a young lieutenant, he had joined the *Scorpion*'s pre-commissioning crew in Groton in 1959 and served aboard the submarine for the next two years, including participation in several top-secret reconnaissance missions along the Soviet northern coast. After a tour aboard the nuclear attack submarine *USS Barb* (SSN 596) in the Pacific Fleet, Baciocco—now a commander—had put the *Gato* into commission on January 25. It was the newest attack submarine in the Atlantic Submarine Force at the time the *Scorpion* went missing. Baciocco and his crew of 127 were west of Bermuda carrying out the "SSBN security exercise" against Ghormley and the *Sam Rayburn* when the *Gato*'s KW-7 encrypted teletypewriter chattered to life in the sub's cramped radio room. "SubMiss came out," Baciocco recalled. "It required all submarines to surface and report in. There was [message] traffic saying *Scorpion* wasn't accounted for. She was last heard from off the Azores." Schade's staff fired off a subsequent message to Baciocco, ordering his submarine to proceed at maximum speed to an area of the eastern Atlantic, where a group of submerged seamounts came within several hundred feet of the surface. The *Scorpion*'s projected homeward track had run through that area, and one of the many theories being considered was that the submarine might have suffered an underwater collision with a seamount.[19]

That night, Admiral Thomas H. Moorer, the chief of naval operations, gave an impromptu press conference at the Pentagon. "The weather is very, very bad out there," the fifty-two-year-old admiral said in his signature Alabama drawl, explaining that the turbulence and lightning might have prevented the submarine from establishing radio contact. "But the weather may abate, the ship may well have been held back and she could proceed into port."

By dawn on May 28, the missing *Scorpion* was banner-headline news across the country. In Norfolk, *The Ledger-Star* proclaimed, "No Trace of Sub Found As Navy Presses Search." "Giant Search Started for Missing U.S. Sub," *The Milwaukee Journal* headline trumpeted. In a slightly less blaring tone *The New York Times* announced, "U.S. Nuclear Submarine with 99 Overdue" but placed the article at the top of the front page.

Schade, who was still aboard the attack submarine *Pargo* at the time of Moorer's press conference, would expand on the navy's degree of concern at that juncture in a speech the following month: "The failure of a submarine to return to port at an appointed hour, while cause for concern, is not normally an immediate cause for alarm. I say this because there are a number of ways in which a submarine can be delayed."[20]

By midnight, navy officials were privately very worried. A consensus had formed in the Pentagon and at Norfolk that the *Scorpion* had likely suffered some form of mishap that made it impossible to return to port or even to send an emergency message.

Three scenarios emerged that dictated the initial rescue response:

As Chief of Naval Operations in 1968, Admiral Thomas H. Moorer formally declared the *Scorpion* "presumed lost" in the Atlantic after a ten-day search found no trace of the submarine.
U.S. Navy Photo

(1) The *Scorpion* was disabled on the surface somewhere in the At-lantic unable to communicate with headquarters;

(2) It had suffered a collision, grounding, or other breakdown and was on the bottom in relatively shallow water with its hull intact and crew alive, but living on a limited supply of air; or

(3) It had gone down with all hands in the deep ocean.

The *Scorpion*'s last message to Norfolk, transmitted between 1:02 A.M. and 3:03 A.M. GMT on May 22, further shaped the navy response. Commander Slattery reported the *Scorpion*'s position as 21:19 North and 27:37 West, about 400 miles southwest of the Azores. Navy officials told reporters that Slattery had plotted a speed of eighteen knots and a Great Circle course of 290 degrees back to Norfolk with the scheduled arrival time of one P.M. EDT on Memorial Day. That information literally defined a narrow search corridor running roughly on a course of 110 degrees from the Thimble Shoal channel entrance to *Scorpion*'s last navigational fix.[21]

The dozens of surface ships and submarines that surged out of Norfolk and the other East Coast navy bases on the afternoon and evening of May 27 converged on the western end of the *Scorpion*'s track along the shallow waters of the continental shelf extending out some fifty-five miles from the Virginia coastline. Ignoring the towering waves and horizontal rain, they began searching the shallows.

On the other end of the search corridor, navy spokesman Captain John F. Davis told Pentagon reporters on Tuesday morning, the submarine rescue ship *USS Kittiwake* (ASR 13) and ballistic missile submarine *USS Simon Bolivar* (SSBN 641) had been dispatched to an area south-southeast of the Azores. The decision stemmed from a May 23rd message from the amphibious transport ship *USS Monrovia* (APA 31) reporting an oil slick in the vicinity.[22]

Meanwhile, the navy's fleet of long-range patrol aircraft was already scouring the *Scorpion*'s track from bases along the East Coast, Bermuda and the Azores. The challenge in locating any sign of the missing submarine was not that the Atlantic Ocean was empty but rather that it was so full of debris—oil drums, stray buoys, pieces of styrofoam plastic, and other unidentified junk—and oil slicks. Larry Bonko, a Norfolk reporter who went out on one seven-hour search flight in a P-2V Neptune early in the *Scorpion* search, saw the difficulty. He quoted one crewman as saying, "There are enough oil slicks out here to report until doomsday." Bonko concluded: "The log would be short: Nothing sighted. Nothing to report."[23]

On the first full day of the *Scorpion* crisis, senior navy officials in the Pentagon and Atlantic Fleet headquarters in Norfolk began clearing their in-trays and setting up twenty-four-hour watch desks. Rear Admiral Philip A. Beshany, the director of submarine warfare on Admiral Moorer's staff, coordinated the navy's response to the missing submarine. One of his first tasks was breaking down some long-held suspicions and rivalries between the elite Submarine Service and the rest of the navy.

"We had a very tightly knit organization in those days," Beshany said of the submarine force. "We had to cooperate with the surface people involved in the search. At that time there was a feeling, 'We've got to work together.'" Beshany spent the first two days of the crisis talking with senior staff members at COMSUBLANT headquarters, since Schade was still out in the *Pargo*.[24]

The *Scorpion* emergency sparked a deluge of calls: messages and letters to the Pentagon expressing sympathy, offers of assistance, unsolicited theories about the disappearance and detailed descriptions of the *Scorpion*'s current location. Callers from other parts of the navy, from other nations' militaries, and from the public at large jammed the phone lines. Beshany and his assistant, Captain Walter N. "Buck" Dietzen, were soon drowning in phone message slips in their small fourth-floor office on the Pentagon's C Ring.

Captain William F. Searle, the navy's supervisor of salvage, prepared a list of resources, including a roster of qualified deep sea divers from the Navy Experimental Diving Unit in Washington, D.C., and the SeaLab underwater habitat in southern California. SupeSalv, as Searle was nicknamed, also noted the availability of specialized rescue gear that could be used should the *Scorpion* be stranded on the bottom in relatively shallow water. A number of companies that owned manned submersibles also contacted the navy to offer their equipment if it was needed.[25]

At the Brooklyn Navy Yard, ten civilian scientists at the Naval Applied Science Laboratory volunteered their expertise and advanced navigational equipment to help with any underwater surveying operations. The navy flew them out to the Azores for the detailed technical search for the *Scorpion*. The navy immediately accepted an offer from the French government to assist the search with one of its diesel-powered submarines, the *Requin*, which was at the time already operating in the Atlantic.[26]

Meanwhile, sighting reports, none very helpful, poured in. Schade's headquarters in Norfolk received a message from the U.S. naval attaché in Portugal: "Father Abel, a Jesuit teacher of a school near Oporto, reported that through ESP he knows *Scorpion* is in area bounded by Lat[itude] 38 to 39 North and Long[itude] 26–27 West." A tips call to the Federal Communications Commission prompted the FCC duty watch officer to recommend the message be passed to the navy with the caveat that the caller's source must have been an "astrology reading, Ouija board, tea leaves, or whatever."[27]

By midday Tuesday, Rear Admiral Bernard and the *Petrel* were about halfway to Norfolk. The admiral had already concluded that the small submarine rescue ship would be inadequate to supervise the *Scorpion* search.[28]

Schade quickly approved Bernard's request to transfer with his staff to a larger ship, the guided missile frigate *USS William H. Standley* (DLG 32). The admiral and his men spent the day organizing the second phase of the *Scorpion* operation: a slow and deliberate surface search of the *Scorpion's* projected course track from the Chesapeake Bay mouth east-southeast across the Atlantic to the submarine's last reported position southwest of the Azores.[29]

As the *Petrel* drew closer to the Virginia Capes, it moved into the storm. In response to a COMSUBLANT message at 3:07 P.M. directing him to rendezvous with the *William H. Standley* at a designated Point Alfa 127 miles off the Virginia coast, Bernard requested that the ships instead move inshore to Norfolk's Lynnhaven Roads because of the extreme sea conditions. The *Petrel,* making eleven knots in the steadily worsening seas, sighted the Chesapeake Bay entrance buoy at 12:15 A.M. on Wednesday, May 30. Fifteen minutes later, its radar located the destroyer 14,000 yards to the southwest. Two hours later, Bernard and his staff were aboard the *William H. Standley* and making twenty-seven knots through the storm to Point Alfa.[30]

Not far away, the *Pargo* was heading west. Having spent over twenty-four hours trying the manage the *Scorpion* search from the submarine, Schade decided to return to his headquarters in Norfolk and directed *Pargo* Commander White to surface for a rendezvous with a navy work boat at the Thimble Shoal Channel entrance. The *Pargo* then proceeded back out to sea to rejoin the search.[31]

As a weak sun broke through the fast-moving clouds several hours later, Bernard found himself in charge of ten submarines, nineteen destroyers, three submarine rescue ships, and two auxiliary ships spread out around the Atlantic continental shelf. He immediately began shrinking the search force, sending several of the destroyers and submarines back to port. The search force, which had peaked at fifty-five ships, would steadily get smaller in the days ahead as the shallow-water hunt off the Virginia coast came to an end. (See the *USS Scorpion* Search Roster, page 393, for a list of the ships and submarines involved in the search.)[32]

At 6:43 P.M. on May 30, Schade—now back in his office at Atlantic Fleet Headquarters in Norfolk—formally established Navy Task Unit 42.2.1 to carry out the fine-grain search. The unit consisted of five destroyers, five submarines, and the fleet oiler *USS Waccamaw* (AO 109). The Special Search Unit would remain under Schade's direct command. This group consisted of three submarines—the *Gato, Pargo,* and *Simon Bolivar*—and six of COMSUBLANT's own surface support ships, including the *Petrel.* Four of them, the *Gato* and *Simon Bolivar, Kittiwake,* and the salvage ship *USS Preserver* (ARS 8), were already in the vicinity of the Azores or heading there directly from the U.S. Navy base at Rota. Schade ordered the *Petrel* and experimental navigation ship *USS Compass Island* (AG 153) to proceed east to meet them. He kept the *Pargo* and *USS Sunbird* (ASR 15) in the western continental shelf to search the littorals.[33]

Bernard's eleven-ship surface and submarine task unit had the responsibility of succeeding where an aerial armada of patrol aircraft had so far failed: to find a sign of the *Scorpion* somewhere on its projected 2,500-nautical mile homeward track. To ensure maximum coverage of every square foot of the area, the admiral evenly spread the five destroyers apart on a line abreast about forty-eight miles wide, with the submarine group following twelve hours behind in a similar formation between thirty-two and forty-eight miles wide. Bernard would later admit that the formation was a compromise, providing total radar coverage of a larger area at the expense of preventing the ships' lookouts from scanning the entire search path with binoculars.[34]

But scarcely had the ships formed up for the long march to the east when a radio transmission burst over the air at 8:28 P.M. Wednesday. "Steady keying—1,2,3,4,5 any station this net," the voice crackled in radio room loudspeakers on more than a dozen ships and submarines and at least one patrol plane. "This is Brandywine."

Brandywine was the *Scorpion*'s classified radio call sign.[35]

The news electrified the searchers and the exhausted *Scorpion* families. For fifty-five long hours, COMSUBLANT headquarters, ships, and aircraft at sea had bombarded the airwaves calling out for the *Scorpion* to respond. News reports had become more and more pessimistic. In Annapolis, Maryland, where the family of Torpedoman Seaman John D. Sweeney, Jr. anxiously waited for any news at all, the front page of *The Evening Capital* had marked the beginning of the third day with the gloomy headline "Hope Ebbs for Submarine." The headline writer for *The Ledger-Star* in Norfolk used the same words: "Hope of Finding Scorpion Ebbs As Hunt Goes on in Rough Seas." In his front-page article Jack Kestner matched the headline's gloom: "So far, the round-the-clock search has produced not a single reliable clue to the whereabouts of the missing submarine."

News of the radio transmission sent admirals from Norfolk to the Pentagon into a frenzy of activity. It triggered wire service bulletin bells in every newsroom across America. At sea, a navy P-2V Neptune aircraft and the submarine *USS Lapon* (SSN 661), one of the five submarines in Admiral Bernard's search unit, succeeded in making a radio direction-finding fix on the signal on a bearing of 074 degrees (east-northeast) from the *Lapon*'s location about 300 miles east of Norfolk. Bernard rushed the ships *Josephus Daniels* (DLG 27), *USS John King* (DDG 3), *USS Eugene A. Greene* (DD 711), and *Robert L. Wilson* to investigate. But no more transmissions came, and the destroyers found only open ocean. Within several hours, navy officials suspected the transmission had been an accident or a hoax.

Back in Norfolk, the *Scorpion* families were whipsawed by the news. Ever since the nightmare had erupted two days earlier, they had clung together, calling one another or gathering in small groups to keep their spirits up. Five wives who sat down with a local reporter that Wednesday morning had expressed hope that the navy would still pull off a miracle and bring home their loved ones. "We're not tough, but we're not weeping and wailing," said Allie Brueggeman, wife of Machinist's Mate First Class James K. Brueggeman. "We could—probably would—break down if we weren't together. . . . We know that everything that could be done is being done. And God bless all those out there in the search."[36]

Word of the Brandywine signal sent the family members' spirits soaring. "I'm absolutely speechless," Theresa Bishop told *The Virginian-Pilot.* "How about if you talk to me in a couple of days?" She was still at home with the children praying for word about Walter. Onboard the *Orion,* Squadron 6 sailors manned a bank of telephones to answer queries from the *Scorpion* families. The Submarine Division 62 commander, Captain Wallace A. Greene, who was also on the *Orion,* later said, "Within minutes [of the radio signal], all eight telephones here virtually jumped off the desk." But the elation faded as navy officials called to caution that the report may have been in error. Judith Brocker, the wife of *Scorpion* crewman Machinist's Mate Second Class Kenneth Ray Brocker, told a reporter, "I wanted so much to believe it, but I was afraid to get my hopes up so high." By the next afternoon, Atlantic Fleet headquarters had concluded the transmission was false, and Bernard's search force resumed its long march down to 21:19 North 27:37 West.[37]

And so it went. For the next six days there was scant news to report. Bernard's little fleet steamed down the longitudes toward 27 degrees West, pausing to refuel and interrupting the eastward voyage only to divert to retrieve yet another abandoned buoy or oil drum. Crisscrossing the continental shelf, the crew of the submarine *Pargo* discovered several sunken hulks. Scores of patrol flights, often in coordination with the surface search, turned up only debris. Far to the east, the *Gato, Kittiwake, Simon Bolivar,* and *Requin* explored the seamounts.[38]

On Thursday, June 5, nine days after the *Scorpion* had failed to reach port, Admiral Moorer released a two-page statement formally declaring the submarine and its crew "presumed lost": "Now, because of the lack of any evidence of *Scorpion's* presence on the surface or in waters which would permit rescue, we must conclude that she was lost in the depths of the Atlantic."

Navy leaders had been gearing up for such an announcement for some time. Experts had calculated to the hour how long the air supply would last if the submarine was trapped on the bottom: The submariners would run out of oxygen around June 1. On June 2, Schade forwarded a memorandum to the Pentagon itemizing the rationale for such a determination. He noted that the search had yielded not a single clue to the *Scorpion*'s location on the surface, and surveys of "areas of possible salvageable depths" had likewise failed to locate the submarine.[39]

A day after the *Scorpion* search began, Navy Captain R. P. Brett, a senior aide to Moorer, had drafted a detailed memorandum bracing the admiral for what he described as likely "rough days" ahead. Assuming the worst, Brett advised Moorer to plan a "chronology of actions" for the coming weeks. The plan included the formal declaration that the *Scorpion* and its crew were lost and a public announcement of that finding; the appointment of a court of inquiry to investigate the sinking; a visit by Secretary of the Navy Paul Ignatius or Moorer himself to Norfolk to meet with *Scorpion* family members; a ceremonial order that flags fly at half-staff for four days; and memorial services in Norfolk and other locations.[40]

These recommendations served as a roadmap for the navy during and immediately after the search. On June 4, Admiral Ephraim P. Holmes, the Atlantic Fleet commander, formally appointed a seven-member court of inquiry. Retired Vice Admiral Bernard L. Austin, a distinguished World War II submariner, agreed to return to active duty to serve as president of the court. It was the second such assignment in five years for "Count" Austin, who had also presided over a court of inquiry into the sinking of the nuclear attack submarine *USS Thresher* (SSN 593) in 1963.

The *Scorpion* inquest was scheduled to begin on June 5. It would continue off and on for the next seven months while the small Special Search Unit under Schade scoured a twelve-by-twelve-mile area of the ocean, two miles deep.

Captain Brett's memorandum had also dictated the final steps that Bernard's surface search unit would take as the *Scorpion* search drew to a close. For the first six days of the unit's hunt down the track from

Norfolk—from May 29 until June 4—Bernard had ordered the ships
to maintain an average speed of advance of 13.2 knots. This was because the submarines and the oiler *Waccamaw,* accompanying the ships
to provide refueling, could not go faster. However, at 10:30 A.M. EDT
on June 4, Schade ordered Bernard to have the search force cross the
Scorpion's last known position at the exact time that Moorer back in
the Pentagon was announcing that the submarine was lost. It would be
a tidy—if inconclusive—end to the long search.

So Bernard sent the order to the five destroyers to increase their
speed to eighteen knots and instructed the rest of the group to meet up
at the *Scorpion's* last identified position as soon as they could. At 2005
GMT, or 4:05 P.M. EDT, Bernard entered a final notation in his logbook.

> 2005Z: TE 42.2.1.1 passed through *Scorpion's* last known position
> and set course 300 [degrees], speed 10 with distance between ships
> 3,000 yards. At 052000Z CNO declared *Scorpion* lost. Search of
> *Scorpion* track from CONUS to *Scorpion's* last reported position had
> been completed.[41]

Everything you have read thus far is documented, verified, and accurate. And almost everything that is part of the official navy account is
a lie.

THE OLD ADMIRAL'S REVELATION

I**T WAS A SUNNY AFTERNOON IN APRIL 1983, AND THE OLD ADMIRAL** was in a reminiscing mood. I had tracked him down to his home in Port Charlotte, Florida, and to my surprise, he had agreed to share his recollections on the loss of the *USS Scorpion.* Nearly fifteen years had passed since the submarine vanished in the eastern Atlantic Ocean, and I was working on an article for my newspaper, *The Virginian-Pilot and The Ledger-Star* in Norfolk, Virginia, commemorating the tragedy. Among the dozens of navy admirals, scores of naval unit commanders, and tens of thousands of sailors who had been involved in the search for the missing submarine, Vice Admiral Arnold F. Schade was the central figure in the story. The decorated World War II submariner had been halfway through his four-year tour as Atlantic Submarine Force Commander when the *Scorpion* disappeared. As the *Scorpion's* operational commander, Schade had supervised its missions, selected the attack submarine for its 1968 Mediterranean deployment, and presided over the massive search beginning with its failure to return to Norfolk on May 27, 1968.

Many things had happened to the U.S. Navy and the Submarine Service since that stormy Memorial Day. The furies of Vietnam were a receding memory. So too was the political backlash against the war that had torn the nation apart in the late 1960s. All but a handful of the

Atlantic Submarine Force commander Vice Admiral Arnold F. Schade controlled the operations of the *Scorpion* during its last five days in the Atlantic in May 1968. *U.S. Navy Photo*

Scorpion families had left the Norfolk area. Many newcomers there had no knowledge of the sinking. The *Scorpion* story rested in a limbo halfway between old news and forgotten history.

But one big thing had not changed: The Cold War was still on. The U.S. Navy and its Soviet counterpart continued to stalk one another from the Mediterranean to the White Sea and from Pearl Harbor to Petropavlovsk. For submariners, the gap between peacetime operations and a shooting war—in 1983 as in 1968—remained a membrane so thin as to seem almost nonexistent.

Naval technology, however, was changing dramatically. In this, the third year of the Reagan administration, defense dollars were pouring into the fleet, heralding a post-Vietnam renaissance that promised a modern navy of 600 warships by decade's end. Shipyards from Maine to California were working overtime in a vast rebuilding of the navy and submarine fleet. For sailors who had endured the dark years of post-Vietnam military life, it was indeed, in their commander-in-chief's words, "morning in America." The Destroyer-Submarine Piers in Norfolk bristled with the silhouettes of new surface warships and submarines that were coming into service. More were on the way. The *Skipjack*-class submarines, once the premier nuclear attack boat in Norfolk, had long given way to more advanced models. Two of the *Scorpion's* surviving sister ships, the *USS Snook* (SSN 592) and *USS Scamp* (SSN 588), were just four years away from scheduled retirement in 1987, and the other three were entering the twilight years of their operational service. In their place, the *Permit-* and *Sturgeon*-class attack submarines that had entered fleet service in the 1960s and 1970s now carried out the lion's share of the missions. Even newer *Los Angeles*-class attack boats—larger, quieter, and significantly more powerful—were emerging from the shipyards to take on the navy's ever-dangerous submarine operations.[1]

The corporate mentality of the navy, however, had changed very little. Schade was typical of the World War II generation of American submariners who had emerged from the rubble of Pearl Harbor to wage war against Imperial Japan. As the postwar era devolved into Cold War confrontation with the Soviet Union, they had steadily risen to positions of command in the navy during the hardest years of the standoff. By 1983, they were living quietly in retirement or resting on "eternal patrol" in military cemeteries around the nation. Accounts of their formative World War II experiences filled library bookshelves, but of the Cold War at sea there was practically nothing. This was no accident: Navy leaders of the 1980s saw the military standoff with the Soviet Union as an ongoing conflict, and so, to them, the wartime information disclosure policy of World War II–era Chief of Naval Operations Admiral Ernest J. King still applied: "Tell them nothing. Then tell them who won."[2]

I didn't embark on a project to revisit the *Scorpion* incident with any particular agenda. I had read of the submarine's disappearance while a twenty-year-old college student in 1968 but recalled few details. To me, it had been one of many bad events that had befallen the U.S. military in that violent year. My goal was to write an in-depth profile of the *Scor-*

pion tragedy on its fifteenth anniversary—a fitting Memorial Day newspaper topic for residents of the "navy capital" in southeast Virginia. My initial plan was to touch on what was known of the *Scorpion* incident and to try to capture the memories of former navy officials and the submarine crew's next of kin. And I would also attempt to provide any new information on the incident that might have emerged since 1968.

At first, the article seemed like a straightforward exercise in reporting. I would review the newspaper coverage in 1968 beginning with the *Scorpion*'s failure to return to Norfolk. I would seek out any relevant evidence the navy had earlier withheld as classified that might, with the passage of time, now be suitable for declassification and release. Finally, I would locate and interview the main characters in the *Scorpion* story.

Not surprisingly, I found when I began my research that there were significant holes in the historical record. News reports on the *Scorpion* were comprehensive when the navy had permitted access to officials and events, and fragmentary and speculative when officials invoked secrecy. That by itself implied nothing unusual or suspicious. Submarine operations are highly classified. Naval tactical communications involve security concerns rivaling that of nuclear weapons. *Nothing* about nuclear weapons is unclassified. I would have to try to obtain more information from the navy archives and to find navy veterans familiar with the *Scorpion* incident who could help fill in the blanks.[3]

At the outset, I had no reason to suspect anything sinister about the sinking of the *Scorpion*. Press accounts of the navy's search for the missing submarine and the formal investigation into its disappearance depicted a disaster and a tragedy but did not suggest a conspiracy or a cover-up.

THE *SCORPION* INVESTIGATION had played out over the summer and fall of 1968. After the open-ocean search ended on June 5, 1968, reporters continued to shadow the navy probe, particularly that by the court of inquiry, which had held an initial round of hearings in Norfolk for seven weeks in June and July. A majority of those hearings were closed due to the sensitive nature of the testimony or evidence, but a few interesting facts had emerged nonetheless.

News reports at the time described a crisis that had erupted over a matter of hours on the afternoon that the submarine was supposed to have returned to port. All of the information available, from official navy announcements to comments by distraught family members and other sailors, agreed on that critical point. The court of inquiry seemed to confirm this theme as it summoned witnesses from all parts of the navy to tell of the submarine's operational history, maintenance records, and final deployment.

From the outset, the court focused on the fact that the *Scorpion* had somehow vanished without the rest of the navy even noticing. While most civilians had a vague awareness that submarines operate by themselves in secret, for a 251-foot-long warship and its crew of ninety-nine to disappear in this manner added an aura of mystery to the crisis. Thus, an immediate issue for the court had been the lack of communications between the *Scorpion* and Norfolk from May 22 to its scheduled return on Memorial Day. The court quickly established that no one in the Hampton Roads navy complex had been surprised that the Atlantic Submarine Force had not heard from the *Scorpion* in the days before its scheduled arrival. Such silences were in no way unusual in the submarine service, officials assured the court. "Polaris subs go on 60-day patrol and never broadcast," Schade testified.

Reporters early on in the investigation also learned that the *Scorpion* had taken part in a classified mission between the time the submarine left Rota, Spain, and its last message to Norfolk early on May 22. Officials declined to elaborate, but this did not seem out of order. In brief testimony, the submarine's division commander revealed that Commander Francis A. Slattery, the *Scorpion*'s commanding officer, had been given the authority to deviate north and south of his projected course track and was twenty-seven miles south of the track at the time he filed what would be his final position report transmitted just after midnight on Wednesday, May 22. Upon further questioning by Vice Admiral Bernard Austin, president of the seven-member court, Submarine Division 62 Commander Captain Wallace A. Greene testified he could say only that the mission involved "a task of higher classification than would permit revealing in open court." At that point, Austin cleared the courtroom. No further details on this mission emerged in the open hearings. The court quickly turned to other subjects, suggesting that the mission—whatever it was—did not play a major role in the loss.[4]

According to other newspaper accounts, several witnesses in the hearing reported minor mechanical flaws and equipment breakdowns on board the *Scorpion* during its deployment, including a faulty exterior radio whip antenna, a minor leak in the propeller shaft seal, difficulty in calibrating the submarine's LORAN (LOng-RANge) navigational receiver, and several minor hull cracks. Another witness revealed that the *Scorpion* had not received a thorough redesign under the navy's Submarine Safety (SubSafe) improvement program ordered in the wake of the 1963 sinking of the nuclear submarine *USS Thresher* (SSN 593). However, the *Scorpion*'s squadron commander, Captain Jared E. Clarke III, testified that experts deemed the submarine safe because its main ballast blow system was adequate and it was operating under a depth restriction that would enable it to recover and reach the surface quickly in event of a major mechanical casualty.[5]

Eight days after the hearings opened, another intriguing fact emerged. Commander George R. Parrish, the Atlantic Submarine Force's operations officer, testified that the *Scorpion* had collided with a mooring barge while in the harbor at Naples, Italy, a month before its deployment ended. The mishap occurred during a squall when the submarine was tied up alongside the aircraft support ship *USS Tallahatchie County* (AVB 2), and the barge was being used as a fender to prevent the two ships from bumping into one another. Parrish added that navy divers inspected the *Scorpion*'s hull five days later and found no damage.[6]

During the hearings, facts began to emerge as well from the search operation. The commander of the open-ocean search for the *Scorpion* returned to Norfolk and told the court of inquiry that his units had failed to detect any uncharted seamounts in the vicinity of the submarine's homeward track that could have posed a navigational hazard. One navy navigational expert had previously disclosed that the submarine lacked the latest ocean-bottom charts showing where such hazards occurred; still, the new reports from the search seemed to rule out the possibility that the sinking had been caused by impact with a seamount. Rear Admiral Lawrence G. Bernard further testified that, in his opinion, had the *Scorpion* been disabled on the surface, his search force and an armada of land-based patrol aircraft would have detected it.[7]

And yet while many theories about the *Scorpion* sinking were seemingly ruled out in the course of the hearings, nothing emerged to take their place. One of the last witnesses to appear confirmed that, as of early July, after thirty-five days of searching, the navy had failed to find a single clue. "Not a single item of flotsam even remotely associated with the *Scorpion* or any other submarine has been located," said the commander of Submarine Squadron 12 in Key West, Captain George C. Ball, who on June 17 had taken over command of the search force from Bernard.[8]

Once the hearings ended, the news media interest in the story subsided. A few press reports mentioned that the navy was still searching for the *Scorpion* in the eastern Atlantic with a handful of research ships. But as the weeks went by, the torrent of articles slowed to a trickle, and then all but ceased.

But then, on October 30, came a stunning navy bulletin: Using a towed underwater sled equipped with sonar, other sensors, and a still camera, the civilian-crewed research ship *USNS Mizar* (T-AGOR 11) had photographed the wreckage of the *Scorpion* in 11,100 feet of water. The announcement caused a fresh outpouring of news articles. The day it was made, navy officials told *The Ledger-Star* that the *Mizar* had been close to calling off the search until the spring of 1969, due to worsening weather conditions. *The Virginian-Pilot* noted that the discovery came on the very day the navy had planned to mail to *Scorpion* family members a sanitized summary of the court of inquiry's findings.[9]

Citing navy sources, the press reports revealed two new elements of the investigation that had enabled the *Mizar* to ultimately locate the stricken submarine: First, unnamed navy officials confirmed that the still-highly-classified Sound Surveillance System, a network of underwater listening devices, had detected acoustic signals from the sinking, allowing the navy to identify an area of special interest measuring several hundred square miles southwest of the Azores in which searchers later found the *Scorpion*. Second, a team of researchers led by civilian navy scientist Dr. John P. Craven constructed a list of ten detailed scenarios for the sinking itself that contained different likely maneuvers the *Scorpion* crew would have taken in response to different types of casualties. Fed into a navy computer, each scenario produced a high-probability area within the overall search grid where the submarine's hull most likely would have come to rest. Officials said the *Scorpion* was found at the edge of one of those small subset areas.[10]

In November, a key member of the *Scorpion* technical search effort revealed to a reporter that the *Mizar* had found another vital clue that finally helped lead the team to the submarine. Early on in its search, the *Mizar*'s sled had photographed a small twisted piece of shiny metal on the seabed. Dr. Chester L. Buchanan of the Naval Research Laboratory, the senior scientist aboard the *Mizar,* said the two-foot-long metal shard was the "first hint" of anything possibly related to the *Scorpion*. The *Mizar* photographed the fragment around June 27–28, but it took another four months of searching to locate the submarine itself, he said. Navy officials at the time still did not know if the piece of metal actually came from the *Scorpion*; they knew only that it was located very close to the wreck site.[11]

With this new evidence in hand, the court of inquiry reconvened on November 6 with the same seven members under Austin's leadership. Again, the hearings were mostly closed to the public and press. The court spent the rest of the month in closed meetings with photographic analysts reviewing the detailed images. Other than one unnamed navy official who described the photographs as "terrific, much better than those they took of *Thresher*" after its sinking, the navy stayed mum about the panel's work. After several news reports noted that the *Scorpion* hull was essentially in one piece, the navy released an announcement that the hull actually was "in several major pieces, completely flooded, and with the obvious damage expected when a submarine exceeds crush depth."[12]

Then on January 31, 1969, the navy tersely made public the court's findings. After eleven weeks of testimony from ninety expert witnesses and the study of 232 separate exhibits—including one that comprised thousands of photographs of the *Scorpion*'s shattered hull—Austin and his fellow panelists had thrown up their hands. Armed with the power to compel sworn testimony and authorized to summon experts on technical subjects as diverse as passive sonar, navy communications, reactor safety, and submarine hull design, the court of inquiry still could not say what had happened: "The certain cause of the loss of *Scorpion* cannot be ascertained by any evidence now available." Years later, one member of the court called the *Scorpion* sinking "one of the greatest unsolved sea mysteries of our era."[13]

It was a major disappointment.

The court of inquiry had, however, been able to eliminate two possible causes for the sinking: collision with an underwater seamount and a mishap involving the *Scorpion's* S5W nuclear reactor. The court effectively ruled out any number of other scenarios as well. It "gave the opinion" that the delay of SubSafe modifications had not contributed to the sinking: "*Scorpion's* overall material condition was excellent and none of the outstanding ship alterations . . . were required for safe operation to her restricted depth."

The court concluded that *Scorpion's* crew was well trained and that Slattery and his men "could be expected to take proper action in event of a ship control casualty in order to prevent the submarine from descending to crush depth." While the *Mizar's* photographs "gave no indication that loss of the submarine was due to one of her own torpedoes," the court "probed this possibility." The panel then seemed to dismiss that scenario as well, noting that "*Scorpion's* torpedomen were well trained and that procedures used in handling ordnance on board were consistent with established safety procedures."

The court also stressed that no wreckage was found other than that of the missing submarine, and that there was no evidence suggesting foul play or sabotage. In the end, the court of inquiry disbanded with as many questions unanswered as when its members had convened seven months earlier.[14]

The court wrestled with the same dilemma that juries, police detectives, historians, and reporters confront every day: proving a theory based primarily on circumstantial evidence. In this case, not only was the evidence circumstantial but also one compelling piece of evidence often contradicted another. Still, anyone with experience in decoding the syntax of navy news releases could not help but notice a curious adjective the court employed in the penultimate sentence of its final report: that the "certain" cause remained elusive. If nothing was "certain," was there not anything else close enough to constitute a plausible reason for the *Scorpion*'s demise? The members of the court held their tongues. The news release did not elaborate. With one small but striking exception, the story was over.

That exception came six years later, in March 1975, shortly after several newspapers revealed an ambitious and highly classified operation by the Central Intelligence Agency to attempt to physically raise a sunken Soviet submarine from the floor of the Pacific Ocean. The CIA-backed ship *Glomar Explorer* employed a massive steel claw and an oil-derrick-like crane to lower the device nearly three miles below the ocean surface to grasp the hulk of the Soviet submarine.

When he saw those reports, *The Ledger-Star*'s military reporter, Jack Kestner, telephoned the *Scorpion* court of inquiry's president to ask if a similar recovery operation might have enabled the inquest to come to a definitive conclusion about the American submarine. Austin's reply came as a shock: "We had a pretty good idea of what happened [although] it was still something we couldn't be 100 percent positive about." Kestner pressed the retired submariner to explain, but the admiral declined. Austin replied that it was "the wisdom of the Navy Department that they released what they did." In his article that appeared the next day, Kestner recounted the navy's public announcement that the "certain cause" of the sinking could not be determined and that he had asked Austin to explain the apparent discrepancy. The retired submariner replied that the court had only managed to establish a theory on the cause of the sinking. However, when Kestner pressed him on whether lifting the *Scorpion* wreckage to the surface might have resolved any uncertainties about its fate, Austin's reply seemed to contradict his earlier comment. "I don't believe so, although one can never be certain about something like that," Austin said. "The information we had from [the *Mizar*'s] pictures was pretty complete." He declined to elaborate, and the navy subsequently refused comment.[15]

It was a tantalizing if frustrating sign that there was still much more to the *Scorpion* story.

The trail on the *Scorpion* went cold after 1975. It was obvious to me that the navy's massive *Scorpion* archives were the best source of any new information. I recalled discovering in an earlier research project that the navy had waited until the late 1960s to declassify the World War II–era patrol reports and other archives of the Submarine Service. One interesting detail was that the navy had not made a public announcement of this declassification, although historians had been quick to learn of the newly accessible documents. By 1983, I thought, perhaps the service might have reviewed the *Scorpion* court of inquiry and declassified some of the 1,334 pages of transcripts and exhibits for public release. Alas, no. Almost four decades after V-J Day, the navy judge advocate general was still operating under Admiral King's "tell them nothing" rule.

My first step was to file a formal request under the federal Freedom of Information Act (FOIA) for a copy of the court of inquiry file. In response, on April 8, 1983 the navy released a sanitized copy of the Findings of Fact, Opinions and Recommendations from the hearings. The document came in two parts: The first comprised the final fifty-four pages of the court's initial seven-week session that ran from June 5 until July 25, 1968. A second, eighteen-page, section stemmed from the panel's final session after it reconvened on November 6 for six weeks of "supplemental hearings" after the announced discovery of the *Scorpion*.[16]

The heavily redacted pages provided additional details here and there, but in terms of the sinking itself, the navy censor had struck far, wide, and deep. Entire sections of the report were blanked out, particularly technical details about the *Scorpion*'s overall operating capabilities, any references to the mission "of higher classification," and details of how the *Mizar* had found the wreckage. The court's fifteen-page opinions section likewise was riddled with deletions, including whatever theory of the cause of the sinking the panel had found. Marine Corps Colonel R. F. Edwards of the Navy Judge Advocate General (JAG) Corps enclosed a cover letter in which he justified the heavy censoring of the *Scorpion* file. Edwards asserted that he had the facts, Navy Department regulations, a recent presidential executive order on declassification procedures, and even the Freedom of Information Act itself on his side: "Except for the sanitized Findings of Fact from the Court of Inquiry . . . the Court of Inquiry is classified as TOP SECRET. This classification is in the interest of national defense. Under the security classification exemption of the Freedom of Information Act [5 U.S.C. 552(b)(1)(1976)], therefore this information is exempt from release."[17]

In an earlier letter to me, the navy had explained some reasons why it would continue to store the *Scorpion* file in a locked, guarded vault:

> Although the Court of Inquiry was convened to determine the precise cause of the loss of the *Scorpion,* few specifics could be determined about the events surrounding her loss. Most of the testimony, therefore, consists of the ship's class [design] characteristics and performance parameters in order to determine possible causes for the loss of the submarine. Since the testimony considered performance of a class of submarine that is still in commission, release of this information could provide invaluable insight into current United States submarine operations and procedures. The damage would far outweigh any benefits to the public from its disclosure.

In terms of the Freedom of Information Act, the navy had partially denied my request, leaving me with the options of abandoning that avenue of inquiry or seeking a formal appeal to have the navy reconsider its denial.[18]

Heavily censored though the court summary document was, it still provided some useful clues. First off, I learned that the issue of radio communications between Norfolk and the *Scorpion* was more complicated than Admiral Schade's testimony had led reporters to believe. During the summer hearings, he had asserted that his command was not expecting to hear from the submarine at all during its transit of the Atlantic to Norfolk between May 21 and May 27, 1968. But according to the court report, the radio silence imposed on the *Scorpion* was by no means absolute. The court found that "the operation order under which *Scorpion* was operating while in transit to Norfolk required electronic silence *except as necessary for safety and certain other specified situations* [emphasis added]." In fact, the *Scorpion*'s command center had tried to make contact with the *Scorpion* unsuccessfully during this time. Between May 22 and May 27, no fewer than nine messages were transmitted on the navy's submarine broadcast to the *Scorpion*. In three cases—on May 23, 24, and 25—the message requested a reply. Two of them were from Submarine Division 62, the *Scorpion*'s administrative command, and the third originated with the Norfolk Naval Shipyard. As the court's report stated bluntly, "No replies were received."[19]

For the first time, the declassified court summary revealed that a Soviet Navy operation was taking place in the eastern Atlantic at the time of the *Scorpion*'s disappearance. The heavily censored pages did not explicitly link the Soviets to the *Scorpion,* although the operation was the only event that conformed to the mission "of higher classification" that Captain Greene had mentioned to the court. The court document stated that the panel heard evidence that "a Soviet [deleted] operation was being conducted southwest of the Canary Islands during the period of *Scorpion*'s return transit from the Mediterranean. The group consisted of two hydrographic survey ships, a submarine rescue ship and an [deleted] nuclear submarine." A Krupny-class guided missile destroyer and a fleet oiler departed Algiers to join this group on May 18 but did not arrive until the *Scorpion* was about 200 miles to the west, the court noted. U.S. Navy patrol aircraft had the Soviet formation under "surveillance coverage" except for a two-day period, May 19–21, and sightings before the *Scorpion*'s last message to Norfolk early on May 22 placed the Soviet vessels "over 200 miles from *Scorpion*'s last known position." The court ultimately concluded that the Soviet presence in the region was irrelevant: "There were no observed changes in the pattern of operations of the Soviet ships, either before or after *Scorpion*'s loss, that were evaluated as indicating involvement or interest in any way."[20]

The report also indicated that the court had examined at length the possibility that the *Scorpion* had been sunk by one of its own torpedoes. Although this section of the report was heavily censored, it was clear that the panel had studied in detail the safety record of three types of torpedoes used by the *Scorpion*. The document revealed that the submarine had experienced the "inadvertent activation of the [propulsion] battery of a MK 37 torpedo" during a training exercise in 1967. This led, the summary continued, to a "hot run" in which the torpedo's electric motor activated and the propeller began to rotate while still inside the submarine. That incident involved a training torpedo that did not have a warhead installed. The torpedo was loaded into one of the *Scorpion's* six torpedo tubes, and when it activated, crewmen flooded the tube, opened the outer shutter doors, and allowed the torpedo to swim out of the tube. It was never recovered. And yet it was impossible to know what conclusions the court members drew from this fact or anything else they learned about the torpedoes on board the *Scorpion*. The first nine pages of the court's opinions section of the document were blank. The information was still classified top secret.[21]

The Findings of Fact from the July hearings confirmed some aspects of the story journalists had reported at the time. Navy officials had informed the court of the *Mizar* discovery of the twisted, shiny metal fragment in late June 1968 and provided update reports of the ongoing search effort. In other cases, the heavily censored pages said nothing.

Completely absent from the sanitized text that the navy provided in 1983 were any references to the underwater acoustic signals that news accounts had stated led the search to the several hundred square miles of ocean near the Azores where the technical search team later found the missing submarine. By 1983, it was common knowledge that the U.S. Navy had long operated the Sound Surveillance System in the Atlantic and other regions, and navy sources as far back as 1968 had told reporters that only by tracking acoustic signals from the sinking was the search effort able to find the *Scorpion*. Officially, however, Sosus remained highly classified. Censors blanked out all references to its involvement.[22]

This threadbare, elliptical, and incomplete set of facts formed the foundation of my first attempt to retell the story of the loss of the *Scorpion*. The trail had gone very cold. The only way I would be able to obtain a fuller account of the incident would be to proceed with the Freedom of Information Act's appeals process. But an attempt to obtain a new declassification review of the *Scorpion* archive could take months, if not years. In the short term, the only promising option was to find and interview those navy officials who had played important roles in the *Scorpion* search and investigation.

I began by setting up a telephone interview with Vice Admiral Schade. In 1983, the seventy-one-year-old Connecticut native and World War II combat hero had been retired for ten years. But Schade was probably the single most important official involved in the *Scorpion* incident. Fortunately, he expressed no hesitation in sharing his experiences with me.[23]

"She had just completed a complete tour in the Med, which was extremely successful—in fact when they were coming out [through the Straits of Gibraltar] we normally diverted them into the Polaris base at Rota, Spain, for a couple of days for a [weapons] load-out and [to pick up] a couple of things they might need before leaving the area," Schade explained in a long telephone interview. "And they reported their condition was so good that they didn't even need to stop. They pulled in to the entrance at Rota . . . discharged two sailors who were due for rotation and would be flown back before they got back. They were transferred and the ship came on by itself, apparently in excellent condition with an outstanding operational record."

The admiral's voice was clear and firm as he searched his memory. When I asked if he had obtained specific information about the *Scorpion*'s performance during its seventy-eight-day tour with the U.S. Sixth Fleet, he paused only a moment. "They would have been reported through the Sixth Fleet and CINCUSNAVEUR, the [Navy's] operational command in Europe. Of course, we saw all of those [reports] and they were outstanding." Thus far, Schade's recollections dovetailed precisely with the chronology of events from newspaper coverage and with as much of the court of inquiry report as had evaded the censor's marking pen. The *Scorpion* was a front-line unit of the Atlantic Submarine Force. The submarine's Mediterranean deployment had been an unqualified success. Its crew was experienced, well trained, and carried out the mission to the letter. The transfer from Sixth Fleet to Atlantic Submarine Force operational control on the night of May 17, as the *Scorpion* reentered the Atlantic, was routine. The cause of the sinking remained an unsolved mystery.

Later in the conversation, Schade also confirmed a link suggested in the court of inquiry summary, that the *Scorpion's* classified mission mentioned by Greene had targeted the Soviet operation southwest of the Canary Islands. "We had general information of a task force operating over in that general area so we advised them to slow down, take a look, see what they could find out," Schade said. "As far as we know they never made contact, they never reported on that." Once again, Schade's recollections seemed to align with the conclusions of the court of inquiry.

But then the elderly submariner began to veer away from the narrative I had been able to reconstruct from the court of inquiry summary and the news reports from the time of the hearings. In 1968, the navy had flatly asserted that the submarine was not expected to break radio silence on the homeward voyage. Schade himself had confirmed this during his own sworn testimony in the open court of inquiry hearing. But now, when I asked him about the *Scorpion's* final message transmitted in the early hours of May 22, Schade seemed to minimize its importance. "We got that position report," he recalled. "That was the basis for our initial search operation. But that was really all we had and we didn't consider that too significant, other than just as the last known position that we actually had." Then Schade flatly contradicted his 1968 statements. "They were due to report in to us shortly thereafter. It was at that time we got a little suspicious, because they did not report, they did not check in, and then when we got to the time limit of their 'check-in' they were first reported as overdue."

Nothing in anything I had read indicated that there had been any expectation that the *Scorpion* would check in by radio message during those final days—just the opposite. I was immediately confused and gently pressed Schade to expand on his comments. "As far as we were concerned all was clear," he responded, "and she should have kept coming and then within about twenty-four hours after that [the May 22 position report] she should have given us a rather long, windy resumé of her operations and what she would need upon her return to port . . . you know, transition from one command to another, homeward bound voyage. We have absolute confidence in our communications, both in the reception and the response, and when they did not respond, almost immediately that's when we first became suspicious, that's when we followed up with other messages, and really, it was just a matter of hours that we became somewhat concerned."

It was possible, I reasoned, that after fifteen years Schade's memory of the episode was either incomplete or wrong. But then the old submariner dropped the verbal equivalent of a hydrogen bomb.

"I happened to be out at sea in the [*USS*] *Ray* [SSN 653]," he said, recalling the moment when he had learned that the *Scorpion* was missing, "which was the—"

I interrupted. "Was this off Connecticut?" I asked, recalling the press reports of Schade aboard the Groton-based nuclear attack submarine *USS Pargo* the morning of May 27.

"No," he replied. "I was out at sea off Norfolk in the *Ray*, which was the flagship of the [Atlantic] Submarine Force, and when we first got the report and it looked like we needed to do something in the way of a search operation, I got [Atlantic Fleet commander] Admiral [Ephraim P.] Holmes on the radio and said, 'Would you place the facilities of CINCLANTFLT at my disposal for the next day or two until we can organize a search operation?'"

For a moment, I was stunned by this unexpected curveball. Schade, on a never-revealed cruise on another submarine off the Virginia Capes five days before the "missing submarine" panic, had asked his superior to approve a secret search for the *Scorpion*? Schade's recollection of that moment seemed too accurate to ascribe to confusion or memory loss. I was instantly aware of two imperatives: to coax the admiral into providing as many details of this as possible, and not to say anything that might cause him to become suspicious of my confusion.

"Was this before the 27th of May?" I asked, attempting to stifle my bewilderment.

"I can't remember the dates. As soon as we were concerned that she had not checked in."

"SubMiss was declared several hours after the *Scorpion's* arrival time on 27 May," I reminded him, trying to prod his memory. "Was this before . . . "

"No—well before her scheduled arrival because we worked back from Norfolk all the way to her last reported position which was in the neighborhood of the Azores."

This was a stunning revelation. The navy had made any number of official statements throughout the *Scorpion* emergency. None of them had deviated from the unequivocal position that Atlantic Submarine Force officials from Schade on down to the lowest yeoman striker knew anything of the *Scorpion*'s fate until the day it failed to arrive at Hampton Roads on Monday, May 27.

"Prior to the day she was supposed to get back," I asked, "you had already asked CINCLANTFLT if he could put some resources at your disposal?"

"Well in advance of that," Schade firmly replied, clearly unaware of the implications of what he was telling me. "And in fact, he had placed them all at our disposal and this was quite an amazing set of operational circumstances because we controlled the entire resources of the Atlantic Fleet from a submarine at sea. Working through CINCLANTFLT headquarters and their communications, but we organized a search from both ends both by air and surface ships and other submarines."

I decided to test his memory some more. "The [newspaper] clips don't tell all of the story. You're saying that you were looking for the *Scorpion* before the 27th of May?"

The admiral rewarded me with a golden sound bite—an on-the-record quote that removed all ambiguity from his revelation of a secret search for the *Scorpion*. "All I know is that long before she was actually due in Norfolk we had organized a search effort," Schade explained. "We had two squadrons of destroyers, a lot of long-range antisubmarine search planes operating out of the Azores, Norfolk and other areas, and we had several ships that were in the Atlantic that were in transit between the Med and the U.S. Some [were] diverted, some of them were just told to come over to the track which we presupposed the *Scorpion* would be on. They searched up and down that. This went on for quite some time until it was quite obvious that she was long overdue arriving in Norfolk."

I needed to ask one last question to clarify this new account. "But you kept this on a classified basis?"

"Well, it was classified more because we didn't know where she was or what had happened and we were just trying to find out," Schade concluded. "It was no sense making a big brouhaha over something we really couldn't explain."

Neither Schade nor I realized at that moment the full implications of what he had just revealed. At the time, the "secret" search for the *Scorpion* seemed to me just one more puzzle in a story that was becoming more confusing by the day. But as I reread the newspaper clips from 1968 after my conversation with Schade, I realized that if the navy had been looking in secret for the submarine before May 27, there was more to the incident than an inexplicable disappearance that led to near-panic on the Norfolk navy base piers that day. It was not until much later that I would come to see that Schade's disclosure was much more than an unexpected vignette in a larger story. Rather, it was the first of many revelations that most of what the American people and even the rest of the navy knew about the *Scorpion* was, in fact, a cover story. And a lie.

Schade's revelation prompted me to change the emphasis of my research and article plans. It had become clear that I couldn't just retell the story of the *Scorpion* tragedy as it had stood for fifteen years. There were too many holes in the historical record, and now I had a senior admiral flat-out contradicting the story he himself had told the court of inquiry under oath. I had to dig deeper.

In addition to writing the already planned fifteenth-anniversary article about the incident, my editors at *The Ledger-Star* authorized me to begin an open-ended investigation into the entire *Scorpion* incident as time and other professional obligations permitted. I decided to pursue several angles simultaneously. I would continue pursuing the Freedom of Information Act appeal for the navy's still-classified *Scorpion* court of inquiry archive and other navy records; I would attempt to obtain through FOIA relevant documents from other federal government agencies; and I would mine other news media sources for additional material. Finally, and most importantly, I would interview principal navy officials involved in the *Scorpion* incident who were willing to speak. And here another surprise lay in wait.

Keepers of the *Scorpion* archive may have locked their windows and barricaded their doors, but most participants in the *Scorpion* incident were willing, even eager, to talk about their experiences.

During the spring of 1983, I conducted interviews with several dozen former navy officers, scientists, and family members of the *Scorpion*'s crewmen. The process was exhausting and, at times, discouraging. Fifteen years had passed, and for many participants, memories had faded. And a number of interview subjects warned that they were still subject to classified information nondisclosure agreements they had signed upon leaving the navy. So even when a vital detail came to mind, the official's response would often trickle to a halt halfway through the first sentence.

Gag orders and memory lapses aside, the *Scorpion* participants I interviewed voiced the same range of theories about the sinking that the navy had apparently investigated during the hearings.

For some officials, a battery explosion seemed the most likely explanation. This theory had first emerged when experts viewed the *Mizar* photographs of the wreckage in November 1968. Then in 1969, when the navy bathyscaph *Trieste II* had recovered from the *Scorpion* site a plastic battery terminal cover with minute bits of metal embedded in it, the piece of debris seemed to indicate that one or more of the *Scorpion*'s batteries—located in the bottom of the hull—had exploded. Other researchers I interviewed were equally adamant that a battery explosion, while serious, could *not* have generated an acoustic signal as large as the initial pulse that later was determined to be of the initial casualty that led to the *Scorpion* sinking. Admiral Bernard A. Clarey, the vice chief of naval operations and the navy's senior submarine officer in 1968, refuted the possibility that an exploding battery could have caused the *Scorpion*'s demise. "Nuclear submarines don't have a big battery like diesel submarines," he explained. "It's a small battery, it's only made for extreme emergencies. . . . One of the reasons that I never thought it would be strong enough [to broach the hull] and cause extreme hull damage was that there was enough room down there, enough air space down there, for the explosion to be spread throughout the boat. I never thought the battery explosion could be it."[24]

Schade put forward a different theory. For him, the most likely scenario involved a physical failure of the *Scorpion's* trash-disposal unit, which could have resulted in flooding severe enough to sink the submarine. The disposal unit, he explained, consisted of a small chamber with one hatchway leading to the outside of the submarine hull and an inner door through which crewmen would load garbage for dumping. Failure of a safety interlock that prevented both doors from opening at the same time could permit a fatal blast of high-pressure water into the submarine.[25]

Others who had played roles in the *Scorpion* incident were content to accept the court's finding that no clear cause of the loss had emerged from the evidence. Having served as commander of the *Scorpion's* sister ship *USS Scamp,* retired Rear Admiral Walter N. "Buck" Dietzen knew a lot about the *Skipjack*-class attack submarine. And as deputy director of submarine warfare in the Pentagon in 1968, Dietzen had become one of the point men for calls from other government agencies and the news media amid the public uproar after the announcement that the *Scorpion* had gone missing. "You had a material casualty, complicated by a personnel casualty," Dietzen said in a 1988 interview. "And that probably caused the loss. . . . The problem was, that [submarine] was a fast little bugger. Their test depth was not nearly as deep as the submarines are today. And you could crank that sumbitch up to thirty knots but in any event if you had a hydraulic system casualty and then you complicate that thing with a personnel casualty on top, go to full dive instead of full rise—you have fifteen seconds to recover before test depth. It's a tight [safety] envelope."[26]

If we set aside for now the contradictory assertions regarding the *Scorpion's* lack of communications with Norfolk, the most plausible theory that emerged from my interviews was that the *Scorpion* had been downed by an accidental torpedo warhead explosion. The court of inquiry, I knew, had rigorously investigated this scenario but seemed to dismiss it in its final report. Nonetheless, a significant number of key of-

ficials in the search and investigation held to this as the most likely explanation. These officials with whom I talked argued that they were only
able to locate the missing submarine because the acoustic signals ema-
nating from its breakup—particularly the initial acoustic signal—were
large enough to have been recorded by sensors over 1,300 nautical miles
away in the North Atlantic. Dr. John P. Craven, chairman of the navy's
Deep Submergence Systems Project, led the Technical Advisory Group
effort to pinpoint the *Scorpion's* resting place using acoustic evidence and
complex "probability analysis" to calculate its most likely location. The
key aspect of that evidence, he said, was that the sinking involved an initial, very large impulse—an explosion—followed after ninety-one seconds of silence by the sounds of various compartments and tanks
imploding within a few seconds.[27]

Interviewed in 1984, Craven still could recall the tiniest details of
the *Scorpion* incident. When he heard over his car radio the bulletin of
the *Scorpion* being overdue on May 27, the retired scientist recalled, he
drove straight to the Pentagon. There senior admirals asked him to conduct an immediate survey to see if there were any underwater recordings
in the Atlantic that might have captured the sounds of the *Scorpion*
breaking up. The idea was to use any acoustic evidence found to triangulate the location of the sinking in the same manner that ground-based
listening antennas can pinpoint the position of a radio transmitter.

"Immediately that evening there were two questions that I was directed to spend all my time on," Craven said. "The first question was,
'Where would the submarine be if it was down in an area where people
could still be alive?' and, 'What assets did we have that we could get out
to that area as fast as possible?' The second question was, 'What acoustic
information or any other kind of information did we have—which included "submarine sunk here" buoys—to find it?'" The navy, Craven
went on, told him that officials had already reviewed records of the Sosus
system without detecting any sign of the submarine.[28]

Craven's husky Brooklyn accent intensified as he continued. "The
other thing is that, in addition to the Sosus nets, there are all sorts of—
everybody's got hydrophones in the water. Oil companies have hydrophones in the water, scientists have hydrophones in the water,

scientific laboratories have hydrophones in the water, there are hydrophones in the water for all sorts of reasons. . . . The sea is just full of sound all of the time." Early in the morning on May 28, Craven said, he reached a navy civilian scientist, Gordon Hamilton, who ran oceanographic research stations in Bermuda and the Canary Islands. It turned out that the Canary Island station still had its reel tape recordings from the previous week. And when Navy Research Laboratory officials listened to the tape for May 22, they heard the spine-chilling recording of the *Scorpion's* death. The tape (and a computer-driven visual printout) showed the massive initial pulse of sound, then silence for ninety-one seconds, then what Craven called a "train wreck" cascade of smaller sound pulses. Several days later, researchers found the same pattern of sounds buried deep within two other recordings from hydrophones in the Atlantic off the Newfoundland coast. That evidence enabled the *Mizar* to focus its search in a roughly twelve-by-twelve-square-mile area of the eastern Atlantic, Craven said. It also made possible finding the *Scorpion* five months after it had failed to reach port.[29]

In reviewing what officials had thus far said, it was clear from Admiral Austin's conversation with reporter Jack Kestner in 1975 that the seven-member panel had identified a likely cause of the sinking that outweighed other scenarios, then verbally put an anchor out to windward by saying it could find no "certain cause" for the loss. Bearing that in mind, I believed that Craven's theory of an accidental torpedo explosion offered the most credible answer to the *Scorpion* mystery. While there was nothing like consensus on this point—not in 1983, and certainly not in 1968—the other scenarios failed to explain the unique pattern of sounds that recorded the *Scorpion's* death.

Still, this was by no means an open-and-shut finding. Retired Captain A. J. Martin Atkins was one of the court's seven members. When I interviewed the career submariner, who had, like Dietzen, once commanded the *Scamp,* he told me that he could not recall the panel opting for one theory over another. "The real significant thing about the whole proceeding was the fact that we . . . actually found that ship or the remains of that ship. Of course, it was just pure luck that that happened. The clarity of some of the photographs taken at that depth of the ocean was to me very significant." Atkins said he had only learned by chance of several follow-on technical studies of the *Scorpion* incident in 1969 and 1970 but had no access to that material. Schade had earlier said essentially the same thing: "They could never establish the cause. . . . It [the evidence] signifies to me that she just sort of cruised on down below her actual [depth] capability and was crushed and kept right on going down from there. . . . We never will know whether she was flooded or steamed down there or what it was."[30]

ON DECEMBER 16, 1984, *The Virginian-Pilot and The Ledger-Star* published my report based on nearly two years of research and interviews. I had managed to pry some additional documents out of the classified navy vaults by appealing the navy's partial denial of my FOIA request, followed by a civil lawsuit in federal court that prompted the navy to conduct an in-depth "security declassification review" of the *Scorpion* archive. The evidence I had compiled clearly pointed to an accidental torpedo mishap as the prime cause of the sinking. In making my case, I described how Craven and his team had developed the scenario of a torpedo warhead accident onboard the *Scorpion*. When I interviewed the retired scientist, now living in Hawaii, in November 1984, he told me that he was able to speak out on the subject because the navy had declassified and released to me two technical reports on the investigation. They revealed enough of the information on the acoustic evidence that he could speak freely about it for the first time. The acoustic signals from the *Scorpion* sinking, Craven said, not only confirmed the time and general location of the event but also gave a strong indication of what had gone wrong with the submarine. That evidence—the sequence of sounds from the *Scorpion* sinking—showed that the submarine was traveling *east* and not west on its homeward transit at the time it went down. Inquiries that Craven and his team had made with navy submariners revealed that a common procedure to disarm a torpedo that had inadvertently become active inside the submarine was to order an immediate 180-degree course reversal. A safety mechanism in the torpedo's guidance system would then shut down the weapon, he added. Moreover, the navy had confirmed to Craven that there had been a problem with the Mark 37 torpedo in recent years involving accidental startups of the battery-powered motor when stray electrical voltage entered a test unit via the fire-control circuit. Under Craven's scenario, the *Scorpion* had suffered a hot run, attempted to disarm the warhead by reversing course, but failed to deactivate it before the weapon detonated. A torpedo warhead explosion inside the submarine, Craven concluded, "is the one scenario that in my opinion fits all of the evidence."[31]

Not for the last time, however, the *Scorpion* story would evade a tidy ending. Within twenty-four hours, it again became clear that the actual *Scorpion* secret still lay in the navy's locked vaults. A chance comment in a hallway of my newspaper building shattered the theory I had developed over the course of the previous twenty-five months, and I realized with dismay that I was back to square one. The torpedo-accident theory had survived only the length of time that passes between reading a headline and wrapping it around a fish.

I now realized that it would take an unprecedented, sustained research and reporting effort to unlock the truth of what had happened to the *Scorpion* and its ninety-nine-man crew. At the time, I didn't realize that it would take something much more, as well: It would take the collapse of the Soviet Union and end of the Cold War, the retirement of the *Skipjack*-class nuclear submarines, and the passage of decades before the U.S. Navy would begin unlocking most—but even then, not all—of the *Scorpion* archive.

All of this came to me the day after my story was published. On December 17, 1984, I was walking down a hallway in *The Virginian-Pilot and The Ledger-Star* building in high spirits when I ran into Jerry Hall, the head of the newspaper's production department. "That was an interesting article about the *Scorpion*," Hall said with a mischievous grin. "Too bad you missed the real cause." I was mildly annoyed; I was proud of the story and believed that I had pried the comprehensive account out of the navy's classified archives.

I asked Hall why he thought he knew what had happened to the submarine.

"This is my second career," Hall replied. "You probably didn't know it. I spent twenty years in the navy—the submarine service, in fact. In 1968, I was Arnie Schade's flag yeoman."

"So it wasn't a torpedo accident?"

"No," Hall said. "The Russians sank the *Scorpion.*"[32]

3

THE SPORTS CAR OF SHIPS

HE *SCORPION* WAS CONDUCTING A ROUTINE EQUIPMENT TEST OUT
in the Atlantic off Long Island Sound one day when Kenneth Carr
discovered what the submarine could really do. It was the fall of 1960,
and the thirty-two-year-old lieutenant commander had just joined the
navy's newest nuclear attack submarine shortly after its commissioning
on July 29. With eleven years of service since graduating from the U.S.
Naval Academy in 1949, Carr was no stranger to submarines. He had
served tours on the diesel boats *USS Flying Fish* (SS 229) and *USS
Blackfin* (SS 322)—both of which had seen combat in the Pacific in
World War II—then transferred to the navy's first nuclear submarine,
USS Nautilus (SSN 571), as engineering officer.

Now, as the *Scorpion's* new executive officer, Carr was helping direct
the crew in a series of exercises to assess the *Scorpion's* overall capability
and to test several new pieces of equipment. One task for the *Scorpion*
this day was to see how effectively an experimental scoop injector
mounted on the front of the *Scorpion's* dorsal-fin-shaped sail would
work as an alternative to the traditional (and noisier) electrical pumps
used to collect seawater for the ship's condensers to make fresh water. At
one point in the drill, Commander Norman G. Bessac, thirty-seven, ordered the submarine to maximum, or flank, speed, followed by a sharp
turn to in order to test how the scoop would work during extreme

maneuvering. Carr said he was shocked by the intensity of the maneuver and its impact on the submarine. "It was a full rudder turn at high speed." The *Scorpion* heeled over sharply like an aircraft banking in the air, then plunged deeper into the ocean. "It was a snap roll," Carr said. "We threw one guy from one bunk on one side [of the berthing compartment passageway] to a bunk on the other side without touching the deck." In the cramped control room, Bessac turned to the shaken shipyard technicians and calmly asked if they needed a repeat of the maneuver. "No," one technician stammered. "We have enough data."[1]

FEW PEOPLE EVER HAD the opportunity to view the extraordinary design of the *Scorpion* in full, and fewer were able to witness the capabilities that this submarine possessed. Submarines in general ride low in the water and offer little of their silhouettes to the human eye. The *Skipjack*-class boats provided even less to see than the older diesel submarines they were replacing: Afloat, the sail structure and only a hint of the hull would emerge above the waterline.

So when 3,000 shipyard workers, sailors, and family members gathered for the *Scorpion* launching in Groton, Connecticut, on December 19, 1959, they were awed by what they saw. Resting on its large construction cradle, the 251-foot-long, 31.5-foot-diameter submarine towered over the crowd in the Electric Boat shipyard. Other than the sail structure with its stubby diving planes jutting up from the top center of the hull, the *Scorpion* was devoid of any exterior features. Every other piece of external gear—anchor, mooring cleats, antennas, and masts—was retracted flush into the hull or sail. Wetted by the chill rain, the *Scorpion*'s black teardrop-shaped hull gleamed menacingly under the floodlights that had been turned on to illuminate the submarine under the dark clouds overhead. Even the bright red-and-white banner capping the *Scorpion*'s bow and colorful navy signal flags and pennants could not diminish this image of naked power.

After sixteen months of construction, the *Scorpion* was ready for her inaugural voyage into the Thames River. Over the past few days, Electric

Several thousand navy officials, family members, and shipyard employees gathered at the Electric Boat Co. in Groton, Conn., on December 19, 1959, to watch the *Scorpion* slide down the shipway into the Thames River. *U.S. Navy Photo*

Boat workers had carefully lowered both submarine and cradle onto a grid of greased timbers resting on the slipway. Only a brake and trigger held back the forces of gravity that would send the submarine swooping stern-first into the Thames. After the obligatory speeches and martial music, the ship's sponsor, Elizabeth Morrison, stepped up onto the edge of the platform under the *Scorpion*. The daughter of the commander of a World War II diesel submarine named *Scorpion* lost at sea with all hands in 1944, Morrison said, "I christen thee United States Ship *Scorpion*," and smashed a bottle of champagne across the bow. Instantly, a shipyard worker hidden below pulled the trigger. With its officers on the tiny bridge and crewmen huddled on the curved hull clinging for dear life, the *Scorpion* hit the river in a towering furrow of water. The crowd cheered.[2]

Seven months later, upon its commissioning as a navy warship on July 29, 1960, the *Scorpion* became the second *Skipjack*-class nuclear attack submarine to join the fleet.

The year 1960 was a busy time at Electric Boat and other shipyards across the nation. Responding to what was perceived as a growing Soviet military threat, the navy undertook a crash buildup of both its nuclear attack submarine force and a new fleet of ballistic missile submarines. As the navy formally welcomed the *Scorpion* into the fleet that summer day, the riverfront at Electric Boat was teeming with workers building the nuclear attack submarine *USS Tullibee* (SSN 597) and a pair of *George Washington*–class missile submarines, the third and fourth to come from their shipyard. Another four *Skipjack*-class submarines and three attack boats belonging to the even more advanced *Thresher* class were under construction at other shipyards, and a follow-on attack boat—the *Sturgeon* class—was in the planning stages. By 1970, Electric Boat would have an unprecedented shipbuilding record: seventeen of the forty-one Polaris missile submarines; two of the six *Skipjacks*; three of the thirteen *Thresher* class; eleven of the modern *Sturgeons*; and the one-of-a-kind *USS Narwhal* (SSN 671), a *Sturgeon*-design attack submarine using a different model of reactor.[3]

The *Scorpion* and the other new submarines represented a quantum leap in technology that the U.S. Navy had been refining since the late 1940s. In fact, the *Scorpion* and the other *Skipjack*-class submarines represented not one revolution in undersea warfare but two—nuclear propulsion and a radical new hull design—that would allow them to excel in what submarine experts called the "holy trinity" of undersea warfare: speed, operating depth, and silence. It had taken years to get there, and the *Skipjacks* remained very much a work in progress.[4]

When *USS Nautilus* was commissioned on September 30, 1954, the U.S. Navy formally launched a revolution in submarine design and operations that dwarfed anything in the 164-year history of the service. It was a bigger technological leap than the shift from sailing vessels to coal- and oil-burning warships. The nuclear reactor transformed the submarine from a small submersible that did most of its maneuvering on the

With its construction finished but not yet a navy warship, the *Scorpion* was underway for builder's trials in the spring of 1960 with a number of guests, including nuclear submarine "godfather" Rear Admiral Hyman G. Rickover, seen here in civilian clothes at left on the port fairwater diving plane.

U.S. Navy Photo

surface with only a limited capability to lurk submerged while running on electric batteries, to a true underwater warship that could hide beneath the wave tops for months at a time.

The revolution had been long in the making. In 1938, Naval Research Laboratory (NRL) scientist Dr. Ross Gunn became intrigued by the idea of using nuclear power for submarines. The next year, navy scientists speculated that uranium fission—at that time more of a scientific theory than established fact—might become a source of propulsion in warships. In a meeting on March 17, 1939, Columbia University physicist Dr. George Pergram proposed to the head of the navy's Bureau of Steam Engineering that navy researchers get together with civilian experts to explore the possibility.

One of the men attending that meeting was Enrico Fermi, the Italian-born scientist who had recently won the Nobel Prize in Physics. In January 1939, Fermi learned about Danish physicist Neils Bohr's discovery of nuclear fission, the process in which radioactive isotopes emit particles and energy. On December 2, 1942, Fermi and his University of Chicago colleague Leó Szilárd became the scientists to build the world's first nuclear reactor and then demonstrate a controlled nuclear chain reaction.[5]

But with the country at war, the U.S. government's interest in nuclear fission quickly turned not to propulsion systems but to atomic bombs. The army was in charge of the super-secret Manhattan Project, and it seized control over all nuclear research and what small quantity of fissile materials then existed. Army generals had no use for submarines, nuclear or otherwise.

But the idea of nuclear-powered ship propulsion did not die. With atomic research expanding as the nation faced a growing postwar rivalry with the Soviet Union, Gunn and another NRL scientist, Dr. Philip H. Abelson, revived the concept of a nuclear-powered submarine. In late March 1946, Abelson, thirty-three, briefed the navy's leadership on the potential of nuclear ship propulsion. Abelson had drafted a twenty-seven-page report examining the feasibility of installing a nuclear pile as the propulsion source for a new submarine loosely modeled after an advanced German design for U-boats (U for *Untersee,* underwater). He concluded that "with a proper program, only about two years would be required to put into operation an atomic-powered submarine mechanically capable of operating at 26 knots to 30 knots submerged for many years without surfacing or refueling." While much of Abelson's findings were vague and theoretical, he predicted the operating capabilities of the *Skipjack*-class nuclear attack submarine a decade before the navy issued its first contract for the class of submarines to the Electric Boat Co. Even more importantly, he fired the imaginations of navy admirals.[6]

Vice Admiral Charles Lockwood, who had commanded the U.S. submarine campaign against Japan during World War II, later recalled his astonishment at hearing Abelson's briefing: "If I live to be a hundred, I shall never forget that meeting on March 28, 1946, in a large Bureau of Ships conference room, its walls lined with blackboards, which in turn were covered with diagrams, blueprints, figures and equations which Phil used to illustrate various points as he read from his document, the first ever submitted anywhere on nuclear-powered subs. It sounded like something out of Jules Verne's *Twenty Thousand Leagues Under the Sea*."[7]

Because of that meeting, the admirals proposed to then-Secretary of the Navy James V. Forrestal that the new civilian-run Atomic Energy Commission (AEC) bring in experienced navy engineering duty officers to begin work on nuclear propulsion concepts at the atomic power pile project at Oak Ridge, Tennessee. The navy selected eight officers and two civilian scientists for the assignment. One of them was an engineering officer, Captain Hyman G. Rickover, a 1922 Naval Academy graduate whose career to date had been mostly a series of technically challenging staff and engineering jobs and whose genius was his ability to get the job done while totally alienating his fellow officers.[8]

The navy's nuclear revolution began in fits and starts. In the chaos of postwar military demobilization and government reorganization, officials abandoned many new ideas simply because the executive branch working committees and government departments that would carry them out were disbanding, consolidating, or fighting for their next budget appropriation, and officials were struggling to keep their jobs. Amidst all this, the navy sent Rickover and a small group of naval engineers to Oak Ridge to explore design options for nuclear propulsion. There, one of the primary nuclear weapons plants that the army's Manhattan Project had constructed during its crash effort to make the atomic bomb was converting for postwar projects, primarily building new types of nuclear bombs. As navy officials dithered over how best to organize the nuclear propulsion venture, the army was planning to get out of the nuclear weapons business by handing over Oak Ridge and other facilities to the AEC.

Meanwhile, Rickover began waging a vigorous bureaucratic campaign to become the navy's point man on nuclear propulsion. In November 1947, after months of struggle and setbacks, Chief of Naval Operations Admiral Chester L. Nimitz endorsed a navy planning committee's recommendation to develop a nuclear submarine. That was a positive step, but not a battle won. Over the next two years, the navy's nuclear advocates struggled against civilian leaders' uncertainty, industrial corporations' ignorance of nuclear technology, and bureaucratic indifference within the AEC. But several corporations that had been deeply involved in the Manhattan Project—notably Westinghouse and General Electric—quietly assigned some of their scientists to begin work on the submarine reactor design challenge. At the same time, Rickover enticed two shipyards—Electric Boat in Groton and the Portsmouth Naval Shipyard in Kittery, Maine—to draft concepts for designing the submarine hulls in which the first reactors would go.

By 1950, Rickover had found a powerful ally in Congress, which had created a Joint Committee on Atomic Energy. On February 28 of that year Rickover convinced the bipartisan group to fast-track the nuclear submarine program, and in April, the navy submitted to Congress its proposed 1952 shipbuilding budget with a new line item: funds for one "SS(N)—submarine, nuclear propulsion."

The navy now proposed developing two different reactor designs. One would employ liquid sodium as the primary coolant that drew heat from the reactor fission process and created steam for driving the submarine's pumps and turbines. The second used pressurized water as the primary coolant. The navy would install the sodium reactor on the second nuclear submarine, *USS Seawolf* (SSN 572), but would ultimately choose the pressurized water design on every submarine it has built to this day.

Despite the major advances that nuclear power promised to bring to submarine design, the characteristics of that design remained essentially the same. In its official history, the Electric Boat Co. notes that it first began working on submarines a half-century earlier when in 1899 the company was established to bring to completion a fifty-four-foot submersible vessel developed by John P. Holland, an Irish immigrant who had pursued a lifelong ambition to design and build boats that could operate beneath the sea. From 1898, when Holland started building the U.S. Navy's first primitive submarine, and a year later, when the Electric Boat Company was founded to complete the project, to nearly a century later, when Electric Boat technicians used CAD-CAM computer software to refine the new *Seawolf*-class attack submarine, submarine design did not change much. Call it a fish, name it after a president, city, or state, the warship was still a steel cylinder with only a fin-shaped sail structure and diving planes emerging from the torpedo-shaped hull. Everything had to fit inside the tube. The nuclear propulsion system had to move its mass through the water. The ballasting system had to be able to submerge the submarine and bring it back to the surface on command. The sensors, navigational gear, weapons, and fire-control systems had to work to bring the boat to the correct spot in the ocean where it could locate, identify, and destroy the enemy. The overall design had to provide it with the speed, depth, and stealth necessary to do all of those things without betraying its presence to the enemy. And the life-support systems—electricity, water, air—had to enable the crew to survive inside the steel tube while doing all that.[9]

Nevertheless, the liberation of navy submarines from diesel-engine-and-battery propulsion was the nuclear reactor's greatest gift. It gave the submarine unlimited heat energy in a sealed system, allowing the boat to operate while submerged for months at a time, limited only by the food supply for the crew.

As Rickover and his staff of engineers and scientists worked with contractors to develop a successful reactor design, other scientists were beginning to realize that the reactor's immense power required a major revolution in the design of the submarine hull. There were a large number of variables at play, and each would create a major headache. A larger propulsion system requires a heavier and larger reactor power plant. This in turn requires a larger hull diameter and length to accommodate it. Yet as the hull increases in length and surface area, it creates more drag in the water, undercutting the increased power that the larger reactor brings to the submarine. More weapons—torpedoes, mines, and, later, submarine-launched cruise missiles—have the same effect. As does a larger crew. Meanwhile, efforts in quieting the submarine remained, according to Rickover, "a bigger job than nuclear power." Just as challenging would be to protect a hundred or so sailors from the nuclear genii sharing that steel tube. So as the reactor revolution picked up speed, another team of scientists was searching for a new submarine hull that could enable submariners to capitalize on nuclear power to its fullest.[10]

At the start of World War II, the German and Japanese navies were technologically superior to the Americans. The Germans with their Type VIIC and later Type XXI and XXIII U-boat designs waged war against enemy shipping from the approaches to Murmansk to the U.S. Gulf Coast and Caribbean. The Japanese, with superiority in torpedo design and their own excellent submarine technology, sank U.S. and Allied ships from mid-Pacific to the Indian Ocean. But the Allies caught up and by 1943 decimated the German U-boats and by 1945 the Japanese Navy. After World War II, American submarine designers did what wartime victors have done throughout the ages: They plundered the wealth of the vanquished.

In the ten years immediately after the war, the United States, Great Britain, and the Soviet Union rushed to exploit German technology they had seized after the Nazi surrender, particularly the Type XXI U-boat design, which had entered the war late, in 1944. The legacy of master submarine designer Helmuth Walter, the Type XXI was state of the art: Its snorkel device allowed the boat to recharge its electric batteries without fully surfacing; its closed-cycle diesel engine reused its exhaust for further combustion; and its streamlined hull enabled the Type XXI to sprint underwater at nearly seventeen knots with a submerged maximum range of 360 nautical miles—three times that of the mainstay Type VIIC U-boat. If Germany had launched a massive fleet of Type XXIs a few years earlier, the outcome of World War II might have been very different.

The boats that dominated undersea naval operations from 1945 until 1954—the American *Tang*-class diesel attack submarine, the British *Porpoise* class, and the Soviet Whiskey-class attack boats—all stemmed from the Type XXI. Even the *Nautilus* and other American nuclear attack submarines of the late 1950s featured hull designs that more closely resembled the German U-boat than anything else.[11]

Walter's design was perfect for diesel-fueled German U-boats, but it proved less effective with the introduction of nuclear propulsion and the significant increase in submerged speed that the reactor provided. To build the *Nautilus* and its immediate successors, the navy inserted a nuclear reactor into a *Tang*-class diesel boat hull—the son of Walter's Type XXI. But they quickly discovered a design flaw: The submarines became unstable at higher submerged speeds: Above eight knots, the submarine would tend to "fly," with the bow pitching sharply up. The resulting loss of control could prove fatal.

The design solution came from an unlikely source: It was inspired not by a type of enemy submarine but by a British blimp. Using the dirigible shape, British scientists produced a shorter, blunter hull design. As submarine design expert Norman Friedman notes, "The new hull was dynamically stable at all speeds, yet easy to dive. For a given displacement it was shorter than a conventional submarine, hence much more maneuverable." While shorter, the new hull offered designers the chance to stack propulsion gear, equipment, weapons, and crew in multiple deck levels. And the new submarine, with a smaller external surface area, required only one shaft and propeller rather than the two that were the norm in World War II.[12]

Designers at Electric Boat embraced the British concept and quickly produced a pint-sized, diesel-powered experimental submarine named the *USS Albacore* (AGSS 569). Like several other diesel boats designed in the 1950s and 1960s, the *Albacore* was a noncombatant built exclusively to test new systems and designs. The navy did not waste a nickel on torpedo tubes or deck guns. The hull was everything, design verification the solitary mission. Only 210 feet in length and twenty-seven feet at maximum beam, the *Albacore* displaced just 1,850 tons submerged, making it half the size of the *Skipjacks* that later would owe it credit for their shape and form.[13]

The *Albacore* first took to sea in 1953, and the admirals were ecstatic. With its 15,000 shaft-horsepower Westinghouse electric motor, it was the little submarine that could: It raced through the deep at twenty-six knots, 2.7 knots better than the nuclear *Nautilus* and other early-model nuclear boats. The four *Skate*-class submarines that followed were close in design and operating limitations to the *Nautilus*. When designers modified the *Albacore* by installing new silver-zinc batteries and a pair of counter-rotating propellers, the effect was even more astounding. The submarine's top speed reached thirty-three knots, the submarine version of supersonic flight. The new *Skipjack* class got a makeover of hull and propulsion reactor design, using the Westinghouse S5W pressurized water reactor inside an *Albacore* hull. The *Albacore* hull went into full production with the *Skipjack* and its five sister ships, of which *Scorpion* was the second built. The hull would also dictate the design parameters of all follow-on submarine classes, from the *Thresher/Permit* and *Sturgeon* fast attack boats of the 1960s, the *Los Angeles* class submarines of the 1970s and 1980s, and the advanced *Seawolf* and *Virginia* attack submarine classes that entered service decades after the *Albacore* itself had retired in 1972.[14]

The interior of the *Scorpion* was as revolutionary as the shape of its hull. The heart of the submarine was the S5W nuclear reactor, a relatively small but extremely powerful source of thermal energy used to create steam to drive the submarine's propeller and electrical generators. Even the "nucs" who operated the *Scorpion*'s S5W rarely touched the actual onboard reactor system, for it was imbedded in a heavily shielded containment structure within the sealed reactor compartment itself. They were familiar with its design and function and had seen mockups and diagrams of the propulsion plant at the navy's Nuclear Power School.

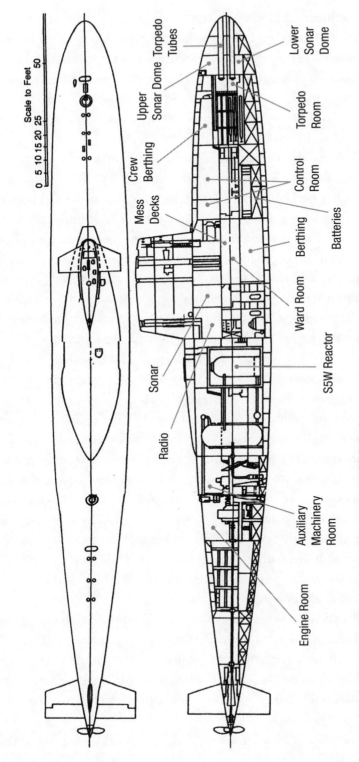

Interior diagram and external bird's-eye view of the *USS Scorpion*

Onboard the *Scorpion,* the reactor compartment was a narrow, twenty-foot-long hull segment located amidships just aft of the sail. It functioned as a physical divider between the torpedo compartment, control room, and berthing spaces at the forward end of the submarine, and the larger machinery and engine compartments at the aft end. Connecting the two halves was a narrow tunnel atop the reactor compartment providing crew access between the two ends.

Despite the lead and other shielding, submariners did not linger in the tunnel, one *Scorpion* crewman recalled. "You could see the reactor through a heavily shielded lead glass window," said Bill Elrod, the submarine's leading sonarman in 1968. "There's an access in the floor of the tunnel . . . all you could see is the top of the vessel. The nucs would make a reactor compartment entry as a routine part of their job of going in there to ensure this and that was okay, but it was a very controlled operation when the plant was shut down." But when the reactor was critical, he added, "You were not supposed to loiter in the tunnel because that was the rule. Don't hang around, why take a chance?"[15]

The S5W appeared to be much larger that it actually was. A pressurized water reactor (PWR) system consists of several major components. These include the reactor vessel itself that contains the fuel core and control rod assembly. The heart of the reactor is the fuel core, a cluster of fuel assemblies containing a number of individual fuel rods. Each fuel rod in the S5W was a zirconium metal alloy tube packed with highly radioactive uranium dioxide pellets and sealed with helium gas. Although the design specifications for all naval nuclear reactors remain classified today, a typical commercial PWR reactor would have several fuel assemblies of 200–300 fuel rods apiece. One submariner explained, "You'd be surprised how small this thing actually is: On a *Trident* [missile submarine], the reactor vessel is actually the size of an office desk. The core itself is the size of a small waste can."[16]

The S5W was nevertheless extremely powerful: The energy from the reactor core was strong enough that it could generate 15,000 shaft horsepower to drive the 3,500-ton submarine through the water at speeds up to thirty-five knots—faster than even the *Albacore* at flank speed. And the core—for that early era of nuclear propulsion—was especially long-lived. The *Nautilus* ran only 62,562 nautical miles on its first reactor core before the submarine required a refueling. A second, improved-design reactor core allowed the *Nautilus* to travel another 91,324 nautical miles. The *Scorpion's* S5W was rated for 140,000 nautical miles. The *Scorpion* ran for seven years on its original fuel core before receiving a new one at Norfolk Naval Shipyard in 1967.[17]

The rest of the *Scorpion's* propulsion system, mounted in the auxiliary machinery room and engine room further aft, translated the reactor's heat into mechanical energy—steam—for propelling the submarine through the water. It also powered two ship's service turbine generators that created electrical energy to run everything else—from the torpedo fire-control circuits to the wardroom refrigerator to the reactor controls themselves. The principle was as simple as the mechanisms to carry it out were complex. The S5W works when its nuclear fuel is engaged in a chain reaction. Unless blocked by absorptive material—in this case, control rods containing boron that when lowered into the fuel core absorb the neutrons and slow down or halt entirely the fission process—the fuel rods would emit a constant shower of neutrons, which, striking other uranium atoms nearby, then released even more neutrons, generating more and more heat inside the core. Unlike an atomic bomb, where the warhead material is designed to engage in a runaway fission reaction within milliseconds to create the nuclear fireball, a reactor fuel core is meant to operate under controlled conditions over an extended period of time.

Nevertheless, submarine reactor operators, like their civilian counterparts, knew well the lethal potential of the heated core. Reactors could easily become bombs themselves. In 1985, at the Soviet Far East port of Chazma Bay during the defueling of a decommissioned Echo-II nuclear submarine, shipyard workers forgot to disconnect the reactor control rods from the roof of the reactor vessel. When they lifted the lid free, the rods all pulled out of the core. In an instant the nuclear fuel went supercritical and exploded. The radiation accident killed ten workers and contaminated fifty square miles of land and water.[18]

The S5W contained two separate but intertwined coolant systems to transfer the heat energy from the reactor vessel while leaving its lethal radiation safely behind. The primary coolant—fresh water heavily contaminated from passing through the reactor core—ran in a sealed network of pipes from the vessel to a larger steam generator, then returned to the reactor vessel in a constant flow. The primary coolant remained locked in its piping system and maintained in liquid form by a pressurizer that kept the liquid at about 2,200 psi. Primary coolant entered the steam generator at a temperature of 600 degrees. Inside the steam generator, which was part of the secondary loop, heat from the primary coolant transferred to the water there, raising its temperature to a point where it flashed into steam. That steam then passed through several turbines in the *Scorpion*'s stern that powered the massive reduction gears that lowered the rotor's speed from hundreds of turns per second to tens of turns per second or slower for the propeller shaft. Other pipes led the steam into the two turbine generators that created electricity to run the ship's equipment. Once it passed through the turbines, the secondary water (steam) then entered a condenser that lowered its temperature and returned the once-again liquid secondary coolant back into the steam generator, again in a constant flow. It ran like a Swiss watch.

***

WHEN SONARMAN Second Class Bill Elrod reported to the *Scorpion* at Norfolk's Pier 22 in May 1964, he already had five years of service in the navy behind him, four of which he had spent as a sonar operator on a destroyer. But the twenty-two-year-old Texas native had never been on a submarine before.

Earmarked for sonar duty while at navy boot camp in 1959, Elrod had attended the navy's "A" school for sonar technicians and formed friendships with several classmates who went directly into the submarine force. While stationed in Pearl Harbor on the radar picket destroyer *USS Forster* (DER 344), Elrod became attracted to both the idea of duty in submarines and the relatively relaxed lifestyle that submariners enjoyed while in port. "I used to hang out with them, go down to the boats," he recalled. "We'd roll the cook out of his rack and fry steaks at three in the morning." While submariners lived like sardines in a can at sea, it was different in port. When the subs were in port, "those guys

The control room of a *Skipjack*-class submarine was a relatively large compartment on the upper deck amidships that was jammed with controls and electronic equipment. Seen from the periscope platform, the ballast control panel is at left and the two planesmen control seats are at the far end. *U.S. Navy Photo*

had a barracks to live in," he said. So when his first four-year term was up, Elrod decided to re-enlist and apply for submarine duty. In early 1964, he breezed through the twelve-week Navy Submarine School course and three weeks of submarine sonar refresher training in Key West, arriving at the Norfolk Destroyer-Submarine Piers on a glorious spring day.[19]

As he clambered down the access ladder into the submarine's control room, Elrod was as mystified as any civilian seeing a nuclear submarine for the first time. Elrod found a labyrinth of crowded steel spaces jammed with incomprehensible pieces of heavy equipment, piping, miles of cable, and electrical wires—with a small collection of government-issue furniture seemingly thrown in as an afterthought. Passageways with temporary electrical cables cluttering the deck and instrument panels torn apart for routine maintenance added to the confusion. If the compressed space didn't trigger claustrophobia, the compact circular hull could easily disorient the newcomer. The outside walls curved tightly in, reflecting the submarine's smooth hull form. The only signs of normalcy were the flat deck and overhead surfaces inside.

To enter the *Scorpion,* sailors passed through a hatchway on the side of the sail where they found a vertical ladder that descended into the control room that was located on the upper deck amidships. There were two other access hatches on the main deck leading down into the torpedo compartment forward or the engine room aft, but those two were used primarily by sailors going topside for line-handling or routine maintenance when the submarine was in port or operating on the surface. To pass through all three hatches required a lot of hunching over and careful footwork on the narrow vertical rungs. The forward and aft access hatches actually entered into small rescue chambers that could hold two crewmen, with a second hatchway then leading down into the submarine itself.

When Elrod reached the control room, a crewman stepped forward to escort him to the enlisted berthing compartment three decks down in the center of the submarine. He found an assigned rack and stashed his seabag. After dropping off copies of his orders at the small ship's office aft of the control room, he met briefly with the commanding officer and his new division officer. Then Elrod followed his escort through the tight passageways on an orientation tour of the boat, beginning with the torpedo compartment.

Located at the very front of the hull, the torpedo compartment was one of the two largest spaces aboard the submarine. The chamber ran 32.5 feet back from a vertical bulkhead at Frame 13 where the six bronze torpedo tube loading hatches jutted out about five feet from the bulkhead. The torpedo tubes themselves emerged from the hull, where their outer shutter doors were flush on the curving outer surface of the bow.[20]

The torpedo compartment was far from empty. Elrod peered at a forest of hydraulic lines, electrical cables, valve handles, and other control mechanisms surrounding the six torpedo tube access hatches where they emerged from the forward bulkhead. On the main deck in the torpedo compartment, a 4.5-foot-wide passageway ran the length of the room. The compartment was crammed with gear, including a pair of bulky torpedo-handling cradles resting on moveable struts.

In port, the torpedoes were absent from the torpedo compartment, making it appear deceptively roomy. In the final weeks before a deployment, the *Scorpion*'s torpedo gang and a working party from the submarine tender *Orion* would load the full complement of weapons through the torpedo access hatch that opened into the torpedo compartment at an angle from the main deck overhead. At sea, the weapons would further fill the space, stacked on storage racks throughout the room. To load a torpedo into a torpedo tube, crewmen would move one of them from a storage rack onto one of the loading trays, then move the weapon horizontally or vertically to align with the open torpedo tube. A moveable ram would then slowly push the weapon into its launcher. In addition to the torpedoes, during normal operations the torpedo compartment was also packed with ancillary equipment and people. During its ill-fated deployment in 1968, the *Scorpion* carried twenty-three torpedoes ranging in size from the mainstay Mark 37, 11.3 feet long and weighing 1,430 pounds, to the nuclear-tipped Mark 45 ASTOR that was 18.9 feet long and weighed 2,217 pounds. Under these conditions, the storage racks on either side of the torpedo compartment would also be full. The compartment also featured a lower-level torpedo storage area accessible by removable deck plates. Throw in the seven-man torpedo gang, and the compartment resembled a subway car at rush hour.[21]

Climbing up an aluminum ladder at the after end of the torpedo compartment, Elrod next toured the mezzanine deck where a snug berthing compartment was tucked up into the top of the hull. Here, about a dozen crewmen slept in metal bunks stacked in threes amidships and in pairs against the inner curve of the hull.

As in the main crew compartment down below, each sailor's space consisted of his bunk and a single 26-by-24-inch metal storage locker. False wood paneling on interior walls and beige floor tiles provided the barest semblance of normalcy. Space efficiency was the rule. The washroom sink folded up out of the way when not in use. A sailor entering the compartment always risked bashing his head on an array of forward ballast tank control valves that jutted down from the overhead.

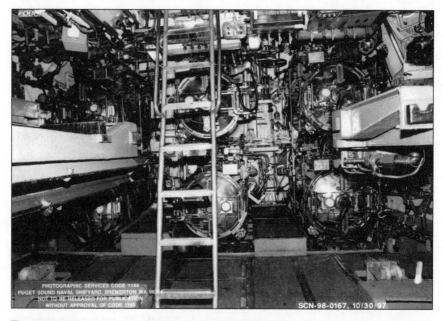

The second-largest compartment on the *Skipjack*-class submarine was the forward torpedo room, which ran nearly 33 feet from the forward bulkhead where six torpedo tube doors jutted out, to the rear bulkhead at Frame 26. The six torpedo tube doors can be seen on the far bulkhead. Large cradles partially visible at left and right were used to move torpedoes from their storage racks for loading into the torpedo tubes. *U.S. Navy Photo*

As elsewhere on the boat, pipes, electrical cables, and other gear sprang out of the steel, further subtracting from the available space.

The rear of the bow compartment ended some 67.5 feet back from the bow at a solid vertical steel bulkhead that plugged the entire hull at Frame 26. To maintain its strength against the extreme hydrostatic pressure while operating submerged, the *Scorpion* consisted of six interior compartments separated by these thick circular steel bulkheads that acted as structural supports. Designers maximized their strength by minimizing the number of holes cut into them. The net result was a series of bottlenecks as one moved through the *Scorpion*. To get from the bow compartment to the rest of the submarine, there was only a solitary access hatch set in the middle of the 1.5-inch steel bulkhead at Frame 26. Crewmen usually left this 20-by-38-inch oval hatch open during routine transit but slammed it shut and locked it during general quarters or in emergencies. Similar constrictions occurred on either end of the reactor compartment access tunnel, and with the hatchways linking the auxiliary machinery room and engine compartment to the rest of the interior. Much of the *Scorpion* was a single-file pathway. Reaching the center part of the *Scorpion,* Elrod noticed that the wider hull diameter amidships permitted four deck levels, an unheard of innovation in submarine design. The German Type XXI U-boat, the U.S. Navy's *Tang*-class postwar diesel boats, and even the first-generation U.S. nuclear submarines all featured the lengthy, slender, two-deck hull that World War II submariners had long known. The second hull segment of the *Scorpion* featured the ship's control room, sonar, and radio rooms on the top level; officer berthing and wardroom and the enlisted crew eating area below; and a larger enlisted berthing compartment down on the third level along with a pair of battery compartments housing the *Scorpion's* emergency propulsion capability at the very bottom.

The torpedo compartment hatchway opened directly onto the middle deck and the *Scorpion's* main living and dining spaces. On the starboard side, the crew's mess and galley enabled several dozen sailors, about one-fourth of the crew, to dine at a time. A half-dozen of the *Scorpion's* crew worked full-time there as cooks or assistants. The crew mess area was a simple, medium-sized space with four dining tables and chairs bolted to the deck, similar to but much smaller than the eating spaces Elrod had known on the *Forster* in Hawaii.[22]

Continuing on, Elrod and his guide paused for a quick glimpse of the officers' wardroom and berthing compartments that took up the port side on the second level. These spaces were also smaller than their counterparts on surface ships, but since there was only one officer for each ten enlisted crewmen on the *Skipjack*-class attack boat, the net result was more privacy and a bit more elbow room. Still, to say that the *Scorpion* officers had better living accommodations than the enlisted men is to acknowledge that oppression can be a relative thing. Three officers shared each of the three four-by-six-foot berthing compartments adjoining a slightly larger, nine-by-twelve-foot wardroom. A tier of three bunks— with the ends obscured by lockers and other wall-mounted items—filled the far wall of each tiny space. To get into bed, an officer would have to sit on the edge in the middle, scrunch up into a ball, and then carefully extend his feet and head to stretch out. Each officer had a small personal effects locker, shared one desk with his two roommates, and like their enlisted subordinates, folded the washbasin sink up and away when it was not in use. When there were more than nine officers plus the captain on board—a common occurrence—the junior-most lieutenants would find themselves temporarily exiled to the small chief petty officers' berthing compartment down below. Only the *Scorpion's* commanding officer enjoyed his own private stateroom, but it, too, was small enough that the skipper slept on a navy version of a Murphy bed—a fold-down bunk that when secured against the bulkhead would allow the skipper use of a small worktable that could seat all of two people.

Back up in the control room, Elrod paid closer attention to the layout and detail, since his duty station in the sonar shack was nearby. This was the submarine's brain, he knew—a combination of the navigation bridge and combat information center located in separate places in a destroyer or cruiser. Whether conning (directing) the submarine, diving or surfacing the boat, or preparing a practice or actual torpedo attack, the *Scorpion's* commander and his duty watchstanders worked in this twenty-foot-wide, thirty-five-foot-long space on the top level of the submarine. Despite its size, this room also would have oppressed the claustrophobic, for it too was jammed with equipment and stuffed with crewmen. Between twelve and sixteen sailors would be crouched over controls and manning the equipment in this living room–sized space. On prolonged missions, it would reek of cigarette smoke and the smell of underwashed men.

Elrod stepped quickly up on the short platform where the two periscope cylinders stood and glanced forward. At the forward-most bulkhead on the port side, two aircraft-type seats indicated where the duty planesmen sat strapped in with four-point seat belts to control the submarine's movement through the water. They faced an instrument panel that depicted the *Scorpion's* course, speed, depth, diving angle, and other key inputs. Each used a control wheel—not unlike a car's steering wheel—and foot pedals to drive the *Scorpion* using the submarine's two

The helmsman of a *Skipjack*-class attack submarine uses an aircraft-like control wheel and foot pedals to handle both steering and vertical movement. The submarines had twin controls side by side in the cramped control room with one crewman normally operating the rudder and the second handling the control planes. Instruments and lights are attached to the curving hull.
U.S. Navy Photo

sets of diving planes. Depending on the situation, the captain could use two planesmen, with one operating the stern planes and rudder, and his partner controlling the fairwater planes mounted on the sail. Or the controls could be transferred so that just one sailor would operate all three systems directly.

Immediately to the right of the platform, facing the starboard side of the compartment, was another workstation where the watchstanders monitored the Mark 15 fire-control panel that provided navigational inputs and firing orders to the torpedoes in their tubes. This included the torpedo's initial course and speed after launching, its initial search pattern, and final attack instructions. A third instrument panel on the port side of the control room just aft of where the planesmen sat featured the ballast controls and sealed-hatch indicators used by the diving officer of the watch to submerge the submarine or send it back up to the surface.

The control room—like every other nook on the boat—conveyed a strange, impersonal intimacy with the exterior bulkhead curving in tightly overhead just a few feet above where the crewmen sat. As everywhere else on the boat, the circular steel frames and bulkheads were adorned with gauges, hydraulic lines, wiring, and instruments.

The officer of the deck (OOD) was the man responsible for conning the submarine under normal underway conditions. He usually stood where Elrod was on the small raised platform, an arm's reach away from where the two chrome periscopes emerged from the lower decks and continued on up to the top of the sail. There was just room for another officer here, and the captain usually had a small chair in which he could sit while monitoring the control room watch. At the rear of the room was the navigational station, where the ship's navigator and duty quartermasters plotted the *Scorpion's* location and future courses and speeds using a variety of pre-GPS navigational technology, including a handheld sextant like the ones used by sailors for the past two centuries.[23]

At the rear of the control room, several small rooms housed sonar operators, radiomen, and administrative yeomen. The tiny ship's office was across a narrow passageway from the sonar shack and radio room on the port side. Elrod and his escort next opened a hatchway door and stepped through the narrow tunnel at the top of the reactor compartment connecting the forward and after halves of the submarine. A small window of heavily leaded glass on the deck marked where the submarine's S5W reactor sat. Aft of the reactor compartment, the *Scorpion's* engineering spaces seemed much roomier than the forward part of the submarine, but it was hotter and much noisier than the forward end of the boat. Despite the reactor's metal shielding and thick layers of insulation covering the machinery, the engineering space temperatures frequently exceeded 100 degrees Fahrenheit. A strong aroma of ozone and lubricating oil came from the electrical motors and pumps.

Just aft of the reactor tunnel was the auxiliary machinery room, a cylindrical hull section thirty-two feet long. It was crammed on two levels with ancillary gear including the reactor steam generator, diesel motor generator, auxiliary seawater pumps, and primary electrical breakers. This compartment then connected with the *Scorpion's* two-story, 67.5-

foot-long engine room, which took up the rear one-third of the hull. This compartment began as a circular space thirty feet in diameter but steadily tapered off to a narrow end only twelve feet across where the propeller shaft exited the hull. It contained the *Scorpion's* propulsion turbines and ship's service turbine generators; the massive reduction gear assembly; the air conditioning plant and ship's condensers; and other equipment. Continuing the tour, Elrod and his escort arrived at a compact, closed-off office space known as the maneuvering room. When underway, the engineering officer of the watch, duty throttleman, reactor plant operator, and electric plant operator sat at workstations here gazing at their assigned array of dials, gauges, and control switches and levers as they kept the reactor burning and the propeller turning. On a typical day underway, about a third of the *Scorpion's* crew would be on watch. From the Mark 14 torpedo tubes in the bow all the way to the pressurized shaft seal more than 250 feet astern, officers and enlisted specialists kept the machinery working, drove the submarine through the dark depths, cooked the meals, and monitored the reactor. This does not mean the other crewmen were lazing about. Many of the junior crewmen were busy in their on-the-job training to earn their Dolphin insignia as qualified submariners. Junior officers likewise were learning the ropes from their seniors. Newly transferred crewmen needed to obtain formal certification as watchstanders. And there were drills and emergency exercises galore: fire, flooding, reactor shutdown, general quarters, and simulated combat. A submarine at sea is a very busy place, and a submarine in port was far from inactive. After the tour, Elrod's guide introduced him to an older man for a formal welcoming conversation. He was Torpedoman Chief Walter Bishop, the chief of the boat. Years later, Elrod recalled this meeting as a pivotal moment in his navy career.

In 1964, Walter Bishop was a thirty-three-year-old torpedoman chief who had served on the *Scorpion* since September 1959, three months before its launching. A New Hampshire native, he had joined the navy in 1948 after graduating from high school and had previously served on two diesel submarines and the nuclear attack boat *USS Sargo* (SSN 583), the navy's fifth nuclear submarine, prior to joining the *Scorpion's* pre-commissioning crew. It was a sign of his leadership potential and maturity, one former *Scorpion* officer recalled, that *Scorpion* skipper Commander Robert "Yogi" Kaufman appointed Bishop chief of the boat even before he had received his promotion to the rank of chief petty officer.

Years later, Elrod said he could not remember the exact conversation they had on his first day as a *Scorpion* crewman, but he remembered the older man's impact. Twenty-one years later, when he himself retired in 1985 as a senior chief with two tours as a chief of the boat under his belt, Elrod recalled Bishop by name to the audience at his retirement ceremony: Bishop, he said, was the sailor "I tried my damnedest to emulate."

The *Scorpion* crew loved their boat, both for what it was and for what it could do. "The 588-class submarine is an extremely maneuverable ship when going ahead either submerged or surfaced," then-Lieutenant Sanford Levey wrote in a 1962 technical paper assessing the boat's ship-handling characteristics based on his experience aboard the *USS Shark* (SSN 591), the fifth *Skipjack*. "It is the 'sports car' of ships and affords a genuine feeling of accomplishment to those who handle it correctly." Levey later joined the *Scorpion* in 1963 as executive officer.[24]

Retired Rear Admiral Walter N. "Buck" Dietzen, who served as commander of the *USS Scamp* when it joined the fleet in October 1960, looked back years later with affection for the *Skipjack* class. "It was great, the Austin Healey of the submarine force. It was a small submarine displacing only 3,000 tons. She could turn on a dime."[25]

To Bill Elrod, it was the submarine's sprint speed that left the deepest impression. "The *Scorpion* with a five-bladed screw [propeller] was a rocket. That thing was fast! It could give you a heart attack." Considering that the fastest surface ship at the time could only race along at thirty to thirty-two knots, the *Scorpion's* flank speed of thirty-five knots—just over forty miles per hour on land—would give the submarine's crew great amusement as they baffled and frustrated their surface sailor comrades during anti-submarine warfare exercises. Retired Vice Admiral Al Baciocco, who served in the *Scorpion's* first crew as a lieutenant and later commanded the *Gato* during the search for the *Scorpion,* said he was awestruck to learn one day that he was traveling faster underwater than he had ever done in his prior service on a navy cruiser.[26]

But speed was a mixed blessing. The modern nuclear fast-attack submarine had unprecedented speed and an operating depth that vastly exceeded its predecessors. But the safety envelope was exceedingly narrow. "They were new, very complex, had capabilities that pushed the limits of the control systems," said retired Captain Robert Pirie, who served on the *Scorpion* as engineering officer during 1962–63 and went on to command the *USS Skipjack* (SSN 585) several years later. "There were a lot of things about the tactics and operations of the ship that you found out by doing. In some cases they hadn't done any theoretical or modeling work to tell you what the limits were. For example, what speed can you shoot what torpedoes out of which tubes? This was something we had to find out for ourselves. What ranges can you detect a snorkeling submarine? Can you expect to outrun a torpedo if you hear it launched—that question never occurred to a diesel submariner—if he heard a torpedo launched, he was already in deep trouble."[27]

One renowned U.S. submariner provided a simple visualization exercise to help a civilian comprehend the actual limited operating environment for nuclear submarines. In his novel *Cold Is the Sea,* retired Captain Edward L. Beach described it this way: Go to a room in your house with an eight-foot ceiling, then imagine it completely full of water—that's the Atlantic Ocean with a two-mile depth. At that scale, a 251-foot-long submarine like the *Scorpion* would be the size of a 2.5-inch wooden matchstick. Despite its tough steel hull and nuclear reactor, the submarine can only operate in the narrow band of water descending thirteen inches from the ceiling (the surface)—that is, only five times the length of its own hull. Diving below that invisible barrier is instantly fatal since it marks the submarine's "crush depth," the point where the hydrostatic pressure of the water reaches the point where it overwhelms the submarine's steel pressure hull.[28]

Beach's exercise illustrated the point all too clearly: The *Scorpion* and other modern nuclear submarines were so powerful that if the captain, officer of the deck, or duty planesman made a miscalculation, it could doom the submarine within seconds.

Dietzen said that, when he was commander of the *Scamp* during 1960–62, concern over exceeding the submarine's safety margin was always on everyone's mind. "The problem was, that was a fast little bugger. Their test depth [the maximum depth that a submarine is permitted to operate at under peacetime circumstances] was not nearly as deep as the submarines are today. If you had a hydraulic system casualty and then you complicate that thing with a personnel casualty on top, [for instance if you went] to full dive instead of full rise [on the control planes], you had only fifteen seconds to recover before test depth. It's a tight envelope."[29]

Pirie said the submarine was never far from danger. "You're in this big thing that displaces 3,500 tons . . . and it's charging along through the water at a rate of speed that isn't much in terms of how fast you can drive your car, but in terms of how fast ships go, pretty impressive. There's associated vibrations. And then this thing takes a thirty-degree down-angle. So you're heading for the bottom at something over ten knots. Well, thirty [degrees] down is a pretty striking angle. It doesn't sound like much, but when you're in this big thing it feels like a lot."[30]

The *Scorpion's* incredible responsiveness was, like its speed, a source of both delight and anxiety. Bill Elrod and other *Scorpion* veterans said the submarine's movements during a high-speed turn required extreme caution by the crew. Once the rudder moved to turn the submarine to the left or right, Elrod explained, the hull would then rotate in the direction of the turn. As it rotated, the rudder would begin to act as a control plane set on dive, pushing the submarine deeper in the water. Pirie noted that even veteran crewmen could be taken by surprise by the swiftness of the *Scorpion's* response. "When you put the rudder over at high speed, the dynamic forces on the sail cause the ship to heel a lot. The *Scorpion* could take a snap roll of fifty degrees when you put the rudder over at high speed. I've been sitting at the wardroom table [and] been flung out through the scuttle into the pantry. Not paying much attention. It was not so much being tossed—the ship heels over and you fall."[31]

So as the *Scorpion* first took to sea in the summer of 1960, its crew had to work hard to master the promise and peril of the technology. Much of that learning lay ahead: When the *Scorpion* formally entered the fleet as the second ship in its class, the *Skipjack* had been in commission for only fourteen months. The navy was still trying to determine not only how the new submarine design would perform but what tactics would work best in a number of new missions. The design engineers at Naval Reactors Branch made the ship's blueprints and the shipwrights at Electric Boat translated them into forged steel, but it would be the crew of the *Scorpion* who would write its operating manual.

ON AUGUST 24, 1960, just four weeks after donning its commissioning pennant, the *Scorpion* cast loose from the pier at the New London Submarine Base for a two-month series of NATO exercises near the United Kingdom. Commander Norman Bessac, who had shepherded the submarine through its final construction, could now boast that he commanded the most advanced nuclear attack submarine in the world. The *Scorpion*'s mission across the Atlantic was a combination of routine drills and public relations: to shake down the submarine and to demonstrate to the U.S. Navy's closest allies its vastly superior capability. Elrod, who joined the *Scorpion* in 1964, recalled similar drills aimed at honing antisubmarine warfare skills. The *Scorpion* would sometimes engage in a little psychological warfare along with the combat drills: "If you're in an exercise . . . [the captain] would say, 'Don't exceed fifteen knots or a fifteen-degree down-angle.' The destroyers would get to feeling cocky because they would find you and run you around. Then the admiral on the carrier would start feeling his oats and say to us, 'Okay, let her rip,' then *pheeewsh*—we'd just vanish. The place we'd hide most of the time was right under the carrier. Its propulsion plant is so noisy and so huge that you get yourself under the carrier and ride along there."[32]

The *Scorpion* impressed NATO and the British news media. During a rare press tour of the nuclear submarine, veteran London military reporter Desmond Wettern sang the *Scorpion*'s praises for the quality of life aboard: "The boat . . . is air-conditioned throughout and so long as the reactor is running and the condenser is operating there is ample water always available. Bunks, in separate compartments from the mess halls, have curtains and reading lights and do not have to be stowed away in working hours." He particularly lauded the lunch served in the crew mess decks: "grilled steak, sautéed mushrooms, O'Brien potatoes . . .

green beans, bread, butter, coffee." Unlike the British Navy, which still allowed alcoholic beverages on board, the reporter noted, "The special duplicating machine ink is the only 'hard liquor' carried."[33]

The only glitch in the *Scorpion*'s visit occurred in mid-September during Exercise Fishplay in the Atlantic west of Ireland when the submarine failed to respond to a radio message from the British admiralty. After twenty-four hours of silence, London issued a precautionary SubMiss alert but canceled it after Atlantic Submarine Force headquarters in Norfolk informed the admiralty that the *Scorpion* was operating on an extended radio silence order.[34]

By the end of 1960, the *Scorpion* was a fully active warship in the Atlantic Submarine Force. In September 1961, it transferred to its new homeport in Norfolk as a unit of Submarine Squadron 6. Crewmen recalled a steady pace of activity focusing on training exercises and research-and-development projects to further refine nuclear submarine warfare tactics in a variety of operations. "In those days we were pioneers," retired Vice Admiral Baciocco recalled of his *Scorpion* tour as a lieutenant during 1959–61. "The procedures were nowhere as detailed as they are now. We were operating on the edge of the envelope."[35]

For the first two years in commission, the *Scorpion* engaged in research cruises and training operations. In training exercises along the Atlantic coast and near Bermuda and Puerto Rico, the submarine took turns hunting U.S. Navy surface ships and being hunted by anti–submarine warfare units. Some assignments did nothing for military preparedness. One chore universally unpopular among the crew was to host day trips off the Virginia Capes for visiting delegations of senior military leaders, members of Congress, and other VIPs. As one *Scorpion* officer put it, "We just took everyone in the world out to sea. The worst thing was to get back after a seventy-day deployment on Saturday and on Monday have to get underway to take some congressman for a ride."[36]

The *Scorpion* was far more than a showboat or a state-of-the-art training vessel, however. Within a year of joining the fleet, the Atlantic Submarine Force in May 1961 dispatched the submarine to the far north. Its mission: spy on the Soviet Northern Fleet.

4

THE SECRET WAR

SONARMAN SECOND CLASS BILL ELROD SAT NERVOUSLY CHAIN-smoking as he listened to the sounds from the Soviet submarine coming through his sweat-stained headset. It was October 13, 1965, and the twenty-three-year-old sailor and two other watchstanders were crouched in the *Scorpion's* tiny sonar shack just aft of the submarine's control room. No one was speaking above a whisper; the *Scorpion* was rigged for ultra-quiet. Its skipper, Commander Ralph Ghormley, thirty-eight, conferred with several other men in a low murmur as the nuclear attack submarine tiptoed through the Barents Sea at periscope depth. Other watchstanders silently monitored their instruments. Behind a drawn curtain in the radio room just aft of the sonar shack, a handful of "spooks"—technical intelligence specialists from the Office of Naval Intelligence—listened carefully for Russian voice transmissions to or from the target submarine.

Ghormley slowly raised the narrow attack periscope until its hood just broke the surface and briefly gazed at the squat bulk of the Soviet submarine on the surface just 250 feet away. "Take her down slowly," he said. The duty planesman pushed his control yoke forward a few inches, and the *Scorpion,* riding under low power, nudged deeper into the water. Ghormley ordered a course to head toward the surveillance target, intending to pass directly under it and take some photographs of its hull with a thirty-five millimeter camera on the periscope viewfinder.

The *Scorpion* had traveled more than 4,200 miles from Norfolk to spy on Soviet naval operations. Running submerged the whole way, the nuclear attack submarine had traveled up the North Atlantic, passed through the Iceland–United Kingdom gap into the Norwegian Sea, and finally turned east beyond Norway's North Cape to enter the Barents Sea north of Scandinavia and the northwestern Soviet Union. The nearly month-long trip from Pier 22 had a single goal: to locate and conduct surveillance on the Soviet Northern Fleet's growing nuclear submarine force. Using the *Scorpion's* bow-mounted BQR-2 sonar in passive listening mode, Elrod and the other sonarmen had recorded hours of the Soviet's acoustic signature—the fluttering rumble from its turning propeller, the sound of pumps and generators reverberating through its steel hull, and the compressed air blast as it expelled garbage into the sea.

What made this deployment special was the presence on board of the communications intercept team from naval intelligence. On these top-secret missions, the submarine served as a covert listening platform. On such trips, Ghormley and his crew were working not for the navy but for the super-secret National Security Agency, which specializes in intercepting foreign military communications. In the White House Situation Room, at NSA headquarters at Fort Meade, Maryland, and at Atlantic Submarine Force headquarters in Norfolk, the operation was known as the Special Naval Control Program. Submariners like Elrod simply called their mission the "Northern run."[1]

Now it was time for pictures. The *Scorpion* silently glided under its prey. Suddenly, a heart-stopping sound penetrated the *Scorpion's* hull from above. With a large *whoosh,* the Soviet submarine flooded its ballast tanks to dive. The steel mass fell in slow motion toward the *Scorpion's* hull.

"One of the things we listened for was a submarine's blade count," Elrod later recalled. Recording the count, or number of the propeller blades as they turned on the shaft, was a major component of the unique acoustic fingerprint that U.S. submariners took of each Soviet submarine and surface ship that they encountered. Over time, the U.S. Submarine Service amassed a database of Soviet submarine sounds that enabled

Like many submariners,
Scorpion Sonarman
Bill G. Elrod opted to
grow a beard while on
patrol. *Courtesy of Bill G. Elrod*

its sonar teams to identify not just the class of the submarine but the identity of the individual boat. "Soviet trawlers and surface ships usually had three blades," Elrod said. "You'd hear, 'One-two-three, one-two-three' as the shaft rotated. Cruise liners normally had four and the sound would be 'one-two-three-four, one-two-three-four,' and so on." Early Soviet nuclear submarines had a pair of six-bladed propellers, with a correspondingly recognizable sound.

This time the *Scorpion* collected a lot more than an audiotaped signal. The collision knocked sailors off their feet as the larger Soviet submarine crashed into the *Scorpion*'s fin-shaped sail, flattening both of its periscopes. The Soviet sub slowly slid off with a dull grinding groan of metal on metal, but then one of its propellers struck the *Scorpion*. "We recorded the blade count this time—on the top of the sail," Elrod said with a laugh: "*WHAM, WHAM, WHAM, WHAM!*" Four of the Soviet submarine's propeller blades had bitten deep into the sail.

Recovering from the blow, Ghormley ordered the *Scorpion* to slip away from the surveillance area and put his damaged submarine on a course back home. Several weeks later, the *Scorpion* entered Hampton Roads. Instead of turning south for the Destroyer-Submarine Piers, it headed west toward the massive Newport News Shipbuilding facility on the James River. There, in a covered drydock, civilian hull technicians began their repair work on the sliced steel where each of the Soviet submarine's blades had bitten deep.

A collision at sea would be an instant career-killer in the rest of the navy, but not in the Atlantic Submarine Force of the 1960s. "Periscopes bent like pretzels," Elrod recalled with a shrug. "There weren't any casualties." As for Commander Ghormley? "He was doing a bold move in the finest traditions of the U.S. Submarine Service," Elrod added with a grin. "He got promoted." In fact, Ghormley went on to command the fleet ballistic submarine *USS Sam Rayburn* (SSBN 635) and would retire as a rear admiral. When asked about the incident years later, he said he could not recall it.[2]

THE COLD WAR was already two decades old at the time of the *Scorpion's* collision, and the highly classified submarine shadowboxing had been going on for practically that entire period. The *Scorpion* had conducted at least three "missions of higher classification" against Soviet naval targets in its first four years of fleet service. As the nuclear submarine force expanded in the 1960s and beyond, there were more and more of these high-risk operations.[3]

The first known U.S. submarine reconnaissance against the Soviet fleet took place in 1948, when the U.S. Pacific Fleet sent two diesel-powered submarines using a new passive sonar system up into the Bering Sea to monitor Soviet Pacific Fleet operations. In late August 1949, a similar attempt involving the submarine *USS Cochino* (SS 345) turned into tragedy when the diesel submarine caught fire and sank off the northern coast of Norway after a brief attempt to spy on the Soviet Northern Fleet headquarters at Murmansk. Another submarine, the

USS Tusk (SS-426), rescued all but one of the Cochino's crew, but lost seven of its own men in the attempt.[4]

By the 1960s, the U.S. and Soviet submariners—sometimes aided by surface warships and naval aviation units—dodged and weaved in dead-serious undersea confrontations. This skirmishing went far beyond the heated political rhetoric on both sides of the Cold War. It was a grim, unrelenting standoff that mirrored the other zones of Cold War military confrontation then spanning the world from Checkpoint Charlie at the Berlin Wall to the Korean Demilitarized Zone.

From the earliest days of the geopolitical rivalry, the U.S. Navy had tracked the production, training, and operations of the Soviet Navy and its growing submarine force. U.S. Navy admirals knew that the Soviets had seized a number of the thirteen surviving Type XXI German U-boats in 1945. More significantly, just two years after the U.S. Navy laid the keel of the *USS Nautilus* (SSN 571) in December 1952, the Soviets began Project 627, the planning and production of its first nuclear attack submarines. The first of what NATO would call the November class entered service in 1958, only four years after the *Nautilus* first went to sea. Moreover, American submariners were well aware by then that encounters in similar intelligence-gathering operations involving U.S. military aircraft had turned violent during the 1950s and early 1960s. Between 1950 and 1964, at least 130 American fliers perished in eighteen identified shootdown incidents involving the Soviets. Most of these missions were flights along the Soviet periphery and even into Soviet airspace to monitor Soviet radars and air-defense systems. Several were major news stories, and the biggest was the downing of a CIA U-2 spy plane piloted by Francis Gary Powers near Sverdlovsk in the central Soviet Union on May 1, 1960.[5]

The undersea version of the aerial showdown did not reach to the level of a declared state of war, but the *Scorpion* and other U.S. submarines in the 1960s operated on a permanent wartime footing. So too did their adversaries. Submariners studied their enemy's capabilities, rehearsed their own tactics, and generally prepared for a shooting war that many of them thought could erupt at any moment—and that some officials feared might go off as a result of the submarines' risky maneuvers.[6]

The dawn of the nuclear submarine era coincided with one of the most ambitious and dangerous intelligence operations of all: using nuclear attack submarines to spy on the Soviet Navy by penetrating its coastal waters. It was a radical innovation to a longstanding U.S. Navy practice of seeking information on current and potential enemies both in war and peace.

Very early on in the Cold War, it became obvious to the U.S. Navy and intelligence community that submarines would constitute an important platform for conducting sensitive surveillance on critical Soviet military operations. As a result, crews of the *Scorpion* and other nuclear attack submarines quickly found themselves serving entirely different masters depending on the nature of the mission.

For traditional naval operations and exercises, the *Scorpion* was just another warship in the fleet. It reported to its division and squadron commanders in Norfolk for administrative and logistical support and routine operational training. The Atlantic Submarine Force, or COMSUB-LANT, also headquartered in Norfolk, controlled the *Scorpion's* overseas deployments to the Mediterranean, Caribbean, and other foreign operating areas as a subordinate command of the U.S. Atlantic Fleet.[7]

But on Special Naval Control Missions, the *Scorpion* reported to an entirely new chain of command. Established in 1952, the NSA had assumed overall responsibility for managing the collection and analysis of intercepted foreign and military communications. Each of the military services in turn had an intelligence-gathering organization that served as a subordinate unit to the NSA. For the navy, it was the secretive communications intelligence branch of the Office of Naval Intelligence, later renamed the Naval Security Group.

The navy's interest in intercepting and decoding foreign communications predated the U.S. entry into World War I in 1917. What was then the Code and Signal section of the Naval Communications Service, later called the Cryptologic Bureau, performed limited code-breaking activities during that conflict. During the interwar years, the navy established a minuscule cadre of radio interception and code-breaking experts within the Office of Naval Intelligence, with a grand total of five full-time personnel under the command of the code-breaking pioneer Lieutenant Commander Laurence F. Safford. In 1924, more than seventeen years before Pearl Harbor, Safford's research desk began a long-term program to break the Japanese diplomatic and naval codes. After Pearl Harbor, the navy drastically expanded the organization. At its peak, there were 8,454 navy code-breakers and analysts serving worldwide. Within a six-month period during late 1941 to mid-1942, naval code-breakers were involved in both the biggest intelligence failure and the most successful intelligence victory in modern history. Poor cooperation between the army and navy code-breaking offices had led in part to the U.S. failure to anticipate Japanese plans to attack Pearl Harbor. However, military historians credit the navy code-breakers' ability to decipher Japanese naval communications for the U.S. Pacific Fleet's successful ambush of the enemy aircraft carrier force at the Battle of Midway in June 1942.[8]

The Cold War led to a major expansion of intelligence-gathering missions for the U.S. military, whose communications intercept and code-breaking efforts now fell under the direction of the NSA. The air force constructed a worldwide array of electronic listening posts using ground-based "antenna farms" to pluck Soviet radio signals out of the air. Other air force units flew aircraft modified to capture radio signals, radar beams, telemetry data from Soviet missile tests, and even samplers to detect traces from nuclear weapons tests. So, too, army, marine, and navy units added intelligence gathering to their worldwide operational requirements.

As the submarine-spying missions escalated in the early 1960s, the Office of Naval Intelligence created a new department, the ONI Collection Directorate. Within the new organization was the directorate's Special Operations Department, later reorganized as the Director of Undersea Warfare, responsible for the details of the inshore reconnaissance missions and even more risky spy operations such as wiretapping undersea communications cables.[9]

By this time, the navy, the top Pentagon leadership, the U.S. intelligence community, and senior national security officials at the White

House coordinated the submarine spy missions through a highly classified chain of command. At the Pentagon, the Joint Chiefs of Staff
scheduled and monitored these deployments through the Joint Reconnaissance Center. Upcoming missions were logged inside a three-inch
black ring binder that formed the monthly reconnaissance schedule
containing the Top Secret/Code Word details. Once the Pentagon's designated manager—usually the deputy secretary of defense—signed off
on the binder, a courier would drive it to the White House, where
another top-secret panel subjected it to a final review and formal
approval.[10]

At his spacious Flag Plot operations center in the Pentagon, the chief
of naval operations (CNO) could look up at a huge world map with col-
ored pins marking the location of all ongoing naval operations, including the Northern run submarine spy missions. From there, the Top
Secret/Code Word orders flowed down the chain of command, from the
CNO to the U.S. Atlantic Fleet to the Atlantic Submarine Force to
squadron, division, and the individual submarine loading food and provisions at pier side.

What mattered to the nuclear submariners on the waterfront was
not where the mission orders originated, but what they portended:
weeks at sea, long hours of tedium, and, occasionally, endless moments
of stark terror. As the CNO watched aides move the pins and his subordinate admirals went about their daily tasks, the submarine commander
and his embarked spooks up north were on their own.

It would always begin with a small convoy of black vans passing through
the guarded gate at the Destroyer-Submarine Piers. Former nuclear submariner David F. Horn recalled one such mission in the spring of 1964
about eight weeks before his submarine went on a Northern run. An engineman first class aboard the Norfolk-based *USS Shark* (SSN 591), the
Scorpion's sister ship, Horn was up on deck one morning when he saw
four black government vehicles slowly driving onto Pier 22. "There were
two black cars and two black vans," he recalled. "Guards came out of the
lead car armed to the teeth. The vans open up and other guys come out
with the black boxes." Then the guards cleared the pier of all unneces-

sary personnel, and the team began loading the gear aboard his submarine. "They carry the boxes onto the submarine and take them to the radio room aft of the control room. Up goes a curtain blocking off the
space—the crew will never see it." For the Special Naval Control Program missions, the *Scorpion* and other submarines would operate under
the tactical control of this intelligence-gathering team.[11]

Horn said that on the day of the *Shark*'s departure, April 5, 1964, he
went forward from the engineering spaces to get a cup of coffee in the
mess decks. Sitting at two of the six tables were eight strangers wearing
nondescript navy uniforms. They ignored the *Shark*'s crewmen, and
Horn poured his coffee in silence.

The secrecy involved in these reconnaissance missions was unusually
severe, even for nuclear submarine operations, former participants say.
But the submariners did not work in a complete vacuum. Because all but
a few non-rated newcomers possessed top-secret security clearances, the
commanding officers would brief their crews on the upcoming schedule
of events. "We knew what was going on," Elrod said of the *Scorpion*
crew. The senior *Scorpion* officers "would get each watch section in the
crew's mess, put the chart on the wall. The CO would brief us on what
the bottom line of the mission was. Because I was in the combat suite, I
was pretty well briefed." The sonar gang and other key enlisted personnel also received a formal briefing from Submarine Squadron 6 officials,
but Elrod dismissed those sessions as "Kabuki theater and stork dancing"
by the administrative staff. If another Norfolk-based submarine had recently returned from a spy mission in the same operating area, a group
of *Scorpion* crewmen would hold an informal debriefing with them.
"Unofficially we'd get guys off the boat who just came back [from Soviet
waters]," Elrod explained. "We'd walk to the end of the pier with them
and have a good off-line chat with them about what really went on."

The transit from Norfolk to the Barents Sea or other target areas
would pass quickly in the brisk routine that constituted a nuclear submariner's life at sea. "The reactor is critical, the steam is up," Horn said,
describing the *Shark*'s 1964 mission. "We cast off lines and we're underway. Once past the hundred-fathom curve we dive deep, then come up
to cruising depth. The order goes out: Set all chronometers to Zulu

[Greenwich Mean Time]; set lights to red; set 'patrol quiet conditions.'" Elrod's description mirrored Horn's: "We'd leave Norfolk. If lucky, we'd get a stop in Scotland on the way up, then straight back home. You'd go to your assigned area. You would be given a choke point to patrol or a bit of ocean to be aware of everything that was operating in it."

The crews would know that they were nearing the target area when their skipper would pass the order. "Rig for one-third speed and rig for 'silent running,'" Horn continued. "That means we're going to get close to the battle. Then the order: 'Rig for ultra-quiet.' What does that mean? It means nothing—no sound—you don't move unless you have to. You listen. You hear nothing." Once in the mission area, the submarine would go on full surveillance mode. Its reed-shaped antennas would pop out of the ocean, sucking in electronic intelligence of all forms, radio traffic, and missile telemetry data. The conning team would use the periscope to photograph Soviet surface ships and submarines.

The submarines' sonar gangs had a heavy workload on these surveillance operations. While the spooks were monitoring the electromagnetic spectrum, the sonar watchstanders were making a continuous recording of all acoustic signals coming in through the BQR-2 passive sonar array in the bow.

The *Skipjack*-class submarine sonars were advanced for their day but still required close cooperation between the sonarmen and the maneuvering watch during these tense reconnaissance operations, said Elrod. Unlike advanced sonar technology developed for subsequent submarine designs that could steer a listening beam 360 degrees using a spherical sonar array, the *Scorpion* had a flat plane array that could only create a cone of listening ahead of the submarine with a maximum range of twenty to thirty miles depending on ambient sea conditions. To listen in any area outside of the cone, the sonarmen would have to direct the maneuvering watch team to turn the *Scorpion* to aim its listening gear in the desired direction. So once the *Scorpion* or its sister ships reached the surveillance area, the sonar gang found itself working in a state of permanent overtime.

"You'd have a sonar supervisor and two sonar watchstanders on watch," Elrod recalled. "Usually six to eight sonarmen plus electronics technician and fire control ratings would occasionally stand in." While listening with their headsets, the sonarmen would consult a paper chart showing significant known contacts or bearings of interest for them to monitor. They would enter all sound contacts in a logbook including the time, bearing to the signal, their initial classification of the sound (as submarine or surface ship), and its movement relative to the *Scorpion.* "Depending on the general interest you would either pursue it or let it fly," Elrod said.

It would be years before the navy developed its fully computerized sonar systems that employed a computer-screen display to visually show the sound signals as frequency lines on a color "waterfall" screen. So too, the modern towed-array sonar that trailed sensitive hydrophones far beyond the submarine and its propeller was years off. During transits, the men would stand four hours on watch and eight hours off, but when on station they would serve six on and six off, a much more grueling schedule. "On some missions it would get very raggedy," Elrod said. "I'd work fourteen to eighteen hours, go collapse in my bunk for a few hours, then come back on again. I used to go into the sonar room with three packs of cigarettes and smoke them up before the watch was over." As for the spooks, they sat behind a security curtain in the radio room manipulating their intelligence-gathering hardware; only occasionally, as the situation dictated, did they pass on maneuvering advice to the submarine commander.[12]

Many former submariners try to downplay the sense of risk or potential crisis inherent in the Northern run operations, which also were known by the code words "Holystone" and "Bollard." Retired Vice Admiral Kenneth Carr recalled one northern deployment that the *Scorpion* carried out in 1960–61 during his tour as executive officer: "It was hours of boredom followed by minutes of excitement. It was routine—you went up, spent your time, you were just watching exercises. Mainly you looked in the ocean to see what was going on. [The Soviet submarines] were operating pretty much the way we were, running exercises in their own operating area."[13]

Many other submariners say differently. They recall constant stress and anxiety as their submarine loitered in the vicinity of Soviet surface warships and submarines that were test-firing live weapons, including ballistic missile launches. And the even more daring missions to deliberately penetrate Soviet territorial waters were worse, because an accident or collision carried the risk of exploding into a violent confrontation, an international incident, even a hot war.

Retired submariner Jerry Hall recalled one hair-raising encounter when he was in the nuclear attack submarine *USS Tullibee* (SSN 597) off the Soviet coast. "I was on a trip across the top of Russia and we were out there playing games with a [Soviet] submarine for four days. It chased our ass all over the place over there," he said. "We weren't sure they could launch submerged. So we set in there and when they did, there were three Russian destroyers and one of their ballistic missile boats. We thought there was this ballistic missile boat and us in this little triangle.

"Well lo and behold," Hall continued, "when that damn missile went up we had to put all of our telemetric data—the scopes, the ECM mast, we had to expose all that—and here came the damn destroyers after us. We pulled down our antenna and went deep, and shit, about that time here goes this [Soviet] boat right across the top of us."[14]

The *Skipjack* was on one such spy mission in late 1960 when it deliberately entered Soviet territorial waters to spy on a new Golf-class missile submarine conducting sea trials. At the time, gathering accurate information on the state of the Soviet ballistic missile submarine force was one of the top intelligence-collecting priorities. Having finished that phase of the patrol, *Skipjack* Commander William "Wild Bill" Behrens proceeded to enter the ship channel that led to the Soviet naval complex at Murmansk to snoop around the cluster of surface ship and submarine facilities, thus violating the Soviet three-mile territorial limit. The *Skipjack* was not detected in this risky gambit but some time later suffered damage to its sail when it accidentally collided with a Soviet destroyer while surfacing. It was forced to flee when other Soviet warships raced to the scene.[15]

Even in the early 1960s, the *Skipjack's* experience was not a rare event. In the summer of 1962, the *Scorpion* barely avoided striking a November-class attack boat. Carrying a spook team and specialized radiation-detecting gear to assess a planned Soviet nuclear weapons test, the *Scorpion* traveled north of Novaya Zemla Island. When the Soviets postponed the blast, the submarine moved over to the Kola Peninsula east of Norway to conduct electronic surveillance on the Soviet Northern Fleet. During that mission, the *Scorpion* nearly collided with the unknown November, at the time the most advanced nuclear attack boat in the Red Banner Fleet. According to John Arnold, a chief petty officer assigned to the naval intelligence team aboard the submarine, "We were trailing, collecting data on its bottom side when it was on the surface. We were smack dab under him. . . . Between the bottom of his sub and the top of the *Scorpion,* sometimes the periscope was only six to twelve inches, closely inspecting underwater appendages, protrusions and so forth, and recording it on television." But when the November suddenly fired off its high-frequency fathometer—in preparation for diving—the *Scorpion* hastily retreated, Arnold said.[16]

Several months later the *USS Nautilus* returned to Novaya Zemla with a spook team and detection gear. Over a six-week period, they tracked more than a dozen nuclear explosions, some of which sent shock waves through the water powerful enough to jolt crewmen off their feet and shatter neon light bulbs.[17]

The *Shark's* 1964 Northern run operation was also far from routine, Horn recalled. But in that instance, the excitement was primarily on the Soviet side. Assigned to monitor a ballistic missile submarine test launch, the *Shark's* crew witnessed a near-fatal accident on board the Soviet boat.

Throughout most of the Cold War, the Soviet Union opted to test-fire submarine-launched ballistic missiles on an easterly course heading from the southern Barents Sea or inside the White Sea to impact points in arctic Siberia, the Kamchatka peninsula landmass, and the Sea of Okhotsk. The best observation point would be from a submerged nuclear attack submarine lurking close to the Soviet missile submarine, so this became a prime reconnaissance target for the U.S. nuclear boats. "We got a target," Horn said. "The captain puts out his night orders: 'Be ever vigilant. We're running alongside the icepack and we have a contact.'"[18]

Horn was passing through the control room as a roving watchstander several hours later when he saw the senior spook onboard, a navy commander, stiffen at the periscope. A fireball had just erupted on the Soviet submarine that the *Shark* was shadowing. "There was a Soviet missile boat running a missile exercise," Horn said. "He tried to fire a missile but when the rocket went off, it hung in the [missile] hatch burning. We went underneath it and took pictures. By the time we got to the periscope depth [on the other side of the Soviet submarine] the Russian sailors were on deck trying to put out the fire. We circled around, and finally, the captain said 'secure from battle stations,' and we headed back to Norfolk."[19]

From the outset of what would become a three-decades-long submarine rivalry with the Soviets, the U.S. admirals clearly recognized the dangers involved in these ambitious inshore spy missions. There was a distinct chance that discovery of a U.S. submarine might lead to a combat incident, but accidents were even more likely. Pentagon leaders and intelligence officials believed, however, that the rewards justified the risk. Because the U.S. military had long been routinely penetrating Soviet airspace with so-called ferret flights designed to force the Russians to activate their radars and air-defense forces and the CIA was engaged in a number of brutal back-alley covert missions in the Third World against its KGB rival, the submarine spying program seemed only a moderate escalation of the global superpower rivalry.

As the Northern run missions and similar operations targeting the Soviet Pacific Fleet expanded throughout the 1960s, the number of collisions, groundings, and other mishaps reached an alarming rate. The U.S. Navy suppressed information about the accidents as part of the overall security blanket cloaking the program, but over the years details began to emerge. The diesel-electric attack submarine *USS Ronquil* (SS 396) suffered an onboard fire on December 31, 1967 while being harassed by Soviet naval forces during an unspecified special operation. That incident remained secret until 1998.

Two years later, on May 15, 1969, the *USS Tautog* (SSN 639) collided with a Soviet Echo-II-class nuclear submarine off Petropavlovsk. The U.S. submarine had been following the Echo-II for several days when the Soviet cruise-missile-firing submarine suddenly submerged on top of the *Tautog* in a replay of the *Scorpion's* 1965 collision. The American crewmen initially thought that the collision had destroyed the Soviet submarine when the *Tautog's* sonarmen tracked it falling to a depth of 2,000 feet below the surface. However, twenty-two years later after the collapse of the Soviet Union, former Captain Boris Bagdasaryan said it was his submarine, nicknamed the Black Lila, that had struck the *Tautog*. Cloaked by a huge mass of air bubbles that blanked the American sonar, Bagdasaryan said he had managed to get his submarine to the surface and limp back to port on one of its two propellers.[20]

Supervisors of the top-secret submarine spy missions came up with one creative tactic to ensure that these confrontations remained hidden: the double reporting system. If a collision or other potentially dangerous encounter occurred, the submarine commander had orders to write two separate top-secret patrol reports: a cover story essentially denying that anything amiss had happened, and a second document stating the facts. When *The New York Times* in 1975 first revealed significant details of the Northern run program, it mentioned a collision in 1969 between the attack submarine *USS Gato* (SSN 615) and a Soviet submarine, later identified as the Golf-class *K-19*. The newspaper cited several former crewmen who said Atlantic Fleet headquarters had directed the *Gato's* commanding officer to prepare twenty-five copies of a top-secret after-action report that falsely stated the submarine had broken off its mission two days before the collision occurred in November 1969. The *Gato's* commanding officer also prepared a second patrol report, also classified top secret, that documented the collision inside Soviet territorial waters. The second, and accurate, report was restricted to six copies and distributed to only a handful of senior government leaders. As a result, many navy and intelligence officials were kept in the dark about the potentially fatal collision, the *Times* noted. The Soviets, of course, knew otherwise. Captain Second Rank Vladimir Lebedko aboard the *K-19* was able to free his submarine and make an "emergency blow" on his ballast tanks.

The *K-19* reached the surface and returned to port, its bow seriously damaged.[21]

The mishaps continued on a regular basis into the 1970s. Some escaped public notice, while others made headlines despite the heavy security. In 1971, the *USS Puffer* (SSN 652) collided with a Soviet diesel-powered submarine during a Holystone mission near Petropavlovsk. The incident remained unknown to the public for twenty-seven more years. In March 1974, another Pacific Fleet submarine, the *USS Pintado* (SSN 672), collided with a Soviet Yankee-class missile submarine that was exiting the Soviet Navy base at Petropavlovsk. This time, a San Diego newspaper revealed details of the incident sixteen months later, including a photograph of the dished-in bow section of the *Pintado* in a drydock at the U.S. Navy base on Guam. The newspaper report noted that while the *Pintado* was operating within Soviet territorial waters when the collision took place, there was no information that the Soviet Union had ever registered a formal complaint.[22]

But it wasn't always the U.S. submarine that was at fault. On November 3, 1974, a Soviet Victor-class nuclear attack submarine struck the *USS James Madison* (SSBN 627), armed with sixteen C-3 ballistic missiles, while the missile submarine was operating in the North Sea. Both submarines apparently escaped without life-threatening damage.[23]

To this day, the history of Cold War encounters between U.S. nuclear attack submarines and the Soviet Navy remains incomplete. Fifteen years after the end of the Soviet Union, the U.S. Navy still refuses to declassify the patrol reports of its attack submarine force including the top-secret spy missions. The Soviet Navy archives also remain locked and sealed. But from what little evidence we do have, it is clear that there were many more dangerous encounters than either side ever admitted.

The Northern run and other risky submarine ventures did not spring out of a vacuum. The U.S.–Soviet standoff was not the first time powerful navies armed with submarines had confronted one another in the first six decades of the twentieth century. In those previous conflicts, submarines on all sides won renown for daring missions in enemy coastal waters. The U.S. nuclear submarines edging up to the littoral areas of the Soviet Union were figuratively following in the wakes of their predecessors: German U-boats that penetrated the Chesapeake Bay in 1918, Japanese mini-subs sent to sneak inside Pearl Harbor as part of the planned 1941 attack, and the U.S. submarines USS *Nautilus* (SS 168) and USS *Argonaut* (SM 1) that penetrated the Japanese-held Gilbert Islands to land Major Evans F. Carlson's Marine Raiders in 1942. The submarine course tracks of American and German submarines in the two earlier wars neatly underlay the plots of U.S. and Soviet Cold War submarine patrols fifty years after the 1918 Armistice and nearly a quarter-century after V-E Day in 1945.

The U.S. submariners of the 1960s were linked to their predecessors by far more than geography, however. They lived and operated within a unique environment, a martial community both physically separated and radically different from the formal and often rigid naval culture from which they came. World War II submarine ace Lieutenant Commander Ignatius Galantin recalled his decision to volunteer for submarines after two years in the surface navy: "I became increasingly restive. . . . I wanted to be free of the dull, repetitious, institutionalized life of the battleship Navy, and to be part of a more personalized, more modern and flexible sea arm." It was a sentiment that submariners of all navies shared. They had long enjoyed a reputation as nonconformists who hated the monotony of fleet service. They disdained the pomp and circumstance of sideboys, buglers, and holystoned teak quarterdecks. They embraced the hardships of life in a steel tube and the go-it-alone missions that submarines were designed to do. They were a fighting elite, and they knew it.[24]

When war came, submariners were among the first to fight. In addition to hunting enemy merchantmen in the deep ocean, they deployed on long-range solitary missions to sink ships or lay mines in distant enemy shoal waters. They ferried commandos in special operations raids. The submarine's design and weaponry and the submariners' aggressive mindset combined into one of the more lethal weapon systems that mankind ever built.

Peace, when it came in 1918 and 1945, offered merely an interlude during which submariners could rearm and prepare for the next fight. They studied the submarine technology of their previous foes. Equally important, they scoured battle after-action records, patrol reports, and other accounts to learn which tactics and strategies had succeeded the most in bringing victory.[25]

Over the course of the twentieth century, warfare became increasingly lethal because of new technologies. Submarines were no exception to the steady growth in combat power. In the case of submarine design and development, the technological gains also dictated that submariners embrace harsher new tactics and strategies and abandon any pretense of chivalry and human compassion. This evolution is crucial to understanding the military environment in which the *Scorpion* and its sister ships operated in the late 1960s. Like soldiers, airmen, and other sailors, submariners were forced to cast off codes of gentlemanly conduct as the century progressed.

The German U-boat campaign of World War I marked the first time that submarines played a major role in modern warfare. In the first three years after war broke out in 1914, the United States was neutral, and Germany tried to avoid any provocation that would create a new enemy. German U-boats had periodically sunk Allied ships in the western Atlantic but not American-flag vessels. Still, several incidents sorely strained U.S. neutrality—especially the sinking of the liner *RMS Lusitania*. On May 7, 1915, the German submarine *U-20* torpedoed the British luxury liner off the coast of Ireland, killing nearly 1,200 people, among them 128 Americans. The international furor over the incident prompted Germany to halt its campaign of unrestricted submarine warfare, the tactic of sinking as many civilian and military ships as possible in order to strangle the enemy's economy.

With the European battlefield stalemated, in February 1917, however, Germany resumed unrestricted submarine warfare in hopes of starving Britain into surrender. British monthly shipping losses soared above 500,000 tons from February until July, peaking at 860,000 tons in April, the month that the United States entered the war. Nearly a year later, in the spring of 1918, the German government unleashed a six-month-long U-boat campaign along the U.S. Atlantic coast in a last-gasp effort to halt the dispatch of several million American troops to Europe.[26]

Compared with the later submarine campaigns of World War II, the Germans didn't deploy much of a fleet—just six diesel-powered U-boats, of which only five would see much action. Still, armed with six-inch and four-inch deck guns, and carrying torpedoes, floating mines, and demolition charges, they outgunned and outran practically everything else in the area. Powered by twin diesel engines, the German U-boats could sprint on the surface at 16.4 knots or maintain a sustained underwater speed of five knots for ten hours. The surface speed enabled them to chase down all but a handful of ships, and later-model U-boats had an unrefueled cruising range of over 6,700 nautical miles at fifteen knots.

The German U-boat campaign was successful in finding and destroying American ships because the U.S. Navy was almost completely absent from its own home waters. Most American warships were escorting troop convoys to France. The U.S. Navy deployments were a sound tactical decision, but they came at the expense of coastal security at home.

The First World War was the last submarine war for gentlemen: Coming upon a freighter or coastal schooner, the U-boat would surface if it wasn't already steaming along that way, fire a shot or two across the target's bow, then dispatch a boarding party to the victim to review the ship's papers. If the boat was deemed a legal target, the U-boat captain would give the crew a half hour to man lifeboats while the boarding team set demolition charges. In several cases, U-boat captains wrote out a formal receipt for the seizure and sinking, then handed it to the forlorn merchant skipper as he wallowed alongside in a lifeboat. Soon, with the ship's crew at a safe distance, the fuses would burn down, the charges would detonate, and the helpless target would sink to the ocean floor. With few exceptions, the German sailors acted with professional courtesy and aplomb. Some offered to let their onboard doctor treat anyone injured. Others shared cigarettes, cognac, and coffee with the bedraggled survivors. Occasionally, the U-boat crew would seize the civilian master or senior officers as prisoners of war to accompany the submarine back to Germany.

The American loss of life was minuscule, largely because of the German U-boat policy of allowing passengers and crew to escape in lifeboats before destroying their ship. Throughout the six-month campaign in U.S. waters, casualties totaled 435 killed, including sixty-seven fatalities that were not combat-related such as accidental sinkings involving ships running without lights to avoid detection. Several hundred people were injured, but U.S. Navy and Coast Guard records on this category were imprecise. These casualties stand in sharp contrast to the slaughterhouse on the Western Front in Europe, where in the month-long Battle of Verdun alone, German and Allied casualties exceeded a million.

The U-boat campaign in U.S. waters was a tactical victory for the Germans and included the sinking of the only major U.S. Navy warship to occur in the conflict. Still, the campaign against U.S. forces had no strategic effect on the war's outcome. It did cause enough concern to the U.S. Navy that its admirals ordered the Atlantic Fleet to retreat inland from Norfolk and lurk in a protected anchorage in the York River. The six U-boats sank ninety-one ships and smaller vessels. Elsewhere in the war, the carnage from the U-boats was staggering. While the U-boats sank a total of 166,907 tons of U.S. shipping, it was a small fraction of British losses during that same period.[27]

In today's era of over-the-horizon targeting, pinpoint satellite navigation, and precision-guided weaponry, the U-boat assault of 1918 seems quaint and weird. It was nothing of the sort: The goal, then as now, was to use the best available technology and weapons to sink enemy ships, disrupt maritime supplies to the enemy homeland, and undermine enemy public support for the war.

But there were some lighter moments, as well. On the morning of June 8, 1918, the *U-151* under the command of Korvettenkapitan Heinrich von Nostitz, Graf von Hendendorf caught up with the Norwegian steamer *Vindeggen* carrying 2,500 tons of copper ingots from Chile to New York. The interception occurred about 102 miles east-southeast of Norfolk on a main shipping lane devoid of any U.S. Navy warships. Aware that Germany desperately needed copper, the skipper decided to transfer the cargo from the steamer to the *U-151* and take it back to Germany as a prize of war.

As von Nostitz later recalled, his crew painstakingly transferred 70,000 kilograms of copper from the *Vindeggen* to the *U-151*. But then the *Vindeggen's* captain asked von Nostitz to do him a favor: The captain of another ship had traveled on board the liner as a passenger. He now wished to travel back to Germany, along with his wife and children. Von Nostitz agreed to take them on board the *U-151*.

"We took the woman on board," von Nostitz recalled. "She was quite a genteel lady, only she used perfume somewhat too freely so that it was not long before the whole ship reeked with it. We wanted to take her below deck but owing to the rough weather this was not agreeable to her. So she stayed on the surface of the [*U-151*], where her husband had some wicker furniture carried to her. The child was treated very considerately by the crew. Milk and chocolate were given to it."[28]

Copper loaded, wicker furniture secured below decks, child sated with chocolate, the *U-151* then blew up the now-empty steamer and released its survivors to a passing ship. Von Nostitz allowed the vessel to retrieve them, and then the *U-151* vanished into the mist.

Even so, by the end of the Great War, such niceties had become a thing of the past. The increasingly desperate German campaign of unrestricted submarine warfare around the British Isles and in the Mediterranean presaged future submarine warfare. As a twenty-seven-year-old lieutenant in World War I, German submariner Karl Donitz was serving on the *U-39* in the Mediterranean under submarine ace Walter Forstmann when their submarine sank an Italian troop ship, drowning over a thousand enemy soldiers (Italy was on the side of the Western allies in that conflict). Forstmann told the younger man, "Every softhearted act of mercy to the enemy would be foul treason to our own striving people." This harsh new approach had become standard policy when the U-boats launched a new war against American shipping along the U.S. East Coast in January 1942.

In a fit of pique four days after the Japanese attack on Pearl Harbor, Adolf Hitler declared war on the United States. The Roosevelt administration promptly reciprocated, setting the stage for what the U.S. Navy would call its "two-ocean war." Unlike the navy—still shell-shocked by

The U.S.–Soviet Cold War submarine rivalry had roots in the vicious submarine conflict of World War II. Here, German submarine *U-701* arrives at its base in German-occupied Brest, France, in late 1941. *Courtesy of Horst Degen*

the Pearl Harbor attack and paralyzed by bureaucratic infighting at its Washington headquarters—the German Kriegsmarine was well positioned to do something once the politicians concluded the formalities of declaring war. Vizeadmiral Karl Donitz, now the commander of Germany's submarine force, quickly dispatched five U-boats across the Atlantic to attack merchant shipping along the U.S. East Coast. His intention in Operation Paukenschlag (Drumbeat) was to have all five launch a simultaneous attack on shipping—from Nova Scotia to Cape Hatteras—on the morning of January 13, 1942.

The U.S. Atlantic Fleet was as unprepared for the onslaught of the second Battle of the Atlantic as it had been in 1918. Unlike 1918, this time the results would be devastating. In the first six months of 1942, German torpedoes, mines, and U-boat deck gun shells sank nearly 400 American and allied merchant ships in U.S. waters from Maine to

Panama. During that campaign, only nine U-boats went down. The 1942 U-boat assault on merchant shipping in U.S. coastal waters and the Caribbean was a greater strategic setback for the Allied war effort than the defeat at Pearl Harbor.

The ferocity of submarine warfare during World War II contrasted sharply with the humanitarian conduct of many submarine commanders in the previous war. The goal of the U.S. submarine service and German U-boats was not merely to sink ships but also to kill as many enemy combatants as possible and starve out the enemy homeland. The Japanese, followers of the Bushido Code, did the same as their navy swept south and west into Southeast Asia and the Indian Ocean in the months after Pearl Harbor. Scores of histories have appeared on the various World War II submarine campaigns, and one looks in vain for another Korvettenkapitan von Nostitz offering chocolate to a child.[29]

In response to the submarine campaigns in Europe during World War I, the major naval powers—the United Kingdom, Japan, France, Italy, and the United States—in 1930 had signed the London Naval Treaty, primarily limiting military shipbuilding to maintain a stabilizing balance of naval power among the major navies. The treaty also banned unrestricted submarine warfare, declaring that international law applied to submarines as well as to surface warships. Submarines could not sink any merchant vessel without first ensuring that the victim's crew and passengers had been delivered to "a place of safety." Only ships that demonstrated a "persistent refusal to stop" or put up an "active resistance" were fair game.

While noble in intent, the treaty was doomed simply because, upon being attacked, any merchantman with a radio transmitter could instantly summon help from aircraft or warships—an act that submarine commanders might reasonably define as "active resistance."[30]

By World War II, advances in submarine design and technology resulted in the construction of submarines on both sides that were far more effective in attacking enemy shipping. Torpedoes had greater range and firepower, allowing submarines to launch them at extended ranges up to eight miles rather than several thousand yards from the target. Sonar, while still primitive in comparison to today's acoustic systems, was effective enough in World War II to aid submarines in tracking targets while submerged—and to assist anti-submarine warfare ships in locating submarines. World War II–era submarines had operating ranges and speeds that were greater, enabling longer patrols thousands of miles from their homeports. It was a combination of this increased capability and the decision by the belligerents in World War II to embrace total warfare against their enemies that finished off once and for all the humanitarian treatment of passengers and crews.

Following the *Laconia* incident in 1942 in which one of his U-boat captains ceased combat patrol to help thousands of passengers from the troopship he had just torpedoed, Donitz dispatched an order to all U-boat commanders prohibiting them from aiding survivors of any ships they sank. "Be hard," Donitz said. "Think of the fact that the enemy in his bombing attacks on German towns has no regard for women and children."[31]

Within hours of the attack on Pearl Harbor, the U.S. Navy ordered its submarine commanders to execute unrestricted submarine warfare against Japan. Years of U.S. diplomatic opposition to the strategy and support for the London Naval Treaty went out the window.

Even if those harsh new orders had not been in effect, in the heat of battle, combatants rarely had time to stop and rescue their now-helpless enemies. When the four-stack destroyer *USS Roper* (DD 147) came upon the *U-85* off the Virginia Capes on the night of April 15, 1942, U.S. gunners could clearly see by their searchlight that the German crewmen were frantically attempting to abandon ship. Nevertheless, the destroyer continued to fire at the sinking submarine and launched a number of depth charges after the submarine had gone down to ensure its destruction. In the process, the destroyer killed several dozen German sailors who had managed to jump into the water. None survived.[32]

Down where it counted—at periscope depth in enemy-infested waters—submarine commanders on all sides quickly adjusted to the realities of their mission. No incident illustrates more clearly the savagery of World War II submarine warfare than the encounter between the *USS Wahoo* (SS 238) and the Japanese transport ship *Buyo Maru* northeast of New Guinea. On January 25, 1943, the *Wahoo* came upon a group of four Japanese ships off New Guinea. The *Wahoo's* commanding officer, Lieutenant Commander Dudley "Mush" Morton, crippled several of the ships with torpedoes, and one, the troopship *Buyo Maru*, began to sink. When Morton surfaced to recharge his ship's batteries, he ordered his gunners to fire on the survivors in the water. He said that there were nearly 10,000 enemy troops in the water (it is now estimated that there were only 1,126 people on the ship, including several hundred Indian Army POWs). Due to wartime security restrictions and press censorship, the episode went unnoticed until long after the war's end.[33]

Shortly after the Japanese surrendered on September 2, 1945, Pacific Submarine Force commander Vice Admiral Charles Lockwood reported that U.S. submarines had sunk over 4,000 Japanese ships totaling over ten million tons, including eight aircraft carriers, one battleship, and twenty cruisers—and thousands of civilian-crewed merchant vessels. German U-boats sank fewer ships, 3,500, but the total tonnage was far more, 18.3 million.[34]

In a rare press conference to discuss the war just ended and the future of the U.S. Navy, Fleet Admiral Chester Nimitz said, "Battleships are the ships of yesterday, aircraft carriers are the ships of today, but submarines are going to be the ships of tomorrow." The old Texan's words implied a profound change: Submariners would lead the future U.S. Navy. The young and middle-ranking submarine officers who had cut their teeth in four years of violent, no-holds-barred warfare would take their experiences with them as they climbed the ranks to preside over the Cold War U.S. Navy. Those harsh lessons would guide them as they sent the growing force of nuclear attack submarines up against their new adversary. The violence they had witnessed and the violence they had wrought would steady their hands as they presided over new submarine technology and weapons whose power dwarfed the imagination even of those who had survived the horrors of unrestricted submarine warfare. They would know how to make the tough calls.[35]

5

THE RUSSIANS ARE COMING

HE WAS LIKE ANY OTHER COUNTRY BOY WHO WANTED TO ESCAPE the tedium of his small town for a more interesting and adventuresome life. That's how Engineer-Seaman Sergei Anatolyivech Preminin came to be sitting at the reactor control panel in Compartment 6 of the Soviet ballistic missile submarine *K-219*. Several hundred feet above him, a brilliant October moon washed the Atlantic wavetops in silver, but for Preminin and his 118 fellow crewmen, the uplifting spectacle might as well have been on the far side of another planet. Standing the evening watch, Preminin's world was a cramped, overheated cubicle of gauges, dials, and switches that controlled the two VM-A nuclear reactors powering the 9,000-ton submarine as it headed for its patrol box several hundred miles east of Bermuda in the fall of 1986.

The son of a mill worker in the village of Skornyakovo in central Russia, Preminin had never seen the ocean before enlisting in the Soviet Navy. But he and his brother had been avid freshwater fishermen in their teens, and Sergei had told friends that the idea of becoming a sailor had originated with his delight in watching the clear waters of the local streams as he and his brother cast their hooks. Sergei not only volunteered for the Soviet Navy but also put in for the far more rigorous training to prepare for the nuclear submarine force. By 1986, the twenty-one-year-old was on his second enlistment tour and a qualified reactor operator.

While the *K-219* was one of the older Yankee-class ballistic missile boats, having entered Soviet fleet service in 1971, its officers and enlisted crewmen were proud to be on it. They were part of an elite submarine service that had struggled to achieve a rough parity with their American rivals during more than a quarter-century of nuclear submarine operations. It had been a tough, relentless fight with major obstacles every step of the way: inferior equipment, inefficient shipbuilders, indifferent politicians, and an American submarine force determined to maintain its superiority in the undersea standoff.

Still, Admiral Sergei Georgyevich Gorshkov was their commander-in-chief, and thirty-one years after he had assumed command of a ragtag fleet with little deep-ocean experience and practically no effective warships, the admiral had forged a "blue-water" navy out of sheer determination. His vision of global Soviet maritime power had dazzled the geriatric Politburo members far away in Moscow. The *K-219*'s ongoing mission was proof of that: A month after leaving port, the submarine was nearing its patrol station 800 miles southeast of New York City, where it threatened the entire U.S. East Coast with its arsenal of thirty nuclear warheads mounted two apiece on fifteen SS-N-6 missiles.[1]

Preminin was well aware of the high cost in lives that had been the price of progress in Gorshkov's forced-march modernization of the Soviet submarine fleet. Every Soviet submariner knew the horror stories of radiation leaks, fires, collisions, and other mishaps that plagued the submarine force in the postwar years, regularly maiming and killing crewmen. So when a violent explosion suddenly tore through one of the *K-219*'s sixteen missile tubes, sending shock waves the length of the 423-foot-long submarine, Preminin instantly knew that it had happened again, that in the next few hours he and his shipmates would face the challenge of their lives.

Several hundred feet in front of Preminin's workstation, one of the missile tubes had sprung a leak. Seawater seeped into the narrow space between missile and launch tube, threatening the survival of the submarine. The hazard was immediate. When water came into contact with the oxidizer in the missile fuel tank, it combined to form deadly nitric acid fumes and violently detonated. The *K-219*'s weapons officer had noticed the leak, but the explosion occurred before he could vent out the tube with high-pressure air. A fatal brew of nitric acid, unexpended missile fuel, and plutonium radiation from the shattered missile warheads quickly filled the center compartments of the *K-219*. At the bottom of the missile compartment, a massive fire erupted.

The *K-219* crew, led by Captain Second Rank Igor A. Britanov, tried every trick in the book to suppress the fire and halt the spread of the deadly nitric acid fumes, to no avail. Flames and poisonous gases spread relentlessly forward and aft until they forced the crew to abandon all but the forward- and after-most compartments. As the hours passed after the submarine broadcast an emergency message to Moscow seeking help, the situation seemed to stabilize. But it was a false hope. The raging fire in Compartment 4 severed the electrical wiring to the two nuclear reactors, which began to overheat as the supply of primary coolant flowing through their fuel cores diminished. In addition to fire and deadly nitric acid fumes—which were steadily eating their way through the rubber seals of the watertight compartment hatches—the threat of a runaway fission reaction and a Chernobyl-type nuclear explosion suddenly loomed. The automatic reactor shutdown systems were immobilized.

In the after end of the *K-219*, Preminin and his reactor officer, Senior Lieutenant Nikolai Belikov, realized that they were the only two crew members who knew how to shut down the reactor by hand. It called for an all-but-suicidal foray into the interior of the shielded reactor chamber at the lowest level of Compartment 7. Suppressing the raging fission reaction inside each reactor would require lowering four quench baffles using a heavy metal wrench to turn large threaded bolts protruding from the red-hot reactor vessels, in air temperatures that by now exceeded 150 degrees Fahrenheit. Belikov went first but was only able to lower one of four baffles on the first reactor before the heat and lethal radiation level exhausted him. He found his way back to where Preminin and other sailors were waiting and collapsed. The young engineer-seaman donned a cumbersome radiation suit, took an oxygen breathing apparatus with the last two oxygen canisters left on the submarine, and crawled into hell.

Somehow, Preminin managed to secure the other seven baffles and averted a nuclear explosion inside the submarine. But when Preminin climbed back out of the pit to rejoin his shipmates, heat and pressurized air had jammed the hatchway door to the last uncontaminated compartment. He and his shipmates on the other side of the hatch tried with all their strength to open the hatch without success. His air supply exhausted, Preminin collapsed and died inches away from the other *K-219* crewmen. The others escaped the following day when a Soviet merchant ship arrived, evacuated the *K-219*'s crew, and attempted to take the stricken missile submarine in tow. The flooding had reached a point beyond recovery, however, and on October 6, *K-219* sank to the floor of the Hatteras Abyss more than three miles down. Preminin and three other crewmen who had been killed in the initial explosion went down with the submarine, but the remaining 115 crew members managed to escape.

To a handful of U.S. sailors on a nearby nuclear attack submarine and aboard several land-based navy P-3C Orion patrol aircraft that were flying overhead, the *K-219* sinking appeared at first glance to be a grisly replay of earlier disasters that had long plagued the Soviet submarine force. After the Cold War ended five years later in 1991, U.S. submariners who had tracked, trailed, and harassed the Soviet submarine fleet would salute Seaman Preminin's sacrifice as an act of humanity that transcended the long conflict between the two navies. His actions not only had saved the rest of *K-219*'s crew but also probably prevented a major radiation accident that could have contaminated the U.S. East Coast. Preminin posthumously received the Red Star banner award for securing the two VM-A reactors that fateful night.[2]

But by the mid-1980s, even such recurring mishaps could not mask some unpleasant facts confronting the U.S. Navy. On the night it suffered the fatal accident, *K-219* was but one of a half-dozen Soviet ballistic missile submarines on patrol that posed a deadly threat to the United States. Upon Moscow's order to fire, the Yankee-class submarine could have in a matter of minutes lobbed its fifteen SS-N-6 missiles with a total of thirty deadly nuclear warheads at targets from Florida to New England.

As Navy Secretary John F. Lehman said in 1986, "What is particularly disturbing about the 'fleet that Gorshkov built' is that improvements in its individual unit capabilities have taken place across broad areas. Submarines are faster, quieter, and have better sensors and self-protection. . . . And the people who operate this Soviet concept of a balanced fleet are ever better trained and confident."[3]

The Soviet Navy had come a very long way since Gorshkov's ascension to supreme command in 1955. For the past two decades, its submarine force had grown both in quantity and quality, emerging in the 1960s as a genuine threat to America's domination of the seas. The year 1968 had become pivotal in this grim rivalry, but the roots of that competition went back much farther. The adversary that the *USS Scorpion* would stalk and hunt in its short, seven-year operational life had its genesis in the rubble of postwar Europe.

———

EMERGING FROM THE Soviet Union's victory against Nazi Germany in 1945, Josef Stalin issued a strange boast: With 229 submarines in service, the Soviet Union had the largest submarine force in the world. In fact, about half of this armada comprised a gaggle of pint-sized coastal patrol submersibles with little to no combat capability. Of 124 Soviet submarines officially certified for deep-ocean patrol, only six were anywhere near effective, and they were German Type VIIC and IXC boats that Stalin had acquired as war reparations.

If the Soviet Union really wanted to have a modern navy in the decades after the war, it would have to create the whole thing—from warships to a trained cadre of sailors to an operational doctrine—out of thin air. Unlike the U.S. Navy, which had two centuries of experience, the Soviet Navy's World War II exploits could be written on the back of a matchbook. The Red Army had toppled the Wehrmacht on the plains of the Soviet Union and throughout Eastern Europe in a titanic Armageddon; the Soviet Navy had puttered around on the sidelines. Nor did the Soviet crews have the battle-hardened experience that their American and British counterparts had won in years of struggle against German and Japanese targets.[4]

Soviet submariners lacked modern equipment and weapons. Their enlisted crewmen were largely uneducated conscripts. And the Soviet Navy had practically no deep-ocean operating experience. Making the challenge even more difficult was geography: Most Soviet naval ports were either frozen solid for most of the year and, if not, were hemmed in by narrow choke-point passages or blocked by hostile military forces close in to shore.[5]

But Stalin wanted a navy capable of exporting Soviet influence all over the world, and Stalin was used to getting what he wanted. As part of Germany's surrender, the Soviets had acquired a wide range of military technology and scientists, including a half-dozen Type XXI U-boats and a cadre of German naval architects. Soviet designers seized upon these German spoils as they implemented Stalin's plans.[6]

The obstacles remained all but overwhelming, however. His country was in ashes from the Carpathians to the Don River, and his only wealth was the former German POWs now used as slave laborers and several million Russians consigned to the Gulag. Stalin faced a struggle of indescribable dimensions to rebuild Soviet society, much less create a navy that could operate worldwide. Most of the Soviet shipyards were still smoking rubble after three years of occupation and battles with the German Army. Worse, endemic corruption, inefficient state-run industries, and the inherent flaws of a command economy all conspired to make a difficult and expensive program all but impossible to execute. And so, in the five years between the end of World War II and the outbreak of the Korean War, the Soviets produced only a small number of modern submarines. Realization of Stalin's grand plan lagged far behind his rhetoric.[7]

The true state of affairs in the Soviet bloc could bring no comfort to the U.S. Navy because neither naval strategists nor intelligence specialists had a clear picture of Stalin's actual military weakness. The Pentagon had neither sophisticated reconnaissance satellites nor other technical intelligence-gathering capabilities to penetrate the Iron Curtain.

Meanwhile, U.S. Navy officials were grappling with their own problems. The American fleet that vanquished Imperial Japan and helped storm the shores of Fortress Europe did not exist anymore. From a wartime high of 3.3 million men and women, the U.S. Navy roster plummeted to 491,663 by December 1946.[8]

In the twenty-seven months between V-J Day and December 31, 1947, the U.S. Navy retired more than 2,000 navy warships and auxiliaries and another 5,000 government-owned merchant ships, either laid up in reserve or broken up for scrap. When the New Year dawned in 1948, the navy could still boast a seagoing fleet of over a thousand warships and support auxiliaries, but like Stalin's submarine fleet, it was a boast best kept on paper. The U.S. submarine force also shrank. Of the 313 submarines operating during World War II, fifty-one were lost in combat or accidents, and the remaining postwar fleet soon dwindled to seventy-three.[9]

These factors combined to lead U.S. military planners and intelligence analysts to fall victim to their own unfounded fears of what the Soviets might be capable of doing. This anxiety thrived amid a matrix of Soviet secrecy, inadequate U.S. intelligence penetration of Stalin's closed political system, excellent Soviet intelligence penetration of the West, and several incidents during the late 1940s that raised the possibility that the Russians were, indeed, coming. When the Soviets set off "Joe 1," their first atomic bomb, at Semipalatinsk in Kazakhstan on August 29, 1949, the blast sent psychological shock waves through the Pentagon. Western experts had predicted such a technological feat would not occur for years to come, if ever. Stalin's backing of the North Korean invasion of South Korea ten months later in June 1950 doused the fire with gasoline. Official U.S. estimates of the planned Soviet submarine fleet exploded from 300 to 2,000. U.S. defense industry stocks headed for the moon.[10]

In reality, the U.S. Navy had little to fear. In 1946, one U.S. intelligence report forecast a fleet of 300 Soviet Type XXI submarine equivalents by 1950, but it took the Soviet Navy until 1949 to send its first Type XXI prototype to sea. In fact, the Soviets did not deploy that model, known as the Zulu-class submarine, in any numbers until the late 1950s, when twenty-one of them were in service. A second knockoff of the German design, the Whiskey class, emerged in larger numbers with 236 of the diesel-electric attack boats in active service by 1958. But these submarines were smaller and designed for coastal patrols rather than deep-ocean operations.[11]

When Stalin died on March 5, 1953, the feelings of the Soviet Navy admirals must have been mixed. Though Stalin was a paranoid, brutally whimsical dictator, he had said all the nice things the navy brass wanted to hear about a future fleet. By the early 1950s, through bureaucratic fiat and at the point of a gun, the Soviets had rebuilt most of their naval shipyards. Plans called for both a massive submarine and surface force and even aircraft carriers in the rosy Red dawn.[12]

But the admirals' dream of a deep-ocean Soviet Navy went with Stalin to the grave. Nikita Khrushchev emerged as the dominant Soviet political leader in the next five years, and he was indifferent, if not outright hostile, to the navy. Khrushchev had risen to power in World War II as a political commissar to the Red Army, which had long regarded the navy with barely disguised contempt. So did Khrushchev. One of his first acts as head of government was to scrap an entire class of cruisers under construction.

The nadir of postwar Soviet Navy ambitions came in October 1955, when some ammunition aboard the flagship of the Soviet Black Sea Fleet, the battleship *Novorossysk*—a former Italian warship seized as a war prize—accidentally exploded, sinking the ship in Sevastopol Harbor and killing 608 of its crew. The disaster drew a rebuke from the new leader: "Navy surface ships are good only for carrying heads of state on official visits. They have outlived their time. They're good only as missile platforms. This year to date we have destined practically all cruisers to the scrap heap."[13]

Then, unexpectedly, came deliverance: Less than a year later, Khrushchev appointed Sergei Georgyevich Gorshkov, a World War II comrade, to command the Soviet Navy. No one at the time recognized the routine personnel move for what it would turn out to be: a major turning point in Soviet—and world—naval history.

Born in 1910, Gorshkov had joined the Soviet Navy in 1927. Before World War II, his career was unexceptional—apart from the fact that he managed to avoid Stalin's purges of so many other military officers. After graduating in 1931 from the Frunze Naval College, the Soviet naval academy, Gorshkov commanded a surface naval force in the Black Sea in 1932. In late 1941 he distinguished himself in amphibious landings that helped wrest control of Ukraine and Romania from the Nazis. In the closing months of the war, as a rear admiral, he commanded a destroyer squadron.[14]

Gorshkov would go on to serve as the Soviet Navy's commander-in-chief for twenty-nine years, during which he created not only a modern navy but a Soviet national security strategy that included naval seapower as a central element. The USSR, he argued, had to be more than a land power to exert its international prerogatives and to serve its global interests. In part, this change reflected Soviet ambitions to lead Third World insurrections and guerrilla movements opposing the political and economic interests of the West. But more directly, as the United States forged the NATO Alliance in Europe and began its policy of containment of the Soviet Union, the Kremlin embraced Gorshkov's call for a navy that could meet these adversaries worldwide, and not just at the harbor mouths of Murmansk or Vladivostok.[15]

As Gorshkov's plan materialized in Soviet shipyards, U.S. naval analysts took note. One navy report in the 1950s exclaimed, "The Kremlin leadership had discovered Sea Power!"[16]

By the early 1960s, Gorshkov had won Khrushchev's support to build a modern nuclear submarine fleet while forgoing for the moment a stronger force of surface warships. But the Soviet leadership would soon face a grim reminder that political events do not always wait for Five-Year Plans to catch up. While U.S. admirals feared the unknown, it was Soviet fear of the U.S. Navy's proven capabilities that had been the driving factor during Khrushchev's early years in power. From the mid-1950s onward, he ordered the Soviet Navy to transform itself into a strategic defensive force centered on modern submarines supported by missile-armed coastal patrol craft "to defend the Soviet Union from possible Western aggression." To Soviet admirals, this was progress, but still far from a mandate to develop a true offensive strike capability, to carry out sustained overseas naval deployments, and to show the hammer and sickle from a flagship jack staff in distant seas. Gorshkov's grand vision would have to wait. Loyal to his political masters, the Soviet CINC pushed hard to build a nuclear submarine force. Meanwhile, the lack of modern naval capabilities would prove a major embarrassment to the Kremlin in two back-to-back Mideast crises.

The admiral had barely settled into his spacious office in Soviet Main Navy headquarters in Moscow in 1956 when Egyptian President Gamal Abdel Nasser, a Soviet ally, on July 26 moved to nationalize the Suez Canal. Israel, backed by Great Britain and France, invaded the Sinai Peninsula and moved west to seize the strategic waterway. Had he commanded a deep-ocean navy, Gorshkov could have steamed his fleet to Alexandria, Egypt, to support his nation's embattled ally. He had nothing, so he did nothing. Although the Eisenhower administration had ordered a full military alert in case the Soviets tried to cause trouble in Europe, a superpower showdown never occurred. You can't have a showdown unless you show up. The incident ended when President Dwight Eisenhower himself became concerned that the Suez crisis would undermine his attempts to persuade the international community to pressure Moscow against cracking down on Hungary, where civil unrest against the Communist government was in full cry.[17]

Two years later, another crisis erupted in that same bad neighborhood. Lebanon went up in flames, prompting direct U.S. intervention. Faced with mounting internal political instability among the various Lebanese ethnic groups fueled by Soviet client states nearby, on July 15, 1958 Eisenhower ordered 14,000 army troops and marines to enter the country to bolster the pro-Western government. President Camille Chamoun was locked in a political struggle with Egypt and Syria, which had formed the United Arab Republic, a Soviet ally. To forestall military action on their part, the U.S. military occupied Beirut International Airport and secured the port of Beirut and approaches to the city. The presence of the troops quelled the opposition; the United States withdrew three months later, its political goals attained. Gorshkov sat out the crisis in his Moscow office and chafed as world events passed him by yet again.

Many Soviet sailors saw the *November*-class nuclear attack submarine as more of a threat to their crews than to the American adversary. *U.S. Navy Photo*

Had there been a modern Soviet Navy with force-projection power, the admiral might have been able to deter the United States from intervening.

By the early 1950s, the two superpowers were in a race to build the first nuclear submarine. The Americans, of course, won. With great fanfare, the U.S. Navy commissioned the *USS Nautilus* (SSN 571) on September 30, 1954, and fifteen weeks later, Commander Eugene P. Wilkinson, the submarine's skipper, transmitted a historic message to the rest of the navy: "Underway on nuclear power." But the Soviets were playing catch-up. Their shipyards launched three separate classes of nuclear submarines during 1958–60: the Hotel-class ballistic missile submarine, which, like the diesel-electric Golf-class, housed three missiles in vertical launching tubes in a massive sail; the Echo-class nuclear cruise missile submarine, designed to attack U.S. aircraft carriers with SS-N-3 Shaddock nuclear-tipped cruise missiles; and the torpedo-carrying November-class nuclear attack submarine.

Hotel, Echo, November: Western naval observers nicknamed them the HEN submarines, and lumped them together, since they shared many common internal systems, notably a pair of VM-A pressurized-water reactors apiece. The submarines also shared a propensity for killing and injuring their own crewmen at an alarming rate. Name any unavoidable challenge in submarine design and construction, and the odds were it posed a threat to the poor devils who took them out to sea. Inept management, faulty design, and insufficient quality control would quickly wreak havoc on the new submarines. With gallows humor, Soviet submariners affixed appropriate nicknames to their submarines. The infamous *K-19*, in which thirty-six crew members perished in two separate accidents in 1961 and 1972—and which was damaged by the *USS Gato* in a collision in November 1969—was dubbed Widowmaker. Later, crewmen renamed it the Hiroshima in honor of its tendency to shower the crew with highly radioactive coolant from its leaky pipes.[18]

At this juncture in the Cold War arms race at sea, Gorshkov—like Stalin—opted for quantity at the expense of quality and the health of his men. Unlike the Rickover-dominated planners in the U.S. Navy's Naval Reactors Branch, who stressed careful incrementalism as they proceeded from *Skipjack*-class to *Thresher/Permit*-class to *Sturgeon*-class attack submarines, Soviet design teams would come up with a set of blueprints and immediately begin cranking vessels out en masse. From 1958 to 1962, they produced five Hotel-class and five Echo-I-class submarines, and between 1959 and 1965, fourteen November-class attack boats slid down the shipways at Severodvinsk deep inside the White Sea. Unlike the U.S. Navy, Gorshkov manned his nuclear attack boats with two crews apiece to take turns underway, and quickly sent them packing off on patrol. Fortunately for Gorshkov, Soviet reporters were disinclined to cover bad news.[19]

The *K-8* was the first to blow a gasket. The 360-foot-long November-class attack submarine was exercising in the Barents Sea on October 13, 1960, when several leaks developed in the secondary coolant loop of its nuclear plant. The submarine reportedly had an emergency system installed that was designed to block such leaks as they occurred. It failed.

In the highest traditions of the Soviet Navy, the crew got out baling wire and chewing gum and tried to plug the leaks themselves while pumping seawater into the reactor loop to prevent a runaway fission reaction, all the while enclosed in a nearly lethal radioactive sauna. They were lucky: Although the radiation quickly spread throughout the interior of the *K-8,* only a handful of sailors developed short-term radiation illness, and they recovered.[20]

Nine months later, on July 4, 1961, another VM-A reactor went bad, this time on the Hotel-class *K-19.* According to an independent analysis of the incident, the *K-19* had suffered a leak in an inaccessible part of one reactor's primary cooling circuit. Since the loss of the highly radioactive primary coolant could lead to an uncontrolled chain reaction, the crew had no choice but to rig an improvised backup to ensure the reactor's stability. As they toiled for hours, radioactive steam and gases spread throughout the *K-19.* Ultimately, the crew evacuated to a diesel submarine.[21]

The submarine was able to return to service, but for many of its crewmen, their enlistments were up—for good. Author Peter Huchthausen, a retired U.S. Navy captain, described their fate: "All eight were exposed to lethal doses of gamma and neutron radiation, and absorbed lethal quantities of alpha and beta contamination. Within minutes they suffered severe nausea, their faces swelled, and their tongues turned black. Within hours they broke out in beads of bloody perspiration and suffered painfully slow deaths, some pleading to be shot to allay the severe pain." Another thirteen sailors later died of radiation illness. That year alone, there were eleven other mishaps aboard Soviet submarines serious enough to force them to return to port.[22]

───

THE FIRST MAJOR naval confrontation between the two superpowers erupted in 1962 with the Cuban Missile Crisis. It could easily have been the last. For thirteen days that October, the United States and the Soviet Union placed their military forces on a nuclear hair-trigger alert as the Soviets attempted to deploy intermediate-range ballistic missiles with nuclear warheads in Cuba, and the United States prepared for a full military invasion of the island if diplomacy and a military show of force failed to induce the Soviets to take the weapons out.

Decades after the event, former leaders on all sides learned to their horror just how close the world had actually come to a global nuclear war. At a conference held in Havana in January 1992 on the fortieth anniversary of the crisis, former Kennedy administration members, Soviet participants, and a Cuban delegation led by President Fidel Castro discussed the superpower encounter. Retired Soviet General Anatoly Gribkov stunned the meeting when he revealed that, in addition to their intermediate-range ballistic missiles, the Soviets had deployed nine tactical nuclear missiles in Cuba to be used against any U.S. invasion force. Even more significant, Gribkov stated that Soviet field commanders in Cuba had the authority to fire those tactical nuclear weapons without further direction from the Kremlin.[23]

In the immediate aftermath of the crisis, however, U.S. Navy officials seem to have learned the wrong lessons. They bragged about how the navy's quarantine, backed up by anti-submarine warfare units, had thwarted the Soviets' ballistic missile deployment and its attempt to build a submarine base in Cuba. The admirals boasted how the threat from the Polaris submarine force was a major reason Khrushchev had backed down. They looked upon the Soviet decision to sneak the missiles into Cuba as proof of a hostile regime dedicated to challenging the United States in its home waters. The Soviet behavior in 1962, many believed, justified even more aggressive U.S. moves in return.[24]

As military analysts would later conclude, the Cuban Missile Crisis had one dangerous unintended consequence: It galvanized Kremlin leaders and Admiral Gorshkov to push even harder for a more effective Soviet Navy and nuclear submarine force. Rather than retreating from harm's way, the Soviet Navy chief was even more determined to stand up to the Americans.

The Cuban crisis did not come out of nowhere. In response to the aborted invasion of Cuba by CIA-backed Cuban rebels at the Bay of Pigs in April 1961, Castro, then prime minister, had formally allied his government with the Soviet Union, expanding on a 1960 accord in which the Soviets loaned Cuba $100 million and agreed to a major trade pact. By 1962, the Cubans were aware—and the American public would not learn of this for many years—that the U.S. government was still secretly planning to dislodge the Castro government through a combination of sabotage and subversion aimed at triggering chaos and unrest among the Cuban population that would ultimately lead to a direct U.S. military invasion. Part of the operation involved the use of U.S. Navy diesel submarines based in Key West, Florida to infiltrate and extract anti-Castro saboteurs and spies from the island.[25]

The Soviets decided that they could not tolerate the destruction of their only major ally in the Western Hemisphere but lacked effective options without a major change in the military balance. Despite their public bluster and frequent bragging of military strength, the Kremlin leaders were actually becoming more and more frantic as they observed the Pentagon steadily encircling the Soviet landmass with strategic nuclear missiles and long-range bombers flying on nuclear airborne alert.

In 1960, Khrushchev had publicly condemned the United States for deploying Polaris missile submarines around the periphery of the Soviet Union. "This is a criminal policy on the brink of war," Khrushchev told a mass rally in Moscow after returning from a stormy session of the U.N. Security Council in New York in early October 1960. "This is the path of cold war that can turn into a hot one." Khrushchev warned that the Soviet Navy also had ballistic missile submarines, referring without name to the Golf-class and Hotel-class missile boats, but he and Gorshkov both knew they were far less effective than the growing Polaris fleet. Moscow knew that there were seven Polaris submarines in service with another thirty-four planned or under construction, so the submarine-based missile threat was bad and heading for much worse. By 1962, the U.S. nuclear encirclement had intensified with the deployments of land-based Thor missiles in the United Kingdom and Jupiter missiles in Italy and Turkey. However, the Polaris submarines were the more troubling development, since they were all but impossible to locate.

Despite the political furor in the 1960 U.S. presidential campaign from Democratic Party candidate John F. Kennedy about a missile gap that favored the Soviets, by 1962 a small group of top-level officials in both Washington and Moscow with access to their nations' deepest intelligence reports had concluded that that there was no balance of nuclear terror. The Air Force Strategic Air Command and Navy Polaris submarine force enjoyed an overwhelming military superiority over the Soviets. One top-secret Pentagon assessment of that era written in 1981 candidly admitted, "By the standards of strategic force, survivability and effectiveness that became commonplace a few years later, the Soviet strategic situation in 1962 might thus have been judged little short of desperate." But even though the balance of nuclear terror was so heavily tilted in favor of the United States, a few nuclear Soviet missiles in Cuba that could threaten Washington, D.C., and most major military bases would go far to counteract American strategic superiority elsewhere.[26]

The Soviets had nothing to lose: By the spring of 1962, both Castro and Khrushchev had strong political and military motives to attempt a single stroke that would neutralize the perceived U.S. military threat to both regimes. In May 1962, they agreed on a plan for the Soviets to secretly deploy to Cuba twelve intermediate-range SS-5 ballistic missiles and twenty-four medium-range SS-4 intermediate-range ballistic missiles with nuclear warheads, defended by a force of 43,000 Red Army troops. For good measure, Khrushchev threw in forty IL-28 Badger medium bombers and a dozen 100-kiloton tactical nuclear warheads for its short-range Luna battlefield rockets. The Soviets ultimately planned to create a permanent forward operating base in Mariel, Cuba for a squadron of seven diesel-powered Golf-class ballistic missile submarines.[27]

It was an audacious plan, and a desperate one—born of Soviet military weakness rather than strength. Once again, Gorshkov would find his navy mostly on the sidelines. He was forced to admit to his superiors that his vaunted nuclear submarine fleet was in no shape to play a meaningful role in the Cuban operation. Reactor design flaws and various malfunctions were requiring extensive refitting. The Hotels, Echoes, and Novembers were sidelined for what would become the gravest superpower military confrontation of the Cold War. Moreover, Khrushchev's earlier decision to scrap much of the Soviet surface fleet now came back to haunt him. He had no major surface warships available to challenge the U.S. Navy's Second Fleet in its own backyard. During the height of the crisis in late October, an angry Khrushchev confronted Gorshkov over the need to provide surface warships to escort the Soviet merchant vessels bearing arms to Cuba. "We need ships with autonomy and long range escorts to Cuba," Khrushchev shouted. "But sir," Gorshkov replied, "you ordered them destroyed." The general secretary of the Communist Party of the Soviet Union, forced to rewrite history, shot back: "I ordered no such thing."[28]

With no nuclear-powered submarines available, the Soviets had to fall back on Plan B: They would send four Foxtrot-class diesel-electric attack boats to the Caribbean. Their goal was to conduct surveillance on the U.S. Navy and score political points by serving as a vanguard for the missile boats that would soon operate from a permanent naval base in Cuba.

By mid-October, events were taking on a life of their own. U.S. Air Force U-2 spy planes spotted the missile sites under construction on October 14, 1962. The Kennedy administration went public eight days later with a campaign of diplomatic maneuvering and military deployments to confront the Soviets over the missile emplacements, beginning with a nationally televised speech on October 22 in which the president ordered a naval blockade of Cuba. (U.S. officials termed the move a quarantine to avoid drawing attention to the fact that a blockade in international waters, after all, constitutes an act of war.) Orchestrated by U.S. Navy surface ships, particularly two "hunter-killer" (HUK) anti-submarine groups built around the aircraft carriers USS Randolph (CVS 15) and USS Essex (CVS 9), the operation halted inbound Soviet shipping to Cuba.[29]

The Soviets were vastly overmatched from beginning to end. If one thing above all others illustrates the Soviets' position of naval inferiority in the Cuban crisis, it would be a comparison of the pivotal meetings that each side's naval leaders conducted at the beginning of the crisis. For the U.S. Navy, it came in the spacious, high-tech Navy Flag Plot spaces in the Pentagon. There, Chief of Naval Operations Admiral George W. Anderson and his staff were able to study a wall-sized map of the world showing the current positions of every American, allied, and Soviet-bloc warship as intelligence bulletins and radio position reports poured in from military and intelligence sources. Immaculately dressed Filipino stewards hovered at elbow's length with freshly brewed coffee for the august flag officers presiding over the U.S. Navy's largest operation since Korea.

In contrast, when the four Foxtrot attack submarines of the Fourth Red Banner Squadron prepared for deployment to Cuba on September 30, 1962, their commanders met with several admirals at 3:30 A.M. in a dimly lit wooden shed at the base of the pier at an icebound base northwest of Polyarnyy. Heated only by a small coal-fired furnace, the shed was dark and cold as the freezing winds from Sayda Bay leaked in through the cracks. The admirals kept their heavy greatcoats and wool *mushanka* hats on throughout the briefing. They stamped their feet on the ice-cold floor to keep the circulation going. Coffee was not served.[30]

The Foxtrots' mission was straightforward: As several other admirals watched from the shadows, submarine squadron commander Rear Admiral Leonid Filippovich Rybalko informed the four submarine commanders that their job was to travel undetected to the Cuban port of Mariel, where they would form an advance party for a Soviet flotilla of surface warships, auxiliaries, and coastal patrol craft. The ultimate goal of the Soviet Navy was to create a permanent operating base for seven Golf-class ballistic missile submarines, providing a forward logistics base identical in function to the Americans' Polaris anchorage at Holy Loch, Scotland.

The plan was as simple as it was unattainable: All they had to do was to slip out of Sayda Bay and after entering the Barents Sea, submerge, poke their air-breathing snorkels above the surface, and trudge down to Cuba on diesel power at a submerged speed of nine knots. Without the Americans noticing. There was no choice of routes. They would first set a westward course for the North Cape. Upon entering the Norwegian Sea, the submarines would quietly proceed south and slightly west for about 850 nautical miles, then cross the GIUK Gap, the geographical line extending from Greenland and Iceland through the Faeroe Islands to the United Kingdom. At this juncture, the flotilla would now find itself in the upper North Atlantic, and its course track would veer southwesterly toward the Grand Banks off Newfoundland nearly 2,000 miles away. Then would come the critical leg of the journey, a 1,500-mile crawl submerged against the northward flow of the Gulf Stream toward the outer Caribbean islands. Finally, there would be the 590-mile westward leg along the north shore of Cuba to Mariel.

The Soviet submarines joined the looming crisis with one wild card that the United States would not learn about for many years: They had the means to set off a global nuclear exchange between the United States and the Soviet Union. The four submarines were armed with one nuclear-tipped torpedo apiece, and the captains held formal rules of engagement that were criminally ambiguous, permitting them to fire the deadly weapon merely if they *thought* they were under attack. Don't write or phone in: Just start a nuclear war.

Rybalko ended the briefing in the freezing shed on an upbeat note. "It is considered highly unlikely that American ASW [anti-submarine warfare] forces will be any more than at their usual state of alert, which isn't much of a threat," he told the four skippers. Fat chance. The submarines had barely reached the Faeroe Islands north of Scotland—barely 1,200 miles into their 5,260-mile trek—when U.S. Navy oceanographic technicians at a base on the Caribbean island of Grand Turk detected the sound signals from their diesel engines and rotating propellers. The submarines hadn't even gone a fourth of the way, and their mission had already become mission impossible.[31]

The U.S. military may have been caught flat-footed by the Soviets' ability to smuggle 40,000 soldiers and nuclear-tipped ballistic missiles into Cuba, but one early-warning system worked just fine. The top-secret Sound Surveillance System, or Sosus, would prove its worth during the Cuban Missile Crisis.

The U.S. Navy had been concerned about the potential Soviet submarine threat since the late 1940s. This time, the admirals did not ignore the menace as they had so famously done at Pearl Harbor or during the initial German U-Boat campaign off the East Coast in 1942. Nor did the service place all of its betting chips on the promise of nuclear propulsion in submarines. Immediately after the war, the navy began assembling a multi-layered anti-submarine warfare defense that during the 1962 missile crisis would quickly overwhelm Gorshkov's initial attempt at deep-ocean naval operations.

First came Sosus. The system was a marriage of pure oceanographic science and modern acoustic technology, driven by the U.S. Navy's nearly irrational fear in the late 1940s of what the Soviet submarine fleet might someday do. Building on World War II sonar technology, Lehigh University scientist Maurice Ewing in the mid-1940s had discovered a new phenomenon in the ocean—a deep sound channel hundreds of feet down that conveyed acoustic signals for extended distances. In 1944, Ewing arranged for a test of the sound layer. A navy destroyer dropped explosive charges at a pre-set depth. Ewing was able to detect the impulses at a distance of 900 miles and theorized that fixed hydrophones at that depth could be used to triangulate the location of sound signals, just as a network of direction-finding antennas could pinpoint the location of a radio transmitter. Ewing originally envisioned that the navy could develop a system called Sound Frequency and Ranging (Sofar) for communicating over long ranges by setting off time-coded explosive charges in the deep sound channel itself.

Sosus, like many advanced military capabilities, began as a pure scientific research discovery. It wasn't until 1946 that the navy realized this phenomenon might help find submerged submarines by the acoustic sounds they generated in their passage under the surface. Physicist Frederick Hunt, a former head of Harvard's Underwater Sound Laboratory, is generally credited with realizing that Ewing's scientific discovery could prove revolutionary in anti-submarine warfare.

The U.S. Navy got the message, and fast. Within months, the Office of Naval Research issued a priority research and development contract to AT&T through its Western Electric laboratory, and the project commenced on a wartime crash basis. The initial concept translated low-frequency acoustic signals into a visual display by use of an electrostatic stylus that etched the signals onto specially sensitized paper. The resulting continuous readout from each hydrophone would depict the propulsion system and propeller of a submerged submarine as discrete frequency images that a trained operator could readily identify as the acoustic signature of a submarine.[32]

By January 1952, the first Sosus hydrophone array was installed near Eleuthera Island in the Bahamas just north of Nassau. A cable-laying ship installed a thousand-foot-long line assembly of forty hydrophone elements in 1,440 feet of water. Tests using an American submarine proved successful beyond the scientists' wildest dreams, and the navy ordered the full-fledged creation of what would be called the Caesar system. In five years, Sosus arrays and the shore-based naval facilities (NavFacs) that processed the signals and monitored their bearing angles stood in a semi-circular arc from the Caribbean to Canada. The navy rapidly opened ASW listening posts at Ramey Field, Puerto Rico; Antiqua and Barbados; Grand Turks and San Salvador in the Bahamas in addition to Eleuthera; Bermuda; Cape Hatteras, North Carolina; Cape May, New Jersey; Nantucket, Massachusetts; and Shelburne, Nova Scotia. A final coastal facility went up in Argentia, Newfoundland in 1959. But the navy didn't stop there. Over the next fifteen years, it developed a Sosus network along the northern Pacific rim with hydrophone arrays along the U.S. West Coast, Aleutian Islands, and down the Kuril Islands off the eastern Soviet Union. It ringed the Hawaiian Islands with a circular array more than 1,300 miles in length called Sea Spider, and later did the same in the eastern Atlantic with the Azores Fixed Acoustic Range, which listened in to sound signals from western Africa to the straits of Gibraltar.[33]

The key to the detection system was the Low Frequency and Ranging, or Lofar, analyzer. Each Sosus array listened along a narrow directional beam of the ocean, like a ship's lookout that sweeps his binoculars in a narrow pre-set angle. The sounds generated within that field would appear as a visual display on scrolls of heat-sensitive paper, called Lofargrams. Using advanced (for that day) computers, the various NavFacs could readily triangulate the location of a suspected submarine. Technicians would relay the intelligence data to anti-submarine warfare units that could then attempt to verify the possible contact with ships, submarines, and land-based patrol aircraft equipped with air-dropped sonobuoys.

In a rare public gathering, in 1999, veterans of the Sosus program described their day-to-day work in those early years. It was hardly glamorous: Holed up in windowless NavFacs, each Sosus technician would spend hours patiently gazing at several dozen gram readers, each one of which represented a single acoustic hydrophone array. The work was critical to national security. It was mostly boring, occasionally exciting, and always reeked of burning paper.[34]

By the mid-1950s, the growing Sosus organization in the Atlantic was scouring the underwater sound channels for signs of Gorshkov's submarines. It was at this time an early warning system that was too far ahead of its time. The first known deep-ocean patrol by a Soviet submarine did not occur until 1956, when the Whiskey-class diesel boat S-91 and two other submarines ventured out from their base on the Kamchatka Peninsula in the Far East for a quick foray into the Pacific. Scanning the other ocean for Gorshkov's vaunted submarines, all the Atlantic-based Sosus techs found were sounds from fishing boats, cavorting sea life, and infrequently, *American* submarines passing by.[35]

There were moments of excitement, however. Edwin Smock, a Sosus technician then assigned at a NavFac at Shelburne, Nova Scotia, recalled that one day in July 1956 all of the gram writers went berserk at the same moment, showing huge noises all across the sound spectrum. Sosus technicians stared at one another in bewilderment as the Lofargrams turned dead black. Then they read the headlines the next day: The Italian ocean liner *Andrea Doria* had collided with a freighter and sank off Nantucket 280 miles to the southwest of their NavFac. "We knew right then exactly what we had been looking at," Smock recalled. "That was [the *Andrea Doria*] when she was breaking up and going down to the bottom, the explosions of her boilers and all." Sosus had registered its first shipwreck.[36]

Five years later, Sosus gave the U.S. Navy's Polaris missile program managers a real jolt. While the underwater arrays had been designed to focus on the signals made by Soviet diesel submarines that were snorkeling—running submerged but using their diesel engines for power—the system turned out to work just as well for tracking deep-diving nuclear submarines. In 1961, when the *USS George Washington* (SSBN 598) crossed the Atlantic on its first nuclear patrol, Sosus successfully tracked the boomer from Charleston, South Carolina to the United Kingdom. The sounds of its main engine, steam turbines, and rotating propeller came sparking through the electric stylus onto Sosus Lofargrams.[37]

It was at the time, of course, classified beyond top secret. Those who served in what became the Ocean Systems Atlantic Command were sworn to a degree of secrecy that was right up there with NSA encryption programs, nuclear weapons designs, and tactical communications. Even nuclear submariners had only the dimmest notion of this scientific breakthrough in ASW. "In those days you couldn't even *say* 'Sosus,'" recalled *Scorpion* sonarman Bill Elrod. "It was so secret the *word* Sosus was [classified] Secret." Attending a submarine sonar course at Key West in the spring of 1964, Elrod became aware of another navy school nearby behind locked and guarded doors. "It was the place where they taught Sosus. They couldn't say 'Sosus,' of course, so they called it 'the Green Door.' It was very, *very* sensitive. Any kind of narrowband or frequency analysis or band shifting was very, *very* sensitive."[38]

By the early 1960s, Sosus had become a critical component of the navy's anti-submarine warfare program, which also included the hunter-killer carrier task groups and land-based patrol aircraft designed to localize and attack enemy submarines from the general position plot that the hydrophones identified as possibly containing a hostile submarine. One problem that had plagued the system in its earlier years was that very few people in the navy were allowed to know of the program's existence, much less its accuracy. As a result, tip-offs from the undersea listening system sometimes arrived too late for the HUK groups or land-based patrol aircraft to reach the suspected submarine position before the intruder was long gone. When the Cuban Missile Crisis erupted in October 1962, many of the officers and enlisted men assigned to the naval quarantine had no idea they were being steered to their targets by the anonymous Sosus teams ashore. This time, however, the surface navy was in position and in a heightened state of alert so the Sosus data arrived in a timely manner and proved valuable.

There is some evidence that the Soviet submariners were aware of the existence of Sosus. There also was nothing the submariners could do about it. Soviet submariners who participated in the Cuban Missile Crisis later gave differing accounts about the extent of their knowledge of the acoustic detection system. Captain Nikolai Shumkov, commander of the submarine *B-130*, told an interviewer he was generally aware of the Sosus network but did not know its actual capabilities. On the other hand, Lieutenant Vadim Orlov, a radio-intercept specialist on the submarine *B-59*, recalled he had no idea about the American ASW capability.

What Orlov and the others *did* know was that their effort to avoid detection while traveling to Cuba failed almost before it began. Huddled in his Foxtrot's tiny communications room about a week after leaving port on October 1, 1962, Orlov's radio-intercept team poked an antenna above the surface of the Norwegian Sea and heard dismaying news. American P-2V Neptune patrol aircraft were flying a focused search pattern overhead, dropping sonobuoy devices that would radio any submarine's sound emissions back up to the plane. Worse, the pilots were talking to one another as if they had a specific search target in mind. Worse yet, their flight paths and sonobuoy patterns precisely matched the Foxtrots' course track. Listening in on the Americans' unencrypted radio chatter, Orlov heard that the aircraft overhead were specifically looking for a half-dozen Soviet diesel submarines.[39]

As the Foxtrots passed Bermuda and headed south toward the quarantine line, the Soviet submariners discovered a massive U.S. naval armada waiting for them. For the next several weeks, the two HUK groups filled the air with fixed-wing aircraft and helicopters that would use their sensors to pinpoint the submarines' locations. Destroyers attached to the HUK groups then aggressively hounded the submarines as they hid submerged under the Atlantic, forcing them to surface after long hours when their storage batteries depleted and their air went foul. Only one of the Soviet Foxtrots, the submarine *B-4*, managed to evade the quarantine force throughout the crisis.[40]

On October 28, 1962, Khrushchev finally relented. He ordered the withdrawal of Soviet missiles from Cuba after the Kennedy administration made a public assurance that it would not invade Cuba and sent a back-channel message confirming its plan to remove U.S. missiles from Turkey after several months. By this time, the Foxtrots already were heading back home to Sayda Bay. One of them, the *B-130,* had to be towed back to the Kola peninsula when its drivetrain broke. In true Soviet fashion, the admirals who had sent the Foxtrots on an impossible, near-suicidal operation quickly reprimanded the four submarine commanders for failing in their mission.[41]

Many years after the crisis, both sides learned that the standoff had actually been far more dangerous than anyone at the time realized. Not only had the Soviets managed to deliver nuclear warheads to Cuba without U.S. detection, but the U.S. Navy did not learn until decades later that the Foxtrot submarines had carried nuclear torpedoes and had astonishingly loose rules of engagement that would have allowed their commanders to fire the weapons if they believed they were under attack. The U.S. Air Force nuclear airborne alert bombers were one Emergency Action Message away from launching total nuclear destruction on the Soviet heartland. It is no speculation to see that a single nuclear detonation would have triggered devastation from Moscow to Chicago.[42]

Immediately after the confrontation, analysts on both sides interpreted the Cuban Missile Crisis as a deep political humiliation for the Soviet Union. As Secretary of State Dean Rusk famously put it, "We were eyeball to eyeball, and the other fellow just blinked." Indeed, a week short of the second anniversary of the crisis, the Soviet Central Committee on October 14, 1964, waited for Khrushchev to leave town on vacation, then sacked him and sent him into internal exile. Among the charges against him was his mishandling of Operation Anadyr, the missile emplacement in Cuba. He would remain a non-person under house arrest and die in obscurity in 1971.

For Gorshkov and the Soviet Navy, the Cuban crisis may have ended in embarrassment, but it turned out to be another godsend. One of the direct consequences of the missile crisis was to persuade Khrushchev and his successors to expand and prolong the nuclear submarine confrontation at sea in the decades that followed. In his account of the missile crisis, former U.S. naval attaché to Moscow Captain Peter Huchthausen described the aftermath of the superpower confrontation as fueling an escalation of the Cold War at sea: "The confrontation was a pivotal moment for the Soviet fleet, leading to a resumption of an aggressive naval construction program, which continued until the implosion of the Soviet Union in 1991. By that time, the USSR had achieved status as the world's largest and second most powerful navy."[43]

The new Soviet leadership under Leonid Brezhnev gave Gorshkov the green light to expand both the Soviet submarine and surface fleets, and warship production immediately accelerated. Even before then, in 1963 the CINC had issued a pivotal order to the Soviet Navy that it should "go to sea." Beginning in 1964 and continuing throughout the 1970s, Soviet submarines, surface warships, oceanographic research vessels, electronic spy trawlers (known as AGIs) and the state-owned merchant fleet suddenly began appearing in oceans and seas that had never before seen the Soviet Navy ensign flying from the jackstaff.

The first major military clash after the Cuban Missile Crisis brought proof that Gorshkov was making progress in building the blue-water Soviet Navy. Immediately before the outbreak of the June 1967 Six-Day War in the Middle East, there were normally a half-dozen Soviet warships cruising around the Mediterranean. When hostilities erupted in June 1967, Gorshkov was able to surge his fleet to an unprecedented seventy ships, forty of which would form a permanent Mediterranean squadron based in Alexandria. Syria and Tunisia also opened their ports to Soviet warship visits. Gorshkov would warn in October of that year, "Now, we must be prepared for broad offensive operations against sea and ground troops of the imperialists on any point of the world's oceans and adjacent territories." In just ten years, the Soviet Navy CINC had reached a major milestone in his plan to match U.S. naval power.

Gorshkov's ambition was far from idle. During the six years after the missile crisis, the ongoing modernization effort steadily changed the face of the Soviet Navy. In particular, Gorshkov's submarine fleet substantially improved: The wheezy November-class attack boats were still deployed, but they were joined in 1967 by the first of the Victor class, a significant advance in design and performance. The Golf- and Hotel-class missile boats still went out on patrol (even the cursed *K-19*), but in 1968, the first Yankee-class SSBN, a visual knockoff of the American Polaris, made its debut with sixteen ballistic missiles in launch tubes in the center hull aft of the sail.[44]

Sitting in his Main Navy headquarters in Moscow at the beginning of 1968, a clearly pleased Admiral Sergei Gorshkov was looking forward to even more ambitious operations. Even though the Soviets had withdrawn their missiles from Cuba in 1962, Soviet Navy and merchant ships continued to call on the island in growing numbers. Between 1964 and 1968, Soviet warships had become regular visitors along the African coast and in the Indian Ocean, and the South Pacific. In 1967, the Soviets conducted extensive oceanographic research trips and exercises testing the concept of establishing replenishment bases at sea to extend their submarines' ability to maneuver and patrol far from home base. These included several anchorages in the Mediterranean, North Atlantic, and Indian Ocean, and plans were in play to repeat the effort in 1968. Gorshkov and his staff were also making preliminary plans for a real showstopper—a massive, global naval maneuver set for the summer of 1970 called Operation Okean, in which he hoped to test a new satellite communications system to exercise direct command-and-control over his expanding force. After years of struggle and setback, the Soviets were on the move.[45]

Another profound change had occurred as well, U.S. and Soviet submarine veterans of that era recall: an attitude change. Soviet submariners weren't going to take any lip from their U.S. adversaries anymore. By early 1968, the Soviet submariners were fed up with the aggressive tactics their counterparts had long used to shadow and hound them. U.S. submariners were well aware of the mood change. One indicator was the sudden emergence of an aggressive submarine tactic called Crazy Ivan, where a Soviet submarine skipper, suspecting he was being tailgated, would make an unexpected hard turn to port or starboard, and in doing so, force the American follower to slam on the brakes. Apart from the fun of spiking a *Sturgeon*-class skipper's blood pressure, there was a concrete objective to the ploy. This maneuver forced the American submarine commander to reveal his own presence by the unavoidable scream of reverse-drive engine turbines as the trailing U.S. submarine desperately tried to avoid a collision by ordering all back full. That noise signal showed up just fine on Soviet sonar.

"They were getting sick and tired of being dogged and not being able to retaliate," retired Vice Admiral Philip Beshany, the U.S. Navy's director of submarine warfare in 1968, later recalled. "They were doing the 'Ivan' by then, it had crept into their repertoire. Our guys were able to get out of the way, but he [the Soviet submarine commander] was pissed off, sick and tired of being put in that category. I can appreciate why they'd be that way," Beshany said with a chuckle. "It's not an easy thing to accept that you are less than the best."[46]

Soviet-era submariners were even blunter. Nearly a decade after the Cold War had ended, one Russian admiral still could not contain his exasperation. "I can produce a mass of examples about our subs' encounters with the American subs," said Admiral Vladimir Ivanovich Bez, who was an assistant division commander in the Pacific in 1968. "The thing is, even when we were in our [local] training range, almost every time we found an American sub. There were collisions. The thing is, that in those years there was an order issued to all the [American] submarine commanders to act with extreme assertiveness against our submarines, in order to record the propeller noises. I remembered, in that order there was this kind of phrase: 'Act extremely assertive and take Russians by surprise with this.'" Bez recalled he was at sea one day on a Soviet attack submarine with Rear Admiral N. F. Gonchar as his guest, when the latter complained, "Everyone at sea runs into American submarines and I have not witnessed that even once." Bez went on, "I was looking through the periscope at that moment and suddenly saw the masts of an American sub, so I said, 'Look, here it is.' So he looks and behold, four cables away from us, the American's masts are sticking out. They are very easy to tell. I'm surprised that with those tactics, there were so *few* collisions." Admiral Valery Ivanovich Alexin, a former chief navigator of the Soviet and Russian navies, agreed. He said that there had been at least two dozen collisions involving U.S. and Soviet submarines during 1967–93. "All those collisions were unpremeditated, were always unpremeditated, since any of them could have been fatal for either one or both subs," the admiral said in a 1998 interview.[47]

Over time, inevitably, Soviet submariners began to amass experience and develop tactics to counter the superior submarine technology of the Americans. By the mid-1960s, their older nuclear submarines remained hot, cranky, and often easily detectable, but they were no longer the pushovers that U.S. submariners and ASW tactical action officers had long known. Three incidents over the course of a fourteen-month period illustrate the slow but steady gains that Soviet submariners were making.

The encounter between the November-class nuclear attack submarine *K-181* and the aircraft carrier *USS Saratoga* (CVA 60) in the Atlantic in 1966 was the first. Under the command of Captain First Rank Vladimir Borisov, *K-181* received orders to conduct a long-range patrol along the U.S. East Coast in the fall of 1966 to study the Sosus hydrophone network. Of course, the first thing that occurred as *K-181* trolled down the coast was that its sound signature began sparking across the U.S. Navy Sosus paper drums at NavFacs from Canada to the Caribbean. Then Northern Fleet commander Admiral Semyon Mikhailovich Lobov came up with a better mission: Aware that a U.S. Navy carrier battle group was heading into the Atlantic from the Mediterranean, he dispatched *K-181* to locate and trail the carrier and its five escorts. Unfortunately, Borisov at that moment was 2,400 miles away, near the entrance to the Caribbean. He ordered the submarine to full speed, retracted his bow diving planes to reduce friction, and hightailed it across the Atlantic at an average speed of twenty-seven knots. One imagines U.S. Navy sonar operators within range yanking their headsets off to avoid hearing loss as the *K-181* howled past.

Three days later, Borisov slowed the *K-181* to a crawl, poked his electronic surveillance (ESM) mast out into the night air, and smiled as he heard the radio chatter of the carrier *Saratoga* and its formation drawing near. *K-181* slipped past the escort destroyers and ensconced itself in the one place where the November-class submarine could easily hide— the boiling wake of the 56,000-ton *avianosnoye udarnoye soyedineniye* (aircraft carrier) itself, an inferno of white noise that would cloak the Soviet submarine's own sound emissions. For several days, *K-181* trailed the carrier and photographed the massive ship as it topped off its escorts with fuel and conducted routine air operations. Just for fun, Borisov made nine simulated torpedo attacks on the *Saratoga* as well.

When sonobuoys from P-3 Orion patrol aircraft began dropping like sleet around his submarine several days later, Borisov concluded that the jig was up and broke contact to head home, his mission an unparalleled success. Once tied up to the pier, Borisov presented Vice Admiral Georgi Egorov and his flotilla commander a photo album of periscope photographs of the *Saratoga* and its escorts. Later, Borisov learned that in response to his trailing mission, the U.S. Navy had issued instructions to warn any submarine that came within 100 miles of a carrier by dropping grenade-sized charges as it had done in the Cuban Missile Crisis and, if the submarine failed to back off, to sink it.[48]

A second Soviet breakthrough—one that does not appear in the unclassified literature of the post–Cold War U.S. Navy—occurred eight months later during the Six-Day War. As Captain Nikolai Shashkov, commanding the Echo-II class submarine *K-172*, prepared his boat for a deployment to the Mediterranean, Fleet Admiral Gorshkov summoned the younger officer to his Moscow headquarters and gave him chilling oral instructions "to be ready to make a rocket strike on the coast of Israel." Originally designed for attacking American carriers, the Echo-II-class submarine could also strike land with its eight SS-N-3 Shaddock cruise missiles armed with either a 200- or a 300-kiloton nuclear warhead and a range of about 360 miles.

Shashkov had a number of serious obstacles to overcome to carry out this deployment. The first two were merely very difficult. First, he had to maneuver the *K-172* from the Soviet northern coastline through the Barents and Norwegian Seas and the North Atlantic Ocean without detection. Second, he had to slip through the Straits of Gibraltar into the Mediterranean without notice. The third was even more of a headache: "I was restricted by the flight distance of my rockets . . . so I was forced to 'loiter' . . . dangerously close to three U.S. aircraft carrier strike groups headed by nuclear carriers *America, Forrestal,* and *Enterprise,*" he recalled years later. "Each had in escort 20–30 ships, almost every one of which was equipped with submarine detection systems. And I was alone. . . . At times there were as many as 17 submarine hunting aircraft hammering the entire eastern Mediterranean with their radar. . . . They were looking for an entire underwater Soviet [submarine] screen, while in fact there was my one *K-172*."[49]

Upon receipt of a coded signal from Soviet Navy headquarters in Moscow, Shashkov was to surface the *K-172* and fire his eight missiles at Israel. The trigger point, Shashkov explained, was if Israel or its Western allies invaded Syria, then a Soviet military ally. "We considered [the *K-172*] a 'one-time' sub, i.e., only fit for firing one salvo," the former skipper said with mordant humor. "After all, we could fire only when surfaced, and the time between surfacing and launching is 20 minutes. This would have been more than enough to find us and destroy us immediately after the salvo was fired." In the end, the fatal order never arrived, and *K-172* ended its patrol without firing a shot.

Shashkov said his greatest satisfaction came in successfully evading superior U.S. Navy surface ships and aircraft throughout the weeks he was on patrol near the Syrian coast. He credited the adverse sound conditions in the Mediterranean and the presence of heavy commercial shipping for his ability to remain undetected. "Our intelligence really put the wind up on us: 'Look out, they [the Americans] can pick up a boat at 200 miles whatever the conditions.' They never picked up a thing. We heard them, but they didn't hear us," Shashkov recalled. "If they had, I wouldn't be talking to you today. . . . If they had discovered me I'd have had half a dozen anti-submarine ships down on me, [SH-3] Sea Kings [helicopters] flying overhead and a[n Israeli] nuclear torpedo boat on my tail ready to launch a full salvo if I so much as opened the lids of my rocket containers. That's why I'm 100 percent sure that we didn't blow our cover."

Shashkov, who retired as a vice admiral in the 1990s, recalled the harsh Cold War reality that his submarine and its top-secret mission— and those of his American adversaries—had come to embody: "I understood perfectly well the whole risk of our venture. But war is war. . . . Do you suppose the Americans didn't behave in exactly the same way? I can name for you the commanders of those American nuclear-powered vessels which had Moscow and the industrial areas of the Urals in their sights. They could also have had the honor, or rather misfortune, to start the Third World War. And the Americans knew . . . the USSR was just as capable of making a nuclear strike as American strategists defending their geopolitical interests."[50]

Shashkov and his crew, on returning to port, were amazed to find Soviet leader Leonid Brezhnev himself on the pier to greet the returning *K-172*. Such public recognition was as rare in the Red Banner Fleet as in any other navy in the world.

Just sixteen months later, a November-class attack boat in the Pacific jolted the U.S. Navy even harder than either the *K-181* or *K-172* had managed to do. The unidentified November gave the U.S. Navy a run for its money that stunned admirals in the U.S. Pacific Fleet and the Pentagon. It began on January 3, 1968, six weeks before the *USS Scorpion's* scheduled departure for the Mediterranean from Norfolk. On the West Coast, navy warships were steadily deploying to an actual shooting war in Vietnam. On that Wednesday morning, the nuclear-powered aircraft carrier *USS Enterprise* (CVAN 65) backed out from the pier in Alameda, California, turned into the shipping channel, and slowly edged under the San Francisco-Oakland Bay Bridge heading for the Golden Gate. "Our eventual destination was to be, of course, Vietnam," then-Captain Kent Lee, the *Enterprise's* commander, later recalled. As the carrier emerged out from under the Golden Gate Bridge into the Pacific Ocean, Lee's lookouts spotted a familiar sight: A Soviet intelligence trawler, bristling with aerials and antennas, lurked several miles offshore. The *Enterprise* snubbed the boxy little spy vessel and steamed out on a great circle course for Hawaii.[51]

Lee described what happened next: "After about two days at sea, we got a message . . . telling us that the Navy's intelligence organization reported that a Russian submarine was coming down from the Aleutian chain. . . . If so, we were to wait until he got into position behind us and then increase our speed slowly to see just how fast the Russian submarine was, or to see at what speed he'd break off."[52] As one account put it, the Naval Security Group—the navy's communications intelligence network—had intercepted the coded transmission from the Soviet trawler and an immediate short-burst transmission from the November-class submarine up in the Bering Sea that apparently acknowledged the trawler's message. Shortly thereafter, the navy's Sosus network along the Aleutians detected the November increasing speed and making a new course to the southeast to intercept the *Enterprise*. Such "signal traffic analysis" enabled the navy's intelligence experts to deduce the Soviets' intentions even if the line-by-line text of their encrypted messages remained undeciphered.[53]

U.S. Navy leaders regarded the November's sudden appearance behind the *Enterprise* as an opportunity and not a nuisance. For months, a behind-the-scenes debate had raged over recent Soviet submarine incidents suggesting that Gorshkov's undersea fleet was closing in on U.S. submarine capabilities. Several months earlier, a new Victor-class Soviet nuclear submarine had startled the Pentagon when it managed to pop up behind an aircraft carrier crossing the Atlantic in a replay of the *K-181* confrontation with the *Saratoga*.

Meanwhile, U.S. officials were still uncertain as to how fast the mass-produced November-class nuclear attack boats could go, with the best estimate at that time a maximum of twenty-five to twenty-seven knots. Navy leaders decided to let the massive *Enterprise* play "electric rabbit" with the November, pretending it was unaware of the Soviet's presence while steadily increasing its speed to goad the adversary into revealing his best stuff.[54]

With eight A1W nuclear reactors powering the *Enterprise*'s four massive propellers, Lee was confident that he could outrun the November by going to maximum speed, an incredible thirty-five knots. But the orders from Washington were to play dumb, act clueless, and simply notch his speed up a few knots at a time so as not to trigger the Soviet submarine captain's suspicions. The alert finally came from a P-3 Orion aircraft that had plotted the November's location with air-dropped sonobuoys. The submarine was a few miles astern of the carrier.

Several hours later, Lee ordered the *Enterprise* to make eighteen knots. The four propellers began turning faster, the wave on the carrier's knife-edge bow became whiter, and the game was on. The Soviet submarine increased speed to hold its position. Two hours after that, Lee ordered the *Enterprise* to make a speed of twenty-four knots. An escort cruiser monitoring the Soviet submarine with its passive sonar soon tracked the November at the same speed. By midnight, the *Enterprise* and its escorts were tearing through the Pacific at twenty-eight knots, and the November was still hanging in. As one account of the incident noted, the Soviet submarine "was breaking all speed records for the November class. He was still back there like a dog snarling on your pants leg, and Lee was troubled because the Russian should have been losing ground by now." The *Enterprise's* skipper in frustration ordered flank speed, and the propeller shafts began spinning at 120 rpm. The *Enterprise* redlined at thirty-one knots, or thirty-seven miles an hour on land. Astonishingly, the November kept the pace at that unheard-of speed.[55]

The November finally broke off the chase, and Lee took the *Enterprise* into Pearl Harbor for a brief stopover before crossing the rest of the Pacific for duty on Yankee Station off the coast of North Vietnam. Back in Washington, D.C., a shaken U.S. Navy, Central Intelligence Agency, and Congress quickly realized that they had seriously underestimated the Soviet Navy's gains in submarine design. Worse, they had failed to understand the implications of Admiral Sergei Gorshkov's ambition to make a world-class Soviet Navy and submarine force. It was official: On January 5, 1968, the Russians had arrived.[56]

6

LEAVING HOME

MIDNIGHT. IN THE WINTER, THE DESTROYER-SUBMARINE PIER complex at Norfolk Naval Station could be a dark, bitterly cold, and lonely place.* The wind cut through the duty sailors' thick peacoats; without gloves, the flesh on their hands would freeze to the polished metal gangway rails. Those standing topside watch on submarines in port knew only the glacial creep of the ship's chronometer toward 0400 and their relief from duty. Except for an unplanned emergency, nothing ever happened during the midwatch.[1]

That was the scene on Pier 22 in the early morning hours of Thursday, February 15, 1968. Moored to the end of the massive concrete wharf several hundred yards from shore, bow pointing toward land, the *USS Scorpion* showed little sign of life. A metal gangway reaching out from the pier rested on the port fairwater plane, the stubby wing-like control blade attached to the submarine's fin-shaped sail. From there, a jury-rigged set of safety lines pointed to a doorway hatch in the side of the sail that provided the sole access to the interior of the boat.

---

* The reconstructions in this chapter come from a number of sources, especially interviews with Bill G. Elrod USN (Ret.). Commands and responses during the reactor start-up conform to procedures of the Naval Reactors Branch. Biographical details of the crewmen are from *USS Scorpion: In Memoriam*; the roster of Submarine Squadron 6 is described in *COMSUBLANT Command History for 1968*.

Fireman Michael E. Dunn, nineteen, standing the topside watch on the *Scorpion's* sail, huddled up against the hatchway door in a vain effort to shelter from the biting wind. The nighttime temperature stood at nineteen degrees. There was little for Dunn to see under the dim fluorescent floodlights mounted on fixed poles high overhead. The pier was all but empty. The other four nuclear attack boats of Submarine Squadron 6—the *Scorpion's* sister ships *USS Shark* and *Skipjack*, and the two newer submarines *USS Ray* and *USS Lapon* (SSN 661)—were away from Norfolk on a variety of missions. Far back down the pier where it met the shore, the massive black silhouette of the submarine tender *Orion* and a few of the squadron's older diesel submarines were faintly visible beneath the security floodlights standing sentinel along the streets and parking lots of the massive naval base. The only sounds carrying on the night air were the low drone of air vents, the background hum of electronic gear, and the murmur of the harbor washing up against the submarine's curved hull. Inside the *Scorpion,* however, things were about to change.

In eight hours, the *Scorpion* would depart Norfolk.

The deployment to the Mediterranean was to last a month longer than the sixty-day spy missions along the Soviet coastline that the *Scorpion* and its sister ships normally carried out. And this time there would be no spooks on board to intercept Soviet radio signals or missile telemetry data. Instead, the *Scorpion* would exercise with the U.S. Sixth Fleet and NATO allies in the Mediterranean. It was a last-minute assignment.

The navy originally planned to send its second oldest nuclear submarine, the *USS Seawolf* (SSN 575), on the mission, but two weeks earlier, the *Seawolf* had had an accident. Posing as a mock Soviet submarine, the *Seawolf* was skirmishing in the Gulf of Maine with the *USS Sturgeon* (SSN 637), one of the newest nuclear attack boats. The exercise required the *Seawolf* to make continuous high-speed runs across the gulf while the *Sturgeon's* sonar team tracked the older submarine and calculated practice torpedo-firing solutions. The exercise came to an abrupt end when the *Seawolf* slammed into an uncharted underwater rock formation. The collision wrecked the submarine's rudder and disabled its bow and stern diving planes. After blowing its ballast tanks and climbing out of the depths, the *Seawolf* wallowed on the surface for twenty-four hours until a submarine rescue ship could arrive to tow it back to base at Groton.[2]

Atlantic Submarine Force headquarters in Norfolk needed to send one of its nuclear attack submarines to the Mediterranean, and officials chose the *Scorpion*. The mission would involve a broad menu of training operations with U.S. and NATO warships. Nuclear submariners usually scoffed at this assignment, describing it as playing electric rabbit—a reference to the moving gadget at greyhound racetracks used to incite the hounds to run. There was an upside, however: The *Scorpion*'s crew could look forward to an inviting array of liberty port visits around the Mediterranean, including Naples and Taranto, Italy, Augusta Bay, Sicily, Athens, and Izmir, Turkey. Since the only liberty port on Northern run missions was the submarine anchorage in frigid Holy Loch, Scotland, having to play electric rabbit wasn't such a bad thing after all.[3]

For the past two weeks, the *Scorpion*'s crew had worked hard making last-minute repairs, fine-tuning equipment, and loading supplies. The submarine's storage compartments now bulged with canned food, fresh fruit, vegetables, and beverages. Officers, chiefs, and enlisted crewmen updated their personal paperwork, obtained new underwater navigational charts, and reviewed the ship's training schedule. The crewmen had personally girded themselves to return to sea once more, reassuring loved ones that they would write often and return with gifts from the Mediterranean. Over the past days, those with homes ashore had lugged their seabags down to the submarine, rigged their bunks, and otherwise prepped for one hundred days in the cramped confines of the submarine's berthing compartments. In the early hours of Thursday morning, many of the *Scorpion*'s sailors were enjoying one last night ashore.

But not all. Nearly a fourth of the crew was already preparing the submarine for getting underway. Since returning to Norfolk from their final exercises at sea several weeks earlier, the submarine's nuclear reactor had been shut down. Thick cables from the pier provided electricity to the boat for light and power. This was about to change. The duty engineering watch was preparing to bring the *Scorpion*'s S5W reactor to life.

The four-hour reactor startup process began at about one A.M. It started in the maneuvering room, the tiny cubicle office on the upper level of the *Scorpion's* massive engine compartment. If the control room was the *Scorpion's* brain, the maneuvering room—seventy-five feet aft of the control room and separated from it by the reactor and auxiliary machinery compartments—was the submarine's heart. This is where highly trained nucs operated the pressurized-water reactor that drove the *Scorpion's* propulsion system and powered its electrical generators.

Section 3 had the post-midnight duty, so the point man for lighting the *Scorpion's* nuclear fires was Lieutenant William C. Harwi, twenty-nine, the ship's duty engineering officer of the watch. With Harwi in the tiny maneuvering room were three assistants manning their control consoles. The duty reactor operator, Electronics Technician First Class Michael Lee McGuire, twenty-four, hunched over his console. Sitting practically elbow-to-elbow with McGuire at two other stations were Electrician's Mate Second Class Ralph R. Huber, twenty-one, the throttleman of the watch, and the duty electrical plant operator, Interior Communications Electrician Second Class Thomas E. Amtower, twenty-two. The atmosphere inside the maneuvering room was professional and brisk. The four men had worked together for long hours in engineering training sessions and actual maneuvering watches over the past year. They knew one another and they were well versed in the complex process of lighting off the *Scorpion's* nuclear fires.

A 1961 graduate of Princeton University, Harwi had obtained his commission through the Naval Reserve Officer Training Corps (NROTC). Immediately entering the nuclear submarine pipeline, he spent twenty-one months as a student at the Navy Submarine School in Groton, followed by nuclear power training at a shore-based reactor prototype at Windsor, Connecticut. From there, the Philadelphia native served a tour on the ballistic missile submarine *USS Alexander Hamilton* (SSBN 617) as supply officer and briefly as assistant engineering officer before returning to Windsor for additional training. Since reporting on board the *Scorpion* seventeen months earlier, Harwi had been the ship's engineer. He had supervised the submarine's propulsion systems through a two-month Northern run spy mission in late 1966 before the eight-month nuclear refueling overhaul and the intense, eleven-week spate of refresher training and at-sea exercises since the *Scorpion* left the shipyard. A former supervisor would later describe Harwi as "an extremely competent engineer. He was especially knowledgeable . . . in theoretical aspects as well as operational aspects of the [reactor] plant."[4]

The engineer's plant operators this night were also experienced submariners. The *Scorpion* was the third submarine for McGuire, a six-year navy veteran. A native Missourian, McGuire had been aboard the *Scorpion* three months longer than Harwi, reporting to the submarine in June 1966. Huber joined the navy in 1964 following high school graduation in Schwenksville, Pennsylvania. After electrician school in San Diego and a tour on the repair ship *USS Markab* (AK 31), he attended nuclear power training in Vallejo, California and Submarine School in Groton. He had been onboard the *Scorpion,* his first submarine, for seven months. Amtower also served a tour on surface ships before applying for the submarine force. A West Virginian, he enlisted in the navy in September 1963 and served on the command ship *USS Northampton* (CC 1) after finishing interior communications electrician school in Great Lakes, Illinois. After submarine school, Amtower served aboard the *USS Sea Leopard* (SS 483) before joining the *Scorpion* in October 1966. Roving the engine compartment outside the maneuvering room was a fourth key member of the engineering team, Machinist's Mate Chief James M. Wells, thirty-seven, the engineering watch supervisor, Harwi's direct assistant. A career submariner with nineteen years of service, Wells spent four years on the *Nautilus* before reporting to the *Scorpion* in January 1965, making him one of the longest-serving sailors onboard.[5]

The other Section 3 crewmen included six engineering watchstanders who manned workstations in the aft end of the submarine: Machinist's Mate First Class James K. Brueggeman, twenty-five, the duty engine room supervisor; Machinist's Mate Second Class Kenneth R. Brocker, assigned to the engine room upper level with Machinist's Mate Second Class Francis K. Carey II down below; and Machinist's Mate Second Class David B. Stone in the engine room feed station. In the auxiliary machinery room just forward of the engine compartment, Electronics Technician Second Class Kenneth R. Martin was assigned to the upper level, and Interior Communications Electrician Third Class Donald R. Powell was down below on the AMR lower level.

Had the *Scorpion* been underway at sea, the Section 3 officers and enlisted specialists assigned to the control room and other areas in the forward half of the submarine would have been present at their stations. However, the submarine was still officially in an in-port status, so most of these duty watchstanders were asleep in their bunks, available in case of an emergency. Given standard submarine procedures, the officer of the deck, Lieutenant John P. Burke, twenty-six, and his junior officer of the deck, twenty-five-year-old Lieutenant (junior grade) John Charles Sweet, were likely taking turns napping while the other quietly relaxed in the small wardroom lounge or made his rounds in the submarine. Both were U.S. Naval Academy graduates, from the classes of 1963 and 1964, respectively. They had thus far enjoyed similar career experiences. Each attended the required submarine and nuclear power training and served a tour on a diesel attack submarine before reporting onboard the *Scorpion.*

The other duty section crewman awake on duty was the below-decks watch, another junior sailor who served as a roving watchstander. His responsibilities included answering the ship's telephone and conducting a range of routine tasks such as blowing the sanitary tanks, lining up the ventilation system, and waking people up for watch. Section 3 personnel assigned to these slots included Machinist's Mate Third Class Robert A. Willis and Torpedoman Seaman Joseph F. Miller Jr., both twenty, and Fireman Apprentice Michael R. Dunn, nineteen.

The rest of the Section 3 Control Room watch was likely enjoying a last few hours of rest before getting underway began in earnest. The assigned chief of the watch was Quartermaster Senior Chief Frank Patsy Mazzuchi, forty-two, a naturalized American born in Italy whose family had emigrated to the United States in the early 1930s. One of only two crewmen with World War II service, Mazzuchi had been aboard the *Scorpion* since January 1962, longer than any other except Torpedoman Chief Walter Bishop. Underway, Mazzuchi was quite busy. As a diving officer of the watch, his responsibility was to operate the *Scorpion*'s ballast-control systems that enabled the submarine to dive below the surface and resurface on command.

The rest of the control room duty section this night included Quartermaster Third Class Dennis P. Pferrer, twenty, the duty quartermaster of the watch; Fire Controlman Seaman William R. Fennick, twenty, the fire controlman of the watch; Sonar Technician Second Class Michael E. Henry, twenty-three, and Sonar Technician Third Class Ronald J. Voss, twenty-one, the duty sonar watchstanders, and Radioman Chief Garlin R. Denney, thirty-one, the radioman of the watch. Elsewhere in the forward section, Interior Communications Electrician Second Class Joseph D. Underwood, twenty-four, was auxiliary electrician forward, responsible for monitoring the atmosphere control system and taking readings on the gyroscopes and electrical storage batteries when underway.

Harwi and the technicians in the maneuvering room began the countdown with a careful monitoring of the reactor control gauges and a cross-check of a highly classified S5W technical manual that charted the calculated core life—that is, how much nuclear energy measured in full power hours of operation remained. From these calculations, Harwi and the maneuvering room watch were able to determine the number of inches that they would have to lift the neutron-absorbing control rods from the bottom of the fuel core for the fission reaction to go critical—that is, to become self-sustaining. (Usually the rods rose between thirty and thirty-six inches from the bottom of the fuel core to attain "criticality.") Now, Harwi picked up a telephone and called Commander Francis A. Slattery at his home in Virginia Beach. The *Scorpion's* commanding officer was expecting this call.

"Captain, Engineer, recommending starting the reactor. Section 3 watches are manned aft. Request to start the reactor."

"Request to start the reactor, aye," Slattery answered, then hung up.

Harwi pulled the 2MC microphone from its stand and clicked on the transmit button. His voice reverberated within the engineering spaces. He first paged Chief Wells: "Engineering watch supervisor, come to maneuvering." In less than a minute, Wells formally announced his presence at the open doorway. Reaching for the reactor safety key on a chain around his neck, Harwi opened a locked cabinet and retrieved three safety fuses the size of flashlights. These were a protection against accidental reactor startup. He handed them to Wells.

Once installed, the fuses completed the power circuit in three inverter cabinets, electronic devices that controlled the mechanisms that moved the control rods in and out of the reactor's fuel core. Harwi addressed the chief: "Engineering watch supervisor, place fuses in inverter cabinets alpha, bravo, and charlie, and shut scram breakers." Wells stepped out of the room, returning just several minutes later. The reactor startup litany continued.

"Sir, fuses placed in inverters alpha, bravo, and charlie. Scram breakers alpha, bravo, and charlie are shut." With that vital electrical circuit closed, Harwi and his team were now free to power up the S5W by raising the control rods out of the core. The engineer turned to McGuire at the reactor plant control panel and issued the next order: "Reactor operator, conduct normal reactor startup." McGuire acknowledged the order and Harwi announced over the 2MC loudspeaker circuit, "Commencing normal reactor startup."

The process continued. McGuire activated the pumps that push the primary coolant through the heavily shielded piping loop that runs from the reactor core to the steam generator and back. He latched the first group of control rods using powerful electromagnets, and then slowly raised the first control rod group to the top of the reactor vessel. He then repeated the process twice with the second and third control rod groups. Inside the heavily shielded S5W vessel, neutron emissions from the fuel core steadily increased. As they struck other elements of the highly enriched uranium fuel, even more neutrons flew free in a steady crescendo of radiation and heat. McGuire's gauges depicted a steady increase in nuclear fission inside the reactor, and when it reached the proper level, he turned to Harwi and reported, "Sir, the reactor is critical."

Harwi's voice echoed throughout the *Scorpion* over the 1MC loudspeakers, the communications circuit that reached every compartment on the submarine: "The reactor is critical." At first, the power level was not yet sufficient to begin heating the primary coolant, but in a short time, McGuire reported, "Reactor is in the power range. Heating up main coolant. . . ." At this stage, Harwi, McGuire, and the other maneuvering room watchstanders were passive observers to the laws of nuclear physics. The S5W reactor was now heating up on automatic, with redundant safety systems in place to scram—that is, to execute an emergency shutdown—in case the nuclear reaction process somehow escalated out of control.

It was nearly two A.M. when the primary coolant reached the correct temperature of about 600 degrees Fahrenheit. At this stage, the reactor began generating superheated steam to drive the submarine's main engines and to create internal electricity by spinning the rotors within each of the two ship's steam turbine generators (SSTGs). Harwi again summoned Wells to the maneuvering room and ordered him to start the steam plant. This procedure involved activating the components of the separate secondary coolant system. They consisted of the steam generator, port and starboard main condensers, and the electrical generators and main engines that turned the *Scorpion*'s massive propeller shaft. The highly radioactive primary coolant was locked inside the closed circuit of pipes running from the reactor vessel to steam generator and back. Inside the steam generator, heat from the primary loop would flash the secondary coolant into steam while avoiding any transfer of radioactivity into the secondary system piping.

Wells and Brocker then got to work in the upper level of the engine room, opening intake valves to the steam headers that created a vacuum on the system to start the flow of steam. A light blinked on McGuire's control panel, and he informed Harwi that the two main steam valves were open. Loud shrieks echoed through the aft end of the *Scorpion* as Wells and Brocker blasted steam through the condenser lines to clear out any water drops that may have collected there.

After about ten minutes, Wells stepped down the ladder to the Engine Room lower level, joining Carey at the two huge steam condensers, which acted to lower the secondary coolant temperature and convert the steam back to water before it returned to the steam generator for additional reheating. The two sailors activated the *Scorpion*'s two main seawater pumps, which cooled the condensers down. They next applied steam pressure from the submarine's auxiliary steam system to "suck down" the condensers. This forced a vacuum that kicked off the back end of the propulsion cycle. The superheated primary coolant entering the steam generator flashed the water in the secondary loop piping into steam, which then passed through the SSTGs and main engine turbines. From there, the secondary steam cooled back down into water in the condensers before returning once again to the steam generator. Once the condensers were all operating, Wells climbed back up to the upper level of the engine compartment. The first turbine generator then added its own earsplitting howl to the cacophony as steam began to spin the turbine blades.

Now it was Amtower's turn. Sitting at the electrical plant control panel, he looked over his shoulder at Wells standing in the doorway for the confirmation. "Portside turbine generator on the governor and ready for loading," the chief announced.

Then Harwi spoke: "Electrical operator, shift the electric plant to a half-power lineup on the port TG [turbine generator]." He monitored the panel gauges that showed the portside SSTG breaker. At this juncture, the dials displayed two important readings: the electrical load that was coming in to the breaker from shore power, and the rising electrical voltage now coming from the steam-powered turbine generator. At the correct moment when the power loads were synchronized, Amtower rotated a control switch and then disconnected the breaker to the shore power supply. For the first time in a month, the *Scorpion* was now generating its own electrical power. After repeating the process for the starboard generator, one more step remained. "Engineer watch supervisor," Harwi said, "remove the shore-power cables." Wells and another engineering watchstander physically disconnected the cables. Finally, Harwi called Burke in the control room and requested the officer of the deck's permission to spin the propeller shaft as necessary to keep the main engines warm. Within several minutes, the harbor water at the *Scorpion's* stern began to undulate from the massive seven-bladed propeller as it made occasional half-turns. The maneuvering room and engineering watchstanders then stood by to answer bells from the control room.

The *Scorpion* had become a living thing. It was ready to return once more to the sea.[6]

THE 1960S WERE NOT easy for the U.S. Navy's submarine force. While the Soviet Navy struggled to overcome its technological inferiority, the Atlantic Submarine Force by 1963 was wrestling with the unintended consequences of its earlier successes. In particular, Navy officials were scrambling to deal with a potentially dangerous shortage of qualified and experienced officers and enlisted technicians.

Soon after he took office in 1961, President John F. Kennedy, a navy veteran himself, decided to accelerate the Polaris missile submarine program while continuing to build a modern nuclear fast-attack submarine fleet. In the late 1950s the Eisenhower administration had endorsed a plan to build nineteen of the giant submarines in response to the feared, but unfounded, missile gap favoring the Soviet Union. Kennedy's Secretary of Defense, Robert McNamara, expanded the force to forty-one submarines. The success of the new solid-fueled Polaris missile and the submarines' ability to survive any Soviet pre-emptive attack drove the decision. Both before and after the 1962 Cuban Missile Crisis, nuclear attack submarines and Polaris missile boats came sliding down the shipways in a constant stream.[7]

The new boats created unprecedented career opportunities for those already in the elite nuclear submarine force and gave migraines to personnel specialists who had to find trained crewmen. During the *Scorpion*'s first seven years, the navy constructed and commissioned twenty-five nuclear attack submarines and thirty-nine Polaris missile boats. Each Polaris submarine had two crews of seventeen officers and 128 enlisted men. The math was brutal: The navy had to recruit and train 103 additional submarine crews during the eighty-four-month period that the shipyards were cranking out Polaris missile submarines and nuclear attack boats.[8]

For submarine officers, it felt like the floor had collapsed. "When I went aboard the *Shark* in 1960, before it was built, in that wardroom of eight officers, everybody was a qualified submariner with at least one [diesel] submarine [tour] behind him," recalled retired Captain Sanford Levey, the *Scorpion*'s executive officer during 1963–66. "Most everybody had two or three [tours]. Everybody had done all of those things before in a submarine."

In 1962, the situation was much the same. Reporting aboard the *Scorpion* in October, shortly before the submarine deployed to the Indian Ocean, then-Lieutenant Robin Pirie found himself "fifth or sixth in seniority" in the small wardroom, surrounded by experienced nuclear submariners. Suddenly, that all changed. "When we went into the ship-yard in May of 1963, I was third officer and I was the only officer in the wardroom other than the captain and the executive officer qualified in submarines. Everybody else had gone. They were all new. They were all very good people but it essentially meant that we had to train the ward-room during the overhaul—train the ship. It was the same with the en-listed people."

The dilution of experience continued over the course of the sixties, according to Levey. "When I left the [Polaris submarine *USS*] *George Bancroft* in 1970 ten years later as CO [commanding officer], hardly anybody had been to sea on any ship before," he recalled in a 1983 inter-view. "I had more time at sea, no matter which way you want to count it—days, weeks, years—than the rest of the wardroom put together, in-cluding the XO [executive officer]. And the wardroom was larger. That was fairly normal. There's no doubt that experience was diluted with that big expansion. We operated a lot of submarines safely without it. We were just fat [with experience] in the early days. We didn't know how lucky we were." Veterans of the nuclear submarine force would endure many sleepless nights worrying whether or not their junior officers and enlisted men were up to the task.[9]

The 1960s were also stressful for those managing the assignment program for nuclear enlisted personnel, submariners recall. One of the witnesses called by the *Scorpion* court of inquiry was Torpedoman Sec-ond Class David L. Tennant, assigned to the Polaris missile submarine *USS Patrick Henry* (SSBN 599). Tennant told the court that he had transferred to the *Scorpion* in November 1967 but less than three weeks later found himself with new orders to the missile submarine because the Polaris program had a higher priority than the attack boats.[10]

On Saturday, June 22, 1963, the navy launched four submarines at three separate shipyards within hours of each other. In terms of the aggressive construction schedule, this was the high-water mark of the nuclear sub-marine program. It should have been a time of celebration and pride.

But the elite world of U.S. nuclear submariners was still in mourn-ing. Three months earlier on April 10, the nuclear attack submarine

USS Thresher (SSN 593) had gone down in the Atlantic, killing its crew of 108 and twenty-one other navy officials and shipyard technicians. The worst peacetime submarine disaster in history had struck without warning.[11]

The *Thresher* loss devastated not only individual sailors and family members who had lost friends and comrades aboard the new submarine but the navy as a whole. For more than a decade, the U.S. nuclear submarine fleet had advanced without setback, seemingly invincible. Nuclear propulsion and submarine designs flowed from scientists' minds to technicians' blueprints and to shipyard fabrication facilities. Gleaming new attack submarines and boomers paraded down the shipways to line U.S. Navy piers and anchorages from Scotland to Guam. The nuclear submarine force was on patrol around the world. While minor accidents and design flaws were inevitable in such complex systems, the U.S. nuclear submarine fleet had enjoyed an unblemished safety record. Then one morning, 129 American sailors and civilian technicians died in an instant.

Commissioned on August 3, 1961, just thirteen months after the *Scorpion*, the *Thresher* was the lead ship of a new class of attack submarines. It was larger, longer, and heavier than the *Skipjack* class. The *Thresher* displaced 4,300 tons submerged to the *Scorpion's* 3,500 tons, was twenty-seven feet longer, and carried a crew of 120, nineteen more than the *Skipjacks*. With the *Thresher*, naval submarine designers had pressed for major advancement in the holy trinity of submarine characteristics: speed, diving depth, and silencing. The new submarine sported a revolutionary sonar design housed in a spherical dome at the tip of the bow that would give it unprecedented ability to detect and track enemy submarines and ships in all directions. The larger, heavier hull, built of HY-80 steel, would provide the *Thresher* a design test depth—the maximum underwater depth at which the submarine could safely operate—of 1,300 feet, nearly twice that assigned to the *Scorpion* and its sister ships. Moreover, designers for the first time mounted the submarine's heavy machinery—including the main engines and propulsion turbines and pumps—on sound-absorbing foundations, requiring an even larger hull diameter.

The *Thresher* design improvements forced a trade-off in other areas, but it was a price the navy was willing to pay: Powered by the same 15,000-shaft horsepower S5W reactor as the *Skipjacks,* the *Thresher* and its thirteen sister ships would be significantly slower than the *Scorpion.* Designers believed that the advances in operating depth and silencing were worth it. The *Thresher* would be even more lethal than its predecessors in the dark underwater knife-fight of modern submarine warfare.[12]

What caused the *Thresher* to go down? Forty years after the sinking, one senior official recounted the disaster in such detail as to suggest its loss still haunted the nuclear submarine community. Testifying before the House Science Committee, Rear Admiral Paul E. Sullivan recalled that after the sinking, a new procedure for testing the effectiveness of pipes joined in the "silver-brazing" process had found an alarming number of faulty connections. Fourteen percent of 145 joints tested showed substandard joint integrity, Sullivan said. Extrapolating these test results to the entire population of 3,000 silver-brazed joints on the submarine indicated that possibly more than 400 joints on *Thresher* could have been substandard. The investigation concluded that one or more of these joints had failed, resulting in flooding in the engine room. The *Thresher* crew was unable to stop the flooding, and saltwater spray on electrical components caused short circuits, reactor shutdown, and loss of propulsion power. Compounding the crisis, the submarine's main ballast tank blow system proved insufficient to bring the *Thresher* back up to the surface. As a result, the *Thresher* fell below crush depth and imploded, killing everyone on board.[13]

The navy's reaction was swift. On May 4, 1963, the chief of naval operations issued a fleetwide message restricting the operating depth of the nuclear submarine force while officials scrambled to devise a long-term assessment and solutions to what had gone wrong. The depth restriction aimed at ensuring that any submarine encountering a flooding casualty or other equipment breakdown would be able to safely reach the surface. For the *Scorpion* and other *Skipjacks,* the navy reduced the authorized operating depth from 750 to 500 feet.[14]

A month later, the navy announced an ambitious, complex, and extremely costly Submarine Safety Program (SubSafe) to prevent such disasters. The program mandated design changes in new submarines; these changes would also be retrofitted into the existing fleet as time and funding permitted. The SubSafe changes included the inspection of hundreds of critical pipe connections, castings, and fasteners on each submarine to ensure that they could withstand the hydrostatic pressure at the depths the boat would operate. Officials reviewed the hydraulic systems that controlled the submarine's diving planes. Plans called for installing an emergency main ballast tank blow system to ensure a submarine in distress would not fail to climb out of danger. For new submarines, the program aimed at minimizing the number of hull penetrations such as seawater cooling pipes.[15]

Just weeks after the announcement of SubSafe in the summer of 1963, the *Scorpion* entered Charleston Naval Shipyard for a long-planned overhaul. The navy was still drafting what would become the detailed SubSafe plan, so the shipyard did not make any major modifications to the *Scorpion*'s hull or operating systems. However, shipyard technicians went over the submarine in minute detail. Retired Rear Admiral Ralph Ghormley, the *Scorpion*'s commanding officer at that time, recalled that the engineers took a microscopic look at every hull penetration, pipe, valve, and fitting that could conceivably cause a future flooding casualty like the one that had destroyed the *Thresher*. "They did ultrasonic testing of bigger seawater lines where nonferrous joints had been 'silbrazed,'" he said. "They checked the main and auxiliary seawater lines, every connection . . . each of those fittings from hull to backup valves was recertified. It was an ambitious overhaul."[16]

The navy's response to the *Thresher* disaster had an immediate and dramatic impact on the nuclear attack submarine fleet and its ability to carry out continuous patrols along the Soviet littoral. Because of the time it took to subject each submarine in the navy's burgeoning fleet to this kind of rigorous inspection and upgrade, shipyards were suddenly jammed with submarines. The SubSafe program swallowed much of the programmed shipbuilding budget. As a result, fleet commanders scrambled to meet the unrelenting operational requirements with a suddenly smaller number of operationally capable boats.[17]

Submariners at the time kept their lips buttoned but quietly groused to one another that the navy was overreacting to the sinking of the *Thresher*. Sanford Levey, the *Scorpion's* executive officer during the Charleston overhaul, later said the service's attitude was excessive. "Part of it was 'Let's look at all of these seawater systems, what are they made of, let's replace them with a system that's less corrosion.' And I am talking about millions and millions of dollars, and months and months of overhaul time." Ralph Ghormley, *Scorpion's* commander, later said the SubSafe repairs for a while threatened to paralyze the submarine fleet altogether. "There was a period [in the *Thresher* aftermath] when we were the only operating nuclear submarine in the Atlantic Fleet. The other subs were all in some form of refit condition."[18]

The navy remains proud of its peacetime safety record in submarines since the implementation of SubSafe. "The SubSafe Program has been very successful," Admiral Sullivan told the House committee in 2003. "Between 1915 and 1963, sixteen submarines were lost due to non-combat causes, an average of one every three years. Since the inception of the SubSafe Program in 1963, only one submarine has been lost. *USS Scorpion* (SSN 589) was lost in May 1968 with 99 officers and men aboard. She was not a SubSafe certified submarine."[19]

Strapped for maintenance funds and pressed to provide as many nuclear attack submarines as possible for Northern run operations and other needs, the navy opted in 1967 to defer full SubSafe upgrades to the *Scorpion*. This fact would spawn lingering questions about whether the lack of SubSafe improvements might have played a role in the sinking. To this day, navy submariners have insisted otherwise. Sullivan in his 2003 testimony said the evidence gathered by the court of inquiry and associated technical reviews "indicates that [the *Scorpion*] was lost for reasons that would not have been mitigated by the SubSafe Program."

The 1968 court of inquiry examined the lack of SubSafe upgrades to the *Scorpion* in minute detail. The panel grilled numerous officials from the two naval shipyards where the submarine had undergone extensive maintenance and repairs in 1963–64 and 1967. Captain Charles N. Mitchell, the deputy chief of staff for logistics at COM-SUBLANT, testified that restricting the *Scorpion's* operating depth to 500 feet guaranteed that it would be able to reach the surface in an emergency with its existing ballast control system. He noted that when the *Scorpion* re-entered the Atlantic in late evening on May 16, 1968, formally back under COMSUBLANT control, the navy's European Command had reported the submarine to be "fully combat ready." The court ultimately agreed, concluding: "The normal main ballast tank blow system, as originally designed and built in *Scorpion,* meets the SubSafe air volume requirements for operation to design test depth and that the blowing capability exceeded the SubSafe requirements for operation to her restricted depth."[20]

As far as the Atlantic Submarine Force was concerned, the *Scorpion* emerged from the Norfolk Naval Shipyard on October 6, 1967, a fully capable submarine. During the three-month period between the end of the overhaul and the submarine's departure for the Mediterranean on February 15, 1968, the submarine's squadron and division commanders cracked the whip to ensure the crew was ready as well. Both ship and crew endured a gauntlet of exercises, drills, and formal examinations from New England to the Caribbean. Two weeks after leaving the shipyard in October, the *Scorpion* arrived at the New London Submarine Base in Connecticut, where it underwent follow-up maintenance and specialized crew training under the supervision of the Navy Submarine School. Immediately afterward, the submarine steamed to the Caribbean for submarine-vs.-submarine combat drills and weapons system accuracy tests.

Upon the *Scorpion's* return to Norfolk, Submarine Squadron 6 commander Captain Jared E. Clarke III and his staff conducted an administrative inspection. The *Scorpion* received an overall grade of "excellent." Equipped to carry the Mark 45 Astor nuclear-tipped torpedo, the *Scorpion* passed a nuclear weapons acceptance inspection required before the weapons could be allowed onboard. More submarine-on-submarine drills occurred off the Virginia Capes in January 1968, followed by one last examination for damage control readiness.

Cmdr. Francis A. Slattery was the *Scorpion*'s fifth commanding officer.
U.S. Navy Photo

The gamut of exercises and inspections not only helped the crew come together as a team but also served to familiarize a new commanding officer and executive officer with the ship and its men. The *Scorpion*'s top two officers had departed for other assignments during that period.

Commander Francis A. Slattery became the new commanding officer on October 17, 1967, and fourteen weeks later, Lieutenant Commander David B. Lloyd, thirty-three, became executive officer. Both newcomers were experienced nuclear submariners. After graduating from the Naval Academy in 1954, Slattery served on a destroyer for a year before entering Submarine School. His first assignment was on the diesel-powered submarine *USS Tunny* (SSG 282), followed by nuclear propulsion training in Groton, Idaho Falls, Idaho, and Pittsburgh. For a year after graduating in 1960, he served as an instructor at the Submarine School before reporting to the *USS Nautilus*. For the next five years,

Lt. Cmdr. David Bennett Lloyd joined the *Scorpion* as executive officer four months before the submarine left on its Mediterranean deployment.
U.S. Navy Photo

Slattery held down five different assignments on the *Nautilus,* including engineer and executive officer.

Lloyd's career was also impressive. Graduating in 1956 from the Naval Academy, where he stood third in his class, Lloyd served a year aboard a destroyer before entering Submarine School. He then served a tour on the diesel-powered attack boat *USS Sea Fox* (SS 402). In 1959, Lloyd attended nuclear power training at three different navy schools. He subsequently served aboard the Polaris submarine *USS Ethan Allen* (SSBN 608), held a tour as instructor at the Nuclear Power School in Bainbridge, Maryland, and served three years aboard the nuclear attack submarine *USS Skate* (SSN 578).

In February 1968, the consensus among Atlantic Submarine Force officials and crewmen was the same: The *Scorpion* was a well-trained submarine, with an experienced crew, under the leadership of two highly qualified senior officers. The Atlantic Submarine Force rated the *Scorpion* as "fully combat ready" and appropriately manned as it prepared to cross the Atlantic.[21]

Shortly after 6:30 A.M. on February 15, by ones and twos, the rest of the *Scorpion*'s crew pulled into the parking lot near the end of the pier, said a last good-bye to loved ones, and made the long walk down to where the *Scorpion* was waiting. Slattery and Lloyd were among them. So too was Torpedoman Chief Walter Bishop, the chief of the boat. Julianne Elrod said goodbye to her husband, Bill, who joined the small exodus of submariners passing through the security gate onto the wharf.

Soon, it was time, and Slattery ordered the *Scorpion* crew to man the maneuvering watch. Section 1 watchstanders proceeded to take position throughout the ship. A small delegation of officers and enlisted men from Submarine Squadron 6 were already standing by on the pier along with a mobile crane. No band played and no dignitaries were present, for submarines did not make noisy departures when they left port.

Slattery climbed up to the bridge cockpit, joining three others in the cramped space: the officer of the deck, a lookout, and the civilian harbor pilot. The submarine's surface-search radar and one periscope raised out of their housings atop the sail. The officer of the deck then formally reported: "Sir, we are answering bells on both main engines . . . the electric plant is in a normal full-power lineup, the ship is divorced from shore power and the cables are removed. We're spinning the shaft as necessary to keep the main engines warm. Maneuvering watch is stationed, and we have Squadron's permission to get underway."[22]

"Officer of the deck, get underway." With the captain's terse order, the crane operator lifted the gangway ladder free, linehandlers took in the mooring hawsers, and a deckhand hoisted a small American flag on the short jackstaff mounted on the aft of the sail. The *Scorpion* slowly edged stern-first away from Pier 22.

Several hours later, as the *Scorpion* neared the 100-fathom curve out past the Virginia Capes, Slattery gave the order to submerge. The officer of the deck and lookout quickly secured their gear and scrambled down the ladder from the cockpit into the control room. The last man down,

Slattery ordered the submarine to make its depth 250 feet and climbed down several rungs of the ladder before dogging the hatch shut. The slate-green swells of the western Atlantic slowly rose up and swallowed the *Scorpion.*[23]

7

A SOVIET SUBMARINE VANISHES

DISASTER STRUCK WITH LITTLE WARNING. ONE MOMENT THE NU-clear-armed submarine was moving quietly through the ocean, and the next, a massive explosion tore through its hull, killing most of the crew within seconds. It was March 7, 1968, and nearly a hundred elite submariners had just perished.

The Soviet Golf II-class *K-129*, a diesel-powered ballistic missile submarine with a crew of ninety-eight officers and enlisted men, had left its homeport of Rybachiy Bay on the Kamchatka Peninsula thirteen days earlier. The missile submarine was thought to be heading for its normal patrol area in the Pacific Ocean northwest of Hawaii when it abruptly ceased transmitting routine position reports back to base. After a brief period of time, officials realized something had gone seriously wrong with the *K-129*, and Soviet Pacific Fleet commander Admiral Nikolai Nikolayevich Amelko ordered a full-fledged search.[1]

Years later, when accounts of the incident finally emerged, the loss of the *K-129* would come to seem like an eerie portent of the *Scorpion* sinking eleven weeks later. The two submarine losses, one American official later said, constituted "an almost unbelievable coincidence of fate." U.S. Navy officials who were involved in investigating both disasters would

Armed with three medium-range nuclear ballistic missiles, the Golf-II class submarine was a mainstay of the Soviet Navy throughout most of the 1960s until it was superseded by the larger Yankee-class submarine carrying 16 missiles apiece. *U.S. Navy Photo*

be struck by the number of similarities between the incidents—although at first glance, any resemblances at all would seem unusual.[2]

The two submarines were totally different in design and mission. The *K-129* was a workhorse Soviet boomer that conducted nuclear deterrent patrols in the north Pacific. It was armed with three SS-N-5 Serb ballistic missiles housed in vertical launch tubes in the submarine's massive sail structure, as well as a load-out of torpedoes in the bow and stern torpedo compartments. A new firing system installed three years earlier gave the *K-129* the capability of launching the three missiles while running submerged. Previously, the submarine would have had to surface in order to launch the missiles, rendering it vulnerable to detection and attack. The *Scorpion,* by contrast, was a nuclear-powered fast-attack submarine engaged in a wide range of surveillance operations and anti-submarine warfare tasks, carrying torpedoes but no missiles. Still, many aspects of their final deployments were similar.

Both the *Scorpion* and the *K-129* had been in service for eight years. While no longer the most advanced in their respective fleets, they were both still considered front-line naval units. The *K-129* was a second-generation boomer that had been, along with the nuclear-powered Hotel-class submarines, the primary Soviet sea-based strategic nuclear weapon for nearly a decade. For its part, by 1968 the U.S. Navy had two newer attack submarine classes in addition to the six *Skipjack*-class submarines and nine older nuclear attack boats. Thirteen *Thresher/Permit*-class submarines were operational, and the first four of what would ultimately become a fleet of thirty-seven *Sturgeon*-class nuclear attack boats were in commission by the spring of 1968.[3]

Neither the *Scorpion* nor the *K-129* was originally scheduled for the deployment that ended with their sinking. The *Scorpion* was a last-minute replacement for the *USS Seawolf* after its grounding in the Gulf of Maine. The *K-129* had been back in port from a previous patrol for only a month when its commander, Captain First Rank Vladimir Ivanovich Kobzar, was told that the *K-129* was needed to replace another boat, which had broken down, for immediate patrol in the northern Pacific.[4]

Senior navy officials on both sides initially reacted in much the same way when the submarine disappeared. When the *K-129* failed to issue a scheduled radio position report, Soviet officials in the submarine's chain of command reacted with minor puzzlement that developed into more significant concern over the next hours and days. Higher-up naval commanders initially speculated that the communications breakdown stemmed from a harmless radio malfunction or other explainable glitch. But as increasingly urgent attempts to raise the submarine proved unsuccessful, senior officials sounded the alarm throughout the fleet. In the case of the *Scorpion,* the public reaction was the same when it failed to reach port on May 27: hours of speculation and slowly dawning concern that sparked the massive open-ocean search.

At this point, however, the responses to the two incidents sharply diverged. Years later, senior U.S. Navy officials from 1968 would inadvertently reveal that they had mounted a secret, highly classified search effort that ended only when the *Scorpion*'s failure to reach port as scheduled made it impossible to conceal the emergency. The Soviets, on the other hand, seem to have had no knowledge of the *K-129* sinking until several days had passed without any word from the submarine. Admiral Amelko then scrambled more than three dozen surface ships and submarines escorted by land-based patrol aircraft down the boomer's projected navigational track. The Soviet submarines blasted away with active sonar and the searchers filled the airwaves with urgent, unencrypted broadcasts to the missing submarine. But the Soviet search came to naught. After fruitless weeks scouring the frigid north Pacific, Amelko recalled his ships and submarines to Vladivostok and Petropavlovsk.[5]

The *K-129* incident was far from over, however. It would reverberate thousands of miles throughout the ocean depths to other places where U.S. and Soviet submarines had been confronting one another for years.

———

THE DISAPPEARANCE of the *K-129* would have been serious enough by itself, given the loss of life and the destruction of a front-line missile submarine under mysterious circumstances. But the submarine went down at a time of increasing tensions between the two superpowers over submarine confrontations. Worse, it occurred during a time of war and political unrest around the world.

In the first four weeks of 1968, the Vietnam War intensified with the beginning of the North Vietnamese siege of Khe Sanh on January 22. There, the Twenty-Sixth Marine Regiment, six thousand strong, found itself surrounded and cut off by three North Vietnamese Army divisions. Eight days later on January 30, during the Tet Offensive, the Viet Cong launched coordinated attacks against Saigon and several dozen provincial capitals in an attempt to decapitate the U.S. and South Vietnamese military leadership.

Complicating any Pentagon response to the sudden flare-up of hostilities was the North Korean seizure of the electronic reconnaissance ship *USS Pueblo* (AGER 2) and its crew on January 23. The *Pueblo* incident forced U.S. military leaders to rush scarce navy and air force reinforcements to South Korea instead of Vietnam. Meanwhile, the South

Korean government pressed Washington to return its three ROK Army divisions from Vietnam to deal with the emergency at home.

On top of the military crises, the Pentagon also faced a major environmental disaster at Thule, Greenland, after the January 21 crash of a B-52 bomber carrying four thermonuclear bombs. The accident dispersed deadly radiation over a large area, sparked a strong diplomatic protest from the government of Denmark, and triggered anti-American demonstrations throughout Europe.[6]

The headlines from those incidents all but buried twin submarine disasters that occurred within several days of one another in late January 1968. In the Mediterranean, two submarines, each with a crew of fifty-two, had gone down with all hands. The Israeli submarine *Dakar* disappeared without a trace in the eastern Mediterranean while steaming from Great Britain to Israel. Originally commissioned in 1943 as the British submarine *HMS Totem* (P 352), the submarine was rebuilt and modernized for inshore patrols and mine-laying operations in the 1950s. The British government sold the submarine to Israel in 1965, but it did not leave for its new home until January 8, 1968, under the command of Lieutenant Commander Ya'acov Ra'anan. The voyage had gone without incident when Ra'anan transmitted a message on January 25 indicating that the submarine was east of Crete and would arrive in the port of Haifa four days later. That was the last message ever sent from the *Dakar.* Upon failing to reach Haifa on schedule, the Israeli Navy with the participation of several U.S. Navy ships launched an extensive search but found no trace of the submarine. A year later, its stern emergency marker buoy washed ashore on the coast of the Gaza Strip. The *Dakar* remained lost at sea until 2000, when a recovery team found the wreckage and retrieved the submarine's conning tower. The cause of the sinking was never definitively determined.

While the search for the *Dakar* began on January 28, the French Navy announced that the diesel-electric submarine *Minerve* (P 26) had failed to return from a routine training operation in the Mediterranean south of Toulon. The *Daphne*-class attack boat was a veteran of the French Navy with over 7,000 hours of submerged operations in its logbook. Like the *Dakar,* there was no evidence of foul play in the sinking—

there was no evidence at all. Searchers never found a trace of the missing boat and its crew.[7]

After the disappearance of the *Scorpion* four months later, the court of
inquiry and other U.S. Navy officials closely re-examined the losses of
the French and Israeli submarines. In its preliminary conclusions, the
court stated: "The possibility of foul play was considered, considerably
in view of the unexpected causes of the Israeli and French submarines in
the Mediterranean where *Scorpion* had so recently been operating." The
court did not mention the *K-129* sinking, which was still a closely
guarded secret within the U.S. naval intelligence community.

The court considered several scenarios of foul play involving the
Scorpion, including an explosive device secretly attached to the exterior
of the hull, an explosive device somehow attached to a torpedo inside
the submarine, and unspecified tampering with a torpedo tube door that
might have precipitated deadly flooding. It ultimately ruled out these
scenarios because of the size of the initial explosion recorded on the Canary Islands and AFTAC hydrophones, and the unlikelihood that an intruder might have succeeded in sabotaging equipment inside the
torpedo compartment. Still, the submarine losses in 1968 obviously
heightened anxieties among U.S. Navy officials investigating the *Scorpion* sinking.[8]

Meanwhile, the Soviet Union was facing a series of challenges to its own
hegemony that the Kremlin leadership found increasingly unacceptable,
although none had yet reached a point of crisis. Topping the worry list
was China. Mao Tse-tung had broken with the Soviet leadership in the
1950s, and in 1964 he matched his increasingly vitriolic rhetoric against
the Soviet Union with the explosion of China's first atomic bomb. While
many Americans still saw the Sino-Soviet alliance as a unified threat, by
1968 some experts thought it more likely that a nuclear war would feature Moscow and Bejing—and not Washington—as the combatants.
Ideology was a major driving factor, but the two communist powers also
had a serious border dispute along hundreds of miles that would ignite
into actual shooting incidents by 1969. Eastern Europe was also becom-

ing a headache for the Kremlin, particularly in Czechoslovakia, where in early 1968 the new government of Alexander Dubcek was experimenting with economic and political reforms. That simmering crisis would come to a boil in August when the Red Army invaded to crush the Prague Spring movement.

The crew of the *Scorpion* did not dwell on these storm clouds far away. No man is an island, and even sailors on a nuclear submarine—while trained for solitary missions deep in the ocean—were still citizens of a country torn by a war and civil unrest. In early 1968, the *Scorpion* sailors focused on the job at hand as they prepped their submarine for the Med, passed through pre-deployment drills and inspections, and finally got underway for Europe. As former Sonarman First Class Bill Elrod said decades later, "What I remember from that time was that there were a lot of things going on in the world. But there were a lot of *other* things going on in *my* immediate world. My wife was expecting a baby. I was due to transfer to a new boat that summer. I was a long way from home." Still, he said, "It was a dark time. We were isolated from the day-to-day details of [events in Vietnam and at home]. But all of those things set a heavy tone."[9]

THE SINKING OF THE *K-129* shocked the Soviet Navy. Despite its age and non-nuclear propulsion system, the stricken Soviet missile boat was a vital part of the Soviet strategic nuclear arsenal. By the late 1960s, the Soviets were trying to narrow the overwhelming U.S. lead in nuclear weapons. They expanded their land-based missile force, which by 1967 included about 700 SS-9 and SS-11 intercontinental-range missiles, and since 1964 they had modernized their missile submarine force, focusing on development of the Yankee-class missile submarine. Similar in design to the American *Polaris,* the Yankee carried sixteen SS-N-6 missiles, which had a range of 1,300 nautical miles, twice the distance of the smaller missiles on board the *K-129*. Its payload was ten times that of the older Golf class, with thirty-two warheads loaded two apiece on its sixteen missiles. But the first Yankee was not scheduled to enter service until later in 1968, so the twenty-two Golf-class boats, including eight assigned to the Soviet Pacific Fleet, were still a critical part of the Soviet strategic arsenal.[10]

The SS-N-5 missiles that were carried three apiece on each Golf-II submarine were unable to reach targets deep within the American land-mass but could be used to threaten U.S. military bases and cities near the coasts. Thus by 1968, American strategists knew from their patrol patterns that the *K-129* and its sister ships based in Petropavlovsk were assigned to threaten the U.S. West Coast, American military bases in the Pacific, and the U.S. Navy complex in Hawaii. On its ill-fated deployment in early 1968, the *K-129* had been assigned to loiter about 750 miles northwest of Oahu, its missiles targeted on Pearl Harbor and other military bases on the island.[11]

Overall, the Soviet Navy had significantly expanded its missile-submarine patrols in the three years since 1965. In the Atlantic, between one and three Golf-class submarines were now continuously on station in patrol boxes southeast of Greenland and northeast of the Azores. In addition, the Soviets kept one of their Echo-class cruise missile submarines in a separate patrol area west of the Azores astride the great-circle route between the United States and Europe to be able to track any U.S. Navy aircraft carriers transiting the Atlantic.[12]

Even today, details of the *K-129* incident remain fragmentary and in many cases subject to debate. For a range of reasons, the U.S. and Soviet governments for decades have kept secret whatever knowledge they had.

The Soviets had more than one reason to bury the *K-129* incident. A combination of legitimate military secrecy surrounding missile submarine operations, political embarrassment over yet another fatal submarine mishap, and the regime's knee-jerk tendency to censor *any* bad news led the Soviet Navy to cloak the *K-129* loss under an impenetrable security blanket. Giving no details or explanations to the missing submarine's family members, in late April the Soviet government tersely declared the submarine lost at sea. Families learned only that their men had been declared dead.

The U.S. Navy kept silent about the *K-129* for even more sinister reasons: Within several months of the sinking, U.S. naval intelligence officials organized and carried out an ambitious operation to locate, explore, and salvage the wreckage using a nuclear submarine that had been reconfigured for deep-sea espionage and object retrieval. Every aspect of the U.S. Navy's response to the *K-129* was classified above top secret. The search itself was extremely sensitive because it was largely directed by the then-top-secret Sosus system. Moreover, a Soviet discovery of the U.S. effort to salvage one of its front-line missile submarines would worsen tensions between the two navies and likely trigger a Soviet attempt to thwart such a mission by force.

The navy in 1965 had converted the *USS Halibut* (SSN 575) into a spy submarine capable of object retrieval three miles down from the ocean surface, and by 1968 had already used it on a highly classified operation called Winterwind to locate and retrieve Soviet nuclear missile re-entry vehicles from the ocean floor. The submarine's new operational specialty was also one of the navy's most critical secrets in 1968, known to only a few senior admirals. The U.S. Navy had even more ambitious and controversial plans for the submarine. In addition to the *K-129* exploration, navy officials were planning what would later become the most risky and sensational submarine spy operation of the entire Cold War. They would send the *Halibut* to sneak inside Soviet coastal waters in the Sea of Okhotsk to lay a massive listening pod on top of an underwater communications cable used for sensitive military communications from bases on the Kamchatka Peninsula to the Soviet mainland. Disclosure of that intelligence operation would likely inflame U.S.-Soviet relations even more than the 1960 shoot-down of the CIA's U-2 spy plane, which had wrecked a planned U.S.-Soviet summit meeting. Finally, discovery of an American nuclear submarine well inside Soviet waters could readily spark a military clash.[13]

The U.S. Navy's decision to go after the *K-129* stemmed from one basic fact that emerged in the weeks after it sank: The Soviets had no idea where the submarine had gone down, but the Americans did. Because the acoustic signal of the *K-129's* fatal explosion had registered on Pacific-based Sosus sensors, U.S. naval intelligence officials were pretty sure where the submarine had gone down. American admirals decided to locate the *K-129* and exploit the wreckage for intelligence information.

They turned the mission over to the navy's Deep Submergence Systems Project, led by Dr. John P. Craven. Originally a part of the navy's Special Projects Office, DSSP had evolved by mid-1968 into a stand-alone organization within the navy bureaucracy that controlled a number of deep-diving manned and unmanned submersibles. The cover story at the time was that the mini-subs would be used for scientific research and submarine rescue operations. In reality, the navy earmarked them for a spate of highly sensitive intelligence operations. The *Halibut* was DSSP's proudest possession.[14]

Commissioned in January 1960, just six months before the *Scorpion*, the *Halibut* had originally been designed to carry and fire the air-breathing Regulus missile, a larger, primitive version of the Tomahawk cruise missile now commonly used by the U.S. Navy. When the Pentagon terminated the Regulus program in 1964 in favor of the Polaris missile, the navy was left with a nuclear submarine whose forward end consisted of a massive watertight hangar compartment fifty feet long, twenty-eight feet wide, and thirty feet high. Craven and his engineers found the space ideal for carrying equipment for spy missions, including a massive cable reel that could lower a sensor sled three miles down to locate and photograph objects on the seabed. Several years later, Craven would add a decompression chamber that would allow navy deep-sea divers to exit and enter the submarine and safely work at depths of several hundred feet for extended periods of time.[15]

In the summer of 1968, the *Halibut* went searching for the *K-129*. After several months of trolling the ocean floor with its towed sled dangling three miles down behind it, the *Halibut* found and photographed the *K-129*'s broken hull in mid-August. That critical discovery later led to an ambitious covert operation where the CIA built a massive ship, the *Glomar Explorer,* expressly designed to lift the *K-129*'s hull fragments off the ocean floor. News of the attempt by the *Glomar Explorer* would remain secret until 1975, and it was only in 1997 that the U.S. Navy's earlier role in finding the Soviet submarine became known.

Soviet Navy officials who had been involved in the *K-129* search broke their long silence in 1998 when for the first time they described the frantic effort to locate the Golf-II-class submarine. Their accounts mirrored the U.S. Atlantic Fleet's desperate attempts to respond to the *Scorpion's* loss after the declaration of SubMiss on Memorial Day. When the *K-129* failed to send a scheduled burst-transmission message signaling its continuing progress toward a patrol box 750 miles northwest of the Hawaiian Islands, Pacific Fleet Commander Admiral Nikolai Amelko ordered Rear Admiral Vladimir Bez to sea to find the missing submarine. Bez, the submarine's assistant division commander at Petropavlovsk, boarded a rescue ship with an acoustic surveillance group, a chemical team, and officers. Within several days, a half-dozen Soviet ships and submarines from Petropavlovsk and Vladivostok joined the search under Bez's command. The group ultimately included more than thirty-six surface ships and submarines.[16]

Many aspects of the *K-129* incident remain in dispute because of lingering secrecy on both sides. The *Glomar* mission succeeded in raising at least part of the submarine's hull containing several nuclear-tipped torpedoes and the remains of eight crewmen, but details on the exact outcome of the covert operation remain muddled by contradictory accounts. Several news reports of the CIA operation to lift the submarine from the ocean floor using a giant claw device lowered from the *Glomar Explorer* claimed the operation was largely a failure. The claw was damaged upon impact with the seabed, and during the lifting operation most of the submarine's hull fell free. However, a subsequent investigation alleged that the "failure" was part of a CIA cover story to conceal the extent of the operation's actual success.[17]

Soviet officials said their response to the *K-129* came quickly when it failed to send its report. "We actually left right away on the eighth of March," Bez recalled. "The weather, the storms made it even more difficult for us. Why did we use the surface vessels for this search? Because there was [the chance] that the sub was left motionless somewhere on the surface, that it could not send a radio signal. We were supposed to rescue it." Retired Admiral Viktor A. Dygalo, the *K-129's* division commander in 1968, put the start of the search mission six days later, on March 14, a week after the sinking: "So, when on March 12th, the radiogram was sent but there was no reply, that signaled that something was going wrong aboard that submarine," Dygalo said. "And for the first 48 hours we were still hopeful that perhaps something had happened to the radio transmitter, that there was no reply for the technical reasons. But after then, we realized that something serious had happened with the sub and the state of alert was declared in the navy, then the sub and above-surface ships and aviation were dispatched."[18]

The U.S. Navy's overt response to the Soviet search for the *K-129* was to mount aggressive surveillance of Bez's flotilla. Soviet participants in the search operation years later recalled with undisguised anger how American submarines and patrol aircraft continuously interfered with their efforts. "Why did we think [that] Americans knew that we had been looking for our lost sub?" Bez asked rhetorically. "Well, as we approached [the search site], their planes were flying faster and lower than usual. In fact, dangerously low. Then, I also noticed that we were followed by an American sub. How did I notice it? I was looking at the radars. The visibility was low. I realized there was a small target [object] about four cable lengths away. Something that looked like a periscope."

Once again, the U.S. Navy had thrust its aircraft and submarines into the middle of a Soviet naval operation. Angered over the Americans' reckless interference, Bez determined to call the submarine's bluff. After confirming that the shadower was an American submarine and not one of his own, Bez alerted another Soviet ship on an encrypted radio channel that he wanted to scare the intruder out of the area. "I called the captain at the hydrographic vessel that was next behind me and said, 'Listen, there is a target that's hanging there behind me. I'm going to give you an order, using the short wavelength, to turn around and ram that target.'" Bez said he knew the Americans were listening in on the uncoded short-wave frequency. So he said over the short-wave channel, "I have this target at my rear. You turn around, full speed ahead and ram it." The hydrographic vessel spun on its rudder and raced toward the periscope contact, which quickly vanished under the surface. "We could not see it afterwards, though once in a while there was a trail underneath us, and we also took some radiological measurements," Bez recalled. "We did establish that definitely there was a sub down there. But obviously it was running at a safe depth, and it was pretty fast."[19]

Soon after, the Soviets' annoyance at the interference of the U.S. Navy erupted into a dangerous rage. For more than a week, the Soviet searchers had dodged the American submarines and aircraft when an agent in Japan flashed an intelligence report that rocketed to the top of the Soviet Navy: Ten days after the *K-129* vanished, a U.S. Navy nuclear attack submarine, the *USS Swordfish* (SSN-579), had slipped into the Seventh Fleet base at Yokosuka with damage to its sail and periscopes— irrefutable evidence to the Soviets of an underwater collision.

At the outset, the Soviet admirals had thought its Golf-II-class submarine had suffered some unknown accident while heading to its patrol area northwest of Hawaii. Given the U.S. Navy's track record of aggressive submarine tactics, Amelko and other Soviet admirals immediately concluded that the *Swordfish* must have been involved in the disappearance of the *K-129*. It is a belief that they hold to this day.[20]

"Among many versions about what caused [*K-129*] to sink," said former Admiral Amelko, "many people including myself are inclined to—out of great understanding and with a probability of 99.9—many more 'nines'—consider that it sank because it was rammed by the submarine *Swordfish*—the American submarine. We thought and still think that the Americans knew well about the location of our bottomed sub from the commander of *Swordfish*." Retired Admiral Valery Alexin agreed: "A week after the disappearance of our sub, an American sub [*USS*] *Swordfish* arrives at the Japanese port of Yokosuka, the foremost base of the Seventh Fleet. The conning tower of the submarine was severely disfigured. And therefore it was docked for repairs. It did not return for patrol for the following one-and-a-half years. This means that the damage was serious and repairs were extensive."[21]

Within several months of the sinking of the *K-129*, the Soviets officially concluded that the *K-129* had been downed by a collision, most likely with the *Swordfish*. A formal commission chaired by Deputy Prime Minister Leonid Vassilievich Smirnov was convened in June 1968 to investigate the circumstances surrounding the loss of the *K-129*. Other commission members included Fleet Admiral Gorshkov himself, his deputy, Admiral Vladimir Afanasievich Kassatotov, and a number of senior navy scientists, project engineers, and representatives of the *K-129*'s manufacturing yard at Severodvinsk.[22]

After a month of hearings, the panel narrowed down the possibilities for the sinking to two alternatives: collision with a surface ship while it was running on the surface or at periscope depth while snorkeling; or collision with another submarine. Dygalo explained: "So we came to a conclusion that the main cause [of the *K-129* loss] was a collision of [the] submarine *Swordfish* with our submarine, when the sub was either surfacing or submerging to carry some missions. . . . All this also convinced us and we still believe in it, that *Swordfish* was the real culprit, that it made a wrong maneuver, thus collided [with *K-129*]."[23]

Even before the commission reached that formal conclusion, in the spring of 1968, the highest echelons of the Soviet Navy strongly suspected American involvement in the *K-129* sinking. But this dangerous new twist in the U.S.-Soviet submarine rivalry remained a closely held secret. Most submariners—American and Soviet alike—went on with their work unaware that everything had changed. As the *Scorpion* engaged in various operations in the Mediterranean with NATO and other U.S. naval units, the Soviet Navy had come to the belief that the American submarine force had Russian blood on its hands.[24]

8

THE LAST VOYAGE

THE *SCORPION*'S DEPLOYMENT TO THE MEDITERRANEAN IN MID-February was a new experience for many of its crew. The schedule of the mission was far more predictable than the solitary Northern run reconnaissance operations that frequently sent the submarine racing after targets of opportunity near the Soviet coastline. Tentative plans called for the ship to visit Taranto and Naples in Italy, Augusta Bay, Sicily, Athens, Greece, and Izmir, Turkey.

However, there was a downside to the deployment in the sunny and alluring Mediterranean. The *Scorpion* would be operating with the U.S. Sixth Fleet and NATO allies and thus would come under almost constant observation from other U.S. Navy commands and units. This meant a series of official visits and inspections that added to the workload, detailed instructions and operational restrictions that complicated even routine tasks such as traveling from one port to another, and strict limitations on where the submarine could visit.[1]

The constant scrutiny and bureaucratic nitpicking became a major annoyance to the crew but would prove a boon to those who later investigated the sinking of the *Scorpion*. The court of inquiry would dissect what became a detailed record of the *Scorpion*'s material condition, performance, and crew morale throughout its final voyage. In their letters home the crew painted in many additional details.[2]

Because of the last-minute call-up to replace the *Seawolf* in the Mediterranean, the *Scorpion*'s crew had lost several months of the time it originally had to prepare for a planned Northern run deployment in the spring of 1968. The surprise change of schedule put the crew under pressure to get themselves and their submarine ready for deployment. Morale problems had emerged earlier, during an eight-month overhaul at the Norfolk Naval Shipyard that had ended on October 6, 1967. Chief Radioman Daniel K. Pettey, thirty-seven, a senior member of the *Scorpion*'s radio gang in 1968—and one of three crew members to leave the submarine before it sank—sensed the problem early on. An eighteen-year navy veteran, Pettey had transferred to the *Scorpion* in early 1967 just as it was beginning the shipyard stay. He had just spent three years as a navy instructor and had finished a forty-two-week advanced training course in radio equipment repair at the navy's Radioman School in Bainbridge, Maryland. "I was disappointed in the general morale on the boat when I arrived," Pettey recalled years later. Pettey received routine transfer orders to the *USS Skipjack* in April 1968 while the *Scorpion* was halfway through the Mediterranean deployment, leaving Radioman Senior Chief Robert Johnson, a thirty-six-year-old West Virginia native, as head of the *Scorpion*'s radio gang.[3]

In early February 1967, Machinist's Mate Second Class Mark Christiansen, a two-year veteran of the *Scorpion* at that point, described the drudgery of life during the overhaul: "We are now in drydock and the [reactor] refueling has begun," Christiansen, twenty-five, wrote his parents in Bellmore, N.Y. "It's a long way [from his Norfolk apartment] to the yard and expensive. We're trying to arrange a carpool. . . . Our daily schedule is as follows: 0630-0730, lecture; 0745, quarters; 0745–1615 work; 1615, liberty. The days are going to be long, as you can see. This schedule doesn't count the time spent traveling to and from." A month later, Christiansen said conditions aboard the *Scorpion* had deteriorated to the point where "in a fit of anger" he formally requested a transfer to another submarine as a pretext to be able to voice his (and other sailors') complaints to Lieutenant William Harwi, the submarine's engineering officer.[4]

The mood aboard the *Scorpion* in 1967 worsened markedly, Pettey recalled, when shipyard officials extended the refueling overhaul another four months, to October. The radio gang came under pressure when two weeks before departure, COMSUBLANT officials installed a new hundred-pound piece of cryptographic equipment in their crowded workspace. Known as the KWR-37, the gear was designed to receive and decrypt in clear language encoded communications sent from COMSUBLANT headquarters. "We were working around the clock to get that thing in there," Pettey said. "We also had to do rapid training on it."[5]

The material condition of the *Scorpion* became a source of frustration for the crew early on. Although certified as fully ready for submerged operations and overseas deployment, the submarine's lengthy overhaul at the Norfolk Naval Shipyard had focused on the installation of a new reactor core. The Atlantic Submarine Force deferred many other maintenance procedures and repairs because of time and budgetary constraints. From the time it left Norfolk on its final voyage, the *Scorpion* kept all hands busy as one component or another short-circuited, failed, leaked, broke down, or sparked into flames.[6]

The first glitch occurred four days out of Norfolk, when the *Scorpion* met up with an anti-submarine warfare hunter-killer group. The aircraft carrier *USS Essex* (CVS 9) and seven destroyers under the command of Carrier Division 20 were also heading out on a six-month deployment to the Mediterranean, North Atlantic, and North Sea. Atlantic Fleet headquarters had ordered the *Scorpion* to train with the ASW ships during the crossing. During one maneuver with the *Essex* and its escorts, the *Scorpion* suffered a problem in the hydraulic system that caused the controls for its massive rudder to fail. The steering device suddenly pulled hard to the left. Only quick action by the duty helmsman to shift rudder control to an emergency backup power system prevented the situation from throwing the *Scorpion* into an unanticipated turn and dive. Within several days, the hydraulic systems for the fairwater (bow) and stern diving planes also malfunctioned.

Several other minor problems appeared during the Atlantic crossing to Europe. Crewmen noticed that there was a hydraulic fluid leak from the system that was losing fifty gallons of fluid an hour. After Slattery surfaced the submarine, crewmen succeeded in isolating the problem in a line inside the submarine's sail. In another part of the *Scorpion*, the radio gang reported that the tuner for the AN/BRA-19 high-frequency antenna was malfunctioning—a pesky but not serious problem. Both *Scorpion* crewmen who left the submarine at the end of the Med cruise just five days before the sinking put these incidents into context in their testimony before the *Scorpion* court of inquiry. Interior Communications Electrician First Class Joseph D. Underwood, who was regularly standing watches in the control room in training as diving officer of the watch, dismissed the idea that the hydraulic failure had any bearing on the submarine's sinking. He testified that learning how to anticipate such problems was an integral part of ongoing instruction: "We had a couple of hydraulic problems . . . on a submarine you have problems as a matter of course, but you correct them and go on." Once repaired, the hydraulic systems posed no more problems during the rest of the cruise. Underwood stressed that under Slattery's command, the control room watchstanders continuously practiced a wide range of casualty drills to ensure the *Scorpion* could quickly overcome any malfunction in the rudder and control planes.[7]

There were also several instances of control plane failure, but the crewmen were trained to instantly correct them, according to Sonarman First Class Bill Elrod. Testifying to the court of inquiry, Elrod, who was already rated as both a chief of the watch and a diving officer in the control room, noted that in one incident, the power to the diving plane hydraulic system failed, throwing the control planes to the full-dive position. Before the *Scorpion* could begin pitching down and diving to a potentially dangerous depth, however, the duty planesman switched the system to emergency mode and hauled back on the controls to maintain the submarine's horizontal attitude. Elrod went on to describe the overall condition of the *Scorpion* as excellent, despite such bugs.[8]

Because of the anti-submarine warfare exercises with the *Essex* carrier group, the *Scorpion*'s Atlantic crossing took two weeks instead of the normal ten days. Despite the equipment problems, navy officials described the submarine and crew, before and after its departure from Norfolk, as fully prepared for the deployment. Captain Wallace A. Greene, commander of Submarine Division 62 and the official responsible for ensuring the *Scorpion* was capable of operating in the Mediterranean, told the court of inquiry: "I considered her to be fully trained. We carried her in top readiness category upon her departure for this deployment."[9]

But rather than proceeding directly into the Mediterranean, the Atlantic Submarine Force took note of the rash of minor equipment problems and diverted the submarine to the Polaris submarine base at Rota, Spain. The sailors were still grumbling as they tied up near the submarine tender *USS Canopus* (AS 34).

In 1968, Rota was the epicenter of the *other* U.S. Navy nuclear submarine revolution. The navy by that year in effect had two entirely nuclear submarine fleets—the sleek attack boats and the larger missile submarines. Just eight years after the *USS George Washington* entered fleet service in 1959, the Polaris missile submarine force was running in full stride. The navy had ordered, the shipyards had built, and the navy had commissioned forty-one of the mammoth submarines by April 1967, outnumbering the thirty-one nuclear attack submarines then in service. Each of them carried sixteen nuclear-tipped Polaris missiles that could fly up to 2,500 miles upon launch from a submerged hiding place to target.[10]

The Rota navy base, which had opened to the Polaris boats in February 1964, was designed to provide everything the missile submarines needed in a tight package. At the end of a large pier, there was the *Canopus,* a 644-foot-long, 85-foot-wide floating repair ship whose 1,252 officers and enlisted technicians carried out support and repairs to the giant boomers—from replacing individual A-3 missiles and inspecting their nuclear warheads to fixing electronic equipment and machinery and coming up with the submarine crews' monthly payroll. Also present were the floating drydock *USS Oak Ridge* (ARDM 1), the submarine rescue ship *USS Tringa* (ASR 16), and a navy harbor tug. At any time, three or four of the nine Polaris submarines assigned to Submarine Squadron 16 would be in port, nestled up against the *Canopus* or moored to the pier.[11]

Still, for one of the more important defense programs running, sailors stationed there described Rota as primitive and lacking amenities. "Rota was OK, but there wasn't much to do really," recalled Tom

The *USS Scorpion* began two months of operations in the Mediterranean at Rota, Spain, followed by port visits in Taranto, Italy, Augusta Bay, Sicily, and Naples, Italy. In addition to various exercises throughout the Mediterranean, the *Scorpion* also monitored Soviet Navy warships near Kithira Island, Greece, and Crete.

© 2007 Jeffrey L. Ward

The Mediterranean
at the time of the
Scorpion's last journey

Carlough, who was an engineman second class assigned to the *Canopus* in 1968. Because its prime mission was servicing the Polaris program, Rota rarely saw anything but the steady parade of missile submarines coming and going on patrol. Even the *Scorpion's* visit was unusual because attack submarines hardly ever used the base, Carlough said.[12]

The *Scorpion* arrived at Rota on February 29 and stayed for five days while technicians removed and repaired its LORAN-C navigational receiver, worked on the hydraulic leak in the dive plane control lines, and tried unsuccessfully to repair the tuner for the AN/BRA-19 antenna. Writing to his wife the day after arriving, Senior Chief Yeoman Leo Weinbeck, thirty-five, was sanguine about the stopover: "This really isn't a recreation stop for us so liberty is kept to a minimum in order that we can get some very necessary work done to the boat. Had about 4–5 feet of official mail when we arrived here—all kinds of rush projects to get done before we get underway on Tuesday. The boat has to be painted—inside and out—and that's a job!" Torpedoman Third Class Robert Violetti, twenty-one, echoed the situation: "Halfway here we lost depth control and had to head for the closest port with a U.S. sub tender (*USS Canopus*). Our hydraulic problem has been repaired so we should pull out by Tuesday [Mar 5], anyway."[13]

Scorpion sailors who did manage to get some brief time off during the visit had mixed feelings about the base and nearby countryside. "Rota, Spain, is just a town built outside the naval base," Yeoman Third Class Richard Summers, twenty-two, wrote his parents, Charles and Hila Summers, back home in Statesville, North Carolina. "There's nothing much there except bars, hotels, cafes and cat houses." Mark Christiansen had a more positive view of Andalusia. "Arrived in Spain 1 March and will leave 5 March," he wrote his parents, Mr. and Mrs. Axel Christiansen, of Bellmore, N.Y. "Yesterday we toured and tasted wine at a bodega (winery) in this city. Then we toured the shops and sights and took pictures. Prices are fairly reasonable although I don't have too much money. We have four more liberty ports before we leave, will be home 24 May."[14]

The first sign that the *Scorpion's* deployment would be far from routine came hours after the submarine left Rota for the Straits of Gibraltar. The

The last sighting of the *Scorpion* occurred at the navy's submarine base at Rota, Spain after midnight on May 17, 1968. The base was home to the submarine tender *USS Canopus* (AS 34), at right with a Polaris missile submarine alongside, and floating dry-dock *USS Oak Ridge*. *U.S. Navy Photo*

Sixth Fleet flashed a message to the submarine that the Soviet Navy was confronting U.S. and NATO naval units all over the Mediterranean. The new orders diverted the submarine on a top-secret mission that one crewman later indicated was to spy on Soviet Navy ships near the Straits of Gibraltar. What had been planned as a quick trip through the straits and on to southern Italy for an initial port visit at Taranto turned into something potentially dangerous.

Details of the *Scorpion's* surveillance operation still remain classified nearly forty years after the event, and there is little evidence available of what the secret mission involved. On board the submarine was the operations officer from Submarine Flotilla 8 in Naples, the U.S. Sixth Fleet's submarine headquarters. Commander Kurt F. Dorenkamp was liaison between his headquarters and the *Scorpion,* which for ten weeks served at the Sixth Fleet's beck and call. In heavily censored testimony to the court of inquiry several months later, Dorenkamp described the operation that took place as time-limited and more of a quick surveillance sweep of a limited part of the Mediterranean than an extended operation against an identified target: "Now during the transit [the *Scorpion*] was delayed because she was asked to make a [deleted] just inside the Straits of Gibraltar in an attempt to [deleted]. There was some [deleted] in that particular area, and the object was to see if it was related with the [deleted]." Dorenkamp asserted that "No significant information was obtained" by the *Scorpion*.[15]

One clue to the target of the reconnaissance mission emerges from a letter that Violetti wrote to his uncle four days later as the *Scorpion* rested at anchor in Taranto: "We are on NATO exercises between ports and have been continually annoyed by Russian [spy] trawlers." Soviet intelligence-gathering trawlers by that time were a common sight outside U.S. submarine bases from the East Coast to Scotland and Spain, so it is probable that the *Scorpion* had been diverted to look for one of them, perhaps loitering around the British Navy base at Gibraltar.

The Soviet trawlers had been a sign of the Soviet Navy's growing aggressiveness for some time. Fleet Admiral Sergei Gorshkov had employed the fleet of intelligence-gathering vessels to snoop around U.S. submarine bases on the East Coast as far back as 1961, even before Rota became operational in 1964. Polaris submariners from that era said the Soviets positioned the surveillance trawlers right at the harbor entrances in an attempt to monitor the missile submarines' movements upon leaving port before they could submerge and evade the followers. American submarine captains devised their own tactics to thwart the surveillance. "It got to be a group game in Rota," said retired Rear Admiral Walter Dietzen, who commanded the Polaris submarine *USS Woodrow Wilson* (SSBN 624) during the early 1960s. Aware of a Soviet spy trawler lurking offshore one night as he prepared to leave on patrol, Dietzen said he instructed his radiomen and the navy tug escort to maintain strict radio silence as the Polaris submarine pulled away from the pier. Running with no navigation lights showing, Dietzen then steered his multi-million-dollar nuclear submarine through a nearby fleet of

USS Scorpion in Naples Bay during its Mediterranean deployment in 1968. *U.S. Navy Photo*

Spanish fishing boats and escaped into the Atlantic without the Soviets ever seeing him.[16]

This cat-and-mouse game intensified throughout the 1960s and would continue well beyond. In response, the Atlantic Submarine Force began assigning submarine rescue ships to run interference as the ungainly Polaris boats slipped out of harbor on the surface. The result was even higher tensions between the U.S. and Soviet navies. The situation got worse when Soviet nuclear attack submarines in 1968 joined the trawlers in attempting to shadow the Polaris missile boats as they left port. In response, the Atlantic Submarine Force ordered its nuclear attack submarines to begin serving as underwater escorts. Their tactics against the Soviet submarines included lashing them with active sonar and making aggressive moves to force the Soviet boats to change course and lose track of the missile submarines. By late spring, the incidents had become violent enough that accounts of submarine encounters began to break through the U.S. Navy's cloak of secrecy.

On May 10, 1968, a *New York Times* front-page story described how American attack submarines were now being used to defend against Soviet submarines harassing the Polaris missile boats leaving on patrol. The newspaper cited a recent incident outside the Polaris submarine base in Scotland:

> A sleek, gray Polaris submarine slipped out of her pen at Holy Loch, Scotland, one day recently and nosed out toward the North Atlantic to take up a secret patrol station from which her 16 missiles could reach targets deep inside the Soviet Union in the event of war. . . . Shortly after the American submarine reached international waters, a Soviet nuclear-powered submarine appeared and fell in behind, at a discreet distance, both craft running deep. . . . Suddenly, two other American submarines appeared. They darted in between the Polaris and her Russian shadow, bouncing sonar signals off the Soviet hull to confuse the craft's detection gear, and by daring maneuvering, forcing her to change course repeatedly.[17]

The confrontations led to potentially fatal collisions. On July 2, a Norfolk newspaper reported that a U.S. nuclear submarine had been severely damaged when it collided with a Soviet submarine near Rota while attempting to help a Polaris missile submarine evade detection as it left the Spanish base sometime that spring. Sources told the Norfolk reporter that the incident had involved not the *Scorpion* but rather another nuclear attack submarine. The collision was later verified by the former *Canopus* crewman, Tom Carlough, who recalled two separate incidents in the summer of 1968 where a heavily damaged nuclear attack submarine had limped into Rota after suffering a collision with a Soviet submarine.

"We had two [attack] boats come in with heavy damage," said Carlough. "One included more than half the sail [conning tower] smashed right down to the deck. That meant all the periscopes were gone and the snorkel tube as well. The rudder post was bent and so was the prop.

They worked on this one for weeks, replaced or repaired everything right there alongside us. It was amazing really." The second boat had severe damage to its bow, he said.[18]

It had been nearly a decade since the Soviets first found themselves hounded by U.S. nuclear submarines penetrating their own coastal waters to spy on submarine operations and missile tests. The Soviets were learning how to play this rough game as well. Gorshkov assigned teams of highly trained, English-speaking personnel to radio intercept groups that went to sea aboard his submarines and spy trawlers. Like their counterparts from U.S. naval intelligence, the Soviet spooks used an array of tactics to monitor the other side. They would activate their radio antennas, scour the frequency bands for U.S. military transmissions, record and sight-translate everything they found, and conduct what code breakers call "signal traffic analysis" to glean hints of the other side's activities when the transmissions were encrypted. Earlier in 1968, it was a radio intercept group on the Soviet trawler off San Francisco that had alerted a November-class attack submarine to dash from the Bering Sea and trail the Vietnam-bound aircraft carrier *USS Enterprise*. Like their American rivals, the Soviet naval teams also received intelligence support from a wide array of land-based radio monitoring sites, which by 1968 included a massive facility in Lourdes, Cuba, and embassy compounds in Washington, London, and other European capitals. Within the Soviet Union itself, vast antenna farms intercepted U.S. military communications throughout the United States.[19]

By the time the *Scorpion* arrived, the Soviets had established a substantial, full-time naval presence in the Mediterranean. Admiral Gorshkov's strategic success came on the heels of what had seemed to be a major military setback the previous summer during the Six-Day War between Israel and the Soviets' Arab allies. The USSR had armed and trained Egypt and Syria with the goal of keeping the United States out of the region—but not to support hostilities against Israel. Nevertheless, Egyptian president Gamal Abdel Nasser set out to attack Israel with the help of Jordan, Syria, and the Soviets' newest Mideast ally, Iraq. Aware of the impending war, Israel launched a pre-emptive attack on June 5, 1967 that shattered the Egyptian military and humiliated its Soviet sponsor. The Israeli Air Force destroyed over 300 Egyptian warplanes. The Israeli Army quickly seized the Sinai Peninsula from Egypt, the Golan Heights from Syria, and the West Bank from Jordan.

When the dust settled, Nasser opened his much-reduced territory to bases for the Soviet Navy and Air Force. Gorshkov's Fifth Squadron promptly set up shop at the port of Alexandria, giving the USSR a permanent foothold in the eastern Mediterranean. As military analyst Norman Friedman later wrote, "This was a major disaster for the West." From mid-1967 onward, the Soviet Navy would have a major presence in the Med.[20]

In that one stroke, Gorshkov's fleet had overcome its geographical barriers. While the Soviet Black Sea Fleet could get to the Mediterranean through the narrow Bosporus and Dardanelles Straits that separate Turkey from mainland Europe, it had long been difficult to carry out sustained naval operations and exercises with its shore bases on the other side of that constricted waterway. It was even harder for the Soviet nuclear submarine force. All of those submarines were assigned to the Northern Fleet and had to travel thousands of miles through the Barents and Norwegian Seas and North Atlantic before entering the Mediterranean through the Straits of Gibraltar.

After the Six-Day War, however, Gorshkov not only secured port access in Egypt, Syria, and Yugoslavia but also won limited access to naval facilities at Malta and Algeria. In addition, his fleet planners were deploying auxiliary support vessels to a number of protected anchorages around the Mediterranean, where they could provide supplies and limited maintenance to the warships without them having to make the long trek back home.

As the Soviet naval shipbuilding program continued, the number of warships assigned to the Mediterranean tripled between 1965 and 1968. In mid-April 1968, U.S. naval intelligence analysts predicted that by the end of the month the Soviet squadron would number forty-five ships, including the new helicopter carrier *Moskva,* sixteen surface combatants, nine submarines, and twelve auxiliary ships. A Defense Intelligence Agency assessment that year noted that access to allied naval bases was helping spark the squadron's expanded presence: "The scale and character of the USSR's naval activities in the Mediterranean leave no doubt that Moscow regards it as an area of major policy interest. Because of convenience and as an extension of mobile logistic support of its forces, the [Soviet] navy is increasing its use of facilities at friendly ports." The Fifth Squadron now threatened to expand the East-West superpower standoff along a major new front.[21]

For nearly two decades, the NATO alliance had contained the Soviet Bloc along the 2,000-mile "Iron Curtain" that ran from the Norwegian-Soviet frontier south to the Black Sea. It had neutralized the larger Soviet Army mainly through naval superiority, which kept the Soviet fleet bottled up in the Barents, Baltic, and Black seas. No longer. Without firing a shot, Gorshkov had broken through the de facto blockade. His warships could now roam along NATO's southern flank from the Levant to Gibraltar and beyond.

Press accounts from the spring of 1968 echoed this ongoing shift in the naval balance. U.S. officials portrayed Gorshkov's fleet as a growing menace that was making particular gains in the Mediterranean. One *New York Times* article in early 1968 put the matter in stark terms: "It was common last summer for Westerners to assert that the Soviet Union had suffered a major setback and loss of prestige as a result of Israel's quick and convincing victory over the Arab armies that Moscow had equipped, trained and politically supported. That point is no longer emphasized by Western diplomats. Now, they are increasingly concerned about Moscow's comeback in the Middle East . . . and the extent to which Washington has been put on the defensive."[22]

When the *Scorpion* finished the brief reconnaissance mission near Gibraltar, it passed south of Sicily and headed for the naval port city of Taranto on the southernmost tip of the Italian peninsula. Crew morale was on the upswing. "The new XO and skipper were doing an excellent job," said Radioman Chief Pettey, referring to Lieutenant Commander Lloyd and Commander Slattery. "Everyone was feeling real good about the boat." And they were looking forward to Taranto, the first real liberty port on their cruise.[23]

Nestled in the arch of the Italian boot, Taranto has long been the headquarters of the Italian Navy. It had become famous briefly in 1940 as the site of the first major aircraft carrier strike in modern naval warfare. On November 11, British carrier-based Swordfish aircraft laden with torpedoes sank two Italian battleships and seriously damaged a third in a surprise raid from the sea; the attack helped keep the Italian Navy from closing the Mediterranean to British warships. (The mission was a turning point in the history of World War II for another reason as well: The British success confirmed to the Japanese Navy the feasibility of their plans to attack Pearl Harbor.)[24]

In the spring of 1968, Taranto was used to the arrivals of friendly foreign warships, but only up to a point. The *Scorpion's* crew quickly learned that there were limits to NATO amity and shared maritime values. The *Scorpion* was the first nuclear-powered warship ever to visit there, and out of political and environmental concerns, the Italians directed that the submarine remain anchored far out in the harbor rather than tying up to a pier.

The decision rankled the crew. "We are anchored out in the tidal basin a few hundred yards from the city, as we aren't permitted to tie up in the harbor (being nuclear powered)," Mark Christiansen wrote his family. "Since we have no shore power, we have had to steam [on reactor power] and are in two-section duty." Robert Violetti also mentioned the policy in a letter back to Broomall. "This is the first time an atomic sub has ever been here, for that reason the city made us anchor out in the harbor rather than tie up [to the pier]." He described how he had adjusted to the restriction: "Right now I am sitting on the deck aft of the sail and plan on staying till the sun goes down. This sunshine is a rare treat so I'm getting all I can. We are anchored in the bay and a 'little old wine maker' is taking guys to the town in his boat. I don't know if I got the point across or not but I asked him to get me some stamps to mail letters. No one seems to know if a U.S. stamp will work so he is getting me 10 Italian ones (I hope). Since he doesn't speak English there is no telling what he'll come back with. One guy sent him for some post cards and he came back with a bottle of Vermouth. It wasn't a wasted trip!"[25]

The Italian government was worried about an accident involving a nuclear warship's reactor. Other countries also expressed similar concerns. On May 7, 1968, the issue of radioactive contamination from an

American submarine sparked international headlines when Japanese scientists reported radioactivity ten to twenty times the normal background level in Sasebo harbor during a visit by the submarine *USS Swordfish* (SSN 579). The Japanese government asked the U.S. government not to send any more nuclear-powered ships to Japan until the cause of the increase was determined. U.S. officials denied that the *Swordfish* caused the instrument readings, and the incident remained a stalemate for some time with the *Swordfish* continuing its port visit.

The *Scorpion's* arrival in Taranto on Sunday, March 10 was, at that time, something of an anomaly: Only a handful of nuclear attack submarines had ever visited a foreign port (apart from the navy's own advanced bases at Holy Loch, Scotland; Rota, Spain, and Guam). There is record of only one Polaris submarine liberty call during that period, when the *USS Sam Houston* (SSBN 609) made a visit to Izmir, Turkey in 1963. Despite the strict safety precautions built into submarine nuclear reactors and the intense training of their operators, navy officials at that time feared that just one accident would destroy public confidence in the nuclear submarine fleet, so they kept port visits to a minimum.[26]

The controversy over nuclear power would hound the *Scorpion* throughout its Mediterranean cruise. The *Scorpion* would find itself unwelcome on the waterfront piers at every other port it visited in the Mediterranean and be forced to remain at anchor far offshore. Nonetheless, many of the crew still managed to enjoy brief stints ashore. While anchored near Taranto, Christiansen wrote his parents that he very much would have liked to have shared his experiences in southern Italy with his wife, Jann, who was back in Norfolk with the couple's young son and infant daughter. "I've sent you a postcard showing the unique architecture of the houses of the region," he wrote. "These houses dot the countryside on small farms only a few acres in size. Supposedly the cone-shaped roofs make the houses cool in summer and warm in winter. The Italian Navy arranged a tour to the area north of Taranto where we saw a grotto (underground cavern). . . . It would be great to get a bike and tour the countryside. What a blast Jann and I would have."[27]

Christiansen was slightly older and more educated than his peers on the *Scorpion.* After graduating from high school in 1960 as a member of the National Honor Society, he went to Lehigh University but dropped out after his first year to join the navy. After boot camp and machinist's mate school, Christiansen attended Submarine School in Groton and naval nuclear power school at Mare Island Naval Shipyard, California, and Idaho Falls, Idaho. He had been in uniform for two and a half years when he joined the *Scorpion* in Norfolk in 1965. "He was not planning to make a career in the Navy," his mother, Adrian Christiansen, recalled years later. "He was planning to return to civilian life at the end of one enlistment, although he wanted to do something useful and interesting in the Navy."[28]

What was supposed to have been a five-day port visit ended up being only a forty-eight-hour pit stop. Dorenkamp's staff sent Slattery instructions to leave Taranto on March 12, and the *Scorpion* put out to sea for ten days of mock combat with—and against—a large group of U.S. and NATO warships. In a letter home, Yeoman Third Class Richard Summers noted, "We are operating with NATO forces this time out. They surfaced this morning and there were about fifteen destroyers all around us. They knew, of course. When I came on watch, they were all gone by then, though." He added in a tongue-in-cheek aside, "However, there were two aircraft buzzing over us. One was a Royal Air Force plane and the other was one of ours. I stood up there [on the lookout platform atop the sail] and waved my hat at them. They were probably saying, 'Look at that stupid ass down there waving that damn hat.' I don't really care, though. If you can't have a little fun once in a while, there's no use living."[29]

Summers grew up in a large family in Statesville, North Carolina, and like Mark Christiansen, attended college for a year before enlisting in the navy. A navy reservist, Summers planned to serve a single two-year active-duty tour and then return to civilian life. "Richard was encouraged to join the navy by his oldest brother, Bill, who had served on the *USS Saint Paul* [CA 73] during 1947–50," recalled his sister, Dorothy Little. "Sometime later, he decided to try for submarine service. His outlook was good, he realized that [submarine duty] was an elite service of the Navy but he also was aware that it was dangerous."[30]

Yeoman 3rd Class Richard Summers, center, relaxes with two *Scorpion* shipmates, IC2 Ronald Byers, left, and IC2 Steven Gleason, during an off-hour on the submarine.
Courtesy of Dorothy Summers Little

At this stage of the Med cruise, Summers was not overly impressed with the two stops the *Scorpion* had made. "So far our liberty ports haven't been anything too great," he wrote on March 20. "Taranto, Italy, is just a halfway typical town you would probably find in Italy. . . . The day we left Taranto it started snowing and got cold as the devil. It probably hadn't snowed there in a hundred years! It seems as though everywhere *Scorpion* goes, the weather turns to crap." He ended his letter with a postscript: "Join the Navy and see the slums of the world!"[31]

On Saturday, March 23, the *Scorpion* pulled into Augusta Bay, Sicily, where a military supply port comprised one part of a small but growing U.S. naval presence on the east coast of the island. The week-long port visit should have been a pleasure for the *Scorpion* crew, but in the spring of 1968, Western Europe was convulsed with anti-American sentiments.

Italy was divided about NATO, and a vigorous, homegrown Italian Communist Party led the opposition to the U.S. war in Vietnam. Unlike Rota and Taranto, where their presence had been politely tolerated, *Scorpion* sailors now found themselves subject to verbal harassment and occasional acts of abuse.

Robert Violetti reported to his family back home, "Well, here we are in 'port' again after 12 days submerged. Again, we are anchored out, but this time for a different reason than before. The Navy says we can't tie up to a pier because of the Communist influence here. The guys that go on liberty have to stay in a group at all times with armed escorts. Sort of like a 5th grade trip to the zoo!" Violetti admitted that he was not much interested in the local culture. "There is nothing in this part of the world for me, I don't even bother going on liberty while in port, only the lifers get a thrill out of patronizing the bars and 'houses.'"

In a letter four days later, he noted how hostile locals were: "We are still here in Augusta Bay. Some of the guys went on a bus tour yesterday and got involved in a Communist demonstration. American sailors are so hated here that most restaurants and stores won't let them in!" he wrote. "Every day a few come back to the boat plastered with eggs! Real incentive for joining the Navy, eh? There isn't much to do here but go swimming off the boat. If the Doc [Hospital Corpsman Chief Lynn Thompson Saville] finds out, he'll go berserk. He said anyone who falls in the water will have to re-take all the vaccinations and shots we got on the way over! I'm trying to get the nerve to dive off the top of the sail (30 feet off the water, a long drop)." Clearly, Violetti was growing frustrated with the voyage: "What I think about mostly is buying the Chevy and a tape player for it. Maybe that will take my mind off counting the days."[32]

Sailors in the Vietnam-era navy did not make much money, and this subject emerged during the Augusta Bay stopover. Violetti complained that the navy had cheated the *Scorpion* crewmen by the way it had managed their payroll in the past three months, jolting the sailors' morale once again. Sailors on overseas deployment not only received an extra bonus in their monthly salary but also could claim tax-exempt status on earnings while in the Mediterranean. Violetti wrote to his mother at one point that the paymasters were manipulating the timing of payday to avoid giving the *Scorpion* crew the bonus and tax-exempt benefit: "We were paid our standard pay for 14 weeks before leaving the states. We won't get paid again until June 1st. Since we are not getting paid now, we can't collect overseas pay. Also the reason they paid us the lump sum in USA is so that our pay during the deployment isn't tax exempt. (The Navy claims they paid us in the states and money earned overseas only is tax exempt.) All this succeeded in doing is demoralize everyone a little more."[33]

Machinist's Mate Chief Robert E. Bryan, thirty-seven, mentioned his lack of funds when he wrote to his parents back in Charleston, West Virginia: "I want to ask a favor of you: Would you order Betty a dozen red rosebuds and have them delivered on Apr. 13? You can call the nearest florist and he can deliver it. I am sending five dollars. It is just about all I have left. You can have them put on the card, 'All my love, Bob.'"

Even though Bryan had served in uniform for twenty-seven years, including tours on two submarines and Submarine Squadron 6 flagship *USS Orion* before joining the *Scorpion,* his letter had the heartrending tone of a young navy recruit far from home for the first time. "Hear you are having some more bad weather. It sure is nice here, but we are anchored out in the bay and nothing to go ashore for. Takes too much money to do anything here. We go to sea again on Saturday for almost two weeks."[34]

The *Scorpion* pulled out of Augusta Bay on Saturday, March 30. In a delicately worded letter to Captain Wallace A. Greene back at Submarine Division 62 in Norfolk, Commander Slattery tacitly admitted that the liberty stopover had been disappointing: "Our visit to Augusta Bay, although much longer than optimum (considering things for sailors to do) passed without incident. Most of my people had a chance to visit Mt. Etna, Catania, Syracuse and other places of interest."[35]

The schedule now called for another period of electric rabbit exercises. Joining the *Scorpion* were two older diesel-electric attack boats from Groton, the *USS Irex* (SS 482) and *USS Blenny* (SS 324). Both submarines were assigned to Submarine Squadron 8 in Groton, and in 1968 were two of ten conventionally powered boats that Admiral Schade's command dispatched to the Mediterranean to train with U.S. and NATO warships.[36]

The exercises kept the crew busy for the next two weeks, then the *Scorpion* detached from the fleet and headed toward its next port visit— a five-day sojourn at Naples. So eager was everyone to return to port after the two weeks at sea that Slattery decided to take an illegal shortcut. The submarine had been operating nonstop for six days when the maneuvers ended south of Sicily. The Sixth Fleet headquarters directed Slattery to take the roundabout track circling Sicily in a clockwise movement because the most direct route passed through the narrow Straits of Messina between Sicily and the Italian mainland. The Italian Navy considered the straits an internal waterway and banned foreign warships from using the passage. If it observed the ban, the *Scorpion* would have had to make a 400-mile trip around the island to get from its position to the Naples anchorage on the west coast of mainland Italy, at least a day and a half more at sea.[37]

Slattery decided to get his men to Naples the fastest way. The crew appreciated the move, as Robert Violetti later explained in a letter home: "We passed through the Straits of Messina the other night secretly. We didn't have permission to do it, were supposed to go the long way around Sicily, but the captain decided to take a shortcut." Alas, the Italian Navy spotted the *Scorpion* and gave chase. Unfortunately for Slattery and the crew, the waterway was too shallow to permit the submarine to submerge, and too narrow to allow evasive action on the surface. Their only option was to floor it. After a "very exciting" hour or two at maximum speed, Violetti recounted, the *Scorpion* reached water that was deep enough for Slattery to submerge the boat. The *Scorpion* escaped. "Seems these people are pretty touchy about who goes through the Straits," Violetti noted.[38]

Naples, the *Scorpion's* third liberty stop in the Med, brought the third snub for the nuclear-powered submarine: Italian Navy officials wanted the submarine to remain far from land. Violetti's mood was glum as he described the Naples scene in a letter to his mother:

Well, here I am again in port again, this time in the harbor of Naples. . . . Again, we are moored two miles from land. This time for two reasons. The Atomic Energy Commission won't let us close to the city, and the Communist activity here poses too much of a threat on us. We are tied up to an anchored U.S. warship in the shadow of Mt. Vesuvius. The ship is supposed to deter any pacifists from coming out here and holding demonstrations. . . . You ask what to do in port. You must remember we haven't been closer than one mile from shore since we left Spain on 6 March. If you call that "in port," OK, but to me "in port" is being tied up to a pier! . . . The next time I touch land will be at Pier 22, Norfolk, Virginia, in 44 days.[39]

While in Naples, a mishap occurred that the court of inquiry later scrutinized. The Sixth Fleet had directed that the *USS Tallahatchie County* (AVB 2), a tank landing ship converted into a naval aviation support vessel, serve as a moorage for the larger submarine. Given the *Tallahatchie County's* thin-skinned hull and the circular cross-section of the *Scorpion's* hull, officials decided to position a partially flooded garbage barge between the two as a fend-off to avoid damage if the two hulls came together. Up until the morning of April 15, when the *Scorpion* got underway for another phase of training exercises, the set-up worked. Then, a squall blew in as the *Scorpion* was preparing to disengage from the *Tallahatchie County*, and before the *Scorpion* cast off its mooring lines the two ships surged together. The barge rode up over the *Scorpion's* hull, tipped, filled completely with water, and sank. Commander Kurt Dorenkamp, the submarine flotilla operations officer, later testified to the court of inquiry, "There appeared to be no damage to the barge [once it was recovered] and, to the best of their knowledge, there was also no damage to the *Scorpion*."[40]

The *Scorpion* returned to sea for another five days of scrimmages with the Sixth Fleet, but sometime around this date the crew's morale took yet another hit: Commander Slattery informed them that the navy had canceled the port visits to Athens and Izmir, because of political unrest in Greece and Turkey. Their final liberty stopover would be a return visit to Naples on April 20 and another week anchored far out in the harbor.[41]

The *Scorpion* moored alongside the *Tallahatchie County* in Naples Bay in April 1968. This is believed to be the last photograph ever taken of the submarine. *U.S. Navy Photo*

The *Scorpion* crew nevertheless threw themselves into the anti-submarine warfare drills with their mock enemy. As Torpedoman Seaman John D. Sweeney, Jr. later boasted in a letter to his parents, "Our time at sea has passed without any particular mishaps. . . . We have been hunting with a hunter-killer anti-submarine warfare group playing war games. They look for us, we try to sink them. About a week ago, we rode under a carrier for about an hour. The sound of his screws was so loud you could count the turns he was making through the pressure hull. Later, we surfaced and signaled him that he had been sunk."[42]

Sweeney was a junior member of a sprawling navy family. His father was retired Rear Admiral John Sweeney, and he had a brother serving in Italy and a nephew in naval aviation. He had enlisted in the Naval Reserve in 1964 before graduating from high school in Annapolis, Maryland. After a year of college, Sweeney volunteered for submarine duty, went on active duty in May 1967, and was assigned to the *Scorpion*. He was in the torpedo gang with Violetti.[43]

The *Scorpion* returned to Naples on April 20 for its second liberty visit there, and several crewmen decided to take a navy-sponsored tour to Rome that Easter weekend. "I managed to get a half-day off to see the National Museum in Naples and go to an opera at night," Mark Christiansen reported in a letter to his parents. "A few days later, [we] went on a two-day tour of Rome where among other things we took a tour of the city, saw the Pope address the crowds outside St. Peter's, visited the magnificent Sistine Chapel . . . and visited a museum downtown. I was interested in seeing as many museums as possible but managed only one. I love Rome. I could spend weeks here pouring over all the masterpieces of architecture and art and ancient ruins."[44]

Richard Summers also planned to tour Rome but told his parents that his first objective had been a more modest one: "We arrived here [Naples] Sunday A.M. I stayed in a hotel room Sunday night just to sleep in a bed. Sounds funny, doesn't it?"[45]

The deployment now took a serious turn. Leaving Naples on April 28, the *Scorpion* headed east for a confrontation with Gorshkov's Fifth Squadron, which was conducting spring training between the southern coast of Greece and Crete. The schedule called for the submarine to operate submerged nonstop for two weeks in the Aegean and Mediterranean before beginning the final westward movement toward Gibraltar and home. While no declassified message exists spelling out the *Scorpion's* assignment, navy records and letters from the crew confirm that the submarine's task was to monitor the training operations that had brought dozens of Soviet warships into the eastern Mediterranean and Aegean. Of particular interest to the U.S. Sixth Fleet was the Soviet squadron's use of a protected anchorage near Kithira Island at the southernmost tip of the Peloponnesian peninsula. The *Scorpion's* patrol assignment to the waters around Crete brought it close to this floating logistics base.

U.S. naval intelligence had already detected a more troubling development than the Soviets' attempt to employ a floating logistics base far from home. The Soviet Navy in the spring of 1968 was practicing sealing off an entire part of the Mediterranean against penetration by the U.S. Navy and its allies. Several weeks before the *Scorpion* left Naples, U.S. naval intelligence analysts reported a Soviet operation to establish a barrier of surface ships and submarines along a 200-mile path from Kithira Island south to the Libyan coast: "Submarines and major surface combatants are apparently cooperating in maintaining the barrier—the first time this tactic has been noted being used in this area," the top-secret assessment concluded. "The operation probably represents a test to isolate a part of the Mediterranean." The report continued that the *USS Essex* ASW Group, which was operating in that area, "has been under constant surveillance" by the Soviets. The analysts also disclosed the presence of a number of Soviet submarines around the *Essex* and its escorts.[46]

No unclassified records are available that say if the *Scorpion* attempted to scout out the Soviet picket line. However, an encounter with a Soviet destroyer on May 10 confirmed the heightened level of confrontation between the two naval forces.

The *Scorpion* was running at about 350 feet down in the eastern Mediterranean on Friday, May 10, when Commander Slattery ordered the boat to surface to rendezvous with a navy helicopter carrying mail for the crew. It was shortly before three P.M. local, and the crewmen were counting days until their homecoming on May 24.

The mail delivery would be a welcome break. They had been operating nonstop since leaving Naples on April 28. This was the submarine's sixth extended at-sea maneuver since leaving Norfolk for the Mediterranean on February 15. For the current exercise, the *Scorpion* had traveled from the west coast of Italy around Sicily—no more high-speed sprints through the Straits of Messina—to the eastern Mediterranean south of Greece and around the island of Crete. This time, Slattery and his crew were shadowboxing with the Soviet Navy.

After twelve days of real-time surveillance and tracking of the Soviet warships, Slattery decided to break off contact and arrange for the mail delivery. Sitting at a worktable in the *Scorpion*'s bow compartment, Robert Violetti sealed an envelope containing a letter to his mother, Luella, back in his hometown of Broomall, in suburban Philadelphia.

A first-term sailor, Violetti had enjoyed a well-rounded youth and high school career—playing football and basketball and rising to the rank of Eagle Scout—before enlisting in the navy in April 1966. His parents were divorced. Like his father, Salvatore, in World War II, Robert volunteered for the Submarine Service and applied for the same rating, torpedoman, that his father had worn on his sleeve. "He didn't want a navy career," Luella Violetti said years later, adding that her son had planned to work in a local plumbing and heating firm that friends of the family owned. "He liked the service and enjoyed his shipmates, but he was counting the days," she said, until his enlistment term ended. His sister Anne Pierce recalled that in 1960, when he was fourteen, Robert's Boy Scout troop had visited Groton, where the *Scorpion* was nearing completion at the Electric Boat Co. shipyard. Robert and his fellow scouts saw the submarine under construction.[47]

Both his mother and sister said Robert was diligent about writing whenever the *Scorpion* was out at sea. "He always let me know where he was," his mother said. On May 10, the young torpedoman third class only had time to describe the *Scorpion's* whereabouts in general terms:

> I didn't expect to be writing anyone for another two weeks but the XO [Lieutenant Commander David Lloyd] says we may be able to get some mail off today. Ever since we left Naples (Sunday a week ago) we've been circling the island of Crete. I can't tell you why, all I can say is that for 13 days now we've been going around it again and again. Today at 3 P.M. we are supposed to transfer classified messages to a helicopter off a carrier. It should prove to be interesting, plus, I'll be able to see the sun again. I saw daylight about five days ago. We were at periscope depth and the OOD [officer of the deck] let me look through the scope. The XO says when they lower the line down to us for the messages we'll just give them our mail along with it. Once they have the mail they "have to" mail it. For this reason I doubt if you'll ever get this, but then again, you might.

Anticipating the remaining two weeks before the submarine's return to Norfolk, Violetti added, "Today was supposed to be our last day of operations but we've been extended three more days here. . . . This info has really disheartened most of the crew. You may think, 'What's three days after you've been gone 100?' Well, those last three are said to be the worst of the whole trip."[48]

Up in the *Scorpion*'s tiny administrative office, just aft of the control room across a passageway from the sonar shack and radio room, Senior Chief Yeoman Leo Weinbeck, thirty-five, and his young assistant, Yeoman Third Class Richard Summers, loaded the outgoing mail and a separate bundle of administrative messages and classified exercise reports into a stiff canvas bag. Included in the pile was Weinbeck's latest letter to his wife, Arliss, and their four children back home in Minneapolis. He had written it eight days earlier when word had come that the mail drop would take place on May 2. However, operational requirements had forced the *Scorpion* to delay the rendezvous. "Here we are, just off the island of Crete playing games with the bad boys," Weinbeck wrote. "It is now 10:30 at night and I've just finished my work for the day—or rather, I quit working today. I've got quite a stack left that must be completed tomorrow morning in order for it—and this letter—to get in the mail. Since we left Naples on the 29th, we have been constantly submerged, operating around and in the Aegean Sea. If you look on the map it doesn't seem like much of an area, but there is an awful lot of water around here. . . . My striker [Summers] and I have finally finished reproducing *Scorpion*'s new Organization and Regulations Manual. I typed 404 pages both sides to finish this monumental task. Now all we have to do is assemble fifteen copies."

Weinbeck was a veteran of both the surface navy and the Submarine Service. He had enlisted in 1950, and served on two mine warfare ships before an assignment ashore at the office of the chief of naval operations. In the late 1950s as a crewman aboard the navy icebreaker *USS Edisto* (AG 89), he participated in an Operation Deep Freeze deployment to Antarctica. Then he did a stint as a navy recruiter in Minnesota. Transferring to the Submarine Service in 1961, he served on the diesel-electric attack submarine *USS Wahoo* (SS 565) and the Polaris submarine *USS Alexander Hamilton* (SSBN 617) before joining the *Scorpion* in March 1967.[49]

As the chronometer ticked closer to 1500 hours local, Slattery ordered the *Scorpion* to prepare for surfacing. The officer of the deck slowly maneuvered the submarine in a lazy circle as the sonar gang listened intently for other submarines or ships on the surface. "Clearing the baffles," as this move is called, is a standard precaution to avoid a collision as the submarine emerges from the depths. Unfortunately for the *Scorpion's* maneuvering watch, they were about to experience an unusual feature of the Mediterranean: Unlike the colder Atlantic Ocean or Barents Sea, where sound waves tend to travel in predictable straight paths, the warm, turbid waters in the Med often bend and twist underwater sound signals. As retired Captain Sanford Levey, a former *Scorpion* executive officer, explained, "You have very weird sound conditions in the Mediterranean. There can be a ship right above you and you won't hear it because of the way the sound curves. The Mediterranean is like a bowl and the water heats up differently than any place else I know of. You just don't hear these guys [on the surface] unless you have special equipment. You go up and there's somebody just right there."[50]

In this case, it was a Soviet destroyer from Fleet Admiral Sergei Gorshkov's Fifth Squadron. The officer of the deck ordered the diving officer of the watch to blow the main ballast tanks, and the 251-foot-long *Scorpion* slowly rose from the depths, breaking free on the surface. Slattery and several lookouts scrambled up the control room ladder to the submarine's cramped bridge atop the sail to find a bright blue sky, a U.S. Navy helicopter clattering in the distance—and the Soviet warship riding close aboard with every one of its guns pointed at them.

Robert Violetti wrote his mother what happened next: "Boy, was that an exciting day. When we surfaced to meet that [mail] helicopter, IVAN was there waiting also. You can imagine how helpless you feel when you go to the bridge and see a Russian destroyer riding alongside 100 feet away with every gun he has trained on you." Once the mail transfer was over, the *Scorpion* submerged and tried to elude the Soviet warship. However, Violetti wrote, the destroyer aggressively tracked the *Scorpion*. Finally, the U.S. Navy launched two fighters from a nearby aircraft carrier, and when they arrived on scene, the Soviet destroyer backed down. "It took us two days to get rid of that 'tin can,'" wrote Violetti.[51]

———

SIX DAYS AFTER its encounter with the Soviet destroyer off Crete, the *Scorpion* was in the western Mediterranean preparing for the final lap of its deployment, a westward crossing of the Atlantic from Europe back to Norfolk. After thirteen weeks at sea broken up by only five port visits, the crew was looking forward to home, even though they already knew that their operating schedule for the summer and fall would be just as busy as the Med cruise had been.

Robert Violetti wrote his mother on the evening of May 16, "The latest dope is that between now and the end of October we will be in Norfolk a total of 30 days!! Of course, this is subject to change but we were told to expect to be at sea from 20 July to about 31 October. Yow!!!" Violetti added that he hoped to visit home for a week in late June.[52]

Navy officials had already selected the *Scorpion* for an unusual and ambitious operation scheduled for the late summer of 1968. They planned to modify the submarine to spy on an upcoming French nuclear test at the island of Fangataufa in the South Pacific. Even before the submarine had left Norfolk back in February for the Mediterranean, senior Atlantic Fleet officials had already earmarked the *Scorpion* for this operation. Then-Lieutenant Commander Les Morcerf, a U.S. naval intelligence officer assigned to monitor the French nuclear test, said the navy planned to install special radiation monitoring sensors on the *Scorpion* upon its return to Norfolk in advance of the next assignment. "This was going to be the first test of the second-generation French nuclear warheads," Morcerf recalled years later.[53]

With Chief Pettey's transfer off the *Scorpion* in April, there were now 101 crew onboard as the submarine reached the Straits. Sometime late in the evening on May 16, a messenger of the watch awoke Sonarman First Class Bill Elrod in his narrow bunk in the crowded berthing compartment down on the fourth deck and escorted him to Commander Slattery's cabin. The commanding officer had bad news: A message had just arrived that Elrod's infant son had died shortly after birth. Since the *Scorpion* was not far from Rota, Slattery said, he was willing to divert there to allow Elrod to catch an emergency flight home.

"He had a Navy message in a clipboard and read the thing off to me. My wife has delivered a baby and the baby is dead. My wife is in satisfactory condition," Elrod recalled. "He said, 'Would you like to go home?' and I said, 'Yes sir, very much.' He said, 'I think I got a tugboat coming out here, I'll get you off tonight.' That was pretty much all that was said. He patted me on the shoulder and sent me on my way. I went and found [Chief of the Boat] Wally Bishop and told him what was going on."

Slattery also wanted to detach a second crewman for follow-up medical tests. Interior Communication Electrician First Class Joseph D. Underwood had undergone a recent medical exam, and an X-ray had shown a spot on his lung that doctors feared might be tuberculosis, which is highly contagious and thus dreaded by submariners.

At that moment, Slattery and his crew still expected to arrive in Norfolk on Friday, May 24. Weinbeck, Christiansen, and Violetti had all written home to that effect. And in his April 18th letter to Captain Wallace Greene at Submarine Division 62, Commander Slattery noted that the Atlantic crossing would take eight days so he was anxious to be released from Sixth Fleet control no later than May 16 to make the scheduled arrival on May 24. Then everything changed.[54]

Sometime in the early morning hours of May 17, 1968, the radio teletypewriter in the *Scorpion's* radio shack came chattering to life. From his Norfolk headquarters, Vice Admiral Schade dispatched a top-secret movement order diverting the submarine from its westward track to Virginia. Instead, the *Scorpion* would proceed west-southwest to a point southwest of the Canary Islands to spy on a group of Soviet Navy ships that included an Echo-II nuclear cruise missile submarine.

Shortly before two A.M. on Friday, May 17, 1968, the *Scorpion*, now traveling on the surface, approached the breakwater at the Rota naval base. Elrod and Underwood climbed up the vertical ladder from the *Scorpion's* control room into the submarine's sail structure. There, they stepped through the small doorway hatch opening out on the portside fairwater diving plane. A navy tug was already nudged along the port side of the submarine's hull, so it was just a matter of taking two steps out on the wing-shaped diving plane and jumping down to the deck of the tug. "I remember looking at the boat from the tug, seeing it in an almost dead astern view," Elrod recalled. "The captain and the lookout were up there. The bridge cockpit on those things is rather small, there's not a lot of room up there, just one lookout and the captain. He called down to me from the bridge and said, 'Take care, good luck.'"[55] It was the last anyone saw the *Scorpion* and its crew. Five days later, they were all dead.[55]

9

A TWISTED, SHINY PIECE OF METAL

1968 WAS AMONG A HANDFUL OF THE MOST EVENTFUL AND SIGNIFI-
cant years of the twentieth century. In the United States, there were
citizen mobilizations for and against the Vietnam War, troops in the
streets, student strikes, and police crackdowns. There was hope and de-
spair. There was the assassination of two moral and political leaders.

In France in May, ten million workers joined a general strike that
threatened to topple the government. In Paris, in a hotel conference
room, U.S. and North Vietnamese negotiators convened for their fourth
session in ten days. For three hours, each side denounced the other for
impeding progress toward a settlement. In Vietnam, Vietcong sappers
launched mortar attacks in Saigon, B-52 bombers blasted enemy targets
thirty miles away, and battles raged near Danang and Quang Tri.

May 22, the day the *Scorpion* went down, was a calm, beautiful,
warm spring day in Norfolk. On that day, the city announced it had received bids to build a new Cultural and Convention Center near City
Hall. The Virginia Beach School Board said that it was proceeding with
plans for a new junior high school and had received state funding for a
new vocational-technical center. And *The Virginian-Pilot* reported that
more than two years after he had stuffed a handwritten message in a
bottle and thrown it into the ocean near the Cape of Good Hope in
southern Africa, Navy Electrician's Mate Third Class Robert Yoachum

had received a letter in reply. A fisherman in Martinique had written to say he had found the bottle, more than 5,623 miles from its deposit location.[1]

For family members of the *USS Scorpion,* including forty-six households in the Norfolk area, there was a sense of anticipation and excitement at the homecoming of their men aboard the submarine. But May 22 was the day that would ruin the dreams of these families forever.

Those aboard the *Scorpion* did not live to see the final moments of their ship. In a letter to a widow of one of the *Scorpion* crewmen, a navy medical expert offered reassurance that her husband had not suffered. "This flooding is accompanied with a massive increase in air pressure within the boat," Navy Captain George F. Bond wrote several weeks after the navy announced the discovery of the wreckage. "It is this high pressure air which is the immediate cause of the death of the crew . . . producing cardiac arrest and death in a matter, not of seconds, but of milliseconds. Under these conditions, no member of the crew would have any knowledge of the disaster prior to instantaneous death."[2]

WITHIN HOURS OF the May 27 SubMiss alert, the navy commenced what would become an ambitious hunt for the submarine involving survey ships at sea and a cadre of scientists back in Norfolk and Washington. Officials alerted a few oceanographic research ships and support vessels to be ready to carry out what would be known as the "focused operations" search, which would depend heavily on the oceanographic research ship *USNS Mizar* (T-AGOR 11), a small Naval Research Laboratory vessel crewed by civilians. This technical search did not begin in earnest until the second week in June, but the navy was setting the stage for it even as it rushed dozens of surface ships and submarines out into the Memorial Day storm. The first challenge was to identify any evidence that might narrow down such a search from millions of square miles of ocean to a smaller, more manageable area.

A converted navy supply ship, the *USNS Mizar* (T-AGOR 11) conducted deep-sea experiments and salvage for the Naval Research Laboratory and was credited with finding the *Scorpion* after a four-month search. *U.S. Navy Photo*

NAVY SCIENTIST DR. JOHN P. CRAVEN recalled almost to the minute how he heard about the *Scorpion* crisis. The news came on his car radio as he was driving home from work on Memorial Day. Craven had worked as a submarine designer and ocean engineering specialist for years. As the director of the Deep Submergence Systems Project in 1966 and 1967, he had been responsible for organizing the development of manned and unmanned submersibles capable of operating in thousands of feet of water, including vehicles designed for rescuing trapped submariners. Unknown to all but a handful of senior admirals and U.S. intelligence officials, the DSSP was also involved in highly classified intelligence operations employing submarines, smaller submersibles, and navy deep-sea divers to exploit the deep ocean environment for information about Soviet military operations.

In January 1967, the navy assigned a navy captain to head the DSSP, and Craven returned to his earlier role as the unit's chief scientist.

Craven immediately drove to the Pentagon and hustled into the Chief of Naval Operations Flag Plot to volunteer the services of his unit. One admiral suggested that they try to find acoustic information that might reveal the location of the submarine if it had suffered a major casualty or had actually sunk. He told Craven that Pentagon officials had already called the Ocean Systems Atlantic Command to see if the Sosus hydrophone arrays had any evidence of the *Scorpion,* and the initial response had been negative. Later, officials said in-depth analysis of the raw tapes revealed that Sosus stations had just barely detected the first of about fifteen major acoustic signals from the sinking, but this fact remained unknown for several weeks.[3]

"When I got involved there was absolutely no acoustic evidence," Craven recalled. "The whole thing was completely hopeless. . . . The first question you ask is, 'What about acoustic signals?' And the answer is, 'None. We've searched everything we could search and we have no signals.' They had already reviewed all of the [Sosus] nets. That's the first thing you do is call up the Sosus nets and say, 'Hey, were you tracking this guy and did you have him, and if you had him did you lose him and did you get a signal associated with the loss?' That was done immediately in knee-jerk reaction."

So as navy ships' sirens continued to sound across Hampton Roads that night with the launching of the massive open-ocean *Scorpion* search-and-rescue operation, Craven sat in a windowless Pentagon office and began calling anyone he could think of "who might have hydrophones in the water that are active." After four hours of dialing, Craven reached Dr. Gordon Hamilton, a civilian scientist at a navy acoustic research station in Bermuda.[4]

Hamilton, who was doing acoustic research for the Office of Naval Research (ONR) and had stations in the Canary Islands and Bermuda, told Craven he had a hydrophone collection in the Canary Islands. Craven asked him if he saved the data, and Hamilton replied, "They save it for about a week and then they erase it." Hamilton called the Canary Islands research station, which confirmed that it still had a continuous-reel recording from the week of May 20.

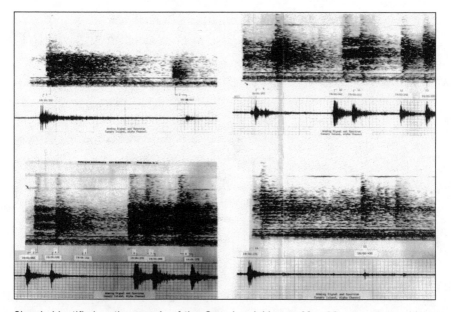

Signals identified as the sounds of the *Scorpion* sinking on May 22 were captured by a research hydrophone at the Canary Islands. *U.S. Navy Photo*

The navy ordered the reel delivered to Washington, and by late Wednesday, May 29, Craven and Hamilton were in a military sound laboratory listening to the acoustic signals. "We went through this record and there were just loads of big spurious signals," Craven said. "We picked up four or five events that looked like they were big enough. And we had the time of the events so we had some rough idea of where the track would be. So this gave us some rough idea of position. Our rush was that we wanted to aid the air search at that time."[5]

The Canary Islands tape contained the first significant clue: a sequence of sharp acoustic signals at 1844 GMT on Wednesday, May 22—most probably the sounds of the *Scorpion* breaking up as it sank. Craven told the court of inquiry that one acoustic expert had told him the initial sound spike "sounds like an explosion, it looks like an explosion," while the train of signals that followed after ninety-one seconds of silence appeared to be the implosion sounds of various compartments and tanks collapsing after the submarine plunged below crush depth. Confirmation soon came from the then-highly classified Air Force Technical Applications Center (AFTAC), a secret military intelligence organization that operated a global array of ground-, sea- and space-based sensors to detect and triangulate the location of nuclear explosions. Two underwater hydrophones that AFTAC controlled near Argentia, Newfoundland also contained the same sound pattern as Hamilton's Canary Islands sensor. The signals were barely recognizable because of the faint signal strength from the event 1,300 miles away. However, detailed analysis confirmed they were recordings of the same series of acoustic events that the Canary Islands station had recorded. The three sites gave AFTAC's position calculation computer a starting point for the scientific search.

The navy's official account of the technical search that began days after the *Scorpion* was pronounced lost on June 5 started on an upbeat note. Two days after Craven and Hamilton huddled over the Canary Islands recording, the AFTAC computers had already plotted a roughly twelve-by-twelve-mile area southwest of the Azores where they calculated the *Scorpion* most likely had gone down. This search square centered on the estimated latitude-longitude plot of the location of the sixth of fifteen sound signals from the *Scorpion* breakup. No one knew it at the time, but officials would later marvel at the accuracy: The estimated position turned out to be only three and a half nautical miles from the actual location of the submarine.[6]

The scientific team was working on many fronts in the first few days after the SubMiss alert. Craven and his associates were not only scrambling for any credible evidence of the *Scorpion*'s resting place but also struggling to assemble the flotilla of survey ships that would try to find the submarine.

That first night, Craven called Naval Research Laboratory civilian scientist Dr. Chester L. Buchanan to alert him to the *Scorpion* emergency and the probability that the *Mizar*, the NRL's principal oceanographic survey vessel, would soon be ordered to participate in the search.

Manned by a civilian crew from the Military Sea Transportation Service, the *Mizar* was an unprepossessing ship. Only 266 feet long, fifty-two feet at the beam, and with a draft of eighteen feet, its primary mission in 1968 was for pure scientific research. Its most notable feature was a specially constructed center well that opened to the sea for lowering and towing an unmanned search sled to a maximum depth of 20,000 feet. In the past five years, the little ship had scored two major operational successes this way. In 1964, it located the major hull fragments of the *USS Thresher* on the Atlantic seabed in 5,500 feet of water, some 220 miles east of Boston. In January 1966, it helped find a missing U.S. Air Force H-Bomb that had fallen into the Mediterranean after a midair collision between a B-52G bomber and KC-135 aerial tanker.

Buchanan later recalled that the second sentence out of Craven's mouth that Monday night was, "Where is the *Mizar?*" Fortunately, the ship was in the Atlantic returning to port after several months at sea. Formal orders to join the *Scorpion* search came on Friday, May 31, when a message arrived in the *Mizar*'s radio shack directing it to proceed at best speed to Norfolk to load out equipment for an ocean-bottom survey search in the "area of special interest" that the navy had now identified southwest of the Azores.[7]

Meanwhile, Pentagon officials were organizing the scientific team that would manage the focused-operations search effort. Chief of Naval Operations Admiral Thomas H. Moorer appointed a *Scorpion* Technical Advisory Group (TAG) with Craven as chairman and mandated it to provide scientific assistance to the operation. Craven's panel would report to Rear Admiral J. C. Donaldson, director of the Fleet Operations Division (OP-33) in the office of the CNO, but its charter instructed the group to coordinate with the Atlantic Submarine Force headquarters, where Vice Admiral Arnold Schade was the officer-in-charge of the overall search.[8]

For the first phase of the *Mizar* search, Buchanan was aboard the ship as lead scientist while Craven remained behind in Washington. The open-ocean search, under the command of Rear Admiral Lawrence G. Bernard, began on May 27 and was still underway on Sunday, June 2, as the *Mizar* departed Norfolk on the 2,126-mile trip to the target area. The group of surface ships and submarines were still sailing down the *Scorpion's* presumed course track from the submarine's last reported position south of the Azores back to Norfolk. In addition to the *Mizar,* three other survey and support ships were heading toward the "area of special interest": the survey ship *USNS Bowditch* (T-AGS 21) from its homeport in Londonderry, Northern Ireland; the experimental navigation ship *USS Compass Island* (AG 153) from Brooklyn; and the submarine rescue ship *USS Petrel* (ASR 14), which had transported Rear Admiral Bernard from Charleston to Norfolk at the start of the open-ocean search. No one anticipated immediate results.

Craven and the *Scorpion* TAG were concerned about the limited capability of the search equipment aboard the *Mizar.* The towed sled contained a magnetometer whose official maximum sweep width was only 220 feet, and a still camera with wide-angle lens that had a visual range width even smaller, 185 feet. Assuming that the *Mizar* could somehow make perfectly aligned sweeps of the search area, such an effort would still require steaming 331 separate twelve-mile legs to blanket the 144-square-mile search area, a task that would have taken more than a year, he said. Even that it could not do. According to Buchanan, *Mizar's* chief scientist, the actual sweep width was only half of the nominal 220-foot sweep width. Compounding the difficulty was the fact that the submarine's hull was not the only object on the ocean floor that would trigger an alert signal from the magnetometer. The seabed was full of underwater rock formations with high concentrations of iron ore that would generate false alarms. Worse, the still camera mounted on the sled would require extremely close-up imaging that restricted the camera's sweep width to just thirty feet. "We didn't have the capability to do several hundred square miles," Buchanan said. "If we had had to do more than a hundred [square miles] somebody would have thought twice" about the whole operation. To track the towed sled as it glided above the seabed, the ship employed three transponders attached to the underside of its hull that could query a fourth transponder unit mounted on the sled to determine its position relative to the ship. Of course, the *Mizar* did not possess the pinpoint navigational capability that ships started having in the 1980s with the advent of the Global Positioning System satellite network. As *Mizar*'s crew began searching, they at any one moment would have only a vague notion of their actual location.[9]

"What would you want if you were given the job of looking for a needle in a four-square-mile haystack from a helicopter?" wrote Journalist First Class Sam Herzog, who was assigned to the *Mizar* for the first two weeks of the search. "Having a good helicopter, accurate navigation, a magnet and a camera would be some of the most desirable tools for a search like that." Craven, monitoring the focused-search operation from the DSSP office in Chevy Chase, Maryland, used a slightly different metaphor: "It was like looking through a soda straw for a contact lens in your front yard at midnight—in the rain."

In a speech to a defense industry trade group on June 27, 1968, Vice Admiral Schade said essentially the same thing: "I can't impress on you enough the magnitude of the job that we have been pursuing. When the *Thresher* went down she was escorted by a submarine rescue vessel that knew her exact position. It still took us two summers to locate her hull. Now we are faced with and are pursuing a search that covers some 2,400 miles of ocean to search, and no clues where that search might begin." As the ships were heading toward the target area, Atlantic Fleet Commander Admiral Ephraim P. Holmes on June 3 voiced his own apprehension in a message to Admiral Moorer. The deep ocean search, he wrote, "will be long and difficult since the only ships capable of deep water search have practically no open ocean search capability and are effective only in small localized areas. It will be a case of try[ing] to localize some areas promising for search." At this point, the two senior admirals actually knew more about the *Scorpion*'s location than their pessimistic tones implied, but it was a very closely guarded secret.[10]

Navy officials had few illusions about the task confronting them. The Technical Advisory Group would later note that the search team struggled with a number of serious shortcomings throughout the hunt. "One must realize that the *Mizar* system did not represent a ready capability in the military sense," the group's after-action report found. "While her scientists are experienced in deep search and underwater navigation techniques, they do not maintain themselves as a ready and proficient team in between ad hoc operations. Nor can one always count on *Mizar*'s technical facilities to be at peak performance levels. Lastly, the *Mizar*'s search system still had many technical faults which her scientific managers could eliminate but had not done so because of lack of time and money. In short, *Mizar*'s search system is a breadboard model."

As a result of these deficiencies, Craven and Buchanan recalled in separate interviews, the search team employed two additional tactics to attempt to shrink the search area to a manageable size. First, they decided to refine the initial estimated location of the *Scorpion* acoustic signals with calibration tests at the scene. Second, the Technical Advisory Group would turn to a proven analytical technique in which possible scenarios that led to the *Scorpion* sinking would be gamed using a probability analysis formula that would result in identifying specific sub-areas of the twelve-by-twelve-mile search square that were more likely to contain the wreckage than others.

From the beginning of the focused-operations search, Schade and his staff kept an iron grip on the day-to-day effort. The admiral first ordered the *Mizar* to join up with the experimental navigation ship *USS Compass Island* southwest of the Azores. Schade had sent the *Compass Island* ahead of Admiral Bernard's open-ocean force anticipating that the technical search effort would need its sophisticated navigational capabilities. On June 5 it arrived in Bahia Praia at the island of Terceira, Azores.

The next day the *Compass Island* was underway for the designated search area about 450 miles south-southwest. Without stopping, *Compass Island* skipper Captain Joseph E. Bonds at three P.M. ordered a brief memorial service in honor of the *Scorpion* and its crew on the ship's main deck. At ten A.M., June 7, it was still steering a course of 230 degrees when it reached a point roughly 400 nautical miles southwest of Punta del Gada and about thirty-five miles northeast of the AFTAC computer's initial calculated position of the *Scorpion* acoustic signals. Even before its rendezvous with the *Mizar*, the *Compass Island* began what would be a week of round-the-clock operations to help the scientists back in Washington, D.C. refine the estimated position where the *Scorpion* had exploded.[11]

The process was relatively straightforward. While steering "various courses at various speeds," as its official deck logs noted, the *Compass Island* carefully marked its location with the array of sophisticated navigational systems on board. Then, crewmen would drop demolition charges off the fantail. The charges were set to explode at predetermined depths according to a schedule that the scientists back in Washington had determined would replicate the sound path that the original *Scorpion* acoustic signals had taken just two weeks earlier. Once the new acoustic pulses appeared on the Canary Islands and AFTAC hydrophones, scientists could compare the computer's estimated location of the blast with the more accurate position plotted by the *Compass Island*. Any discrepancy between the two positions would create an offset that would allow the scientists to identify a more accurate estimate of the submarine's location.[12]

The scientific theory might have been simple, but poor communications between the search vessels at sea and the scientists and admirals in the United States quickly hampered the effort. The results of the calibration shots carried out in the first four days were a failure, largely because of a communications breakdown between the ship and the AFTAC sensor operators. The shore-based signal-processing stations in Canada and the Canary Islands failed to record all of the shots. In testimony on June 13 to the court of inquiry, which remains heavily censored to this day, Craven said,

> The *Compass Island* conducted a first [calibration shot] series on, I believe it was, Friday [June 7]. The operation was partially successful in that the [deleted] were not operating for the second half of the *Compass Island* sequence of events, which were the [deleted]. And the [deleted]. Due to a failure in communication the *Compass Island* conducted the exercise earlier than we had intended. . . . a message was sent to the *Compass Island* requesting her to reschedule her event from 1400Z to 2000Z. The message was not received by *Compass Island*. . . . I do not know whether she has yet received the message. [Deleted]. We therefore attempted on Sunday evening [June 9] to carry out in a more favorable location the [deleted].

The *Compass Island* planned a second series of demolition charge drops over the weekend of June 15–16, Craven told the court.

Deck logs for the *Compass Island,* finally declassified in 1998, show that the ship conducted round-the-clock "special operations" in the search area for seven days starting Friday, June 7 then broke off for a quick trip back to the Azores for supplies. The ship returned to the datum area two days later on June 16 and resumed special-operations calibration shots for another five days through Friday, June 21.[13]

Craven and the other scientists had figured that with the series of explosions and computer calculations they could hone in on the *Scorpion's* most likely location, but the results from the June 16–21 series came as a real surprise: They showed that the events of the sinking had probably been far more violent than originally suspected. They also showed the submarine traveling in the wrong direction at the time it went down. The first shocker was the magnitude of the sixteen "acoustical events" corresponding to the initial explosion and collapse of the *Scorpion's* hull. Navy scientists monitoring the acoustic signals coming in to the Canary Islands and AFTAC hydrophones from the calibration shots were perplexed when smaller-sized demolition charges failed to register at all. "They're dropping a series of charges then they wanted to know whether we heard them," Craven recalled in 1984. "We used charges of one size, that didn't work, then we doubled the charges, that didn't work, then we doubled them again. Then we had a dilemma—how do we get charges that are big enough to go down there and do the thing? Very, very large charges."

During that period, the *Compass Island* dropped fifty-one individual demolition charges ranging in size from 1.8 pounds of TNT to seventy pounds. They included nine 1.8-pound charges, five twenty-pound charges and two seventy-pound charges set to detonate at sixty feet; seven 1.8-pound charges, thirteen twenty-pound charges, and one forty-pound charge set off at 800 feet; three seventy-pound charges detonated at 1,000 feet; three seventy-pound charges set off at 1,500 feet; five seventy-pound charges triggered at 2,000 feet; and three seventy-pound charges fired at 3,000 feet. In its final report, not declassified for more than twenty-five years after the event, the court of inquiry noted that the seventy-pound charges detonated at 1,500 feet below the surface finally generated "similar energy levels" to that of the acoustic impulses from the stricken submarine. This allowed the scientists to calculate that the cascade of sounds that followed the initial explosion after ninety-one seconds occurred at the *Scorpion's* estimated collapse depth around 1,300 feet down.[14]

The revelation that the *Scorpion* was heading east amazed the scientists. When they processed the *Compass Island's* calibration tests into the AFTAC computer and replayed the original acoustic recordings, they found that the position of the train of signals—the initial explosion, followed after ninety-one seconds by the multiple sounds of the submarine imploding—clearly showed the *Scorpion* heading in the wrong direction. "We looked at those signals," Craven said of the initial AFTAC–Canary Island recordings. "We didn't have an absolute location, we had a relative location and that relative location indicated the submarine was going in the wrong direction." At first, Craven and his colleagues thought the results might be an anomaly caused by changes in the water temperature or other variables that threw off the timing of the signals' arrival, but subsequent demolition charge measurements confirmed the submarine's easterly heading. Additional demolition shots not only underscored the *Scorpion's* eastward movement but showed the submarine was moving extremely fast at the time of the first explosion.

Craven and the other scientists now had the first important piece of evidence that they believed would help them both pinpoint the location of the *Scorpion* wreckage and identify a credible theory about the cause of the sinking. Convinced that the computer data showing the submarine's eastward heading was accurate, Craven asked Atlantic Submarine Force officials a critical question: What sort of an emergency or malfunction would prompt a submarine to suddenly reverse course? That's when he learned about the hot run.

The Mark 37 torpedo was a mainstay submarine weapon in the 1960s. With 330 pounds of HBX-3 explosive, each torpedo was 11.3 feet long and 21 inches in diameter and weighed 1,430 pounds. On its

1968 deployment the *Scorpion* carried fourteen of the torpedoes, including ten wire-guided models that enabled the *Scorpion's* fire-control technicians in the control room to transmit targeting data to the torpedo over a thin monofilament wire even after it had been launched from the tube. The data initially traveled from the fire control panel to the torpedo via a pair of coaxial cables, including one that ran from the control room to the torpedo tube. A second cable inside the watertight torpedo tube linked the first cable and the torpedo itself. Before firing the torpedo, the crew would upload instructions that would dictate the torpedo's search pattern after launching, its operating depth, and whether the sonar transducer on the nose of the weapon would passively listen for sounds of the target or would emit active sound pulses and guide to the target from the reflected sound echoes. With the weapon running free, the fire controlman could change its search pattern, speed, or depth by transmitting new instructions over the slender wire still linking submarine and torpedo.

On occasion, through crew error or mechanical malfunction, the navy had experienced Mark 37 hot runs, in which a torpedo accidentally activated inside the torpedo tube, with its propulsion system engaged as if the launch order had arrived. Even though there was a mechanical lock to prevent the torpedo propeller from turning, the activation of a Mark 37 battery would instantly create tremendous heat inside its body. Whether inside the torpedo compartment or in one of its six torpedo tubes, a hot-running torpedo constituted a serious emergency. Significantly, in 1967 the *Scorpion* had experienced a hot run with a training version of the Mark 37 that did not contain an explosive warhead.

The navy had a simple fail-safe system to overcome a hot-run incident. Simply turning the submarine 180 degrees from its course at the time the torpedo became live would activate an anti–circular-run device that would automatically shut down the torpedo. Craven said he became convinced that this had happened on the *Scorpion* minutes before the sinking, since it offered a plausible reason for the submarine to have been heading in the opposite direction of its homeward course track. At first opportunity, Craven decided to test the hot-run scenario with a former *Scorpion* officer who had left the submarine just before its Mediterranean deployment.

Lieutenant Commander Robert R. Fountain sat at a worktable in a laboratory at the navy's David Taylor Model Basin in Bethesda, Maryland. As part of a simulation of the *Scorpion* sinking Craven gave the submariner course, speed, and other operating conditions as if he were conning the submarine at sea. One of the scenarios they tested was the following: "You have a 'hot running' torpedo in the torpedo room." Craven explained that he wanted to know what Fountain's immediate reaction would be to that event: "We told him what depth he was at, what speed he was going. And his response was this [snapping his fingers], he said, 'Right standard rudder.' He turned the whole submarine around." Craven went on, "If you want my personal scenario, this is it: They had a hot-running tube, they had it going, that instead of jettisoning it, somebody in the boat, for one reason or another, decided to pull it back into the torpedo room. They pulled it back into the torpedo room and dropped it before the turn was completed."[15]

The hot-run theory would spark fierce debate within the navy. Admiral Schade and his COMSUBLANT staff said safety procedures and training made such an accident all but impossible. Even with Fountain's response seemingly strengthening the hot-run scenario, some scientists still cautioned that the evidence was far from airtight. "They looked at the stuff," Craven said of the acoustic evidence. "They were experienced guys, and they thought we were smoking opium." The court of inquiry would later accept the hot-run theory but with a twist. It concluded that instead of the torpedo detonating inside the torpedo compartment, the *Scorpion* crew had launched the weapon but failed to disarm it before the Mark 37 warhead went active. The torpedo then homed in on the submarine and sank it.[16]

The focused operations search for the *Scorpion* officially began on Monday, June 10, when the *Mizar* and *Compass Island* rendezvoused in the "area of special interest" southwest of the Azores. Navy journalist Sam Herzog, on the smaller ship, later described the scene: "As we reached the search starting point, a strange light appears on the horizon—a ship.

It is the first ship that has been seen since leaving the Norfolk area, although several Navy P-2Vs [patrol aircraft] have been spotted flying overhead. The ship is identified as the Navy's oceanographic survey ship *USS Compass Island,* which dwarfs the *Mizar.* The *Compass Island* gives some added help as it transfers aboard some supplies and personnel." The *Bowditch* and *Petrel* arrived shortly thereafter.[17]

As the focused-operations searchers began organizing their first attempt to locate the *Scorpion* wreckage, back in Washington disagreement between the submariners and the scientists over the acoustic evidence raged on. Unbeknownst to Buchanan on the *Mizar* and Bonds on the *Compass Island,* Schade's disbelief in the Craven scenario had fostered a breakdown in communications between the *Scorpion* TAG and the Atlantic Submarine Force that nearly aborted the focused-operations search.

The *Compass Island*'s demolition drops had enabled Craven's team to refine the calculated estimate of the submarine's location to a remarkable degree. Between May 30 and June 22 the scientists shifted the estimated position of the *Scorpion* sinking no less than five times within a sub-area of the search zone spanning approximately seven by three miles. Since this marked the beginning spot for the *Mizar*'s fine-grain sweep using its towed sled, Craven's staff was essentially telling Buchanan and his team where to start looking. However, Schade stepped in on at least three occasions with orders that ignored the refined acoustic evidence and sent the *Mizar* off in the wrong direction.

The initial AFTAC estimate on May 30, plotted from the raw *Scorpion* sound signals, was located at 32:54 North 033:06 West. Later that day, the scientists refined the computer results and shifted the estimate to a point identified as Rev. 1A. This was about three nautical miles to the west-southwest of the original plot, located at 32:53.1 North 033:09.55 West. After the first, and only partially successful, *Compass Island* demolition charge drops during June 7 and 8, the experts moved the estimate to the east by 1.5 nautical miles to a third point marked Rev. 1B, at 32:53.1 North 033:08.5 West. Eight days later, the *Compass Island* resumed its demolition charge drops, and the scientists recali-

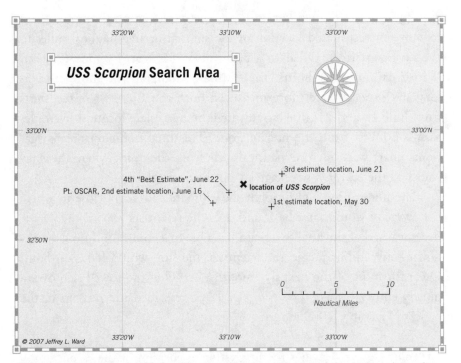

This composite map of *USS Scorpion* search area southwest of the Azores shows four initial estimated plots of the submarine's location calculated by acoustic signals, and the submarine's actual location. Due to a misunderstanding, the *USNS Mizar* continued to search around Point Oscar rather than explore around the 3rd and 4th estimates, which officials said prolonged the search.

Sources: Scorpion *TAG Report,* CINCLANTFLT Annual Report for 1968–69

brated the signals once more. They identified the fourth—and most plausible estimated position—at Point Oscar, at the same latitude as the two previous estimates but now 2.5 miles to the west from the mean of Rev. 1A and Rev. 1B.

This calculated plot of the May 22 acoustic signals, at 32:53.1 North 033:11.5 West, would remain the benchmark for the *Scorpion* search over the next five months. The official after-action report on the *Mizar* search later called the miscommunication a major mistake that almost caused the search to fail.

On June 21, scientists plotted a fifth revised position based on magnetic tape playback of the AFTAC and Canary Island signals considered even more accurate than Point Oscar. The recalculation prompted them to move the estimated location of the submarine five nautical miles to the northeast from Oscar to a point at 32:56 North 033:06.5 West. Within twenty-four hours, the estimate changed one more time as Craven's experts once more measured both the *Compass Island* shots from June 16 and 21, moving this final best estimate location five miles west-southwest from the previous one. This final point on the navigational chart was only one nautical mile from the point where the navy later said the *Scorpion* wreckage lay on the ocean floor.

The fine-tuning had brought the estimate extremely close to where the *Scorpion* would later be found, but the scientists aboard the *Mizar* never learned of the final two revisions. Due to a communications breakdown between Shade and the scientists, the ship would focus on Point Oscar for most of the next five months, dragging the towed sled over a mostly empty seabed. The *Scorpion* TAG described the mix-up in the panel's November 1969 report:

> Point "Oscar" was not the best estimate position of the "acoustic events" associated with *Scorpion's* breakup. However, through a misunderstanding, this position was used as the search datum and was a major assumption in calculating target location probabilities. . . . [On June 21] the TAG received a new estimate of the position of the acoustical events from Mr. Gordon Hamilton, the Columbia University scientist who was responsible for the majority of the analysis of the acoustic events. . . . Apparently the significance of this evaluation never came through to the TAG or COMSUBLANT. . . . In retrospect, this new position should have been treated as the most likely position of Event #6 [of the *Scorpion* sinking]. Instead, Point Oscar was used in calculating target location probabilities and as the major point of reference for the search team aboard *Mizar*.[18]

Even as the *Compass Island* continued with the demolition shot series, the *Mizar* began trolling the Atlantic seabed with its towed sled at the end of a three-mile cable. Schade had directed Buchanan and his civilian technicians to first conduct a "coarse grain search" in a circular area one mile in radius centered on the Rev. 1B spot.

The *Mizar's* actual hunt for the *Scorpion* wreckage was a complex and tedious ballet of navigation, seamanship, and engineering that tested the skills and the patience of the dozens of experts aboard. The little ship first had to identify its intended search corridor using an ad hoc array of navigational equipment that provided only intermittent fixes to define its location in the search area. Once satisfied that the *Mizar* was operating in the correct location, the technicians then had to safely lower the 1,400-pound sled and its coaxial cable miles below and at least a mile behind the ship.

Navy Journalist Sam Herzog described a typical launching of the sensor platform, which crewmen dubbed "the fish": "Ready to lower the fish into the hole, it is first raised up to the top of its silvered cradle. Then the deck-level [well] doors slide ponderously open, revealing foam-capped, translucent blue water rising and falling within the well. . . . With the ship barely moving, the fish is lowered down the hold into the water until it approaches the bottom, over 1,500 fathoms [9,000 feet] down." Back in the control room, one *Mizar* technician carefully monitored an instrument panel showing the sled's height above the seabed, continuously raising or lowering the cable to keep it at a precise height above the ocean floor. As the sled glided along in the lightless depths, it transmitted continuous sonar and magnetometer signals back to the ship that would indicate the possible presence of the *Scorpion*. Meanwhile, a pair of powerful strobe lights regularly flashed to illuminate the seabed as the still camera took a succession of photographs.[19]

The *Mizar* crew quickly fell into a search routine that was physically and mentally exhausting. The thirteen-man scientific team split into two sections and worked back-to-back twelve-hour shifts as the sled slowly glided over the ocean floor down below. "We'd take photographs for about eight hours; we had enough film to take that many photographs," Buchanan recalled. "They were overlapping photographs about thirty feet in diameter, so this gave you a line thirty feet wide on the ocean floor you photographed. And of course we're looking for debris, not a submarine. We're looking for some indication that something unusual was happening."

During the search, the *Mizar* crept through the water at one nautical mile per hour. A technician in the control room carefully monitored the sled's onboard sonar and other sensors for signs of debris or underwater obstructions that would require him to command the winch to raise the sensor platform to prevent the sled from colliding with the bottom. "So we would in any eight hours, travel about eight miles," Buchanan said. "We had to search the whole area around [Point Oscar]. It's hard to realize when you're doing a search with a thirty-foot-wide camera and maybe one-hundred-feet range for the magnetometer, who knows what the sonar can see? You have to make some decisions on how fine the search grain should be, how close you should try to make your tracks. If you make the tracks a couple hundred feet apart, you won't search very much area in the eight hours—you're only going eight miles."

The prolonged sweep of the towed sled was only a part of the task. At the end of each search track, the *Mizar* would haul in the sled and technicians would remove the large reel of film from the camera for immediate processing. "We processed the film twice," Buchanan said. "We made a negative and then copied it to a positive." Then, as the little ship trudged on photographing its next narrow slice of Atlantic seabed, the senior navy officer or his military assistant would load the film strip into a viewer and gaze intently at the screen as some 4,000 separate images flickered past. "The film would just continuously go on as long as you held the switch," Buchanan explained. "With this you could review the film very rapidly, because most of the time you don't see anything."

Between June 10 and 28, when the initial search phase ended, the *Mizar* conducted ten runs around Point Oscar with its sled in contact with the ocean floor for a total of about 270 hours. During this first cruise, only three objects appeared on the viewer screen: a bottle, a tin can, and a twisted piece of shiny, torn metal about two feet long. The other 40,000 negative frames were identical: featureless images of mud and clay silt. The scientists had not expected any miracles. And they didn't get any.

In the last five days of the first cruise, Schade's headquarters in Norfolk on June 23 ordered the *Mizar* to expand the coarse-grain search out to a two-mile radius around Point Oscar using eleven parallel path sweeps. This tactic, a consultant to the search later explained, "was designed for simplicity while at the same time allowing near optimal search effort to be placed in the area." It also quadrupled the search area from 3.1 square miles to 12.5 square miles. But the only clue to appear was a sonar contact identified by *Mizar* scientist Gordon Roessler and located five miles to the northeast of Point Oscar, where the terrain was extremely steep and dense with rock outcroppings. The sonar image was intriguing since it showed an object roughly 20-by-300-feet in size lying on the seabed that might be the *Scorpion's* hull.[20]

At the end of June, Craven flew out from Washington to the Azores with a new on-scene commander, Captain H. R. Hanssen, commander of Submarine Squadron 4 in Charleston, South Carolina, rendezvousing with Buchanan aboard the *Mizar* in Terceira. After a close review of the *Mizar's* track charts, photographs, and sonar contacts, the three agreed that the next search phase should be to reacquire the twisted piece of metal found near the end of the first cruise and to search in that general area. Given the total absence of any other physical clues, Buchanan recalled, the scientists thought that the piece of metal was the "least unlikely" piece of evidence and deserved a closer look. Craven agreed, saying, "We had these long, long discussions and arguments as to whether or not in the middle of the ocean you would or would not find these random pieces of metal . . . just as a result of ships going by." They had nothing else to go on. Ironically, the piece of twisted metal was later determined to be from the *Scorpion,* and it lay only 200 feet from the submarine's debris field.

The *Mizar* left for the search area on July 10 for the second cruise. The ship was less than two weeks into the new search phase when Schade for a second time intervened to change the search pattern. He ordered the *Mizar* to focus on the Roessler sonar contact instead of the piece of metal. It was another major misstep. Schade's order moved the *Mizar* even further away from the actual site of the *Scorpion* than the earlier error that he and the Technical Advisory Group had made assigning Point Oscar as the best location and ignoring Hamilton's two later revisions of the *Scorpion* acoustic signals.[21]

Craven described the decision as one of simple human nature. "The problem you have with a search of this kind is that everyone comes up with his own conclusion as to what is the best search pattern to carry out," he recalled. "Even yourself, and your team, end up going on wild-goose chases that in retrospect you realize if you had just kept your cool, you wouldn't have gone on." Craven's scientific team would also cite the lack of accurate navigation that made it hard to even find an object that had previously appeared on the *Mizar*'s sensors. Obeying the admiral's orders, the *Mizar* abandoned its plan to search for the twisted metal and spent two days in a futile effort to reacquire the Roessler sonar contact before giving up and returning to the two-mile radius search around Point Oscar. With tens of thousands of additional photographs of seabed mud, the *Mizar* skulked back to the Azores on August 6 for some more R&R.[22]

After two months of fruitless searching, Craven and his fellow scientists were ready to provide the *Mizar* with an additional tool to use in the hunt for the *Scorpion*. When the ship arrived back in the Azores after the end of the second cruise on August 6, a representative from the scientists arrived with Craven's "a priori location probability" assessment model. This was a complex series of formulas based on the calculations of mathematician Thomas Bayes in 1763 to determine the probability of random events. For the *Scorpion* search, Craven had brainstormed with other scientists in the Technical Advisory Group to compile a list of all possible events that conceivably could have caused the *Scorpion* sinking, and the most likely movement of the submarine or its fragments away from the best-known location of the hull collapse as it fell to the seabed. Then, the group of experts would bet on the likelihood of one scenario over the others, Craven explained.

The first step in the process is to devise a list of possible causes for the sinking, Craven said: "The method is to get a group of experts together to dream up all of the scenarios that you can dream up and for each scenario to get a location—a most probable location." Since most of the information was imprecise, this resulted not in a pinpoint location for each scenario, but instead, a circle drawn on the search area chart in which there is a fifty-percent probability that the *Scorpion* debris was located. The second step involves calculating relative odds for the entire list. "Then the group sits down and gives a likelihood that each scenario is correct. With that likelihood you add all of the scenarios, all of the probability curves together, weighted by the likelihood, and you make up one great big probability map." Once the computers cranked out the results, the searchers had a probability map of the twelve-by-twelve-mile search area, divided into one-by-one-mile sub-areas, each of which contained an individual "a posteriori" probability that the *Scorpion* was inside its borders. According to Craven, this step shrank the likely location of the *Scorpion* from the entire 144-square-mile area to a half-dozen individual one-by-one-mile sub-areas, offering the *Mizar* a much more useful range of search choices. "You search on the basis of that probability map."[23]

The *Scorpion* Technical Advisory Group drew heavily on the *Scorpion*'s own maintenance history and testimony from former crewmen to the court of inquiry to devise a list of possible fatal mishaps and how the submarine would have likely moved during its last minutes from the estimated location of the acoustic events. "We did have a complete history of all malfunctions on the *Scorpion* that had been logged or reported, or even anecdotal from those who were on the boat who had left" before its 1968 cruise, Craven explained. "Most scenarios [involved] malfunctions that had occurred on *Scorpion* which if they had occurred in a different way would have been fatal."

The navy kept the *Scorpion* scenarios classified until 1993, when it released the information. With one exception, they all involved a string of unspecified accidents that produced a certain rate of flooding at different depths and operating speeds. The exception, and the most likely scenario, Craven said in a 1983 interview with me, was one that postulated a torpedo warhead accidentally detonating, ripping open a hole in the pressure hull, and causing fatal flooding of the *Scorpion* in ninety-one seconds. "It's the one scenario that in my opinion fits all of the evidence."[24]

The *Mizar* set out on its third cruise on August 14, with the Craven search model as a guide. But the scenarios, and Craven's grid map identifying the most promising search areas, would again have to wait. Once again, Schade stepped in to divert the *Mizar* in an entirely new direction. In a message from Norfolk, Schade directed the *Mizar* to hunt down a clue that the ship had detected toward the end of the second cruise. On August 3, the magnetometer on the *Mizar*'s towed sled had suddenly spiked, indicating the presence of a substantial magnetic field on the seabed that the scientists thought might be from the *Scorpion*'s HY-80 steel hull. The location of what would be known as the M8/3 contact (for Magnetometer-August 3) was about two miles southeast of the erroneous Point Oscar—still the search team's center of operations. This time, the *Mizar* had good luck in finding the target, because it had successfully dropped an acoustic transponder nearby during the initial discovery. The pinging from that device enabled the search team to reacquire it "almost at will," the *Scorpion* Technical Advisory Group later reported. Alas, M8/3 turned out not to be a *Skipjack*-class submarine hull, but rocks. The magnetometer needle had spiked from the high iron ore content and not from the submarine's hull.

The third cruise, like the others, ended with photos of rocks and mud. Years later, officials from the *Mizar* search would document Schade's multiple interventions to me in interviews, but no one explicitly criticized COMSUBLANT for keeping a tight leash on the search. It was a naval operation, and he was the man in charge. However, in bureaucratically correct sentences, the *Scorpion* Technical Advisory Group in 1969 gently chided Schade in its after-action report for insisting that the *Mizar* focus on the M8/3 contact instead of proceeding with the search of the high-probability grid areas on Craven's map. Contributing to the error, the report admitted, was the inadequacy of radio communications between the ship and Atlantic Submarine Force headquarters. As a result, the *Mizar* wasted more than a week trolling southeast of Point Oscar before the scientists were able to persuade Norfolk to let them look elsewhere. The rest of the third cruise focused on a sweep of the ocean to the east and northeast of the M8/3 location.[25]

As if Schade's micromanagement weren't hurting the search enough, mechanical malfunctions now set in like a gang of poltergeists. First the ship's acoustic tracking computer—used to determine where the towed sled was in relation to the ship—crashed. Then the SRN-9 navigational computer went bad. Transponders didn't work. Several weeks later, the *Mizar* returned to the Azores, empty-handed once more.

Back home, the leaves were changing color, football season was kicking off, college students were demonstrating against the war, and the *Scorpion* court of inquiry had adjourned to write a report based mainly on navy officials' testimony, maintenance records, and the few acoustical signals that had recorded the *Scorpion*'s demise. Southwest of the Azores, the *Mizar* continued plodding over a trackless ocean with the sled trailing far below, photographing mud. Its crewmen and scientists were beginning to wonder if they weren't just wasting their time.

Its fourth cruise began on September 18, and for the first time, the *Mizar* team planned to use the "a priori" map with its specific sub-areas earmarked for close scrutiny. When the ship arrived in the search area two days later, the sled rumbled through the open well and glided into the black depths. Armed with Craven's grid squares, the team went looking for the twisted metallic artifact that the sled camera had photographed on June 27. Seven long runs of the sled later, zilch: The *Mizar*'s navigational accuracy was not precise enough to clearly identify the artifact's location. The after-action report's tone at this point was one of despond: "Perhaps one should not be surprised at the lack of success up to this point."

The mood was just as gloomy back in the Pentagon and down in Norfolk. The admirals were starting to consider putting off the search until the spring of 1969. There was even talk of canceling it altogether. At this point, Craven and Buchanan devised a bit of sleight of hand to fend off the nay-sayers. They proposed a final research cruise in which the *Mizar* would experiment with different search techniques and fine-tune its equipment, looking ahead to a resumption of the search the following spring. In fact, Craven later said, he and Buchanan had been sitting on a little secret of their own: a mutual optimism that the overall search technique would ultimately succeed.

"We cooked up a 'research phase' because if we hadn't, the search would have been over," Craven said.[26]

But time was running out. Buchanan said the autumn weather patterns in the eastern Atlantic posed a threat to the search effort. They would have to start off as soon as possible. "We really didn't expect to make that fifth cruise once the weather gets so bad in the fall," he said. "I had argued and fussed about it and they finally let me go."

On Wednesday, October 16, the *Mizar* pulled out of Terceira and arrived on station two days later. Buchanan was on board the ship for his third stint in the focused-operations search, with an ambitious list of equipment checks to keep the *Mizar* crew busy for weeks. Captain James T. Traylor, commanding officer of Submarine Squadron 10 in Groton, had reported as on-scene commander, but as one after-action report noted, he decided to let the scientific team run the show on this cruise since the main goal was to work out the technical difficulties and recalculate the accuracy of the sensors.

For the first week, the *Mizar* team fine-tuned the underwater tracking system used to monitor the towed sled's relative position to the ship, deployed a number of seabed transponders to enable a more accurate search pattern, and undertook several noise-reduction efforts to enhance the ability of the three hull-mounted hydrophones to receive signals from the sled marking its position relative to the ship. By October 23, the ship was ready to make a series of fine-grain sensor sweeps near the last-known estimated position of the piece of torn metal.[27]

Meanwhile, stateside, the *Scorpion* families knew almost nothing of the *Mizar* and the months of frustration that had plagued its crew. Many of the wives said that the navy's response in May had been thorough. Casualty assistance officers assigned to each family had helped with general information and access to military pensions through the Veterans Administration and Social Security Administration. Moorer, Schade, and other admirals had personally written parents and wives to assure them that the search and investigation would be comprehensive. However, after the *Scorpion* was declared "presumed lost" on June 5, the information flow slowed to a trickle, and then stopped.

By October, about half of the forty-six *Scorpion* families in Norfolk had left the area. Some who were originally from the Hampton Roads area stayed, while others were still weighing their options. Allie Brueggeman, the wife of Machinist's Mate First Class James Brueggeman, told a *Virginian-Pilot* reporter she planned to stay in Virginia Beach with their three young children despite the constant reminders of her late husband. "I have my bad days and my good days," she said. Theresa Bishop, wife of Chief of the Boat Walter Bishop, said many of the young wives still had problems handling the loss. "They can't accept it." Bonnie Lou Peterson, wife of Electrician's Mate Chief Daniel Peterson, said that many of the younger wives were still in denial over their husbands' deaths. "They keep on hoping that the crew can live as long as that reactor's intact. But then, why didn't they send up signals?"[28]

Some family members later recalled how angry they were with the way the navy had treated them. Adrian Christiansen, the mother of Machinist's Mate Second Class Mark Christiansen, was critical of what she said was the navy's insistence that the *Scorpion* wives move on: "My daughter-in-law recalled that the *Scorpion* families were told to leave Norfolk and to forget about everything and to get on with their lives. The navy wanted no one related to the *Scorpion* to stay in Norfolk." This prompted Christiansen's widow, Jann, to move her two children to another home out of state, she said. Barbara Foli Lake, the wife of Interior Communications Electrician Third Class Vernon Foli, said, "While they were still searching [for the *Scorpion*], the navy arranged Bekins moving service to come to my Norfolk home and pack everything to send back to my home town. I couldn't believe how quickly they wanted to get me out of there. In one way it felt like the Navy was caring for its families, but in other ways it felt like they were just putting sacks over our heads."[29]

"They don't know anything," said Bonnie Lou Peterson, wife of Electrician's Mate Chief Daniel Peterson, speaking of the navy probe. "They're going on assumptions, same as the newspapers." But Peterson and the other *Scorpion* relatives did not know how close the *Mizar* crew was to finding the *Scorpion*.[30]

EVEN AS THE *MIZAR* had set out on its fifth search cruise on October 16, senior navy officials were preparing to close out the *Scorpion* investigation, which had gone on throughout most of the summer. After the court of inquiry completed its hearings in early July, the seven members spent three weeks reviewing testimony and evidence before submitting the final report to Atlantic Fleet commander Admiral Ephraim P. Holmes on July 25. Since then, a series of senior navy officials in Washington had been formally reviewing the court's verdict and adding their comments. By late September, Chief of Naval Operations Thomas H. Moorer and Navy Secretary John Chafee had signed off on the inquest, and navy lawyers were preparing an unclassified summary to release to the *Scorpion* families, news media, and public. Navy officials in Washington and Norfolk told reporters on October 24 that the navy planned to release an unclassified summary of its findings around October 30–November 1 but would first notify families of the submarine's crew by mail.[31]

The navy was also taking steps to forestall any rigorous investigation of the *Scorpion* by the House or Senate Armed Services Committees. On Friday, October 25, Captain Walter N. Dietzen, deputy director of the Submarine Warfare Division, met with Joint Committee on Atomic Energy Staff Director John Conway and his designated successor, Ed Bauser. They discussed the *Scorpion* investigation, the status of the focused-operations search, and the impending release of the court of inquiry report. Dietzen summarized the meeting in a memorandum classified secret: "I described the plan for release of the *Scorpion* press release and the unclassified summary to the dependents. Both Messrs. Conway and Bowser [*sic*] read these documents. Mr. Bowser's only comment was that 'It sure doesn't say much.' I explained the need to protect the sensor [the top-secret AFTAC nuclear detonation monitoring system] involved in the court's findings, and Messrs. Conway and Bowser stated they understood the need for proceeding as we are."

During the rest of the discussion, according to Dietzen, the three men brainstormed ideas on how to ensure that the Joint Committee on Atomic Energy—and not either of the two Armed Services Committees—would control any possible congressional investigation of the

Scorpion loss. The joint committee had long worked with the Naval Reactors Branch and nuclear submarine force and was regarded as a much
more friendly panel than the two Armed Services Committees.

Then came the news that few had ever expected to hear. The *Scorpion*
had been found. At three A.M. GMT on Tuesday, October 29 (eleven
P.M. EDT on October 28 in Washington and Norfolk), Captain Traylor
had been viewing the filmstrip of the *Mizar's* Run 75 in the photolab
when he bolted upright in his chair: The ghostly bow section of the
missing submarine had appeared on the screen.[32]

Within twenty-four hours, the navy announced that the *Mizar's*
towed sled had found and photographed the *Scorpion* wreckage, and that
the court of inquiry would reconvene to examine the new photographic
evidence, which was being rushed back to the United States. The news
made headlines around the country.

For the families, the revelation did not bring an end to their grief
but did promise the prospect of providing answers to their questions and
closure to their suffering.

BUT IT WAS ALL A LIE.

A few senior U.S. Navy officials knew the truth.

Searchers had located the *Scorpion* on June 9, four days after the
navy had pronounced it "presumed lost." The entire focused-operations
search involving the *Mizar* and the other research ships was an elaborate, time-consuming and expensive cover-up. Just as navy officials had
known about the *Scorpion* sinking within hours of the actual event—
and not five days later when it failed to reach port—the senior admirals
dispatched the *Mizar* to the search area knowing exactly where to look
for it. Rather than a frustrating detective hunt that had taken five
months from beginning to end, the navy survey ships had steamed to
the search area with the latitude-longitude coordinates of the wreckage
already in hand. The entire affair was again cloaked in the tightest security classification possible. That was because the Russians had told them
where to look.

10

WHAT WERE THEY TRYING TO HIDE?

TWENTY-ONE-YEAR-OLD HUGH BREMNER WAS STRETCHED OUT ON the hood of his car enjoying a drive-in movie in Linden, N.J., his hometown, when the sound track abruptly fell silent. Then a voice crackled over the loudspeaker system: *"Your attention please. Will Hugh Bremner please call home at once. The matter is urgent."* It was Friday, May 24, 1968.

The navy boiler technician third class walked over to a pay phone at the snack bar and dialed his parents' house. His mother answered on the first ring. "Your ship just phoned, Hugh," she said breathlessly. "It's an emergency recall. You're to get back as soon as you can." Bewildered, he glanced at his watch as he hung up. It was 6:30 P.M., and he had been enjoying weekend liberty since returning from sea that morning. Bremner quickly calculated that it would take fifteen minutes to get back to the house and change into his uniform, and another hour to make the drive into Manhattan via the Holland Tunnel before crossing over the East River on the Brooklyn Bridge to the naval station, where his ship, the *Compass Island*, was moored. Trying not to interrupt the other patrons, Bremner climbed into his car, turned on the motor, and edged his way to the drive-in's exit.[1]

Neither Hugh Bremner nor the other 217 officers and enlisted men knew at the time that their ship was about to assume a crucial role in a highly classified search for the *USS Scorpion*. Three days before the navy would announce the *Scorpion* as missing on Memorial Day 1968, the *Compass Island* had received crash orders to get underway to hunt for the submarine. And it was the crew of the *Compass Island* that, only two weeks later, would find the wreckage of the *Scorpion* two miles down on the Atlantic seabed.

This secret discovery in early June 1968, nearly five months before the navy officially announced that the survey ship *USNS Mizar* had located the wreckage on October 28, does more than expose the official navy account of the search as a coverup. The secret voyage of the *Compass Island*—obscured by a navy disinformation campaign, then overlooked by journalists, and finally concealed by a process of deliberate records falsification—provides a key to unlocking the truth of what really happened to the submarine and its ninety-nine men.

The navy made no attempt to conceal the *Compass Island*'s involvement in the open-ocean search that began late in the afternoon of May 27. Declassified navy messages and situation reports listed the ship as one of nearly five dozen surface ships and submarines in that highly publicized operation. However, to conceal the fact that they had ordered the ship to sea on May 24, Atlantic Submarine Force officials took such draconian measures as altering the *Compass Island*'s official records to falsely show that the ship was in port throughout the Memorial Day weekend. The ship's own 1968 Command History and deck logs for May 27 and 28, 1968, state that it did not begin preparations to get underway for the search until ten P.M., Monday, when the captain ordered the crew to set the special sea and anchor detail. Forty-one minutes later, the logs report, the ship was underway for the search.

According to official records, on June 5—the day the navy declared the *Scorpion* presumed lost and terminated the open-ocean search—the *Compass Island* arrived at Bahia Praia at Terceira, the Azores, to load cargo and passengers before steaming to the focused-operations search area southwest of the Azores. The ship's assignment was to provide support for the *Mizar* as the smaller ship began scouring the seabed with its towed sensor sled. Officials reported that upon arrival, the *Compass Island* spent most of its time helping navy scientists calibrate the accuracy

The experimental navigation ship *USS Compass Island* passes down the East River in New York from its homeport at the former Brooklyn Naval Shipyard. The ship searched for the *Scorpion* in early June using a powerful imaging sonar installed in its bow.
U.S. Navy Photo

of the underwater hydrophones that had recorded the sounds of the submarine sinking. On June 25, the Atlantic Submarine Force then detached the *Compass Island* from the focused-operations search, and it returned to New York.

That was the official record of the *Compass Island*'s activities during the four weeks between May 27 and June 25. The reality is something quite different.

In 1968, the *Compass Island* was an eleven-year-old Atlantic Submarine Force support ship whose primary mission was to serve as a test platform for navigational systems developed for the Polaris ballistic missile submarine fleet. While seemingly a prosaic research topic, navigational accuracy went to the heart of the effectiveness of the Polaris nuclear missile system. Without knowing *exactly* where they were at any given moment on undersea patrol, the forty-one Polaris submarines would be unable to strike their designated targets with the sixteen nuclear-tipped missiles they carried in vertical launching tubes. Precision navigation thus became a prime component of the navy's crash program during the 1960s to build and deploy forty-one Polaris missile submarines.

Converted from a civilian cargo freighter to a navy test-bed for submarine navigation equipment, the *Compass Island* carried several systems onboard that proved invaluable in the hunt for the *Scorpion*. Among them was a unique star-tracker optical system for plotting its position by triangulating the location of stars, as well as an advanced version of the Ships Inertial Navigation System, or SINS, used by the Polaris submarines. The latter was a self-contained array of accelerometers, gyroscopes, electronic servo units, and early computers that made a moving plot of a submarine's location by calculating its movement through the water from a known latitude-longitude starting point. These two devices allowed the *Compass Island* to provide its location on any spot of the ocean with unparalleled accuracy. Also on the ship was the Sonar Array Sounding System (SASS), a state-of-the-art underwater mapping system that enabled it to create detailed topographic charts of the seabed several miles down. For much of 1968, the ship had been undergoing repairs and equipment upgrades in a New Jersey shipyard, including installation of a new SINS navigational system for the navy's new Poseidon ballistic missile. Finally, on May 13 the ship had departed for an operational area north of the Bahamas to test out the new navigational equipment.[2]

Captain Joseph E. Bonds, the *Compass Island's* popular and respected skipper, was a firm believer in a non-military concept: the weekend off. Under his command, unless a particular task at hand required the ship to be at sea for an extended period, the skipper held his ship to a Monday-to-Friday work schedule with weekends free for rest and recreation. "We came in from operations on Fridays—we always did that," said former Boiler Technician Second Class William A. Sebold, a twenty-one-year-old crewman in 1968. "When we pulled in sometime that morning, we would usually shut everything down and go on shore power. Usually half the crew would leave at that time because most of them lived in Brooklyn." May 24th was no different. The ship tied up to Pier J at the Brooklyn Naval Station shortly before 9:30 A.M., and Bonds announced liberty call. Half the crew, including Hugh Bremner, hit the bricks. Two shipmates, Electronics Technician Third Class Bill D'Emilio, nineteen, and Bill Sebold, remained aboard with the rest of the duty section.[3]

Then, toward evening, an emergency message from Submarine Flotilla 2 headquarters rocketed in to the *Compass Island* radio shack and the weekend liberty routine slammed to a halt. Sebold recalled he was relaxing in one of the fire rooms down below with several other sailors when about six P.M. the internal communication panel buzzed. "We were told, 'Light the boilers back off, we are getting underway right away.'" Captain Bonds had received urgent orders to get the *Compass Island* to sea as fast as possible to join the search for the *Scorpion,* Sebold said. It normally took three to four hours to raise the steam pressure in the ship's boilers to the level where they could drive the propulsion system, but by breaking every rule in the book, Sebold and his engineering gang had the *Compass Island* underway in just an hour.[4]

Less than ninety minutes after the emergency call came in at the drive-in movie, Bremner passed through the old shipyard gates and drove down to the pier. "The ship had already left," he recalled with a chuckle. "I was standing there with probably half the crew. They had pulled out with a skeleton crew on board." Referring to his shipmates unlucky enough to have been on duty when the alarm sounded, he said, "The guys standing watches were working 'six on and six off.'" Navy documents declassified twenty-five years later confirmed that forty crewmen failed to get back in time. Led by the ship's engineering officer, the motley group of homeless sailors ended up in a temporary barracks at the naval station until the navy could figure out a way to get them out to their ship. The sun was low in the western sky over New Jersey as the *Compass Island* passed under the Brooklyn Bridge for the second time that day and turned left into the main ship channel for the Verrazano Narrows and the open Atlantic. As darkness fell on Friday, May 24, the ship was steaming south at flank speed for the Virginia Capes area to join the secret search for the *Scorpion*.[5]

Meanwhile, *Scorpion* wives and children in forty-five homes throughout the Norfolk area were coping with their own last-minute changes of plans. At midday, Atlantic Submarine Force officials informed them that the *Scorpion* would not be returning in late afternoon after all. Instead, the submarine's estimated time of arrival was now one P.M., Monday, May 27. The delay was particularly upsetting to Julie Sue Smith, wife of Machinist's Mate Second Class Robert B. Smith. "I was due to have our first child on May 26," she recalled years later. "Bob and I were both filled with anticipation at the prospect of him being home for the delivery." Her sister, Dee Ann Wright, had flown in from St. Louis to help out, so the two women prepared for a long weekend, unsure of which would be the first to arrive: Julie's husband or their baby. Nine days later, officials would pronounce Robert Smith and his ninety-eight crewmates lost at sea.[6]

THE RECORD OF the *Scorpion*'s final days was corrupted even before the submarine exploded and sank on Wednesday, May 22, 1968. The secrecy, disinformation, and outright lies escalated for five months as the Atlantic Fleet mounted its massive open-ocean hunt for the submarine and then as the Atlantic Submarine Force commander, Vice Admiral Arnold Schade, assembled the small flotilla of navy survey ships that carried out the focused-operations search southwest of the Azores. To this day, the navy's falsified account of the *Scorpion* search—and the cover-up of the actual events—remains the official version of the incident.

In theory, a formal court of inquiry seemed the perfect instrument for the navy to determine what had happened. In his message appointing retired Vice Admiral Bernard L. Austin president of the *Scorpion* court of inquiry, the Atlantic Fleet commander, Admiral Ephraim P. Holmes—Schade's superior officer in the navy chain of command—set out the inquest's mission: "The Court is directed to inquire into all the facts and circumstances connected with the disappearance of the *Scor-*

pion; death of, or injuries to personnel aboard . . . and to fix responsibility for the incident. After deliberation, the Court shall submit its findings of fact, opinions and recommendations." The seven-member panel had legal authority equal to that of a civilian grand jury, although its mandate did not include deciding criminal guilt or innocence. Its chief function was to determine the facts by the sworn testimony of witnesses and the review of evidence, including material classified as high as top secret. But evidence of the navy's efforts to manipulate pertinent information runs throughout the transcripts of the court's investigation.[7]

The court of inquiry's first day, June 5, was also the day the navy declared the submarine presumed lost, and the first witness to take the stand was Vice Admiral Schade. He was, of course, in the best position to provide the seven-member court of inquiry with a comprehensive account of the *Scorpion's* final days. He had originally decided to send the *Scorpion* to the Mediterranean after the *USS Seawolf* accident on January 30. His operations staff controlled the *Scorpion's* every movement before and after it formally joined the Sixth Fleet. His intelligence section provided the submarine with vital information to carry out its mission, and his communications center sent messages to and received them from the *Scorpion*. And it was his headquarters that ordered the *Scorpion* to divert from its homeward track on a final, top-secret mission in the Atlantic. If anyone could unlock the mystery of the *Scorpion's* disappearance, it was Schade.

Schade presented himself as a "friendly" witness anxious to set the record straight and eager to provide the court whatever it needed to get to the truth. There was no reason for anyone to doubt the fifty-six-year-old three-star admiral. A distinguished World War II combat veteran, he held one of the critical jobs in the Atlantic Fleet, and he enjoyed an excellent reputation among his subordinates as a firm but fair commander.

Schade had taken over the Atlantic Submarine Force eighteen months earlier on November 19, 1966, assuming command of 30,256 officers and enlisted men, eighty-four attack submarines (including twenty-one nuclear-powered boats), thirty-five of the navy's forty-one Polaris missile submarines, and nineteen surface support ships. But unlike his three-star counterparts in Norfolk who provided administrative support to the fleet, Schade also held the designation as an *operational* commander under the four-star admiral who presided over both the U.S. Atlantic Fleet and NATO's Atlantic combat force. As a result, Schade's headquarters had separate operations, communications, and intelligence sections whose handpicked staffs assessed the intelligence, prepared the operations orders, and assigned missions for the submarines in the command's eight submarine squadrons. Schade's office in-tray contained the full spectrum of administrative letters, files, reports, and memorandums generated by this range of activity. It also held some of the most volatile and sensitive military secrets of the Cold War.[8]

Schade's military record was impressive: Schade graduated from the U.S. Naval Academy in 1933 at the age of twenty and after three years on a cruiser joined the Submarine Service. By the time the United States entered World War II, Schade had already served on two submarines and two more surface warships. In February 1942 as a lieutenant commander, he became executive officer of the submarine *USS Growler* (SS 215) under Commander Howard W. Gilmore.

A year later, in February 1943, the *Growler,* operating out of Brisbane, Australia, went on patrol to attack Japanese merchant shipping and warships traveling between the two fortified ports of Truk and Rabaul, New Guinea. On the night of February 7, the *Growler* became involved in one of the most dramatic submarine combat incidents of World War II. Sighting a Japanese cargo ship, Gilmore ordered a night surface attack. However, the Japanese vessel saw the submarine and turned toward it, leading to a collision that damaged the forward eighteen feet of the submarine. The Japanese ship swept the *Growler's* decks with heavy machine-gun fire, killing two men and seriously injuring Gilmore and two others. Gilmore ordered the survivors back down inside the submarine. As Schade and the other men on the bridge dropped down the hatch into the conning tower, they waited for Gilmore to join them. But to their horror, he remained topside, and shouted, "Take her down!" Seriously injured in the machine-gun attack, Gilmore realized that he could not get below in time before the Japanese ship crippled or sank his submarine. Schade followed his captain's last command and ordered the *Growler* to dive.

The navy posthumously awarded Gilmore the Medal of Honor for giving his life to save his submarine and crew. Schade received the Navy Cross, the second-highest naval award for combat valor, for that incident.[9]

Many of Schade's subordinates referred to him not as Admiral, or Admiral Schade, but simply as Arnie. Retired Admiral Joe Williams, who served under him on the Atlantic Submarine Force staff as a captain and returned six years later himself as COMSUBLANT, recalled, "Schade was a hell of a good guy to work for. He was a good diesel skipper during World War II. I liked Arnie, he treated everyone very well." As a relatively junior officer in the COMSUBLANT communications division and one of nearly a hundred commissioned officers in the sprawling submarine force headquarters compound on Blandy Road in Norfolk, Lieutenant Harold Meeker said it would have been normal to regard the submarine force commander as a remote and austere figure— but he was nothing of the kind. "Arnie Schade was a great guy," Meeker said years later. "Everybody liked him, he was straightforward, firm and friendly."

As Schade stood before the court of inquiry in the SACLANT (Supreme Allied Commander Atlantic) headquarters conference room on June 5, raised his right hand, and swore to tell the whole truth, no one in attendance imagined that the three-star admiral would give false and misleading testimony.

Launching into his testimony, the admiral quickly reviewed the submarine's reactor refueling overhaul in 1967, summarized the various inspections, examinations, and drills required before ship and crew would formally be certified as ready for deployment, and sketched out the Mediterranean cruise itself in a handful of sentences. Then, as he reached the point in his testimony where the *Scorpion* left the Mediterranean for its homeward transit of the Atlantic, the admiral started tap-dancing around the full story. When asked whether Atlantic Submarine Force headquarters was in radio contact with the *Scorpion* while it was crossing the Atlantic, Schade stated that the submarine was operating under "restricted communications" during the last six days of its scheduled transit, May 22–27. "We do not expect to hear from them," Schade said of submarines operating under this condition. "We did expect to hear from her on arrival at 1700Z, which was one o'clock in the afternoon local time, Monday, the 27th." He added that his staff initially believed that the Memorial Day storm had interfered with radio communications from the submarine and had delayed its arrival.[10]

On June 5, what did Schade know that he did not tell the court? Of course he knew that he himself had diverted the *Scorpion* from its homeward journey onto a top-secret mission. He knew by June 5 that the *Scorpion* sank at 6:44 P.M. GMT, on Wednesday, May 22. He knew that navy scientists had already pinpointed the area where the submarine went down. He had already ordered the *Mizar, Compass Island,* and other ships to the vicinity to begin the focused-operations search. But on that first day of testimony, Schade revealed none of this to the court. On that day he failed to tell the court the whole truth.

Once the *Scorpion* left the Mediterranean close to midnight on May 17, he testified, the submarine reverted from Sixth Fleet to Atlantic Submarine Force operational control. He said that on May 16 he had sent *Scorpion* commander Francis A. Slattery what he termed "exercise instructions" for the next five days, after which he directed the submarine to transmit a message on May 21 providing a position report and homeward course track. The *Scorpion* duly reported shortly after midnight on May 22, providing its location, homeward course, and estimated time of arrival in Norfolk. Schade assured the panel that this was the only time that he had heard from the *Scorpion* since it left Rota on May 17.[11]

Schade explained to the court that the *Scorpion* was operating under a COMSUBLANT operational order that required radio silence unless specifically directed to communicate with his headquarters. He had further ordered Slattery to resume radio silence after transmission of the May 22 position report. Schade explained: "I might point out that submarines operating under special order, once they give their departure report, their course and speed, and indicate their arrival report—when they are operating under restricted communications—we do not expect to hear from them." In short, Schade assured the court that there was nothing unusual or troubling about the lack of communications from the submarine during that five-day period.[12]

The court went over that critical point in detail with the Atlantic Submarine Force commander. Captain Nathan Cole Jr., a navy lawyer assigned as counsel to the inquest, pressed Schade with several follow-up questions over communications with the submarine:

Q. Now, I believe you did state that it would be normal, you would not expect to hear from *Scorpion* after she filed her posit[ion] report and got underway returning home until she got here. Is that correct, sir?

A. That is correct.

Q. Is this normal, Admiral?

A. It is quite common practice. As you know, our Polaris submarines go out for 60-day patrols and never broadcast except in most extraordinary circumstances. And frequently, our submarines are sent out on exercises which eliminate any requirement for reporting. It is only normal to expect check reports and continuous communications both ways when submarines are operating in the local areas when the exercise ground rules so provide.[13]

Later on in the hearing, court member Captain Thomas Moriarty, a non-submariner serving on the staff of the Cruiser-Destroyer Force headquarters in Newport, Rhode Island, returned to the communications issue, asking Schade if his headquarters had transmitted any messages to the submarine during the six-day period it was heading home. Schade replied that his command had sent a total of eight administrative messages to the submarine over the Fleet Broadcast System between May 22 and May 27. "There were two messages that required an answer but not necessarily by radio while at sea, sir," Schade added. He subsequently identified the two messages as Submarine Division 62 message 211337Z May 68 (May 21 at 1:37 P.M. GMT), first transmitted over the Fleet Broadcast System at four A.M. GMT on May 23, and a follow-up message, Submarine Division 62 message, 242006Z May 68 (May 24 at

8:06 P.M. GMT), transmitted at 2:17 A.M. GMT on May 25. Both referred to routine post-deployment maintenance work the *Scorpion* was
scheduled to undertake. These messages sparked a protracted discussion
among the court members and several witnesses as to whether the *Scorpion's* failure to respond to them as requested should have sparked concern among the submarine force staff.

The court soon discovered that things were not as clear-cut as
Schade had described. Testifying a week after Schade on June 12, Commander George R. Parrish Jr., the COMSUBLANT operations officer,
told the court in closed session that Slattery might have reasonably interpreted the two messages, which were from Captain Wallace A. Greene at
Submarine Division 62, as allowing him to break radio silence to re-
spond. However, Parrish reassured the panel that there had been "no
cause for concern" at COMSUBLANT when the *Scorpion* did not reply.
And Greene himself testified the next day that he was not troubled about
Slattery's failure to respond to his two messages. This was because neither he "nor COMSUBRON 6 [commander Captain Jared E. Clarke
III] had been informed that the ship had been taken off of COMSUB-
LANT OpOrder 2-67, which prohibits her transmitting," Greene said.
In its final report, the court would accept the testimony, concluding that
"the operations order under which *Scorpion* was operating while in tran-
sit to Norfolk required electronic silence except as necessary for safety
and other specified situations."

However, the court remained silent on the issue that would ultimately undermine its ability to determine the fate of the *Scorpion*. It was
not the ongoing security of the submarine force that led navy officials to
mislead the court of inquiry. Rather, it was an even stricter body of classified information known as Special Intelligence that drove the cover-up.[14]

There is little information in the open literature even today about Special
Intelligence and how the U.S. military and the intelligence agencies managed and guarded such sensitive information during that phase of the
Cold War. Special Intelligence is a unique and little-known category of
intelligence information involving the interception of foreign military
communications to which even the most senior admirals might not have

As director of the Deep Submergence Systems Project for the navy, Dr. John P. Craven headed a scientific research effort to locate the *Scorpion* while also supervising several top-secret intelligence operations using submarines.
Ed Offley Photo

access. The navy, other military services, and the U.S. intelligence agencies handled this particular skein of intelligence material with draconian protective measures. In his memoirs, published in 2001, Dr. John P. Craven describes how the navy and particularly the Defense Intelligence Agency (DIA) controlled Special Intelligence material: "The activities of the DIA are highly compartmentalized. Most activities are categorized as Special Intelligence projects. Even the code name of each project is highly classified. A list of individuals with a need to know is designated for each project. The list is as short as possible. Information acquired under the program is kept in tightly guarded security spaces and nothing may be removed except when transferred to another secure facility. . . . Participants can tell no one, not even their families or closest professional colleagues, of their involvement in a Special Intelligence project."[15]

The security measures didn't stop there. Deception is a fundamental element in safeguarding Special Intelligence, Craven explains: "Every project must have a cover project that must be true. Thus is formed a hierarchy of projects, with one or more Special Intelligence projects at the top of the pyramid. Most participants in a cover project do not know that it is a cover project. . . . Those who understood the system appreciated the fact that the project they were working on was real and significant but at the same time might be a cover for a project whose mission was more sensitive. You would never know whether you had penetrated the 'seventh veil' except by the length of the clearance list."[16]

From the first day, the *Scorpion* court of inquiry grappled with two contradictory goals: telling the truth and protecting the security of Special Intelligence surrounding the submarine loss. The Atlantic Fleet commander had charged the inquest with finding out the cause of the sinking of the *Scorpion*. On paper, the court had the legal authority to compel witnesses to provide a full accounting of every aspect of the loss. But the navy, particularly the Atlantic Submarine Force, was also involved in numerous Special Intelligence operations that were so highly classified that officials had the authority to conceal them under cover stories—officially sanctioned lies—to prevent their disclosure. This included the loss of the *Scorpion* itself. The court and its parade of witnesses wrestled with that conundrum for the next six months. Secrecy won out over disclosure.

Thus, one of the prime elements of the navy's initial cover story concerning the *Scorpion* disappearance was the absence of any sign of an emergency or danger. Schade's overall testimony stressed that the *Scorpion* vanished while engaged in the most routine of activities—steaming toward Norfolk on a preset course and speed that would bring the submarine to the mouth of the Chesapeake Bay on the morning of May 27. As if to emphasize the absence of crisis or alarm, Schade told the court that he had left Norfolk on May 27 for a previously scheduled cruise on the *USS Pargo*, one of his command's newer attack submarines based in Groton.

According to Schade, it was not until the *Pargo* was about 100 miles south of Block Island off the Connecticut coastline that the first sign of trouble appeared. The *Pargo* received the SubMiss alert from Norfolk at 4:25 P.M. EDT. In response to the alarm, Schade told the court, he ordered the *Pargo* to proceed south at high speed to the area just east of the

Chesapeake Bay entrance where the "first intensive operation" of the search began early Tuesday morning, May 28.[17]

Schade stated his claims about the *Scorpion*'s radio silence in another venue besides the court of inquiry. On June 27, Schade returned to the navy submarine base in Groton to give a speech to the local chapter of the National Security Industrial Association. In his remarks to the defense industry trade group, replete with new details and personal observations on the *Scorpion* incident, Schade fleshed out a narrative in which the emergency had erupted suddenly without warning that Memorial Day:

> Now the failure of a submarine to return to port at an appointed hour, while cause for concern, is not normally an immediate cause for alarm. I say this because there are a number of ways in which a submarine can be delayed. An extremely bad storm had been centered about the Norfolk area that morning and it was only natural to assume that the submarine upon surfacing had been delayed by high seas, and, because of atmospheric interference caused by the electrical nature of this storm, it is also reasonable to assume that she might be experiencing some communications difficulty. This is a not unusual occurrence in the Virginia Capes area. It soon became apparent that neither of these [conditions] were true. While *Scorpion* dependents waited patiently at her assigned berth throughout the afternoon, one of the largest and most extensive search efforts ever manned by the United States Navy began to swing into full motion. . . . [18]
>
> Let me review for you at this time the information that was available to my chief of staff at SUBLANT headquarters who was in the best position to immediately take charge of the search effort and direct it. *Scorpion* had last reported on the 21st of May [referring to the 212354Z message transmitted several hours after midnight on May 22]. She was not required to transmit again until the 27th of May. She had not reported in as she was required to do upon entering port. She had not been heard on the local harbor frequency. And obviously, she had not reported to port. Any

submariner at this point can probably think of a dozen reasons why a submarine might be having difficulty communicating. Communication transmissions have always been somewhat difficult in submarine operations due primarily to the configuration of the antenna arrangement of submarines in general. As I said before, the initial reaction was that she was delayed by the storm and was having communication difficulties. . . .

You will recall that *Scorpion* was returning from approximately three months deployment to the Mediterranean and while *Scorpion* was not required to communicate, it is normal after a deployment of this length for a submarine commanding officer to have several areas where problems may have arisen. Repairs might be required or equipment may [illegible text] originate communications [illegible text]. In fact, it had been anticipated that *Scorpion* would originate such communications. Her failure to do so has led us to believe that the cause of her disappearance may have occurred within a day or two of her last reported position.[19]

This, then, was the story that Schade and other admirals put out during the months of searching for the missing submarine, and it has remained the navy's official account for nearly four decades: A submarine's routine homecoming suddenly flared into crisis when it failed to make port, catching everyone by surprise. The story likely would have remained unchallenged, except for Schade's apparently inadvertent disclosure of a strikingly different narrative of the *Scorpion* loss that he gave in an unguarded moment during an interview with me fifteen years after the sinking.

As told in Chapter 2, in April 1983, I was interviewing the retired three-star admiral for a fifteenth-anniversary article on the *Scorpion* when he described a series of events far different from his testimony and speech in 1968. I had asked Schade simply to recount his experiences from the spring and summer of 1968, and he began recalling how and when he had first learned that something might be amiss. In this interview Schade said that rather than operating under conditions of radio silence during May 22–27, as he had told the court of inquiry, the

Scorpion was supposed to send in at least one additional message to COMSUBLANT after the May 22 position report. "They did not report, they did not check in, and then when we got to the time limit of their 'check-in' they were first reported as overdue," Schade said in 1983.

When I asked him about the *Scorpion's* May 22 position report—the only transmission from the submarine between the time it departed Rota, Spain, until its scheduled arrival date in Norfolk on May 27, his response was again starkly different from his original contention. Commander Slattery's May 22 position report message to Norfolk now held no value at all in terms of helping navy officials assess whether the submarine was in trouble. In 1968, Schade and other officials had cited the May 22 position report as proof that the *Scorpion* was homeward bound and engaged on the most routine of activities. In 1983, Schade all but dismissed that last message as incidental to the events that followed. "We got that position report," he said. "That was the basis for our initial search operation. But that was really all we had and we didn't consider that too significant, other than just as the last known position that we actually had."[20]

Likewise in 1968, Schade had reassured the court of inquiry and the public that the *Scorpion's* radio silence between May 22 and May 27 was no cause for alarm. In his 1983 interview, Schade reversed course: "We have absolute confidence in our communications, both in the reception and the response and when they did not respond, almost immediately that's when we first became suspicious. That's when we followed up with other messages, and really, it was just a matter of hours that we became somewhat concerned."

I realized that Schade was recalling a series of events completely different from the *Scorpion* narrative that he and other senior admirals had presented to the court of inquiry and to the public in 1968. My instinct was not to challenge him over the difference, but as gently as possible, to press him for as much detail as he would be willing to provide. I remembered that the navy had consistently stated that it was the *Scorpion's* failure to arrive as scheduled at one P.M. that Memorial Day that had triggered the SubMiss alert. So I asked Schade if he could recall what had sparked the first anxiety or concern over the submarine. His reply was detailed and unequivocal: "As far as we were concerned all was clear and she should have kept coming and then within about 24 hours after that [the May 22 position report], she should have given us a rather long, windy, resumé of her operations and what she would need upon her return to port . . . you know, transition from one command to another, homeward bound voyage."

I reminded Schade of the messages that COMSUBLANT had transmitted to the *Scorpion* including the two from Submarine Division 62 that requested information on the planned post-deployment maintenance. However, he brushed that issue aside and repeated that it was Slattery's failure to send a follow-up message on the termination of the *Scorpion*'s deployment—and not the maintenance requests—that had sparked concern. "We anticipated getting a full report," he repeated. "When we did not get that, that's when we first became suspicious . . . in a matter of hours."

By now, Schade was fully immersed in his memories of that fateful week in May 1968. With little prompting from me, he continued recounting his experiences with the *Scorpion*—and dropped a major bombshell. Unsolicited, he revealed that he had been out at sea on another one of his command's nuclear submarines when the *Scorpion* emergency began—at least five days earlier than anyone had previously admitted.

Schade said that he was on the Norfolk-based attack submarine *USS Ray* the week of May 20, operating off the Virginia Capes, when he learned that the *Scorpion* had failed to communicate with COMSUBLANT. Schade said that he had reacted with alarm: "When we first got the report and it looked like we needed to do something in the way of a search operation, I got [Atlantic Fleet commander] Admiral [Ephraim P.] Holmes on the radio and said, 'Would you place the facilities of CINCLANTFLT at my disposal for the next day or two until we can organize a search operation?'. . . And in fact, he had placed them all at our [COMSUBLANT's] disposal and this was quite an amazing set of operational circumstances because we controlled the entire resources of the Atlantic Fleet from a submarine at sea."

With Holmes's approval, Schade said, Atlantic Fleet headquarters organized a quick search across the Atlantic using land-based aircraft and any navy ships and submarines that were underway close to the *Scorpion's* last known position.

At this point, I interrupted Schade to make sure he wasn't confusing his account of the *Ray* with the previously publicized account that he had been embarked on the *Pargo* off Groton, when the actual SubMiss alarm went off on the afternoon of May 27. Schade was unequivocal in his response: "No—I was out at sea off Norfolk in the *Ray,* which was the flagship of the submarine force, and when we first got the report and it looked like we needed to do something in the way of a search operation, I got Admiral Holmes on the radio."

"Was this before the 27th?" I asked. His response was unambiguous: "Well before her scheduled arrival."

In another interview in early 1986, I asked Schade to repeat the story of his experience aboard the *Ray.* Again, his memory was acute and his account unwavering from what he had told me several years earlier. "I'd been out for two days when we got concerned. That's when we notified CINCLANTFLT that we thought we ought to start looking around. That maybe she might be disabled out there someplace on the surface or proceeding slowly on her diesel engine which would give her about four knots," he said. "It was the week of the 20th [of May] and I know as soon as I became aware and concerned I called CINCLANT-FLT, which was Admiral Holmes, and I said, 'How about giving me a couple of patrol squadrons and some destroyers that can go from Gibraltar going west and from Norfolk going east.' Which he did—he assigned them to us and we started them off down the most likely track hoping we would find her with a power failure or something like that."[21]

The *Scorpion* mystery was far deeper than I had imagined. It was now obvious that something radically different had occurred in the last nine days of May 1968 than the press, public, and even most of the U.S. Navy had long believed. With the vast bulk of the *Scorpion* archive still formally classified secret or higher, I would need to find additional sources from the original incident who would be willing to confirm and amplify Schade's disturbing revelation.

Fortunately, one potential source was very close at hand: former Chief of Naval Operations Admiral Thomas H. Moorer. Since his retirement as chairman of the Joint Chiefs of Staff nine years earlier in 1974, Moorer was still active in the national security community, and I had covered him at a major military event in Norfolk less than a year earlier. When I tracked him down at the Center for Strategic and International Studies in Washington—a conservative but respected think-tank focusing on military affairs and foreign policy—he agreed to an interview.

My encounter with the former CNO in April 1983 was a pivotal event in what would become a quarter-century effort to uncover the truth of the *Scorpion* incident. Gruff, acerbic, and impatient over being interrupted from important work by an out-of-town reporter, Moorer responded to my thanks for him agreeing to see me with a hand chop and a dismissive reply: "This won't take long." But ninety minutes later, we were deep in conversation, and I could tell that the admiral was torn between an impulse to evict me from his office as quickly as possible and his curiosity over just what I had been able to learn about the *Scorpion* loss from other sources. During the course of that conversation, Moorer confirmed beyond any doubt that Schade's recollection of a classified search for the missing submarine prior to its May 27 arrival date was neither a false memory nor a factual error.

As the navy's top admiral in 1968, Moorer told me, he would meet every morning with his senior staff at the Navy Flag Plot in the Pentagon to receive a daily briefing on operations, intelligence summaries, and other information from around the fleet. It was either on Thursday, May 23 or Friday, May 24, that he first got word of concern that the *Scorpion* was in trouble. He confirmed Schade's revelation that the submarine had failed to respond to a message from Atlantic Submarine Force transmitted over the Fleet Broadcast System following its May 22 position report. "It was progressive . . . a matter of hours," Moorer said in his thick Alabama drawl. "I immediately picked up the telephone and called [Atlantic Fleet Commander Admiral Ephraim] Holmes discussing the incident. Holmes called back to reaffirm the *Scorpion*'s non-response."

Like Schade, Moorer downplayed the secret search for the *Scorpion* as a routine precaution that did not warrant alarming the public or the *Scorpion* families: "We didn't release anything until it was certain that the ship was in trouble," Moorer said. "We didn't want to tell the families she was missing only to have her show up." Moorer's contention that the navy was acting out of concern for the families struck a false note because neither he nor any other senior navy admiral had ever clarified that foreknowledge to the court of inquiry or to the families themselves.

But then Moorer said something else that seemed to contradict his assertion that the navy had been uncertain about the submarine's condition. Having confirmed that the navy had taken action to locate the submarine three to four days before Memorial Day, Moorer dropped a major bombshell of his own: "Within twenty-four hours" of first learning that the *Scorpion* may have been in trouble, Moorer said, "the conclusion was made that she was lost." That is, at least forty-eight hours before the families gathered at Pier 22 on Memorial Day, he and other senior navy admirals had become convinced that the submarine was lost at the bottom of the Atlantic. Moorer declined to specify what information had prompted this dire assessment.

The navy succeeded in keeping secret this initial response to the *Scorpion* throughout the crisis and for years afterwards. Confronted by this new version of events, I went back and carefully reviewed press accounts and the small number of navy documents then available on the *Scorpion* incident. Not a single article or navy document from the week of May 20–27 mentioned a thing about the *Scorpion* before its failure to arrive in Norfolk on May 27.[22]

During my first five years of research into the *Scorpion* incident, I interviewed many former navy officers who had held command positions in the navy's Pentagon headquarters or in Norfolk during the months that the *Scorpion* incident occurred. When I showed them the statements by Schade and Moorer disclosing the classified search before May 27, they reacted with shock, surprise, and disbelief. To them, the crisis had started only with the SubMiss alert that Monday afternoon.

Even the man the navy credits with ultimately helping the searchers locate the missing submarine said that he was never told of the pre–May

27 crisis and secret search for the *Scorpion.* In several interviews, retired navy civilian scientist John Craven insisted that he had only learned of the *Scorpion* from his car radio when the SubMiss alert spilled over into the news on Monday, May 27. "I know nothing about that," Dr. Craven said of Schade's admission that he had controlled a classified hunt for the *Scorpion* days before Memorial Day.

Craven insisted to me that when he turned his car around and went directly to the Navy Flag Plot spaces in the Pentagon, he neither saw nor sensed any evidence of concealment or suppression of evidence among the admirals there. "You're up there dealing with a roomful of guys with the top level admirals in the United States Navy with one motivation in mind—to find that damn submarine using everything they could use," Craven recalled. "At that point, there's no reason to hold back from people in that room. We're all cleared [to receive classified information], and we all have a 'need to know.'"

Craven suggested that the entire recollection of a secret search might have been an inadvertent mistake on the part of Schade and Moorer, a false recall attributable to fading memory on the part of two admirals who were involved at that time in many highly classified operations. "All of us were engaged in one way or another in different compartmented operations," he explained. "It's very standard that you just don't reveal in the submarine service what goes on in compartment A to compartment B. So that comes to me as no surprise. What would come to me as a surprise is that information [was] withheld from me relevant to the search scenario. We were charged to find out why the damn thing was lost." Craven concluded, "In my mind, I've put that story [of the secret search] as a fairly low probability event that might be within the reconstruction of minds of people like Schade who like all of us get old and as we get old, have fading memories."[23]

Senior navy officials said they, too, were kept in the dark. Interviewed fifteen years later, former Atlantic Fleet chief of staff Vice Admiral Frederick L. Ashworth, the senior navy officer in Norfolk on Memorial Day 1968, was adamant that his knowledge of the *Scorpion* crisis came only when it failed to appear in port as scheduled that Monday afternoon: "They didn't expect to hear anything from her. When she didn't show up on time, people began to wonder. Retired Capt. James C. Bellah, who as acting Submarine Squadron 6 commander on May 27, had to deal with the distraught family members when the *Scorpion* failed to arrive at one P.M. as planned, said he was never informed of the secret search effort."[24]

Captain Wallace A. Greene, the *Scorpion's* immediate administrative supervisor as commander of Submarine Division 62, insisted that a secret search for the *Scorpion* was impossible. "Either he is mistaken or you misunderstood him," Greene said when I told him about Schade's disclosure of the classified search. Greene added that on Memorial Day in 1968, "there was no reason for us to have been the slightest concerned for her safety." He scoffed at the notion that a failure on Slattery's part to respond to the two COMSUBDIV 62 messages might have triggered the alarm, as Moorer had asserted. "They were innocuous, strictly routine matters on which I wanted some information," Greene said, "and it was information that she would *not* have had to break communications silence to provide it prior to her arrival."[25]

Within the guarded COMSUBLANT communications center, few had known of the secret search. Lieutenant Harold Meeker, assistant submarine force communications officer in 1968, said the first time he learned of a brewing crisis was early in the morning of May 27 when he reported to work: "I vaguely remember [COMSUBLANT Communications Officer Lieutenant Commander] Chuck Garrison mentioning they were having communications problems with the *Scorpion*. . . . I had some pretty good [security] clearances, but this 'need to know' thing, when it worked, it worked very well."

The COMSUBLANT communications center was manned around the clock seven days a week, and its highly trained staff members were cleared up to top secret for handling and decrypting tactical communications with submarines at sea. Retired Warrant Officer First Class Howard Sparks, who was one of three communications watch supervisors at the message center, said he did not learn of the crisis until the morning of May 27 when he spoke by telephone with Lieutenant John Rogers, director of the message center. "I wasn't on duty the morning she was supposed to be in," Sparks said. "I called in to speak with Rogers.

He said, 'We've got something going on here.'"[26] Ultimately, I realized
that these responses did not challenge the truth of what Schade and
Moorer had revealed. Rather, they confirmed that knowledge of the secret search during May 23–27 had been limited to an incredibly small
number of senior navy officials.

Despite its mandate and legal power to collect all of the facts surrounding the *Scorpion* disappearance and to determine what had happened to
the submarine, the court of inquiry never learned about the growing
concern among senior navy admirals during May 23–27, or their decision to launch the secret search. Neither Moorer nor any senior CNO
staff members testified before the court, and Schade in his appearance
on June 5 said nothing about events prior to May 27.[27]

Even more significant, four of the seven court members confirmed
in interviews with me years after the fact that Atlantic Submarine Force
officials had told them nothing about the secret search that went on during May 23–27. Rear Admiral Charles D. Nace, the senior ranking court
member after Vice Admiral Bernard Austin; Captain A. J. Martin
Atkins, who had previously commanded the *Scorpion*'s sister ship *USS
Scamp;* retired Captain Dean Horn, an engineering expert picked for assignment to the court because of his background in submarine design;
and retired Rear Admiral Harold G. Rich, all were unequivocal on this
point.[28]

Rear Admiral Nace was one of Schade's senior Atlantic Submarine
Force subordinates, yet he knew nothing of the secret search. "To the
best of my knowledge we the Court were not formally advised of that,
and I was not informally advised or aware of any such search," Nace told
me in a 1997 interview. Speaking of Austin, Nace added, "It's possible a
senior member of the court was advised, but I can't say he was or was
not." Nace indirectly raised the possibility that the navy had decided to
prevent the court from knowing the full account of the submarine. "I'm
a great believer of 'need to know,'" he said. "There may have been something in existence that they felt all of us did not need to know."[29]

By preventing the court of inquiry from learning of the navy's
mounting concern on May 23–24 and the secret search for the *Scorpion*,

and by suppressing evidence of messages after May 22 explicitly request-ing the submarine to break radio silence, Schade and the small number of COMSUBLANT officials in the know helped convince the inquiry that the *Scorpion* was engaged in a routine homeward transit from May 22 to 27. This then set the stage for COMSUBLANT to manipulate the evidence available to steer the court toward a "safe" conclusion that an unidentified mechanical malfunction was the most likely cause of its sinking on May 22.

Nevertheless, since 1968 a growing body of evidence has contradicted the official navy story while underscoring the strict secrecy under which the pre–May 27 concern over the *Scorpion* was kept. Admiral Schade's Memorial Day trip from Norfolk to Groton for an orientation ride aboard the nuclear attack submarine *Pargo* provides the starkest evidence of just how tightly guarded was any information on the *Scorpion* before the formal SubMiss alert later that day.

Shortly after seven A.M. that Monday morning, Schade and three of his personal staff members drove from the submarine force headquarters building to the nearby Norfolk Naval Air Station to catch a plane for the ninety-minute flight up to Connecticut to ride on the *Pargo*. Three staffers who accompanied him on the trip were among the small number of headquarters personnel who worked at the admiral's side every day: Captain Allison L. Maynard, the COMSUBLANT plans officer; Com-mander Jack Klinefelter, the admiral's flag secretary; and Yeoman Senior Chief Jerry Hall, his senior flag yeoman. During my extended research on the *Scorpion*, I interviewed two of the three. Maynard refused to dis-cuss the *Scorpion* incident. Klinefelter told me what so many others al-ready had said: that he did not learn of the *Scorpion* crisis until the SubMiss alert came chattering out of the *Pargo's* secure radio receiver at 4:25 p.m. EDT on May 27.[30]

Then there was Jerry Hall. In December 1984, I knew Jerry only as a coworker at my newspaper. After I'd published my first story about the *Scorpion*, he had told me about his earlier career. As a senior chief petty officer, it was Hall who managed the admiral's classified papers. As flag yeoman, he worked closely with the Atlantic Submarine Force commander every day. A career submariner who had served on several nuclear attack submarines prior to that assignment, Hall handled documents classified top secret and even higher that included details of the most sensitive submarine operations of the day. Some eight years after our initial conversation about the *Scorpion,* I called him in February 1993 for an extended interview as part of an article on the incident following the navy's decision to release hundreds of pages of newly declassified information from the court of inquiry files.

"I was the chief in charge of the flag office," Hall told me. "We did all the admin work for the admiral, we took care of all of his correspondence, Top Secret, Cosmic Top Secret [a NATO security designation], all the reports. Everything that came in we routed it to the right offices to get the answers, assigned action, made sure all of the letters were sent to the right places." Hall said his job with Schade provided him with access to the most highly classified operational information in the Atlantic Submarine Force. "I rode the fast attacks, and on the fast attacks we had the—we called them spooks—the surveillance people. They gave you an extra clearance in order to type up their trip reports, their patrol reports. Almost all the SSN yeomen had an additional [security] clearance. They really, really looked into our backgrounds. They spent a small fortune investigating me."

Despite his unprecedented access to Schade and the Atlantic Submarine Force's classified records, Hall told me that on the morning of Monday, May 27, 1968, he was totally unaware of the *Scorpion* crisis, now in its sixth day. As far as he was concerned, Hall said, the trip to Connecticut was purely routine. "We were going up to ride the *Pargo,* " Hall explained. "[The trip had been scheduled] for about a week. We were going up to get our sub time in. You had to go to sea for forty-eight hours a month [to qualify for the extra money]." The only thing unusual was the weather. "It was one hell of a morning, it was really bad. I didn't think that damn airplane was going to get airborne out of Norfolk. It was terrible weather."

Then I read Hall the interview transcript where Schade spoke of learning that the *Scorpion* was in trouble while he was out on the *USS Ray* the week of May 22, and I repeated Moorer's confirmation of the secret search. I expected Hall to confirm the operation and perhaps add some details from his eyewitness vantage point. Instead, there was a stunned silence. He finally stammered, "I did not know it." He paused a long moment and repeated, "I did not know it. They sure as hell don't want this to come out." Then Hall repeated what he had told me in 1984: Sometime in the first weeks immediately after the Sub-Miss alert on May 27, he learned in whispered conversations with COMSUBLANT officials that the Soviets had been involved in the sinking. Hall said he had tried to recall the names of the officials but could not.[31]

THE *SCORPION* COVER-UP did not end on Memorial Day when the submarine's disappearance could no longer be hidden. Schade, by his own admission in 1983, was fully aware by that day that not only had something gone wrong with the submarine but in all likelihood it was already lost at sea and the crew dead. He had kept the information from two of his most trusted aides and dozens of other COMSUBLANT officials. As navy ships, submarines, and aircraft began racing out into the Atlantic in strength on the evening of May 27, Schade and other senior admirals were implementing a plan that would significantly expand the deception to create an entirely false account of the search for, and ultimate discovery of, the missing nuclear submarine. In particular, Schade ordered a highly technical search for the *Scorpion* with a small flotilla of scientific research ships to further conceal what a handful of senior navy officers already knew had happened to the submarine. The truth about what really took place out in the Sargasso Sea 400 miles southwest of the Azores would remain a secret for more than a quarter century—until a handful of participants in the highly technical search for the submarine wreckage decided to break their silence.

The focused-operations search for the *Scorpion* wreckage was not itself a secret but received almost no publicity during the five months it went on. After the as-yet-unrevealed secret search for the submarine during May 23–27, and the highly public open-ocean search that ran from May

27 until June 5, the scientific hunt began on June 6 as the small group of oceanographic survey ships and support vessels staged out of the Azores to quarter a 144-square-mile search area identified by the hydro-acoustic signals from the submarine's sinking. As described in Chapter 9, it was a tedious and frustrating effort that nearly came to failure before a last-minute discovery of the *Scorpion* wreckage on October 28.

That, too, was a cover story concocted by Schade and other senior admirals to hide the actual discovery of the *Scorpion* nearly five months earlier. That successful discovery of the *Scorpion* on June 9, 1968, had to be hidden from the public and even the rest of the navy at all costs, because the timing and the nature of the actual discovery would directly lead to other, darker secrets of the *Scorpion* loss.

Despite the high security that surrounded the actual discovery of the *Scorpion*, it was impossible to keep the event a secret. There were nearly a thousand U.S. Navy personnel serving aboard the five ships that took part in the focused-operations search for the *Scorpion* wreckage between early June and late October. Five former sailors who had eyewitness roles in the secret search and discovery on two of the ships came forward decades later to tell of the actual events that had occurred in the spring and summer of 1968. Their accounts, which dovetail to a remarkable degree despite the fact the five men were from two different ships and did not know all the others, tell a story that is radically different from the navy's official report.[32]

The following is an account of the discovery, in early June, of the *Scorpion,* largely based on interviews with *Compass Island* crewmen Bill Sebold, Bill D'Emilio, and Hugh Bremner.

When their ship began its "special operations" after entering the focused-operations search area for the first time at mid-morning on Friday, June 7, its orders called for much more than merely dropping calibration charges for the benefit of pinpointing the acoustic signals from the *Scorpion,* as recounted by Schade and the official navy after-action report. The ship also had orders to search directly for the submarine wreckage two miles down using its powerful Sonar Array Sounding System (SASS) imaging sonar, the three former crewmen said.

William A. Sebold was a witness to the secret discovery of the *Scorpion* in early June 1968. Here, commander Capt. Joseph Bonds congratulates Sebold on his promotion during a ceremony on the *Compass Island* in 1969. *Courtesy of William A. Sebold*

The *Compass Island* had several unique capabilities that made it the right ship to employ in this critical phase of the *Scorpion* search. In addition to testing navigational gear for the Polaris submarine force, the ship also regularly conducted ocean-bottom sonar mapping to create accurate underwater navigational charts for the missile submarines, the former crewmen said. In 1963, the General Instrument Corp. had devised SASS, an advanced active sonar system that used multi-beam sounding instruments to create detailed contour maps of the deep-ocean floor. The company installed the prototype on the *Compass Island*. Instead of a single sonar transducer, the SASS system employed sixty-one individual sonar units mounted in a line perpendicular to the keel of the ship inside its massive bow sonar dome. Each transducer would emit a highly focused, narrow beam of sound that would touch bottom and bounce back, delivering a detailed image of the seabed that an onboard computer would then translate into a visual display printed out as a continuous bathymetric map of the ocean floor.[33]

Navy records declassified during the 1990s confirmed that officials intended the *Compass Island* to use its SASS sonar to conduct a bathymetric survey of the seabed and to create a detailed underwater topographical chart of the ocean floor to assist the *Mizar* with its towed sled operations. Those Navy records confirm this support mission to map the seabed in the focused-operations search area: In a memorandum for Secretary of the Navy John Chafee on June 26, 1968, Rear Admiral J. C. Donaldson noted, "*Compass Island* has completed her bottom survey" in the search area. The court of inquiry's January 1969 report noted that the *Compass Island* had conducted "a bathymetric survey of the area of special interest." In its after-action report of November 1969, the *Scorpion* Technical Advisory Group wrote, "*Compass Island* provided a bottom chart which was subsequently used throughout for bottom navigation. . . . and proved satisfactory for *Mizar* use in the areas immediately adjacent to Point Oscar."[34]

What none of those navy documents revealed was that the *Compass Island*'s sonar-mapping capability could be—and was—used to hunt for the *Scorpion* directly. It was a secret hidden in plain sight. The SASS sonar mounted in the *Compass Island*'s massive bow dome was accurate enough to capture a recognizable silhouette of the *Scorpion* two miles down on the ocean floor. Neither Donaldson nor the court of inquiry nor the *Scorpion* TAG ever expressly mentioned that capability. Instead, they described the ship's surveying capability in limited and general terms that concealed its potential. It is impossible in retrospect to say whether this was a deliberate omission or whether those officials—like the majority of the navy—were kept in the dark.

The three former *Compass Island* crewmen knew otherwise. The SASS imaging system was incredibly accurate even in water nearly two miles deep, said Bill D'Emilio: "We had the best in the navy at that time. We were doing our three-dimensional plots in sonar and trying to look for stuff on the bottom of the ocean floor. That was what our purpose was at the time, to try and find debris from the submarine or something. Our sonar was supposed to be the key reason we were in the search because it was three-dimensional and it could pick up such small objects on the ocean floor without having to lower the camera."

D'Emilio said he had friends in the ship's sonar gang and would occasionally visit them to watch the SASS imaging system at work. "I'd go in sonar every once in a while when I was off duty. I knew the sonar guys down there." D'Emilio described how the multiple sonar beams generated a detailed image of the seabed: "It was actually a continuous roll chart and it was a three-dimensional plot. It would actually show you the bottom, the floor of the ocean and it would show you rocks and different things," he said. "You could actually see three-dimensionally, as good as you could do three dimensionals at the time on a piece of paper [including] different rock formations, how high they went, where the depth of the ocean was and all, and you could pick up some pretty small objects on the bottom. That was what our purpose was at the time, to try and find debris from the submarine." While D'Emilio did not work on the SASS sonar himself, he recalled technicians telling him the system was accurate enough that it would be able to easily detect the actual silhouette of the missing submarine within its imaging swath. "Oh yeah, they were picking up rocks," he noted. "The submarine would have stood out like a sore thumb."

It was the *Compass Island,* and not the *Mizar,* that found the remains of the *Scorpion* two miles down in the eastern Atlantic, the three former crewmen asserted without hesitation. And the discovery did not occur in late October. Their ship found the submarine within days of beginning its sonar-imaging operation on June 7, 1968. "We found that submarine . . . in the early part of June," Sebold said. D'Emilio, who worked in a separate part of the ship and did not know Sebold or Bremner, made the identical point: "I was on board the *Compass Island* when we found the *Scorpion*," he said, emphasizing that the SASS array had actually sighted the submarine. "If they had *not* found it they would have kept us there," Bremner said.

The crewmen said that they were aware of the navy's announcement in late October that year of the *Scorpion* discovery but did not realize the implications of the delayed announcement or the fact that officials credited the *Mizar* with the discovery. Sebold told me that it wasn't until he

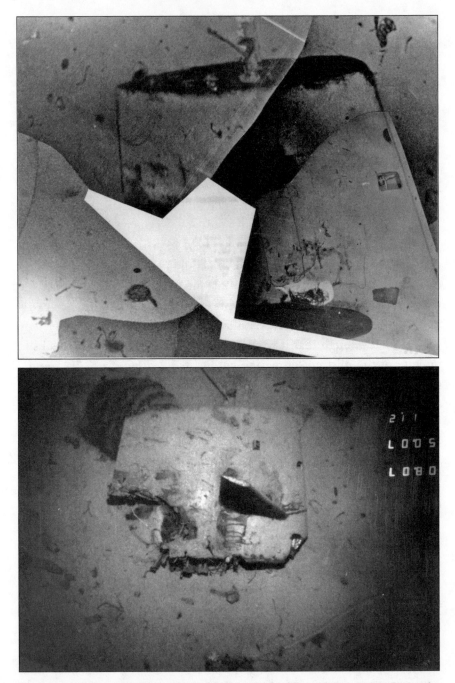

The navy obscured signs of damage to the *Scorpion*'s sail in a 1968 "montage" taken by the *USNS Mizar*, but the damage later appeared in full clarity in a photograph taken by a survey team led by Dr. Robert Ballard in 1986. *U.S. Navy Photos*

read a 1998 article of mine on the navy's cover-up of the secret search that he realized the same deception had occurred during the focused-operations search. That discovery led him to contact me and tell me about his and Hugh Bremner's roles on the crew. I located Bill D'Emilio independently from the other two from a *Compass Island* veterans website, and he provided essentially the same account as the other crewmen.

A navy technical analysis of the SASS sonar published in the 1980s confirmed the system's imaging resolution capability, indicating that the array of bow-mounted sonar transducers could capture a swath of the seabed two miles wide at a depth of 11,100 feet, the depth where the *Scorpion* lay. The resulting imagery would also have one-degree accuracy at that depth, which meant that sound impulses could capture objects smaller than 190 feet in size, well below the length of the *Scorpion's* hull.[35]

Ironically, Schade himself had already publicly confirmed the SASS system's ability to spot the *Scorpion* wreckage. In his June 27, 1968 speech on the search to the defense trade group in Connecticut, Schade revealed that SASS technology was being used because it had the necessary accuracy and resolution. "I cannot speculate at this time how long we will continue the search, but I can say we will continue it for a while longer," Schade told the group. "The search is currently being conducted by the oceanographic vessel *Bowditch,* which has very fine bottom charting capability, and therefore, may be able to spot unusual irregularities in the ocean floor such as a submarine hull." Schade did not mention SASS or the *Compass Island* by name, but navy documents confirm that the *Bowditch* had an SASS array onboard that was the same as the sonar installed on the *Compass Island.* This was an important disclosure (though the speech received no press coverage at the time), since neither Schade nor anyone on his staff ever mentioned the SASS system's imaging capability to the court of inquiry.[36]

Further evidence supporting the former *Compass Island* crewmen on their ship's discovery of the *Scorpion* can be found in the ship's own deck logs from June 1968. The ship conducted operations in the search area southwest of the Azores during June 7–14 and June 16–21, 1968. Three times a day—at eight A.M., twelve noon, and eight P.M.—the duty quartermaster of the watch entered the ship's exact location by latitude and longitude. During its surveying of the seabed, the former crewmen said, the *Compass Island* would travel in a straight line at speeds less than five knots as the imaging sonar mapped the undersea terrain. At least four times, once on June 9 and 12 and twice on June 19, the ship's course track passed less than a mile from the precise latitude-longitude position of the *Scorpion* wreckage later confirmed by the *Mizar* (see map on following page). All four of those course tracks brought the *Scorpion* wreck site well within the imaging swath of the SASS sonar array.[37]

The *Compass Island*'s participation in the search ended after only nineteen days. Navy officials in Washington in early June 1968 had reported that the *Compass Island* was slated to remain with the focused-operations search until it concluded, but those plans suddenly changed when Admiral Schade at COMSUBLANT headquarters ordered the ship to return to Brooklyn on June 25. There is no record of Schade's rationale for the decision, which stripped the search team of the one ship with the navigational accuracy to ensure a precise mapping of the area. However, to the three former *Compass Island* sailors, the move made perfect sense: The ship was no longer needed in the search area, because it had already found the *Scorpion*.

Two days after the *Compass Island* set a course back to Brooklyn, the *Mizar* photographed the now-famous two-foot-long piece of twisted metal that subsequently was located at the very edge of the submarine's debris field. According to the *Scorpion* Technical Advisory Group's after-action report in 1969, "A piece of distorted metal perhaps two feet by two feet was photographed by [*USNS*] *Mizar* on 27 June 1968. Several serious attempts to re-photograph this contact were made as the search progressed. *All failed due mainly to poor underwater navigation* [emphasis added]." As a result, the official navy report conceded, the *Mizar* and its scientists would labor for another four months before finally stumbling across the submarine wreckage on October 28.[38]

Two former crewmen from another ship, the *USS Petrel* (AS 14), also came forward to corroborate what Bill Sebold, Bill D'Emilio, and Hugh Bremner told me. In 1993, I interviewed former Boatswain's Mate Seaman Gregg Platte and Boatswain's Mate Second Class Craig F. Nelson,

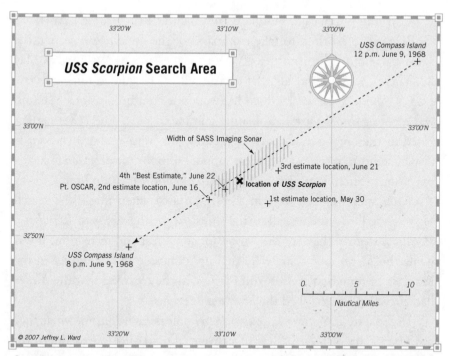

Graphic shows location of *Scorpion* wreckage site and three initial estimates of the location, along with the plotted course track of the *USS Compass Island* that ran overtop the spot on June 9, 1968.

who said that in late June they saw photographs of the *Scorpion* taken from the camera on the *Mizar's* sled.

In 1968, the *Petrel* was no stranger to naval disasters. In fact, the *Scorpion* search was the fourth emergency-response mission that the submarine rescue ship had conducted that year alone. In late January, it helped search the eastern Mediterranean for the Israeli submarine *Dakar* then within days raced to the southern French coast to join the search for the French submarine *Minerve*. And if that wasn't enough excitement, in mid-February, the *Petrel* attempted to salvage the *USS Bache* (DD 470) after a storm blew the Norfolk-based destroyer onto the rocks near Rhodes, Greece. The *Petrel* had only been back in Charleston a few weeks when the *Scorpion* SubMiss alert sent it back to sea.[39]

Carrying Submarine Flotilla 6 commander Rear Admiral Lawrence G. Bernard to Norfolk to take command of the open-ocean search, the *Petrel* arrived in the storm-tossed Virginia Capes area on Wednesday, May 29. There, Bernard and his staff transferred to the guided missile frigate *USS William H. Standley,* which had superior communications gear and was a better ship to use as a floating command post. The *Petrel* participated in the open-ocean search that ended on June 5, and then Schade dispatched it to serve as a logistical support ship for the *Scorpion* focused-operations search, joining the *Compass Island* and *Mizar* on June 17.

After spending ten days in the search area when the initial search phase ended on June 28, all of the ships except the *Compass Island* and *Bowditch* steamed back to the Azores for some rest and recreation. It was while the *Mizar* and *Petrel* were tied up alongside the same pier in the last days of June that Nelson and Platte said they learned that the *Mizar* had already photographed the *Scorpion* wreckage.[40]

In separate interviews, the two *Petrel* sailors each told me what they saw aboard the *Mizar.* "A few of us went aboard and toured the ship," Nelson said. "We went into a room full of electronic gear and talked to one of the men responsible for the search operation with the sled. We asked him if he had found the *Scorpion.* He not only said that he had, but showed us pictures of it and said it was at about 2,500 fathoms. I was astonished to see her lying on her side in nearly one piece. . . . I have not, and am sure could not have seen this anywhere else."

Platte echoed Nelson's comments. "We were based out of Terceira in the Azores," Platte said. "We'd go out at night on the *Mizar* [while in port] and hang out. I remember seeing pictures of it. We knew that we had found it."

Cut off from home and news reports of the ongoing search, the two sailors said they did not immediately suspect anything unusual in the *Mizar* photographs. It was only years later, after reading several accounts of the *Scorpion* incident that I had written, that Nelson contacted me to say that the navy's official position that the *Mizar* had not located the *Scorpion* until late October 1968 was inaccurate.

Both sailors acknowledged that they could not precisely recall the exact dates. "I regret to this day that I did not keep a detailed journal of what I heard, saw and did at the time," Nelson said. However, both men were able to locate records containing operational details from their experience on the *Petrel* that indirectly confirmed their stories and narrowed the time frame of their encounter aboard the *Mizar* at Terceira to a four-day period the ships were in port during June 30 to July 3.

It was not difficult to match the two sailors' accounts with the chronology of the focused-operations search contained in the official after-action report published in 1969. Their encounter in the *Mizar* photolab happened during the port visit between the end of the *Mizar's* first cruise and the second search phase, which began on July 10. Nelson recalled that the encounter with the *Mizar* technician who showed them the *Scorpion* photographs occurred several days before a change-of-command ceremony on their ship. The *Petrel's* own deck logs for June 1968 confirm that Lieutenant Commander Lewis M. Tew relieved Lieutenant Commander Robert L. Miller as skipper of the ship on Wednesday, July 3. The after-action report on the focused-operations search also confirmed that the *Petrel* left the Azores for the search area on Wednesday, July 10, and operated with the other ships for only another five days after receiving orders on July 12 to proceed back to its homeport in Charleston.[41]

In response to the official navy account that the scientific team led by Dr. John Craven had found the *Scorpion* in late October 1968, Nelson said, "One thing is certain. Mr. Craven and anyone else that say they found the *Scorpion* five months after she disappeared is dead wrong. They may have gone back and *confirmed* it, but *Mizar* had already found her, and I know what I know. There are a lot of other sailors out there that know this too." Craven has always asserted that the *Mizar* discovered the *Scorpion* wreckage on October 28, as the navy announced. Whether the scientist was involved in the deception or was deliberately excluded from knowing of the actual discovery in early June cannot be determined.[42]

Nelson also underscored a basic reality of shipboard life: An operation may be designated with the highest secrecy classification, but sailors carrying out their daily watchstanding duties and other assignments see and hear what is going on. Unlike classified documents and tapes, a ship's mission cannot be hidden from those who carry it out.

Moreover, sailors like to talk. "Why would a deckhand see and know these things?" Nelson asked rhetorically. "Nobody tried to keep anything a secret from those involved, and overall, there wasn't much to know anyway. We knew exactly where we were and what we were doing there. Everybody knew that *Scorpion* was lost and the only speculation was where and why. . . . So what's to hide? We were simply told not to discuss it with the public. Not just until just prior to our return to Charleston were we told not to say anything to *anybody*—period."

<hr>

FOR FIVE MONTHS in 1968 from late spring to late autumn, the U.S. Navy was engulfed in a crisis over the *Scorpion,* but it was a crisis far different than the one that the Atlantic Submarine Force and senior Pentagon admirals portrayed. The navy mounted a secret search for the submarine between three and five days before anyone was supposed to be aware that anything was amiss. When the *Scorpion's* disappearance could no longer be concealed, the Atlantic Fleet mounted a massive open-ocean search that not only attempted to find the missing submarine but also concealed the existence of the earlier, classified hunt. After the navy pronounced the *Scorpion* presumed lost on June 5, the scientific search operation got underway to pinpoint the wreckage in several hundred square miles of ocean. In secret, however, searchers found the *Scorpion* within days of beginning their effort, only to conceal that momentous accomplishment for another four months before announcing the discovery on October 30.

For the most part, the *Scorpion* cover-up worked. The court of inquiry never learned of the secret, pre-May 27 search or of the discovery of the *Scorpion* in early June. The public and press accepted the navy's story that the submarine was on a routine homeward voyage when it vanished in the depths of the Atlantic, and acceded to the court of inquiry's conclusion that the "certain cause" of the loss would remain unknown.

It would take years before a small number of participants in the *Scorpion* search came to realize that what they had seen and heard did not match the official navy version of events and finally stepped forward to recount their experiences. It would take countless hours of research to find navy documents that had escaped the top-secret stamp, the shredder, or the censor's marker pen to confirm that the mystery of the *Scorpion* was instead a deadly secret.

Inevitably, the next question must be: "What were they trying to hide?"

11

BURN BEFORE YOU READ

I T WAS IN SEPTEMBER OF 1982 THAT VINCE COLLIER LEARNED THE darkest secret of the *Scorpion*.

Behind the barred windows and cipher-locked doors of their classroom at the Anti-Submarine Warfare Training Center in Norfolk, Collier and his fellow students in Class 82–22 were finishing up a course in the top-secret Sound Surveillance System (Sosus). The students were in a festive mood. For the past sixteen weeks, they had sweated through what officials consider the toughest technical course in the navy after nuclear reactor operator training. At the Ocean Systems Technician "A" School, in the training center just off Hampton Boulevard near the Norfolk Naval Station, young sailors fresh out of boot camp came to master Sosus theory and practice.

Like their Air Force counterparts who managed the nation's array of reconnaissance satellites, or others who manned a global array of signals intelligence-gathering antenna farms, those striking for the Ocean System Technician, or OT, patch were a cut above the ordinary. Navy OTs had the responsibility of tracking the movements of the growing Soviet submarine fleet worldwide.

At that time, Sosus technology still translated underwater sounds into a visual display on electrostatically sensitive paper. Making sense of the arcane patterns burned into the paper took college-level science and math skills, an acuity in electronics and acoustics, and the ability to spend hours quietly gazing at the continuous-print readouts while keeping a clear head. Nearly thirty years after the navy had planted the first Sosus array off the Caribbean island of Eleutheria, the OTs of the early 1980s were still on the front lines of the Cold War, though they sat at consoles in windowless rooms hundreds of miles from the nearest fleet.

A California native, Vince Collier chose this challenging but peculiar military specialty when he signed up for a four-year navy hitch. After graduation from boot camp in San Diego in early 1982, Collier, then nineteen, flew to Norfolk where he joined several dozen other students on April 18. Collier and his classmates studied the history of the worldwide deployment of hydrophone arrays beginning with the continental shelf of the East Coast. They scribbled notes in notebooks that were gathered up and locked away after each session because their scrawled handwriting and crude graphs on the pages were, like the instructors' presentations, classified top secret. They mastered the details of reading submarine turbine signatures and propeller blade counts, watching the actuator spark sweeping back and forth as it painted each machine's "gram" display from a separate hydrophone in each Sosus sonar array. They became intimate with the YNK–20 computer and DSA-grams. They lingered long hours huddled over the electro-sensitive rolls of paper, analyzing the significance of Sosus recordings of actual submarines captured in real-time and kept in a locked storage cabinet for instructional review. They became used to the burned-tire odor that filled the air from the actuator sparks etching the sound signals into a visual display. They became resigned to the sooty smudges from the printouts that blackened their fingers and stained their uniforms.

With just a day or two left before graduation and orders to their fleet assignments, Collier recalled, one of the senior instructors announced he had a surprise for the class. Ocean Systems Technician (Analyst) First Class Richard Falck walked into the classroom and held up what appeared to be another Sosus training tape and said, "Watch this. You're going to love this one." He started the tape, and the actuator started painting a detailed image on the paper. The students watched intently as

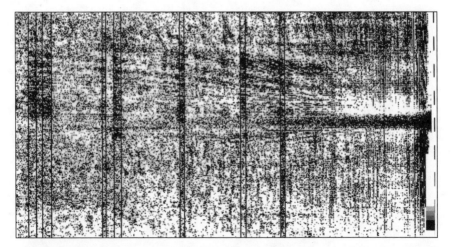

Darkened vertical columns on a Sosus Lofargram depict various sounds at different frequencies being generated by a submerged submarine. Former Sosus technician Vincent Collier said his Sosus class saw a tape actually showing the encounter between the *Scorpion* and a Soviet submarine. *U.S. Navy Photo*

the lofargram writer began to re-create the acoustic signals from an underwater confrontation.

"From the beginning of the tape we saw noise, a blade rate. We saw two intertwined blade rates, and two intertwined turbines. We were watching these two submarines. We saw 'sprint and drift,' we saw 'Crazy Ivan,'" Collier said, referring to submarine tactical maneuvering techniques. The students were mesmerized as they translated the patterns on the electrostatic paper into a mental image of two submarines in an underwater dogfight. The presentation went on for more than twenty minutes when, suddenly, the students gasped: The gram writer clearly showed a torpedo launch from one of the submarines.

"The next thing we saw was a high-speed torpedo signature," Collier said. "The blade rate for the torpedo is steady." For another five or six minutes, the paper scrolled out of the printer as the signal showed the torpedo racing through the water. On a different frequency path, they watched the signature of the targeted submarine shifting in size and width as it tried one evasive maneuver after another. "It's possible the torpedo missed a few times," Collier recalled. "It explains the turning effect. That submarine was ducking and dodging. As [the submarine] turns stern on, all you get is its blade count because it [the propeller] masked the turbine signature."

The encounter ended in sudden violence: "When the torpedo hit, the seismic explosion blackened the paper," he said. The tape reel turned, the actuator spark kept on marking the paper, and when the visual display returned to normal, there was only one submarine signature left. Collier recalled the babble of voices erupting from his classmates when Falck turned off the tape.

"Are we seeing an American submarine biting the bullet?" one student asked.

"This is the death of the *USS Scorpion*," Falck replied. "That was a Russian torpedo signature. Officially, it's not."

"Why not?" a student asked.

"Officially, the *Scorpion* sank because of a mechanical failure," the instructor said.

Collier said he and his classmates were flabbergasted by the classroom incident. Nowhere in their navy training had anyone ever mentioned the loss of the *Scorpion*, much less its death at the hands of a Soviet submarine. "No one had ever heard of a Russian submarine sinking an American sub," Collier recalled. In fact, Collier said, he himself had never even known of the *Scorpion* incident, which had occurred when he was only five years old. "The tape was top secret and the instructor wanted us to see how we would react," he explained. "We analyzed it correctly. He told us exactly what the tape had shown. The Russian fired a torpedo and sank our submarine."

Discussing the classroom incident with me seventeen years later, Collier said he could still recall details that had convinced him and the other students that the OT instructors were on the level and not playing a graduation-eve prank. First, he said, the length of the tape was unusual. Most of the training tapes ran for about twenty minutes, but this one was more than twice as long. The second factor that convinced Collier that the tape was genuine was the presence of additional sound sources on the Sosus tape. The students had seen the visual depiction of a number of Soviet surface ships within detection range of the Sosus hydrophone array,

Collier said. "There were a boatload of surface ship signatures as well, but they weren't on top of the action. They weren't exactly right there." That extra detail dovetailed with other actual Sosus recordings that captured not only the sound from the target submarine but pulled in background noise from other ships as well. Finally, Collier recalled that when the classroom presentation came to an end, he walked up to Falck as he was placing the tape reel back in its container. "I looked straight down on the cover of the tape, and it said '*USS Scorpion*,'" he said.[1]

Nearly a decade after our telephone interviews, in early 2007 I was able to locate retired Ocean Systems Technician Chief Richard Falck, who had played the Sosus tape to Collier and the other students that late summer day in 1982. Falck, who retired in May 1993 after a twenty-two-year Navy career, confirmed that the Sosus tape had depicted a Soviet Echo-II class nuclear submarine, the *Scorpion* and a torpedo firing that led to the sinking of the American submarine.

Falck specifically recalled that the tape depicted an Echo-II class Soviet nuclear submarine. He even remembered the exact propulsion mode that the Soviet submarine was using at the time of the encounter. "An Echo-II runs in modes, and one of the modes is called 'split plant,'" he recalled. "It runs its turbines in turbine-electric and uses an electrical motor to run the props, rather than going through a reduction[-gear] system to run the props. That was their silent version. The trouble with the Soviets was that they never thought to sound-dampen their turbines, so we could see it for miles—you could hear it if you were close to it."

While cautioning that it was physically quite easy to dub false signals onto a Sosus tape that could create the false impression of a submarine-vs.-submarine encounter, Falck said that in his assessment the *Scorpion* tape was genuine. "It played right," he recalled. "I can believe it. I was told it was real" by senior instructors at the Ocean Systems Technican "A" school. Falck said he recalled the tape had originally come from a naval facility in Bermuda but could not say if it had been generated on a Sosus hydrophone or an aircraft-launched sonobuoy.[2]

Collier's initial disclosure of the *Scorpion* tape in a June 1999 interview marked a milestone in my search for answers about the submarine's loss. For the first time, someone with access to the deepest secrets of the *Scorpion* from the navy's anti-submarine warfare community had voluntarily stepped forward to challenge the official version of the sinking. But he was not the only source to come forward at that point.

One fascinating backstory of the *Scorpion* incident has been the gradual but profound change in the attitudes of former navy people toward discussing what they knew. Since the navy had branded the vast majority of information about the *Scorpion* with secret or top-secret security stamps, most navy veterans I contacted for my initial research during the 1980s and early 1990s were extremely reluctant to discuss the *Scorpion* in any detail. Those who had played key roles in the *Scorpion* search and investigation were still bound by security regulations and nondisclosure agreements that applied even after their retirement. In many cases, these officials consented to talk only after I personally showed them that the navy had declassified information about a specific topic I wanted to discuss.

A number of events pertaining to the *Scorpion* occurred in the early 1990s that would help diminish this overall reluctance to talk. The first one, of course, was the end of the Cold War and the Soviet Union on December 31, 1991. Even the most conservative, play-by-the-book navy veterans with whom I spoke during that time now accepted that the tenets of operational security and classified information that had framed their military careers no longer held sway.

The second event came in October 1993, when the navy conducted a comprehensive security declassification review of the *Scorpion* archive twenty-five years after the sinking. For the first time, the navy released hundreds of pages of previously classified *Scorpion* material, including transcripts of many closed sessions from the court of inquiry. The documents provided a wealth of new information from the navy inquest into the submarine, although huge gaps in the record still remained. Most material concerning the *Scorpion*'s operations in the Atlantic from May 17 through the time of its sinking on May 22, 1968, remained classified. Information from the navy's intelligence community and most details of communications between the *Scorpion* and COMSUBLANT remained heavily censored. In fact, most of that material remains top secret to this day, nearly forty years later. But as the *Scorpion* incident, like the Cold

War itself, passed into history, many participants and witnesses arrived at the personal realization that it was no longer a security threat to discuss the pieces of the story that they had long concealed in navy documents, personal papers, or their own memories.

The third event was the personal computer revolution of the late 1990s, particularly advances in the Internet, email, and search-engine technology. For the thirtieth anniversary of the *Scorpion* loss in May 1998, I had assembled the best evidence into four articles for my news-paper, *The Seattle Post-Intelligencer*. Several wire services distributed a condensed version nationwide, and *The Post-Intelligencer* archived the *Scorpion* report on its website. It is natural that any investigative news report will elicit responses from people interested in adding new details to the story or in challenging it. To my amazement, however, the news-paper's routine decision to post my 1998 *Scorpion* report on its website sparked a constant stream of emails and telephone calls from former navy personnel who had come upon the articles and who were now willing and anxious to share their own experiences. More than eight years after the articles first appeared, I am still hearing from veterans of the *Scorpion* incident.[3]

Like many former navy sailors who had seen a small piece of the *Scorpion* puzzle, Vince Collier said he had wondered for years about the unbridgeable gap between the navy's official conclusion that the sinking stemmed from a mechanical mishap, and the hard evidence that the OT School instructor had shown him and his classmates in 1982 of a Soviet attack on the *Scorpion*. Like so many others, Collier had decided by 1999 that it was time to tell the truth.

Still, there was something that Collier himself did not know about this key new evidence showing the *Scorpion* attacked and sunk by a So-viet torpedo. The Sosus tape had apparently escaped a massive operation by naval intelligence officials in May 1968 to confiscate and destroy all documentation of the hostile encounter between the *Scorpion* and the Soviet submarine on May 22, 1968.

A former senior Sosus technician who had also read my thirtieth-anniversary articles on the *Scorpion* incident contacted me in June 2002 with disturbing details about the navy's effort to seize and quash that explosive evidence. "I have only discussed this once in thirty-some years knowing the security surrounding this incident," said the source, who agreed to provide information only on grounds of total anonymity. The retired senior Sosus operator said he decided to contact me because of a reference in my 1998 articles to the navy's decision to declassify the recording from the Canary Islands research station that had recorded the clearest signal of the *Scorpion* sinking.

The navy released what it said was the visual depiction of the train of acoustic pulses that corresponded to the initial explosive "event" followed after ninety seconds of silence by the "train wreck" sounds of the submarine hull imploding as it fell below crush depth (see figure on page 215). The retired Sosus technician said the tape segment the navy had released was deliberately inaccurate. "The acoustic tracking tape of the area where the *Scorpion* went down was incomplete. Tracks of the Soviet torpedo in the water were, I believe, destroyed," he said. (This source had no knowledge of my then-ongoing talks with Collier.) The retired Sosus technician also challenged the navy's public narrative that no one suspected any harm had come to the *Scorpion* until its failure to reach Norfolk five days after the May 22 incident: "Within *hours*, Naval Intelligence came aboard the respective Sosus facilities and confiscated all tapes and evidences. All members of the Sosus teams were debriefed with all the usual threats. The guys believed they had read the tracks as Soviet fish in the water," he said, using the navy's slang term for a torpedo. The retired Sosus operator's revelation sent me searching deep into my filing cabinet, where I finally retrieved an interview transcript that I had collected, filed, and forgotten nearly twenty years earlier.

In late 1982, a former navy ocean systems technician had told me the identical story of a knock-the-door-open raid of his Sosus station by U.S. naval intelligence agents soon after the *Scorpion* went down. I had met the former sailor by chance as tens of thousands of military veterans gathered in Washington to dedicate the Vietnam Veterans Memorial on November 13, 1982. While in the nation's capital to cover several days of ceremonies formally opening the Wall to public display, I had also undertaken my first stint of researching the *Scorpion* incident by visiting the U.S. Navy's operational archives. After the Veterans Day ceremony ended, I was standing on a corner waiting for the light to change when I noticed a stocky man about my own age wearing a navy flight jacket adorned with a dozen unit patches. A quick glance confirmed that they were all Sosus facilities or commands, so I introduced myself and asked him if he had been on duty during the *Scorpion* incident in 1968, and if so, did he recall anything unusual about the event. His reply was intriguing.

Stationed at a Sosus facility on the island of Guam in 1968, the former sailor said he and his colleagues were shocked when shortly after May 22, naval intelligence agents arrived unannounced at his station. He recalled that they confiscated all messages and documents that might contain reference to the *Scorpion* from the files. He told me that he and the others were stunned by the raid because Sosus technicians themselves were all cleared for top-secret information. "That was a very strange event," he said, shaking his head slowly. "They never did that before—or after, as far as I knew."[3]

SINCE 1968, the U.S. Navy has denied that the Soviets were involved in any way with the loss of the *USS Scorpion*. In its final report released on January 31, 1969, the court of inquiry concluded, "There were no known Soviet or [Warsaw] Bloc surface warships, merchant ships, submarines or aircraft within 200 miles of *Scorpion's* last reported position" while it was transmitting what would be its final message to Norfolk shortly after midnight on May 22. The court also concluded that "available intelligence estimates indicate that there was no evidence of any Soviet preparations for hostilities or a crisis situation such as would be expected in the event of a premeditated attack on *Scorpion*." As related in earlier chapters, many of the key navy officials in the *Scorpion* search and investigation took pains to insist to me that a thorough analysis of the evidence had ruled out a hostile Soviet act.[4]

Those court of inquiry conclusions and official denials are no longer credible. Just as senior navy officials blocked any evidence of the navy's foreknowledge of the sinking and its pre–May 27 search from reaching the court, it now appears certain, based on the accounts of Vince Collier,

Richard Falck and the two other Sosus technicians, that the court never got the hydro-acoustic evidence of the Soviet attack on the *Scorpion* that the naval intelligence agents had impounded within hours of the sinking. The navy, in short, not only seized the Sosus evidence to prevent it from becoming public but also suppressed it to manipulate the *Scorpion* court of inquiry deliberations from ever finding out what had actually happened to the submarine.

The seizure of the Sosus evidence was not the only troubling revelation that I received in the years since *The Seattle Post-Intelligencer* published my thirty-year retrospective. Thanks to Internet and email technology, a steady stream of reliable sources who were involved in the *Scorpion* search, serving in the Pentagon, assigned to navy ships in the focused-operations search, and even on Polaris missile submarines on strategic nuclear patrol in 1968, stepped forward to provide even more startling allegations about the final days of the nuclear attack submarine. In face-to-face interviews, telephone calls, emails, and regular letters since 1998, dozens of former naval officers and enlisted men have provided new information that, in the aggregate, depicts a steadily growing crisis over the *Scorpion* that began at the time it re-entered the Atlantic on May 17, 1968 and culminated in the confrontation five days later that left the Norfolk-based submarine at the bottom of the ocean.

Having confirmed beyond doubt that navy officials had continuously lied about the origin of the *Scorpion* crisis, covered up their concern over the submarine before May 27, blocked information of the secret search for the submarine, and suppressed the truth of the actual discovery of the wreckage, I finally came to realize that the official navy stance was a deliberately crafted fiction. It was now becoming clear that the disparate accounts from these new *Scorpion* sources, examined as parts of a new narrative, were far more credible than the navy's official position. And when viewed as a whole, they provided a remarkably coherent and convincing account of the loss of the submarine and its crew.

With that assessment in mind, I returned to the court of inquiry records to examine any testimony or information pertaining to the *Scorpion*'s final five days in the Atlantic before it went down on May 22. Assuming that there had been a successful attempt on the part of naval intelligence and senior admirals to conceal evidence from the court, I was still surprised to discover a number of revealing nuggets of information in hundreds of pages of testimony that further demonstrated how carefully senior navy officials had acted to steer the court away from the truth.

Atlantic Submarine Force officials who testified before the court were unable to completely conceal the fact that the *Scorpion* in its last days had been on a highly classified mission to spy on a formation of Soviet Navy warships that included a nuclear submarine. The first hint of this emerged in the opening session on June 5, when Vice Admiral Arnold Schade, the Atlantic Submarine Force commander, testified about the *Scorpion's* scheduled return to Norfolk.

After summarizing the *Scorpion's* preparations for deployment and its three-month assignment in the Mediterranean under the control of the U.S. Sixth Fleet, Schade explained to the court that the submarine had formally transferred, or "chopped," to Atlantic Submarine Force operational control several hours after entering the Atlantic in the early hours of May 17. Here, Schade threw out a quick sentence laden with submariners' verbal shorthand: "She out-chopped from the Straits of Gibraltar and into COMSUBLANT operational control," Schade told the inquest. "She was given exercise instructions during this period and on the 16th of May she was directed by COMSUBLANT to report her position on or about the 21st of May."[5]

"Exercise": Submariners instantly understand that this word means not "routine practice" but rather "operational mission." And so, without mentioning by name the top-secret message that he had flashed to *Scorpion* commander Francis Slattery on May 16, Schade signaled to those who knew the verbal code that the *Scorpion* was engaged on a highly classified operation. The verbal sleight-of-hand seemed to work. Schade did not amplify, the court did not ask, and as a result journalists did not report any details of the "exercise." Twenty years later, discussing this aspect of Schade's testimony with the author, retired Rear Admiral Walter N. "Buck" Dietzen, who had commanded the *Scorpion's* sister ship *USS Scamp,* chuckled dryly at the way submariners employed

the word "exercise" to cover a host of real-world activities: "We also called it 'training operations,'" he said of the ruse.[6]

On the second day of the inquest, Submarine Division 62 commander Captain Wallace A. Greene let slip a bit more information, telling the court that the submarine was on "a mission of higher classification" south of the Azores before transmitting its last message. Greene said he could not discuss details in open session, so court president Vice Admiral Bernard L. Austin ordered the hearing closed and directed reporters to leave the room. The disclosure generated newspaper stories the next day about a "secret mission," but few details emerged because Greene's presentation took place behind locked doors. To this day, his full testimony remains classified top secret. Except for a highly censored exchange between the court and an Atlantic Fleet intelligence official over the Soviet activity, the only other reference to that group of Soviet ships appeared in the court's summary conclusions that were declassified in 1983. Most details of the Soviet operation were kept in "Annex A" to the court archive, a repository of top-secret evidence that still remains classified.

In its Findings of Fact section, the court identified the Soviet Navy activity without explicitly stating that the *Scorpion's* mission was to spy on it. The court identified "a Soviet hydro-acoustic operation" southwest of the Canary Islands that was taking place at the time of the American submarine's Atlantic transit during May 17–21. The Soviet ships included two hydrographic survey ships, a submarine rescue ship, and an Echo-II class nuclear cruise missile submarine. A *Krupny*-class guided missile destroyer and a fleet oiler later joined the Soviet group from a port in Algeria.[7]

The navy's paper trail on the Soviet warships and the *Scorpion's* mission to conduct surveillance on them remains extremely limited because of the top-secret security designation draped on all aspects of the matter. Greene provided the court with a briefing memorandum on highlights of the *Scorpion's* 1968 deployment that included confirmation that Schade's top-secret message to Commander Slattery on May 16 had resulted in "*Scorpion* [being] diverted from transit to Norfolk . . . to oper-

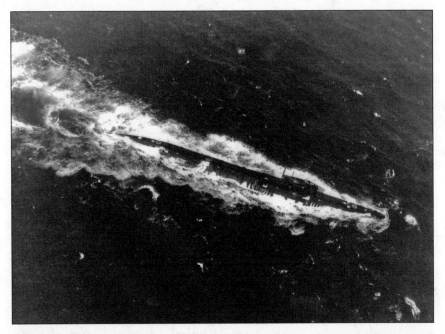

The *Scorpion* was sent to spy on a Soviet naval group that included an Echo-II nuclear cruise missile submarine, and some later claimed the *Scorpion* was pursued and sunk by the submarine. *U.S. Navy Photo*

ate under COMSUBLANT operational control." The memorandum provided no details of the mission.[8]

Any attempt to confirm a connection between the *Scorpion's* classified surveillance of the Soviet warships and the stunning allegations by the former Sosus technicians of a torpedo attack on the American submarine would require interviewing U.S. Navy officials who most likely had been in the know. The difficulty was that most of those officials continued to argue years later that it was an innocuous oceanographic research venture by the Soviet ships of no real concern to the U.S. Navy. In his 1983 interview with me, Admiral Schade acknowledged that he had dispatched the *Scorpion* to spy on the Soviet formation, but he downplayed the significance of the operation. "We had general information of a task force operating over in that general area, so we advised them to slow down, take a look, see what they could find out," the admiral explained. He made no mention either in his interview or court of inquiry testimony of the fact that to make its covert rendezvous with the Soviet formation, Commander Slattery was forced to divert at least 900 miles south of his homeward course track or that the sudden change in orders delayed the submarine's planned homecoming by nearly three days. In a follow-up interview in 1986, Schade attempted to put the Soviets' operation in historical context as a relatively innocent activity. "That was the time that they were moving out into the blue water instead of just staying in their own home waters for training," he said of the Soviets. "They were sending ships and submarines out into operational areas including the Mediterranean."

A second key official in the *Scorpion* investigation likewise minimized the significance of the Soviet ships operating off the Azores, even though they included an Echo-II class nuclear cruise missile submarine and at least one missile-armed destroyer. When I presented him with the court's evidence of the Soviet ships, Dr. John Craven, the navy civilian scientist who headed the *Scorpion* Technical Advisory Group, also dismissed the formation's military significance. Their presence in the formation, Craven said, suggested a research effort to improve submarine operating capabilities in that part of the Atlantic. "U.S. ASRs [submarine rescue ships] are at sea in operations all the time and they're *not* there for submarine rescue," Craven explained. "ASRs in the Soviet Navy and the U.S. Navy are submarine workboats. . . . What are they doing there? Not only playing the same game we're playing, but one of the things they're looking for is places in the ocean where their submarines can operate without being heard. The point is that they send their scientific-oceanographic research ships out . . . to do scientific research entirely in Polaris operational areas, things of that kind." The Echo-II submarine, Craven went on, "may have been there as a target submarine, they may have been listening to the submarine to see what it sounds like, they may be interested in the topography, the sound channels. The Soviet Navy operates all over the world. I never did regard this as a particularly significant Soviet operation."[9]

It was immediately clear that the same senior navy officials who presided over the secret search and discovery of the *Scorpion* were also the ones who most adamantly denied anything sinister about the Soviet formation that Schade had sent the *Scorpion* to spy on. Admiral Thomas H. Moorer, the chief of naval operations in 1968, was no exception. Moorer during 1968 had given a number of speeches and congressional testimony on the rising threat posed by the Soviet Navy and the escalating showdown at sea throughout the world. In one congressional appearance that year, Moorer put the situation in stark terms: "The Soviets' ocean operations are becoming unmistakably more aggressive, more varied and are being conducted at ever-increasing distances from their home base." But when I asked him in 1983 about the *Scorpion's* mission to spy on the particular group of Soviet ships operating off the Azores, the former CNO's response was strangely muted. "I didn't consider it [the composition of the Soviet ships] of any particular significance, especially since the group was operating off a third-country coastline," Moorer said. "When Soviet ships get too far from home, they send a submarine rescue fleet."[10]

Not all officials downplayed the navy's degree of interest in the Soviet formation. In fact, the officer at navy headquarters who had pressed Atlantic Submarine Force officials to organize the *Scorpion* mission stated that the *Scorpion* surveillance was a high-priority mission from the very top. Retired Rear Admiral Dietzen, in 1968 a captain and the deputy director of the Submarine Warfare Branch at navy headquarters, confirmed to me in a 1988 interview that the Soviet operation was far from routine. "I knew what the operation was. We recognized the high desirability of getting some ship over there and taking a look at them. The CNO wouldn't direct something like that, but I was salivating in the [Pentagon] corridors to find out what they were doing."[11]

While former navy officials and the court of inquiry report both alluded to the Soviet warships and support vessels as participating in a vaguely described "hydro-acoustic operation," the navy at that time had a totally different interpretation of the presence of the Echo-II nuclear submarine in that part of the world. The Soviet Navy by 1968 continuously deployed at least one Echo-II submarine in the eastern Atlantic at all times as a contingency force to attack U.S. aircraft carrier battle groups crossing the ocean between the United States and Europe if war were to erupt. Armed with eight SS-N-3 Shaddock nuclear-tipped cruise missiles with a range of over 250 miles, the Echo-II was deemed a major potential threat to the U.S. Navy surface fleet and would have been an obvious surveillance target with or without the presence of any hydrographic research vessels.[12]

Nevertheless, evidence showing a connection between the Soviet ships and the *Scorpion* loss remained tentative at best. Former navy officials with whom I talked about the *Scorpion's* surveillance operation of the Soviets during May 19–21 could not even agree about whether the mission had been a success, or if it had even occurred.

Schade told me in 1986 that his orders diverting the *Scorpion* to hunt down the Soviet ships were not ironclad. "In some of the informative messages that we gave her, there was the possibility that if these other [Soviet] units changed course, she was then to conduct a modified surveillance. That's about as far as I can go," he said. "It was a contingency. If it happens, it does." Schade then tried to cast doubt on whether the surveillance had taken place at all. "As far as we know they never made contact [with the Soviet ships], they never reported on that. As far as I know, they never made a report on it. And on their track it does not appear that they ever made contact with them, but I don't have any way of knowing it and nobody else does."

Other navy officials painted a completely different picture. According to court of inquiry testimony from a senior staff officer in the Atlantic Fleet's anti-submarine warfare command (COMASWFORLANT), the *Scorpion* did carry out surveillance on the Soviet ships. Commander Deming W. Smith, operations officer for the ASW command, testified that before and after the *Scorpion* was operating in the vicinity, his command's P-3 Orion aircraft staging out of the Azores had conducted daylight and nighttime flights to track the Soviet ships, using the code word "Bravo 20" for their airborne surveillance. Based primarily on Smith's testimony, the court concluded that the aircraft broke off surveillance on May 19 and resumed it on May 21, suggesting the specific time frame for the submarine's surveillance effort. This timeline dovetailed with Schade's earlier testimony on June 5, 1968, that he had directed the submarine to report back by radio to Atlantic Submarine Force headquarters on May 21 after the "exercise" on which he had sent the submarine.

Speaking of May 21—the day before the submarine went down—Smith explained to the court: "At that time it was our understanding that *Scorpion* had departed the area [of the Soviet ships] slowly to avoid detection and would come up and put out a report. So there were aircraft in the vicinity of the Bravo 20 operations shortly after she departed."[13]

Classified Secret at the time, one COMSUBLANT situation report also stated that the surveillance had taken place. Updating events in the *Scorpion* search on May 28, 1968, the report tersely noted, "On the 21st the *Scorpion* completed a reconnaissance of the Soviet units operating in the Cape Verde Islands [*sic*] area and departed enroute Norfolk. . . . Her last reported position of 220001Z is as shown." Twenty years later, Dietzen agreed: "The *Scorpion* got there, finished her operation, and was on her way back."[14]

A careful review of various navy officials' comments on the *Scorpion* surveillance mission does not indicate that the starkly differing accounts stemmed from incomplete information in their possession or confusion because of dim memories of an event long ago. The former Norfolk-based officers and Pentagon staff members with whom I talked all remembered the issue of the *Scorpion* surveillance mission quite clearly. It was just that some recalled that the operation occurred, while others denied that it had.

Several former navy officials declared that the submarine came, saw, conducted surveillance, and departed. Schade, having initially confirmed in 1983 that he had dispatched Slattery and his crew to sniff around the Soviet Navy group, several years later attempted to dismiss the entire venture as a contingency plan that had never been carried out.

In retrospect, the most likely scenario is that Schade and other officials were describing two separate accounts. One reflected what had really happened, and the other was the navy cover story that they concocted to conceal how close the *Scorpion* was to the Soviet warships. This became even more obvious when Schade and Moorer inadvertently revealed to me in 1983 that the navy had been searching in secret for the *Scorpion* as early as May 23, four days before its failure to reach Norfolk was supposed to have triggered the SubMiss alert. Disclosure of the secret, pre–May 27 search undermined the veracity of *all* their public statements on the *Scorpion* incident, including the submarine's surveillance mission that supposedly had ended just twenty-four hours before the sinking.

The *Scorpion's* final message to Norfolk in the early hours of May 22 is another element of the story that remains clouded in controversy and contradictory accounts. Officials such as Smith and Dietzen said that Slattery's message included the report on his surveillance of the Soviet formation. The navy identified the message by its date-time group of 212354Z May 68, or 11:54 P.M. GMT on May 21. It was transmitted between one and three A.M. GMT on May 22, just fifteen hours before the *Scorpion* exploded and sank at 6:44 P.M. GMT. But very little is publicly known of the message today because it remains classified top secret thirty-nine years after the incident, and the navy refuses to release the full text.

Still, bits and pieces of information about it have come out in the succeeding years. The court's roster of exhibits did describe the message as a "situation report." Newspaper reports from the start of the open-ocean search on May 27 included remarks from unnamed navy officials who said the message had provided the *Scorpion's* position as of midnight on May 22 at 31:19 North and 27:37 West, a point in the eastern Atlantic about 450 miles south-southwest of the Azores and about 1,160 miles west-southwest of the naval base at Rota. The message, the officials added, also included the *Scorpion's* projected Great Circle course track to Norfolk and the submarine's estimated time of arrival at one P.M. EDT on May 27. Submarine Division 62 commander Captain Wallace A. Greene told the court that upon receipt of the May 22 message, COMSUBLANT operations officer Commander George R. Parrish Jr. informed Submarine Squadron 6 that the *Scorpion's* arrival time had been changed from Friday, May 24, to Monday, May 27 at one P.M. EDT. Parrish then authorized squadron commander Captain Jared E. Clarke to declassify this new arrival time on Friday, May 24, primarily to let the families of the crew know of the change, Greene added.[15]

The *Scorpion*'s May 22 message lies at the heart of the entire cover-up. COMSUBLANT communications officer Lieutenant Commander Charles Garrison testified to the court on June 11, 1968, that the May 22 message was the last one that the *Scorpion* had transmitted before its sinking. He added in words that echoed Schade's previous testimony that the command was not expecting to hear from the *Scorpion* again until it surfaced just off the Virginia Capes. Schade himself in the 1983 interview essentially disavowed his own sworn testimony and that of several of his former aides, including Garrison. The retired admiral insisted that the final message merely provided the submarine's position as of midnight on May 22, its homeward course, and speed and time of arrival. On several occasions in that interview, Schade denied that he had ever received the detailed after-action report on the spy mission that he had expected from the *Scorpion,* and that it was this failure to report that triggered the spasm of concern that led to the secret search.[16]

UNRAVELING THE NAVY cover-up of the *Scorpion* loss was one challenge. Confirming the graphic description by Vince Collier and Richard Falck of the *Scorpion*'s destruction would prove to be a far more difficult task.

Senior navy officials who had testified before the *Scorpion* court of inquiry had clearly done everything they could to convince the panel that the submarine was *not* involved in any potentially dangerous spy mission against the Soviet Navy formation; that its final message to Norfolk headquarters on May 22 was *only* a routine position report; that they were *not* anticipating any further communications from Slattery before his expected arrival on Monday, May 27; and that the crisis had erupted *only* after the submarine failed to reach port that Memorial Day afternoon. The growing body of evidence I had acquired from participants in the *Scorpion* investigation thus far—including the disturbing remarks from Schade and Moorer revealing the secret pre–May 27 search—clearly showed that this narrative was a lie. The challenge now was to locate credible sources who could describe what had indeed taken place that resulted in the destruction of the submarine and the deaths of its crew.

The first glimpse of Soviet complicity in the sinking of the *Scorpion* had occurred in December 1984 when retired Yeoman Chief Jerry Hall, my co-worker at *The Virginian-Pilot*, came up to me in the hallway of the newspaper's building to dispute an article I had written about the *Scorpion*. As Admiral Schade's flag yeoman in 1968, Hall had been in a position to see and hear sensitive details of ongoing submarine operations, including the *Scorpion* incident. His description of a hostile Soviet encounter with the *Scorpion* was unequivocal and unwavering. "The operations that they were asking her to do," Hall said, "were such that . . . to have the navy's version that a torpedo [from the *Scorpion*] ran hot, I don't believe that." He added that Soviet involvement in the *Scorpion*'s demise was common knowledge in the inner halls of the Atlantic Submarine Force headquarters compound, but the security classification on the incident was so tight that people discussed it only in whispers.

"Do you believe the *Scorpion* went down in a hostile encounter?" I asked Hall directly in a follow-up interview some eight years later. "Yes," he replied. "I wasn't just shooting from the hip. I do not believe that the *Scorpion* sank itself. I believe it was sunk by some other submarine."[17]

Hall's allegation of a Soviet submarine attack served as a marker for me in my subsequent research. It was a specific accusation unclouded by ambiguity or uncertainty: The two submarines found themselves in close proximity in the eastern Atlantic, and the Soviet submarine attacked and sank the *Scorpion*. I had no reason to doubt either Hall's sincerity or the fact that he had been in a position in 1968 to learn about such a disturbing revelation. Even so, confirming beyond a reasonable doubt that the *Scorpion* sinking had stemmed from a Soviet torpedo attack would require ample confirmation and details from additional sources of equal credibility. In late 1984, the prospect seemed daunting. But one by one, I began to find those sources.

———

PHILIP A. BESHANY was not on my original short list of navy officials to ask about the *Scorpion*. A rear admiral in 1968, the submariner occupied a staff slot at navy headquarters in the Pentagon that at first seemed far removed from the drama that had unfolded at Atlantic Submarine Force

Nearly 30 years after the *Scorpion* sinking, retired Navy Vice Admiral Philip A. Beshany revealed that there was intelligence information before the *Scorpion* sinking to prompt fears that the Soviets were planning to attack the submarine. *U.S. Navy Photo*

headquarters in Norfolk. His job as director of submarine warfare on the surface made Beshany a senior-level bureaucrat responsible for budgeting and long-range planning on submarine issues, a point that he confirmed when I finally tracked him down for what I thought would be a fill-in conversation in 1997. By that time, I had interviewed his deputy, then-Captain Walter Dietzen, at great length, and had the overall impression that both officers had been on the sidelines for most of the *Scorpion* incident.

Beshany quickly disabused me of that notion as he dropped yet another major bombshell. It turned out that as director of submarine warfare on the CNO staff that year, he was involved in much more than submarine procurement debates and long-range planning. In fact, he was the navy's supervisor of a number of highly classified operations where the submarine service and U.S. intelligence community worked hand-in-hand against the Soviet target. In particular, Beshany was privy to submarine operations involving Special Intelligence, a unique and little-known category of intelligence information involving the interception of foreign military communications to which even the most senior admirals might not have access. And it was at this nexus of the submarine force and the highly secret world of communications intelligence-gathering where Beshany said he had first learned of the *Scorpion's* encounter with a Soviet submarine.[18]

During the interview, Beshany became the third senior navy official after Admirals Schade and Moorer to confirm that the service quickly came to suspect that something deadly had happened to the *Scorpion* during the week of May 20—and not when it failed to arrive back in Norfolk on May 27. He confirmed that Atlantic Submarine Force commander Schade had been at sea on the nuclear attack submarine *Ray* when Schade contacted his immediate boss, Admiral Ephraim P. Holmes, to request a secret search for the *Scorpion*. Beshany also confirmed Schade's admission to me in 1983 that the *Scorpion* had failed to respond to a COMSUBLANT message directing the submarine to break radio silence and report in. "COMSUBLANT alerted me to the fact that they were having a problem raising *Scorpion*," Beshany recounted. "She should have reported at a certain time and date . . . which is a normal way we do operationally. She had completed her work as far as we were concerned in what she was doing and she was heading home. She was to report about that time."

In addition to the submarine and the ongoing P-3 patrol aircraft flights, Beshany disclosed for the first time that the navy had been using a third surveillance tool to keep the Soviet warships under close watch: radio communications intercepts from land-based listening posts. In 1968, the Office of Naval Intelligence—the same organization that provided Russian-speaking linguists and communications intercept operators to the Northern run submarine spy missions—also operated the Atlantic High Frequency Direction Finding network of land-based antenna farms that could pluck Soviet radio transmissions out of the ether, triangulate their location, and conduct signal traffic analysis to glean operational implications from the adversary's pattern of messages.

Then Beshany added a critical piece of the puzzle that neither Schade nor Moorer had ever revealed: In all likelihood, the *Scorpion* surveillance mission had been blown, he said. "There was a lot of classified material relating to the Soviet group [circulating in the Pentagon at the time]," Beshany told me. "In fact, there was some concern that the *Scorpion* might have been trailed and sunk by them, that they had tracked our submarine and decided he had seen things they didn't want divulged. . . . They had been alerted to the presence of *Scorpion*. They [U.S. intelligence and Navy officials] had reason to believe at that time . . . that they might have detected her, trailed her and decided they would just eliminate her." Beshany said the information was at a level of classification so high that he and his colleagues would sometimes jest it was a "burn before you read category."[19]

In the case of the electronic monitoring of the Soviet warships off the Canary Islands, the navy and various U.S. intelligence agencies were linked by a special communications circuit known as Spintcomm, for Special Intelligence Communications. Operated by specially cleared communications specialists, the mission of the Spintcomm centers was to pass on highly classified electronic intelligence information such as intercepts of Soviet warship and submarine communications. This network, physically separated from the Navy Fleet Broadcast System and other conventional communications facilities, offered the perfect means by which senior admirals and intelligence officials could exchange alerts and pass intelligence-related messages with a minimum of exposure to the rest of the navy.

In 1968, both the U.S. Atlantic Fleet headquarters off Terminal Boulevard and the Atlantic Submarine Force headquarters in the same complex had a dedicated Spintcomm communications center to handle the torrent of electronic intelligence pouring in from submarines, surface ships, aircraft, and ground listening stations. The Atlantic Fleet's annual report for that year confirmed that a naval intelligence detachment maintained a full-time Spintcomm Communications Center at the fleet headquarters compound in Norfolk that provided intelligence to the various naval commands there. The Norfolk-based Atlantic Fleet intelligence section in 1968 also operated an around-the-clock "all-source naval plot" that showed the presence of all Soviet Navy warships and submarines in the Atlantic Ocean, Mediterranean Sea, and the Indian Ocean. The staff of intelligence specialists provided a daily intelligence summary to the Joint Chiefs of Staff, National Military Command Center, Defense Intelligence Agency, and specified military commands such as the Strategic Air Command and North American Aerospace Defense Command. The secrets of the Soviet Canary Island operation would have most likely originated from that closely guarded space.

Beshany confirmed that the Spintcomm network was the likely secure communications channel over which the emergency warnings about the *Scorpion* traveled up and down the navy chain of command, protected by a degree of compartmentalization that kept it from disclosure to the rest of COMSUBLANT, the other navy commands in Norfolk, and ultimately, the *Scorpion* court of inquiry. Thanks to the secure Spintcomm communications network, Schade, Holmes, Moorer, and other Pentagon admirals were able to assess the *Scorpion* situation and to launch the secret, pre–May 27 search in a few hours—despite the fact that Schade was at sea in one of his submarines, Holmes was in Washington on administrative duty, and Beshany and Moorer were working at their normal tasks in the Pentagon.[20]

The picture of the *Scorpion's* last days and hours was coming more and more into focus as a result of Beshany's new information. In their 1983 interviews with me, Moorer and Schade admitted that the navy had become suddenly concerned about the submarine either on Thursday, May 23 or Friday, May 24, three or four days before its failure to reach Norfolk triggered the SubMiss alert and massive open-ocean search. The two admirals left a clear implication that it was the sinking of the submarine on May 22 that resulted in that communications breakdown. Still, both admirals refused my repeated requests to explain in detail how the sequence of events had actually played out. Schade would only say that while out on the *Ray* he had received "a report" that the *Scorpion* had not established radio communications as directed, and this prompted him to contact Holmes and Moorer to request the secret search.

Now, Beshany provided two more vital pieces of the puzzle that described an even more sinister situation. First, he contradicted Schade,

Moorer, and many more navy officials when he said that communications intercepts led U.S. intelligence officials to fear that the *Scorpion* was in danger because the Soviets had become aware of the submarine's surveillance mission against them off the Canary Islands. Second, Beshany revealed for the first time that U.S. Navy officials were concerned that the *Scorpion* was in danger *even before it exploded and sank on May 22.*

U.S. Navy foreknowledge that the Soviets were aware of the *Scorpion's* presence off the Canary Islands, and were trailing the submarine with one of their own just hours or even days before it sank, added an entirely new dimension to the overall incident. If that was the true situation, the *Scorpion* loss was not a mystery that the U.S. Navy subsequently solved and suppressed. Rather, it had been a running confrontation known to the admirals well before the loss of the *Scorpion.* Corroborating Beshany's explosive revelation of that foreknowledge became my primary research task in the months after his 1997 interview.

Because of the severe restrictions on the Special Intelligence information pertaining to the *Scorpion* and the Soviet warships, few officers in Norfolk or Washington I interviewed knew of the Special Intelligence warning to which Beshany had referred. His former deputy, Dietzen, freely admitted in several interviews that he had been cut out of that information loop entirely. So, too, the officers in the *Scorpion's* administrative command in Norfolk and even members of the COMSUBLANT communications staff said they were totally in the dark about any aspect of the secret search before May 27 and what had triggered such an operation.

But in subsequent years, I began hearing from ordinary sailors who had been drawn into the *Scorpion* search at sea the week of May 20, 1968. In interviews with them and other former sailors whom I tracked down through various navy ship websites, I found explicit and repeated confirmation of Beshany's disclosure. When at Schade's request, Holmes ordered surface ships and submarines to hunt for the *Scorpion* during the week of May 20, his alert message apparently included specific reference to the fact that the Soviets were trailing the *Scorpion* and that the American submarine had sent a message to Norfolk saying it was unable to elude its shadower. On surface ships, in submarines, and in squadron ready rooms, sailors of all ranks and duties were aware of the ongoing encounter between the *Scorpion* and the Soviet submarine.

Bill D'Emilio, the *Compass Island* crewman, recalled that as his ship headed across the Atlantic toward the focused-operations search area southwest of the Azores in the last week of May 1968, commanding officer Captain Joseph Bonds told the crew of the *Scorpion*'s attempt to evade Soviet surveillance. D'Emilio recalled that the trailing vessel was described as a Soviet spy trawler and not a submarine: "And [the *Scorpion*] was reporting that it was being followed by a Soviet trawler. That was its last communication—again this is was what I was told. There was a Soviet trawler following it around. And it wasn't unusual back then to have Soviet ships following our subs or other ships."[21]

Word that the *Scorpion* had reported its inability to shake the Soviet submarine was so hot that it rocketed over the Navy Fleet Broadcast System to Polaris submarines on patrol. Ron Rule was a storekeeper on the *USS Nathanael Greene* (SSBN 636) patrolling in the North Atlantic the week of May 20, when his commanding officer made an announcement over the ship's 1MC loudspeaker. "What I remember about the incident is the announcement over the 1MC that the *Scorpion* was missing. Obviously, this was a very sobering announcement and it had an immediate effect on all of us," Rule said. "A very somber mood immediately came over all of us. I recall one of my shipmates, an electrician, had recently served in *Scorpion* and therefore had personal friends onboard." Rule remembered that the information relayed to the *Nathanael Greene*'s crew was explicit and detailed. "The announcement continued that what was known about *Scorpion* was that she was in transit back to the U.S. after her mission and that she thought she was being tailed and asked for instructions as to what to do, e.g., go check it out, or simply continue in transit." Rule continued, "We were told that that was the last that was heard from her. I remember thinking and talking about the possible scenarios, 'Russian submarine' being foremost on most (if not all) of our minds."

In a separate interview, another *Nathanael Greene* crewman confirmed Rule's account. Frank Greene said he learned of the *Scorpion* even before the formal announcement. "I was a Quartermaster and all information generally flowed through us pertaining to navigation. Word spreads quickly amongst a crew of 130." The *Nathanael Greene* was returning to its homeport in Charleston, South Carolina, from a seventy-day patrol when the message about the *Scorpion* came in, Greene recalled. "We were nearing Bermuda, when we received orders from Subflot Six to plot new courses in order to assist in the search for the *USS Scorpion*. They were sunk by a Soviet torpedo. The U.S. Navy has listening devices all over the floor of the ocean and taped everything."

Other participants in the secret search revealed yet another stunning disclosure: The crisis apparently began not on May 21, when the *Scorpion* reportedly terminated surveillance of the Soviet Navy ships, but five days earlier—even before the submarine had passed through the Straits of Gibraltar. Three sources from widely disparate branches of the U.S. and Canadian militaries provided essentially the same story in telephone interviews and emails with me in 2006: The encounter began sometime before May 17 and steadily escalated in the days after both submarines entered the eastern Atlantic. Sometime during that period—either early in the morning hours of May 22 or earlier—Commander Slattery sent a message to COMSUBLANT reporting his inability to break away from the Soviet submarine.

Frank Greene said he learned from friends on a nuclear attack submarine, the *USS Haddo* (SSN 604), that the showdown between the *Scorpion* and the Soviet submarine had been long in the making. Greene told me that these friends said that the *Haddo* also had had an encounter with the Soviet submarine in the far western Mediterranean around the time that the *Scorpion* passed through the Straits of Gibraltar the night of May 16–17. "They closed in, played games (harassment) and were generally becoming a major annoyance to the Soviet sub commander," Greene recounted in an email to me. "The *Haddo* apparently lost sonar contact with the Soviet sub and radioed the *Scorpion*, which was patrolling off Gibraltar in the Atlantic Ocean. They suspected that the Soviet sub was heading in their direction and to continue the harassment if located." Heavily censored *Scorpion* court of inquiry records confirm that the *Haddo* was indeed operating in the Mediterranean at that time. It was one of a half-dozen submarines whose movements were being watched by the Sosus operators from the Ocean Systems Atlantic Command at the time of the *Scorpion* sinking.[22]

A Canadian Air Force officer told essentially the same story. Vic Furney, a fourteen-year veteran of the anti-submarine warfare patrol aircraft community in 1968, was involved in the ongoing aerial surveillance of the Echo-II nuclear submarine that the U.S. Navy later said was part of the Soviet Navy formation operating near the Canary Islands.

Assigned to the 404 Maritime Patrol Squadron out of Greenwood, Nova Scotia, then-Captain Furney was senior "tacco," or tactical operations officer, for an eleven-member aircrew operating a CP-107 Argus ASW patrol plane. The Argus, a four-engine, propeller-driven aircraft, was capable of extremely long-range missions and held the world's record for the longest unrefueled flight, at thirty-one hours, for more than twenty years. Furney said that he and his crew were flying routine ASW patrols from Lajes airbase in the Azores when the *Scorpion* vanished. "The Canadian Forces and the U.S. Navy were one and the same in this [search] operation," Furney said. "At Lajes we had the same intel briefings."

Furney sent me a detailed memorandum he had written of his experience in the aerial patrol surveillance of the Soviet ships to preserve his memories of the event. Furney's aircraft had flown down from its base in Nova Scotia to the airbase at Lajes in the Azores for a stint of ASW patrols. Upon arrival, the Argus aircrew received orders to report for a special briefing the next morning, when they were directed to join the aerial hunt for the *Scorpion*.

What was unusual, Furney said, was the specific intelligence information U.S. Navy officials provided him and his aircrew: "We found out that the submarine *USS Scorpion* was missing. It had been on patrol in the Mediterranean and had stopped at the U.S. Navy base at Cadiz, Spain. . . . It departed Cadiz with the intention of shadowing a Soviet submarine which was en route to its North American 'on station' position, and was never seen again. The fear was that there had been an underwater collision." Furney told me that after each search mission, U.S. Navy intelligence officers would gather the crew and collect reports of all visual debris sightings and any acoustic signals picked up by the aircraft-dropped sonobuoys. "We were also brought up to date, daily, on the latest intelligence information concerning what was known about the *Scorpion's* known movements after Cadiz and those of the Soviet submarine," Furney said.

Furney was adamant that the U.S. Navy intelligence officers who briefed his crew had told them the *Scorpion* had been engaged in a running encounter with the Echo-II submarine even *before* its May 17 stopover at Rota. "I do know that the *Scorpion* was assigned to shadow a Soviet submarine coming out of the Med," Furney said. "He had been shadowing it prior to reaching the Straits of Gibraltar. There was an intelligence officer there and those were the words he used." In short, Furney confirmed Frank Greene's account that the Soviet encounter began even before May 17.[23]

A third confirmation that the *Scorpion*–Soviet submarine encounter began well before the day it sank comes in the recollections of two crewmen assigned to the Norfolk-based guided missile frigate *USS Josephus Daniels* (DLG 27) in 1968. Surprisingly, the ship's own official command history for that year specifically confirms their allegations. The two crewmen, in separate interviews in 2006, said that their ship had received emergency deployment orders to join the secret search on Saturday, May 18. That was a full four days before the submarine went down.

George Stermer, a helmsman on the *Josephus Daniels,* described an emergency crew recall and departure from port similar to the one that the *Compass Island* crew experienced in Brooklyn six days later on May 24. Stermer remembered that the *Josephus Daniels* got the assignment because it was one of only a few navy warships equipped with the newest and most advanced sonar system at the time, the SQS-26 bow-mounted array. On Friday, May 17, the *Josephus Daniels* had just returned to Norfolk from a thirty-day training exercise in Newport, Rhode Island, where it served as an engineering test ship for the navy's Destroyer School. Because of the month-long operation, upon arrival in Norfolk, commanding officer Commander E. L. Cochran granted leave to many of the crewmen. The next day, Stermer said, the ship received emergency orders to get underway to join the search for the *Scorpion*. "Many of the crew could not be reached," Stermer recalled. "We were pretty much a skeleton crew when we left port." For days, the short-handed crew had to work a "four-on, four-off" shift—manning their watch stations for four hours, then free to eat or sleep during the next four hours before returning to their duty posts once again.

A second *Josephus Daniels* sailor, Bill Palmer, gave an account that was virtually identical to Stermer's. A nineteen-year-old quartermaster third class on the ship at the time of the *Scorpion* alert, Palmer said his memories of the search operation remain vivid nearly forty years later. Like the crewmen on the *Nathanael Greene* and *Compass Island,* Palmer also remembered his commanding officer informing the *Josephus Daniels* crew that the *Scorpion* had radioed the submarine force headquarters to say a Soviet submarine was trailing it. "I recall hearing that the *Scorpion's* last known communication with [COMSUBLANT] was that they were being followed by a Russian submarine—and then they [Norfolk] lost communications." Palmer said he could not remember if Commander Cochran announced the information over the ship's 1MC speakers or whether it was a topic of conversation between the skipper and his watchstanders on the bridge, but in any event, the entire crew quickly became aware of the development. "They were being followed by a Russian submarine," he said. He added that the *Josephus Daniels* traveled at flank speed from the Virginia Capes eastward to a point just south of the Azores when the ship finally received orders calling off the search and ordering it to return to Norfolk.[24]

The navy's own written records for the *Josephus Daniels* provide starkly contradictory versions of the missile frigate's involvement in the *Scorpion* incident, strongly indicating that someone in authority altered key records to conceal the ship's involvement in the pre–May 27 search.

The *Josephus Daniels's* official command history for 1968 confirms details of the two former crewmen's account: The ship was indeed operating out of Newport from April 16 until May 16, when it returned to Norfolk, as the two former crewmen recalled. The history added: "During the period of 17 through 28 May, the ship remained in Norfolk, undergoing an RAV [restricted availability for repairs] in preparation for the forthcoming UNITAS IX deployment [to South America], on which the ship was to be flagship for Commander South Atlantic. The intended RAV was interrupted on May 18 when the ship got underway for SAR [search-and-rescue] operations for the *USS Scorpion*. Returning to Norfolk on 31 May, the ship continued the RAV." A separate chronology of major events in the 1968 command history also stated that the warship joined the *Scorpion* search on May 18.

But the daily quartermaster deck logs for the *Josephus Daniels* during May 15–31, 1968, tell a different story. Maintained by the duty quartermaster on watch with the navigation team when underway, and on the quarterdeck when the ship is in port, a navy ship's deck logs provide a minute-by-minute journal of the ship's operating conditions, movements, and locations when underway. These, too, showed the *Josephus Daniels* in Newport for a month, then steaming for Norfolk and arriving at 4:53 P.M. on Friday, May 17. At that point, the command history and deck logs tell radically different accounts. While the command history shows the ship joining the *Scorpion* search on May 18, the deck logs report the guided missile destroyer remained tied up at Pier 23 at the naval station for a ten-day period until 5:30 P.M. on Monday, May 27, when the ship initiated a general recall of personnel in anticipation of getting underway. At 10:48 P.M. on May 27, the logs state that the ship was underway for "special search and rescue operations" in the Atlantic.

The command history, deck logs, and two former sailors all agreed that the *Josephus Daniels* returned to port on May 31.[25]

Weighing the credibility of one document against another can be an all-but-impossible task. However, in the case of the *Josephus Daniels's* involvement in the *Scorpion* search, two factors strongly suggest that the command history narrative and chronology showing a thirteen-day search at sea are more credible than the deck logs that indicate the ship was out in the hunt for only four days between May 27 and 31. First, when former crewman George Stermer recounted his experiences on the *Josephus Daniels* from memory in June 2006, he noted without prompting, "Approximately two days before we went looking for the *Scorpion*, we had returned from New England." When I compared his statement with the ship's command history, which I had obtained from the Naval Historical Center in Washington, D.C., the two-day interval that Stermer remembered matched exactly the chronology of events showing the ship being mobilized for the search on May 18. Second, in an interview in November 2006, Bill Palmer recalled several details of the ship's participation in the *Scorpion* search that conformed to the longer deployment described in the ship's command history. "We were at sea long before that submarine was due back in Norfolk," Palmer said of the May 27 ETA for the *Scorpion*. "We were steaming for the Azores and were out quite a while with no ports of call. We were out longer than three to four days."

OTHER DETAILS of the *Scorpion* sinking and its aftermath remain subject to debate. While former navy crewmen at sea in the Atlantic in 1968 paint an unequivocal picture of the *Scorpion* engaged in a prolonged cat-and-mouse game with the Soviet submarine that culminated in the American submarine's destruction, other aspects of the incident are less clear. In particular, there is strong disagreement among those who claimed to have heard the true story as to whether or not the *Scorpion* it-self fought back. Several sources have alleged that there was at least some evidence that the *Scorpion* had fired at least one of its own torpedoes at the Soviet submarine. Others disagree.

During a civilian orientation tour aboard the Trident submarine *USS Alaska* (SSBN 732) on April 30, 1997, my wife, Karen T. Conrad, fell into discussion with several sailors about the Cold War and encounters between the U.S. and Soviet submarines. Aware of my prolonged research into the navy cover-up of the secret pre–May 27 search and other contradictions in the official account of the *Scorpion* loss, Karen was stunned when one *Alaska* crewman without prompting bluntly stated that the Soviets had destroyed the American submarine. She later wrote down a description of the conversation:

> Somehow we started chatting about submarines during the Cold War and the submariner started talking about the *Scorpion* and its mission. He stated that a Russian submarine sank the *Scorpion*. The *Scorpion* had just finished a routine deployment in the Mediter-ranean and was headed back to the states when it met with the Russ-

ian sub somewhere off the coast of Portugal. He said the *Scorpion* heard the sound of the Russian torpedo doors opening and launched a torpedo of their own . . . and somehow the Russian sub, after opening their torpedo [doors] maneuvered into a position to avoid being hit by [the torpedo from] the *Scorpion*. The *Scorpion,* in turn, was maneuvering and apparently the torpedoes simultaneously found their respective marks, despite both boats' efforts to avoid being hit.

Karen said she was struck not only by what the submariner had told her, but by his tone of voice and the unspoken agreement that the disclosure elicited among a handful of other crewmen. "He spoke with authority concerning the *Scorpion's* fate."[26]

The *Alaska* crewman wasn't the only source to assert the *Scorpion* had tried to defend itself. One of the two former Sosus technicians who spoke of the naval intelligence agents' effort to seize all records of the encounter recalled, "I believe we also fired, damaging the Soviet sub in question."

Former Sosus technician Vince Collier, on the other hand, said the Sosus tape replay that he and his classmates had seen at the Ocean Systems Technician "A" School in 1982 clearly showed that only the Soviet submarine had fired a torpedo. "There was no evidence whatsoever that the *Scorpion* fought back," he said.[27]

There is, however, evidence that the Soviet submarine did not emerge from the *Scorpion* encounter unscathed. Canadian Air Force Captain Vic Furney added one additional—and very intriguing—detail to the incident. Because of its superior flight range to that of American P-2V and P-3A patrol aircraft, he and his CP-107 Argus aircrew received new mission orders after a week or so of searching the *Scorpion's* track from the Azores. In his memorandum on the incident written down several years later, Furney told of an overflight they had made of the Soviet submarine some days after the *Scorpion* was publicly reported missing: "After a couple of days, the Soviet sub was approaching the limits of prolonged search by the U.S. P-3 Orions, so we were asked to continue tracking it and the P-3s would concentrate on the *Scorpion* search. Our next search was in the vicinity of Cape Verde, some 1,500 miles away from Lajes," Furney wrote. "We did find a Soviet Elint vessel, probably the [intelligence-collecting ship] *Teodolit,* with an unidentifiable submarine alongside and welding sparks coming out from under a tarpaulin which covered the front of the submarine. All of a sudden, the 'Crazy Ivan' theory seemed to have great credibility. . . . We had been in Lajes for nine days and although we were disappointed in not finding *Scorpion* or survivors, we were pleased that we had at least shed some light on the probable cause, the submarine repair event just off the big bulge in Africa."[28]

The retired Canadian Forces officer told me in May 2006 that the activity that he and his aircrew had observed onboard the Soviet submarine was far more intensive than a routine mid-ocean rendezvous for supplies and minor repairs. "There were a *lot* of sparks coming out from under that canvas." Whether the damage stemmed from a near-fatal torpedo warhead explosion, a collision, or some other malfunction remains unknown.[29]

A second eyewitness to evidence that the Soviet submarine was damaged in the encounter contacted me out of the blue in December 2006. In late May 1968, U.S. Navy Lieutenant (j.g.) Tom Corcoran was serving on the destroyer *USS John Willis* (DE 1027) when he saw a raw naval intelligence file that included an aerial photograph of a heavily damaged Soviet submarine being towed by a support vessel. Homeported in Newport, the eleven-year-old destroyer was operating with other U.S. Navy ships in the Norwegian Sea just south of the Arctic Circle when the intelligence report arrived as part of a routine dispatch of new material for the ship's officers to study.

Assigned as the destroyer's Combat Information Center officer, Corcoran had access to current intelligence information on the Soviet Navy. Sometime in early June, he said, "We received aerial photos of a USSR submarine tender towing a damaged Soviet sub northward from the vicinity of the Azores. . . . The photo showed it being towed alongside the tender's starboard (rear) quarter, a standard Soviet towing arrangement. But its hull was not at standard surface cruising height—it looked as if only the sail and minimal topsides rode at sea level as if to hide damage."[30]

Given the extraordinary secrecy in which the navy buried all details of the *Scorpion's* final hours and suppressed evidence that would have pointed to a hostile encounter with the Soviet submarine, it is understandable that many details of the incident still remain unclear and in conflict with each other. Nevertheless, multiple witnesses from a broad spectrum of the Atlantic Fleet in 1968 provide a clear and compelling account of what actually destroyed the *Scorpion*.

Absent signed, notarized affidavits from the senior navy admirals who carried out the cover-up, however, the best narrative must be a synthesis of the individual accounts provided by those who were in a position to see, hear, or learn about the incident either as it unfolded in 1968, or afterwards. Despite the U.S. Navy's diligence in confiscating evidence, burying records under top-secret security stamps, and even falsifying documents to conceal the submarine's fate, it is clear beyond a reasonable doubt that the nuclear attack submarine was the victim of an attack by a Soviet submarine.

From those sources, we now know that the standoff between the *Scorpion* and the Soviet submarine did not occur over several hours, but rather, was a running confrontation that began before May 17 and lasted until the American submarine sank on May 22. Senior navy officials were aware for several days before it sank that a Soviet submarine had been trailing the *Scorpion*. Multiple sources in the Pentagon, on surface ships, and on submerged submarines at sea all heard the essence of a message that Commander Slattery had sent to COMSUB-LANT reporting that the *Scorpion* could not shake off the Soviet submarine. Shortly after that, communications between the *Scorpion* and Norfolk suddenly broke off. Senior Pentagon officials with access to the most sensitive intelligence on the Soviet Navy voiced concern about the possibility of an attack on the *Scorpion*. In response, the Atlantic Submarine Force scrambled aircraft, ships, and submarines in a frantic secret search to locate the *Scorpion* at least four days before its failure to make port on May 27 triggered the public alarm. To that end, the bootleg Sosus tape of the final confrontation between the *Scorpion* and the Soviet submarine must be regarded as a credible narrative of the final minutes of the life of the submarine and its crew: Locked in an underwater dogfight, the *Scorpion* heard the Soviet submarine launch a torpedo, tried valiantly for about six minutes to evade the marauding weapon, and perished when it struck.

U.S. Navy officials since 1968 have stuck to the company line: Not only was there no attack on the *Scorpion,* but even if the Soviets had attempted one, U.S. submarine technology and the level of professional competence of American submariners were so superior in 1968 that the outcome would have been preordained—the *Scorpion* would have been the victor. It would not be for another two decades that navy insiders would learn just how wrong they had been on that point. Unknown to the U.S. Navy or intelligence agencies, the Soviets in 1968 possessed the means to penetrate the most closely guarded secrets of the Atlantic Submarine Force, and used that knowledge with deadly effect against the *Scorpion* and its ninety-nine-man crew.

12

THE FATAL TRIANGLE

T WAS DEATHLY QUIET ON THE SEVENTH-FLOOR HALLWAY OF THE Ramada Inn as the two FBI agents in bulletproof vests waited to spring the trap.

One glanced at his watch: 3:30 A.M., Monday, May 20, 1985. Down in the lobby, a third agent posing as the hotel's night clerk called the guest in Room 763 to tell him that an unknown motorist had struck and damaged his blue and white Chevrolet van in the parking lot. He needed to come down to fill out an accident claim report, the agent said.

Around a corner near the hotel elevators, FBI Special Agents Robert W. Hunter and James Kolouch heard the phone ring in Room 763. A few seconds later, they heard the door open, but then close again. They drew their guns and waited. A few minutes later, the sound repeated itself as the occupant again stepped out of his room but retreated back inside.

Fifteen minutes later, the door opened a third time, and suddenly the middle-aged suspect was standing in front of them, clutching a manila envelope in one hand and a .38 caliber revolver in the other.

"FBI! Drop it!" the agents shouted. For a long moment, the suspect stood frozen, and then dropped his weapon. As Kolouch slammed the man against a wall and quickly frisked him for any hidden weapons, Hunter said, "You are under arrest for violation of the espionage laws of the United States." Retired Navy Warrant Officer John Anthony Walker Jr., forty-seven, did not reply.[1]

For nearly three months, dozens of FBI agents from Boston to Norfolk, Virginia, had been quietly but diligently amassing evidence that the retired navy submariner was a spy for the Soviet KGB. Officials had opened the investigation after Walker's divorced wife, Barbara Crowley Walker, contacted an FBI agent in Boston in late 1984 to accuse her ex-husband of selling military secrets to the Soviets. On February 25, 1985, FBI headquarters gave its Norfolk office approval to launch a probe. Agents quietly interviewed Barbara Walker again, along with one of their four children, Laura Walker Snyder. Obtaining federal court approval, the FBI tapped John Walker's home and office telephones and placed him under close surveillance. They quickly learned that Walker was a licensed private detective who worked out of a modest Virginia Beach office complex. In addition to his house, Walker also owned a single-engine Grumman Tiger airplane and a houseboat on which he frequently entertained guests—mainly single women in their twenties. For weeks, the agents monitored his movements and listened in on his calls, but nothing suspicious happened.

Then, on May 18, the agents heard Walker telling friends and relatives that he planned to spend the weekend on an out-of-town business trip. Curiously, he told one person he was going to Nags Head, N.C., but then told another his destination was Charlotte. Their suspicions on full alert, the agents readied a massive surveillance plan.

The next day, Walker climbed into his blue Chevy van and backed out into the street in Norfolk's Ocean View neighborhood. Within minutes, he was driving westbound on Interstate 64 with an FBI aircraft and a half dozen surveillance cars tailing him. At Richmond, Walker headed north toward Washington, where he then got on the Capital Beltway and crossed the Potomac River into Maryland. By late afternoon, the agents lost Walker as he drove in seemingly random directions through a tangle of narrow and winding two-lane country roads in rural Maryland between Rockville and Poolesville. Then several hours later, they reacquired their target in a shopping center several miles away. After dark, they followed him back down into the same area where he had earlier vanished.

Navy Warrant Officer John A. Walker, saluting at right, participates in an honor guard ceremony for Atlantic Submarine Force communications officer Lt. John S. Rogers in 1968. Walker had been a spy for the Soviet KGB for at least three years at this time and would not be caught for another 17.
Courtesy Bernice Rogers

Then Walker did something strange that immediately confirmed the agents' suspicions. He drove to an intersection and placed a 7-Up can on the side of the road, then drove to a spot a mile or so away where he picked up another 7-Up can. To the FBI agents, it was clear that he was engaged in a "dead drop," a venerable espionage tool where a spy and his handler exchange material or information without ever meeting face to face. The dead drop involves using pre-selected locations to cache the goods for the other to retrieve and a complex choreography of planting signals to inform the other side that the attempt is underway. As the FBI would later explain in court documents, the 7-Up cans signaled that each person was in the area and now ready to make the exchange—documents from Walker, and a large cash payment from his handler.

The drop now arranged, Walker got out of his van carrying a white garbage bag and walked into thick underbrush. As soon as he left the scene, agents emerged from hiding and searched through the underbrush for the bag. Later, it was found to contain 129 highly classified U.S. Navy documents.

Upon discovery of the documents, a Justice Department official authorized the agents to take the retired officer into custody at the Rockville hotel. Walker's arrest set the stage for the unmasking of the most damaging spy ring the U.S. Navy had experienced in its history.[2]

Within days, U.S. Navy officials were panicked over the potential security implications from the Walker arrest. Submariners and naval communications experts began to realize that the Soviets had most likely penetrated the navy's most closely guarded secrets. What neither the FBI nor the U.S. Navy knew at the time was that the balding little man in the prison jumpsuit in the Baltimore city jail held the key that would unlock the final mystery of the sinking of the *USS Scorpion:* How the Soviets could have successfully tracked and ambushed the submarine. Most navy officials had long dismissed the possibility of a successful Soviet attack on the grounds that Admiral Sergei Gorshkov's submarine force was simply incapable of such a feat. American nuclear attack submarines were simply too quiet, their sensors too superior, and the crews too well trained. This then was the last secret: John Walker knew how the Soviets could have surprised and attacked the submarine, for he had given them the tools to do it. His espionage had triggered a major Soviet intelligence operation against the U.S. Navy that culminated in the attack on the *Scorpion.*

THE FBI ARRESTED WALKER "on suspicion of espionage and conspiracy to commit espionage," and within days information about the case began to appear in news reports. Then the FBI arrested two more members of the spy ring, Walker's brother, retired Lieutenant Commander Arthur Walker, and son, Yeoman Seaman Michael L. Walker, who was then serving onboard the Norfolk-based aircraft carrier *USS Nimitz* (CVN 68), deployed in the Mediterranean. More arrests were expected, officials said.

In Norfolk, the scandal struck with particular force. Admirals, ordinary sailors, and civilians were shocked that a navy retiree with deep roots in the local community was accused of espionage. At that time, I was living in Norfolk and working for *The Ledger-Star*, the city's afternoon newspaper, as an editorial writer and columnist specializing in military issues. I was just as stunned as everyone else at the news. When federal officials revealed that Walker had been a career submariner and communications expert, I immediately realized that the espionage, if it had happened, would have had a major impact on the navy's security.

I read with fascination Walker's work history, which the navy had released. He had enlisted in the navy on October 25, 1955, attending boot camp and Radioman "A" School, the initial training for that communications specialty. After five years on active duty including service on two submarine support ships, he had been accepted into Submarine School at Groton, and served aboard the diesel-electric attack submarine *USS Razorback* (SS 394) during 1961–62. At that point, Walker won admission to the nuclear submarine force when in 1962 he reported to Mare Island Naval Shipyard, California, as part of the pre-commissioning crew of the *USS Andrew Jackson* (SSBN 619). After its commissioning on July 3, 1963, the *Andrew Jackson* transferred to its homeport of Charleston. During part of that year, Walker—by then a radioman first class—was detached to attend a special navy technical school for operating the cryptographic gear employed by submarines to encrypt and decrypt messages. During the rest of 1963 and the following year, he served on several seventy-day strategic missile patrols on the *Andrew Jackson* before transferring to another Polaris submarine, the *USS Simon Bolivar* (SSBN 641), in 1965.

Promoted to radioman chief later in 1965, Walker for the next two years led the Polaris submarine's radio shack during several seventy-day strategic missile patrols out of Charleston and Rota, Spain. In March 1967, Walker won promotion to warrant officer and reported to the Atlantic Submarine Force headquarters in Norfolk. He served as a senior watchstander at the communications center there for three years. The last seven years of Walker's career were spent outside of the Submarine Service but still within the naval communications field. He transferred to San Diego in 1970 for a two-year tour as an instructor, then served three years aboard a navy cargo ship. In 1974, Walker returned to Norfolk, where his final duty station was at the Atlantic Fleet's amphibious warfare command. He retired in 1976.[3]

Walker's tour at Atlantic Submarine Force communications came during a tumultuous time for the command. Norfolk-based navy ships had suffered major casualties in two separate wars that raged during that period. In an eleven-month interval between June 1967 and May 1968, 267 Norfolk sailors died at sea in three separate disasters.

Walker had been at his new duty post for only two months when the Six-Day War between Israel and some of its neighbors erupted on June 5, 1967. Three days into that conflict, Israeli air force and naval units attacked the Norfolk-based electronic reconnaissance ship *USS Liberty* (ATGR 5) off the coast of Egypt, killing thirty-four of its crewmen and wounding another 174. Then, a month later, the Norfolk-based aircraft carrier *USS Forrestal* (CVA 59) was preparing for combat operations in the Gulf of Tonkin off North Vietnam when a fire erupted on its flight deck. The ship was preparing to launch a major air strike when an air-to-air missile on one aircraft accidentally fired and slammed into the fuel tank of a second plane, igniting a conflagration that quickly engulfed the flight deck as more bombs and rockets exploded. The accident killed 134 sailors and injured several hundred others. And then the *Scorpion* disappeared.

In those early days after the Walker arrest story broke in the week of May 20, 1985, there was no immediate information explicitly linking the retired warrant officer's alleged espionage to the loss of the *Scorpion* or the other two naval disasters. In fact, in the first week, the actual extent of the security breach was completely unknown to the navy or FBI. Walker had been incarcerated in Baltimore for only a few days. His brother and son were also in custody but only starting their passage through the federal court system. FBI officials released few details on the suspects. It appeared to me and other journalists that the espionage ring may have gone back as far as the mid-1970s, but even that suspicion was unconfirmed. Nevertheless, this was still a very big story that was unfolding by the hour.

From my experience in covering the navy, it was clear that the potential security breach was much larger than most people realized. Walker's career had placed him at the center of the most highly classified aspects of naval communications and submarine operations. If the accusations were indeed true, John Walker's spying would likely have had profound consequences for the navy.

When federal officials released a synopsis of Arthur Walker's navy career, it was obvious to me that his service as a career submariner meant that the Submarine Service had probably been a major target of the spy ring. Enlisting in 1953 after high school graduation and commissioned in 1960, Arthur Walker rose to the rank of lieutenant commander, held a top-secret clearance, and later served as the executive officer of a diesel-electric attack boat. Like his brother, Arthur's final billet was shore duty in Norfolk: He served as a senior instructor at the navy's Anti-Submarine Warfare School in Little Creek, Virginia, before retiring in 1973. Arthur Walker had possessed many critical secrets about submarine operations and anti-submarine warfare over the years.

Less was known of the potential security threat from Michael Walker, a relatively junior enlisted man serving his first tour in the operations department aboard the USS Nimitz. From what few details were available on Michael's brief navy experience, it did not seem likely that he had had much access to classified material. We would learn otherwise in the months ahead. Assigned to the ship's operations department, he regularly had the assignment of taking classified documents in a burn bag to the ship's incinerator for destruction. Instead, he stole over 1,000 classified papers and stashed them in various places on the carrier for future delivery to his father.[4]

With the scandal deepening, I embarked on research for a news analysis article that would identify the worst-case scenario: just how extensive the damage to naval security might be if the charges were true. I had few expectations that the navy or FBI would be officially willing to help me. The FBI had its hands full with the investigation and arrests. Navy officials were stung and embarrassed, and it was unlikely they would do anything to publicize such a disastrous situation. Moreover, during the mid-1980s reporters and navy officials in general did not enjoy a cordial relationship.

And so I was hardly surprised when navy and FBI spokesmen declined my request for interviews. Still, as I set out to coax Atlantic

Submarine Force officials to outline the possible dimensions of the Walker spy ring betrayal, I discovered an unexpected factor that helped break down the old barriers: rage. Submariners, like infantrymen in close-quarters combat or fighter pilots flying in formation, must rely on their comrades to carry out the mission. In the undersea confrontation between U.S. and Soviet submarines, the bonds were even tighter. To a man, retired submariners I spoke with were choking with anger at Walker's betrayal of the navy and the Submarine Service. Within several days, I tracked down two retired navy chief radiomen who had served with Walker in Norfolk seventeen years earlier. Their assessments were grim, and they wanted the public to fully realize just how serious the security breach had been.

As a communications watch officer in the Atlantic Submarine Force headquarters, they said, Walker had unprecedented access to highly classified details of ongoing submarine operations. "He had the ability to share with them the movement orders of every one of our damn boats—the missions, the timing of operations, everything," one said. This included the patrol areas of both the U.S. and British strategic missile submarines. Walker would have known the assigned operational areas of the attack submarine force, including the top-secret Northern run spy missions. He would have had ongoing access to the entire order of battle of the Atlantic Submarine Force, the roster of which submarines were ready for combat and which ones were not.

One ex-radioman gave a chilling example of just what a breach in security could do: When an attack submarine deployed on one of the sensitive surveillance missions, headquarters would issue strict parameters and limits governing its activities. "How far north and south of its track is the submarine allowed to roam?" the chief asked. "What is the overall size of the patrol area? Does he run a pattern or does he have total initiative within that sector? How long will he be there?" Such operational details were readily available to the communications staff at COMSUBLANT, the chief said. The second retiree, who had also served in the communication section with Walker, said the likely disclosures went even farther than that: "For eight out of every 24 hours he was privy to *everything* that went on in the command." And it would have been easy for Walker to glean any information of importance that had come in while he was off-duty.

The two veterans grew hesitant, however, when I asked if Walker might have given the KGB information that would have allowed them to break the navy's closely guarded encrypted communications. At this, the two former radiomen balked. They told me that it was impossible even to explain how a communications expert could compromise the top-secret encryption machinery and cipher procedures without revealing highly classified information in the process. While they agreed that Walker might have partially compromised secure naval communications, the two former radiomen declined to offer any specifics. I didn't pursue this issue in the article I ultimately published. Like most civilians and even many navy people, I knew little about the navy's worldwide communications broadcast system, particularly the technology and procedures by which it encrypted and decrypted messages as they passed from sender to receiver. Inevitably, my subsequent news analysis on the case focused on John Walker's access to top-secret information—the *content* of the thousands of messages that passed through his fingers each month—instead of the even more critical subject of how Walker might have betrayed the navy's process for encrypting those messages to keep its secrets safe in transmission.[5]

Two days after my column appeared, a new development brought the espionage scandal back into the headlines. Retired Radioman Chief Jerry Whitworth had come to the attention of the FBI early on in the investigation in March when Walker's ex-wife had told agents that a navy friend of John's from California was probably involved in the spying. FBI agents confronted Whitworth several hours after John's arrest and placed him under twenty-four-hour surveillance as they assembled evidence to secure an arrest warrant. Whitworth finally turned himself in on June 3.[6]

In the wake of the arrests, the FBI and other federal officials quickly amassed compelling evidence that charted the spy ring's trail in chilling detail. They were able to construct a detailed chronology of how Walker—first by himself, then later with his three accomplices—copied classified documents and sold them to the KGB. Through patient back-tracking, witness interviews, and John Walker's penchant for keeping detailed travel records and retail sales receipts, the government determined that the Soviets had paid the spy ring over $1 million from start to finish.[7]

Within three months of the initial arrests, prosecutors took the first case to trial. On August 5, 1985, Arthur Walker sat in a Norfolk federal courtroom as prosecutors made their opening arguments. In repeated interviews with the FBI and subsequent grand jury testimony, the older Walker brother had cooperated with the government to the point of voluntary self-incrimination. This greased the skids of justice: Only four days after his non-jury trial began, the retired lieutenant commander sat listening to U.S. District Judge J. Calvitt Clarke Jr. pronounce him guilty on seven espionage-related counts. Three months later, Clarke sentenced Arthur Walker to three life terms plus forty years in confinement.

Arthur Walker's belated and limited contribution to the spy ring came while he was an employee of a local shipyard that repaired navy ships. The evidence against him, like that against his nephew Michael, involved classified navy documents but not encryption procedures, so the subject of any possible penetration of the navy's classified communications system was never raised during his trial.

While Arthur Walker's trial was on, the federal government was preparing to try John Walker and his son in Baltimore. John Walker's defense attorney, aware that Arthur Walker's conviction stemmed from government evidence of John Walker's espionage, realized the feds had a slam-dunk case against his client. Both John Walker and federal prosecutors knew that the only leverage the government had over him was the fate of his son. Both sides also knew that the only leverage John Walker had over them was his knowledge of the spy ring's long operation. Given the imperative for U.S. counterintelligence officials to learn the extent of the security breach down to the last detail, and the prosecution's need for John Walker as a trial witness against Whitworth, it did not take long for the two sides to reach a plea agreement.

In late October 1985, John Walker agreed to plead guilty to three espionage-related charges that carried multiple life sentences with no

chance of parole. Michael Walker would agree to plead guilty to five espionage-related charges. John Walker also agreed to cooperate fully with
a multi-agency "damage assessment" team charged with a comprehensive
review of the case. He agreed to be a prosecution witness against Whitworth. The government in turn would recommend that Michael
Walker's sentences run concurrently, setting a likely maximum prison
term of twenty-five years.[8]

By the end of 1985, the Walker spy ring had mostly faded from the
headlines. The navy and FBI were releasing no information on the John
Walker security debriefing or on prosecutors' planning for the trial of
Jerry Whitworth. The prosecutors were amassing a mountain of evidence and a witness list of more than 170 people as they prepared to try
Whitworth in a San Francisco federal courtroom in the spring of 1986.
Meanwhile, the team of navy, FBI, and other intelligence officials had
begun an intensive series of meetings with John Walker with the goal, in
John le Carré's phrase, of "walking back the cat"—retracing his espionage activities down to the last detail. Any information on what the retired warrant officer might be telling the navy damage assessment team
behind closed doors remained highly classified.

In the fall of 1985, I left Norfolk to take up a new editorial-writing
job with *The Seattle Post-Intelligencer*. From this new vantage point, the
spy scandal in Norfolk seemed remote and obscure, a dormant volcano
on the other side of the country. Back on the East Coast, the navy was
doing everything it could to downplay the significance of the spy ring
and the damage it had caused to fleet operations, communications security, and wartime contingency plans. A *Washington Post* article in late
July quoted unnamed senior navy officials who described the impact as
"serious" but "not disastrous." The article continued, "Other high-rank-
ing Pentagon officials said yesterday they shared that assessment." Senator David Durenberger (R-Minnesota), chairman of the Senate
Intelligence Committee, echoed the sentiment after a navy briefing. "I'm
not that worried about the [stolen] information. It certainly wasn't of
much significance that there's any kind of alarm." A *Time* magazine article relying on unnamed navy officials several weeks after the arrests took
the same tack.

But some naval intelligence officials recognized the actual dimensions of the breach to the navy's classified communications, and they were horrified at the self-deception among the top admirals. After a spate of articles inaccurately minimized the damage, sources that were obviously within the naval intelligence community struck back by leaking information to *Time* and other publications confirming that the Walker espionage had actually been a very serious breach of security.[9]

My interest in the still-unresolved accusations against John Walker and Jerry Whitworth was rekindled in early 1986 when I learned that Walker would likely be a prosecution witness against his alleged co-conspirator. When the U.S. Justice Department announced in February 1986 that Whitworth's trial would begin the next month in San Francisco, I briefed my editors on my earlier coverage of the spy scandal in Norfolk and volunteered to cover the proceeding and write an analysis of the case. The trial was expected to last several months with scores of witnesses and hundreds of exhibits, so the best approach would be to focus on the testimony of the government's star witness.

On April 28 and 29, I sat in the courtroom of U.S. District Judge John P. Vukasin in San Francisco as John Walker made his one and only public appearance since his arrest. During two days of testimony, he seemed to revel in his notoriety. For the first time, he spoke directly of his dead drops in the Maryland countryside, of midnight strolls in the streets of Vienna with his Soviet handler, of his recruitment of family members and a close friend to commit treason for money.

At one point in his testimony, I felt the hairs on the back of my neck actually stand up. For the first time, Walker publicly revealed a central aspect of his spying that no U.S. government official had acknowledged. Walker and later Whitworth had compromised specific pieces of navy radio gear used to encrypt and decrypt highly classified messages to and from ships and submarines at sea.

I also learned a crucial piece of technical information bearing on the navy's communications system and the spy ring's betrayal of classified messages. The U.S. military does not use codes to hide its secrets. Codes employ the simple process of swapping key words with others to mask the identity of a word or phrase. In a coded message, the sender might refer to the pending arrival of "stopsign." A classified codebook would inform the recipient that stopsign actually means "battleship." While secure in their own right, codes were too ungainly and cumbersome to use in the Navy Fleet Broadcast System, which transmitted thousands of messages worldwide each day. So the navy, like most military organizations, used cipher cryptography to protect the content of classified messages. In this system, electro-mechanical transmitters and receivers automatically substituted each letter or numeral in the message with a randomly generated replacement using a special encryption device. If intercepted, the text would appear to be a random set of letters that would read as gibberish. Only with a proper receiver set to the same encryption "logic" could someone "break" the encrypted message back into plain English.

John Walker testified that he and Jerry Whitworth had long worked as classified materials custodians in the navy communications system, responsible for safeguarding the encryption gear and highly classified operating and repair manuals. In addition, they were in charge of daily keylists that provided more security by adding another level of encryption when inserted into each machine. I was shocked. John Walker and Jerry Whitworth had held the very keys to the navy's operational communications networks. The material that had passed through their hands would enable the Soviets to read the navy's most highly classified operational messages. This disclosure suddenly brought into sharp focus a question that I had been mulling over for nearly a year: Could there have been a connection between Walker's espionage and the *Scorpion* incident? In the weeks after his arrest, I had assumed that Walker as a COM-SUBLANT communications watch supervisor might have known details of the *Scorpion*'s surveillance of the Soviet warships and other operational information from its 1968 deployment. I had suspected his espionage probably would have given the other side confirmation of events months after they had occurred, but not the ability to influence naval operations as they were actually taking place. Nor did Walker's courtroom admission of when he actually began spying for the KGB paint a clear picture. During the Whitworth trial, Walker testified that he began passing secrets to the Soviets "in early 1968" with several deliveries of material every few months or so. The timeline of events in 1968 did not suggest a credible connection between Walker's spying and the *Scorpion* sinking: There was only a four-month interval between his confessed start as a spy and the loss of the submarine.

Walker's testimony did not focus on his tour at Atlantic Submarine Force headquarters for long. The prosecutors were after Jerry Whitworth, after all, and as a result focused their examination of the star witness on events that occurred after Whitworth agreed to join the conspiracy in the autumn of 1974.[10]

Another reason that a Walker-*Scorpion* connection seemed unlikely to me was that, at that time, I still believed that the submarine loss was from a torpedo accident and not a hostile confrontation, so I felt that any connection between Walker and the *Scorpion* most likely would have involved him telling the Soviets what the U.S. Navy knew or suspected about the sinking. Former Yeoman Chief Jerry Hall's assertion about the Soviets sinking the *Scorpion* remained an enticing, but unproven, allegation.

After listening to Walker's version of events for two days, I became curious as to whether his testimony against Whitworth confirmed or contradicted what he had been telling the damage assessment team, so I decided to see if navy officials might be willing to reveal whether Walker was living up to his side of the plea deal by revealing the full extent of his spying. On returning to Seattle, I contacted the Office of Naval Intelligence in the Pentagon and requested a background interview with a senior member of the damage-assessment team. Surprisingly, the response was yes, and one afternoon in early May a team member, whom I was allowed to publicly identify only as Jack, called me. Our conversation led to a major revelation about John Walker's espionage that would help me solve the mystery of the *Scorpion* sinking.

BY MAY 1986, my research into the *Scorpion* incident was on indefinite hold. And so when I picked up the phone to speak with Jack, the topic of the *Scorpion* was far from my center of attention. Walker's presence as a KGB agent working at Atlantic Submarine Force headquarters in May 1968 had initially struck me as a coincidence. The evidence that had emerged so far suggested that Walker's job in the message center would only have enabled him to tell the Soviets what the U.S. Navy had known or not known of the *Scorpion's* disappearance, and not play a direct role in the sinking itself.

The first thing that Jack told me was that the damage-assessment team had already spent four months debriefing John Walker before his appearance as a government witness against Whitworth. Experts from FBI counterintelligence, the CIA, the Submarine Service, naval intelligence, communications, and other experts tried to retrieve every detail of his spying, Jack said. The topics ranged from technical details of submarine communications to Walker's modus operandi in identifying potential recruits for his spy ring. The team organized each interview session along a specific topic and sat with Walker in an unadorned conference room for up to eight hours at a stretch.

The first question I asked Jack was whether John Walker was cooperating with the investigators as he had promised in the plea deal. The damage-assessment team, Jack answered, felt that Walker was still hiding a secret from the beginning of his espionage. Jack explained that despite Walker's pledge to tell everything about his activities, there was one area where he refused to go. "From about 1970 on, we feel that he is telling the truth as best as he can remember it," Jack said. "He's very reluctant to talk about anything that has taken place prior to 1970. He retreats mentally. He looks very careful in any question, in any discussion relative to any incident that may have taken place prior to 1970. He's extremely reluctant to zero in on that. He becomes very curt, very short in his answers, saying, 'I don't remember. I don't know.'"

After weeks of this pattern of responses, Jack continued, the damage-control experts sensed that there was something lurking in John Walker's memory so sinister that he would risk abrogating the plea bargain to prevent it from becoming known. The team had been forced to set aside the issue of this troubling reticence to prepare Walker for the court testimony against Whitworth. "We intend to pursue that with him when the trial is over," Jack said. "We are not giving up on that at all."[11]

Suddenly, I grabbed a chronology of Walker's navy career from the pile of papers on my desk and stared at it. As far as anyone knew, Walker began spying during his assignment at the Atlantic Submarine Force communications center. Could he be hiding something related to the *Scorpion?* As calmly as possible, I said to Jack, "I know something that happened in 1968 when Walker was at COMSUBLANT."

"Me too," Jack replied. "It's pretty obvious what happened on January 23, 1968."

This was not what I had expected to hear. On that day, the North Korean Navy seized the *USS Pueblo* (AGER 2) and its eighty-three-man crew off the east coast of North Korea, half a world away from Norfolk, where John Walker was working in the Atlantic Submarine Force communications center. What could these two things possibly have to do with one another?

THE *PUEBLO* INCIDENT was the other navy catastrophe in 1968. The seizure of the *Pueblo* by North Korean forces in international waters marked the first time a U.S. Navy ship had been captured without a fight since June 22, 1807, when the British warship *HMS Leopard* attacked the frigate *USS Chesapeake* off the Virginia Capes, killing twenty-one of its crew and seizing four men believed to be British deserters.

The *Pueblo* was a small, minimally armed former army freighter that the navy in 1966 had converted into an electronic intelligence-gathering ship. By the mid-1960s the National Security Agency and the military had established a global network of ground stations, orbiting satellites, and aircraft to intercept all forms of intelligence on the Soviet Union and other hostile regimes. The navy's prime contribution was in using the nuclear attack submarines to spy on Soviet Navy exercises and sea-based ballistic missile tests, but in 1959 the NSA became interested in using navy surface ships as "platforms" to carry listening gear and a cadre of trained technicians to operate the equipment. The admirals were unenthusiastic. Such operations would divert expensive warships such as destroyers and frigates from their primary missions at sea. In addition, combat ships had little extra room in which to place the bulky antenna arrays and listening gear. The navy's compromise was to emulate the Soviets and build a small flotilla of reconnaissance ships similar to the Soviet spy trawlers. Their prime mission was to loiter innocuously out in international waters for extended periods while the "spooks" on board recorded and studied a wide array of electronic signals and radio transmissions from the target: military and civilian communications, missile telemetry signals, even radar pulses.[12]

The *Pueblo* was part of a small but growing fleet of electronic spy ships the navy created during that decade. Between 1960 and 1968, the navy converted seven World War II–era *Liberty* ships into electronic listening platforms. These were much larger than the *Pueblo* and its two sister ships, displacing about 10,000 tons against the *Pueblo*'s 950. Originally built in 1944 as an army cargo vessel, the *Pueblo* was tiny, 176 feet long, 32 feet wide, and with a draft of only 11.5 feet below the waterline. Its crew of eighty-three consisted of fifty-one navy sailors to operate the ship and thirty NSA intelligence specialists. The navy arranged for two civilian oceanographers to join the crew for cover. Its only armaments were two .50-caliber machine guns mounted amidships and at the bow, and several dozen submachine guns and handguns in a safe.

The navy had ambitious plans for the *Pueblo*. After its recommissioning in 1967 in Bremerton, Washington, officials ordered the ship to Yokosuka, Japan, where it would work with a sister ship, the *USS Banner* (AGER 1). Pacific Fleet officials had already approved a six-month deployment schedule for the two reconnaissance ships under the title of Operation Icthyic. Beginning with the *Pueblo* on January 5, 1968, each ship would conduct thirty-day patrols along a designated corridor just outside the twelve-mile limit. With a slight overlap in deployment dates, fleet officials had earmarked nine separate reconnaissance missions along a 2,500-mile swath of the Pacific Rim during the first seven months of 1968. The *Pueblo*'s mission in Operation Icthyic I would run from January 5 until February 4 off the Soviet and North Korean east coasts. For this first mission, the *Pueblo*'s operational objectives included determining the nature and extent of naval activity at various North Korean ports, sampling the "electronic environment" of the entire North Korean east coast, and conducting surveillance of Soviet naval units in the region.[13]

Mission planners had compiled a ream of top-secret paperwork in the weeks before Commander Lloyd Bucher and his crew set sail from

Sasebo for Icthyic I on January 11. One of the documents later came
back to haunt navy leaders. The U.S. Pacific Command on December
23, 1967, had issued an "estimate of risk" on the upcoming *Pueblo* operation. It acknowledged a number of troubling signs in the region. The
North Korean Air Force "has been extremely sensitive to peripheral reconnaissance flights in this area since early 1965." The message cited an
incident on April 28 of that year when North Korean MiGs attacked
and seriously damaged an air force RB-47 flying more than thirty-five
miles off the coast. The CINCPAC message further warned that the
North Korean Navy had regularly attacked South Korean naval vessels or
civilian fishing boats found near its eastern coastline. Finally, the message warned that North Korea had the habit of ignoring "internationally
recognized boundaries" throughout the region including the twelve-mile
limit.

Nevertheless, the top navy command in the Pacific concluded that
the "risk to *Pueblo* is estimated to be minimal since operations will be
conducted in international waters." Mission planners in the Hawaii
headquarters apparently ignored what had happened to the *USS Liberty*
just seven months earlier when Israeli aircraft and gunboats attacked the
ship in international waters off the Sinai Peninsula under mysterious and
still controversial circumstances. Nor did the Pentagon or Pacific Command consider aborting the mission when on January 21—just two days
before the *Pueblo* hijacking—a large team of North Korean infiltrators
attempted to assassinate South Korean President Park Chung Hee at his
official residence in Seoul.[14]

Unarmed, alone, and plagued by spotty communications with the
naval intelligence listening station at Kamiseya, Japan, the *Pueblo* was an
enticing target. On January 23, the North Koreans dispatched a force of
patrol boats and sub-chasers out of the east coast port of Wonsan at mid-
morning. They surrounded the small ship, ordered it to heave to, and
opened fire when Bucher attempted to flee. After a two-hour standoff,
several dozen North Korean soldiers boarded the ship and took its crew
prisoner.

The seizure caught the entire U.S. military flatfooted. No land-based
air force fighters were on alert to bring help in an emergency, and by the

time confirmation of the hijacking had reached senior air force commanders in Japan and South Korea in late afternoon, it was too late to do anything about it. Worse, the aircraft carrier *USS Enterprise* was only 470 miles from the incident and could have had its combat jets reach the scene of the hijacking within an hour. But the orders never came. Thanks in large part to the U.S. military's cumbersome and multiple chains of command, and a worldwide communications network that proved too slow and inefficient to get the right information to the right commanders in time, the *Pueblo* was a walkover for the North Koreans.[15]

But what did the *Pueblo* have to do with the Walker spy ring? I was intrigued by Jack's hint that they were connected. I had vivid but fragmentary memories of the *Pueblo* seizure but had never studied it in detail. Fortunately, there was plenty of material at hand. Most political histories of that era contained substantial segments on the incident, and there were a half-dozen books about it, including three written or co-authored by former *Pueblo* officers.

The *Pueblo* seizure dominated the news in late January 1968, and it had major political and military ramifications. It probably derailed a plan by the U.S. command in Vietnam to break the North Vietnamese siege of the marine base at Khe Sanh by staging a diversionary attack into lower North Vietnam. It also threatened to significantly undermine the U.S. and South Vietnamese defense against the Tet Offensive throughout South Vietnam that intelligence officials in Saigon now knew was imminent. The South Korean government's response to the Park assassination attempt and *Pueblo* incident added to the stress. Seoul officials told their American counterparts they wanted to redeploy its crack South Korean Army divisions serving in South Vietnam back to Korea.

At home, the seizure of the *Pueblo* was yet another massive political headache for President Lyndon Johnson. The incident seemed to paint the entire U.S. military as incompetent and paralyzed. Frustrated and helpless, U.S. government officials and citizens watched the grim newsreel footage of U.S. Navy officers and sailors being marched down a Wonsan street at gunpoint with their hands in the air.[16]

U.S. military experts and political leaders were also genuinely baffled at why North Korea had made such a dangerous move. President Johnson himself would write in his 1971 memoirs that the *Pueblo* seizure had been the first of what he called "a chain of crises that appeared to be carrying [the United States] downhill at an ever-increasing pace" that year. The president recalled his own confusion and dismay upon being told of the incident: "The unanswered question was *why* the North Koreans had seized the *Pueblo*," Johnson wrote. "Piracy on the high seas is a serious matter. Why had North Korea flagrantly risked stirring up an international hornet's nest and perhaps starting a war?" He attempted to supply the answer to that question several pages later in his book: "Our best estimate then, and one that I believe holds up well in the light of subsequent events, is that they were aware of the Tet offensive in Vietnam, which was scheduled to take place eight days later. They were trying to divert U.S. military resources from Vietnam and to pressure the South Koreans into recalling their two divisions from that area. . . ." In short, the former president agreed with most of the political and military experts of the day that North Korea had seized the *Pueblo* simply as a diversionary move to thwart its enemies and help North Vietnam at a critical juncture in the war.

No one, including Johnson, seemed to have considered that the *Pueblo* and its crypto gear were themselves a target of great value.[17]

Cloaked in secrecy, the *Pueblo*'s spy mission was unknown to most Americans. Most news accounts of the hijacking focused on the drama of the eighty-three-man crew suddenly finding itself in captivity, and of the political and military fallout from the seizure. Some U.S. intelligence officials surely suspected that seizing the *Pueblo*'s intelligence-collecting equipment was the actual goal of the North Koreans, but they never said so publicly. For obvious reasons, the U.S. Navy did not want to confirm the compromise of highly classified communications-gathering equipment with the loss of the *Pueblo*.

Before communication satellites became a mainstay of naval message traffic in the 1970s, the U.S. Navy relied on the same technology to send messages to and from ships and shore stations that it had employed for the previous seven decades: direct high-frequency radio transmission. Because the signals were easy to intercept and monitor, the navy used a wide array of encryption machines to translate the English text into an unreadable jumble of seemingly random characters. During World War II, the process had been laborious and slow, since encrypting machines used a series of mechanical rotors to transpose the original characters into the secure text. Decrypting the message at the other end required an identical machine whose rotors were set to the same position. By the late 1960s, the communications architecture remained essentially the same, but the machines were now faster and more efficient. Most navy ships and submarines in the 1960s contained several different devices used to encrypt outgoing messages and translate incoming ones back into English at 100 words per minute.

I was sitting in a Seattle restaurant on a cold, rainy afternoon in May 1986, reading an obscure congressional report from 1969, when the connection between John Walker's espionage and the *Pueblo* leaped off the pages. For weeks, I had pored over my notes from the interview with Jack, trying to discern why his team suspected that Walker's theft of secrets might have been connected with the *Pueblo*. I knew it most likely had something to do with navy communications—but what? Walker had been a nuclear submariner. The *Pueblo* was a motley little ex-army freighter converted into an electronic listening post.

I obviously needed to know more. After inquiries with several experts I knew in Washington, D.C., I obtained a 1969 report by a House Armed Services subcommittee that had investigated the *Pueblo* incident along with the North Korean shoot-down of a navy EC-121 reconnaissance aircraft in April 1969. The partially declassified transcript of the panel's hearings and conclusions cited the equipment carried aboard the ship that had fallen into the hands of the North Koreans. I began to tremble with excitement. The roster showed that the *Pueblo* had almost a dozen different encryption systems on board at the time it was hijacked. Three of them were the KLB-47 tape-fed transmitter/receiver, the KWR-37 Jason receiver unit, and the KW-7 Orestes secure send/receive teletypewriter. Just weeks earlier, John Walker had calmly described to the Whitworth trial how he had compromised those three systems while assigned to the Atlantic Submarine Force communications center!

The compromise of the three systems confirmed the extent of the potential damage from his espionage, for they were used throughout the navy during that period. While the three reflected differing stages of encryption technology available in the late 1960s, all followed the same general principle. The sender would type out a clear-text version of the message or document with the device's teletypewriter keyboard. The text would pass through special cryptographic circuits that encrypted them into seemingly random blocks of text. This then would be transmitted over the navy's high-frequency radio network, where an identical device would retrieve the jumbled text and, with the same internal encryption circuitry, print out the document once again in plain English. Of the three, the KW-7 Orestes was the most advanced and widely used model in 1968. The navy used Orestes as a primary communications system for its shore stations, ships, and submarines. In addition, the KW-7 was a mainstay device for the other U.S. armed services and allied military units.[18]

As I stared at the roster of *Pueblo* crypto gear, I realized that navy officials had known from the outset that the *Pueblo* seizure potentially compromised more than a half-dozen separate encryption systems used on board. Further confirmation came from transcripts of radio communications between the ship and shore. As the North Koreans were physically boarding the ship at 2:15 P.M. local time on January 23, a radio operator at the Kamiseya naval listening post sent this query: "What status of classified material left to destroy?" The cryptic reply from Communications Technician First Class Don Bailey left no doubt: "We have the KW-7 and some cards in the [KRW-]37 and [KG-]14 to smash. I think that just about [does] it." Sixteen minutes later, as North Korean soldiers pounded on the locked door to the communications space, Bailey dispatched a final message: "Destruction of [classified] pubs have [*sic*] been ineffective. Suspect several will be compromised." Two minutes later the *Pueblo* was off the air.

In 1998, more than ten years after discovering the roster of *Pueblo* crypto gear in the congressional report, I located Don Bailey in his hometown outside of Indianapolis. The former naval communications technician was polite but extremely hesitant to discuss his experiences from 1968, citing his concerns over revealing still-classified information. Bailey did confirm to me that the North Koreans had captured at least one KW-7 unit intact—the one he was using at the end. "I was on the [KW-7] teletype operating it," he recalled. "We got some of it destroyed but not all of it. It was pretty much intact when they got us."

Although he had retired from the navy in 1973, Bailey said he still was constrained from discussing the highly classified equipment he had operated on the *Pueblo* and, prior to that, at the listening post at Kamiseya. However, he did confirm the gist of the radio transcripts of his frantic final minutes communicating with the shore station in Japan. "I was busy trying to destroy everything I could," Bailey recalled. "The destruction was ineffective." Lloyd Bucher, commander of the *Pueblo,* had requested explosive demolition charges to be used in the event the equipment was threatened with seizure, but the navy turned down the request on grounds of safety to the crew. As a result, Bailey said, all the sailors had at hand when the North Koreans boarded their ship were sledgehammers. "You can't beat it up with a sledge," he said of the reinforced steel boxes containing the encryption gear. "The way they were built, it can't be done."[19]

Although U.S. Navy and intelligence officials were aware of the loss of the *Pueblo's* encryption gear and the potential risk to communications security, they believed that U.S. military communications on the whole were still protected from penetration. There was an additional level of encryption protection for each system: the daily crypto keylist. In addition to the internal circuits built into each machine that provided the "logic" to scramble the text into random characters, radio operators each day would insert a top-secret keylist, or cipher key, that gave an additional encryption layer to each message. In the case of older devices such as the KLB-47, the keylist was actually a printed instruction on how the operator should set a series of mechanical rotors in the machine to generate the random blocks of text. In more modern systems such as the KWR-37 and KW-7, the keylist was an IBM punchcard that the radioman inserted in a slot in the machine.

Because of that additional layer of security, navy officials believed that any advantage to the enemy from gaining the communications gear would quickly erode with the passage of time and the immediate obsolescence of the dated cipher keylists. The *Pueblo* had carried keylists for the month of January 1968 and reserve onboard keylists for February and March, so the theory was that any communications breach would be limited and temporary.

And so, by the summer of 1986, I had learned that the navy's secure communications relied on a combination of the encryption gear and the daily keylists. The North Koreans had seized the three critical navy communications units in varying degrees of destruction, including at least one intact KW-7. Still, the limited compromise of the daily keylists persuaded the navy and National Security Agency that it was not necessary to embark on a crash effort costing hundreds of millions of dollars to replace tens of thousands of individual encryption devices. Future upgrades and improvements to the machines would also strengthen their protection against penetration.

But unknown to them, John Walker in early 1968 was already providing the KGB with a constant stream of keylists, repair manuals, and technical documents with design improvements for the navy's encryption machines. And he would continue to do so for the next seventeen years.

It seemed banal, almost boring at the time, but John Walker's testimony in April 1986 completely rewrote the history of the *Pueblo* incident. His espionage, first and foremost, had involved selling the Soviets the ever-changing crypto keylists for U.S. Navy communications encryption systems. He had spent two days in Judge Vukasin's courtroom recounting nearly two decades of espionage that centered around photographing and delivering keylists from communication center vaults to his KGB handlers. As he admitted to federal agents after his arrest, "If I had access to it, color it gone."

The double whammy of the seizure of the *Pueblo* and John Walker's espionage allowed the Soviets to unlock the navy's most secret communications channels.

Of course, my discovery of the Walker-*Pueblo* connection led me to wonder if the Soviets could have used this capability against the *Scorpion*. Had they actually gained the ability to break and read classified navy message traffic by the time the *Scorpion* left the Mediterranean on May 17, 1968? The *Pueblo* seizure, after all, had occurred only four months before the *Scorpion* went down.

During the three years after the unmasking of the Walker spy ring in 1985, more details of the *Pueblo*-Walker connection emerged as a number of journalists and authors published books on the scandal. Additional accounts would also follow during the 1990s. One account of the *Pueblo* incident that appeared during this period added a major new twist to the story. Two civilian naval analysts, Norman Polmar and Thomas B. Allen, cited U.S. intelligence officials to reveal that Soviet and Chinese intelligence specialists swarmed over the *Pueblo* several days after its capture, and that the crypto gear had been rushed to Moscow for study and possible exploitation by the KGB.[20]

As each new detail emerged, I realized that the issue of when John Walker's espionage had begun would be critical to determining if the spy, the *Pueblo* seizure, and the *Scorpion* loss were linked. Jack mentioned Walker's insistence that he had only begun spying "in early 1968" and that Jack and his colleagues were extremely suspicious of the truthfulness of Walker's statement. Soon, more information would emerge that suggested the spying had begun in 1967, or even earlier.

John Walker himself provided new details of his Norfolk spying to *Washington Post* reporter Pete Earley, and these, I believe, clinched the connection between the spy ring and the *Pueblo*. Walker told Earley that he had impulsively copied the keylist for the KLB-47 system sometime during a late-night watch in December 1967. The next day, he drove to Washington, D.C., walked in the front door of the Soviet Embassy, and volunteered to spy for the Soviets. After several hours discussing his background and access to naval communications, Walker took an envelope containing $1,000 from the Soviet officer and returned to Norfolk. Two weeks later, Walker said he drove back for a second face-to-face meeting with his Soviet handler in a suburban shopping center just across the Potomac River from Washington. Walker came with what he later described as a small packet of classified documents and a detailed list of the classified systems in his workspace. Two of them were the KWR-37 and KW-7. At a third exchange in early January 1968, this time a dead drop, Walker said he slipped the Soviets a current keylist for the KW-7.[21]

The more the FBI agents and navy damage-assessment team interrogated Walker, the more they believed he was lying when he said his spying began "in early 1968." FBI Special Agent Robert Hunter, who headed the investigation leading to Walker's arrest and later participated in the damage assessment, said the FBI was able to prove that Walker had *not* made the visit at that time because his description of a wrought-iron fence in front of the Soviet Embassy was inaccurate. "He told us there was a wrought-iron fence around the embassy compound when he walked in. In fact, there was no wrought iron fence around the Soviet embassy until June 1974," Hunter recalled. "However, John's description of the inside of the embassy was on the money, which seems to show that he was in there at some later time." Or earlier. Barbara Crowley Walker told federal investigators after his arrest that her ex-husband had actually started spying for the Soviets earlier, most probably in the spring of 1967, during his 1965–67 assignment aboard the *USS Simon Bolivar* in Charleston, when the couple were experiencing serious financial difficulties. However, Barbara Walker also revealed that years earlier, Arthur Walker had confessed to her that *he* had sold secrets to the Soviets for a brief period during an assignment at the New London Submarine Base sometime during the mid-1960s. Arthur Walker denied the charge but failed lie detector questions regarding the subject.[22]

After himself repeatedly failing lie-detector tests on the question of when his spying had begun, John Walker during a meeting with FBI officials on August 28, 1986, finally attempted to clear the air with a vague but titillating concession: "I know you believe I'm lying about the beginning of the operation because of [his failing] the polygraph and the [Soviet embassy] fence story. Let me give you a scenario: Arthur got in some type of financial trouble, probably in New York, and became involved with a number of New York loan sharks. Art needed money desperately, and I gave him some classified documents to sell. After Art sold the documents and got some money, he became frightened and wanted to drop out. I saw no harm in selling the information to the Soviets, as the countries were not at war and would never go to war. I felt it was an easy chance to make some money, so I walked into a Soviet embassy somewhere in the world."[23]

The implications of this admission that John and Arthur Walker had already been involved in espionage—even if for a brief period—were especially significant in terms of positing the Soviets' ability to capitalize in minimal time on John Walker's espionage while at COMSUBLANT in 1968. If Walker had begun spying for the KGB as early as 1965 as he had now seemed to admit, the Soviets would have already known of his background as a submariner and communications officer well before his arrival at the Atlantic Submarine Force communications center in the spring of 1967. In all likelihood, they probably would have received advance notice from Walker of his pending new responsibilities in Norfolk, inasmuch as he later revealed the KGB's intense interest in any change of jobs or responsibilities by spy ring members within the navy. By Walker's new admission, he was already a known and proven espionage asset to the KGB several years before he entered the locked communications center at COMSUBLANT. The possibility that the KGB could have combined the seized *Pueblo* encryption gear with Walker's stolen keylists in time to use them against the *Scorpion* now appeared to be a distinct possibility.

The final piece of the Walker-*Pueblo-Scorpion* puzzle fell into place for the navy damage-control team the following year, but it did not come to my attention for another decade.

By 1998, the *Scorpion* incident and Walker spy scandal had become old news, but with the thirtieth anniversary of the sinking coming up, *The Seattle Post-Intelligencer* approved my request to write an in-depth retrospective on the entire affair. I contacted another member of the Walker damage-assessment team to see if any new information had emerged in the ensuing years that might clarify Walker's connection to the *Pueblo* and/or the *Scorpion*. Like his former colleague, Jack, the senior official would consent to talk only on grounds of anonymity. He said that the panel of experts had continued meeting with Walker for several years after his first and only public testimony, at the Whitworth trial in 1986.

The question of when he actually began spying remained one of the thorniest issues, the analyst said. "When Walker got started was always a problem," he explained. "My recollection is that Walker always wanted to put it after the *Pueblo* [seizure on January 23, 1968]. We pushed hard on this, and the FBI always believed he was quite deceptive on the point." On the issue of the *Scorpion* incident itself, Walker would say little, although it was agreed he was a paid KGB spy on the day the submarine vanished.

And then my source dropped another bombshell.

One day, he said, Walker blurted out that the Soviets had once congratulated him on his spying and told him that as a result of his delivery of navy crypto keylists from the Atlantic Submarine Force communication center, they had engineered the North Korean seizure of the *Pueblo*. "After a long and hard day of debriefing, Walker was frustrated and popping off," the intelligence official recalled. "He 'wise guyed' himself into a discussion of the *Pueblo* and claimed the Russians got the DPRK [North Korea] to grab the ship to make full use of his stuff." The members of the assessment team concluded that this time Walker was telling the truth, he said.[24]

THE WORLD OF intelligence-gathering is often described as a "wilderness of mirrors" where facts and information are elusive and contradictory. Despite the inconsistencies and many unknowns that permeated the Walker spy ring investigation, the U.S. Navy was uncharacteristically blunt when in late 1986, it formally described the general extent of John Walker's espionage and the damage that he had done to the navy's secure communications system.

On November 4 of that year, during the sentencing phase of Jerry Whitworth's espionage trial, Rear Admiral William O. Studemann, the newly appointed Director of Naval Intelligence, signed a thirteen-page affidavit to the U.S. District Court in Baltimore summarizing the U.S.

Navy's assessment of the damage. The unclassified document was unusually harsh: "In my professional opinion," the admiral wrote, "the harm caused to the national security by John Anthony Walker is of the gravest nature." Studemann cited the comments made by a prominent KGB official who had defected to the United States in July 1985, only two months after Walker's arrest in May of that year. As security officer for the Soviet Embassy in Washington during 1975–80, Vitaly Yurchenko had received formal briefings from the KGB on the ongoing Walker espionage. Studemann recounted Yurchenko's description of the Walker spy ring to American security experts after his defection: "From his [KGB] briefings, Yurchenko learned . . . the KGB considered the Walker/Whitworth operation to be the most important operation in the KGB's history." The keylists and other cryptographic material John Walker and his associates provided allowed the Soviets to decipher over a million messages, an average of about 150 a day, over the span of the spying. Yurchenko also informed his American handlers that the information Walker had passed to them would have been "devastating" to the United States in time of war.[25]

"Not even the formidable cryptosystems of the United States are safe when an adversary can employ a trusted agent to covertly obtain the protective logic and key which protect national security information," Studemann continued. "John Walker not only provided the Soviets with details to cryptologic and key, he also provided classified documents which included information on communications architecture [and] future communications systems" including technical manuals that detailed modifications to the communications gear. In addition, the admiral said, during Walker's 1967–69 tour at Atlantic Submarine Force headquarters, the spy had access "not only to the communications received and transmitted during his watch, but also to a great variety of classified information" including emergency procedures for nuclear war planning.[26]

THE STEADY ACCUMULATION of evidence now showed a clear link between the Walker spy ring and the *Pueblo* hijacking. By the late 1980s, it appeared plausible that as early as May 1968, the Soviets already had the potential to break at least some of the U.S. Navy's codes. Specific evidence underscoring the *Scorpion*'s own vulnerability to Soviet intercepts of its own encrypted messages finally appeared in late 1993, eight years after Walker's arrest. Again, it was a handful of seemingly innocuous sentences buried in a mass of navy paperwork.

In October 1993, the navy declassified a major portion of the *Scorpion* court of inquiry's hearing transcripts. Included in the trove of documents was explicit confirmation that the *Scorpion* had employed the same three encrpytion systems that Walker had betrayed at COMSUBLANT and that had been lost on the *Pueblo*. During its last voyage, the *Scorpion* had communicated with Atlantic Submarine Force headquarters via three different cryptographic systems: the KLB-47, KWR-37, and KW-7. And the evidence now strongly indicated that for nearly a year before it sank, John Walker had been delivering the daily cipher keylists for those three communications devices to the Soviets. In his 1986 affidavit, Studemann had stated that the cumulative impact of the Walker spy ring had enabled the Soviets to decipher an average of about 150 classified messages a day. While not yet ironclad, the evidence now showed Soviet interception and breaking of the *Scorpion*'s messages to be to be a distinct possibility.

By now, I was privately convinced that the Soviets indeed had been able to decipher at least part of the *Scorpion*'s messages by late May 1968. Even harder confirmation soon emerged in yet another revelation that brought chills up and down my spine.

In 1994, a key Soviet official in the Walker spy ring stepped forward to recount his experiences as one of John Walker's original case officers. Oleg Kalugin was deputy KGB station chief—or *rezident*—in the Soviet Embassy when he claimed Walker made his walk-in approach to spy for them in the fall of 1967. In his memoirs published in 1994, Kalugin wrote that the volume of material Walker provided required a special team of experts in the KGB's Department 16—the Soviet equivalent of the National Security Agency codebreakers—to handle and process it. "Walker got his hands on an astonishing amount of material," Kalugin wrote. "First, there were documents on the movement and activity of the Atlantic Fleet. Then there was information that enabled us to break the United States' codes."

In a subsequent interview in early 2001 with CBS that was never televised, Kalugin said that the KGB did not orchestrate the *Pueblo* hijacking but confirmed that the Soviet intelligence agency immediately jumped to exploit the harvest of classified documents and encryption systems that the North Koreans had seized. "John Walker's information, on top of *Pueblo,* definitively provided the Soviets with the final solutions to whatever technical problems [in breaking U.S. codes] they may have had at the time. . . . We certainly made use of the equipment from the *Pueblo.*"[27]

From senior intelligence officials on both sides of the Cold War—Studemann and Kalugin—there was now formal confirmation that the KGB early on in the Walker spying was able to read classified U.S. Navy messages in "realtime." Kalugin strongly suggested in his memoirs and the CBS interview that success in breaking the navy codes came quite early, raising the odds that even within a matter of four months the espionage windfall was being put to use at sea. This received further confirmation when I learned from a former U.S. naval attaché to the Soviet Union in 1998 that a retired Soviet admiral had told him that as early as March 1968, the Soviets were intercepting and deciphering U.S. Navy encrypted communications thanks to the Walker-*Pueblo* intelligence operation.[28]

Experts with whom I have discussed the Walker-*Pueblo* espionage operation raise one point that is of critical importance to understanding the degree of vulnerability that the *Scorpion* would have been in during the last two weeks of May 1968: It is not necessary to break an adversary's encrypted communications 100 percent to be able to prevail in a military showdown. In 1942, the U.S. Navy could read only one-tenth of the Imperial Japanese naval code. Even that fragmentary capability led to the decisive U.S. victory at the Battle of Midway, where the Pacific Fleet ambushed a larger Japanese carrier force and sank four flattops. Thus, John Walker's keylists and the *Pueblo*'s encryption gear most likely helped betray the *Scorpion*'s pattern of operations in the final weeks of May 1968.

One footnote to the submarine's Mediterranean deployment further underscores the credibility of this scenario: Sometime in early March 1968, a member of the *Scorpion's* radio gang made a grievous error while preparing to transmit a top secret message from Commander Slattery to COMSUBLANT. Retired Radioman Chief Daniel K. Pettey, who transferred off the submarine to the *USS Skipjack* in April, told me in a 2006 interview that another radioman had accidentally transmitted the top secret message without encrypting it first on the KW-7 Orestes transmitter. "He just wasn't thinking what he was doing and sent it out in the clear," Pettey said. "That was a pretty bad breach of security." The unencrypted message would have not only given the Soviets the knowledge of what the message itself contained but also provided them with a template with which to "break" other messages from the submarine, Pettey said.[29]

For years, U.S. Navy officials had argued that it would have been impossible for the Soviet Navy to be able to attack and sink a front-line American nuclear submarine. Despite its technological inferiority and poorer training, the Soviet Navy by the spring of 1968 had obtained the means to neutralize the U.S. nuclear submarine fleet's overall superiority by breaking its adversary's communications and anticipating the submarine's operational objectives and intended movements.[30]

Throughout the Cold War rivalry at sea, the Soviet Navy led by Admiral Sergei Gorshkov had striven to attain parity with the U.S. Navy. The Soviets had built nuclear submarines that because of poor workmanship and inferior personnel training frequently were more of a threat to their crews than to the "main enemy." By ruthless bureaucratic maneuvering, Gorshkov built a massive submarine and surface navy that in the mid-1960s went to sea to challenge the American adversary in every ocean. American admirals publicly registered alarm over the growing size of the Soviet Navy while privately still reassured they had the qualitative edge. What the Americans did not learn for nearly two decades was that the Soviets, in an intelligence victory nearly unparalleled in history, had broken the U.S. Navy's codes. And we now can conclude that the Soviets wielded that weapon to set up an ambush that destroyed the *Scorpion* and its crew in a secret battle that climaxed beneath the Atlantic on May 22, 1968.

13

WITH MAXIMUM PUNISHMENT

APTAIN PETER HUCHTHAUSEN WAS PREPARING FOR HIS NEXT DUTY station as U.S. naval attaché in Moscow in June 1987, when a chance encounter with a senior Soviet submariner pitched him head-first into the long-running mystery of the *USS Scorpion.*

His superiors in the Pentagon had directed Huchthausen to serve as an escort for a visiting delegation of ten senior Soviet Navy officers. The group was coming to Washington to attend an annual conference by representatives of both navies to review encounters between naval warships and aircraft on both sides over the previous twelve months.

For the past fifteen years, both sides had worked to avoid dangerous confrontations through an accord known as the Incidents at Sea Agreement, which both navies had signed in 1972 in the early years of détente between the superpowers. Throughout the 1950s and 1960s there had been a series of U.S.–Soviet encounters at sea that could have easily escalated into a shooting incident as ships and aircraft carried out mock attacks against the other side. On June 4, 1966, a Soviet warship collided with the electronic reconnaissance ship *USS Banner,* a sister ship to the *USS Pueblo,* in the Sea of Japan in what appeared to be an act of harassment by the larger Soviet ship. The following year, a two-day confrontation occurred between the *USS Walker* (DD 517) and the Soviet Kotlin-class destroyer *Bessledny* in the Sea of Japan during a U.S. Navy anti-submarine warfare exercise. Twice in two days the Soviet warship brushed up against the American destroyer despite repeated radio calls warning it not to approach too closely. On May 24, 1968, a mock attack turned fatal when a Soviet Badger bomber crashed after conducting several low-level mock attacks against the *USS Essex* (CVS 9) and its escorts operating in the Norwegian Sea. Eyewitnesses said the Soviet aircraft cartwheeled into the ocean after a wingtip brushed the water as it was making a turn after buzzing past the carrier. The crew of seven perished instantly.

After three years of negotiations, the two sides reached an agreement, and the naval accord was signed during a meeting in Moscow on May 25, 1972, by Secretary of the Navy John Warner and Soviet Navy commander-in-chief Admiral Sergei Gorshkov. The agreement had helped tone down tensions between the two navies, but one limitation in the accord deeply rankled the Soviets: It did not apply to submarines.[1]

BY THE TIME HUCHTHAUSEN was selected to be the next naval attaché in Moscow, overall relations between the United States and Soviet Union had recovered from a serious setback following the 1979 Soviet invasion of Afghanistan. The early 1980s had been a period when American leaders characterized the Soviet Union—in Ronald Reagan's words—as an "evil empire." With the accession of Mikhail Gorbachev in 1985 as Soviet leader, superpower relations once again began to thaw, but the two navies still found themselves regarding their counterparts with lingering suspicion and mistrust.

A 1962 Naval Academy graduate, Huchthausen had served primarily as a surface navy officer for most of his twenty-five years in uniform. He was no stranger to the decades-long Cold War rivalry at sea. Huchthausen had been a junior officer on the destroyer *USS Blandy* (DD 943) during the 1962 Cuban Missile Crisis. During the thirteen-day showdown in the Atlantic, Huchthausen and the rest of the *Blandy's* crew had spent long hours at general quarters battle stations as their ship hunted for the Soviet submarines that had deployed into the western Atlantic as part of the Kremlin's effort to ship ballistic missiles into Cuba. At one point, the *Blandy* on October 30 actually forced the Soviet Fox-

As U.S. Naval Attaché in Moscow during 1987–90, Capt. Peter Huchthausen learned from several Soviet admirals that the two governments had secretly agreed to suppress all evidence of the *Scorpion* sinking. Here, Huchthausen (at left) and Rear Admiral Vladimir Khuzhokov, then director of the Ministry of Defense Foreign Affairs Directorate, confer after a meeting in the ministry building in 1990. *Courtesy of Peter Huchthausen*

trot-class submarine *B-130* to the surface after hours of tracking it. The next year, Huchthausen's ship would take part in the search for debris from the *USS Thresher*. When the *Scorpion* vanished five years later, Huchthausen—like many U.S. Navy men—heard rumors that the Soviets might have had something to do with the sinking.

During the 1970s, Huchthausen, who was fluent in Russian, served as an analyst of Soviet naval submarine forces and in anti-submarine warfare staff assignments in the European Command, the Atlantic Fleet, and U.S. Pacific Command. Then, in the early 1980s, he entered the strange world—half-diplomat half-spy—of the military attaché. By 1987 he had served as the senior U.S. naval attaché to Yugoslavia and Romania, and also as chief of attaché and human intelligence collection operations in Western Europe for the Defense Intelligence Agency.[2]

When the Soviet naval delegation arrived in Washington for the June 1987 gathering, Huchthausen and the other American navy hosts found themselves welcoming an angry group of Soviet Navy flag officers. As a relatively junior member of the U.S. delegation, he later recalled in a letter to the author, his job was to serve as little more than an escort for the Soviet group. "I had to do the care-and-feeding of the ten officer delegation, live in the same hotel, take all meals with them, and be with them the entire ten-day period."

The Soviet delegation members had one overriding topic on their minds as they sat down for the first session. A year before, on October 3, 1986, the Soviet Yankee-class missile submarine *K-219* had sunk in the Atlantic after an explosion and fire in one of its missile tubes (as discussed in Chapter 5). Three crewmen died in the initial explosion, and a fourth, Sergei Preminin, perished while valiantly attempting to shut down the two nuclear reactors. The remaining 115 crew members survived and were evacuated to a Soviet freighter that came to the scene. Senior Soviet Navy officials believed that the explosion was caused by a collision with a U.S. nuclear attack submarine, and this accusation recurred during the conference.

The Soviet admirals were in a foul mood as the conference got underway. Huchthausen was standing in the background during the first session of the conference when he saw Admiral Pitr Navoytsev, the senior Soviet admiral, step up to his U.S. counterpart, Vice Admiral Henry C. Mustin, and begin berating him. Huchthausen waited for the right moment and asked a colleague what the confrontation had been about. Navoytsev, he was told, had condemned what he called the "irresponsible and dangerous" actions of American submarine commanders. Huchthausen recalled that the Soviet officer then "threatened specifically that next time a similar submarine incident occurred, the Soviets would retaliate with hostile action."

As the meeting went on, Huchthausen saw that whatever Mustin had said in reply to Navoytsev did little to ease the tension. Essentially, it was the same response that U.S. Navy admirals had been giving their Soviet counterparts for the previous fifteen years since the Incidents at Sea Agreement had gone into effect: As negotiated and signed, the pact applied only to aircraft and surface ships—*not* to submarines. "Each year, the Soviet side tabled a motion to include submarine operations," Huchthausen recalled. "Each year the U.S. side vetoed the motion, stating that we did not want to hamper our submarine commanding officers."[3]

After that inauspicious first session of the conference ended, Huchthausen escorted the delegation to their hotel in Crystal City, Virginia, just down the road from the Pentagon. It had been a long and tiring day, he said. At the hotel, Captain Valentin Serkov, the delegation's Law of the Sea expert, told him that Admiral Navoytsev wanted to take a swim and relax in the sauna to get rid of his jet lag before a scheduled reception that evening. Huchthausen said he met with the two officers at five P.M. at the hotel pool, which the hotel management had closed so the three officers could meet in private.

Curious over the Russian's earlier outburst, Huchthausen asked Navoytsev to explain why the Soviets were so upset. The admiral repeated his charge that the Soviets were concerned because of the alleged collision by an American nuclear attack submarine that had led to the loss of the *K-219* eight months earlier. Huchthausen decided to take the initiative in the conversation: "I replied, trying to be appropriately aggressive myself, that we had questions as well about aggressive Soviet submarine operations, specifically during the *Scorpion* event in May 1968."[4]

What had been an almost idle conversation at the side of the pool suddenly escalated into another face-to-face standoff like the one the American officer had witnessed just several hours earlier. Huchthausen was stunned by the senior Soviet admiral's reply. Navoytsev instantly and angrily revealed a link between the sinking of the Golf II-class missile submarine *K-129* on March 7, 1968, and the loss of the *Scorpion* eleven weeks later on May 22: His jaw clenched, the Soviet officer shot back, "Captain, you are very young and inexperienced, but you will learn that there are some things both sides have agreed not to address, and one is that event and our *K-129* loss, for similar reasons."

Huchthausen was baffled and intrigued by the Soviet officer's virulent response. Like many Americans, he had read the news reports in 1975 of the CIA operation involving the *Glomar Explorer* attempting to salvage the Soviet Golf-II submarine but was unaware of any substantial details of the *K-129* loss. The next day, Huchthausen reported the gist of the poolside encounter to his superiors as required by standing navy regulations. Then came another jolt. Instead of a pat on the back for standing up to Navoytsev, a senior American member of the Incidents at Sea delegation reprimanded Huchthausen "for conducting private talks with the Soviets."

After arriving in Moscow several months later, Huchthausen said, there were many outstanding issues to master and a multitude of tasks to accomplish as he settled in at the U.S. Embassy. But one unofficial thought kept coming back to him: What had the Soviet admiral meant about a connection between the loss of the Soviet submarine and the sinking of the *Scorpion?* He decided that if it were at all possible, he would try to find out.

Two years later, in October 1989, Huchthausen was well established as the U.S. naval attaché in Moscow when Admiral Carlisle A. H. Trost, the U.S. chief of naval operations, made a historic first visit to the Soviet Union by the U.S. Navy's senior officer. At the time of the CNO's long-planned visit, a different climate permeated the Soviet capital that few veteran diplomats could have predicted just a few short years earlier. Eastern Europe was in a ferment of democratic reforms. The Soviet leadership under Gorbachev was turning away from superpower confrontation with the United States, and a series of breakthrough nuclear arms treaties had added substance to the thaw in superpower relations. The Kremlin earlier that fall had announced a unilateral force reduction of over 500,000 men in its military ranks. Trost's visit promised to be the harbinger of a new working relationship between the U.S. and Soviet navies. Officials on both sides were working hard to make the admiral's visit productive and successful.[5]

As naval attaché, Huchthausen was a principal go-between for the upcoming CNO visit and spent hours talking with his Soviet counterparts planning the schedule and itinerary for Trost. One day several months before the event, Huchthausen received a request from the Soviet Navy to come straight to Soviet Naval Headquarters. Ushered into the chief of main navy staff's office, Huchthausen listened politely to a formal request from Admiral Konstantin Markarov, the Soviet Navy chief of staff. Markarov said that the Soviet Navy wanted the exact location of the wreckage of the *K-129*. The Soviet admiral also asked Huchthausen to forward a request for a list of names of the Soviet submariners whose remains had been recovered and to confirm that the remains had been properly disposed of. In a personal aside, Markarov explained to the American attaché that the request stemmed from a resurgence of religion in his country as communist philosophy was gradually being replaced by a return of Russian Orthodox religious values. Returning to the embassy, Huchthausen recalled, "I dutifully forwarded their request via a personal, eyes-only, message to Admiral Trost."

Unlike the confrontation two years earlier with Admiral Navoytsev in the Crystal City hotel swimming pool, Huchthausen saw nothing sinister or mysterious in Admiral Markarov's request. "Military-to-military cooperation was in full blossom," he told me.

The U.S. Navy's response, Huchthausen said, was a major disappointment that, in his opinion, made little sense. What possible intelligence loss would result from telling the Soviets where their submarine had gone down nineteen years earlier? Or confirming that American intelligence officials had acted with respect in burying at sea the remains of the *K-129* sailors that had come up with the hull section? Trost never directly replied to Huchthausen's message. The attaché tried several follow-up phone calls and messages, but there was only silence from navy headquarters in the Pentagon. As an alternative, Huchthausen sent a similar message forwarding Markarov's request up the chain of command of the Defense Intelligence Agency. More silence. "I finally received a short reply from an obscure DIA office, stating that any inquiries concerning deceased local nationals of my host country should be referred to the embassy's consular section," Huchthausen told me years later. "It was an attempt to shut me up."

Aware of the Soviet Navy's deep interest in finding answers to the *K-129* incident, Huchthausen decided to give the matter one more try. By pre-arrangement, he flew to Helsinki, Finland, to meet Trost for preparatory briefings before the official visit to the Soviet Union by the

U.S. chief of naval operations. When the two officers found themselves alone, Huchthausen privately asked the U.S. Navy's senior admiral why the Soviet request over the *K-129* had caused such a problem. Trost's reply was puzzling, Huchthausen recalled: "The U.S. Navy can never answer that question," said Trost. Huchthausen cautioned the chief of naval operations that Soviet Navy Commander-in-Chief Admiral Vladimir Chernavin would likely raise the question directly when the two navy chiefs met for a planned private session. Speaking of the encounter ten years later, Huchthausen shook his head in dismay. "Trost responded in words to the effect that he would take care of that," Huchthausen recalled, "and that, since I was not a submariner, I could never know the reasons behind the silence on that subject." Huchthausen said he was struck by the CNO's dismissive phrase, "since I was not a submariner"—as if the American and Soviet submarine forces were both separate and independent military fiefs. However, a mere navy captain knows better than to argue with a four-star admiral, so the attaché let the matter drop. Nevertheless, Huchthausen would soon find that the mysterious connection between the *Scorpion* and the *K-129* was deeper and more bizarre than he had ever thought possible.

During his tour as naval attaché in Moscow, Captain Huchthausen and another senior Soviet officer, Vice Admiral Ivan M. Komarov, established a close work relationship. In 1988, Komarov replaced Navoytsev as head of the Incidents at Sea delegation, and he met with Huchthausen one day while Soviet and U.S. navy officials were traveling together in the Crimea. "I had not been present for all their one-on-one discussions between the two senior admirals," Huchthausen said of the formal meeting between Trost and Chernavin the previous month. In a casual conversation with Komarov, Huchthausen asked if the subject of the *K-129* had come up between Trost and Chernavin during their private meeting. Komarov's response surprised the American.

Both the United States and Soviet navies had agreed to cover up the truth of both submarine losses, the Russian admiral said. Huchthausen a decade later recounted to me his diary entry that summarized their startling conversation. On whether the two senior admirals had talked about

Scorpion crewmen get a rare break to work abovedecks as they prepare to tie the submarine up to the *Tallahatchie County* in Naples Bay in April 1968. *U.S. Navy Photo*

the *Scorpion* and *K-129,* "Komarov shook his head and said he didn't know, but he *did* know that the subjects of *Scorpion* and *K-129* were agreed never to be discussed by both sides, especially now when our relations were improving. Since there was egg on both our faces, it was in both sides' interests to insure that full disclosure of those events never fell into the hands of those elements who were opposed to the thaw, on both sides." Komarov cautioned Huchthausen that the submariners involved, and those few in the know, on both sides, "were sworn, with the threat of maximum punishment" should they disclose what had actually happened to either submarine.

Huchthausen said he came away from that encounter convinced that the sinking of the *K-129* and the loss of the *Scorpion* had a deadly connection. He added that this assessment was even further reinforced in 1995—five years after his retirement from active duty—when he traveled to Moscow to interview retired Soviet Navy officers for a book he was writing on the Cold War naval confrontation. One of his contacts was retired Admiral Viktor A. Dygalo, who in 1968 had commanded the Soviet submarine division to which the *K-129* was assigned. Dygalo warned Huchthausen, he told me, that there was "an unofficial agreement by senior submariners on both sides" that would prevent anyone from ever learning the full account of what had caused the two submarine sinkings.[6]

BY THE LATE 1990S, I had accumulated enough evidence to establish a plausible scenario that the Soviet Navy had the motive, means, and opportunity by May 1968 to attack and sink the *Scorpion*. The very fact that senior Soviet Navy admirals would confide to U.S. Naval Attaché Captain Peter Huchthausen that a secret, mutual agreement to suppress the facts of both submarine losses was still in effect decades after the event convinced me beyond a reasonable doubt that the *Scorpion* sinking was an act of reprisal by the Soviets for their belief that the U.S. Navy was responsible for the loss of the *K-129*.

Additional confirming evidence remained elusive. There were additional pieces to the puzzle, but not enough to answer some basic questions about why the deadly undersea confrontation had actually started, and how the two superpower navies had managed to de-escalate the situation before it spun entirely out of control.

In 1995 Dygalo made one additional disclosure to Huchthausen that reinforced the credibility of the overall allegation that the John Walker spy ring and the Soviet intelligence coup in recovering the *Pueblo*'s crypto gear had given the Soviets the means to track, locate, and ambush the *Scorpion*. During his meeting with Huchthausen, the Soviet admiral said his service had gleaned details about the U.S. Navy hunt for the *K-129* from communications intercepts. "Dygalo asserted that they had learned of the incident by reading U.S. Pacific Fleet submarine communications," Huchthausen told me. "Look at the timing: the Walkers were already giving submarine [crypto] key material to the Russians in 1968." If the Soviets indeed were already penetrating encrypted U.S. Navy messages in early March of that year, they could have done the same thing two months later when COMSUBLANT ordered the *Scorpion* to divert to the Canary Islands to spy on the Soviet warships there.

It was at this time in the late 1990s that I stumbled upon an even more bizarre allegation concerning the *Scorpion* incident: A retired U.S. Navy admiral had publicly stated that the Soviet Navy had told the Americans the exact location of where the *Scorpion* had gone down with all hands.

For decades, the nonprofit U.S. Naval Institute has conducted an oral history program in which retired naval commanders provide detailed reminiscences about their careers and the issues with which they were involved while on active duty. In 1977, the institute commissioned an interview with retired Rear Admiral Ralph K. James. Relatively unknown to the American public, James had served most of his thirty-five-year career as an engineering duty officer with a specialty in shipbuilding and design. As chief of the Navy Bureau of Ships from 1956 until his retirement in 1963, James had played a pivotal background role in the crash program to build the navy's nuclear submarine fleet. While day-to-day control of the nuclear reactor development effort—and the lion's share of publicity—went to his nominal deputy, then-Rear Admiral Hyman G. Rickover at the Nuclear Reactors Branch, James still had earned widespread respect in the service for his leadership role in that program.

It was midway through a series of interviews that James spoke about the *Scorpion*. James had also been a key—but unheralded—official in the navy investigation into the sinking of the *Thresher* in April 1963. During a discussion of that disaster, James without prompting changed the subject to the *Scorpion:* "The only other submarine accident to boats built in my era was to the *Scorpion* that was lost in the South [*sic*] Atlantic," James recalled. "We located the *Scorpion* rather quickly, primarily through the help of the Russians, which leads you to ponder whether or not they didn't have a hand in her destruction. That's a possibility, but here again, we'll never know unless indeed it was a Russian incident and someday we are able to unearth in the archives of the Russian Navy an admission to this effect. We would have to be victors in a major cataclysm, however, in order to accomplish that."

The implications of what James had said were enormous. First, since he had retired in 1963, this information must have come to him from a friend or former colleague still on active duty and with access to the most highly classified intelligence information surrounding the *Scorpion* incident. Second, yet another senior navy admiral in retirement had blown a gaping hole through the navy's official story. The details of James's revelation were incredibly precise. Not only did he confirm that the Soviets knew about the sinking, but his remarks—if true—showed that they physically were close enough to pinpoint the spot where the *Scorpion* sank. And his comments obviously meant that the Soviets had quickly decided that it was in their national security interests not to conceal their knowledge of the *Scorpion* loss, but instead to reach across a gaping chasm of fear, suspicion, and mistrust to inform their adversaries of the *Scorpion's* death. Was this a psychological warfare ploy to figuratively twist the dagger a bit? Could it have meant remorse over complicity in the *Scorpion's* destruction? Or was it a cool-headed decision to defuse the crisis before it escalated into open warfare? Alas, the admiral and his interlocutor changed subjects back to submarine safety in general and did not address the *Scorpion* incident again.[7]

BETWEEN 1947 AND 1991, the United States and the Soviet Union argued at the United Nations, fought proxy wars in Korea, Vietnam, and Afghanistan, and aided combatants on both sides in dozens of Third World brushfire conflicts. Military intelligence-gathering operations added to the violence and tensions. The Soviet shoot-down of the CIA's U-2 spy plane wrecked a peace summit in the summer of 1960. The 1962 Cuban Missile Crisis brought the world the closest it has ever been to nuclear war. Aggressive U.S. Air Force and Navy reconnaissance flights in the mid-1950s through the early 1960s routinely violated Soviet airspace and prompted the Russians to fire back, downing dozens of aircraft and killing scores of airmen.

But it was out in the great darkness of the ocean depths that the most dangerous military confrontation took place. For nearly five decades, submariners on both sides hunted and trailed, stalked and harassed their adversaries. They carried out espionage missions so secret that the two governments still deny their existence decades after the great standoff finally ended. They monitored naval exercises, spied on

missile launches, and shadowed the other side's ballistic missile submarine force. Carried out with no publicity and the highest security, this
long, gray conflict—not quite a shooting war, rather a peacetime rivalry
in near-combat conditions—was always just a hairsbreadth away from
torpedo action, missile launches, and death.

By the spring of 1968, military leaders in both the United States and
Soviet Union had reason to want to lash out at their main adversary. The
U.S. military believed that Soviet support of the North Vietnamese and
Viet Cong was prolonging the war in Vietnam. In North Korea, eighty-
one American sailors remained hostages after the hijacking of the *Pueblo*
(they would finally be freed after eleven months in captivity when the
U.S. military command in South Korea made a public apology for the
Pueblo, which it immediately repudiated after the sailors' release). Elsewhere across the globe, Admiral Sergei Gorshkov's fleet was on the move,
seeming to grow larger and more threatening each month. For the Soviets, the mirror image was just as frightening. The United States held
overall military superiority in strategic nuclear weapons and seapower.
The Pentagon maintained a network of military bases worldwide that
the Soviets saw as a threat encircling their nations. And the Soviet Navy's
leaders believed that the *K-129,* one of their strategic missile submarines,
and its crew of ninety-eight lay dead on the Pacific ocean floor because
of over-aggressive actions by the American submarine force. The death
of the *K-129,* Gorshkov and other Soviet admirals believed, was a major
escalation in violence against their submarine fleet. The U.S. Navy had
crossed a line.

And so the Soviets must have regarded the *Scorpion* as a proper target
as it entered the Atlantic on its way home on May 17, 1968. When the
Commander, Submarine Force, U.S. Atlantic Fleet sent top-secret messages diverting the *Scorpion* to the Canary Islands to spy on Soviet warships, the Soviets would have known the submarine was on its way. John
Walker had given them the most secret communication codes of the
U.S. submarine force.

One of the last unknowns remains the origin of any decision for the
Soviet submarine to attack the *Scorpion.* While there is substantial evidence that the attack occurred, no evidence has yet to appear that points

to specific Soviet orders to target and sink the *Scorpion*. At this juncture, the precursor events that led to its destruction remain hidden. It is possible that the confrontation between the *Scorpion* and the Soviet submarine may have begun as an isolated and local encounter that spun out of control as the two submarines shadowboxed their way across the eastern Atlantic. In any event, once the *Scorpion* lay on the Atlantic seabed, both sides reached an unprecedented agreement to bury the truth about the *K-129* and the *Scorpion* as deeply as their shattered hulls far beneath the ocean surface.

One critical aspect of the *Scorpion* incident is now beyond dispute. The U.S. Navy took drastic and immediate steps to hide the truth of the loss of the submarine. U.S. officials confiscated key documents, altered critical files and logs, and buried key information under a top secret classification to prevent the full truth from ever getting out. They ordered participants in the secret search and discovery of the *Scorpion* to forget what they knew and to never speak of what had happened. If what the Soviet admirals told Peter Huchthausen is correct, the Soviets did the same.

The men with stars on the uniform collars who presided over the *Scorpion* loss and engineered the cover-up believed they were acting properly. It is obvious that their deception aimed at a greater good—preventing the incident from flaring up into a general war at sea. Still, a number of questions still demand answers: Did the U.S. Navy by accident or design contribute to the sinking of the *K-129?* Or did the atmosphere of mutual mistrust between submariners on both sides lead the Soviets to make a deadly but inaccurate conclusion that, in turn, led to an act of violent revenge, submarine for submarine and blood for blood?

The men who moved to suppress the facts of the *K-129* and *Scorpion* were the same ones who organized, planned, and sent the "mission execute" orders for those submarines to carry out. They were the military commanders who encouraged and rewarded the over-aggressive tactics and clandestine submarine operations that continuously risked a combat incident erupting between two superpowers armed to the teeth with nuclear weapons. They were the national security experts who believed that the intelligence "take" always justified the danger in which the submarine crews were forced to operate.

In the end, the U.S. admirals consoled the grief-stricken families of the *Scorpion* crew while promoting a false cover story on how the submarine was lost. Their Soviet counterparts did even less for the families of the men of the *K-129*, merely announcing weeks after the loss that the submarine and its crew were gone. The men who were lost, the ninety-nine men of the *Scorpion* and the ninety-eight men of the *K-129*, gave their lives in the service of their country. In return, their military leaders robbed the families of a full accounting of how their men had perished.

The men of the *USS Scorpion* fell in combat.

Machinist's Mate 2nd Class Mark Christiansen, second from right, poses with four other shipmates during the *Scorpion*'s 1968 Mediterranean cruise. *Courtesy of Christiansen family*

EPILOGUE: ON ETERNAL PATROL

B Y EARLY 1969, THE *SCORPION* INCIDENT APPEARED OVER. THOSE who had suffered the loss of fathers, husbands, sons, lovers, or friends tried to pick up the pieces of their shattered lives and move on. Behind closed doors, however, navy officials were still very much engaged with the crisis.

The *Scorpion* cover-up did not end with the court of inquiry. Senior navy officials privy to the Soviet attack on the submarine continued their behind-scenes campaign to manipulate the evidence and bury the truth. This effort would continue for the next eighteen months as the service launched two investigations of the sinking—a 1969 exploration of the submarine wreckage by the deep-diving bathyscaph *Trieste II,* and an analysis of the *Scorpion* sinking by a panel of experts in submarine design.

So far, the effort by top navy officials to bury the truth of the *Scorpion* loss had been a success. The senior admirals in the Pentagon and Norfolk had concealed the secret pre–May 27 search and the actual discovery of the wreckage in early June. A trove of critical evidence that may have pointed toward Soviet involvement had been locked away. Elsewhere, naval intelligence had buried other evidence concealed from the court such as the Sosus tapes and messages showing the Soviet submarine attack on the *Scorpion.* The same group of navy insiders—Admirals Thomas H. Moorer, Ephraim P. Holmes, and Arnold F. Schade and a small number of their handpicked senior aides and naval intelligence officials—now took steps to add extra layers to the security cloak that concealed the facts of the *Scorpion* sinking.

Their first step was to obscure and diffuse the court of inquiry's conclusion as to the most likely cause of the submarine's loss. Acting on the best evidence available, the court had found that the "certain cause" of the *Scorpion* sinking remained unknown. However, the seven members identified what they called the "most probable scenario" for the loss after examining the acoustic evidence and studying thousands of photographs taken by the *Mizar*. They found that a "cataclysmic" initial event had occurred that led to uncontrollable flooding. Based on acoustic analysis by expert witnesses (who were not part of the cover-up), the court concluded that the initial acoustic event most likely stemmed from "an explosion of large charge weight external to the pressure hull" in the area of the control room. Given that U.S. naval intelligence officials had assured the court that there were no Soviet submarines or surface warships in the vicinity, the court logically assumed that the source of the fatal explosion had to have come from the *Scorpion* itself. So the panel had constructed a hypothesis of the sinking that involved an inadvertently armed Mark 37 torpedo that when expelled from the *Scorpion* became armed and homed in on the submarine, detonating and sinking it.[1]

Classified Secret or not, even this finding was too risky for navy leaders to support. In a formal endorsement review of the inquest on December 31, 1969, Atlantic Fleet Commander Admiral Holmes disavowed the court's conclusion. He cited in particular the strong disagreement by Atlantic Submarine Force Commander Vice Admiral Schade with that scenario. Schade himself had argued to the court that the most likely cause of the sinking was an "undetermined" flooding casualty that led the *Scorpion* to fall to crush depth, and that the piston-like collapse of the engine compartment into the hull had generated the initial massive acoustic signal that preceded the submarine's collapse by 91 seconds. The court had considered Schade's theory and then rejected it, concluding that, "while the sequence of events postulated by the Commander Submarine Force, U.S. Atlantic Fleet is considered possible, the weight of evidence leads to the conclusion that such a sequence of events was not probable." The court agreed with navy scientist John P. Craven that a torpedo "hot run" triggered the series of events that led to the sinking but disagreed with the scientist that the torpedo explosion had occurred inside the torpedo compartment.

In an endorsement memorandum that the navy initially classified top secret and did not declassify and release for twenty-five years, Holmes wrote of the court's external explosion scenario: "Although this explanation of the cause of the loss of the *USS Scorpion* is relatively well documented, it is not the only explanation of the manner in which the submarine could have been lost. . . . Therefore, the Commander-in-Chief U.S. Atlantic Fleet, while not an expert in many of the areas which were considered by the Court, is of the opinion that the conclusions of the Court concerning the most probable cause of the loss of the *USS Scorpion* although logical cannot be confirmed and therefore, the cause of the loss cannot be definitely ascertained." In effect, Holmes upheld Schade's argument that the sinking stemmed from some unknown mechanical malfunction and not a torpedo-warhead mishap. The Atlantic Fleet commander's action formally certified the official navy narrative that the *Scorpion* sinking would remain unidentified while also sparing the service from a vicious internal debate that would have ensued from placing blame for the loss on the navy's ordnance bureau.[2]

The whitewash of the court of inquiry report continued five months later when Chief of Naval Operations Admiral Moorer on May 28, 1969, added his own endorsement and submitted the court of inquiry report to Secretary of the Navy John Chafee for final review. Moorer likewise embraced Holmes's disavowal of the torpedo-warhead explosion, tersely writing: "With data available to date, the exact cause of the loss of *Scorpion* has not been determined."

On September 24, 1969, Chafee himself accepted the admirals' retreat on the cause of the *Scorpion* sinking. In his endorsement of the court's findings, Chafee wrote, "The basic correspondence and prior endorsements have served the purposes for which they were submitted directly to the Secretary of the Navy. They are forwarded for such disposition as may be appropriate." Chafee recommended that the navy provide a full copy of the court of inquiry file to the congressional joint committee on atomic energy for review in case the panel considered hearings into the *Scorpion* loss. Neither the JCAE nor the armed services committees ever held hearings on the loss of the *Scorpion*.[3]

The navy sponsored two subsequent studies on the *Scorpion* incident in 1969 and 1970 that drew the the service's formal position on the sinking even further away from the court of inquiry's central finding of a massive explosion external to the submarine hull.

In the summer of 1969, John Craven's Deep Submergence Systems Project brought the bathyscaph *Trieste II* to the eastern Atlantic and made nine dives on the *Scorpion* wreckage. While the manned submersible was able to take a number of additional photographs of the submarine wreckage, it failed in a second task, to send a primitive remote operating vehicle into the bow compartment to photograph the torpedo room. The *Trieste II* task unit report asserted that the operations compartment showed signs of failing from hydrostatic pressure rather than an "explosion of large charge weight" as the court had concluded. Holmes, the Atlantic Fleet Commander, subsequently endorsed the *Trieste II* report without changes, noting that "no new evidence has been developed which will materially affect the conclusions of the original and supplementary Courts of Inquiry. . . ." It remains unknown whether or not Craven's DSSP group was part of the cover-up.

Finally, in 1970, the Structural Analysis Group, a panel of submarine design experts, reviewed the court of inquiry and *Trieste II* reports and photographs. This panel backed even further away from the court's conclusion, saying that a hull implosion had been the most likely cause of the sinking. Despite many experts' assertions that a battery explosion aboard the submarine could not have generated sufficient force to rupture the hull or to create the acoustic pulse detected on hydrophones as far away as Newfoundland, the panel concluded that this scenario constituted "a plausible contributing cause" for the sinking. The group's report in June 1970—classified Secret and not substantially declassified until 1998—also dismissed the relevance of the acoustic evidence that had led searchers to the submarine wreckage in the first place. The panel concluded there was "no positive evidence" of either a large external explosion or an internal explosion. Again, there is insufficient evidence to conclude that the structural committee was part of the cover-up.[4]

The best evidence strongly indicates that the *Scorpion* cover-up was the product of a very small number of senior navy officials at key locations in the operational chain of command that ran from the Atlantic Submarine Force to the office of the chief of naval operations, aided by members of naval intelligence and other U.S. intelligence agencies. From the moment the *Scorpion* court of inquiry first convened on June 5, 1968 until the completion of the Structural Analysis Group report on June 29, 1970, navy officials charged with determining the cause of the *Scorpion* disaster operated under a significant number of false premises and assumptions that helped skew their findings away from any conclusion that would have identified a hostile Soviet act against the submarine. These false premises and assumptions included the navy account that the *Scorpion* disappearance was unknown to all until Monday, May 27, 1968 with the submarine's failure to reach port on schedule. The follow-up studies were silent on the top navy admirals' fears that the Soviets had been tracking the *Scorpion* in the eastern Atlantic for as many as five days before the sinking on May 22, 1968. Likewise, they contained no reference to Schade's own fears the week of May 20 that the submarine had failed to transmit a situation report on the Canary Islands surveillance. They all accepted COMSUBLANT's public—and inaccurate—assertion that the *Scorpion* was operating under radio silence and therefore no one was anticipating further messages after May 22. The follow-up probes did not cite the secret search that Schade requested from Holmes and that Moorer approved on May 23, just hours after the sinking and four days before the SubMiss alert. The *Trieste II* and structural analysis reports likewise said nothing of the *Compass Island*'s secret discovery of the *Scorpion* in early June and the subsequent four-month charade that the *Mizar* had carried out before announcing the discovery at the end of October. Finally, none of them included references to the Sosus tape that showed a submarine-vs.-submarine encounter that climaxed with a torpedo launch that struck and killed the *Scorpion*. In short, the two post-1968 analyses of the *Scorpion,* like the court of inquiry itself, never possessed the substantial body of facts that would have led to a far different conclusion than that the sinking was a mere accident.

In short, the navy by mid-1970 seemed to have buried the *USS Scorpion* for good.

During the next two years, many officials involved in the search and discovery of the *Scorpion* had already gone on to new tasks and assignments.

When Admiral Thomas H. Moorer finished his second tour as chief of naval operations in June 1970, President Richard Nixon appointed him Chairman of the Joint Chiefs of Staff. He would serve as the nation's most senior military commander for four years, retiring in 1974 after forty-one years of distinguished service. As a four-star admiral during the 1960s and early 1970s, Moorer had been the man in charge when a number of controversial events occurred: As Pacific Fleet commander during 1964–65, he oversaw all navy units in the Pacific when the United States entered major combat in Vietnam. While he served as Atlantic Fleet commander during 1965–67, Israel attacked the *USS Liberty*. Moorer was the navy's top officer when North Korea seized the *Pueblo* and when the *Scorpion* vanished at sea. As chairman of the joint chiefs of staff, Moorer presided over the entire U.S. military as the United States attempted to extricate itself from Vietnam.

Thomas Moorer died on February 5, 2004 at the U.S. Naval Hospital in Bethesda, Maryland, at age ninety-one. He was buried with honors in Arlington National Cemetery. In a long oral history for the U.S. Naval Institute released after his death, Moorer had much to say about his experiences during World War II, Korea, and Vietnam, and about the *Liberty* and *Pueblo*. About the *Scorpion,* he said nothing.

Vice Admiral Arnold F. Schade, on whose watch the *Scorpion* went down, finished his tour as Atlantic Submarine Force commander in December 1969. He then served as vice chairman of the U.S. delegation to the United Nations military staff committee before retiring in 1972. He and his wife lived in retirement in Port Charlotte, Florida, for thirty years before moving to San Diego in 2000. Schade died at the age of ninety-one on February 12, 2003. He was buried with military honors at Fort Rosecrans National Cemetery in San Diego.

Dr. John P. Craven left government service in 1970 after a decade and a half of research and development work involving nuclear submarines, the Polaris missile project, the Deep Submerged Systems Project, SeaLab, and the top-secret intelligence operations using submarines and deep-sea divers for underwater espionage. He served as a founder of the International Law of the Sea Institute and formed the Common Heritage Corporation in Hawaii to serve as a research platform for alternative energy sources. In 2006 at the age of eighty-two, he was still active in technology projects and civic affairs in Hawaii.

Captain Peter Huchthausen retired from the navy in 1990 after twenty-eight years as a surface warfare officer and naval attaché. Since then, he has written extensively on Cold War naval operations. Two of his books, *Hostile Waters* and *K-19: The Widowmaker,* became motion pictures. He currently lives in Normandy, France.

Many of the officers assigned to the *Scorpion* before 1968 went on to distinguished careers. Robert Pirie retired as a navy captain but later served in several senior civilian positions in the Pentagon. As assistant secretary of the navy in 1998, Pirie presided over the thirtieth anniversary ceremony commemorating the loss of the *Scorpion.* A number of *Scorpion* officers made flag rank, including Vice Admiral Yogi Kaufman, the submarine's second skipper, and Rear Admiral Ralph Ghormley, Kaufman's successor as *Scorpion* commander. Four other *Scorpion* officers became rear admirals: Robert R. Fountain, who served on the *Scorpion* in two tours; James Lewis, the *Scorpion's* commander during 1966–68; and Thomas Evans and William J. Holland, both of whom were junior officers on the submarine. Former *Scorpion* executive officers Kenneth Carr and Carlisle A. H. Trost would go the farthest. Carr went on to four-star rank and served as Atlantic Fleet commander before retiring. He later served as chairman of the Nuclear Regulatory Commission under President George H. W. Bush. Trost went even farther, earning four stars and serving as the Atlantic Fleet commander, and then chief of naval operations, in the mid-1980s.

Sometime after he became CNO on June 30, 1986, Trost—the *Scorpion's* second executive officer—visited the navy's operational intelligence center, and in a secure reading room, spent an afternoon poring over the still-classified *Scorpion* archive. "I came away with an inconclusive feeling of what had caused it," he said of the submarine's destruction years later. On one point, however, Trost's memory was clear: The navy records all showed that the crisis had begun only after the submarine failed to reach Norfolk on May 27, 1968.[5]

Former Yeoman Chief Jerry Hall, who served alongside Admiral Schade as flag yeoman during the *Scorpion* crisis, retired from *The Virginian-Pilot* in 1993. He and his wife, Dottie, bought a second home in Bonita Beach, Florida, where they still spend part of the year.

Many other key players in the *Scorpion* saga have since passed away. Vice Admiral Bernard Austin, who came out of retirement for the second time to serve as president of the *Scorpion* court of inquiry, died in 1975. Rear Admiral Charles D. Nace, the senior ranking member of the court, died in 2000. Admiral Bernard Clarey, the senior navy submariner in 1968 and holder of three Navy Crosses for heroism during World War II, passed away in 1996. Commander Norman Bessac, the *Scorpion*'s first commanding officer, died in 2005 and Vice Admiral Yogi Kaufman in 2006. Rear Admiral Walter N. "Buck" Dietzen, who commanded the *USS Scamp* and served as a key Pentagon aide during the *Scorpion* incident, died in 2005. Captain J. C. Bellah, the acting Submarine Squadron 6 commander on May 27, 1968, passed away in 2006 after an unprecedented fifty-two-year career with the Submarine Service—thirty years in uniform and another twenty-two as a senior civilian staffer at Atlantic Submarine Force Headquarters.

The navy did not entirely forget the *Scorpion* and its crew. At least three times since discovering the wreckage—in 1979, 1983, and 1986—the navy has surveyed the *Scorpion* for any evidence of radioactive contamination from its S5W reactor or the two Mark 45 nuclear torpedo warheads aboard. In all three instances, the navy states there has been "no significant impact" on the environment. Over the years, the *USS Scorpion* has also been added to a number of submarine memorials that honor the memory of the fifty-two submarines still on "eternal patrol" since World War II. There are also three memorials to the submarine itself: A flagpole and modest pedestal bearing the names of the ninety-nine crewmen has stood on the foot of Pier 22 in the Destroyer-Submarine Pier Complex for nearly four decades, outlasting the submarine pier itself, which the navy demolished and re-placed in 2000. A larger memorial to the *Scorpion* stands in Hunting-ton Park in nearby Newport News, Virginia. Dedicated in 1992, its polished granite face also records the final crew roster of the *Scorpion*. A third memorial to the *Scorpion*, along with the *USS Thresher*, is at the U.S. Naval Academy in Annapolis, Maryland, where nine of the twelve *Scorpion* officers had trained as midshipmen. A similar plaque honoring the *Scorpion* crew can be found at the National Submarine Memorial West located in Seal Beach, California. A modest display commemorating the *Scorpion* can also be found at the Submarine Force Museum in Groton, Connecticut, several miles upriver from where the submarine took shape on the Electric Boat Co. shipways during 1958–60. That memorial duly attributes the sinking to an un-specified mechanical malfunction. In 1997, the service changed the enlisted barracks at the naval facility in Guam to Scorpion Hall, in memory of the lost submarine.

The navy also honored the memory of a number of individual *Scorpion* crewmen. In 1970, officials dedicated Walter Bishop Hall at the Ballast Point Submarine Base in San Diego in memory of the *Scorpion's* chief of the boat. In 1976, the navy renamed the enlisted dining facility at its New London Submarine Base as Cross Hall, in honor of *Scorpion* crewman Steward First Class Joseph Cross. The navy also created the David Lloyd Award for excellence in leadership during the Submarine Officer Advance Course in honor of the *Scorpion's* executive officer, Lieutenant Commander David Lloyd.

Most of the families of the *Scorpion's* lost crew left Norfolk in the summer and fall of 1968 to try and put their lives back together. The family of Chief of the Boat Walter Bishop stayed behind at the family's comfortable home on Johnston's Road. Theresa Bishop never remarried but remained active in her church and community. She died at the age of seventy-three in 2000. Two of their three children went on to serve in the navy. Mary Etta Bishop Nolan, ten years old at the time of her fa-ther's death, became a nurse and an officer in the U.S. Navy Reserve. In 1998, she helped organize the thirtieth-anniversary commemoration of the *Scorpion*. John Bishop, nine years old in 1968, followed his father into the Navy and became a submariner, serving twenty years before his retirement in 1999.

Following the loss of the *Scorpion*, Bill G. Elrod continued his navy career, transferring from Norfolk to the Charleston-based submarine *USS Chivo* (SS 341), which had participated in the massive open-ocean search for the *Scorpion*. His twenty-five-year navy career also included tours aboard the *USS Cavalla* (SSN 684), *USS Billfish* (SSN 676), and *USS Dallas* (SSN 700). He retired as a senior chief sonarman in 1985 after back-to-back tours on the *Billfish* and *Dallas* as the chief of the boat, like his mentor and best friend, Walter Bishop.

In 1993, Bill Elrod learned that John Bishop had been selected for the rank of chief petty officer in the Submarine Service. Twenty-nine years earlier, when Elrod had formally qualified in submarines, Walter Bishop had taken one of his own Dolphin insignia and pinned it on the young sonarman's chest. Elrod went into his den and removed the older Bishop's Dolphin insignia from its place of honor on a wall plaque and mailed it to John Bishop's wife, Darlene. On the day of his promotion ceremony, Darlene Bishop pinned his father's own Submarine Service insignia on her husband's chest.

Bill Elrod and his wife Julianne raised five children including an adopted son they named Gordon in memory of their infant son who had died at birth in May 1968. Julianne Elrod passed away in 2005. Today, Bill is active in various Submarine Service veterans' organizations, and is proud to represent the *USS Scorpion* during formal memorial services to submariners lost in action.[6]

The U.S. Navy and Central Intelligence Agency never publicly confirmed the extent of their knowledge of the sinking of the Soviet submarine *K-129* and the two highly classified intelligence operations to exploit the submarine wreck involving the spy submarine *USS Halibut* and later the CIA-built *Glomar Explorer*. In October 1992 while visiting Russian leaders in Moscow, then-CIA Director Robert Gates presented President Boris Yeltsin with a videotape and a Soviet Navy flag. The videotape showed a formal burial at sea ceremony for the remains of six sailors from the *K-129* recovered from the submarine by the *Glomar Ex-*

plorer. The flag that Gates gave the Russian president had covered their coffins before they were remanded to the deep.[7]

John Walker is serving a life sentence for espionage in the federal "supermax" penitentiary in Florence, Colorado. His accomplices, Arthur Walker and Jerry Whitworth, likewise remain behind bars in federal prison. Michael Walker, who joined the spy ring after he entered the navy in 1982, was released from prison on parole in 2000.

Former KGB deputy *rezident* Oleg Kalugin, who helped run the Walker spy ring for many years and became the youngest general in the KGB as a result of the espionage operation's success, later turned against the Soviet system and in 1990 was stripped of his rank and pension on orders of then-Soviet Communist Party General Secretary Mikhail Gorbachev. He became a strong supporter of Boris Yeltsin and served a single term in the Russian Parliament following the collapse of the Soviet Union. In 1995, Kalugin accepted a teaching position at Catholic University in Washington, D.C., and became a U.S. citizen in 2003. He is a director of the International Spy Museum in Washington, D.C.

Forty years is a very long time in military history. By 2006, the officers and enlisted men, civilian scientists and family members alike who had a connection with the *USS Scorpion* had long since left the stage—with one exception. As this book went to press, there still was one member of the U.S. military on active duty who could claim to have served on the nuclear attack submarine.

In the summer of 1965, Bob Magnus was a young Navy Reserve seaman apprentice from Brooklyn, who was working toward qualification as an electronics technician. Magnus reported to Submarine Squadron 6 in Norfolk for his mandatory two-week summer training and received orders to join a repair and working party onboard the *Scorpion* moored alongside Pier 22. While not formally assigned to the submarine's crew roster, Magnus recalled his brief but intensive duty on the submarine with pride and affection. "I distinctly remember laying and bracketing in a wrist-thick cable from a large . . . structure in the top of the sail superstructure down into the [Control Room] area where one or two other ETs were doing the connections," Magnus recalled.

One day, when no one was looking, as he toiled in the enclosed space in the submarine's sail, Magnus dabbed heavy waterproof grease on a fingertip and reached out to write on the cable the name of his high school sweetheart, Rose.

In the end, Magnus became neither an electronics technician nor a qualified submariner nor even a sailor. His military career took a different turn. Winning an NROTC scholarship, in his junior year at the University of Virginia, he chose a career in the marines. In 2006, General Robert Magnus was serving as assistant commandant of the U.S. Marine Corps, his association with the *USS Scorpion* unrecorded in his official marine biography.

A personal endnote: Over the years as I researched and studied the fate of the *USS Scorpion,* I was repeatedly surprised to see how many elements of the story were hidden in plain sight. This was one of them: Bob Magnus was my best friend throughout four years of college and roommate for the last two of them. We have been in close contact for more than forty years, yet I never learned of his involvement with the *USS Scorpion* until a chance conversation over dinner with Bob and his wife, Rose, in the twenty-first year of my research into the fascinating life and tragic death of this American nuclear submarine.[8]

ACKNOWLEDGMENTS

WHEN YOU SPEND NEARLY A QUARTER OF A CENTURY RESEARCHING a particular story, the number of people deserving thanks for helping you along the way can practically fill a manuscript in itself. Nevertheless, I want to salute those in the U.S. Navy, in other federal government agencies, and in the profession of journalism and other colleagues and friends without whose help this book would never have come to pass.

First and foremost, I want to thank my wife, Karen Conrad, and our daughters, Elaine and Andrea, for their loving support during my long stint of researching and writing about the *USS Scorpion*.

I also want to express my deepest gratitude to Executive Editor Lara Heimert, Managing Editor Robert Kimzey, Associate Publisher John Sherer, and the other people at Basic Books for their willingness to support and shepherd this lifelong project into reality. My agent, Deborah Grosvenor, not only made that possible, but was invaluable in transforming a reporter's jumbled notes into a marketable book.

I also want to thank my colleagues at *The Ledger-Star* in Norfolk, Virginia, during 1982–85 who supported my first efforts to research the *USS Scorpion,* particularly the late Perry Morgan, publisher, and my editor and lifelong friend, George J. Hebert. In addition, Military Reporter Jack Dorsey not only aided me in my on-the-job training as a military writer but also has been a constant source of help as I wrestled with the complexities of the story. Chief Librarian Ann Johnson was invaluable in helping me launch the project in 1983, and just as helpful in tracking down a number of last-minute details twenty-three years later. In Seattle, where I continued my *Scorpion* research during a fifteen-year stint from 1985 to 2000, I owe a debt of gratitude to my two publishers during that time, Virg Fassio and the late J. D. Alexander. Both men gave me material support and time to chase a story that in the mid-1990s was already decades old and had occurred nearly 5,000 miles from the shores of Puget Sound. National Editor Robert Schenet was a thorough professional as he refined and improved my reporting. In Panama City, Florida, Publisher Karen Hanes, Executive Editor Phil Lucas, and Managing Editor Mike Cazalas of *The News Herald* were strongly supportive of this project and graciously allowed me to disappear from the newsroom for seven months to write the book.

I owe particular thanks and appreciation to those family members who lost loved ones on the *Scorpion* and who opened their family archives to me years later despite the risk that this would reopen their old wounds. In particular I want to thank the families of Chief of the Boat Walter Bishop, Machinist Mate Second Class Mark Christiansen, Torpedoman Third Class Robert Violetti, and Interior Communications Electrician Third Class Vernon Mark Foli for their help and support.

Former officers and crewmen of the *Scorpion* were the key to my effort in bringing the submarine "back to life" in words, and I owe much to them for their patience and help. In particular, I want to thank Bill G. Elrod for his assistance in what was for him often a difficult effort to relive a particularly traumatic period of his navy career and life. Just as much, I want to thank scores of former navy sailors, aviators, and submariners who stepped forward over the years to share their personal experiences in the *Scorpion* search and investigation. Each of them provided a piece of the mosaic and without their inputs much of this book could not have been written.

Despite the U.S. Navy's unyielding stance that "the certain cause of the loss of the *USS Scorpion* cannot be ascertained by any evidence now available," many navy people of all ranks and assignments during 1983–2006 proved willing to go the extra mile to help me in my research. In particular, retired Captain Peter Huchthausen has been a source of knowledge about the Soviet Navy during the Cold War. Over the years, navy scientist John P. Craven consented to numerous interviews to explain and provide context for newly declassified information about the *Scorpion*.

Other navy people who provided help when I needed it included public affairs officers in Norfolk, at navy headquarters at the Pentagon, and at the Naval Sea Systems Command. The five men who held the job as chief of naval information during the two decades I worked on the story were helpful in many ways to open doors that I thought were permanently shut: Rear Admirals Jimmie Finkelstein, Brent Baker, Kendall Pease, Tom Jurkowsky, and Steve Pietropaoli. I also want to thank Rear Admiral Craig Quigley for his help while at CHINFO. Admiral Frank Bowman at the Naval Reactors Branch in 1997 opened a critical door for me when he approved my tour aboard the decommissioned *USS Sculpin* (SSN 590) at Puget Sound Naval Shipyard; and a special thanks to retired Captain Mark van Dyke, who helped steer me through the halls of U.S. naval intelligence.

A rich and diverse cast of other journalists and professionals added their talents on request. This includes attorney Robert C. Burns of the law firm Cohn and Marks in Washington, D.C. in 1984, who shepherded the civil lawsuit filed on behalf of Landmark Communications that prompted the navy to release the first meaningful portion of the *Scorpion* court of inquiry transcripts and other documents. Demolishing the stereotype of journalists as ruthless rivals, reporters Chris Drew and Sherry Sontag, the co-authors of *Blind Man's Bluff,* were helpful in many ways despite the fact that my *Scorpion* reporting arrived at a different conclusion than their own. I also wish to thank Stephen Johnson of *The Houston Chronicle* for his effort in *Silent Steel* to examine the "screen door" theory of the *Scorpion's* loss. Kenneth Sewell, author of the nonfiction novel *Red Star Rogue,* was an inspiration for me to do my best on this book. Tobias Naegele, first as editor of *Navy Times* and later as executive editor of the *Army Times* Publishing Co., has been a longtime supporter of my *Scorpion* research. Chris Cavas at *Army Times* was exceptionally generous in sharing hard-to-find images of the navy in the 1960s from his private photo archive.

Research into some of the military aspects of the *Scorpion* story was significantly helped by advances in computer technology, the Internet, and data-storage programs. Several commercial websites and software producers provided computational assistance and archival data retrieval that otherwise would have been extraordinarily difficult, if not impossible. I owe several of these organizations my appreciation for their help. In particular, the firm Jeppesen Marine (formerly Nobeltec) provides a comprehensive nautical eChart Planner that enabled me to rapidly create a detailed and accurate chart description of the U.S. Navy's search for the *Scorpion* (http://www.nobeltec.com). The software easily converted position reports that each navy ship compiles in its daily quartermaster deck logs into accurate course tracks on an electronic chart of the Atlantic and Mediterranean. Nobeltec devised this excellent software program to assist boaters to create sailing routes, but it is also an excellent tool for researchers attempting to visualize the complicated movements of dozens of ships over an extended period of time. My personal thanks to Ms. Devon Mandaleris of the W. T. Brownley Company in Norfolk, Virginia, who alerted me to the Nobeltec eChart Planner software program. A second powerful research tool comes from the Internet-based travel company, Indo.com, which serves as a reference website for people planning to visit the Republic of Indonesia and the island of Bali. For reasons I can only describe as serendipitous, the folks at Indo.com provide a user-friendly web tool called "How Far Is It" (http://www.indo.com/distance) that allows you to calculate the distance between any two locations on earth by latitude-longitude inputs. While the Indo.com website designers intended this to be a source of fun for tourists from the Midwest to calculate how far the beaches of Bali are from downtown Peoria, the tool also enabled me to rapidly calculate the nautical mileage and bearing azimuths for key waypoints and ship locations as the navy carried out the *Scorpion* search, making a task almost too complex to undertake a simple and enjoyable job. Finally, if you ever need to know whether it was raining or snowing on a specific day nearly forty years ago, a number of online commercial weather database archives can provide you the details for a reasonable fee. Thanks to The Weather Source (www.weather-source.com), I was able to determine this obscure but relevant information while writing the narrative of the *Scorpion*'s 1968 deployment.

Finally, while the credit for this book belongs in great part to all of the men and women who have helped me over the years, responsibility for its accuracy is mine alone.

ED OFFLEY
Panama City Beach, Florida, 2007

GLOSSARY

1MC   Internal communication speaker system on U.S. Navy ships and submarines used to make announcements to the entire crew.

"A" School   A formal navy school where a sailor out of basic training receives special instruction for his rate, such as machinist's mate or engineman.

AFTAC   An abbreviation for *Air Force Technical Applications Center,* the scientific intelligence unit that employed ground- and sea-based acoustic sensors, specially configured aircraft, and orbiting satellites to track and locate nuclear explosions anywhere in the world.

AG   U.S. Navy designator for an auxiliary ship (AGER/AGOR: environmental research/oceanographic research).

AO   U.S. Navy designator for a fleet oiler.

APA   U.S. Navy designator for a troop transport ship.

ARS   U.S. Navy designator for a salvage ship.

ASR   U.S. Navy designator for a submarine rescue ship.

ASW   An abbreviation for *Anti-Submarine Warfare.*

ASWEX   An abbreviation for *Anti-Submarine Warfare Exercise.*

blade count   Term used by navy sonar operators to identify a ship or submarine by counting the number of propeller blades by their sound.

boomer   Navy nickname for a ballistic missile submarine.

BQR–2   Sonar system used on the *Skipjack*-class submarines.

Brandywine   Classified radio call-sign for the *USS Scorpion* in 1968.

Chief of the Boat Senior chief petty officer on a submarine.

CIC An abbreviation for *Combat Information Center* (later Combat Direction Center), the compartment on a Navy warship where operational specialists control the ship's information-gathering sensors and weapons fire-control equipment.

CINCLANTFLT An abbreviation for *Commander-in-Chief, U.S. Atlantic Fleet.*

CINCPAC An abbreviation for *Commander-in-Chief Pacific*. Headquartered at Camp H. M. Smith in Hawaii, it was a major multi-service military command that controlled the U.S. Pacific Fleet, Pacific Air Forces, U.S. Army Pacific, and Marine Forces Pacific during the Cold War. It was also the superior headquarters for U.S. military forces in South Korea and Vietnam at the time.

CINCUSNAVEUR An abbreviation for *Commander-in-Chief, U.S. Navy Europe.*

cipher cryptography A form of safeguarding classified messages by using special communications encryption devices to substitute each letter or numeral with a randomly generated replacement.

COMASWFORLANT An abbreviation for *Commander, Anti-Submarine Forces, Atlantic Fleet*, a subordinate command under Atlantic Fleet control.

COMNAVSHIPYD NORVA An abbreviation for *Commander, Norfolk Naval Shipyard.*

COMSUBLANT An abbreviation for *Commander, Atlantic Submarine Force*, a subordinate command under Atlantic Fleet Control. In 1968, the command included 30,256 officers and enlisted men, 84 attack submarines (including 21 nuclear-powered boats), 35 of the navy's 41 Polaris missile submarines, and a fleet of 19 surface support ships.

control room Compartment in a submarine where the commanding officer or officer of the deck manages the operation of the ship while underway. The submarine's periscopes, ballast control panel, control plane stations, and fire-control systems are all located here.

CORTRON   Destroyer Escort Squadron.

court of inquiry   An administrative, fact-finding panel convened to investigate serious incidents. It is not a court in the usual sense but rather a formal investigative board. The court of inquiry has a long history in the U.S. military, dating to the 1786 Articles of War.

Crazy Ivan   U.S. submariners' term for a Soviet submarine tactic of making sudden, radical turning movements to force a trailing American submarine to break off surveillance because of the increased threat of a collision.

CVA/CVAN   U.S. navy designator for an attack aircraft carrier.

CVS   U.S. Navy designator for an anti-submarine warfare aircraft carrier.

damage assessment   A formal investigation into unauthorized release of classified information with the goal of identifying compromises in secure communications and operations as a result of the security breakdown.

DE   U.S. Navy designator for a destroyer escort.

DD   U.S. Navy designator for a destroyer.

DDG   U.S. Navy designator for a guided missile destroyer.

dead drop   An espionage tool where a spy and his handler exchange material or information without ever meeting face to face. The procedure usually involves using preselected locations to cache the goods for the other to retrieve and a complex choreography of planting signals to inform the other side that the attempted exchange is underway.

deck log   Contemporaneous record of a ship's operating conditions, course, speed, location, and other information kept on a minute-by-minute basis, usually by the duty quartermaster of the watch.

Deep Submergence Systems Project (DSSP)   A special navy office established in the mid-1960s to spearhead research and development into manned and unmanned submersibles capable of operating at great depths in the ocean. The DSSP later became involved in several top-secret intelligence operations against the Soviet military.

DESRON   An abbreviation for *Destroyer Squadron.*

DESSUB Pier   Piers at the Norfolk Naval Station used by destroyers and submarines.

DLG   U.S. Navy designator for a guided missile frigate.

Fleet Broadcast System   A worldwide U.S. Navy communications network using high-frequency or low-frequency radio signals to send messages to aircraft, ships, and submarines at sea. For security, the messages were encrypted to prevent unauthorized disclosure.

focused-operations search   Technical search for the *USS Scorpion* during June 10 to October 30, 1968, employing a fleet of survey ships and other support vessels.

FOIA   An abbreviation for the *Freedom of Information Act*, a federal law first enacted in 1966 that provides regulations and procedures for the release of government information to the public, including the review of classified information for possible declassification and release.

HBX–3   Explosive material used in the Mark 37 torpedo warhead.

hot run   Unofficial term for a torpedo that accidentally activates prior to receiving a legitimate launching order due to operator error or malfunction.

HY–80   A high-strength steel used for the pressure hull plating on the *USS Scorpion* and other submarines during the 1960s.

Incidents at Sea Agreement   A formal agreement between the U.S. and Soviet navies to minimize confrontations at sea involving naval aircraft and warships. The 1972 accord does not apply to submarine operations.

Joint Reconnaissance Center   Pentagon office that supervised and scheduled top-secret reconnaissance missions involving U.S. military units, including submarines.

KGB (*Komitet Gosudarstvennoy Bezopasnosti*)   Committee for State Security, a Soviet-era intelligence organization that held both domestic and foreign intelligence-gathering responsibilities for the Kremlin.

keylist   A daily cipher code inserted into an encrypted transmitter or receiver to add an additional layer of protection to the message traffic.

KLB–47   Tape-fed secure naval transmitter/receiver first operational in the late 1940s.

KW–7 "Orestes"   Encrypted secure send/receive teletypewriter used by the U.S. Navy, other American military services, and U.S. allies during the 1960s.

KWR–37 "Jason"   Encrypted naval communications receiver unit used during the 1960s.

Lofargram   An abbreviation for *Low Frequency and Ranging Gram*, a graphic printout of a SOSUS or sonobuoy sound signal of a surface ship or submarine.

LORAN   An abbreviation for *Long Range Navigation*, a navigation system using low-frequency radio transmitters that employ the time interval between radio signals received from three or more stations to determine the position of a ship or aircraft.

LST   U.S. Navy designator for a tank landing ship.

maneuvering room   Engineering control station on a submarine located in the engine room. The engineering officer of the watch, reactor control operator, electric plant operator, and throttleman of the watch work here.

message header   U.S. Navy messages are identified by a date-time group (Greenwich Mean Time) at which the message is cleared for transmission. Example: *USS Scorpion* message 212354Z May 68 was prepared for sending at 23:54 hours "Z," or GMT, on May 21, 1968. The actual time of transmission lagged by a number of hours, according to the urgency of the message.

movement order   A formal and detailed set of instructions for a ship or submarine commander setting out details of the timing, course, speed, and (in case of submarines) depth at which the vessel will operate during a prescribed period of time.

NATO   An abbreviation for *North Atlantic Treaty Organization*.

NavFac   An abbreviation for *Naval Facility*, the informal title of shore-based information processing stations in the Sosus system.

Northern run missions   See **Special Navy Control Program**.

NRL   An abbreviation for *Naval Research Laboratory.*

NSA   An abbreviation for *National Security Agency,* the U.S. intelligence agency responsible for intercepting foreign communications and electronic intelligence, and for developing and safeguarding U.S. encrypted communications.

ONR   An abbreviation for *Office of Naval Research.*

OPCON   A contraction of *operational control,* the duty office of a naval shore command.

Operation Icthyic   A series of planned U.S. Navy electronic reconnaissance missions in 1968 along the Soviet Pacific coastline and eastern littorals of North Korea and China that were canceled after the North Korean seizure of the *USS Pueblo* (AGER 2).

Point Oscar   A latitude-longitude spot in the eastern Atlantic for the estimated location of the sixth of fifteen acoustic signals generated by the sinking of the *USS Scorpion.*

PWR   An abbreviation for *Pressurized Water Reactor,* a standard propulsion reactor design used by the navy since 1955. Its main characteristic is that it uses highly pressurized water in the primary coolant that passes in sealed pipes through the reactor fuel core. The primary coolant transfers heat from the fission reaction to the propulsion system without contaminating it with radiation. Other naval reactors have used liquid sodium metal as the primary coolant.

Radioman   A formal navy rate for personnel trained to operate various naval communications systems including voice and data transmissions.

RAV   Abbreviation for *restricted availability,* a limited repair or overhaul period for a navy ship or submarine in between operational missions.

Rezident   Senior KGB official in a Soviet foreign embassy.

ROE   Abbreviation for *rules of engagement,* formal instructions to military commanders setting conditions of how they can act in a crisis or combat.

S5W   Designator for the nuclear propulsion reactor used on the *USS Scorpion* and other submarines. It signifies the fifth naval submarine reactor design by the Westinghouse Corp.

SACLANT An abbreviation for *Supreme Allied Commander, Atlantic,* a major NATO command headquartered in Norfolk that controlled all alliance warships in the Atlantic Ocean, held by the four-star admiral who also had the responsibilities as commander of the multi-service Atlantic Command, and the navy's Atlantic Fleet.

SASS An abbreviation for *Sonar Array Sounding System,* a highly sophisticated active sonar system installed on several U.S. Navy ships in the late 1960s. Using several dozen individual sonar transducers mounted in a massive dome on the bow of a ship, it translated the sound echoes returning from the seabed far below into a topographic chart depicting the underwater landscape.

SCI An abbreviation for *Special Compartmented Information,* a form of security restriction that limits access to specific classified information to a hand-picked roster of personnel. A dedicated facility for handling and storing such material is a SCIF, for *Special Compartmented Information Facility.*

shaft horsepower A measure of the actual mechanical energy per unit time delivered to a turning shaft. One shaft horsepower = 1 electric horsepower = 550 ft.-lb./second.

SINS An abbreviation for *Ship's Inertial Navigation System,* a navigational system used from the 1950s through the mid-1970s in U.S. missile submarines. It consisted of a self-contained array of accelerometers, gyroscopes, electronic servo units, and early computers that made a moving plot of the submarine's location by calculating its movement through the water from a known latitude-longitude starting point.

Sixth Fleet One of four numbered U.S. Navy fleets during the 1960s; its operational area was the Mediterranean Sea.

Skipjack A class of six nuclear attack submarines commissioned during 1959–61 that first combined the *Albacore*-design hull and the Westinghouse S5W nuclear reactor.

sonar An abbreviation for *sound navigation and ranging,* any one of a number of systems that use underwater acoustics to help navigate or locate objects moving submerged or on the surface. "Passive" sonar systems listen without transmitting impulses to illuminate the target, while "active" sonar generates a sound whose reflection off the target can then be analyzed for its range and bearing.

sonobuoy   Device dropped from an anti-submarine patrol plane to track submerged submarines. It includes an active and/or passive sonar sensor, power supply, and transmitter to send the signal back to the aircraft overhead.

Sosus   An abbreviation for *Sound Surveillance System*, the top-secret array of underwater hydrophones and signal processing stations used to detect and track submarines by their acoustic signals. Elements of the system were also known as Caesar and Colossus.

Special Intelligence   A highly classified category of intelligence related to electronic interception of foreign military communications. The U.S. military and intelligence agencies developed a separate network of communications centers, transmission facilities, and encryption gear dedicated to handling this form of classified information, with emphasis on physical isolation of the equipment and information from unauthorized personnel.

Special Navy Control Program   A top-secret intelligence program using nuclear submarines to conduct inshore reconnaissance on Soviet Navy operations and missile tests, informally known as Northern run missions.

Spintcomm   An abbreviation for *Special Intelligence Communications*, dedicated military communications centers that handled only Special Intelligence.

spooks   Navy nickname for intelligence technicians who were aboard submarines for Northern run and other reconnaissance operations.

sprint and drift   An undersea tactic in which a submarine dashes at high speeds (during which time it loses much or all of its ability to listen in to potential enemies using passive sonar), followed by a period of ultra-quiet operation at slow speeds in order to reacquire the target.

SS   Designator for diesel-electric-powered attack submarine.

SSB   Designator for diesel-electric-powered ballistic missile submarine (Soviet).

SSBN   Designator for nuclear-powered ballistic missile submarine.

SSGN   Designator for nuclear-powered cruise missile submarine.

SSN   Designator for nuclear-powered attack submarine.

SUBDIV   An abbreviation for *submarine division,* two or more of which are assigned to each submarine squadron with four to eight submarines and/or support ships assigned.

SUBFLOT   An abbreviation for *submarine flotilla,* administrative headquarters managing two or more submarine squadrons.

SubMiss   Contraction of *Missing Submarine.* The formal designation of the alert in event of a submarine's failure to contact headquarters or arrive at a designated time.

SUBRON   An abbreviation for *submarine squadron.*

SUBSAFE   An abbreviation for *Submarine Safety Improvement Program,* a multi-million-dollar program to improve various equipment components on U.S. Navy submarines in the wake of the 1963 sinking of the *USS Thresher.*

SUPESALV   An abbreviation for the *Supervisor of Salvage,* a Navy official in charge of all salvage and diving operations in the service.

Type XXI   Advanced World War II German U-boat design that could operate submerged for significantly longer periods of time than other contemporary submarines. Its design innovations included an effective snorkel that would deliver air to the diesel engines while the submarine ran submerged at periscope depth, a more efficient hull design, and diesel engines that could recycle exhaust air into the combustion cycle.

Winterwind   Code word for a U.S. Navy intelligence operation to secretly retrieve Soviet missile nosecone fragments from the ocean floor by the spy submarine *USS Halibut* to analyze their sophistication and design.

USS SCORPION SEARCH ROSTER

The U.S. Navy never compiled an authoritative roster of ships and submarines that took part in the search for the *USS Scorpion*. Navy officials have also never officially confirmed that the Atlantic Submarine Force orchestrated a classified search for the submarine during the ten-day period between the time it left the Mediterranean and its scheduled arrival in Norfolk on Monday, May 27, 1968. The following roster of search participants compiled by the author is based on declassified navy messages, situation reports, and other documents as well as interviews with dozens of officers and enlisted men involved in the search. Ships that participated in both the classified and overt search are listed in both categories.

CLASSIFIED PRE–MAY 27 SEARCH

Confirmed participants (participation confirmed by former crewmen and/or navy documents)

USS Ray (SSN 653)
USS Josephus Daniels (DLG 27)
USS Compass Island (AG 153)

Likely participants (evidence exists confirming the ship was underway in the Atlantic during May 17–27, 1968 and likely would have been ordered to take part in the secret search)

USS Shark (SSN 591)
USS Simon Bolivar (SSBN 641)
USS Haddo (SSN 604)
USS John King (DDG 3)
USS Charles F. Adams (DDG 2)*
USS Semmes (DDG 18)*
USS Tattnall (DDG 19)*
USNS Norwalk (T AK 279)*
USS Hyades (AF 28)*
USS Monrovia (APA 31)*
USS Shasta (AE 33)*
USS Sagacity (MSO 469)*
USS Skill (MSO 471)*
USS Walworth County (LST 1164)*

OPEN-OCEAN *SCORPION* SEARCH:
MAY 27–JUNE 5

COMCRUDESLANT Ships

Norfolk, Virginia
USS Beale (DD 471)
USS Douglas H. Fox (DD 779)
USS Eugene A. Greene (DD 711)
USS John King (DDG 3)
USS Josephus Daniels (DLG 27)
USS New (DD 818)
USS Robert A. Owens (DD 827)
USS Robert L. Wilson (DD 847)
USS William M. Wood (DD 715)

Charleston, South Carolina
USS Soley (DD 707)

Mayport, Florida
USS Allen M. Sumner (DD 692)
USS Forrest Royal (DD 872)
USS Sarsfield (DD 837)
USS William H. Standley (DLG 32)

Newport, Rhode Island
USS Hugh Purvis (DD 709)
USS Julius A. Furer (DEG 6)
USS Koelsch (DE 1049)
USS Talbot (DEG 4)

Philadelphia
USS Purdy (DD 734)

COMSUBLANT Submarines and Ships

Norfolk, Virginia
USS Lapon (SSN 661)
USS Skipjack (SSN 637)
USS Argonaut (SS 475)
USS Cubera (SS 347)
USS Requin (SS 481)
USS Sea Leopard (SS 483)

New London, Connecticut
USS Gato (SSN 615)
USS Greenling (SSN 614)
USS Pargo (SSN 650)
USS Skate (SSN 578)
USS Hoist (ARS 40)
USS Skylark (ASR 20)
USS Sunbird (ASR 15)

Brooklyn, New York
USS Compass Island (EAG 153)

Charleston, South Carolina
USS Nathanael Greene (SSBN 636)
USS Simon Bolivar (SSBN 641)
USS Chivo (SS 341)
USS Sennet (SS 408)
USS Petrel (ASR 14)
USS Ozark (MCS 2)

Rota, Spain
USS Kittiwake (ASR 13)
USS Preserver (ARS 8)

Amphibious/Other (Homeports Unknown)

USS Sagacity (MSO 469)*
USS Skill (MSO 471)*
USS Suffolk County (LST 1173)
USS Walworth County (LST 1164)*

Service/Support (Homeports Unknown)

USS Hyades (AF 28)*
USS Monrovia (APA 31)*
USS Shasta (AE 33)*
USS Waccamaw (AO 109)

Military Sea Transportation Service (Homeports Unknown)

USNS Mizar (T AGOR 11)
USNS Norwalk (T AK 279)*
USNS Bowditch (T AGS 21)

French Navy

FNS Requin

FOCUSED OPERATIONS SEARCH: JUNE 7 TO OCT. 31

USNS Mizar (T AGOR 11)

USNS Bowditch (T AGS 21)

USS Compass Island (EAG 153)

USS Petrel (ASR 14)

USS Ozark (MCS 2)**

USS Douglas H. Fox (DD 779)

USS Sturgeon (SSN 637)***

---

* Ships in routine transit across the Atlantic at the time of *Scorpion* search that were directed to watch for the *Scorpion* or signs of debris along their track.

** Joined later phase of *Scorpion* search on June 13, 1968 as flagship of Special Search Unit.

*** Joined search on June 7, 1968, replacing *USS Lapon.*

Sources: Atlantic Submarine Force Command Histories, 1967 and 1968; Report of Search Operations for *USS Scorpion* (SSN 589) by Commander Task Unit 42.2.1 (CO Submarine Flotilla 6, June 28, 1968; various Navy messages and *Scorpion* search situation reports May 27–June 25, 1968.

USS SCORPION
CHRONOLOGY OF EVENTS
MAY 14 TO OCTOBER 30, 1968

All times are in Greenwich Mean Time, identified as "Zulu," or "Z" (four hours ahead of Eastern Daylight Time) unless stated otherwise.

Boldface type indicates key events and incidents that were suppressed by the navy and never shown to the court of inquiry.

THURSDAY, MAY 14

2037Z

Submarine Squadron 6 message announces *USS Scorpion* (SSN 589) departing the Mediterranean with a time of arrival in Norfolk at 1330Z (9:30 A.M.) on Friday, May 24. ETA subsequently moved back to 1900Z (3 P.M.) on May 24.

FRIDAY, MAY 15

USS Haddo **(SSN 604) reportedly harassing a Soviet submarine in the western Mediterranean near the Straits of Gibraltar. The Soviet submarine enters the Atlantic.**

THURSDAY, MAY 16

1947Z

COMSUBLANT top secret message diverts *Scorpion* from its homeward track to investigate Soviet navy warships operating southwest of the Canary Islands.

FRIDAY, MAY 17

0001Z

Departing the Mediterranean, the *USS Scorpion* formally "chops" from Sixth Fleet control to COMSUBLANT control.

0130Z

Scorpion arrives at entrance to Rota naval base and transfers two crewmen and mail to a navy tug, then heads out into the Atlantic.

SATURDAY, MAY 18

USS *Josephus Daniels* (DLG 27) in Norfolk is scrambled to sea to search for the *Scorpion*.

Sometime before May 22 senior U.S. Navy admirals become concerned about hostile Soviet intent toward the *Scorpion*.

Sometime during May 18–22 *Scorpion* radios COMSUBLANT that it is being followed by a Soviet submarine and is unable to elude the shadower.

SUNDAY, MAY 19

U.S. Navy curtails ongoing patrol aircraft surveillance of Soviet Navy ships in Canary Islands area, resuming flights on May 21.

MONDAY, MAY 20

Vice Admiral Arnold F. Schade, Atlantic Submarine Force commander, is at sea off the Virginia Capes on the submarine *USS Ray* (SSN 653).

TUESDAY, MAY 21

212354Z *Scorpion* message gives position report of 31:19 North 27:37 West with an arrival time in Norfolk of 1700Z on Monday, May 27.

WEDNESDAY, MAY 22

1844Z

Scorpion explodes and sinks 400 miles southwest of the Azores.

Within hours, U.S. naval intelligence agents raid Sosus facilities worldwide to seize all evidence of *Scorpion* sinking.

THURSDAY, MAY 23

Senior U.S. Navy admirals become more concerned over status of *Scorpion* when it fails to reply to messages. Schade onboard the *Ray* requests a classified search of the Atlantic for the submarine involving navy ships, submarines, and aircraft.

0414Z (12:14 A.M. EDT)

First of three routine messages to *Scorpion* sent during May 23–25 requesting replies (but not necessarily while operating at sea) is transmitted over Fleet Broadcast System.

FRIDAY, MAY 24

1330Z (9:30 A.M. EDT)

USS Compass Island (AG 153) arrives in Brooklyn from operations in the western Caribbean.

1600Z (12 noon EDT)

Submarine Squadron 6 officials tell *Scorpion* family members the submarine's arrival has been delayed from May 23 until Monday, May 27 at 1 P.M.

2230Z (6:30 P.M. EDT)

Compass Island ordered underway as part of secret *Scorpion* search. CNO Admiral Thomas H. Moorer believes that *Scorpion* has sunk with all hands.

MONDAY, MAY 27

1130Z (7:30 A.M. EDT)

Admiral Schade and three aides depart Norfolk to embark on the Groton-based submarine *USS Pargo* (SSN 650).

1352Z (9:52 A.M. EDT)

Pargo underway from New London with Vice Admiral Schade.

1400Z (10 A.M. EDT)

Families of *Scorpion* crew begin gathering at Pier 22 at Norfolk Naval Station.

1640Z (12:40 P.M. EDT)

Submarine Squadron 6 contacts COMSUBLANT headquarters asking if the *Scorpion* has broken radio silence.

1700Z (1 P.M. EDT)

Scorpion's scheduled arrival time at Pier 22.

1915Z (3:15 P.M. EDT)

COMSUBLANT headquarters transmits SubMiss alert for *Scorpion*, ordering all submarines under its control to surface and radio in.

2015Z (4:15 P.M. EDT)

Pargo copies SubMiss message from COMSUBLANT headquarters.

2200Z May 68 (6 P.M. EDT)

WTAR broadcasts CBS bulletin that the *Scorpion* is overdue.

TUESDAY, MAY 28

Open-ocean search for *Scorpion* is underway in earnest with several dozen ships and submarines at sea. Search force will grow over the next three days to 55 surface ships and submarines and over three dozen land-based patrol aircraft.

WEDNESDAY, MAY 29

0715Z (3:15 A.M. EDT)

Rear Admiral Lawrence G. Bernard on board *USS Petrel* (ASR 14) arrives in Lynnhaven Roads, Virginia from Charleston, transfers to *USS William H. Standley* (DLG 32) as Senior Officer Search Force.

0746Z (3:46 A.M. EDT)

USS Pargo reports Admiral Schade has departed the submarine to return to his headquarters.

Daytime

Scorpion Technical Advisory Group under John P. Craven forms at navy headquarters.

2315Z (7:15 P.M. EDT)

Scorpion search force begins to shrink as all but a dozen ships and submarines are directed to return to port.

THURSDAY, MAY 30

0028Z (8:28 P.M. EDT May 29)

Search units respond to a radio transmission from "Brandywine," which is the *Scorpion*'s call sign. The transmission is later determined to be operator mistake or a hoax.

1749Z (1:49 P.M. EDT)

Admiral Bernard orders five submarines and six surface ships to follow down *Scorpion's* projected course track from the Azores area to Norfolk with the two groups each in a line abreast 50 miles wide and with the submarines and *USS Petrel* following twelve hours behind the surface ships for continuous daylight coverage of the corridor.

Navy scientists plot initial estimate of *Scorpion* location from acoustic signals.

SATURDAY, JUNE 1

Sometime around June 1, crew of Canadian CP–107 patrol plane spot a heavily damaged Soviet submarine on the surface near the Cape Verde Islands.

EARLY JUNE

U.S. Navy ships receive intelligence report including photograph of damaged Soviet submarine being towed by a larger Soviet surface ship.

SUNDAY, JUNE 2

1945Z (3:45 P.M. EDT)

Open-ocean search force is now about halfway between Norfolk and the Azores.

2000Z (4 P.M. EDT)

USNS Mizar leaves Norfolk for "focused operations" search area southwest of the Azores.

MONDAY, JUNE 3

2000Z (4 P.M. EDT)

Compass Island completes survey of *Scorpion* course track and heads for Azores.

WEDNESDAY, JUNE 5

0800Z (4 A.M. EDT)

Compass Island anchors at Bahia Praia, Terceira, Azores for pickup of personnel (crewmen and scientists) and supplies; underway at 1035Z for Punta del Gada, mooring at 1624Z.

1739Z (1:39 P.M. EDT)

Scorpion court of inquiry convenes in Norfolk with Schade as the first witness.

2000Z (4 P.M. EDT)

CNO formally declares *Scorpion* "presumed lost."

2005Z (4:05 P.M. EDT)

Open-ocean search force passes over *Scorpion's* last known position at 31:19 North, 27:37 West.

2340Z (7:40 P.M. EDT)

Admiral Moorer publicly announces *Scorpion* lost.

THURSDAY, JUNE 6

0645Z

Compass Island departs Ponta Delgada, Azores, for *Scorpion* focused-operations search area.

FRIDAY, JUNE 7

1000Z (10 A.M. local)

Compass Island begins dropping demolition charges to calibrate accuracy of calculated hydrophone positions of the *Scorpion* sinking location.

SUNDAY, JUNE 9

Compass Island passes within detection range of Scorpion wreckage location at 32:54.9 North 33:08.89 West. Three former crewmen say this is most likely date of the actual Scorpion discovery.

MONDAY, JUNE 10

Mizar rendezvous with *Compass Island* in focused-operations search area to transfer supplies and personnel.

THURSDAY, JUNE 13

Compass Island completes seven days of demolition charge drops and departs search area for Bahia Praia, Terceira, Azores.

Scorpion TAG Chairman John P. Craven testifies to *Scorpion* court of inquiry concerning ongoing demolition charge drops.

FRIDAY, JUNE 14

Compass Island anchored at Bahia Praia to transfer medical patient and to take on provisions; departs Bahia Praia for search area.

SUNDAY, JUNE 16

1338Z

Message from COMSUBLANT to search force identifies Point Oscar (32:52.2 North 33:11.5 West) as most accurate estimate of *Scorpion* location, superseding earlier estimates.

MONDAY, JUNE 17

1932Z (3:32 P.M. EDT)

Petrel arrives Bahia Praia, Terceira, Azores.

FRIDAY, JUNE 21

Conference of ship commanders aboard *Mizar*.

SATURDAY, JUNE 22

1248Z (8:48 A.M. EDT)

Petrel underway for *Scorpion* search area.

SUNDAY, JUNE 23

1756Z (1:56 P.M. EDT)

Mizar rendezvous with *USS Ozark* (MCS 2) in search area for personnel transfer and return to Azores.

TUESDAY, JUNE 25

Compass Island detached from search to return to New York.

1000Z (6 A.M. EDT)

Petrel arrives at Bahia Praia, Terceira, Azores, moored to pier.

WEDNESDAY, JUNE 26

0853Z (4:53 A.M. EDT)

Petrel underway for search area.

THURSDAY, JUNE 27

Mizar's towed sled photographs twisted metal fragment that later is identified as part of *Scorpion* but is unable to relocate it in subsequent attempts.

FRIDAY, JUNE 28

First *Mizar* search cruise ends, ship proceeds to Azores.

SUNDAY, JUNE 30

0858Z (4:58 A.M. EDT)

Petrel returns from search area, arriving in Bahia Praia, Azores, moored next to *Mizar* and *Ozark*.

Sometime between *Petrel* arrival and change of command ceremony on July 3, a *Mizar* crewman shows two *Petrel* crewmen photographs of the *Scorpion* wreckage taken by the *Mizar*'s towed sled camera.

WEDNESDAY, JULY 3

Change of command ceremony aboard *Petrel*.

MONDAY, JULY 8

Mizar leaves Azores for second search cruise.

TUESDAY, AUGUST 6

Mizar second search cruise ends.

MONDAY, AUGUST 12

Mizar departs Azores for third search cruise, arriving on station on August 14.

SUNDAY, SEPTEMBER 8

Mizar third search cruise ends.

FRIDAY, SEPTEMBER 20

Mizar departs Azores for fourth search cruise.

TUESDAY, SEPTEMBER 24

Vice Admiral Schade recommends to CNO Admiral Moorer that *Scorpion* search operations be suspended until the spring of 1969 if no new artifacts are found in ongoing *Mizar* search period.

MONDAY, OCTOBER 7

Mizar fourth search cruise ends.

WEDNESDAY, OCTOBER 16

Mizar departs Azores for fifth search cruise ("research phase").

FRIDAY, OCTOBER 18

Atlantic Fleet officials preparing planned news release for November 8 announcing suspension of the *Scorpion* search.

MONDAY, OCTOBER 28

Mizar towed sled magnetometer and still camera detects wreckage of *Scorpion*.

WEDNESDAY, OCTOBER 30

U.S. Navy publicly announces discovery of *Scorpion*.

NOTES

CHAPTER 1: "WE MAY HAVE LOST A SUBMARINE"

1. This chapter draws on various sources, most notably the official U.S. Navy account, news reports, and interviews with *Scorpion* family members and other members of the Submarine Service and the navy.

2. Descriptions of the scene at the Destroyer-Submarine Piers were compiled from interviews with various *Scorpion* family members and navy officials who were there as well as articles in *The Virginian-Pilot* and *The Ledger-Star* newspapers, particularly "Patience Turned to Alarm," *Virginian-Pilot,* May 29, 1968, and Larry Bonko, "Ordeal of Hope and Fear," *Ledger-Star,* May 29, 1968.

3. Commander Submarine Force, U.S. Atlantic Fleet, Command History 1968, pp. 4–5 and 11.

4. From *USS William M. Wood* (DD 715), deck log for May 27, 1968.

5. George Williams interview with the author, May 31, 2006.

6. Bill Elrod interview with the author, Nov. 13, 1997.

7. The *Scorpion's* last reported message was identified as *Scorpion* message to COM-SUBLANT 212354Z May 68, *Record of Proceedings of a Court of Inquiry Convened by Commander-in-Chief, United States Atlantic Fleet . . . to Inquire into the Loss of* USS Scorpion *(SSN-589),* Exhibit 73. While news reports at the time cited this message in detail, noting the *Scorpion's* last-recorded position several hundred miles southwest of the Azores, as well as the Great Circle track from there to Norfolk and the estimated time of arrival at 1 P.M. on May 27, 1968, the actual text of the message itself remains classified top secret to this day. The formal SubMiss alert on May 27, 1968 was in the 272200Z May 68 COMSUBLANT "SUBMISS SITREP 1" message to all search units. Capt. Bellah's comments in an interview with the author, Jan. 9, 1998.

8. COMASWFORLANT, "Report on the Air Search for *Scorpion,*" July 16, 1968; also, "*Scorpion* SAR Narrative" briefing to the *Scorpion* court of inquiry, June 11, 1968.

9. Navy message headers come in a six-digit format combining the day of the month (the first two numbers) followed by a four-digit sequence denoting the time of day using the twenty-four-hour clock. Most include the suffix Z for Greenwich Mean Time. Thus,

271915Z corresponds to 1515Q, or Eastern Daylight Time (four hours earlier), on May 27. Declassified Navy message 271955Z May 68 CSL ADMINO.

10. NDDC Memorandum for the Record, May 27, 1968, declassified.

11. President's Daily Diary, May 27, 1968, p. 13, released by the Lyndon Baines Johnson Library, Oct. 7, 1983.

12. John Bishop interview with the author, May 9, 1998; Theresa Bishop interview with the author, April 25, 1983; other *Scorpion* wives in "Patience Turned to Alarm," *Virginian-Pilot,* May 29, 1968.

13. Details on *USS Pargo* from author interview with Vice Adm. Arnold F. Schade, April 21, 1983; text of Schade's speech to the National Security Industrial Association in Groton, Conn., on June 27, 1968; author interviews with YNC Jerry Hall (Ret.) May 15, 1983; Cmdr. Jack Klinefelter (Ret.), May 20, 1983; also, report from CO *USS Pargo* on *Scorpion* Search Operations, June 7, 1968.

14. John P. Craven interviews with the author, April 21, 1983, Nov. 29, 1984, and Jan. 15, 1985. Craven's role in the undersea intelligence operations revealed in detail in Sherry Sontag and Chris Drew, *Blind Man's Bluff: The Untold Story of American Submarine Espionage* (New York: PublicAffairs, 1998), and his own memoir, *The Silent War: The Cold War Battle Beneath the Sea* (New York: Simon & Schuster, 2001).

15. The "quarantine" of Cuba in October 1962 and related operations involved three aircraft carrier battle groups and initially 117 Atlantic Fleet warships. The total number of vessels that took part over the next two months was 223 as various ships rotated back to homeport. See Dino A. Brugioni, *Eyeball to Eyeball: The Inside Story of the Cuban Missile Crisis* (New York: Random House, 1991), pp. 221 and 273. Also see *USS Scorpion* Search Roster, page 393.

16. Ship movements are described in a series of navy messages and situation reports issued in the days after the *Scorpion* SAR exercise.

17. The three "unions" of the U.S. Navy of that era—the aviation branch, surface fleet, and submarine force—were unofficially described by the uniform shoes they wore. Aviators wore brown, surface sailors wore black, and submariners, to minimize noise, often wore felt slippers. For *William M. Wood* departure, see deck log, *USS William M. Wood,* May 27, 1968. *USS Shark* report cited in "Giant Search Started for Missing U.S. Sub," Associated Press, *Milwaukee Journal,* May 28, 1968.

18. Ghormley interview with the author, Dec. 10, 1998.

19. Baciocco interview with the author, Dec. 4, 1997.

20. Schade speech to the National Security Industrial Association.

21. Navy officials in subsequent declassified search messages and "hydrolant" advisories to commercial shipping described the course track as: Last reported position 21:19 N 27:37 W, course 290 degrees, speed 18 knots ETA Submerged Submarine Operating Area 36:50 N 65 W at 26 May 1000Z. The course track described was: 21:19 N 27:37 W to 31 N 25 W, then to 32:25N 30 W, then to 33:50 N 35 W, then to 34:45 N 40 W, then to 35:28 N 45 W, then to 36:12 N 50 W, then to 36:38 N 55 W, then to 36:45 N 60 W, then to 36:50 N 65 W, then to Lanes Kent and Whiskey to Norfolk.

22. "Oil Slick Seen on Lost Sub's Course," Associated Press, May 29, 1968.

23. Larry Bonko, "Splendid View of Nothing Filled *Scorpion* Hunters' Eyes," *Ledger-Star,* May 30, 1968.

24. Beshany interview with the author, Dec. 9, 1997.

25. Capt. W. F. Searle, "Assets and Status for *Scorpion* (SSN 589) Salvops," May 27, 1968. The navy ultimately flew the Deep Diver and a Mark IV diving capsule to the Azores in event the *Scorpion* were to be found in water shallow enough to rescue the crew, but the systems were never needed. See "Two Deep-Diving Rigs Flown to Azores," *Ledger-Star,* June 2, 1968. Adm. Maurer offer, see 282014Z MAY 68 ADMINO COMSUBPAC message to COMSUBLANT.

26. 292049Z May 68 message from NASL to COMSUBLANT; 291430Z May 68 message from COMSUBLANT to CNO; 291549Z May 68 message from COMASWFORLANT to CSAF (Air Force Chief of Staff).

27. 301320Z May 68 message from ALUSMA Lisbon to COMSUBLANT; FCC Memorandum for the Record, June 5, 1968.

28. Rear Adm. Lawrence G. Bernard, Commander Submarine Flotilla 6, "Report of Search Operations for USS *Scorpion* (SSN 589) during period 271915Z May 1968 to 052000Z June 1968," June 28, 1968, Narrative, p. 2.

29. The *William H. Standley* and eight other ships in its class were reclassified from guided missile frigates (DLG) to cruisers (CG) in 1975. This included another ship that played a prominent role in the *Scorpion* search, the *USS Josephus Daniels* (DLG 27).

30. *USS Petrel* deck log, May 29, 1968; Bernard report, Narrative, p. 2.

31. *USS Pargo* SAR (search and rescue) summary June 7, 1968.

32. "Hope of Finding Scorpion Ebbs As Hunt Goes on in Rough Seas," *Ledger-Star,* May 29, 1968.

33. Bernard report, Narrative pp. 5–6.

34. Bernard testimony, *Record of Proceedings of a Court of Inquiry,* vol. 3, pp. 612–13.

35. Bernard report, Narrative p. 6.

36. Frank Creasy, "*Scorpion* Grapevine Silent but Quintet Keeps Hoping," *Ledger-Star,* May 30, 1968.

37. Richard C. Bayer, "False Hopes Plague *Scorpion* Crew's Kin," *Ledger-Star,* June 3, 1968; Wayne Woodlief, "Wives Wait for News," *Virginian-Pilot,* May 30, 1968.

38. Two submarines named *Requin* were in the *Scorpion* search. The Norfolk-based USS *Requin* (SS 481) also took part in the initial SAR operation.

39. Memorandum, "Statements and Rationale to Support 'Presumed Loss,'" Vice Adm. Arnold F. Schade, June 2, 1968.

40. Memorandum for the Chief of Naval Operations, May 28, 1968.

41. Bernard report, p. 8 and Narrative, p. 14.

CHAPTER 2: THE OLD ADMIRAL'S REVELATION

1. For the Submarine Service, the Reagan administration wanted 100 nuclear-powered submarines, including 52 of the new *Los Angeles*–class attack boats and 18 Trident missile submarines carrying 24 Trident (C4) missiles with eight warheads apiece. At this

juncture the navy was also planning for the new *Seawolf*-class nuclear attack submarine in the mid-1990s, but that program was terminated after only three hulls were launched. In 2006, the navy was struggling to maintain a fleet of 50 submarines including 14 Trident missile boats and four Tridents converted into a cruise missile-carrying configuration.

2. Submarine war patrol reports from World War II were not fully declassified until the late 1960s. Cold War–era nuclear submarine patrol reports remain classified top secret to this day. Adm. King's "advice" recited in "Observers Shocked and Awed at Media Savvy," *Advisor* newsletter on communications, June 2003, found online at http://www.ammermanexperience.com/newsletters/june03/index.html.

3. While the national news media reported on the *Scorpion* incident in great detail during its first weeks, the two Norfolk newspapers provided the most in-depth and sustained coverage throughout the summer and fall of 1968. In 1968, *The Virginian-Pilot* and *The Ledger-Star* were both owned by Landmark Communications Inc. but operated as separate newspapers. The two newspapers merged into a single publication in the late 1980s.

4. Schade testimony cited in Lawrence Maddrey, "Sub Lost, Navy Declares," *Virginian-Pilot*, June 6, 1968; Greene comments on classified mission cited in "Scorpion Mission Secret," *Ledger-Star*, June 7, 1968. Unbeknownst to the court members or spectators, Capt. Greene's disclosure sparked a small kerfuffle in the Pentagon. On June 8, Cmdr. C. P. Barnes attached two UPI articles to a memorandum to his superior noting that the testimony had been "misinterpreted" by the press. This, he said, "led to a report that *Scorpion* was on a 'secret mission.' In fact, her operation order was classified as are most operation orders for ships and the press used this as a 'sensation item.'"

5. Flaws reported in "Sub Faulty, Ex-Crewmen Tell Court," *Virginian-Pilot*, June 7, 1968; lack of post-*Thresher* modifications cited in "Sub Was Safe, Officer Testifies," *Virginian-Pilot*, June 9, 1968; Clarke testimony reported in "Two Debate Scorpion's Safety During Navy Court of Inquiry," *Ledger-Star*, June 10, 1968.

6. "No Damage Done Sub by Bump," *Ledger-Star*, June 13, 1968.

7. Bernard testimony cited in "No Peaks Found at Scorpion's Depth," *Ledger-Star*, June 20, 1968; testimony over absence of seamounts cited in "Court Advised 'Scorpion' Lacked Latest Charts," *Virginian-Pilot*, June 20, 1968.

8. "Nothing Remotely Connected with *Scorpion* Found by Navy," *Ledger-Star*, July 3, 1968.

9. The *Mizar's* sled first detected the *Scorpion* with an onboard sonar and magnetometer, but photographic confirmation did not occur until 0300 GMT on Oct. 30 (11 P.M. EDT on Oct. 29). The navy withheld a public announcement of the discovery until Oct. 31. Disclosure of planned termination of search revealed in Jack Kestner, "Scorpion Found Near End of Search," *Ledger-Star*, Nov. 1, 1968. Notice of planned navy announcement to families reported in John Greenbacker, "*Scorpion* Found About 400 Miles from the Azores," *Virginian-Pilot*, Nov. 1, 1968.

10. John Greenbacker, "*Scorpion* Found by Deductive Reasoning," *Virginian-Pilot*, Nov. 4, 1968.

11. Fred Hoffman, "Small Piece of Metal Led Navy to Ill-Fated *Scorpion*," Associated Press (published in *Virginian-Pilot*), Nov. 21, 1968.

12. Account of closed court sessions cited by John Greenbacker, "Court Views Pictures of *Scorpion* Debris," *Virginian-Pilot,* Nov. 8, 1968; disclosure of wreckage condition reported in "Navy Says *Scorpion* Is in Several Major Pieces," *Virginian-Pilot,* Nov. 16, 1968.

13. Rear Adm. Charles D. Nace, member of the *Scorpion* Court of Inquiry, letter to the author, June 1, 1998.

14. "Navy Reports Findings of the Court of Inquiry on the Loss of the USS *Scorpion*," News Release, Office of the Assistant Secretary of Defense (Public Affairs), Jan. 31, 1969.

15. "Likely Cause of Scorpion Loss Still Being Kept Secret by Navy," *Ledger-Star,* March 26, 1975. Also see Jack Kestner, "Navy 'Stonewalls' Sub Talk," *Ledger-Star,* March 27, 1975.

16. The Freedom of Information Act was first passed by Congress and signed into law by President Lyndon B. Johnson on July 4, 1966. Amended many times over the past 40 years, the law remains a primary means for journalists, historians, and ordinary citizens to obtain records from the federal government, including the military and intelligence agencies. A "Citizen's Guide" on using the FOIA released by the House Committee on Government Reform on September 20, 2005 reviewed the history and legislative intent of Congress in passing the much-amended law: "The Freedom of Information Act (FOIA) establishes a presumption that records in the possession of agencies and departments of the executive branch of the U.S. Government are accessible to the people. This was not always the approach to Federal information disclosure policy. Before enactment of the FOIA in 1966, the burden was on the individual to establish a right to examine these government records. There were no statutory guidelines or procedures to help a person seeking information. There were no judicial remedies for those denied access. With the passage of the FOIA, the burden of proof shifted from the individual to the government. Those seeking information are no longer required to show a need for information. Instead, the 'need to know' standard has been replaced by a 'right to know' doctrine. The government now has to justify the need for secrecy. The FOIA sets standards for determining which records must be disclosed and which records may be withheld. The law also provides administrative and judicial remedies for those denied access to records. Above all, the statute requires federal agencies to provide the fullest possible disclosure of information to the public."

The full text of the "Citizen's Guide" can be viewed at: http://www.fas.org/sgp/foia/citizen.html.

The navy judge advocate general released the "sanitized" court summaries to the author under the FOIA on April 8, 1983. Testimony from witnesses ended on July 3, but the court of inquiry spent another three weeks deliberating over the evidence and writing its report, which the panel then turned over to Atlantic Fleet commander Adm. Ephraim P. Holmes on July 25, 1968. Upon reconvening in November after the *Scorpion* discovery, the court drafted a supplementary report that also included "findings of fact, opinions and recommendations."

17. Executive Order 12356, issued by President Reagan on April 2, 1982, dictated the handling, security, and declassification procedures for all classified information. For the full text, see http://www.epic.org/open_gov/eo_12356.html; letter of partial denial of FOIA request from Col. R. W. Edwards USMC, Office of the Navy Judge Advocate General, April 29, 1983.

18. Letter to the author from Capt. T. K. Woods, Jr., Deputy Assistant Judge Advocate General (Investigations), April 8, 1983.

19. *Record of Proceedings of a Court of Inquiry Convened by Commander-in-Chief, United States Atlantic Fleet . . . to Inquire into the Loss of* USS Scorpion *(SSN–589)*, excerpted "Findings of Fact, Opinions and Recommendations" released to the author by the Navy Judge Advocate General, April 8, 1983 (with redactions), p. 1043.

20. Ibid., p. 1046.

21. The Mark 37 was the mainstream conventionally armed submarine torpedo during that era. *Skipjack*-class attack submarines also carried the older Mark 16 torpedo, and some deployed with a small number of the nuclear-tipped Mark 45 ASTOR. Ibid., pp. 1046 and 1058. Confirmation of Mark 45 nuclear torpedoes from memorandum to navy officials from James G. Whiteaker, director, Atomic Energy Division, May 28, 1968, declassified. Ibid., pp. 1079–89.

22. The navy would not declassify the role of Sosus and other acoustic systems in the *Scorpion* search until ten years later, in 1993, as discussed later in the book.

23. Schade telephone interview with the author, April 27, 1983.

24. Clarey interview with the author, Nov. 30, 1984.

25. Schade interview.

26. Dietzen interview with the author, Feb. 23, 1988.

27. Calculations of the distance between the *Scorpion* debris location and two underwater hydrophones near Argentia, Newfoundland, disclosed in Craven interview with the author, Nov. 29, 1984.

28. Craven and other technical experts explained that Sosus at that time was programmed to track the continuous sounds made by ships and submarines moving through the water, including the noise from their propulsion gear. The computers in the system filtered out "stray" sounds such as oil drilling or explosives. It took a detailed review of the audiotapes before experts later detected hidden sounds from the sinking.

29. For years, Craven and other navy officials declined to identify the source of the other recordings, but in 2000, newly declassified documents showed that they were part of the then–top-secret Nuclear Detection System (formerly the Atomic Energy Detection System) managed by the Air Force Technical Application Center based at Patrick Air Force Base, Florida.

30. Atkins interview with the author, April 22, 1983; Schade 1983 interview.

31. Ed Offley, "Mystery of Sub's Sinking Unravels," *Virginian-Pilot and The Ledger-Star,* Dec. 16, 1984.

32. Conversation between the author and retired YNC (SS) Jerry Hall, Dec. 17, 1984, later transcribed.

CHAPTER 3: THE SPORTS CAR OF SHIPS

1. Carr interview with the author, March 14, 1998.

2. Description of *Scorpion* at launching ceremony from "*Scorpion* Goes for First Dip As Onlookers Brave the Cold," *New London Day*, Dec. 19, 1959, and various news photographs of the event, courtesy of the Submarine Force Library and Museum, Groton, Conn.

3. The first five Polaris missile submarines were essentially *Skipjack* designs with a 130-foot-long missile section grafted into the center of the hull. The *Tullibee* was a one-of-a-kind hunter-killer submarine proposed for shallow-water missions. The navy later opted to build the *Thresher/Permit* class to carry out that mission and others. In mid-1960, the *USS Skipjack* (SSN 585) and *USS Scorpion* (SSN 589) were already in commission. While the hull number of the *USS Scamp* (SSN 588) indicated an earlier construction contract than the *Scorpion,* in fact Electric Boat began work on the *Scorpion* on Aug. 20, 1958, nearly five months before construction commenced on the *Scamp* at Mare Island Naval Shipyard in California on Jan. 22, 1959. The U.S. Navy enjoyed a diverse and widespread industrial base for its early nuclear submarine program, with seven shipyards—five privately owned and two naval shipyards—working on the early generations of nuclear submarines. From construction of the *USS Nautilus* (SSN 571) on June 14, 1952 until commissioning of the last Polaris submarine, *USS Richard B. Russell,* on Aug. 16, 1975, the navy constructed 106 nuclear attack and ballistic missile submarines. In addition to Electric Boat, the other shipyards and number of nuclear submarines built included Newport News (Va.) Shipbuilding, 23; Mare Island Naval Shipyard, Calif., 17; Litton Ingalls, Miss., 12; Portsmouth (N.H.) Naval Shipyard, 9; New York Shipbuilding, 3; and General Dynamics Quincy, Mass., 3. See Norman Polmar, editor, *The Ships and Aircraft of the U.S. Fleet,* 11th ed. (Annapolis, Md.: Naval Institute Press, 1978), pp. 20–23 and 31–32.

4. See in general, Norman Friedman, *Submarine Design and Development* (Annapolis, Md.: Naval Institute Press, 1984). For a focused perspective on Soviet submarine design see Gary E. Weir with Walter J. Boyne, *Rising Tide: The Untold Story of the Russian Submarines That Fought the Cold War* (New York: New American Library/Caliber, 2004).

5. See Norman Polmar and Thomas B. Allen, *Rickover: Controversy and Genius* (New York: Simon & Schuster, 1982), pp. 118–120. Also see profile of Enrico Fermi at http://en.wikipedia.org/wiki/Enrico_Fermi.

6. Dr. Philip A. Abelson, "Atomic Energy Submarine," Naval Research Laboratory, March 29, 1946, quoted in Polmar and Allen, *Rickover,* pp. 121–22.

7. Quoted in Polmar and Allen, *Rickover,* p. 122.

8. Three in-depth biographies of Rickover have appeared in the past quarter century: Polmar and Allen is considered the most objective. Two others were compiled and written with navy support: Francis Duncan, *Rickover and the Nuclear Navy* (Annapolis,

Md.: Naval Institute Press, 1990) and Theodore Rockwell, *The Rickover Effect* (Annapolis, Md.: Naval Institute Press, Annapolis, 1992).

9. See Jeff Rodengen, *The Legend of Electric Boat* (Fort Lauderdale: Write Stuff Syndicate, 1994), pp. 17–21 and 156.

10. Rickover comment on silencing cited in Polmar and Allen, *Rickover,* p. 369.

11. Friedman comments on the Type XXI U-boat, cited in *Submarine Design and Development,* Chapter 4. During the Cold War, NATO assigned a phonetic letter designation for each class of Soviet submarines. The Soviet Navy identified each class by a Project number, and the long-serving Whiskey class, of which 236 in differing models were built between 1949 and 1958, actually came from three: Projects 613, 644, and 665. Prior to the *Skipjack* class, the navy constructed three one-of-a-kind nuclear submarines: the *Nautilus;* the USS *Seawolf* (SSN 575) with a prototype S2G reactor using liquid sodium rather than pressurized water as a coolant; and the massive USS *Triton* (SSN 586), the only U.S. nuclear submarine equipped with two nuclear reactors. Subsequent submarines also followed closely after the *Nautilus* design, including four *Skate*-class attack submarines and the USS *Halibut* (SSN 587), originally designed with a massive forward compartment to house the air-breathing Regulus attack missile but later converted into a spy submarine capable of retrieving objects from the ocean floor thousands of feet below.

12. See Friedman, *Submarine Design and Development,* p. 82.

13. Vice Adm. Charles Bowers "Swede" Momsen, renowned for his earlier development of submarine rescue gear, was the *Albacore's* godfather. As the navy's director of undersea warfare in a postwar navy dominated by aircraft carrier admirals, Momsen won support for the submarine by telling the aviators he wanted to build a small submarine that they could use as a practice target. For a concise history of the *Albacore,* see http://www.ussalbacore.org/html/albacore_story.html.

14. Details on the *Albacore* cited in Polmar, *The Ships and Aircraft of the U.S. Fleet,* p. 44, and Friedman, *Submarine Design and Development,* p. 82. Submarine shaft-horsepower is defined as a measure of the actual mechanical energy per unit time delivered to a turning shaft. 1 shaft horsepower = 1 electric horsepower = 550 ft.-lb./second. The navy also built three *Barbel*-class advanced diesel submarines—the last non-nuclear attack submarines in the U.S. Navy—which served until the late 1980s.

15. Elrod interview with the author, Nov. 13, 1997.

16. Confidential source. The S8G reactor used in the 18,700-ton *Ohio*-class submarines, with an estimated 60,000 shaft horsepower, is much larger than the *Scorpion's* S5W. An unclassified schematic diagram of the reactor and auxiliary machinery room compartments of a *George Washington*–class missile submarine—which used the same propulsion system as the *Scorpion*—suggested that the containment vessel was actually larger, about eight feet in diameter and 18–20 feet high.

17. For the *Scorpion's* maximum speed, confidential source. For reactor steaming ranges, see Polmar and Allen, *Rickover,* p. 416.

18. See Ed Offley, "Russian Warships Pose Threat—to Russians," *Seattle Post-Intelligencer,* Feb. 26, 1993. Additional details of the Chazma Bay accident can be

found in Suzanne Kopte, "Nuclear Submarine Decommissioning and Related Problems," Bonn International Center for Conversion, August 1997, available online at http://www.bicc.de/publications/papers/paper12/paper12.pdf.

19. Elrod interview.

20. The submarine hull plating was affixed to a series of circular girder-like frames about 30 inches apart that ran the length of the submarine, beginning with Frame 1 at the bow and Frame 100 at the stern.

21. The *Scorpion's* torpedo "loadout" for its 1968 Mediterranean deployment consisted of ten Mark 37-1 wire-guided conventional torpedoes; four Mark 37-0 models; seven Mark 14-5 conventional torpedoes, and the two Mark 45 ASTORs. *Record of Proceedings of a Court of Inquiry Convened by Commander-in-Chief, United States Atlantic Fleet . . . to Inquire into the Loss of* USS Scorpion *(SSN-589),* vol. 4, p. 1057.

22. Elrod interview.

23. When the deep-diving bathyscaph *Trieste* II surveyed the *Scorpion's* wreckage in the summer of 1969, one of the few pieces of gear that it managed to retrieve with its robotic arm was the submarine's hand-held sextant.

24. Sanford N. Levey, Lt. USN, "Handling Characteristics of the 588-class Submarine, a Qualification for Command Thesis," June 6, 1962, provided to the author. While the *Scorpion* and her sister ships were known as *Skipjack*-class attack submarines after the *USS Skipjack*, the navy also termed them "588 Class" boats after the *USS Scamp* because of several design changes incorporated in the two-year period between the *Skipjack's* commissioning and that of the *Scamp*. This was in part a result of the navy's decision in 1958 to convert three planned *Skipjacks* into what became the first three Polaris missile submarines.

25. Dietzen interview with the author, Feb. 23, 1988.

26. Elrod interview; Baciocco interview with the author, Dec. 4, 1997.

27. Pirie interview with the author, April 13, 1983.

28. See Capt. Edward L. Beach Jr., *Cold Is the Sea* (Bluejacket Books, 2002).

29. Dietzen interview.

30. Pirie interview.

31. Ibid.

32. Elrod interview.

33. From an unidentified newspaper tearsheet in the Submarine Force Library and Museum, Groton, Conn. Wettern covered military conflicts from the Cold War through the 1982 Falklands War and Operation Desert Storm for a variety of military newspapers and magazines.

34. "Sub *Scorpion* Safe; Breaks Radio Silence," *New London Day,* Sept. 16, 1960.

35. Baciocco interview.

36. History of *USS Scorpion* (SSN 589), from the *Dictionary of American Naval Fighting Ships,* Naval Historical Center, at http://www.history.navy.mil/danfs/s7/scorpion-vi.htm; Levey interview with the author, April 15, 1983.

CHAPTER 4: THE SECRET WAR

1. The communications intelligence program was formally renamed the Naval Security Group on July 1, 1968. For a background overview of the SNCP program, see Jeffrey T. Richelson, *The U.S. Intelligence Community*, Fourth Edition (Cambridge, Mass.: Ballinger Books, 1999), pp. 203–5; also Bob Woodward, *Veil: The Secret Wars of the CIA* (New York: Simon & Schuster, 1987), p. 30. For a detailed history of the SNCP element involving the tapping of undersea communications cables, see Sherry Sontag and Chris Drew, *Blind Man's Bluff: The Untold Story of American Submarine Espionage* (New York: PublicAffairs, 1998).

2. Elrod interview with the author, Nov. 13, 1997; Ghormley interview with the author, Dec. 10, 1998.

3. Cited by several former *Scorpion* crewmen. Nuclear submarine patrol reports remain classified top secret even fifteen years after the end of the Soviet Union. An unclassified history of the *Scorpion* in the Naval Historical Center's "Dictionary of American Naval Fighting Ships" does cite several "special operations" by the *Scorpion* in 1966 but is silent on others, including at least two in 1961–62 and another pair in 1964. This is not uncommon in the ship's histories archives. See http://www.history.navy.mil/danfs/s7/scorpion-vi.htm.

4. The fire occurred in the submarine's after battery compartment and spread throughout the *Cochino* for fifteen hours before its commander ordered the crew to abandon ship. A civilian sonar expert onboard the *Cochino* and six crewmen from the submarine *USS Tusk*, which accompanied the *Cochino* on its mission, drowned during a rescue operation to transfer the stricken submarine's crew to the *Tusk*. See Sontag and Drew, *Blind Man's Bluff*, Chapter 1.

5. For Type XXI U-boat transfers, see Gary E. Weir with Walter J. Boyne, *Rising Tide: The Untold Story of the Russian Submarines That Fought the Cold War* (New York: New American Library/Caliber, 2004), p. 19. Of 117 Type XXI U-boats that were built, 104 were scuttled and only thirteen came into the hands of the U.S., British, and Soviet navies. For November-class submarines, see Weir, *Rising Tide*, pp. 290 and 302. The Cold War spy flights were exceptionally dangerous. By one estimate, the Air Force and CIA flew nearly a thousand of these flights every year during that period. These incidents led to one of the darkest chapters of Cold War history: Nongovernmental researchers have estimated that scores of American military fliers were taken alive and vanished into the Soviet Gulag prison system never to be seen again. In 1992, Russian President Boris Yeltsin said twelve downed American aviators were known to have been in secret captivity in the Soviet Union but none were alive in 1991, when the USSR dissolved. See Mark Sauter, with John D. Sanders and Cort Kirkwood, *Soldiers of Misfortune: Washington's Betrayal of American POWs in the Soviet Union* (Washington, D.C.: National Press Books, 1992); also Norman Polmar and Thomas B. Allen, *Spy Book, the Encyclopedia of Espionage* (New York: Random House, 1997), pp. 11–16.

6. Woodward, *Veil*.

7. Once the submarine formally crossed a designated "chop" line it would then report to the Commander, U.S. Naval Forces in Europe and would be under the operational con-

trol of that headquarters or the U.S. Sixth Fleet until returning to COMSUBLANT control when returning into the Atlantic. Unlike the Atlantic Fleet's cruiser-destroyer or aircraft carrier organization, *COMSUBLANT* also had an operational command responsibility under the North Atlantic Treaty Organization. The four-star in command in Norfolk was triple-hatted as Supreme Allied Commander Atlantic (NATO), commander of the U.S. Atlantic Command (all U.S. military combat forces in that region), and commander of the U.S. Atlantic Fleet (Navy). The three-star at COMSUBLANT not only directed operational control over all submarines in his command but under the NATO Alliance would direct all NATO submarine operations in the Atlantic as well. See *COMSUBLANT Command History for 1968,* Dec. 16, 1969, declassified, pp. 2–4.

8. See Norman Polmar and Thomas B. Allen, *Spy Book: The Encyclopedia of Espionage* (New York: Random House, 1997), pp. 390–92.

9. See Richelson, *The U.S. Intelligence Community,* pp. 84–85. Also Sontag and Drew, *Blind Man's Bluff,* pp. 65–67.

10. Joint Reconnaissance Center described in James Bamford, *Body of Secrets: Anatomy of the Ultra-Secret National Security Agency* (New York: Doubleday, 2001), pp. 245–46. For White House supervision of these missions, see John Ranelagh, *The Agency: The Rise and Decline of the CIA* (New York: Touchstone/Simon & Schuster, 1987), pp. 514–15. The White House used this panel to monitor and control extra-sensitive covert operations and intelligence-gathering missions such as U-2 and SR-71 flights, the ill-fated 1968 *Pueblo* sortie to North Korean waters, and the Holystone submarine missions. Organized in the early 1950s, it went through a series of name changes, including Special Group 10/2, 5412 Panel, NSC 5412/2 Special Group, Special Group (until 1964), and 303 Committee. In 1969 when the Nixon administration took office, the group was renamed yet again to the 40 Committee under the direction of National Security Adviser Henry Kissinger.

11. Horn interview with the author, Dec. 30, 2005. Naval intelligence also managed a number of shore-based SIGINT collection operations including the "High Frequency/Direction Finding" antenna arrays located in the United States and several overseas locations. It also was responsible for naval Communications Security programs, the safeguarding of secure U.S. communications. The Army Security Agency and the Air Force Electronic Security Command (formerly the Air Force Security Service) are the counterparts to the Naval Security Group. All three commands conduct a variety of intelligence and communications functions for their respective parent services as well as gathering intelligence for the NSA. See Richelson, *The U.S. Intelligence Community,* pp. 74–100.

12. Elrod interview.

13. Carr interview.

14. Hall interview with the author, Feb. 10, 1993.

15. See Sontag and Drew, *Blind Man's Bluff,* pp. 42–43; also Seymour M. Hersh, "Submarines of U.S. Stage Spy Missions Inside Soviet Waters," *New York Times,* May 24, 1975, p. A-1; and Seymour M. Hersh, "A False Navy Report Alleged in Sub Crash," *New York Times,* July 6, 1975, p. A-1.

16. Bamford, *Body of Secrets,* pp. 104–105.

17. Ibid., p. 106.

18. For missile-launch surveillance tactics, see William M. Arkin and Richard W. Fieldhouse, *Nuclear Battlefields: Global Links in the Arms Race* (Cambridge, Mass.: Ballinger Books, 1985), pp. 70–71.

19. Horn interview.

20. Given the top-secret nature of the Holystone missions, differences exist in details and exact dates for many of the incidents. One of the more detailed rosters of U.S.-Soviet submarine encounters was compiled by retired submarine Engineman Master Chief (SS) Jim Christley in 1994 and donated to the Submarine Force Library and Museum in Groton, Conn. For the *Tautog* collision with the "Black Lila," see Sontag and Drew, *Blind Man's Bluff,* pp. 146–154.

21. Hersh, "A False Navy Report Alleged in Sub Crash." A second incident of alleged false record-keeping emerged in 1989, when several crewmen aboard the nuclear attack submarine *USS La Jolla* (SSN 701) filed a complaint with the navy's inspector general accusing their senior officers of altering the submarine's navigational records during 1986–88 to conceal encounters with Soviet submarines and violations of Soviet territorial waters. In this incident, the officers allegedly moved to conceal from their chain of command several mistakes that allowed a Soviet submarine to counter-detect the *La Jolla.* The navy later said the accusations were unsubstantiated, prompting several crewmen to leak the incident to a San Diego newspaper. See Tom Burgess, "Cover-up Aboard Nuclear Sub Alleged," *San Diego Union,* Aug. 6, 1989.

22. *Neptune Papers No. 3: Naval Accidents 1945–1988,* by William M. Arkin and Joshua Handler, Greenpeace/Institute for Policy Studies, p. 47. The report cites a 1975 *San Diego Tribune* article "U.S.–Russ Atom Sub Collision Revealed," in July 3, 1975 that first disclosed the *Pintado* collision with the Soviet submarine.

23. Christley incident roster.

24. Galantin quoted in Peter Padfield, *War Beneath the Sea: Submarine Conflict During World War II* (New York: John Wiley & Sons, 1995), p. 16.

25. See Colin Simpson, *The Lusitania* (Boston: Little, Brown and Company, 1972).

26. Ibid. For a description of the U-20, see http://www.firstworldwar.com/atoz/u20.htm. For trends in the war, see "World War I: The First Three Years," extracted from *American Military History,* Army Historical Studies, Office of the Chief of Military History, online at http://www.army.mil/cmh-pg/books/AMH/AMH-17.htm

27. William Bell Clark, *When the U-boats Came to America,* (Boston: Little, Brown and Co., 1929), pp. 302–5. Few U.S. Navy archives refer to the Atlantic Fleet's retreat to Yorktown in 1918. This generally unreported incident was still a topic of conversation among longtime residents along the Yorktown waterfront in the mid-1970s. Clark noted from U.S. Navy records that when the battleship *USS Minnesota* (BB 22) struck a mine near the mouth of the Delaware River, it was "under convoy of the U.S. destroyer *Israel* and on its way from Base 2 (York River) to the Philadelphia Navy Yard. . . ."

28. News report, Cologne *Volks Zeitung,* translated and reprinted in *New York Times,* Sept. 14, 1918.

29. The *Laconia* affair illustrates the conundrum faced by submarine captains in rendering humanitarian aid to their victims. After the submarine *U-156* (not to be confused with the U-boat of the same designation from World War I) sank the British troop ship *Laconia* in the South Atlantic on Sept. 12, 1942, *Korvettenkapitan* Werner Hartenstein discovered the ship was carrying over 2,200 passengers including 1,800 Italian prisoners of war captured by the British in North Africa. Unable to carry more than a handful aboard, Hartenstein sent an emergency radio report to Donitz summoning two other U-boats and an Italian submarine to the scene, where they remained on the surface caring for the civilians in lifeboats. Hartenstein also broadcast in clear English his location and pledged not to attack any allied ship that would come help rescue the civilians. Suspecting a ruse, none came, and a U.S. Army bomber attempted to sink the U-boat several days later. The Vichy French government managed to send several ships from Dakar, and 1,370 of the passengers from the *Laconia* ultimately survived. While Donitz supported Hartenstein's decision not to abandon the *Laconia* survivors, he ordered all U-boat commanders to make no similar attempt in the future.

30. See "London Naval Treaty" at http://en.wikipedia.org/wiki/London_Naval_Treaty.

31. The text of Donitz's order of Sept. 17, 1942 would be included in the Nuremberg International War Crimes Tribunal proceeding against the admiral after Germany's surrender in May 1945. See Document 650 v.35, p. 304.

32. David C. Poyer, "Death of a U-boat," *Virginian-Pilot*, April 8, 1982.

33. For one assessment of the *Wahoo* attack, see James DeRose, *Unrestricted Warfare: How a New Breed of Officers Led the Submarine Force to Victory in World War II* (New York: John Wiley & Sons, 2000), p. 56. The details of the *Wahoo*'s encounter did not appear until author and Submarine Service veteran Clay Blair revealed the incident in *Silent Victory* (New York: J. B. Lippincott Company, 1975).

34. A subsequent report from the Joint Army-Navy Assessment Committee reduced Lockwood's totals to 1,314 ships and 5.3 million tons. This report was disputed by navy officials at the time. See Blair, *Silent Victory,* vol. 2, pp. 851–52.

35. Quoted in Peter Padfield, *War Beneath the Sea: Submarine Conflict During World War II* (New York: John Wiley & Sons, 1995), p. 479.

CHAPTER 5: THE RUSSIANS ARE COMING

1. One of the *K-219*'s sixteen missile tubes had been permanently sealed after a mishap during the 1970s that rendered it unable to safely house a missile.

2. The heroic actions of Engineer-Seaman Sergei Anatolyivech Preminin were first disclosed by Peter Huchthausen, Irog Kordin, and R. Alan White in their book, *Hostile Waters* (New York: St. Martin's Press, 1997). Additional details of the *K-219* sinking appeared in "Loss of a Yankee SSBN," by Captain First Rank Igor Kurdin MVF (Ret.) and Lt. Cmdr. Wayne Grasdock, USN, *Undersea Warfare,* Fall 2005 (Vol. 7, No. 5) posted at http://www.navy.mil/palib/cno/n87/usw/issue_28/yankee.html.

3. Norman Polmar, *Guide to the Soviet Navy* (Annapolis, Md.: Naval Institute Press, 1988), p. ii.

4. There were few Soviet naval successes at sea during World War II. One exception was the submarine *S-13,* which in two separate attacks on January 30 and February 10, 1945, sank two German ships evacuating military personnel from the Baltics. More than 7,000 German soldiers, civilian technicians, and refugees went down, and the submarine's captain, Capt. Third Rank A. I. Marinesko, received the title Hero of the Soviet Union. See Gary E. Weir and Walter J. Boyne, *Rising Tide: The Untold Story of the Russian Submarines That Fought the Cold War* (New York: New American Library/Caliber, 2004), pp. 27–33.

5. *Soviet Naval Developments,* Second Edition, prepared at the direction of the Chief of Naval Operations and Director of Naval Intelligence and the Chief of Information (Annapolis, Md.: Nautical and Aviation Publishing Co. of America, 1981), p. 1.

6. Stalin's naval ambitions cited in John E. Moore, Capt. RN (Ret.), *The Soviet Navy Today* (New York: Stein and Day, 1976), p. 19.

7. Weir and Boyne, *Rising Tide*, p. 37.

8. Michael T. Isenberg, *Shield of the Republic,* vol. 1 (New York: St. Martin's Press, 1993), pp. 93–96; also Norman Polmar and Thomas B. Allen, *World War II: America at War* (New York: Random House, 1991), pp. 853–53.

9. Norman Polmar, *The American Submarine,* Second Edition (Annapolis, Md.: Nautical & Aviation Publishing Co. of America, 1983), pp. 58–75.

10. Reaction to Soviet atomic bomb cited in Curtis Peebles, *Shadow Flights: America's Secret Air War Against the Soviet Union* (Novato, Cal.: Presidio Press, 2000), pp. 9–10; estimated Soviet submarine strength cited in Norman Polmar and Jurrien Noot, *Submarines of the Russian and Soviet Navies, 1718–1970* (Annapolis, Md.: Naval Institute Press, 1970), p. 139; also cited in Weir and Boyne, *Rising Tide,* p. 34.

11. Dr. Owen R. Cote Jr., "The Third Battle: Innovation in the U.S. Navy's Silent Cold War Struggle with Soviet Submarines," March 2000, posted at the U.S. Navy web site at http://www.chinfo.navy.mil/navpalib/cno/n87/history.html.

12. *Soviet Naval Developments,* pp. 4–5.

13. Quoted in Peter A. Huchthausen, *October Fury* (Hoboken, N.J.: John Wiley and Sons, 2002), p. 4.

14. Dr. Donald Chipman, "Admiral Gorshkov and the Soviet Navy," *Air University Review,* July-August 1982, posted at the Air University web site at http://www.airpower. maxwell.af.mil/airchronicles/aureview/1982/jul-aug/chipman.html

15. While Gorshkov's service span was nearly five years shorter than the extraordinary tenure of Adm. Hyman G. Rickover as head of U.S. Naval Nuclear Propulsion during 1949, Rickover did not have operational command of the nuclear submarine fleet nor the rest of the navy, as Gorshkov did in the Soviet Union. During Gorshkov's time as commander-in-chief, the U.S. Navy had nine chiefs of naval operations; also Chipman, "Admiral Gorshkov."

16. *Soviet Naval Developments,* p. 6.

17. Weir and Boyne, *Rising Tide,* pp. 48–49. For a detailed description of the 1956 Suez Crisis, see Daniel Yergin, *The Prize: The Epic Quest for Oil, Money, and Power* (New York: Simon & Schuster, 1991), Chapter 24.

18. Weir and Boyne, *Rising Tide,* p. 64. Unsafe conditions were not limited to Soviet nuclear submarines. The old Quebec-class diesel-electric submarines had such a penchant for violent fires in their diesel engines that their crewmen commonly referred to them as "cigarette lighters" in the Soviet fleet.

19. The Hotel-class nuclear submarine *K-19,* touted as the Soviets' answer to the more powerful American Polaris submarine, in July 1962 was supposed to launch several missiles while operating submerged. Soviets watching TV at home duly saw a missile rise from the ocean depths where the *K-19* lay submerged, ignite, and streak off toward a distant land-based target. Credit for the shot went to the Soviet Navy's propaganda office, which spliced in a land-based Strategic Rocket Force missile in place of the submarine's SS-N-5 missile, which had indeed been fired but abruptly veered off course and self-destructed. See Huchthausen, *October Fury,* pp. 11–12.

20. Bellona Foundation report, "Soviet Nuclear Submarine Accidents and Casualties," posted at http://spb.org.ru/bellona/ehome/russia/nfl/nfl8.htm#O17b.

21. Bellona Foundation report, "Soviet Nuclear Submarine Accidents and Casualties," posted on its web site at http://www.bellona.no/en/international/russia/navy/northern_fleet/report_2–1996/11084.html.

22. Huchthausen, *October Fury,* p. 13; also Weir and Boyne, *Rising Tide,* p. 65.

23. *The Cuban Missile Crisis 1962, a National Security Archive Documents Reader,* edited by Laurence Chang and Peter Kornbluh (New York: New Press, 1998). In *October Fury,* Peter Huchthausen, former U.S. Naval Attaché to Moscow, disclosed for the first time that four Soviet diesel submarines attempting to break through the naval quarantine in 1962 were armed with nuclear-tipped torpedoes and their commanders had permission to fire them if they thought their submarines were coming under attack.

24. Retired Vice Adm. Philip A. Beshany said in a 1977 oral history, "Polaris was one of the main considerations in his [the Soviet leader's] pulling back in the Cuban crisis. He said . . . the fact that that they had Polaris missiles at sea close to his homeland gave him a lot of pause for thought." Beshany, USNI oral history.

25. The central plot was called Operation Mongoose, and it had the full attention of both President John F. Kennedy and his brother, Attorney General Robert Kennedy, along with the Joint Chiefs of Staff, CIA, and State Department. This was no rogue operation à la Hollywood director Oliver Stone. Members of the White House's "Special Group (Augmented)," the panel that oversaw Operation Mongoose, included besides the Kennedy brothers presidential military assistant (and later Joint Chiefs Chairman) Gen. Maxwell Taylor, CIA Director John McCone, then-JCS Chairman Gen. Lyman Lemnitzer, National Security Adviser McGeorge Bundy, Undersecretary of State U. Alexis Johnson, and Deputy Secretary of Defense Roswell Gilpatric. See Anatoli Gribkov, Gen. USSR Army (Ret.) and William Y. Smith, Gen. USA (Ret.), *Operation Anadyr, U.S. and Soviet Generals Recount the Cuban Missile Crisis,* edition q (Berlin: Verlags-GmbH, 1994), pp. 89–90. U.S. diesel submarine operations cited in Ernest R. May and Philip D. Ze-

likow, editors, *The Kennedy Tapes: Inside the White House During the Cuban Missile Crisis* (Cambridge, Mass.: The Belknap Press of Harvard University Press, 1997), p. 442.

26. *Strategic Arms Competition,* pp. 471–75. The classified study revealed that at the time of the missile crisis, the Soviets had only forty-four operational ICBMs and about 100 submarine-launched ballistic missiles that were vulnerable because the land-based sites were "soft"—physically undefended—and the submarine missiles were range-limited, which would force their launchers to come close to the U.S. coastline to hit their intended targets. The United States, on the other hand, had 160 land-based missiles and another 100 medium-range missiles in Europe, as well as a massive strategic bomber fleet of 1,300 aircraft and another 112 Polaris missiles on the seven operational submarines.

27. Early models of the Golf-class submarine carried three SS-N-4 or SS-N-5 liquid fueled ballistic missiles. The later Golf-III submarine carried five SS-N-5 missiles. See Siegfried Breyer and Norman Polmar, *Guide to the Soviet Navy,* 2d ed. (Annapolis, Md.: Naval Institute Press, 1977), pp. 120–21. Also see Huchthausen, *October Fury,* pp. 3 and 18–19 for a description of the Soviet submarines' role.

28. Huchthausen, *October Fury,* p. 5.

29. While historians generally mark the period Oct. 16–28, 1962, as the time of the Cuban Missile Crisis, the U.S. Navy maintained a massive force of ships at sea for two months after the Soviets agreed to remove the missiles. The navy deployed an initial force of 117 ships in the first forty-eight hours after President Kennedy announced the naval quarantine on Oct. 22. A total of 223 ships and five land-based naval aviation squadrons formally received the Armed Forces Expeditionary Medal for service in the missile crisis during the official period Oct. 24 to Dec. 31, 1962. This reflects the Atlantic Fleet's decision to keep the force in place well after the Soviets removed the missiles, and a policy to rotate new ships into the area as some warships returned to port after weeks at sea. Sixteen of these ships would participate in the search for the *USS Scorpion* in 1968. See "U.S. Navy Ships and Units Which Received the Armed Forces Expeditionary Medal for Participating in the Cuban Missile Crisis, 1962," online at http://www.history.navy.mil/ faqs/faq90–3.htm#anchor156376. The two antisubmarine units were later relieved by the *USS Lake Champlain* (CVS 39) and *USS Wasp* (CVS 18) HUK Groups.

30. Descriptions of the two meeting locales from Dino A. Brugioni, *Eyeball to Eyeball: The Inside Story of the Cuban Missile Crisis* (New York: Random House, 1991), pp. 384–85, and Huchthausen, *October Fury,* pp. 49–54.

31. Edward C. Whitman, "SOSUS: The Secret Weapon of Undersea Surveillance," *Undersea Warfare* magazine, Winter 2005 (Vol. 7., No. 2), posted online at http://www.navy.mil/palib/cno/n87/usw/issue_25/sosus.htm.

32. Whitman, "SOSUS."

33. Ibid.; also Jeffrey T. Richelson, *American Espionage and the Soviet Target* (New York: William Morrow, 1987), pp. 168–69.

34. Dave Mayfield, "Their Mission: To Find Submarines," *Virginian-Pilot,* Sept. 20, 1999.

35. Weir and Boyne, *Rising Tide,* pp. 43–47.

36. Mayfield, "Their Mission."

37. Whitman, "SOSUS."

38. Elrod interview with the author, Nov. 13, 1997.

39. Huchthausen, *October Fury,* p. 75.

40. The Foxtrots were further plagued by equipment breakdowns and insufficient electric storage batteries, which made it even harder to operate submerged while being tracked by the U.S. Navy armada. See Weir and Boyne, *Rising Tide,* pp. 94–94.

41. Huchthausen, *October Fury,* p. 241.

42. Ibid., pp. 53–54.

43. Ibid., pp. 2–3.

44. Moore, *Soviet Navy Today,* pp. 29–31.

45. Ibid., pp. 29–36; also *Soviet Naval Developments,* pp. 6–8, and Weir and Boyne, *Rising Tide,* pp. 120–21.

46. Beshany interview with the author, Dec. 9, 1997.

47. Bez interview with Cinenova Productions Inc. editorial team, March 1998. The author was a consultant to this project; Alexin interview with Cinenova.

48. *K-181* mission described in Weir and Boyne, *Rising Tide,* pp. 114–18.

49. Question-and-answer interview with former Capt. Nikolai Shashkov: Nikolai Cherkashin, "On Moscow's Orders," *Russian Life* magazine, Oct. 1996. The former submarine commander erred in his identification of two of the U.S. Navy carriers in the Mediterranean in June 1967: The *USS America* and *USS Saratoga* were on deployment in the Mediterranean during the Six-Day War, but the *USS Enterprise* and *USS Forrestal* were not; see James M. Ennes, Jr., *Assault on the Liberty* (New York: Random House, 1979), pp. 116 and 237–41.

50. Cherkashin, "On Moscow's Orders."

51. The intelligence trawlers, known as AGIs, were a ubiquitous sight at the channel entrance to every U.S. Navy port from Holy Loch, Scotland to Guam. They stayed outside the three-mile limit and normally did not interfere with U.S. Navy operations, being content to soak up electronic communications and relay them to other Soviet Navy units. By the mid-1970s, the U.S. Navy and NATO had identified fifty-four intelligence-collecting trawlers in active service. See Moore, *Soviet Navy Today,* pp. 173–78.

52. Vice Adm. Kent Lee USN (Ret.) USNI oral interview, vol. 5, pp. 394–99 (undated), on file with the Naval Historical Center, Washington, D.C.

53. Former Soviet submarine officers later confirmed that their boats employed "burst" transmissions lasting only a few milliseconds to confirm orders in an attempt to avoid detection by U.S. radio direction-finding networks; also Patrick Tyler, *Running Critical: The Silent War, Rickover and General Dynamics* (New York: Harper & Row, 1986), pp. 17–19.

54. Tyler, *Running Critical,* p. 25. Navy officials say the Sosus stations on the U.S. East Coast and in the Caribbean reportedly could only cover sound signals as far as the mid-Atlantic, where the undersea mid-Atlantic Ridge ran north and south like a submerged mountain chain, blocking the long-range sound signals that flowed in the SOFAR channel. For this reason, the navy constructed the Azores Fixed Acoustic Range sonar array near the Portuguese island group in 1969. The incident where the Victor I

nuclear attack submarine reportedly surprised a navy carrier group in the Atlantic in 1967 is eerily similar to that of *K-181* and the *USS Saratoga* the previous fall.

55. Ibid., p. 44.

56. The navy used the intelligence report of the *Enterprise*-November incident to obtain congressional approval to begin work on a new and faster submarine design that would become the *Los Angeles*-class nuclear attack submarine, of which fifty-nine were built between 1976 and 1996. For more information on the *Los Angeles* SSN, see http://www.globalsecurity.org/military/systems/ship/ssn–688.htm.

CHAPTER 6: LEAVING HOME

1. The reconstruction of the scene at Pier 22 and the *USS Scorpion's* reactor start-up come from a number of sources: Former *Scorpion* crewman STCS (SS) Bill G. Elrod USN (Ret.) provided the author the Section 3 watch, quarter, and station bill during the submarine's 1968 deployment; commands and responses during the reactor start-up conform to the strict checklist of procedures mandated by the Naval Reactors Branch. Biographical details of the crewmen are from *USS Scorpion: In Memoriam*, U.S. Navy, 1969; the roster of Submarine Squadron 6 is described in *COMSUBLANT Command History for 1968*, and weather data for Norfolk, Va., on February 14–15, 1968 provided by www.Weather-Source.com.

2. *USS Seawolf* mishap described in William M. Arkin and Joshua Handler, "Naval Accidents: 1945–1988," Neptune Papers No. 3, Greenpeace and the Institute for Policy Studies, pp. 35–36.

3. The Izmir and Athens port visits were subsequently canceled. See personal letter from Cmdr. Francis A. Slattery to Capt. W. A. Greene, commander Submarine Division 62, April 18, 1968, Exhibit 32, Scorpion *Court of Inquiry*, vol. 5.

4. For the *Scorpion's* operations, see "*USS Scorpion* (SSN 589), Command History 1966," declassified in 1993. In 1966, the submarine conducted two separate "operations of higher classification" presumably against the Soviet Navy with port visits to Holy Loch, Scotland, preceding each deployment. The missions occurred during Feb. 20–Apr. 20, 1966, and during Oct. 12–Dec. 6, 1966. The remainder of the *Scorpion's* operational activities during its eight-year service life are found in *Record of Proceedings of a Court of Inquiry Convened by Commander-in-Chief, United States Atlantic Fleet . . . to Inquire into the Loss of* USS Scorpion *(SSN-589)*, Findings of Fact, vol. 4, pp. 1042–1043. For assessment of Lieutenant Harwi, see *Court of Inquiry*, vol. 2, p. 335 (declassified with redactions), testimony of former *USS Scorpion* Executive Officer Lieutenant Commander Robert R. Fountain, June 11, 1968.

5. Wells was 12th in service longevity among the 101 *Scorpion* crewmen in 1968. The longest-serving crewman was Torpedoman Chief Walter W. Bishop, who joined the submarine's pre-commissioning crew in 1959 and had served aboard it nonstop since then.

6. Michael DiMercurio and Michael Benson, *The Complete Idiot's Guide to Submarines* (Indianapolis: Alpha Books, 2003), pp. 191–203, and Norman Friedman,

Submarine Design and Development (Annapolis, Md.: Naval Institute Press, 1984), pp. 134–136. The narrative of the *Scorpion's* reactor startup process is a reconstruction of the procedures for a normal reactor startup in DiMercurio and Benson using the Section 3 Watch roster provided by Elrod, with additional background information on the S5W reactor design in Friedman.

7. Ernest R. May, John D. Steinbruner, and Thomas W. Wolfe, *History of the Strategic Arms Competition: 1945–1972,* Office of the Secretary of Defense, March 1981 (Top Secret, selectively declassified in 1996), Chapter IX, pp. 438–440.

8. Norman Polmar, ed., *The Ships and Aircraft of the U.S. Fleet,* 11th edition (Annapolis, Md.: Naval Institute Press, 1978), pp. 20–37.

9. Levey interview with the author, April 15, 1983.

10. Tennant testimony, *Court of Inquiry,* Vol. 4, p. 861.

11. The submarines launched on June 22, 1963, were the Polaris missile submarines *USS Ulysses S. Grant* (SSBN 631), *John C. Calhoun* (SSBN 630), and *Daniel Boone* (SSBN 629) at Electric Boat, Newport News, and Mare Island Naval Shipyard, respectively, and the nuclear attack boat *USS Flasher* (SSN 613), also at Electric Boat. The *Thresher* sinking still holds the sorrowful record of the most lives lost in a single submarine mishap. When the Russian Oscar II (Project 649A) submarine *Kursk* exploded and sank in the Barents Sea on August 12, 2000, there were 118 crewmen and technicians aboard.

12. The operating depth of nuclear submarines at the time was highly classified, but the figures for the *Skipjack* and *Thresher/Permit* classes have become publicly known in the years since their retirement from operational service. For Thresher details, see Norman Polmar, *The Death of the USS* Thresher (Guilford, Conn.: Lyons Press, 1964, 2001, 2004), pp. 3–10.

13. Statement of Rear Admiral Paul E. Sullivan USN, Deputy Commander, Naval Sea Systems Command, to the House Science Committee, Oct. 29, 2003, posted online at: http://www.house.gov/science/hearings/full03/oct29/sullivan.pdf#search=%22subsafe% 20program%20submarines%22.

14. Confidential source.

15. For a detailed description of the SubSafe program, see Francis Duncan, *Rickover and the Nuclear Navy* (Annapolis, Md: Naval Institute Press, 1990), pp. 96–98.

16. Ghormley interview with the author, Dec. 10, 1998.

17. Evidence of the SubSafe backlog is clear in the program history of the *Thresher/Permit-* and *Sturgeon-*class submarine programs. It took thirty-two months for Mare Island Naval Shipyard in California to build the *USS Permit* (SSN 594) from keel-laying on July 16, 1959 until its commissioning on May 29, 1962. The last four submarines of that class of attack boats, which were still under construction at the time of the *Thresher* sinking, took more than twice as long to construct because of the SubSafe program modifications the navy imposed. The *USS Flasher* (SSN 613) took sixty-three months from keel-laying on April 14, 1961 until it joined the fleet on July 22, 1966. The other three took even longer. The *USS Greenling* (SSN 614) needed seventy-five months, the *USS Gato* (SSN 615) took seventy-three months, and the *USS Haddock*

(SSN 621) required eighty months—nearly seven years from start to finish—because of SubSafe. The follow-on *Sturgeon* class also suffered, with eleven of the thirty-seven nuclear submarines requiring more than four years of SubSafe-certified construction, including two that took more than seven years from keel-laying to commissioning. See Norman Polmar, ed., *The Ships and Aircraft of the U.S. Fleet,* 11th edition (Annapolis, Md.: Naval Institute Press, 1978), p. 30.

18. Levey interview; Ghormley interview with the author, Dec. 10, 1998.

19. Rear Admiral Sullivan, statement.

20. A detailed recitation of the improper maintenance theory appears in Stephen Johnson, *Silent Steel: The Mysterious Death of the Nuclear Attack Sub* USS Scorpion (Hoboken, N.J.: John Wiley & Sons, 2006), which meticulously examines every reported equipment failure and malfunction looked at by the navy or cited by crewmen in letters to relatives. Nevertheless, the author concludes, "Despite the expenditure of millions of dollars and the earnest efforts of some of America's most talented scientists and naval personnel, the *Scorpion*'s demise remains unexplained." Details of the court's probe of the *Scorpion*'s material condition in *Record of Proceedings of a Court of Inquiry Convened by Commander-in-Chief, United States Atlantic Fleet . . . to Inquire into the Loss of* USS Scorpion *(SSN-589)*, Volume 1, pp. 29 and 32–33; also Findings of Fact 80–95, vol. 4, pp. 1051–52 and related testimony and exhibits.

21. In the seven months between the time it left Norfolk Naval Shipyard until sinking on May 22, 1968, the *Scorpion* had thirty enlisted crewmen leave the submarine. These included twenty-eight sailors who transferred off the boat for other assignments (such as Radioman Chief Daniel K. Pettey who left the ship while in the Mediterranean in April 1968) and two crewmen who left the submarine as it passed Rota, Spain en route to the Atlantic. Sonarman First Class Bill Elrod was on emergency leave to return to Norfolk, and Interior Communications Electrician First Class Joseph D. Underwood was sent ashore for a medical checkup. A number of them subsequently testified before the Court of Inquiry. See Exhibit 44, *Court of Inquiry*, Volume 6.

22. *Guide to Submarines,* pp. 206–208.

23. Reconstructed from interviews with former *Scorpion* crewmen; also see ibid.

CHAPTER 7: A SOVIET SUBMARINE VANISHES

1. Several accounts of the *K-129* incident have appeared in the past decade, including William J. Broad, *The Universe Below* (New York: Simon & Schuster, 1997); Sherry Sontag and Chris Drew, *Blind Man's Bluff: The Untold Story of American Submarine Espionage* (New York: PublicAffairs, 1998); John P. Craven, *The Silent War: The Cold War Battle Beneath the Sea* (New York: Simon & Schuster, 2001); and Kenneth Sewell, with Clint Richmond, *Red Star Rogue: The Untold Story of a Soviet Submarine's Nuclear Strike Attempt on the U.S.* (New York: Simon & Schuster, 2005). In the summer of 1968, the *Halibut* went searching for the *K-129*. After several months of trolling the ocean floor with its towed sled dangling three miles down behind it, the *Halibut* found and photographed the *K-129*'s broken hull in mid-August. That critical discovery later led to an ambitious

covert operation where the CIA built a massive ship, the *Glomar Explorer,* expressly designed to lift the *K-129's* hull fragments off the ocean floor. News of the attempt by the *Glomar Explorer* would remain secret until 1975, and it was only in 1997 that the U.S. Navy's earlier role in finding the Soviet submarine became known. Most details of the two operations remain classified to this day, including the exact intelligence bonanza that the submarine provided. When news of the *Glomar Explorer* project first leaked to the U.S. news media in 1975, most accounts portrayed the operation as a straightforward attempt to retrieve the submarine, its nuclear warheads, and Soviet codes. It was not until the publication of *The Universe Below* by *New York Times* reporter William J. Broad in 1997 that the earlier Navy intelligence operation involving the *Halibut* was revealed. Many navy participants including scientist Dr. John P. Craven portrayed the CIA as having usurped the navy's operation out of a combination of bureaucratic rivalry and political interference. One theory had it that the Nixon administration awarded Howard Hughes's company a multi-million-dollar contract to build the *Glomar Explorer* as a political payoff for his support of Richard Nixon's 1968 presidential campaign.

2. "Unbelievable coincidence" in Craven, *The Silent War,* p. 199.

3. The Soviet's first ballistic missile submarine was the Zulu class, a variant on the Whiskey-class diesel-powered attack boat. Ten Zulus were converted to the "Zulu-V" design with a pair of vertical launch tubes that carried SS-N-4 ballistic missiles. By the mid-1970s, all but one had been decommissioned. For information on the Yankee class, Siegfried Breyer and Norman Polmar, *Guide to the Soviet Navy,* 2d ed. (Annapolis, Md.: Naval Institute Press, 1977), pp. 118, 72, 122–24. For U.S. submarines in service in 1968, Norman Polmar, ed., *The Ships and Aircraft of the U.S. Fleet,* 11th ed. (Annapolis, Md.: Naval Institute Press, 1978), pp. 28–32.

4. Sewell, *Red Star Rogue,* pp. 55–56, citing a former submarine commander who spoke on grounds of anonymity.

5. Sontag and Drew, *Blind Man's Bluff,* p. 75.

6. Description of the *Pueblo* incident from Norman Polmar and Thomas B. Allen, *Spy Book, the Encyclopedia of Espionage* (New York: Random House, 1997), pp. 452–54; impact on Vietnam war plans, see Robert Pisor, *The End of the Line: The Siege of Khe Sanh* (New York: Ballantine Books, 1982), pp. 110–12; B-52 accident cited in Jaya Tiwari and Cleve J. Gray, *U.S. Nuclear Weapon Accidents,* Center for Defense Information, posted at http://www.cdi.org/Issues/NukeAccidents/accidents.htm

7. From William M. Arkin and Joshua Handler, *Naval Accidents: 1945–1988,* Neptune Papers No. 3, Greenpeace and Institute for Policy Studies, Washington, D.C., p. 35. The Neptune report listed different dates for the two mishaps.

8. Sabotage investigation cited in *Record of Proceedings of a Court of Inquiry Convened by Commander-in-Chief, United States Atlantic Fleet . . . to Inquire into the Loss of* USS Scorpion *(SSN-589),* chap. 4, pp. 1085–86.

9. Bill Elrod interview with the author, Sept. 22, 2006.

10. *Soviet Strategic Attack Forces,* National Intelligence Estimate 11-8-68, Central Intelligence Agency (declassified from Top Secret) revealed that the initial Yankee-class missile submarine had been launched at the Severodvinsk shipyard in September 1966 and

was scheduled to begin initial operations by the fall of 1968. The top-secret intelligence estimate also formally confirmed without naming it the loss of the *K-129* in March of that year; Soviet nuclear expansion cited in Ernest R. May, John D. Steinbruner, and Thomas W. Wolfe, *History of the Strategic Arms Competition: 1945–1972,* Office of the Secretary of Defense, March 1981 (top secret, partially declassified); also, "The Developing Soviet Submarine Force," *Special Report Weekly Review,* CIA Directorate of Intelligence, Sept. 13, 1968 (top secret, partially declassified July 28, 1994); also Breyer and Polmar, *Guide to the Soviet Navy,* pp. 120–125.

11. Craven, *The Silent War,* p. 204.

12. National Intelligence Estimate 11-8-68, also Craven, *The Silent War,* p. 204.

13. Details of Operation Winterwind and the *Halibut's* conversion into a spy submarine cited in Broad, *The Universe Below,* pp. 70–71. The first news report disclosing the cable-tapping missions did not include details on how or where the intercepts occurred. See Seymour M. Hersh, "Submarines of U.S. Stage Spy Missions Inside Soviet Waters," *New York Times,* May 24, 1975, p. A-1. Six years later, the Soviets acted on a tipoff from turncoat Ronald W. Pelton, a former National Security Agency staffer, locating and retrieving the six-ton cable-tapping pod. It was not for another five years after that, in 1986, that the *Washington Post* first publicly revealed details about Operation Ivy Bells, the cable-tapping missions to the Sea of Okhotsk, after the FBI charged Pelton with selling secrets of the program to the KGB. See Bob Woodward, "Eavesdropping System Betrayed, High-Technology Device Disclosed by Pelton Was Lost to Soviets," *Washington Post,* May 21, 1986.

14. Other submersibles developed by the Deep Submergence Systems Project included the nuclear-powered mini-submarine NR-1; the deep-diving submersible Alvin, and later, two more models, the *Turtle* and *Sea Cliff*; two Deep Submergence Rescue Vehicles that could ride piggyback on a specially configured submarine, the *Mystic* and *Avalon*; and the unmanned CURV (for Cable-controlled Underwater Recovery Vehicle).

15. The cable-tapping operation in the Sea of Okhotsk began in 1971 and continued for a decade. Other cable-tapping missions continued until the early 1990s. Sontag and Drew, *Blind Man's Bluff,* pp. 167 and 257–62.

16. Bez interview with Cinenova, March 1998.

17. The *Glomar Explorer* mission to raise the *K-129* was first reported in detail in several news reports. The two "inside" accounts were Clyde W. Burleson, *The Jennifer Project* (College Station, Tex.: Texas A&M University Press, 1977); and Roy Varner and Wayne Collier, *A Matter of Risk: The Inside Story of the CIA's Glomar Explorer Mission to Raise a Soviet Submarine* (New York: Random House, 1978). For examples of the debate of Sewell's "rogue submarine" theory, see "customer reviews" at http://www.amazon.com/Red-Star-Rogue-Submarines-Nuclear/dp/074326112.

18. Adm. Viktor A. Dygalo interview with Cinenova production team, March 1998.

19. Bez interview.

20. The commander of the *Swordfish*, Cmdr. John T. Rigsbee, later said the damage had come from the submarine striking an ice floe while on patrol off the North Korean coastline. Other U.S. Navy officials have long denied the *Swordfish* had any involvement

in the *K-129* sinking. Sontag and Drew, *Blind Man's Bluff,* pp. 79–80; also Sewell, *Red Star Rogue,* pp. 118–19.

21. Adm. Nikolai Nikolayevich Amelko interview with Cinenova production team, March 1998; Alexin interview.

22. Dygalo interview. For the Severodvinsk shipyard's role in constructing the Golf-class submarine fleet, see Breyer and Polmar, *Guide to the Soviet Navy,* 2d ed., p. 548.

23. Dygalo interview.

24. Sewell in his account of the *K-129* cited several fragments of circumstantial evidence to theorize that the submarine was on a rogue mission to launch its nuclear warheads at Hawaii. Sewell, *Red Star Rogue,* p. 105.

CHAPTER 8: THE LAST VOYAGE

1. Luella Violetti interview with the author, April 18, 1983; Anne Pierce interview with the author, April 18, 1983.

2. Violetti letter to his mother, dated May 10, 1968.

3. Weinbeck letter to his wife, dated May 1, 1968; additional biographical information provided by his brother, Ben Weinbeck.

4. Sanford Levey interview with the author, April 15, 1983.

5. Violetti letter to his mother, dated "May 16, midnight," 1968, actually early May 17.

6. Weinbeck letter to his wife, dated Feb. 26, 1968.

7. The most informative witness was Cmdr. Kurt Dorenkamp, operations officer for Submarine Flotilla 8 headquarters in Naples, who rode aboard the *Scorpion* from Rota to Taranto and provided detailed testimony to the court of inquiry on the material condition of the submarine and performance of its crew. *Record of Proceedings of a Court of Inquiry Convened by Commander-in-Chief, United States Atlantic Fleet . . . to Inquire into the Loss of* USS Scorpion *(SSN-589),* Findings of Fact, vol. 3, pp. 665–79.

8. Pettey transferred from the *Scorpion* to the *Skipjack* in late March 1968 while the *Scorpion* was halfway through the Mediterranean deployment; of the two crewmen transferred at Rota, both Interior Communications Electrician First Class Joseph D. Underwood and Sonarman First Class Bill G. Elrod testified before the court of inquiry. Underwood left the navy in late 1969 when his enlistment was up and returned to his home state of Iowa. He later joined the Iowa Army National Guard and was on a march in 1988 when he died of heart failure. Elrod stayed in the navy for another eighteen years, retiring in 1986 as chief of the boat of the *USS Dallas* (SSN 700); Pettey interview with the author, Aug. 5, 2006. Another *Scorpion* crewman, Steward's Mate Second Class Frederico L. DeGuzman, had been temporarily reassigned to a shore billet during the first five months of 1968 and so missed the submarine's Mediterranean cruise.

9. Christiansen letters to his parents, dated Feb. 2, 1967 and March 7, 1967.

10. Pettey interview.

11. The *Scorpion's* material condition during its 1968 deployment was the focus of one book that raised the possibility that an unknown mechanical failure was the most

likely cause of the submarine's sinking on May 22, 1968. But in *Silent Steel* (Hoboken, N.J.: John Wiley & Sons, 2006), Stephen Johnson concluded that none of the breakdowns could be linked to the sinking itself.

12. *Record of Proceedings of a Court of Inquiry Convened by Commander-in-Chief, United States Atlantic Fleet . . . to Inquire into the Loss of* USS Scorpion *(SSN-589)*, vols. 1–12, Underwood testimony, vol. 1, pp. 55 and 61. Pettey was unable to appear before the court because his new submarine, the *Skipjack*, was on a Northern run operation.

13. Ibid., p. 71.

14. Ibid., p. 93.

15. By 1968, a majority of the Polaris submarines had converted to the Polaris A-3 missile, which carried three separate warheads on a maximum flight range of 2,500 miles. The earlier A-1 and A-2 missiles could carry only a single nuclear warhead a maximum distance of 1,200 and 1,500 miles, respectively. See Norman Polmar, *The American Submarine*, 2d ed. (Annapolis, Md.: Nautical and Aviation Publishing Company of America, 1983), p. 169. Nuclear submarines in service in 1968, *The Ships and Aircraft of the U.S. Fleet*, 11th ed. (Annapolis, Md.: Naval Institute Press, 1978), pp. 20–37.

16. The Polaris submarines assigned to Submarine Squadron 16 in March 1968 were the *USS Andrew Jackson* (SSBN 619), *USS John Adams* (SSBN 620), *USS Casimir Pulaski* (SSBN 633), *USS Henry L. Stimson* (SSBN 655), *USS George C. Marshall* (SSBN 654), *USS John C. Calhoun* (SSBN 630), *USS Von Steuben* (SSBN 632), and *USS Will Rogers* (SSBN 659). The squadron's submarine roster was in a continuous state of flux as various Polaris submarines returned to the United States for scheduled overhauls and conversions to the new A-3 missile. See *COMSUBLANT Command History for 1968*, Dec. 16, 1969, p. 8, and *Submarine Squadron 16, Command History*, 1968, declassified and released to the author under the Freedom of Information Act.

17. Interview with former *Canopus* crewman Tom Carlough, June 11, 2006.

18. Weinbeck letter to his wife, dated March 2, 1968; Violetti letter to his family, dated March 3, 1968.

19. Summers letter to his family, dated March 20, 1968; Christiansen letter to his parents, March 5, 1968.

20. Dorenkamp testimony, *Court of Inquiry*, vol. 3, p. 667.

21. Soviet trawlers cited in Jeffrey T. Richelson, *Sword and Shield, Soviet Intelligence and Security Apparatus* (Cambridge, Mass.: Ballinger Books, 1986), pp. 98–103; Dietzen interview with the author, Feb. 23, 1988.

22. William Beecher, "U.S. and Soviet Craft Play Tag Under Sea," *New York Times*, May 11, 1968, p. A-1.

23. Jack Kestner, "U.S.-Red Subs in Collision Months Ago, Report Indicates," *Ledger-Star*, July 2, 1968; Carlough interview.

24. Soviet radio intercepts of the *USS Enterprise* from Vice Adm. Kent Lee USN (Ret.), USNI oral interview, vol. 5, pp. 394–399 (undated), on file with the Naval Historical Center, Washington, D.C.; land-based Soviet listening posts described in Richelson, *Sword and Shield*, pp. 99–100.

25. Norman Friedman, *The Fifty-Year War: Conflict and Strategy in the Cold War* (Annapolis, Md.: U.S. Naval Institute Press, 1999), pp. 325–31; also *Understanding Soviet Naval Developments,* 5th ed. (Office of the Chief of Naval Operations, 1985), p. 21.

26. "Naval Buildup in Mediterranean," *DIA Intelligence Summary,* April 11, 1968; "Significant Repair and Support Facilities in the Mediterranean," *DIA Intelligence Bulletin,* July 3, 1968.

27. Hedrick Smith, "Soviet Comeback as Power in Middle East Causes Rising Concern in West," *New York Times,* Jan. 14, 1968; also, Martin Arnold, "Admiral Says Soviet Is Striving to Rule the Seas," *New York Times,* Jan. 24, 1968.

28. Pettey interview.

29. Norman Polmar and Thomas B. Allen, *World War II: America at War* (New York: Random House, 1991), pp. 793–94.

30. Christiansen letter to his family dated March 10, 1968; Violetti letter to his mother, dated March 10, 1968.

31. FBM Facts/Chronology: Polaris-Poseidon-Trident, Department of the Navy, 1990; COMSUBLANT's command history chronology for 1967 noted that the Norfolk-based *USS Shark* (SSN 591) made a port visit to Halifax, Nova Scotia, marking "the first visit by a U.S. nuclear powered submarine to a Canadian port."

32. Christiansen letter, March 10.

33. Adrian Christensen letter to the author, April 1998.

34. Summers letter.

35. Dorothy Little letter to the author, Nov. 24, 1997.

36. Summers letter.

37. Violetti letters to his mother, dated March 24 and 28, 1968.

38. Violetti letter, March 28.

39. Bryan letter to his parents, dated March 28, 1968.

40. Slattery letter to Submarine Division 62 commander Capt. W. A. Greene, dated April 18, 1968.

41. Blenny and Irex ship's histories at the Naval Historical Center's *Dictionary of American Naval Fighting Ships* online at http://www.history.navy.mil/danfs/index.html; for Mediterranean deployments, see COMSUBLANT 1968 Command History, Page 15.

42. Calculation of the length of the two routes made using Nobeltec eChart Planner digital map of the Mediterranean, with the Latitude-Longitude calculator provided by the Indonesian travel web site, www.Indo.com.

43. Violetti letter to his mother, dated April 10, 1968.

44. Ibid.

45. Dorenkamp testimony, *Court of Inquiry,* vol. 3, pp. 670–71.

46. Cited by Machinist's Mate Second Class Mark Christiansen in a postcard dated April 28, 1968.

47. Sweeney letter to his parents, dated April 20, 1968.

48 Frances Welch interview with the author, April 14, 1983.

49. Christiansen letter to his parents, April 27, 1968.

50. Quoted in Dorothy Little letter.

51. There is no record in the declassified court of inquiry records explicitly confirming the *Scorpion's* mission to observe the Soviet warships, but several crewmen in letters home referred to extended submerged operations in the area that the DIA intelligence reports said the Soviet squadron was operating; also, "Naval Buildup in Mediterranean."

52. Violetti letter to his mother, dated "May 16, midnight."

53. Morcerf interview with the author, April 16, 1998; France on Aug. 24, 1968, detonated a 2.6 megaton hydrogen bomb code-named Canopus at Fangataufa. The *Scorpion's* sister ship, *USS Shark,* was on hand to monitor the nuclear test.

54. Date citations in letters previously cited.

55. Elrod interview with the author, Nov. 13, 1997.

CHAPTER 9: A TWISTED, SHINY PIECE OF METAL

1. News and weather information obtained from *New York Times* and *Virginian-Pilot* editions of May 22 and May 23, 1968.

2. Letter from Capt. George F. Bond to Ruthann Hogeland, wife of Electronics Technician 1st Class Richard Hogeland, quoted in Stephen Johnson, *Silent Steel: The Mysterious Death of the Nuclear Attack Sub* USS Scorpion (Hoboken, N.J.: John Wiley & Sons, 2006), pp. 123–24.

3. DSSP organization and Craven role from Robert C. Herold, "The Politics of Decision-making in the Defense Establishment: A Case Study," Ph.D. diss., George Washington University, Washington, D.C., 1969. There is a minor contradiction between Craven's public statements over the years regarding how he learned of the *Scorpion* alert and his sworn testimony to the court of inquiry on June 13 on that subject. In interviews with the author and in his 2001 memoirs, *The Silent War,* he hewed to his account of learning of the *Scorpion* on his car radio as he drove home from work around 6 P.M. However, Craven told the court that his office "was notified of the loss of the Scorpion at approximately 2000 [8 p.m. EST] on the 27th of May. We were notified by Captain [William F.] Searle, the Supervisor of Salvage. . . . Several members of the [Deep Submergence Systems Project] office, myself included, then reported to Flag Plot in the Pentagon at approximately 2100 . . . "; *Supplementary Record of Proceedings of the Court of Inquiry,* vol. 2, pp. 438–39. Regarding the Sosus system, the court initially noted that "no contact that could be identified as *Scorpion* was held on the Sound Surveillance System Atlantic (Sosus) at any time after she departed Rota, Spain, on 17 May"; Finding of Fact 42, p. 1046. However, a detailed analysis of the Sosus tapes, which filtered out stray sounds such as explosions, later showed eight separate arrays had in fact recorded the initial explosion. The *Scorpion* Technical Advisory Group in its 1969 report noted, "The Sosus data did serve as a consoling assurance that the hydro-acoustic data received by [other] hydrophones could indeed be associated with a unique event like *Scorpion's* loss." *The* Scorpion *Search—1968, An Analysis of the Operation for the CNO Technical Advisory Group,* prepared for the Chief of Naval Operations, Nov. 5, 1969; declassified with redactions, pp. 38–39.

4. Craven interview with the author, Nov. 15, 1986.

5. Ibid.

6. See *Operations Analysis During the* Scorpion *Search,* report to the Chairman, Technical Advisory Group, *Scorpion* Search, by Daniel H. Wagner Associates, July 31, 1969, p. 73; also *The Scorpion Search—1968,* fig. 4, p. 37 visually depicts the distance between the initial estimated location and the actual location of the *Scorpion.*

7. Official history of *USNS Mizar,* Dictionary of American Naval Fighting Ships, posted online at http://www.history.navy.mil/danfs/index.html; Buchanan's conversation with Craven, see Herbert Shuldiner, "Strange Devices That Found the Sunken Sub *Scorpion,*" *Popular Science,* April 1969; message to *Mizar* in *The* Scorpion Search—*1968,* p. 8.

8. *The* Scorpion Search—*1968,* pp. 18–21.

9. *Mizar* equipment described in *Operations Analysis During the* Scorpion *Search,* p. viii; Buchanan comments from interview with the author, April 18, 1983; the ship used a combination of intermittent satellite fixes to refine its own position several times a day, but this effort was hampered by the absence of an effective inertial navigation gear such as the SINS system onboard the *Compass Island.* See *Operations Analysis During the* Scorpion *Search,* p. 3.

10. Journalist 1st Class Sam Herzog USN, "*Scorpion* Search: Eyewitness Account," News Release, Military Sea Transportation Service, Nov. 22, 1968; Craven description of difficulty, Ed Offley, "*Scorpion:* Tale Can Be Told 25 Years Later," *The Day,* New London, Conn., May 23, 1993; Schade comments from "Remarks by Vice Adm. A. F. Schade USN, commander Submarine Force U.S. Atlantic Fleet to Members of the National Security Industrial Association," Naval Submarine Base, Groton, Conn., June 27, 1968, released under the FOIA Act; Assessment of *Mizar, The* Scorpion Search—*1968,* p. 23; Adm. Holmes's worry over search in CINCLANTFLT message 032136Z June 68 to CNO. This message formally requested that the navy declare the *Scorpion* as "presumed lost" on June 5, with formal notification of crew families several hours before the public announcement.

11. *Compass Island* 1968 history; also deck logs for June 3–7, 1968. Distances and bearings calculated from the Nobeltec eChart Planner software and the Latitude-Longitude calculator at www. Indo.com.

12. Craven 1984 interview and Buchanan 1983 interview.

13. Craven testimony, *Supplemental Record of Proceedings of a Court of Inquiry,* vol. 2, pp. 431 and 445–48.

14. Craven comments from 1984 interview; Buchanan remarks from 1983 interview; roster of explosive drops from *Supplemental Record of Proceedings of a Court of Inquiry,* Findings of Fact 10 and 13, pp. 243–44.

15. Craven 1984 interview.

16. *Supplemental Record of Proceedings of a Court of Inquiry,* vol. 4, Opinion 7, p. 1083.

17. Herzog, "*Scorpion* Search: Eyewitness Account."

18. *The* Scorpion Search—*1968,* pp. 30-31.

19. Herzog, "*Scorpion* Search: Eyewitness Account."

20. Buchanan remarks from 1983 interview; runs around Point Oscar from "Memorandum for the Secretary of the Navy," from Capt. A. T. Nicholson Jr., OP-33, July 1, 1968; no debris sighted, from Scorpion *Search—1968,* p. 68. Sonar image from *Operations Analysis During the* Scorpion *Search,* p. 40.

21. Craven 1984 interview; Buchanan 1983 interview; Scorpion *Search—1968,* Cover Letter from Chairman, Scorpion Technical Advisory Group.

22. Adm. Schade at COMSUBLANT handpicked his on-scene search commanders from his roster of submarine squadron commanders. They included Rear Adm. L. G. Bernard, COMSUBFLOT 6, May 27–June 17 (the open-ocean search and first seven days of the *Mizar* search); Capt. G. C. Ball Jr., COMSUBRON 12, June 17–30; Capt. H. R. Hanssen, COMSUBRON 4, June 30–July 26; Capt. J. E. Clarke II, COMSUBRON 6, July 26–Aug. 12; Capt. W. H. Knull, COMSUBRON 2, Aug. 12–Sept. 10; Capt. C. C. Brock Jr., COMSUBRON 8, Sept. 10–Oct. 11; and Capt. J. T . Traylor, COMSUBRON 10, Oct. 11–Nov. 7. Also see Craven 1984 interview; Buchanan 1983 interview; *Mizar* returns to Azores, Scorpion *Search—1968,* pp. 71–72.

23. Craven had previously used Bayes's theory to devise the underwater search for the missing air force H-bomb at Palomares, Spain, in 1966. Craven interview with the author, April 21, 1983.

24. Ibid.

25. M8/3 contact from Scorpion *Search,* fig. 7, p. 47; criticism of COMSUBLANT, Scorpion *Search,* pp. 77–78.

26. Craven 1984 interview.

27. Scientists directing search, from Scorpion *Search—1968,* p. 83.

28. *Scorpion* wives' comments in John Greenbacker, "22 *Scorpion* Families Still in Area," *Virginian-Pilot,* Oct. 21, 1968.

29. Christiansen letter to the author, March 15, 1998; Foli Lake email to the author, April 4, 1998.

30. Peterson comments in "22 *Scorpion* Families."

31. CNO and Chafee review of court report, endorsements to *Supplemental Record of Proceedings of a Court of Inquiry;* Don Hill, "Navy to Release *Scorpion* Data Next Week," *Virginian-Pilot,* Oct. 25, 1968.

32. Discussion with JCAE staff, Dietzen Memorandum; Traylor discovery of *Scorpion* image, *Supplemental Record of Proceedings of a Court of Inquiry,* Finding of Fact 19, p. 244.

CHAPTER 10: WHAT WERE THEY TRYING TO HIDE?

1. Bremner interview with the author, Oct. 18, 2004. In 1968, the ship's designator had been changed from EAG 153 to AG 153. The *Compass Island* was one of only two navy ships homeported at the 167-year-old Brooklyn base in 1968, the other being the USS *John R. Pierce* (DD 753), a twenty-three-year-old Naval Reserve destroyer. See "New York Naval Shipyard," profile at the Federation of American Scientists web site at http://www.fas.org/man/company/shipyard/new_york.htm.

2. *Compass Island* description, Norman Polmar, ed., *The Ships and Aircraft of the U.S. Fleet,* 11th ed. (Annapolis, Md.: Naval Institute Press, 1978), p. 176; also see *USS Compass Island* (EAG 153) history at http://www.ion.org/newsletter/v10n2.html; D'Emilio interview with the author, May 24, 2006; special operation, in *Command History 1968.*

3. Arrival in Brooklyn from deck log for *USS Compass Island,* May 24, 1968.

4. Alert for emergency departure from interviews with Bremner, Sebold, and D'Emilio interviews.

5. "Forty crewmen" cited in COMSUBLANT message 311500Z May 68 to CNO, declassified in 1993.

6. Julie Smith gave birth to the couple's daughter, Sarah Dee, on Saturday, May 25. Smith letter to the author, March 15, 1998; Sebold, Bremner, and D'Emilio interviews.

7. CINCLANTFLT message 031654Z Jun 68 marked "personal for Vice Admiral Bernard L. Austin." The members of the court were retired Vice Adm. Bernard "Count" Austin, president, who had led a similar inquest into the loss of the *USS Thresher* (SSN 593) in 1963; Rear Adm. Charles D. Nace, commander of Submarine Flotilla 2 in Groton, Conn.; Capt. Thomas J. Moriarty, staff officer, Cruiser-Destroyer Force, Newport, R.I.; Capt. Dean Horn, Portsmouth Naval Shipyard, N.H.; Capt. Harold G. Rich, Fleet Air Wing 3, Brunswick Naval Air Station, Maine; Capt. Ernest R. Barrett, commanding officer *USS Ethan Allen* (Blue) (SSBN 608), homeported in Rota, Spain; Cmdr. A. J. Martin Atkins, commanding officer *USS Daniel Webster* (Gold) (SSBN 626), homeported in Charleston, S.C. Apart from Rich, a naval aviator, and Moriarty, a surface line officer, the court members were all submariners. Schade's testimony, and that of other COMSUBLANT staff officers, was classified secret until September 1993, when the navy declassified most of the court of inquiry transcripts. See *Record of Proceedings of a Court of Inquiry Convened by Commander-in-Chief, United States Atlantic Fleet . . . to Inquire into the Loss of* USS Scorpion *(SSN-589)* (hereafter *Court of Inquiry),* vols. 1–3. *Scorpion* "presumed lost," in CNO Statement to the Press, June 5, 1968, entered as Exhibit 103, *Court of Inquiry.*

8. Ships and submarines described in *COMSUBLANT Command History for 1968,* Dec. 16, 1969, pp. 4–9; when Schade relieved Vice Adm. Vernon L. "Rebel" Lowrance as COMSUBLANT on Nov. 19, 1966, his immediate superior was then–Atlantic Fleet Commander Adm. Thomas H. Moorer. Nine months later, in August 1967, Moorer was sworn in as Chief of Naval Operations, replaced in Norfolk by Adm. Ephraim P. Holmes. During that era, the top admiral in Norfolk actually wore three hats: He was the Supreme Allied Commander Atlantic, responsible for all NATO naval operations in that theater of operations in wartime; he was commander-in-chief of the U.S. Atlantic Command, with command of all U.S. military units in the region in the event of a unilateral U.S. military operation, such as the 1965 intervention in the Dominican Republic or Operation Urgent Fury in Grenada in 1983; and he was U.S. Atlantic Fleet commander in charge of all U.S. Navy ships, aircraft, and shore stations east of the Mississippi. Likewise, the duties of the Atlantic Submarine Force commander involved specific operational responsibilities, including to "exercise operational control of forces . . . plan for and, when directed, conduct offensive submarine patrols. Plan for and, when directed, conduct special submarine

operations. Plan for and, when directed, conduct submarine, anti-submarine and other operations . . . for the defense of the continental United States." Under the NATO Treaty, COMSUBLANT also held the responsibility to "perform additional NATO duties, as directed by higher authority, as commander Submarines Allied Command, Atlantic, and commander Submarine Force, Western Atlantic [and to] act as submarine operational advisor to SACLANT. . . ." In August 1968, the submarine force commander took on yet another responsibility when the NATO Atlantic Submarine Organization realigned to assign Schade's headquarters responsibility for the eastern Atlantic as well. See *COMSUBLANT Command History for 1967*, Feb. 23, 1968, pp. 2–3, and *COMSUBLANT Command History for 1968*, pp. 3–4; command activities in *COMSUBLANT History for Command 1968*, pp. 1–16; "Northern run" operations in *COMSUBLANT Command History for 1968*, pp. 13–20. The number of special surveillance operations was extrapolated from a chart of "submarine week" totals for various operational functions, in which 181 weeks were designated for "special operations." Participants in those missions universally agree that they lasted an average of 60 days, giving a projected total of 22.6 deployments.

9. *Growler* incident, in Edward Whitman, "Submarine Hero—Howard Walter Gilmore," *Undersea Warfare* magazine, Summer 1999, posted online at http://www.chinfo.navy.mil/navpalib/cno/n87/usw/issue_4/sub_herohoward.html. As commander of the *Growler* in four subsequent war patrols, Schade went on to earn a Silver Star and Bronze Star and a second Bronze Star during a fourteen-month tour as commanding officer of the submarine *USS Bugara* (SS 381) from July 1944 until the end of the war. While the majority of World War II submarine officers left active duty in the immediate postwar years, Schade joined a number of veteran submariners who continued on with a navy career. For the next twenty-one years, he held down a number of increasingly responsible positions both in the submarine force and surface fleet, including tours as executive officer of the submarine tender *USS Bushnell* (AS 15); operations officer of the amphibious command ship *USS Mount McKinley* (AGC 7); commander of Submarine Division 12; commander of Submarine Group 1; commander of the amphibious cargo ship *USS Seminole* (AKA 104); and commander of Submarine Squadron 6 in Norfolk during 1958–59, leaving just two years before the *USS Scorpion* transferred to that unit in September 1961. After a tour as commander of the navy's Middle East Task Force during 1963–64, followed by several Pentagon staff assignments, Schade pinned on his third star and appointment as commander, U.S. Atlantic Submarine Force on Nov. 19, 1966, becoming one of a handful of World War II submariners to rise to the very top of the Navy's ranks. One of the ships in his new command was the 22-year-old submarine tender *USS Howard W. Gilmore* (AS 16), based in Charleston, S.C., supporting the 13 attack boats of Submarine Squadron 4; see Schade biography. The admiral's shore assignments and staff jobs during the postwar years also reflected his cultivation by navy leaders as a rising future leader of the service. He attended the Armed Forces Staff College in Norfolk during 1949–50; served as undersea warfare officer for the Commander, Naval Forces Eastern Atlantic and Mediterranean in 1952; attended the National War College during 1954–55, returning as an instructor during 1956–58; and attended a program for senior government and mili-

tary leaders at Harvard University during 1959–60 before becoming head of the Navy Plans Branch, and then director of the Politico-Military Policy Division in the office of the chief of naval operations in the Pentagon. During 1963–64 as a rear admiral, Schade commanded the navy's Middle East Task Force, followed by a two-year stint as deputy commander of U.S. Naval Forces Europe. After a brief tour back in the Pentagon in early 1966 as assistant chief of naval operations for plans and policy, he received his third star and appointment as COMSUBLANT on Nov. 19, 1966. See Schade biography, and *COMSUBLANT Command History for 1966*, chronology, p. 10. Commissioned on May 24, 1944 in honor of its namesake, the *USS Howard W. Gilmore* served the U.S. submarine force for 36 years, beginning in the Majuro Atoll, Marshall Islands, Brisbane, Australia, and Subic Bay, the Philippines during the final 18 months of World War II. Postwar service included 13 years at Key West, Fla., during 1946–59, Charleston, S.C. during 1959–70, and a three-year return assignment to Key West during 1970–73. The tender's last assignment was at La Maddeleina, Sardinia from 1973 until its decommissioning in 1980.

10. *Court of Inquiry,* vol. 1, p. 2.

11. This is the *Scorpion* message 212354Z May 1968, which is still classified top secret nearly 40 years after the fact.

12. Schade testimony, *Court of Inquiry,* pp. 5–7.

13. Ibid., p. 10.

14. In addition to the eight COMSUBLANT messages, the court identified a ninth message to the *Scorpion* that was sent from the Norfolk Naval Shipyard, identified as COMNAVSHIPYD NORVA 212157Z first transmitted at 0400 GMT on May 24. This message also requested a reply. The messages were entered as Exhibit 88. See *Court of Inquiry,* pp. 405–6; Finding of Fact No. 18, *Court of Inquiry,* vol. 4, p. 1043.

15. John P. Craven, *The Silent War: The Cold War Battle Beneath the Sea* (New York: Simon & Schuster, 2001), pp. 130–31.

16. Ibid.

17. Details of *Scorpion* message transmission, *Court of Inquiry,* vol. 2, p. 425; "no other message," *Court of Inquiry,* vol. 2, pp. 294–308; the comments on the messages' length are on p. 300; Schade's presence aboard the *Pargo* May 27, 1968 is cited in an official report and chronology of the submarine's participation in the *Scorpion* search, by Cmdr. Steven A. White, identified as "Enclosure 1 to SSN650:DNS:ht 03000 Ser: 017-68," June 7, 1968. Also see *Court of Inquiry,* vol. 1, p. 7.

18. Weather reports published in *The Virginian-Pilot* during May 22–27 show that the Memorial Day Nor'easter was a rapidly-developing storm that erupted after midnight on Sunday, May 26. In the five days prior to that, weather conditions in eastern Virginia had been unseasonably cool with only isolated rain showers reported between Wednesday, May 22 and Friday, May 24. Weather conditions then became warm and sunny on Saturday and Sunday, May 25–26.

19. The National Security Industrial Association in 1997 merged with the American Defense Preparedness Association and the combined organization was renamed the National Defense Industrial Association; Schade comments from "Remarks by Vice Adm. A.

F. Schade USN, commander Submarine Force U.S. Atlantic Fleet to Members of the National Security Industrial Association," Naval Submarine Base, Groton, Conn., June 27, 1968, released under the FOIA Act.

20. Schade telephone interview with the author, April 27, 1983.

21. Ibid. and Schade interview, 1986.

22. Former Submarine Squadron 6 commander Capt. Jared E. Clarke III and Submarine Division 62 commander Capt. Wallace A. Greene separately told the author that they were never informed of the pre-May 27 search for the *Scorpion*. Both men were interviewed in April 1983.

23. Craven 1986 interview; Craven, *Silent War*, p. 201.

24. Ashworth interview with the author, April 21, 1983.

25. Bellah interview with the author, Jan. 9, 1998; Greene interview with the author, April 20, 1983.

26. Meeker interview with the author, Jan. 16, 1998; Sparks interview with the author, Feb. 23, 1998.

27. *Court of Inquiry,* Finding of Fact 19, p. 1043.

28. Nace "youngest" World War II submarine commander, from obituary, Rear Adm. Charles D. Nace, Feb. 8, 2000; ships from Submarine Flotilla 2 identified in a roster of the *Scorpion* search operation included the submarines *Gato, USS Greenling* (SSN 614), *Pargo, Skate, Sturgeon,* and the surface support ships *Skylark, USS Sunbird* (ASR 15), and *Compass Island*. See *COMSUBLANT Command History for 1968,* pp. 4–6; Nace comments from interview with the author, Dec. 8, 1997; court member comments: Horn interview with the author, March 16, 1998; Atkins interview with the author, April 22, 1983; and Rich interview with the author, March 16, 1998. A fifth member of the *Scorpion* court, retired Adm. Ernest R. Barrett, interviewed in April 1983, said his memories of the inquest had faded to the point he could not discuss any details of the probe. Attempts to locate Capt. Thomas J. Moriarty, the sixth panelist, were unsuccessful. Court president Vice Adm. Austin died in 1975.

29. As commander of Submarine Flotilla 2 in Groton, Nace was responsible for over 51 submarines and surface support ships in Submarine Squadrons 2, 8, 10, and 14, as well as Submarine Development Group 2. Like Schade, Nace was a decorated combat veteran of submarine warfare in World War II. Graduating from the U.S. Naval Academy in 1939, six years after Schade and Moorer.

30. Maynard telephone call with the author, Jan. 14, 1998; Klinefelter interview with the author, Aug. 25, 1985; Hall interview with the author, Feb. 10, 1993; the alert message, ADMINO COMSUBLANT message 271955Z May 68, was actually released for transmission over the Fleet Broadcast System at 3:55 P.M. EDT but did not go out until about 30 minutes later, according to a chronology of events on the *Pargo* included in White, "Enclosure 2 to SSN650." The SubMiss message was entered as Exhibit 87 in *Court of Inquiry.*

31. Hall 1993 interview.

32. The five ships and manning rosters participating in the "focused operations" search for the *Scorpion* during June-October 1968 included the *USS Compass Island,* 218

crewmen; *USS Petrel,* 63 crewmen; *USNS Mizar,* 42 civilian crewmen; *USS Ozark* (MSC 2), 562 crewmen; and *USNS Bowditch,* 100 crewmen and technicians (approx.).

33. As one history of the project noted, "Such sounding arrays, coupled with accurate navigation, allow the immediate generation of accurate sea-floor maps. . . . The SASS [system] mapped a swath of seafloor by using beam-forming techniques to obtain up to 61 individual depths for each emission of the sonar system and, by so doing, developed a high resolution contour map of the seafloor." In 1968, SASS was installed aboard seven other research ships including a second vessel operating in the focused-operations search, the *Bowditch*, whose civilian crew also conducted various underwater surveying missions for the navy. SASS use in the *Scorpion* search from Sebold and D'Emilio interviews. SASS history in "Three Great Tools of the 1960s," in "History of NOAA Ocean Exploration," National Oceanic and Atmospheric Administration web site at http://www.oceanexplorer.noaa.gov/history/electronic/1946_1970/electronic_middle.html; a 2001 roster of military and civilian seafloor mapping systems compiled by the National Oceanic and Atmospheric Administration listed eight Military Sealift Command vessels including the *Compass Island* and *Bowditch* that had been equipped with a variant of the SASS sonar-mapping system. All had been retired from active service at the time of the survey. See "Worldwide Seafloor Swath-Mapping Systems," posted at http://www.ngdc.noaa.gov/mgg/gebco/scdbxxiannex20.pdf.

34. "Memorandum for the Secretary of the Navy: *Scorpion* Sitrep," June 26, 1968, classified Secret; also, *Court of Inquiry,* Finding of Fact 62, vol. 4, p. 1047, and *Scorpion Search,* p. 66.

35. Sebold, D'Emilio, and Bremner interviews; the SASS sonar cast a 60-degree imaging swath downward from the bow dome, aiming 30 degrees to port and 30 degrees to starboard from the vertical. At an ocean depth of two miles—the reported depth in the eastern Atlantic where the *Scorpion* sank—that translates into a roughly two-mile-wide image pathway.

For description of the SASS imaging capability, see "Three Great Tools." The *Scorpion* debris field is described in *Supplemental Court of Inquiry,* Findings of Fact, pp. 24–25, and in the report, "1984–1987 Investigation of *Thresher* and *Scorpion* Sites by the Deep Submergence Laboratory," Department of Ocean Engineering, Woods Hole Oceanographic Institution, Sept. 30, 1987, declassified 2000.

36. The court of inquiry noted in its Findings of Fact that the *Compass Island* had conducted "a detailed bathymetric survey" of the "focused operations" search area but the court was silent on the SASS system or its imaging resolution capability. See *Court of Inquiry,* Finding of Fact 34, p. 1045.

37. Schade's omission of any mention of the *Compass Island* in his June 27 speech was accurate in the narrowest sense; he had detached the experimental navigation ship from the *Scorpion* search on June 25, 1968, just two days before his address. The SASS installation aboard the *Bowditch* in 1968 is confirmed in "Worldwide Seafloor Swath-Mapping Systems." Computations of the *Compass Island*'s individual course tracks during its involvement in the *Scorpion* search are necessarily estimates, since the deck logs highlight only three timed position reports each day while also noting that the ship was steaming

"at various courses and speeds" as it dropped the demolition charges and mapped the seabed. The deck log position reports were plotted on a representative chart of the region, then compared with the latitude-longitude locations of Point Oscar and the various revised estimates, as well as the exact location of the *Scorpion* wreckage—which no one was supposed to know prior to its "official" discovery on Oct. 29.

38. Keeping *Compass Island* in search, "Memorandum for the Secretary of the Navy: *Scorpion* Sitrep 190800Q," by Rear Adm. J. C. Donaldson USN, classified Secret; "mission was over," Sebold interview; "lowering the cameras," D'Emilio interview; inability to relocate twisted metal, Scorpion *Search,* introductory memorandum from John P. Craven, Nov. 15, 1969.

39. *USS Petrel* Command History for 1968.

40. Ibid.; Nelson interview.

41. "Toured the ship": Craig F. Nelson letter to the author, Nov. 25, 1993; "seeing the pictures": Platte interview; Nelson interview; *Petrel* departure confirmation, Gregory L. Platte, BUPERS Record of Transfers and Receipts, furnished to the author. Difficulty of search effort in COMSUBLANT message 011155Z July 68, "Submiss Sitrep 32," declassified in 1993; also *Petrel* 1968 Command History.

42. Comment on Craven, Nelson letter; Nelson 1996 interview.

CHAPTER 11: BURN BEFORE YOU READ

1. The author interviewed former Ocean Systems Technician Vince Collier extensively over a five-month period beginning on June 11, 1999, and in a second session on Apr. 2, 2002. Collier broke his long silence over the Scorpion incident after reading a series of articles by the author published in *The Seattle Post-Intelligencer* on May 21, 1998, commemorating the 30th anniversary of the sinking that is posted online at http://seattlepi.nwsource.com/awards/scorpion/. In late February 2007, with Collier's help, the author located and interviewed retired OTC Richard Falck who confirmed the details of the Sosus tape played in the Navy classroom in 1982.

2. Falck interview with the author, Feb. 16, 2007.

3. The 1998 *Scorpion* report in *The Seattle Post-Intelligencer* is still accessible online at: http://seattlepi.nwsource.com/awards/scorpion/.

4. *Record of Proceedings of a Court of Inquiry Convened by Commander-in-Chief, United States Atlantic Fleet . . . to Inquire into the Loss of* USS Scorpion *(SSN-589)* (hereafter *Court of Inquiry),* vol. 4, Findings of Fact 39 and 53, pp. 1045 and 1047.

5. Schade testimony, ibid., vol. 1, p. 5.

6. The COMSUBLANT message to *Scorpion* identified as 161947Z May 68 was entered as Exhibit 72 and remained classified top secret in 2006. Also see *Court of Inquiry,* vol. 1, pp. 3–6; Dietzen comments from interview with the author, Feb. 23, 1988.

7. *Court of Inquiry,* Findings of Fact 45–50, vol. 4, p. 1045.

8. Even this limited information on the Soviet naval operation off the Canary Islands took years to become public knowledge: In 1983, the navy judge advocate general's office released a "sanitized" version of the court's "Findings of Fact, Opinions and Recommen-

dations." As released 15 years after the event, Finding of Fact 46 read: "That a Soviet [deleted] operation was being conducted southwest of the Canary Islands during the period of *Scorpion's* return transit from the Mediterranean. The group consisted of two hydrographic survey ships, a submarine rescue ship and an [deleted] nuclear submarine." It would not be for another ten years, until 1993, that the navy lifted those two redactions to reveal that the Soviets were involved in a "hydro-acoustic" operation and that the submarine involved was an "Echo-II class" nuclear submarine. *Court of Inquiry,* vol. 4, Findings of Fact 46; Soviet ships described, *Court of Inquiry,* vol. 4, Findings of Fact 46 and 48, p. 1046; most of Greene's testimony surrounding that operation was still classified in 2006. It spanned three pages of court transcripts. See *Court of Inquiry,* vol. 1, pp. 104–107; "*Scorpion* diverted" in "Brief on *USS Scorpion* (SSN 589)," memorandum to the *Scorpion* Court of Inquiry by Capt. W. A. Greene, commander Submarine Division 62, entered as Exhibit 21.

9. Craven interview with the author, Nov. 29, 1984.

10. Moorer testimony on Soviet naval expansion in *New York Times,* "Admiral Moorer Terms Soviet More Aggressive on High Seas," Reuters report, Oct. 9, 1968, p. A-6.

11. Moorer interview with the author, Apr. 15, 1983; Dietzen interview.

12. Schade comments in interviews with the author, Apr. 27, 1983 and March 14, 1986; Craven interview with the author, Nov. 29, 1984. Echo-II deployments in *Soviet Strategic Attack Forces,* National Intelligence Estimate 11-8-68, Central Intelligence Agency (declassified from top secret).

13. Schade 1983 and 1986 interviews; *Scorpion* reporting on May 21 from *Court of Inquiry,* Finding of Fact 50, vol. 4, p. 1046; Smith testimony from *Court of Inquiry,* vol. 3, p. 567.

14. "Completed reconnaissance" in COMSUBLANT Scorpion SAR Situation Report, May 28, 1968, declassified; Dietzen interview.

15. Contents of May 212354Z message paraphrased in Jack Kestner, "No Trace of Sub Found as Navy Presses Search," *Ledger-Star,* Norfolk, Va., May 28, 1968; approval to declassify the message in *Court of Inquiry,* testimony of Capt. W. A. Greene, vol. 2, p. 415.

16. Schade 1983 interview. Contents of May 212354Z message paraphrased in Kestner, "No Trace of Sub Found as Navy Presses Search"; approval to declassify the message in *Court of Inquiry,* testimony of Capt. W. A. Greene, vol. 2, p. 415.

17. Hall interview with the author, Feb. 10, 1993.

18. Beshany interview with the author, Dec. 9, 1997.

19. Beshany recalled that the intelligence indicators were taken very seriously at the time, but he said he never saw any subsequent confirmation of Soviet hostility toward the *Scorpion.* Once the navy located the submarine wreckage and the court of inquiry subsequently concluded that an accidental torpedo warhead explosion by one of the *Scorpion's* own weapons was the most likely cause of the sinking, Beshany said he surmised that the initial spasm of concern had likely been unfounded. Beshany interview with the author, Dec. 9, 1997.

20. Spintcomm described in *Atlantic Fleet* 1968 report, pp. 42 and 111–13. Schade 1983 and 1986 interviews; Moorer 1983 interview; Beshany 1997 interview.

21. D'Emilio interview with the author, May 24, 2006.

22. Greene 2006 interview; testimony of Capt. Allen E. May, Commander, Oceanographic Systems, U.S. Atlantic Fleet, *Court of Inquiry,* vol. 2, p. 434. According to May, the following U.S. submarines were operating at sea at the time of the *Scorpion* sinking: *USS Haddo, USS Skate* (SSN 578), *USS Gato* (SSN 615), *USS Sturgeon* (SSN 637), and *USS Simon Bolivar* (SSBN 641). He made no mention of the *USS Ray* (SSN 653), which Vice Adm. Arnold F. Schade said was operating off the Virginia Capes during the week of May 20, 1968.

23. Memorandum by Vic Furney, provided to the author, Dec. 28, 2005; Furney interview with the author, Nov. 14, 2006.

24. Stermer email interview with the author, June 5, 2006; Palmer email and telephone interviews with the author, July 5 and Nov. 15, 2006, respectively.

25. This is not the only instance where accounts by former sailors and navy records clash with a ship's deck log. The three *Compass Island* sailors quoted in Chapter 10 provided detailed, precise accounts of how their ship was ordered to sea just hours after returning to port on Friday, May 24. Moreover, navy messages confirm that several dozen *Compass Island* crewmen left behind on the pier had to fly out to the Azores on military aircraft to rejoin the ship on June 5, 1968. The deck logs for the *Compass Island,* however, state that the ship did not join the *Scorpion* search until close to midnight on Monday, May 27. The ship's command history reports a different date, noting the ship's participation in the *Scorpion* search began on May 28. *Josephus Daniels* cited in the following documents declassified by the navy: Atlantic Fleet message titled "SAR Operations" released at 2350 GMT, or 7:50 p.m. EDT, on Monday, May 27, with copies to navy headquarters in the Pentagon, the Atlantic Submarine Force, and a number of cruiser-destroyer flotillas. The news release likewise is dated on May 27. Rear Adm. Bernard's order to the *Josephus Daniels* and other ships to investigate the "Brandywine" radio transmission (see Chapter 1) is in his daily log entry for May 30, 1968, in *Court of Inquiry,* vol. 10. The roster of 11 ships and submarines participating in the open-ocean search that omits the *Josephus Daniels* was transmitted several times, including a COMSUBLANT message at 1940 GMT (5:40 P.M.) on Wednesday, May 29.

26. The author was onboard the *Alaska* along with about 20 other civilian guests, but was in another part of the 560-foot-long submarine and did not take part in the conversation in which the *Scorpion*'s fate became a subject. And the *Alaska* sailors did not realize that they were chatting with someone whose spouse had been researching the *Scorpion* incident for 15 years.

27. Collier 2002 interview.

28. Furney Memorandum.

29. Furney said he had long believed there had been a collision between the two submarines. Furney 2006 interview.

30. During the week of May 20, the *John Willis* was part of the anti-submarine formation led by the carrier *USS Essex* (CVS 9). This was the same formation that the

Scorpion had exercised with during its crossing of the Atlantic to the Mediterranean in February that year. The ASW group was 200 miles west of Norway when a Soviet land-based bomber shadowing the group crashed while making a low-altitude pass over the *Essex.* Corcoran recalled that the pilot of the Tu-16 Badger initially flew "so close to our mast top that it cast a shadow over our ship's bridge," then buzzed a second destroyer before approaching the *Essex.* "The plane made numerous mock-attacks on the *Essex.* Finally, it got so low that, on pulling out from its fourth or fifth attack run, it dipped a wing tip in the ocean," Corcoran recalled. The plane then cartwheeled and exploded. There were no survivors. See "Soviet Bomber Falls After Pass Near U.S. Carrier," *New York Times,* May 26, 1968. Corcoran email to the author, Dec. 27, 2006. Corcoran contacted me in response to my 1998 articles that are still posted on *The Seattle Post-Intelligencer* website at http://seattlepi.nwsource.com/awards/scorpion/.

CHAPTER 12: THE FATAL TRIANGLE

1. Description of the investigation and arrest of John A. Walker as a KGB agent primarily drawn from *Spy Hunter: Inside the Investigation of the Walker Espionage Case,* the memoirs of the case agent, retired FBI Special Agent Robert W. Hunter (Annapolis, Md.: Naval Institute Press, 1999). Additional information derived from three other accounts of the Walker spy ring: Jack Kneece, *Family Treason: The Walker Spy Case* (Briarcliff Manor, N.Y.: Stein and Day, 1986); John Barron, *Breaking the Ring* (Boston: Houghton Mifflin, 1987); and Pete Earley, *Family of Spies: Inside the John Walker Spy Ring* (New York: Bantam Books, 1988).

2. The arrest of John Walker came after an FBI screw-up that nearly derailed the entire operation. Due to a communications foul-up, one of the FBI surveillance agents on scene retrieved Walker's first 7-Up can too early. As a result, when a Soviet consular official later identified as Aleksey G. Tkachenko drove through the area and failed to spot Walker's "I am ready" signal, he quickly aborted the handoff and drove back to Washington. Meanwhile, another FBI agent who saw Walker deposit the garbage bag in the woods picked it up, finding the classified navy documents. Walker, returning to the original spot, saw that his can was gone, indicating that the Soviet had left a package with money for the spy ring. After several fruitless attempts rooting around in the woods for the bag containing the money, a visibly frustrated Walker drove back to the hotel, where the agents arrested him several hours later. The navy documents they had seized provided sufficient evidence for the arrest. See Hunter, *Spy Hunter,* pp. 54–60.

3. Walker's career assignments after 1969 included instructor at the Radioman School at the Naval Training Center, San Diego, 1969–71; classified materials systems custodian, supply ship *USS Niagara Falls* (AFS 3), 1971–74; communications staff, U.S. Atlantic Fleet amphibious force, 1974–76.

4. Hunter, *Spy Hunter,* pp. 205-6.

5. Ed Offley, "If Spy Charges Are True, Damage to Navy Is Substantial," *Ledger-Star,* June 1, 1985, quoting two retired navy communications chief petty officers.

6. Barron, *Breaking the Ring,* pp. 69–76.

7. The Walker spy ring's financial profile resulted in a cynical assessment among Norfolk lawyers who monitored the investigation: John Walker and Jerry Whitworth split most of the million dollars; Michael Walker got a measly grand, and Art Walker got just enough money from his brother to buy a barbecue grill and a new toupee.

8. Some navy officials were furious over the plea agreement, including Navy Secretary John F. Lehman, but the Reagan administration supported the move. Hunter, *Spy Hunter*, pp. 170–74. Michael Walker ended up serving just under 15 years in prison before he was paroled in February 2000. John Walker, Arthur Walker, and Jerry Whitworth remain in prison to this day.

9. "Very Serious Losses," *Time,* June 17, 1985; *Washington Post* article and senator's comments cited in Barron, *Breaking the Ring*, p. 136.

10. Ed Offley, "Secrets of the Deep: The John Walker Spy Case," *Seattle Post-Intelligencer,* May 18, 1985.

11. Background interview, U.S. Navy intelligence official, May 6, 1986.

12. "Inquiry into the *USS Pueblo* and EC-121 Plane Incidents," House Armed Services special subcommittee report No. 91-12, 1969, partially declassified, pp. 1630–32.

13. Ibid., p. 1639.

14. CINCPAC risk assessment message 230239Z December 1967, partially declassified and released by the director, National Security Agency to the House Armed Services Subcommittee on the *Pueblo* and EC-121 Incidents. A review of dozens of military and intelligence documents declassified during the House subcommittee review turned up no mention of the Israeli attack on the *Liberty.*

15. "Inquiry into *Pueblo* and EC-121," various sections. The House subcommittee investigation concluded: "If nothing else, the inquiry reveals the existence of a vast and complex military structure capable of acquiring almost infinite amounts of information but with a demonstrated inability in these two instances to relay this information in a timely and comprehensible fashion to those charged with the responsibility for making [national security] decisions."

16. Proposed U.S. landings in North Vietnam cited in Robert Pisor, *The End of the Line: The Siege of Khe Sanh* (New York: Ballantine Books, 1982), pp. 113–14; president's reaction to *Pueblo* seizure in Lyndon B. Johnson, *The Vantage Point: Perspectives of the Presidency* (New York: Holt, Rinehart and Winston, 1971), pp. 532–37.

17. The vast majority of books dealing with military or political events in 1968 include in-depth treatment of the *Pueblo* incident. These include political accounts such as Jules Witcover, *1968: The Year the Dream Died* (New York: Warner Books, 1997) and *The Making of the President 1968* (New York: Atheneum Publishers, 1969). President Johnson himself devoted a chapter to the series of catastrophes that struck in the final days of January 1968, including the *Pueblo.* (Johnson, *The Vantage Point,* pp. 532–37). Subsequently, there were a half-dozen accounts of the incident, including three written or co-authored by *Pueblo* officers: Lloyd Bucher, *My Story*, by the *Pueblo* commanding officer (New York: Dell Books, 1971); former Lt. Edward R. Murphy Jr. with Curt Gentry, *Second in Command: The Uncensored Account of the Capture of the Spy Ship* Pueblo (New York: Holt, Rinehart and Winston, 1971); former Lt.j.g. F. Carl Schumacher Jr. and

George C. Wilson, *Bridge of No Return: The Ordeal of the USS* Pueblo (New York: Harcourt Brace Jovanovich, 1971).

18. COMNAVFORJAPAN message 042304Z Jan 68 to *USS Pueblo* listed the Registered Publications System (cryptographic gear) that the ship would carry on its surveillance mission. Partially declassified and released by the House Armed Services Committee. The ship was authorized to carry two KW-7, three KWR-37, one KLB-47, and four KG-14 units.

19. Chronology of transmissions from the *USS Pueblo*, "Inquiry into *Pueblo* and EC-121," p. 1661; denial of the *Pueblo* commander's request for a "destruct system" for encryption equipment in a Naval Ship Systems Command message of July 18, 1967, cited in "Inquiry into *Pueblo* and EC-121," p, 729; Bailey interview with the author, April 9, 1998.

20. Norman Polmar and Thomas B. Allen, *Merchants of Treason: America's Secrets for Sale* (New York: Delacorte Press, 1988), p. 210.

21. Earley, *Family of Spies,* pp. 74–83.

22. Inaccurate embassy description, Hunter, *Spy Hunter,* p. 122; spying began in 1967, confidential interview, senior U.S. Navy intelligence official, Feb. 20, 1998, also Kneece, *Family Treason,* p. 47, and Barron, *Breaking the Ring,* pp. 220–21; Arthur Walker confession, Hunter, *Spy Hunter,* p. 33.

23. Kalugin's recollection in Oleg Kalugin, Maj. Gen., KGB (Ret.), *The First Directorate: My 32 Years in Intelligence and Espionage against the West* (New York: St. Martin's Press, 1994), p. 83; interview with Kalugin on recruitment of Walker recounted in *Spy Hunter,* p. 215; Walker description of pre-1968 spying in Hunter, *Spy Hunter,* p. 122.

24. The next day Walker denied he meant what he had said regarding the *Pueblo* but subsequently failed multiple lie detector tests on that denial. Confidential interviews, senior U.S. Navy intelligence official, Feb. 20 and April 4, 1998.

25. In a bizarre turnabout, Yurchenko "redefected" back to the Soviet Union in November 1985, publicly charging that he had been kidnapped by the CIA. However, U.S. officials have said he later changed his mind. Yurchenko at Soviet Embassy, Barron, *Breaking the Ring,* p. 138; redefection, pp. 154–57.

26. "Affidavit of William O. Studemann, Director of Naval Intelligence," Nov. 4, 1986, U.S. District Court, District of Maryland Case H-85-0309.

27. Kalugin writing in *The First Directorate,* pp. 87–89; CBS interview transcript cited in James Bamford, *Body of Secrets: Anatomy of the Ultra-Secret National Security Agency* (New York: Doubleday, 2001), pp. 275–77.

28. Interview and email from retired Capt. Peter A. Huchthausen to the author, Sept. 4, 2006. This is further discussed in the next chapter.

29. Roster of *USS Scorpion* cryptographic equipment in *Record of Proceedings of a Court of Inquiry Convened by Commander-in-Chief, United States Atlantic Fleet . . . to Inquire into the Loss of* USS Scorpion *(SSN-589),* testimony of Lt. Cmdr. R. D. Burgert, COMSUBLANT Electronics Material Officer, vol. 2, pp. 460–63. U.S. breaking of Japanese naval codes cited in W. J. Holmes, *Double-Edged Secrets: U.S. Naval Intelligence Operations in the Pacific During World War II* (Annapolis, Md.: Naval Institute Press,

1979), pp. 88–90; also Norman Polmar and Thomas B. Allen, *Spy Book: The Encyclopedia of Espionage* (New York: Random House, 1997), p. 368; Daniel K. Pettey interview with the author, August 5, 2006.

30. Studemann affidavit.

CHAPTER 13: WITH MAXIMUM PUNISHMENT

1. Collisions at sea described in William M. Arkin and Joshua Handler, *Naval Accidents: 1945–1988,* by Neptune Papers No. 3, Washington, D.C., Greenpeace and Institute for Policy Studies, pp. 32–34; Badger crash in "Soviet Bomber Falls After Pass Near U.S. Carrier," Associated Press, *New York Times,* May 26, 1968.

2. *Blandy* and the *B-130* in Peter A. Huchthausen, *October Fury* (Hoboken, N.J.: John Wiley & Sons, 2002), pp. 213–18; Huchthausen background in official navy biography.

3. Huchthausen letter to the author, Sept. 4, 2006; a full text of the Incidents at Sea agreement can be read online at http://www.state.gov/t/ac/trt/4791.htm.

4. Huchthausen letter.

5. Soviet trends cited in "A Soldier Talks Peace Marshal" (interview with Soviet military leader Sergei Akhromeyev), *Time,* Nov. 13, 1989.

6. The Soviets, like the rest of the world, learned in 1975 of the CIA operation to build a massive lift ship, the *Glomar Explorer,* which allegedly tried to lift the entire *K-129* hull from the Pacific seabed in June 1974. Some accounts have described the operation as a failure, with the lifting device recovering only the bow compartment containing two nuclear torpedoes and remains of several sailors. Other reports have said the mission "failure" was actually a cover story to conceal the *Glomar Explorer's* success in actually recovering the critical *K-129's* midships hull section containing its three nuclear missiles, the ship's code machine and various code books. Soviet admirals' comments in Huchthausen letter.

7. Oral history, U.S. Naval Institute interview with Rear Adm. Ralph K. James USN (Ret.), by John Mason, undated, p. 395. It was not until three years after James died on March 31, 1994, that I learned of his oral history comments about the *Scorpion.* In 1997, I contacted James's son, Rick, who confirmed that his father had made the same general comments to him and other family members about the Soviet's knowledge of the *Scorpion* location. The younger James added that his father had never discussed the incident in any detail.

EPILOGUE: ON ETERNAL PATROL

1. *Record of Supplementary Proceedings of a Court of Inquiry Convened by Commander-in-Chief, United States Atlantic Fleet . . . to Inquire into the Loss of* USS Scorpion *(SSN-589),* Opinions, pp. 251–55.

2. Schade theory, *Record of Supplementary Proceedings,* Finding of Fact 43, p. 249; court rejection of Schade theory, *Record of Supplementary Proceedings,* Opinion 16, p. 255.

3. The endorsement documents are: Adm. Holmes's disavowal of explosion as cause, "First Endorsement on Vice Adm. Bernard L. Austin, U.S. Navy (Retired), 058722/1103 (TS/RESDATA) ltr of 19 December 1968," declassified from top secret in 1998; Moorer comments, "Third Endorsement on Vice Adm. Bernard L. Austin, U.S. Navy (Retired), 058722/1103 (TS/RESDATA) ltr of 19 December 1968," declassified from top secret in 1998; Chafee comments, "Fourth Endorsement on Vice Adm. Bernard L. Austin, U.S. Navy (Retired), 058722/1103 (TS/RESDATA) ltr of 19 December 1968," declassified from top secret in 1998. Chafee replaced Paul Ignatius as secretary of the navy in January 1969, when the Nixon administration took office.

4. In several interviews, former Navy scientist John Craven said that one of the few unambiguous pieces of evidence from the Scorpion incident was the magnitude of the initial acoustic event that precipitated the sinking. "That's why I don't feel comfortable with the battery [scenario] because I've got to have . . . an event which is big." Adm. Bernard Clarey, the Navy's senior submariner in 1968, said, "Nuclear submarines don't have a big battery like diesel submarines. . . . It's a small battery, it's only made for extreme emergencies. I personally never thought it was the battery explosion." Trieste II findings from Second Endorsement on "Report of Scorpion Phase II On-Site Operations," Commander Task Unit 42.2.1, Aug. 7, 1969, partially declassified from Secret in 1998; battery explosion scenario from "Evaluation of Date and Artifacts Related to USS Scorpion (SSN 589)," Structural Analysis Group, June 29, 1970, partially declassified from Secret in 1998, pp. 7.1, 7.5, and 8.2.

5. Trost interview with the author, July 18, 2006.

6. Interior Communications Electrician 1st Class Joseph D. Underwood, the other crewman who departed the Scorpion in Rota on May 17, transferred to the USS Orion and left the navy in 1969 when his enlistment ended. He moved back to his hometown of Clinton, Iowa, and later joined the Army National Guard. He died at the age of 50 in 1988. Radioman Chief Daniel K. Pettey, who transferred off the Scorpion midway through the Mediterranean deployment, is retired and living in Pensacola, Fla.

7. Described in Robert M. Gates, From the Shadows: The Ultimate Insider's Story of Five Presidents and How They Won the Cold War (New York: Simon & Schuster, 1996), pp. 553–54.

8. Gen. Robert Magnus conversation with the author in June 2003, and subsequent email.

BIBLIOGRAPHY

BOOKS

Ackland, Len and McGuire, Steven, editors, *Assessing the Nuclear Age,* Bulletin of the Atomic Scientists/Educational Foundation for Nuclear Science, 1986

Allen, Thomas B. and Polmar, Norman, *Code Name Downfall, the Secret Plan to Invade Japan and Why Truman Dropped the Bomb*, Simon & Schuster, New York, 1995

Arkin, William M. and Fieldhouse, Richard W., *Nuclear Battlefields, Global Links in the Arms Race*, Ballinger Books, Cambridge, MA, 1985

Ballard, Robert D., *The Discovery of the Bismarck*, Madison Publishing Co., New York, 1990

Ballard, Robert D., *Explorations*, Hyperion, New York, 1995

Bamford, James, *Body of Secrets: Anatomy of the Ultra-Secret National Security Agency*, Doubleday, New York, 2001

Bamford, James, *The Puzzle Palace,* Houghton Mifflin Company, Boston, MA, 1982

Barlow, Jeffrey G., *Revolt of the Admirals: The Fight for Naval Aviation, 1945–1950*, Naval Historical Center, Washington, DC, 1994

Barron, John, *Breaking the Ring*, Houghton Mifflin Company, Boston, 1987

Beach, Edward L. Jr., Capt. USN (Ret.), *Cold Is the Sea,* Bluejacket Books (Paperback), September 2002

Beach, Edward L. Jr., Capt. USN (Ret.), *Salt and Steel: Reflections of a Submariner*, Naval Institute Press, Annapolis MD, 1999

Beschloss, Michael, *Mayday: Eisenhower, Khrushchev and the U-2 Affair,* Harper & Row, New York, 1986

Bivens, Arthur C., Capt. USN (Ret.), *Of Nukes and Nose Cones*, Gateway Press Inc., Baltimore, 1996

Blackman, Raymond V.B., editor, *Jane's Fighting Ships*, 1970–71, Jane's Publishing Co. Ltd., London, 1971

Blair, Bruce G., *Strategic Command and Control, Redefining the Nuclear Threat*, The Brookings Institution, Washington, DC, 1985

Blair, Clay, *Hitler's U-Boat War, 1939–1942*, Random House, New York, 1996

Blair, Clay, *Silent Victory*, J. B. Lippincott Company, New York, 1975

Brandt, Ed, *The Last Voyage of USS Pueblo*, W. W. Norton & Co., New York, 1969

Breyer, Siegfried, and Polmar, Norman, *Guide to the Soviet Navy*, Second Edition, Naval Institute Press, Annapolis, MD, 1977

Broad, William J., *The Universe Below*, Simon & Schuster, New York, 1997

Brown, Anthony, *Bodyguard of Lies*, Harper & Row, New York, 1975

Brugioni, Dino A., *Eyeball to Eyeball, the Inside Story of the Cuban Missile Crisis*, Random House, New York, 1991

Bucheim, Lothar-Gunther, *Das Boot*, R. Piper & Co., New York, 1973

Bucher, Lloyd, *My Story*, Dell Books, New York, 1971

Burleson, Clyde W., *The Jennifer Project*, Texas A&M University Press, College Station, TX, 1977

Burroughs, William E., *Deep Black, the Startling Truth Behind America's Top-Secret Spy Satellites*, Berkley Books, New York, 1988

Calvert, James F., Vice Adm. USN (Ret.), *Silent Running, My Years on a World War II Attack Submarine*, John Wiley & Sons Inc., New York, 1995

Carter, Ashton B., Steinbruner, John D. and Zraket, Charles A., editors, *Managing Nuclear Operations*, The Brookings Institution, Washington, DC, 1987

Clark, William Bell, *When the U-boats Came to America*, Little, Brown and Co., Boston, 1929

Cochran, Thomas B., Arkin, William M., Norris, Robert S. and Hoenig, Milton M., *Nuclear Weapons Databook*, Volumes I and II, Ballinger Books, Cambridge, MA, 1986 and 1987

Cockburn, Andrew, *The Threat: Inside the Soviet Military Machine*, Random House, New York, NY, 1983

Coleman, Fred, *The Decline and Fall of the Soviet Empire*, St. Martin's Press, New York, NY, 1996

Corson, William, Trento, Susan B. and Trento, Joseph J., *Widows: Four American Spies, the Wives They Left Behind and the KGB's Crippling of American Intelligence*, Crown Books, New York, 1989

Craven, John P., *The Silent War: The Cold War Battle Beneath the Sea*, Simon & Schuster, New York, 2001

Dalgleish, D. Douglas and Schweikert, Larry, *Trident*, Southern Illinois University Press, Carbondale, IL, 1984

Davis, Jacqueline, Sweeney, Michael J. and Perry, Charles M., *The Submarine and U.S. National Security Strategy into the Twenty-first Century*, Institute for Foreign Policy Analysis, Washington, DC, 1997

DeMercurio, Michael and Benson, Michael, *The Complete Idiot's Guide to Submarines*, Alpha Books, New York, 2003

DeRose, James, *Unrestricted Warfare: How a New Breed of Officers Led the Submarine Force to Victory in World War II*, J. Wiley, New York, 2000

Drosnin, Michael, *Citizen Hughes*, Holt, Rinehart & Winston, New York, 1985

Duncan, Francis, *Rickover and the Nuclear Navy*, Naval Institute Press, Annapolis, MD, 1990

Dunham, Roger C., *Spy Sub, a Top Secret Mission to the Bottom of the Pacific*, Naval Institute Press, Annapolis, MD, 1996

Dunnigan, James F. and Nofi, Albert A., *Dirty Little Secrets*, William Morrow, New York, 1990

Dunnigan, James F. and Nofi, Albert A., *Victory and Deceit, Dirty Tricks at War*, Quill/William Morrow, New York, 1995

Earley, Pete, *Family of Spies: Inside the John Walker Spy Ring*, Bantam Books, New York, 1988

Ennes, James M. Jr., *Assault on the Liberty*, Random House, New York, 1979

Eschmann, Karl J., *Linebacker: The Untold Story of the Air Raids Over North Vietnam*, Ivy Books, New York, 1989

Friedman, Norman, *The Fifty-Year War: Conflict and Strategy in the Cold War*, U.S. Naval Insitute Press, Annapolis MD, 1999

Friedman, Norman, *Submarine Design and Development*, Naval Institute Press, Annapolis, MD, 1984.

Friedman, Norman, *The U.S. Maritime Strategy*, Jane's Publishing Co. Ltd., London, 1988

Galantin, I.J., Adm., USN (Ret.), *Submarine Admiral*, University of Illinois Press, Champaign, 1995

Gallery, Daniel V., Rear Adm. USN (Ret.), *The* Pueblo *Incident*, Doubleday & Co., New York, 1970

Gannon, Michael, *Operation Drumbeat,* Harper & Row, 1990.

Garthoff, Raymond L., *Reflections on the Cuban Missile Crisis*, The Brookings Institution, Washington, DC, 1989

Gates, Robert M., *From the Shadows: The Ultimate Insider's Story of Five Presidents and How They Won the Cold War*, Simon & Schuster, New York, 1996

Gervasi, Tom, *The Myth of Soviet Military Supremacy*, Harper & Row, New York, 1986

Gibson, James W., *The Perfect War: Technowar in Vietnam*, Atlantic Monthly Press, New York, 1986

Gottfried, Kurt and Blair, Bruce G., editors, *Crisis Stability and Nuclear War*, Oxford University Press, New York, 1988

Gribkov, Anatoli, Gen. USSR Army (Ret.) and Smith, William Y., Gen. USA, (Ret.), *Operation Anadyr, U.S. and Soviet Generals Recount the Cuban Missile Crisis*, edition q, Verlags-GmbH, Berlin, 1994

Hastings, Max and Jenkins, Simon, *The Battle for the Falklands*, W. W. Norton & Co., New York, 1983

Hayes, Peter; Zarsky, Lyuba; and Bello, Walden, *American Lake, Nuclear Peril in the Pacific*, Viking Penguin, New York, 1986.

Herold, Robert. C., "The Politics of Decision-making in the Defense Establishment: A Case Study," Ph.D. Dissertation, George Washington University, Washington, DC, 1969

Hersh, Seymour M., *The Price of Power: Kissinger in the Nixon White House*, Simon & Schuster, New York, 1983

Hersh, Seymour M., *The Target is Destroyed: What Really Happened to Flight 007 & What America Knew About It*, Vintage Books, New York, 1987

Hobbs, David, *Space Warfare*, Prentice Hall, New York, 1986

Holmes, W. J., *Double-Edged Secrets: U.S. Naval Intelligence Operations in the Pacific During World War II*, Naval Institute Press, Annapolis MD, 1979

Howarth, Stephen, *To Shining Sea, a History of the United States Navy, 1776-1991*, Random House, New York, 1991

Huchthausen, Peter A., *October Fury*, John Wiley & Sons, Hoboken, NJ, 2002

Huchthausen, Peter A., Kurdin, Igor and White, R. Alan, *Hostile Waters*, St. Martin's Press, New York, NY 1997

Hunter, Robert W., with Hunter, Lynn Dean, *Spy Hunter: Inside the Investigation of the Walker Espionage Case*, Naval Institute Press, Annapolis MD, 1999

Isenberg, Michael T., *Shield of the Republic*, Volume 1, St. Martin's Press, New York, 1993

Johnson, Lyndon B., *The Vantage Point: Perspectives of the Presidency*, Holt, Rinehart and Winston, New York, 1971

Johnson, R. W., Shootdown, *Flight 007 and the American Connection*, Viking Penguin, New York, 1986

Johnson, Stephen, *Silent Steel: The Mysterious Death of the Nuclear Attack Sub USS Scorpion*, John Wiley & Sons, Hoboken NJ, 2006

Kalugin, Oleg, Maj. Gen., KGB (Ret.), *The First Directorate: My 32 Years in Intelligence and Espionage against the West*, St. Martin's Press, New York, NY, 1994

Karnow, Stanley, *Vietnam: A History*, Viking Press, New York, 1983

Kaufman, Yogi and Stillwell, Paul, *Sharks of Steel*, Naval Institute Press, Annapolis, MD, 1993

Kneece, Jack, *Family Treason: The Walker Spy Case*, Stein and Day, Briarcliff Manor, NY, 1986

Lee, Bruce, *Marching Orders, the Untold Story of World War II*, Crown Books, New York, NY, 1995

Lehman, John F. Jr., *Command of the Seas*, Scribners, New York, 1988

Lewis, Flora, *One of Our H-Bombs Is Missing*, McGraw-Hill, New York, 1967

Maas, Peter, *The Terrible Hours: The Man Behind the Greatest Submarine Rescue in History*, HarperCollins Publishers, NY, 1999

Manchester, William, *The Glory and the Dream, a Narrative History of America, 1932–1972*, Bantam Books, New York, 1975

Marchetti, Victor and Marks, John, *The CIA and the Cult of Intelligence*, Alfred A. Knopf, New York, 1974, with *The Consequences of Pre-publication Review*, monograph on court-ordered security deletions by the Center for National Security Studies, Washington, DC, 1983

Matlock, Jack F. Jr., *Autopsy on an Empire*, Random House, New York, 1995

May, Ernest R., and Zelikow, Philip D., editors, *The Kennedy Tapes: Inside the White House During the Cuban Missile Crisis*, The Belknap Press of Harvard University Press, Cambridge, MA, 1997

May, John, editor, *The Greenpeace Book of the Nuclear Age*, Pantheon Books, New York, 1989

Middleton, Drew, *Submarine*, Playboy Press, New York, 1976

Miller, David, *The Cold War: A Military History*, St. Martin's Press, New York, 1998

Miller, David and Miller, Chris, *Modern Naval Combat*, Crescent Books, New York, 1986

Moore, John E., Capt. RN (Ret.), *The Soviet Navy Today*, Stein and Day, New York, 1976

Murphy, Edward R., *Second in Command*, Holt, Rinehart and Winston, New York, 1971

Nutter, John J., *The CIA's Black Ops: Covert Action, Foreign Policy and Democracy*, Prometheus Books, Amherst, NY, 2000

Oberg, James E., *Uncovering Soviet Disasters*, Random House, New York, 1988

O'Kane, Richard H., Rear Adm. USN (Ret), *Wahoo, the Patrols of America's Most Famous World War II Submarine*, Presidio Press, Novato, CA, 1987

Ostrovsky, Victor, *The Other Side of Deception*, HarperCollins, New York, 1994

Padfield, Peter, *War Beneath the Sea: Submarine Conflict During World War II*, John Wiley & Sons, New York,1995

Peebles, Curtis, *Dark Eagles: A History of Top Secret U.S. Aircraft Programs*, Presidio Press, Novato, CA, 1995

Peebles, Curtis, *Shadow Flights: America's Secret Air War Against the Soviet Union*, Presidio Press, Novato, CA, 2000

Pisor, Robert, *The End of the Line: the Siege of Khe Sanh*, Ballantine Books, New York, 1982

Polmar, Norman, *Chronology of the Cold War at Sea: 1945–1991*, Naval Institute Press, Annapolis, MD, 1998

Polmar, Norman, *Guide to the Soviet Navy*, Fourth Edition, Naval Institute Press, Annapolis, MD, 1986; also Sixth Edition, 1988

Polmar, Norman, *Merchants of Treason: America's Secrets for Sale*, Delacorte Press, New York, 1988

Polmar, Norman, *The American Submarine*, Second Edition, The Nautical & Aviation Publishing Co. of America, 1983

Polmar, Norman, *The Death of the USS Thresher*, Lyons Press, Guilford, CT, 1964, 2001, 2004

Polmar, Norman, editor, *The Ships and Aircraft of the U.S. Fleet* 11th edition, Naval Institute Press, Annapolis, MD, 1978

Polmar, Norman, and Allen, Thomas B., *Rickover: Controversy and Genius*, Simon & Schuster, New York, 1982

Polmar, Norman, and Allen, Thomas B., *Spy Book: The Encyclopedia of Espionage*, Random House, New York, 1997

Polmar, Norman, and Allen, Thomas B., *World War II: America at War*, Random House, New York, 1991

Polmar, Norman, and Noot, Jurrien, *Submarines of the Russian and Soviet Navies, 1718–1970,* Naval Institute Press, Annapolis, MD, 1970

Powers, Francis Gary, with Gentry, Curt, *Operation Overflight,* Tower Publications, New York, 1970

Prange, Gordon W., with Goldstein, Donald and Dillon, Katherine, *Miracle at Midway,* McGraw-Hill Book Company, New York, 1982

Ranelagh, John, *The Agency: The Rise and Decline of the CIA,* Touchstone/Simon & Schuster, New York, 1987

Richelson, Jeffrey, T., *American Espionage and the Soviet Target,* William Morrow and Company Inc., New York, 1987

Richelson, Jeffrey, T., *Foreign Intelligence Organizations,* Ballinger Books, Cambridge, MA, 1988

Richelson, Jeffrey, T., *Sword and Shield, Soviet Intelligence and Security Apparatus,* Ballinger Books, Cambridge, MA, 1986

Richelson, Jeffrey, T., *The U.S. Intelligence Community,* Fourth Edition, Ballinger Books, Cambridge, MA, 1999; also First Edition, 1985

Rockwell, Theodore, *The Rickover Effect,* Naval Institute Press, Annapolis, MD, 1992

Rodengen, Jeff, *The Legend of Electric Boat,* Write Stuff Syndicate, Fort Lauderdale, FL, 1994

Roscoe, Theodore, *Pig Boats,* Naval Institute Press, Annapolis, MD, 1949

Sauter, Mark, with Sanders, John D. and Kirkwood, Cort, *Soldiers of Misfortune: Washington's Betrayal of American POWs in the Soviet Union,* National Press Books, Washington, DC, 1992.

Schemmer, Benjamin F., *The Raid,* Harper & Row, New York, 1976.

Schumacher, F. Carl and Wilson, George C., *Bridge of No Return, the Ordeal of the USS Pueblo,* Harcourt Brace Jovanovich, New York, 1971

Sewell, Kenneth, with Richmond, Clint, *Red Star Rogue: The Untold Story of a Soviet Submarine's Nuclear Strike Attempt on the U.S.,* Simon & Schuster, New York, 2005

Simpson, Colin, *The Lusitania,* Little, Brown and Company, Boston, 1972

Sontag, Sherry, and Drew, Chris, *Blind Man's Bluff: The Untold Story of American Submarine Espionage,* PublicAffairs, New York, 1998

Soviet Naval Developments, Second Edition, prepared at the direction of the Chief of Naval Operations and Director of Naval Intelligence and the Chief of Information, The Nautical and Aviation Publishing Co. of America, Annapolis, MD, 1981

Suvorov, Viktor, *Inside Soviet Military Intelligence,* Macmillan Publishing Co., New York, 1984

Tactical and Strategic Antisubmarine Warfare, monograph, Stockholm International Peace Research Institute, MIT Press, Cambridge, MA, 1974

Tyler, Patrick, *Running Critical: The Silent War, Rickover and General Dynamics,* Harper & Row, New York, 1986

Understanding Soviet Naval Developments, Fifth Edition, Office of the Chief of Naval Operations, 1985

Van der Vat, Dan, *Stealth at Sea: The History of the Submarine*, Houghton Mifflin Company, Boston, 1994

Varner, Roy and Collier, Wayne, *A Matter of Risk, the Inside Story of the CIA's Glomar Explorer Mission to Raise a Soviet Submarine*, Random House, New York, 1978

Vistica, Gregory L., *Fall from Glory: The Men Who Sank the U.S. Navy*, Simon & Schuster, New York, 1995

Weiner, Tim, *Blank Check: The Pentagon's Black Budget*, Warner Books, New York, 1990

Weir, Gary E., *Forged in War, the Naval-Industrial Complex and American Submarine Construction, 1940–1961*, Naval Historical Center, Washington, DC, 1993

Weir, Gary E. with Boyne, Walter J., *Rising Tide: The Untold Story of the Russian Submarines That Fought the Cold War*, New American Library/Caliber, New York, 2004

White, Theodore P., *The Making of the President, 1968*, Atheneum Publishers, New York, 1969

Wise, David and Ross, Thomas, *The Invisible Government*, Vintage Books, New York, 1974

Witcover, Jules, *1968: The Year the Dream Died*, Warner Books, New York City, 1997

Woodward, Bob, *Veil: The Secret Wars of the CIA*, Simon & Schuster, New York, 1987

Yergin, Daniel, *The Prize: The Epic Quest for Oil, Money, and Power*, Simon & Schuster, New York, 1991

Zumwalt, Elmo R. Jr., Adm. USN (Ret.), *On Watch*, Quadrangle/The New York Times Book Co., New York, 1976

GOVERNMENT REPORTS AND DOCUMENTS

USS Scorpion *Reports*

Deep Sea Radiological Environmental Monitoring Conducted at the Site of the Nuclear-powered Submarine Scorpion *Sinking*, Knolls Atomic Power Laboratory, 1986.

Evaluation of Data and Artifacts Related to USS Scorpion *(SSN-589), prepared for the CNO Technical Advisory Group by the* Scorpion *Structural Analysis Group*, June 29, 1970; declassified with redactions

"Investigation of *Thresher* and *Scorpion* Sites by the Deep Submergence Laboratory, 1984–1987," Department of Ocean Engineering, Woods Hole Oceanographic Institution, Sept. 30, 1987, declassified 2000

Operations Analysis During the Scorpion *Search*, report to the Chairman, Technical Advisory Group, *Scorpion* Search, by Daniel H. Wagner Associates, July 31, 1969

Record of Proceedings of a Court of Inquiry Convened by Commander-in-Chief, United States Atlantic Fleet . . . to Inquire into the Loss of USS Scorpion *(SSN-589),* Volumes 1-12 and *Supplementary Record of Proceedings of the Court of Inquiry;* declassified with redactions

Record of Proceedings of a Court of Inquiry Convened by Commander-in-Chief, United States Atlantic Fleet . . . to Inquire into the Loss of USS Scorpion *(SSN-589),* Volume 4, Page 1057 1–12 and *Supplementary Record of Proceedings of the Court of Inquiry;* declassified with redactions

Scorpion *Phase II On-Site Operations*, a Report by Commander, Task Unit 42.2.1, Aug. 7, 1969; declassified with redactions

The Scorpion *Search—1968, An Analysis of the Operation for the CNO Technical Advisory Group*, prepared for the Chief of Naval Operations, Nov. 5, 1969; declassified with redactions

USNS Mizar (T-AGOR 11), "Daily Operations Summary Log," Sept. 16–Oct. 1, 1968, partially declassified

Miscellaneous USS Scorpion *and Navy Documents*

"Continuing [*USS Scorpion*] Search Operations; Cost Estimates," NRL Memorandum, by C. L. Buchanan, July 25, 1968

"Handling Characteristics of the 588-class Submarine, a Qualification for Command Thesis," by Sanford N. Levey, Lt. USN, June 6, 1962

"Memorandum for the Record: Meeting with Mr. Ed Bowser [sic] and Mr. John Conway of Joint Committee on Atomic Energy (JCAE), report of," by Capt. Walter N. Dietzen USN, classified Secret, Oct. 28, 1968.

"Navy Reports Findings of the Court of Inquiry on the Loss of the USS *Scorpion*," News Release, Office of the Assistant Secretary of Defense (Public Affairs), Jan. 31, 1969

"Remarks by Vice Adm. A. F. Schade USN, commander Submarine Force U.S. Atlantic Fleet to Members of the National Security Industrial Association," Naval Submarine Base, Groton, CT, June 27, 1968

"Report of Search Operations for USS *Scorpion* (SSN 589) during period 271915Z May 1968 to 052000Z June 1968," by Rear Adm. Lawrence G, Bernard, Commander Submarine Flotilla 6, June 28, 1968

"*Scorpion* SAR Narrative" briefing to the *Scorpion* Court of Inquiry, June 11, 1968, declassified

"*Scorpion* Search: Eyewitness Account," by Journalist 1st Class Sam Herzog USN, News Release, Military Sea Transportation Service, Nov. 22, 1968

"*Scorpion* Search—Investigation Operations Period 14 October–7 November 1968," report of Commander Task Unit 42.2.1 to Commander Submarine Force, U.S. Atlantic Fleet, undated

"Statements and Rationale to Support 'Presumed Loss,'" memorandum for the Chief of Naval Operations, Vice Adm. Arnold F. Schade, June 2, 1968, declassified

Other Reports

"An Analysis of the Systemic Security Weaknesses of the U.S. Navy Fleet Broadcasting System, 1967–1974, as Exploited by CWO John Walker," thesis, by Maj. Laura J. Heath USA, 2005, online at http://www.stormingmedia.us/03/0396/A039634.html

Annual Report of the Commander in Chief, U.S. Atlantic Fleet, declassified, for 1967, 1968, 1969, and 1970

Bellona Foundation report, "Soviet Nuclear Submarine Accidents and Casualties," posted at http://www.bellona.no/en/international/russia/navy/northern_fleet/report_2-1996/11084.html

Central Intelligence Agency, Intelligence Information Cables: "Soviet Submarine Accidents," 1971–73 and 1968–72, declassified with redactions, Aug. 9, 1984.

COMSUBLANT Command History for 1968, Dec. 16, 1969. (Also *Command History* for 1967 and 1969)

Foreign and Military Intelligence, Book I, Final Report of the Select Committee to Study Governmental Operations with Respect to Intelligence Activities, United States Senate, Apr. 14, 1976

History of the Strategic Arms Competition, 1945–1972, prepared for the Office of the Secretary of Defense, published 1981 (Top Secret), declassified with redactions

Inventory and Source Term Evaluation of Russian Nuclear Power Plants for Marine Applications, by Ole Reistad and Povl L. Ølgaard, Nordic Nuclear Safety Research Center, April 2006, posted online at http://130.226.56.167/nordisk/publikationer/1994_2004/NKS-139.pdf#search=%22Soviet%20submarine%20S-176%22

Keeping the Nation's Secrets, a Report to the Secretary of Defense by the Commission to Review DOD Security Practices and Policies, Gen. Richard G. Stilwell USE (Ret.), Chairman, 1985

Naval Accidents: 1945–1988, by William M. Arkin and Joshua Handler, Neptune Papers No. 3, Greenpeace and Institute for Policy Studies, Washington, DC

Report to the President by the Commission on CIA Activities Within the United States, U.S. Government Printing Office, June 1975.

The Russian Navy, Federation of American Scientists, online at http://www.fas.org/nuke/guide/russia/agency/mf-intro-r.htm

Soviet Capabilities for Strategic Attack, National Intelligence Estimate 11-8-66, Central Intelligence Agency, declassified from Top Secret

Soviet Capabilities for Strategic Attack, National Intelligence Estimate 11-8-67, Central Intelligence Agency, declassified from Top Secret

Soviet Military Power 1988: An Assessment of the Threat, Department of Defense, 1988

Soviet Military Power 1989: Prospects for Change, Department of Defense, 1989

Soviet Military Power 1990, Department of Defense, 1990

Soviet Strategic Attack Forces, National Intelligence Estimate 11-8-68, Central Intelligence Agency, declassified from Top Secret

Supplementary Detailed Staff Reports on Foreign and Military Intelligence, Book IV, Final Report of the Select Committee to Study Governmental Operations with Respect to Intelligence Activities, United States Senate, April 23, 1976

Supplemental Reports on Intelligence Activities, Book VI, Final Report of the Select Committee to Study Governmental Operations with Respect to Intelligence Activities, United States Senate, April 14, 1976

Transmittal of Documents from the National Security Council to the Chairman of the Joint Chiefs of Staff, Hearings before the Senate Armed Services Committee, Part I and II, Feb. 6, 1974 and Feb. 20–21, 1974

Unauthorized Disclosures and Transmittal of Classified Documents, Report, Senate Armed Services Committee, Dec. 19, 1974

U.S. Nuclear Weapon Accidents, by Jaya Tiwari and Cleve J. Gray, Center for Defense Information, posted at http://www.cdi.org/Issues/NukeAccidents/accidents.htm

Pamphlets and Documents

Around the World, Around the Clock, Always Ready—U.S. Navy Submarine Force, Department of the Navy, 1992

America's Next Submarine, General Dynamics Corporation, 1997

America's Nuclear Powered Submarines, Department of the Navy, 1992

America's Strength Runs Deep, General Dynamics Corporation, 1997.

The Nuclear Navy: 1955–65, General Dynamics Corporation, 1966

The Submarine Force, Department of the Navy, 1992

The United States Naval Nuclear Propulsion Program, Department of the Navy, June 1997

U.S. Naval Nuclear Powered Submarine Inactivation, Disposal and Recycling, Department of the Navy, March 1995

U.S. Navy Nuclear Submarine Lineup, General Dynamics Corporation, 1997

NEWSPAPER AND MAGAZINE ARTICLES

The Chicago Tribune and *The Newport News Daily Press*, "A Risky Game of Cloak-and-Dagger—Under the Sea,*"* by Christopher Drew and Michael L. Millenson, Jan. 7, 1991

The Day, New London, Conn., "*Scorpion* Goes for First Dip As Onlookers Brave the Cold," Dec. 19, 1959

The Day, "Sub *Scorpion* Safe; Breaks Radio Silence," Sept. 16, 1960

The Day, "*Scorpion*: Tale Can Be Told 25 Years Later," May 23, 1993

The Ledger-Star, Norfolk, Va., "Sub Commander's Spouse Perfecting Champagne Aim," by Peggy Saunders, Aug. 30, 1967

The Ledger-Star, Norfolk, Va., "No Trace of Sub Found as Navy Presses Search," by Jack Kestner, May 28, 1968

The Ledger-Star, "Ordeal of Hope and Fear," by Larry Bonko, May 29, 1968

The Ledger-Star, "Hope of Finding *Scorpion* Ebbs as Hunt Goes on in Rough Seas," May 29, 1968

The Ledger-Star, "Splendid View of Nothing Filled *Scorpion* Hunters' Eyes," by Larry Bonko, May 30, 1968

The Ledger-Star, "*Scorpion* Grapevine Silent but Quintet Keeps Hoping," by Frank Creasy, May 30, 1968

The Ledger-Star, "Divers Checking Unidentified Hull, Navy Doesn't Think It Is *Scorpion*," by Richard C. Bayer, May 31, 1968

The Ledger-Star, "False Hopes Plague *Scorpion* Crew's Kin," by Richard C. Bayer, June 3, 1968

The Ledger-Star, "*Scorpion* Mission Secret," by Jack Kestner, June 7, 1968

The Ledger-Star, "*Scorpion*'s Mission Far From 'Routine,'" by Jack Kestner, June 8, 1968

The Ledger-Star, "Two Debate *Scorpion*'s Safety During Navy Court of Inquiry," June 10, 1968

The Ledger-Star, "No Damage Done Sub by Bump," June 13, 1968

The Ledger-Star, "No Peaks Found at *Scorpion*'s Depth," June 20, 1968

The Ledger-Star, "U.S.-Red Subs in Collision Months Ago, Report Indicates," by Jack Kestner, July 2, 1968

The Ledger-Star, "Nothing Remotely Connected with *Scorpion* Found by Navy," July 3, 1968

The Ledger-Star, "*Scorpion* Found Near End of Search," by Jack Kestner, Nov. 1, 1968

The Ledger-Star, "Likely Cause of *Scorpion* Loss Still Being Kept Secret by Navy," March 26, 1975

The Ledger-Star, "Navy 'Stonewalls' Sub Talk," by Jack Kestner, March 27, 1975

The Ledger-Star, "Wartime Foes Reunite as Friends," July 7, 1982, by Ed Offley

The Ledger-Star, "Chesapeake Bay Mined, War Came Close to Home," July 8, 1982, by Ed Offley

The Ledger-Star, "Confrontation in the Atlantic: The Death of U-701," July 9, 1982, by Ed Offley

The Ledger-Star, "If Spy Charges Are True, Damage to Navy Is Substantial," by Ed Offley, June 1, 1985

Metro magazine, "The Ghost U-boats of Hampton Roads," by Ed Offley, July 1977

The Milwaukee Journal, "Giant Search Started for Missing U.S. Sub," by the Associated Press, May 28, 1968

New Review magazine, "The Last Seven from U-701" (translated from the German), by Eberhard J. Fuchs

The New York Times, "Soviet Comeback as Power in Middle East Causes Rising Concern in West," by Hedrick Smith, Jan. 14, 1968

The New York Times, "Admiral Says Soviet Is Striving to Rule the Seas," by Martin Arnold, Jan. 24, 1968

The New York Times, "Soviet Sea Moves Disturbing to U.S.," by Benjamin Welles, Apr. 17, 1968, p. A-8

The New York Times, "U.S. and Soviet Craft Play Tag Under Sea," by William Beecher, May 11, 1968, p. A-1

The New York Times, "Soviet Bomber Falls After Pass Near U.S. Carrier," Associated Press, May 26, 1968

The New York Times, "U.S. Fears Threat to Polaris Craft," by William Beecher, Nov. 19, 1968, p. A-1

The New York Times, "Submarines of U.S. Stage Spy Missions Inside Soviet Waters," by Seymour M. Hersh, May 24, 1975, p. A-1

The New York Times, "A False Navy Report Alleged in Sub Crash," by Seymour M. Hersh, July 6, 1975, p. A-1

The New York Times, "Navy Has Long Had Secret Subs for Deep-Sea Spying, Experts Say," by William J. Broad, Feb. 7, 1994, p. A-1

Oceans Magazine, "When Incidents Are Accidents: The Silent Saga of the Nuclear Navy," by David B. Kaplan, August 1983

The Philadelphia Inquirer, "Soviets Confronted *Scorpion*," May 29, 1968

Popular Science, "Strange Devices That Found the Sunken Sub *Scorpion*," by Herbert Shuldiner, April 1969

Proceedings, U.S. Naval Institute, "Why they called the *Scorpion* 'Scrapiron,' " by Mark A. Bradley, July 1998

Proceedings, U.S. Naval Institute, "Real story of *Scorpion*?" by C. A. K. McDonald, June 1999

The San Diego Union, "Cover-up Aboard Nuclear Sub Alleged," by Tom Burgess, Aug. 6, 1989

The Seattle Post-Intelligencer, "Secrets of the Deep: The John Walker Spy Case," by Ed Offley, May 18, 1985

The Seattle Post-Intelligencer, "Russian Warships Pose Threat—to Russians," by Ed Offley, Feb. 26, 1993

The Seattle Post-Intelligencer, "Navy Says Sinking of the *Scorpion* Was an Accident; Revelations Suggest a Darker Scenario," by Ed Offley, May 21, 1998

The Seattle Post-Intelligencer, "Secrecy of Disappearance Compounded Families' Pain," by Ed Offley, May 21, 1998

The Seattle Post-Intelligencer, "Spy Net May Have Doomed *Scorpion* Before It Set Out," by Ed Offley, May 21, 1998

The Seattle Post-Intelligencer, "Two Men Are Forever Linked by Tragedy of the *Scorpion*," by Ed Offley, May 21, 1998

The Virginian-Pilot, Norfolk, Va., "Oil Slick Seen on Lost Sub's Course," by The Associated Press May 29, 1968

The Virginian-Pilot, "Patience Turned to Alarm," May 29, 1968

The Virginian-Pilot, "Wives Wait for News," by Wayne Woodlief, May 30, 1968

The Virginian-Pilot, "*Scorpion* Hunt Moves Eastward," by James Harper, May 31, 1968

The Virginian-Pilot, "*Scorpion* Search Continues With Lab Ship to Hunt for Sub," by Ken Wheeler, June 1, 1968

The Virginian-Pilot, "Navy to Widen Sub Hunt," by James Harper, June 2, 1968

The Virginian-Pilot, "*Scorpion* Search Centers at Hyeres Bank Near Azores," June 4, 1968

The Virginian-Pilot, "Sub Lost, Navy Declares," by Lawrence Maddrey, June 6, 1968

The Virginian-Pilot, "Sub Faulty, Ex-Crewmen Tell Court," June 7, 1968.

The Virginian-Pilot, "Mission of Sub Secret," June 8, 1968

The Virginian-Pilot, "Sub Was Safe, Officer Testifies," June 9, 1968

The Virginian-Pilot, "Secret of *Scorpion* Lies in the Depths," by Lawrence Maddrey, June 10, 1968

The Virginian-Pilot, "Court Advised 'Scorpion' Lacked Latest Charts, June 20, 1968

The Virginian-Pilot, "22 *Scorpion* Families Still in Area," by John Greenbacker, Oct. 21, 1968

The Virginian-Pilot, "Navy to Release *Scorpion* Data Next Week," by Don Hill, Oct. 25, 1968

The Virginian-Pilot, "*Scorpion* Wreckage Found," by Wayne Woodlief, Oct. 31, 1968

The Virginian-Pilot, "*Scorpion* Found About 400 Miles from the Azores," by John Greenbacker, Nov. 1, 1968

The Virginian-Pilot, "*Scorpion* Found by Deductive Reasoning," by John Greenbacker, Nov. 4, 1968

The Virginian-Pilot, "Small Piece of Metal Led Navy to Ill-Fated *Scorpion*," by Fred Hoffman, The Associated Press, Nov. 21, 1968

The Virginian-Pilot, "Court Views Pictures of *Scorpion* Debris," by John Greenbacker, Nov. 8, 1968

The Virginian-Pilot, "Navy Says *Scorpion* Is in Several Major Pieces," Nov. 16, 1968

The Virginian-Pilot, "Death of a U-boat," by David C. Poyer, Apr. 8, 1982

The Virginian-Pilot, "Their Mission: To Find Submarines," by Dave Mayfield, Sept. 20, 1999

The Virginian-Pilot and The Ledger-Star, "Mystery of Sub's Sinking Unravels," by Ed Offley, Dec. 16, 1984

The Washington Post, "U.S. Subs Spying in Soviet Waters," by Laurence Stern, Jan. 4, 1974

The Washington Post, "Eavesdropping System Betrayed, High-Technology Device Disclosed by Pelton Was Lost to Soviets," by Bob Woodward, May 21, 1986

World Book Science Service, "*Scorpion* Believed Found," by William Hines, July 19, 1968

ONLINE ARTICLES

Air University Review, "Admiral Gorshkov and the Soviet Navy," by Dr. Donald Chipman, July-August 1982, posted at http://www.airpower.maxwell.af.mil/airchronicles/aureview/1982/jul-aug/chipman.html

Air University Review, "Admiral Rickover and the Cult of Personality," by Paul K. Schratz, July 1983, online at http://www.airpower.maxwell.af.mil/airchronicles/aureview/1983/jul-aug/schratz.html#schratz

Army Historical Studies, "World War I: The First Three Years," extracted from *American Military History*, Office of the Chief of Military History posted at http://www.army.mil/cmh-pg/books/AMH/AMH-17.htm

Naval War College Review, "The Employment of Antiship Missiles," by Lt. Cmdr. Asen N. Kojukharov, Bulgarian Navy, Autumn 1997 (Vol. L, No. 4)

Submarine Warfare Division History website, U.S. Navy, *The Third Battle: Innovation in the U.S. Navy's Silent Cold War Struggle with Soviet Submarines*, by Dr. Owen R. Cote Jr., March 2000, posted at http://www.chinfo.navy.mil/navpalib/cno/n87/history.html

Undersea Warfare magazine, "Cold War Strategic ASW," by Norman Polmar and Kenneth J. Moore, Spring 2005 Vol. 7, No. 4, posted at http://www.navy.mil/palib/cno/n87/usw/issue_27/asw2.html

Undersea Warfare magazine, "Loss of a Yankee SSBN," by Captain 1st Rank Igor Kurdin MVF (Ret.) and Lt. Cmdr. Wayne Grasdock, USN, Fall 2005 (Vol. 7 No. 5) posted at http://www.chinfo.navy.mil/navpalib/cno/n87/usw/issue_28/index.html.

Undersea Warfare magazine, "SOSUS—The Secret Weapon of Undersea Surveillance," by Edward C. Whitman, Winter 2005 (Vol. 7., No. 2), posted online at http://www.navy.mil/palib/cno/n87/usw/issue_25/sosus.htm

Undersea Warfare magazine, "Submarine Hero—Howard Walter Gilmore," by Edward Whitman, Summer 1999, posted online at http://www.chinfo.navy.mil/navpalib/cno/n87/usw/issue_4/sub_herohoward.html

INDEX

Abelson, Philip H., 58–59
Acoustic recordings. *See also* Sosus
  Caesar system, 129
  Canada, 129, 137, 221
  Canary Islands, 49, 214–216, 221–223
  listening posts, 129
  SASS, 244, 268–273
  Scorpion sinking, 283–285
  search by, 12, 40, 48–51, 213–216, 221–235, 295–296
  Soviet identity tracked by, 84–85
AEC. *See* Atomic Energy Commission
Afghanistan, Soviet invasion of, 350
Air Force Technical Applications Center (AFTAC), 216, 220–223, 226
Aircraft
  antenna farms constructed by, 89
  North Korean shoot-down of, 337
  patrol by, 112, 132, 141, 295–296, 308
  search by, 8–9, 19, 22, 295–296, 308, 313–314

Soviet reconnaissance missions, 87, 89, 96, 308
  U–2 spy, 87, 125, 360
Alaska, USS, 312–313
Albacore, USS, 63–64, 66
Alexander Hamilton, USS, 146, 207
Alexandria, Egypt, 118, 134, 192
Alexin, Valery Ivanovich, 136, 177
Allen, Thomas B., 341
Amelko, Nikolai Nikolayevich, 165, 168, 175
America, USS, 138
Amtower, Thomas E., 146, 152
Anadyr, Operation, 133. *See also* Cuban Missile Crisis
Anderson, George W., 125–126
Andrea Doria, 130
Andrew Jackson, USS, 321
Antenna farms, 89, 191, 281, 302
Anti-submarine warfare. *See* ASW
Anti-Submarine Warfare School, 281, 323
Archives, declassification, 29, 37–38, 50
Argentia, Newfoundland, 129

Argonaut, USS, 99
Argus patrol plane, 308, 313
Armed Service Committees, 238–239
Arnold, John, 95
Ashworth, Frederick L., 262–263
ASW (anti-submarine warfare), 131. *See also* Warfare, submarine
Atkins, A. J. Martin, 49–50, 264
Atlantic crossing, 182–183, 209
Atlantic High Frequency Direction Finding network, 302
Atlantic Sosus network, 129, 130
Atlantic Submarine Force (COMSUBLANT)
  chain of command, 90
  crew shortage, 152–154
  espionage while at, 343, 344–345
  responsibilities of, 88
  search miscommunication with, 226–229, 234
  situation reports, 297
  Soviet interference tactics by, 189–190
  Special Intelligence operations of, 254
  SubMiss communications with, 7–11, 263–264

SubSafe assessment by, 149, 161–162
Atomic bombs, 115
Atomic Energy Commission (AEC), 59-60
AT&T, 128
Attitude
  submariner crew's, 99–100
  veterans', 285–287, 293–295
Augusta Bay, Sicily, 185, 197–200
Austin, Bernard L., 25, 31–32, 36, 246, 292, 371
Austin Healey, 78
Azores
  final message from, 14, 17, 19–20, 40
  listening post, 129
  Mizar's travel near, 217–218, 220
  search area around, 19–22, 216
  secret search in, 44
  surveillance flights in, 296–297
Azores Fixed Acoustic Range, 129

B–4, 132
B–59, 131
B–130, 131, 133
Bache, USS, 275
Baciocco, Al, 16–17, 78
Bahia Praia, Terceira, 220, 241
Bailey, Don, 338–339
Ball, George C., 33
Ballard, Robert, 272
Ballast Point Submarine Base, 373
Baltimore, Maryland, 320, 322, 326, 344
Banner, USS, 349
Barb, USS, 16
Barents Sea, 83, 95, 120
Battery
  explosion theory, 46–47
  technology, 62, 64
Battle of Midway, 89, 347
Battle of Verdun, 102
Bauser, Ed, 238
Bay of Pigs, 122–123

Bayes, Thomas, 232
Beach, Edward L., 79
Behrens, William "Wild Bill," 94
Beirut, Lebanon, 118
Belikov, Nikolai, 111
Bellah, James C., 6–7, 263, 372
Bering Sea, 86
Berlin Wall, 87
Bermuda, 8, 19, 132, 214
Bernard, Lawrence G.
  search efforts of, 13, 21–26, 217–218, 276
  testimony, 33
Berthing compartments, 71–74
Beshany, Philip A.
  background on, 300–301
  interview with, 136, 300–305
  responsibilities of, 19–20
  Soviet tactics recalled by, 136
Bessac, Norman, 54, 81
Bessledny, 349–350
Bez, Vladimir Ivanovich, 136, 175–176
Billfish, USS, 374
Bishop, Darlene, 374
Bishop, John, 10, 373, 374
Bishop Nolan, Mary Etta, 373
Bishop, Theresa, 2, 12, 24, 237, 373
Bishop, Walter
  background, 2, 77–78
  family, 2, 10, 237, 373, 374
  memorial, 373
Black Fin, USS, 53
Black Sea Fleet (Soviet), 116, 192
Blade count, 84–85
Blandy, USS, 350–351
Bledsoe, Charlice, 10
Blenny, USS, 199–200
Bohr, Neils, 58
Bollard missions, 93. *See also* Reconnaissance missions
Bond, George F., 212
Bonds, Joseph E., 220, 226, 244–245, 269, 306
Bonko, Larry, 19
Borisov, Vladimir, 137–138

Bowditch, USS, 218, 226, 273
BQR–2 sonar, 84, 92
Brandywine call sign, 23–24
Bremner, Hugh, 241, 245, 268, 271, 273
Brest, France, 104
Brett, R. P., 25
Brezhnev, Leonid, 134, 140
Britanov, Igor A., 111
British. *See* Great Britain
Brocker, Judith, 24
Brocker, Kenneth Ray, 24, 147
Brooklyn Naval Yard, 20, 243, 245
Brueggeman, Allie, 24, 237
Brueggeman, James K., 24, 147
Bryan, Robert E., 199
Buchanan, Chester L.
  final search efforts, 235–236
  initial search efforts, 216–220, 228–230, 231
  interview with, 220
  as lead scientist, 217–218
Bucher, Lloyd, 333–334, 339
Bureau of Steam Engineering, 58
Burke, John, 4, 148, 152
Bush, George H. W., 371
Bushido Code, 105
Buyo Maru, 106–107
Byers, Ronald, 197

CAD-CAM software, 61
Cadiz, Spain, 308–309
Caesar system, 129
Canada, listening posts in, 129, 137, 221
Canadian Air Force, 308, 313
Canary Islands
  acoustic recordings, 49, 214–216, 221–223
  diversion to, 209
  map, 14–15
  Soviet operation near, 39, 42
Canopus, USS, 183, 186, 187, 190
Carey, Francis K., II, 147, 151
Carlough, Tom, 183, 186, 190–191
Carlson, Evans F., 99

Carr, Kenneth
  background on, 53, 371
  Scorpion testing by, 53–54
  in Soviet reconnaissance
    mission, 93
Castro, Fidel, 122–123, 124
Cavalla, USS, 374
CBS news, 9–11
Central Intelligence Agency.
  See CIA
Chafee, John, 238, 270, 367
Chains of command, 88,
  90–91
Chamoun, Camille, 118
Charleston, South Carolina,
  13
Chazma Bay radiation
  accident, 67
Checkpoint Charlie, 87
Chernavin, Vladimir, 356
Chesapeake Bay, 99
Chesapeake, USS, 332
Chief of Naval Operations
  (CNO), 90
China, 170
Chivo, USS, 5, 373
Christiansen, Adrian, 196,
  237
Christiansen, Axel, 186
Christiansen, Jann, 9, 195,
  237
Christiansen, Mark, 363
  background on, 195–196
  complaints from, 180
  family of, 9, 186,
    195–196, 203, 237
  letters from, 180, 186,
    194, 195
  port visits of, 186, 194,
    195, 203
CIA (Central Intelligence
  Agency), 374
  Glomar Explorer operation
    of, 36, 174–175
  reconnaissance activity by,
    87, 96
CINCUSNAVEUR (Navy's
  operational command in
  Europe), 41
Clarey, Bernard A., 46–47,
  371
Clarke, J. Calvitt, Jr., 326
Clarke, Jared E., III, 252, 298
  background, 7

SubSafe inspection, 159
testimony, 32
CNO. *See* Chief of Naval
  Operations
Cochino, USS, 86–87
Cochran, E. L., 309
Code. *See also* Cryptography
  breaking, 88–89, 181
  words, 291–292
Cold is the Sea (Beach), 79
Cold War, 28, 29, 51, 86
communications affected by,
  89–90
  declassification after, 286
  reconnaissance missions,
    83–88, 95–96
  submarine warfare, 86–100
Cole, Nathan, Jr., 251
Collier, Vince, 287, 289–290,
  313
  background on, 281–282
  Scorpion sinking recalled
    by, 283–285
Collisions, 83–86, 94, 97–98,
  136–137, 144, 177–178
COMASWFORLANT
  (Atlantic Fleet Anti-
  Submarine Warfare
  Forces Command), 7–8,
  296. *See also* Warfare,
  submarine
Common Heritage
  Corporation, 371
Communications
  Brandywine, 23–24
  Cold War effect on, 89–90
  cryptographic, 88–89, 181,
    336–340
  final message, 7, 14, 17,
    19–20, 40, 42, 289–299
  foreign, intercepting and
    decoding, 88–89
  Pearl Harbor, 89
  Pentagon, 8–9, 19, 23, 25,
    214, 303–304, 315
  Pueblo, 334–340
  satellite, 135
  search, 221, 226–229, 234,
    242
  Special Intelligence,
    303–304
  strength of, 325, 339
  SubMiss, 7–9, 11, 18,
    263–264

top secret, 97–98
Communist hostility, 198,
  201
Compass Island, USS
  capabilities, 243–244,
    269–270
  official records of,
    242–243, 369
  Scorpion finding by,
    268–278, 271–273
  search by, 22, 218,
    220–223, 225–228,
    241–243, 245–246,
    268–278
  on Terceira Island, 220
COMSUBLANT. *See* Atlantic
  Submarine Force
Congress Joint Committee on
  Atomic Energy, 60
Conrad, Karen T., 312–313
Construction, 56, 60, 61–62.
  See also Design
Control rooms, 69–70,
  74–76, 146–149
Conway, John, 238
Coolant systems, 60, 68
Corcoran, Tom, 314
Course track
  conclusions, 50–51, 223
  map, 14–15
Court of Inquiry. *See also*
  Testimonies
  appointment of, 25
  censoring, 37–38, 40, 188,
    221
  Compass Island search
    questioning by,
    221–222
  conclusions, 238–239,
    278, 289–290, 292,
    366–367
  documentation, 366–369
  Findings of Fact, 40, 292
  foul play considerations,
    170
  goals, 246–247, 254
  ignorance of, 264–265,
    278
  initial hearings, 25, 30–33
  investigation into, 34–36,
    37–40
  Schade's part in, 31, 38,
    246–247, 249–252,
    254–255, 291

secondary hearings, 33–34,
170
SubSafe questioning by,
158–159
theory, 36, 47, 49–50, 225,
366
Cowan, Joan, 10
Cowan, Robert James, 10
Craven, John P.
background on, 11–12,
253, 370–371
interview, 48–49, 220,
262, 294
K–129 search by, 174
Scorpion search efforts by,
12, 48–49, 213–236,
277
search area probability map
of, 233–234
Soviet downplay by, 294
Special Intelligence views
of, 253–254
theory, 50–51, 223–225,
233
Crazy Ivan tactic, 135–136,
283, 314
Crete, 203–206
Crew, *Scorpion*, 357, 363. *See
also* Letters; *specific
names of Crew*
Atlantic Submarine Force
shortage, 152–154
attitude of, 99–100
berthing compartments,
71–74
complaints, 179–186, 188,
194–201
death of, 2–5, 9–11, 16,
212
future of surviving,
370–376
pay, 198–199
performance admiration,
78
responsibilities, 77
Section 3, 146–149
Cross, Anna, 4
Cross, Joseph, 4, 373
Crowley Walker, Barbara,
318, 342
Cruises, day, 82
Crush depth, xiii, 50, 79
Cryptography. *See also* Secret
information

code *v.*, 329
development, 336–337
equipment, 181, 337–340
history of, 88–89
keylists, 339–340
Pueblo's, 337–340
Cryptologic Bureau, 88
Crystal City, Virginia, 353
Cuban Missile Crisis, 12,
121–127, 131–134, 350
Czechoslovakia, 171

Dakar, 169, 275
Dallas, USS, 374
Danang, Vietnam, 211
Daphne-class submarines, 169
David Taylor Model Basin,
225
Davis, John F., 19
"Dead drop" espionage,
319–320
Deep Freeze, Operation, 206
Deep Submergence Systems
Project (DSSP), 11,
174, 213–214, 253, 368
Defense Intelligence Agency.
See DIA
D'Emilio, Bill, 245, 268
interview with, 270–273,
306
Soviet tracking recalled by,
306
Demolition drops, 221–223,
226
Denney, Garlin R., 149
Depth
crush, xiii, 50, 79
restrictions, operating, 156,
159
test, 47, 80, 155
Design
Albacore, 63–64, 66
hull, 61–62, 63, 73
Nautilus, 56–57, 63, 64,
66–67
new class, 29
nuclear propulsion, 59–68
Scorpion, 54–56, 57,
64–68
Skipjack, 54, 56, 64, 73, 75
Soviet submarine, 120
Structural Analysis Group,
368
SubSafe, 157

Thresher, 155–156
torpedo, 62, 70–71, 72,
105, 223–224
U-boat, 58, 62, 63
World War II, 106
DIA (Defense Intelligence
Agency), 253–254, 351,
355
Diesel power, 62–63
Dietzen, Walter N. "Buck,"
20, 78, 297, 372
interview, 47, 78,
291–292, 295
loss summary by, 238–239
Rota stop recalled by,
188–189
safety opinion, 79–80
Director of Undersea Warfare,
89
Donaldson, J. C., 217
Donitz, Karl, 103, 104
Dorenkamp, Kurt F.,
187–188, 201
Douglas H. Fox, USS, 13
DSSP. *See* Deep Submergence
Systems Project
Dubcek, Alexander, 171
Dunn, Michael E., 144, 148
Durenberger, David, 327
Dygalo, Viktor A., 175–176,
178, 357–358

Earley, Pete, 341
Echo-II-class submarines, 67,
97, 119–120, 138,
295–296
Edwards, R. F., 37–38
Egorov, Georgi, 138
Egypt, 118, 134, 191–192,
322
Eisenhower administration,
153
Eisenhower, Dwight, 118
Electric Boat Co.
Scorpion launch from,
54–55
submarines built at, 56, 60,
61, 63
Electric rabbit tactic,
141–142, 145, 199–200
Eleuthera Island, 129
Elrod, Bill G., 85, 131, 171
background, 68–69,
373–374

family of, 5–6, 10–11,
208–210
homecoming, 5–6, 10–11,
208–210
NATO exercises recalled
by, 81
Scorpion tour recalled by,
66, 68–78, 80
in *Scorpion's* recon mission,
83–86, 91, 92–93, 182
Elrod, Gordon Vincent, 5, 6,
374
Elrod, Julianne, 5–6, 374
Encryption systems, 337–338,
346. *See also*
Cryptography
Engine room, 77
Enterprise, USS, 138,
140–142, 335
Espionage
arrests and trials for,
317–330, 339–340,
344–345
Atlantic Submarine Force,
343, 344–345
downplay of, 327
news reports, 327–328,
341
Pentagon's damage control,
327, 330–332, 344–345
secret information affected
by, 324–325, 327–328,
339–340
Simon Bolivar, 321, 342
Essex, USS, 125, 181, 204,
350
Ethan Allan, USS, 161
Eugene A. Greene, USS, 23
Evans, Thomas, 371
The Evening Capital, 23
Ewing, Maurice, 127
Exercise, double-meaning of,
291–292

Faeroe Islands, 127
Falck, Richard, 290, 299
Falk, Peter, 283–284
Family. *See also* Letters
Bishop's, W., 2, 10, 237,
373, 374
Brandywine response,
23–24
Christiansen's, M., 9, 186,
195–196, 203, 237

Elrod's, B., 5–6, 10–11,
208–210
homecoming response,
2–5, 9–12
service enlistment of, 373
Fangataufa Island, 208
Farrin, George, 4
FBI (Federal Bureau of
Investigation)
Walker spy ring
investigation and arrest
by, 317–320, 322, 342,
344
Whitworth investigation
and arrest by, 325–326
FCC (Federal
Communication
Commission), 21
Federal Bureau of
Investigation. *See* FBI
Federal Communication
Commission. *See* FCC
Fennick, William R., 148
Fermi, Enrico, 58
Ferret flights, 96
Fishplay, 82
Flying Fish, USS, 53
"Focused operations" search.
*See also Compass Island,
USS; Mizar, USNS*
after-action report, 219,
227, 234–236, 268,
270, 277, 299
as cover up, 239
start of, 212, 220,
225–226
FOIA. *See* Freedom of
Information Act
Foli, Holli, 2
Foli, Vernon, 2, 237
Foli-Lake, Barbara, 2, 10, 237
Foreign communications,
intercepting and
decoding, 88–89
Forrestal, James V., 59
Forrestal, USS, 138, 322
Forster, USS, 68, 73
Forstmann, Walter, 103
Fort Meade, Maryland, 84
Fountain, Robert R., 225,
371
Foxtrot mission, 125,
126–127, 132–133
France, 104, 169–170

assistance from, 20
nuclear testing by, 208
political turmoil in, 211
Freedom of Information Act
(FOIA), 37, 38
appeal, 45, 50
Fresh water production, 53
Friedman, Norman, 63, 192
Furney, Vic, 308–309,
313–314

Galantin, Ignatius, 99
Garrison, Charles "Chuck,"
263, 299
Gates, Robert, 374
Gato, USS, 16, 22, 97, 120
General Electric, 60
General Instrument Corp.,
269
George Bancroft, USS, 154
George Washington, USS, 131,
183
George Washington-class
submarines, 56
German U-boats
about, 58, 62–63, 73
Soviet control of, 87
World War I campaign,
100–103
World War II campaign,
103–107
Ghormley, Ralph, 16, 83–86,
157, 371
Gibraltar, Straits of, 186–188,
307–309
Gilbert Islands, 99
Gilmore, Howard W.,
248–249
Gleason, Steven, 197
Global Positioning System,
219
Glomar Explorer, USNS, 36,
174–175, 353–354, 374
Golf-class submarines, 97,
119, 171
Golf-II-class submarines, 166,
171–172
Gonchar, N. F., 136
Good Hope, Cape of, South
Africa, 211–212
Gorbachev, Mikhail, 350,
354, 375
Gorshkov, Georgyevich, 125,
177

accord signed by, 350
expansion under, 133–134
grand vision of, 110,
   116–117, 134–135, 142
intelligence-gathering
   strategy of, 191
Israel attack directed by,
   138
submarine design under,
   120
Government. *See also specific
   administrations*
French, assistance from, 20
nuclear energy dealings
   with, 59, 60
Grand Turk, Turks and Caicos
   Islands, 127, 129
Great Britain
   NATO exercise impression
   of, 81–82
   submarines of, 63, 169
   U.S. Navy attacks by, 332
   WWI U-boat campaign
   against, 100–103
"The Green Door," 131
Greene, Frank, 306–308
Greene, Wallace A., 24, 209,
   252
   interview with, 263
   testimony of, 31, 182–183,
   292–293, 298
Greenwood, Nova Scotia, 308
Gribkov, Anatoly, 122
Groton, Connecticut
   Electric Boat Co. of,
   54–56, 60, 61, 63
   Navy Submarine School, 2,
   146, 147, 159
   Pargo in, 11, 259, 265
   Schade's speech at, 219,
   255–256, 273
   Scorpion launch, 54–56
   Submarine Force Museum
   of, 373
Growler, USS, 248
Guam, Sosus facility in, 289
Gunn, Ross, 58
Gyatt, USS, 4

Haddo, USS, 307–308
Halibut, USS, 173–175, 374
Hall, Dottie, 372
Hall, Jerry
   background on, 372

interview with, 51–52, 94,
   265–267, 299–300
Hamilton, Gordon, 49,
   214–216, 228, 232
Hanssen, H. R., 231
Harwi, William, 4, 146–147,
   149–152, 180
Hatteras, Cape, North
   Carolina, 112, 129
Havana conference, 122
Hawaii, 371
   listening station, 129
   Pearl Harbor activity near,
   172
Hee, Park Chung, 334
Helsinki, Finland, 355–356
HEN submarines, 120, 125
Henry, Michael E., 148–149
Herzog, Sam, 219, 225–226,
   229
"Hiroshima," 120. *See also
   K–19*
Hitler, Adolf, 103
Holland, John P., 61
Holland, William J., 371
Holmes, Ephraim P.
   Court of Inquiry appointed
   by, 25, 246–247
   Schade's contact with, 43,
   258–259
   theory, 366, 367
Holy Loch, Scotland, 126,
   190
Holystone missions, 93, 98.
   See also Reconnaissance
   missions
Homecoming, 1–12, 212,
   246, 298
   Elrod's, B., 5–6, 10–11,
   208–210
   family's response to, 2–5,
   9–12
   at Norfolk Naval Station,
   1–11
Horn, David F., 90–92,
   95–96, 264
Hostile Waters (Huchthausen),
   371
Hotel-class submarines,
   119–120
House Armed Services, 337
Huber, Ralph R., 146
Huchthausen, Peter

background on, 350–351,
   371
Dygalo's interview by,
   357–358
Incidents at Sea Agreement
   recalled by, 349–354
interview with, 121, 134
K–19 recalled by, 121
K–129 questioned by,
   353–357
Komarov's interview by,
   356–357
as Naval Attaché in
   Moscow, 349, 351–357
Trost's interview by,
   354–356
HUK ("hunter-killer")
   Groups, 125, 131, 132
Hull design, 61–62, 63, 73
Hungary, 118
Hunt, Frederick, 128
Hunter, Robert W., 317–318,
   342
"Hunter-killer." *See* HUK
Huntington Park, 372
Hydrophones, 48–49,
   127–129

Icthyic, Operation, 333
Ignatius, Paul, 25
Incidents at Sea delegation,
   349–354, 356
Intelligence-gathering. *See also*
   Espionage;
   Reconnaissance
   missions; Secret
   information
   antenna farms for, 89, 191,
   281, 302
   K–129 search, 172–178
   NSA networks for, 332
   Soviet, 114–115, 188–191
   tactics, 88–90
International Law of the Sea
   Institute, 353, 370
Internet, information by,
   286–287
Interviews
   Ashworth's, 262–263
   Atkins's, 49–50
   Bailey's, 338–339
   Beshany's, 136, 300–305
   Buchanan's, 220
   Clarey's, 46–47

Collier's, 283–285
Craven's, 48–49, 220, 262, 294
D'Emilio's, 270–273, 306
Dietzen's, 47, 78, 291–292, 295
Dygalo's, 357–358
Furney's, 308–309, 313–314
Greene's, Frank, 306–308
Greene's, Wallace A., 263
Hall's, 51–52, 94, 265–267, 299–300
Huchthausen's, 121, 134
James's, 359–360
Komarov's, 356–357
Meeker's, 263
Moorer's, 260–261, 295
Palmer's, 310, 312
Pentagon, 330–332, 343–344
Pettey's, 180–181, 193, 348
Rule's, 306
Schade's, 41–45, 47, 50, 256–259, 293–294, 296
Sosus confiscation, 287–289
Stermer's, 309–310, 311–312
Trost's, 354–356
Walker spy ring, 324–325, 330–332, 343–344
Investigation, 30–50
Iraq, 191
Irex, USS, 199–200
Iron Curtain, 193
Israel, 118, 138–139, 191–192, 322
Israeli submarines, 169
Italy
casualties suffered by, 103, 116, 130, 194
liberty stops in, 185, 187–189, 193–197, 200–203, 357
map, 185
Naples, 185, 187, 189, 200–203, 357
radiation concerns of, 194–195
Rome, 203
Taranto, 185, 188, 193–197

Ivan, 203–208
Izmur, Turkey, 195

JAG Corps, 37
James Madison, USS, 98
James, Ralph K., 359–360
Japan. *See also* Pearl Harbor
Buyo Maru attack, 106–107
code-breaking, 89, 347
Growler attack, 248
K–129 report by, 177
Pueblo help from, 333, 334–335, 338, 340
radioactivity reports by, 195
torpedo design, 62
U.S.-Soviet encounters near, 349–350
Japan, Sea of, 349–350
"Joe 1" atomic bomb, 115
John King, USS, 23
John Willis, USS, 314
Johnson, Lyndon B., 9, 335–336
Johnson, Robert, 180
Johnson, Tom, 9
Joint Committee on Atomic Energy, 238–239
Joint Reconnaissance Center, 90
Josephus Daniels, USS, 23, 309–311
Judge Advocate General. *See* JAG Corps
Jupiter missiles, 123

K–8, 120–121
K–19, 97–98, 120, 121
K–19: The Widowmaker (Huchthausen), 371
K–129
amends, 374
cover-up, 353–356
Craven's search for, 174
Huchthausen's questions on, 353–358
Japan's report on, 177
Scorpion connection to, 165–168, 353–358, 361–363
secret search for, 172–178
wreckage, 173–178, 355
K–172, 138–139

K–181, 137–138
K–219, 109–112, 352, 353
Kalugin, Oleg, 346–347, 375
Kamchatka, Russia, 95, 130, 165
Kamiseya, Japan, 334, 338, 340
Kassatotov, Vladimir Afanasievich, 177
Kaufman, Robert "Yogi," 78, 371, 372
Kennedy administration, 125, 132–133, 153
Kennedy, John F., 123–124
Kestner, Jack, 23, 36, 49
KG–14 encryption system, 338
KGB spies, 318–319, 326, 340, 341–344, 346–347, 375
Khe Sanh, Vietnam, 168, 335
Khrushchev, Nikita, 116, 117, 123–125, 132–133
Khuzhokov, Vladimir, 351
King, Ernest J., 29
Kithira Island, 185, 204
Kittery, Maine. *See* Portsmouth Naval Shipyard
Kittiwake, USS, 19, 22
KLB–47 encryption system, 337, 339, 346
Klinefelter, Jack, 265
Kobzar, Vladimir Ivanovich, 167
Kola Peninsula, 95, 133
Kolouch, James, 317–318
Komarov, Ivan M., 356–357
Korean Demilitarized Zone, 87
Korean War, 115
Kotlin-class submarines, 349
KW–7 Orestes teletypewriter, 346
hijacking of, 337–338, 339, 340
keylist for, 341
KWR–37 Jason receiver unit
hijacking of, 337, 338, 339
keylist for, 341, 346
purpose of, 181

Laconia, USS, 106
Lajes airbase, 308, 314

Lamberth, Charles, 4
Lapon, USS, 23, 144
le Carré, John, 327
Lebanon, political struggles of, 118
Lebedko, Vladimir, 97
The Ledger-Star, 17, 23, 27, 45, 50, 321
Lee, Kent, 140–142
Lehman, John F., 113
Leopard, HMS, 332
Letters
    Christiansen's, M., 180, 186, 194, 195
    found, 211–212
    Summer's, R., 186, 196–197, 203
    Violetti's, R., 186, 188, 194, 198–201, 204–206, 207–208
    Weinbeck's, L., 186, 206
    Yoachum's, 211–212
Levey, Sanford, 78, 153, 154, 158
Lewis, James, 371
Liberty, USS, 322, 334
Liberty-class submarines, 333
Little, Dorothy, 196
Lloyd, David B., 160–161, 193, 205, 373
Lobov, Semyon Mikhailovich, 137
Lockwood, Charles, 59, 107
Lofar (Low Frequency and Ranging) analyzer, 129
    Scorpion sinking recorded by, 283–285
London. *See* Great Britain
London Naval Treaty, 105
Long Island Sound, testing, 53
Los Angeles-class submarines, 29, 64
Lost declaration, 18, 24–26
Low Frequency and Ranging analyzer. *See* Lofar
Lusitania RMS, 100
Lynnhaven Roads, 21

M8/3 contact, 234
Machinery room, 76–77
Magnus, Robert, 375–376
Maine, Gulf of, collision near, 144

Manhattan Project, 60
Map
    Canary Islands, 14–15
    course track, 14–15
    Mediterranean, 184–185
    SASS underwater technology, 244
    search area, 227, 233–234, 275
    wreckage site, 275
Mare Island Naval Shipyard, California, 321
Mariel, Cuba, 124, 126
Marine Raiders, 99
Mark 15 fire-control panel, 75
Mark 37 torpedo, 223–224.366
Markab, USS, 147
Markarov, Konstantin, 355
Martin, Kenneth R., 147
Maryland
    bases, 219, 225
    Walker spy ring in, 318–320, 322, 326, 344–345
Masterson, Paul, 8
May 17, 1968 search, 307
May 22, 1968 position report, 211–212, 257
May 27, 1968 position report, 1–3, 5–17, 212, 257, 298–299
Mazzuchi, Frank Patsy, 148
McCann Rescue Chamber, 13
McGuire, Michael Lee, 146, 147, 150
McNamara, Robert, 153
Mediterranean. *See also specific countries in Mediterranean*
    Dakar in, 169
    K–172 in, 138–139
    map, 184–185
    radiation concern in, 194–195
    Scorpion's mission to, 144–145, 179–189, 193–210, 250
    sonar conditions, 207
    Soviet presence in, 192–193
    usual activity in, 134
Meeker, Harold, 249, 263

Memorial Day, 1–3, 5–17, 212
Memorials, 372–373
Mess area, 73, 81–82
Messina, Straits of, 200
Midway, Battle of, 89, 347
Military Sea Transportation Service, 217
Miller, Joseph F., Jr., 148
Miller, Robert L., 277
The Milwaukee Journal, 17
Minerve, 169–170, 275
Missiles
    Pentagon's programs for, 174
    Polaris, 11, 123, 153, 183
    Regulus, 174
    Soviet, 95–96, 110–111, 166, 171–172
    Tomahawk, 174
    US deployment of, 123
"Missions of higher classification," 86. *See also* Reconnaissance missions
Mitchell, Charles N., 159
Mizar, USNS, 33, 40, 49, 369
    in Azores, 217–218, 220
    credit, 271
    cruise 1 search by, 212, 213, 216–220, 225–231
    cruise 2 search by, 231
    cruise 3 search by, 234–235
    cruise 4 search by, 235
    cruise 5 search by, 235–236
    Petrel's encounter with, 274–277
    photographs by, 239, 274
    on Terceira Island, 236, 242
Monrovia, USS, 19
Moorer, Thomas H., 25, 26, 219, 236, 238
    background on, 370
    interview with, 260–261, 295
    press release by, 17, 18, 24, 238
    search arrangements by, 217
    Soviet downplay by, 295
    theory, 367

Morcerf, Les, 208
Moriarty, Thomas, 251
Morrison, Ann, 3, 10
Morrison, Dale, 3
Morrison, Elizabeth, 55
Morrison, Florence, 10
Morton, Dudley "Mush," 107
Moscow, Russia, 118, 138, 341
  Huchthausen in, 349, 351–357
  naval accord signed in, 350
Moskva, 192
Murmansk, Russia, 86
Mustin, Henry C., 352

Nace, Charles D., 264, 371
Naples, Italy, 185, 187, 357
  stopover in, 189, 200–203, 357
Narrative, xi–xiv
Narwhal, USS, 56
Nasser, Gamal Abdel, 118, 191–192
Nathanael Greene, USS, 306–307
National Security Agency (NSA), 333
  encryption keylist decision by, 340
  intelligence networks of, 332, 333
  responsibilities of, 84, 88
National Submarine Memorial West, 373
NATO, 81–82, 117, 179, 188, 193
Nautilus, USS, 53, 87, 99, 147, 160–161
  commissioning of, 119
  design, 56–57, 63, 64, 66–67
  Soviet recon missions by, 95
Naval Communications Service, 88
Naval Reactors Branch, 81
Naval Research Laboratory (NRL), 58, 213, 216
Naval Reserve Training Corps (NROTC), 146
Naval Security Group, 88. *See also* Office of Naval Intelligence

NavFacs (shore-based naval facilities), 129, 130, 137
Navigation systems, 219
Navoytsev, Pitr, 352–353, 356
Navy. *See* Soviet Union; U.S. Navy
Navy Fleet Broadcasting System, 306, 328
Navy Submarine School, 2, 146, 147, 159
Nazi surrender, 62, 114
Nelson, Craig F., 274–278
New Guinea, 106–107
New London Submarine Base, 81, 159, 342, 373
The New York Times, 17, 97, 190
Newfoundland, 129
Newport News, Virginia, 372
News reports
  Brandywine, 23–24
  espionage, 327–328, 341
  holes in, 30, 36
  investigating, 30, 32, 45–46
  NATO, 81
  press releases, 17, 18, 24, 238
  Pueblo hijacking, 335
  reconnaissance missions, 97–98
  Scorpion wreckage, 33–34
  secret mission, 292
  Soviet, 190, 193
  SubMiss, 9–12, 17, 213
  Vietnam War, 168–169
Nimitz, Chester L., 60, 107
Nimitz, USS, 320, 323
Nitric acid, 111
Nixon, Richard, 370
Nolan, Mary Etta Bishop, 373
Norfolk ASW Group, 8
Norfolk Naval Station
  casualties of, 322
  homecoming at, 1–11, 212
  memorial at, 372
  post-Vietnam changes, 29
  Scorpion overhaul at, 143–144, 179–182
Norfolk, Virginia
  1968 happenings in, 211–212
  training schools in, 281

North Korean hijacking, 168–169, 332–340, 361. *See also Pueblo, USS*
Northampton, USS, 147
Northern run missions. *See* Reconnaissance missions
Norway
  Cochino sinking near, 86–87
  Scorpion Soviet recon mission by, 95
Norwegian Sea, 84, 350
Novaya Zemla Island, 95
November-class submarines, 87, 95, 119–120
  Enterprise chase, 140–142
Novorossysk, 116
NRL. *See* Naval Research Laboratory
NROTC. *See* Naval Reserve Training Corps
NSA. *See* National Security Agency
Nuclear power. *See also* Radiation
  development, 56, 58
  government involvement in, 59, 60
  hazards of, 67
  propulsion concepts, 59–68
  S5W reactor, 64–68, 76
  Soviet *vs.* US race to, 119–120
  testing, 208
Nuclear Power School, 161

Oak Ridge, Tennessee, nuclear propulsion research in, 59–60
Oak Ridge, USS, 183, 187
Ocean Systems Atlantic Command, 131, 214, 308
Ocean Systems Technician "A" School, 281–282
Office of Naval Intelligence (ONI), 83, 87, 89, 302. *See also* Pentagon
Office of Naval Research (ONR), 128, 214
Officer of the deck (OOD), 76

Offley, Ed. *See also* Interviews
articles, 287, 290
findings, 290, 376
goal of, 29–30
initial research, 30–41
spy scandal coverage by,
327–328
theories of, 297, 315–316,
358
Oil slicks, 19
Okean, Operation, 135
Okhotsk, Sea of, 95, 173
ONI. *See* Office of Naval
Intelligence
ONR. *See* Office of Naval
Research
OOD. *See* Officer of the deck
Open-ocean search, 12–15,
18–26, 217–220, 276
Orestes teletypewriter. *See*
KW–7 Orestes
teletypewriter
Orion, USS, 1, 2, 5, 24, 71,
144
Orlov, Vadim, 131
Oscar, Point, 227–228,
230–231, 232, 234

P–2V Neptune patrol aircraft,
132
P–3C Orion patrol aircraft,
112, 138, 141, 296
Pacific Fleet
Battle of Midway success
of, 89
Soviet reconnaissance
missions, 86–87, 98
Pacific Sosus network, 129
Palmer, Bill, 310, 312
Pargo, USS
in Groton, 11, 259, 265
Schade commanding from,
11, 13, 21, 22, 43,
254–255, 265–267
Paris, France, 211
Parrish, George R.
arrival time notice by, 298
testimony, 32, 252
Passive sonar, 86, 142
Patrick Henry, USS, 154
Paukenschlag (Drumbeat),
Operation, 104
Pearl Harbor
code-breaking, 89

Enterprise at, 142
K–129 aim at, 172
Soviet involvement in, 172
submarine warfare, 99,
103–107
Pentagon
communications, 8–9, 19,
23, 25, 214, 303–304,
315
espionage damage control
by, 327, 330–332,
344–345
interview, 330–332,
343–344
missile programs, 174
press conference, 17
reconnaissance organized
by, 90
scientific search team, 217
Soviet assessment by, 124
Vietnam War crises,
168–169
watch, 12, 19–20, 48
Performance, 67, 78–80
Pergram, George, 58
Periscopes, 86, 92
Permit-class submarines, 29,
64
Peterson, Bonnie Lou, 237
Peterson, Daniel, 237
Petrel, USS, 13, 21, 22, 218,
226
Mizar's encounter by,
274–277
on Terceira Island, 277
Petropavlovsk Soviet Navy
base, 98, 168, 175
Pettey, Daniel K.
background on, 180
interview with, 180–181,
193, 348
transfer of, 208
Pferrer, Dennis P., 148
Photographic evidence
Mizar's, 239, 274
Scorpion, 239, 272, 274,
368
Soviet tracking, 314
Pierce, Anne, 205
Pintado, USS, 98
Pirie, Robert, 78, 80,
153–154, 371
Plate, Douglas, 13
Platte, Greg, 274–276

Polaris missiles, 11, 123, 153,
183
Polmar, Norman, 341
Porpoise-class submarines, 63
Portsmouth Naval Shipyard,
60
Portugal, sightings reports
from, 20–21
Powell, Donald R., 148
Powers, Francis Gary, 87
Prague Spring movement, 171
Preminin, Sergei Anatolyivich,
109–112, 351
Preserver, USS, 22
Press releases, 17, 18, 24, 238.
See also News reports
Pressurized water reactor
(PWR) system, 66
"Presumed lost" decision, 18,
24–26, 236, 239, 261
Project 627 (Soviet attack
submarine production),
87
Propulsion. *See* Nuclear power
Pueblo, USS
communications, 334–340
cryptography equipment
on, 337–340
hostages of, 361
Japan's assistance to, 333,
334–335, 338, 340
North Korean hijacking,
168–169, 332–340, 361
Scorpion connection to,
343–344, 346–347,
358–359
sister ship to, 349
Walker spy ring connection
to, 340–341, 343, 347
Puffer, USS, 98
Punta del Gada, Azores, 220
PWR. *See* Pressurized water
reactor

Quang Tri, Vietnam, 211

Ra'anan, Ya'acov, 169
Radiation
accidents, 67, 97–98,
120–121, 169
concern for, 194–195
detection, 95, 208
Radio. *See* Communications

Radio signal interception, 89, 302

Randolph, USS, 125

Ray, USS, 43, 144, 258–259

Razorback, USS, 321

Reagan administration, 28–29

Reagan, Ronald, 350

Reconnaissance missions
aerial, 87, 89, 96, 308
antenna farms, 89, 191, 281, 302
breach of, 304–306
chain of command, 88, 90–91
CIA, 87, 96
code words, 291–292
collisions, 83–86, 94, 97–98, 144
debriefing, 91
double-reporting system for, 97–98
electronic listening platforms for, 332–333
expansion of, 89–90
French nuclear testing, 208
mishaps, 96–98
Nautilus', 95
news reports, 97–98
North Korean, 332–336, 337–340
orders, 91–92
Pacific Fleet, 86–87, 98
Pentagon organized, 90
photography from, 92, 96
post-Cold War, 83–88, 95–96
Scorpion's, 83–86, 91, 92–95, 144–145, 179–189, 193–210, 250
Shark's, 90–92, 95–96
Skipjack's, 94

Red Army, 113, 116, 171

Red Banner Fleet, 95, 126, 140

Red Star banner award, 112

Regulus missiles, 174

Reports
aerial patrol, 308–309
Atlantic Submarine Force, 297
"focused operations" after-action, 219, 227, 234–236, 268, 270, 277, 299

Josephus Daniels', 310–312

K–129, 177
May 22, 1968, 211–212, 257
May 27, 1968, 1–3, 5–17, 212, 257, 298–299
Spintcomm's, 303–304
Trieste's Scorpion wreckage report, 368

Requin, USS, 20

Rescue response. *See* Search, *Scorpion*

Rich, Harold G., 264

Rickover, Hyman G., 57, 359
nuclear propulsion research of, 59–62

Robert L. Wilson, USS, 4, 13, 23

Rockville, Maryland, 318–320

Roessler, Gordon, 231–232

Rogers, John, 263–264, 319

Rome, Italy, 203

Ronquil, USS, 96

Roosevelt administration, 103–104

Roper, USS, 106

Rostow, Walt W., 9

Rota, Spain, 15, 22, 41, 183–188

Rule, Ron, 306

Rusk, Dean, 133

Russia. *See* Soviet Union

Rybachiy Bay, Russia, 165

Rybalko, Leonid Filippovich, 126–127

S5W nuclear reactor, 64–68, 76
startup, 145, 149–152

SACLANT (Supreme Allied Commander Atlantic), 249

Safety
considerations, 79–80
inspections, 32

Safford, Laurence F., 89

Saigon, Vietnam, 168

Sail structures, 54

Saint Paul, USS, 196

Sam Houston, USS, 195

Sam Rayburn, USS, 16, 85

San Francisco, California, 328

Saratoga, USS, 137–138

Sargo, USS, 77

Sasebo harbor, Japan, 195

SASS (Sonar Array Sounding System), 244, 268–273

Satellite communications, 135

Sayda Bay, Russia, 126

Scamp, USS, 29, 47, 49

Scenarios. *See* Theories

Schade, Arnold F., 28, 236
background on, 11, 27, 247–249, 370
Court of Inquiry testimony of, 31, 38, 246–247, 249–252, 254–255, 291
Groton speech of, 219, 255–256, 273
Holmes's orders from, 43, 258–259
interview with, 41–45, 47, 50, 256–259, 293–294, 296
on *Pargo,* 11, 13, 21, 22, 43, 254–255, 265–267
press announcements, 17
search diversion orders of, 26, 43, 209, 226–234, 258–259, 274
Soviet downplay by, 293–294, 296, 299
theories of, 47, 225, 226, 366
World War II efforts of, 248–249

Science. *See* Technology

Scorpion, USS, 2, 187, 202, 293. *See also* Crew, *Scorpion;* Search, *Scorpion*
archives, 29, 37–38, 50, 346, 351
capabilities, 53–54
control room, 69–70, 74–76, 146–149
course track, 14–15, 50–51, 223
cover-up, 242–262, 267–299, 368–369
design, 54–56, 57, 64–68
encryption systems, 346
final message, 7, 14, 17, 19–20, 40, 42, 298–299
final message from, 14, 298
finding, 33–34, 40, 46, 239, 268–278, 271–277

flaws, 32, 35, 39–40, 179–183
homecoming, 1–11, 212
interior layout, 64–68, 69–77
K–129 connection to, 165–168, 353–358, 361–363
last voyage, 144–145, 179–189, 193–210
launch, 54–56
maneuvering room, 145–146
Mediterranean mission, 144–145, 179–189, 193–210, 250
memorials, 372–373
narrative, xi–xiv
NATO exercises, 81
Norfolk docking pre-mission, 143–144
official account of, 242–257, 267–278, 289
performance, 67, 78–80
photographic evidence of, 239, 272, 274, 368
preparations, 145–152, 179–181
"presumed lost," 18, 24–26, 236, 239, 261
Pueblo-Walker connection to, 343–344, 346–347, 358–359
Section 3 officers of, 146–149
sinking, xi–xiv, 49, 50–51, 212–236, 283–285, 288
sonar, 92
Soviet help to, 359–360
Soviet recon missions by, 83–86, 91, 92–95, 144–145, 179–189, 193–210, 250
Soviet tracking of, 186–188, 201–208, 304–316
SubSafe overhaul, 157–159
tours, 66, 68–78, 81–82
wreckage, 33–34, 40, 46, 228, 231, 239, 271–277, 368
Scotland, 126, 190
Sea Fox, USS, 161
Sea Leopard, USS, 147

Sea Spider, 129
Seal Beach, California, 373
SeaLab underwater habitat, 20
Search, Scorpion. See also "Focused operations" search; Secret search
acoustic, 12, 40, 48–51, 213–216, 221–235, 295–296
aircraft, 8–9, 19, 22, 295–296, 308, 313–314
area, 18–22, 216, 220, 226–229, 233–234, 275
Bernard's, 13, 21–26, 217–218, 276
Buchanan's, 216–220, 228–230, 231, 235–236
cameras, 218–219, 229–230
communications, 221, 226–229, 234, 242
Compass Island assisted, 22, 218, 220–223, 225–228, 241–243, 245–246, 268–278
concluding, 24–26
course track, 14–15, 18–19
Craven's efforts, 12, 48–49, 213–236, 277
demolition drops for, 221–223, 226
May 17th, 307
May 22nd, 211–212, 257
May 27th, 1–3, 5–17, 212, 257, 298–299
Mizar assisted, 212, 213, 216–220, 225–236, 239, 242, 271, 274–277
official account of, 242–262, 267–278
open-ocean, 12–15, 18–26, 217–220, 276
Schade's diversion from, 26, 43, 209, 226–234, 258–259, 274
scientists, 217–218, 219–221
secret, 43–45, 172–178, 241–242, 247–278, 307–314
Sosus used for, 12, 40, 48–51, 213–216, 221–235, 295–296
Special Search Unit, 21, 25

tools, 218–219, 232
underwater, 20
Searle, William F. "SupeSalv," 20, 21
The Seattle Post-Intelligencer, 287, 290, 327, 343
Seawolf, USS, 144, 167, 247
Seawolf-class submarines, 61, 64
Sebold, William A., 244–245, 268, 271–272
Secret information
confiscation, 287–290, 323, 365–366
Court of Inquiry censoring of, 37–38, 40, 188, 221
"dead drop" for, 319–320
declassification, 29, 37–38, 44, 50, 98, 270, 286
double-reporting system, 97–98
espionage effects on, 324–325, 327–328, 339–340
fear to provide, 285–288
Internet, 286–287
leaks, 190, 284, 306–307
news reports about, 292
post-Cold War, 286
Sosus, 40, 131–132, 282, 284, 287–290
Soviet, 172–178
Special Intelligence, 252–254, 302, 303–304
Secret search
K–129, 172–178
Scorpion, 43–45, 172–178, 241–242, 247–278, 307–314
Semipalatinsk, Kazakhstan, 115
Senate Intelligence Committee, 327
Seoul, South Korea, 334, 335
Serkov, Valentin, 353
Severodvinsk, Russia, 178
Shark, USS, 13, 78, 144
Soviet recon missions by, 90–92, 95–96
Shashkov, Nikolai, 138–139
Shelburne, Nova Scotia, 130
Ships Internal Navigation System (SINS), 244

Shore-based naval facilities.
See NavFacs
Shumkov, Nikolai, 131
Siberia, 95
Sightings reports, 20–21
Silver-brazed joints, 156
Simon Bolivar, USS, 19, 22
espionage on, 321, 342
Sinai Peninsula invasion, 118,
192, 334
Sinkings. *See also*
Reconnaissance
missions; Theories;
Wreckage
acoustic recordings of, 12,
40, 48–51, 213–216,
221–235
collisions, 83–86, 94,
97–98, 136–137, 144
Dakar, 169
K–129, 165–168, 172–178
K–219, 109–112
Minerve, 169–170
narrative, xi–xiv
Scorpion, USS, xi–xiv, 49,
50–51, 212–236,
283–285, 288
simulation, 225
Thresher, 156
Sino-Soviet alliance, 170
SINS. *See* Ships Internal
Navigation System
Six-Day War, 134, 138,
191–192, 322
Skate, USS, 161
Skipjack, USS, 79, 80, 94,
144, 180, 347
Skipjack-class submarines, 29,
47
construction, 56
control room, 69, 75
design, 54, 56, 64, 73, 75
sonar technology in, 92
torpedo room, 72
Skornyakovo, Russia, 109
Slattery, Francis A., 31, 193,
207, 252, 258, 307,
348
Augusta Bay comment by,
199
background, 160–161
crew management by, 209
final message by, 7, 18, 298
Harwi's call to, 149

Mediterranean recon
mission orders, 200,
204, 208–209, 250
Soviet tracking messages
from, 307, 315
Smirnov, Leonid Vassilievich,
177
Smith, Deming W., testimony
of, 296–297
Smith, Julie Sue, 3, 9, 246
Smith, Robert B., 3, 4, 246
Smock, Edwin, 130
Snap rolls, 67, 80
Snapp, Bob, 5
Snook, USS, 29
Snorkel device, 62–63
Snyder, Laura Walker, 318
Sodium coolant, 60
Sofar (Sound Frequency and
Ranging), 128
Sonar, 92–93. *See also*
Acoustic recordings
bypassing tactics, 135–140
gangs, 92–93
Mediterranean conditions,
207
passive, 86, 142
technology, 92–93,
105–106, 128–129,
244, 268–270, 282
towed-array, 93
Sonar Array Sounding System.
See SASS
Sosus (Sound Surveillance
System)
Atlantic, 129, 130
capabilities of, 282
confiscation, 287–290
development, 127–129
facilities, 128, 289
first tracking by, 130–131
Lofar analyzer, 129,
283–285
networks, 129, 130, 332,
333
search using, 12, 40,
48–51, 213–216,
221–235
secrecy of, 40, 131–132,
282, 284, 288–290
sinking recorded by, 12,
283–285
training, 281–282

Sound Frequency and
Ranging. *See* Sofar
Sound Surveillance System.
See Sosus
South Korea, 334, 335, 336
Soviet Central Committee,
133
Soviet Embassy, 342–343,
346–347
Soviet Union. *See also*
Moscow, Russia;
Reconnaissance missions
acoustic signature of,
84–85
Afghanistan invasion by,
350
amends, 374
American spies for,
317–327
Black Sea Fleet, 116, 192
Canary Islands operation
of, 39, 42
Chazma Bay radiation
accident, 67
China's break from, 170
collapse, 51
collision with, 85–86
Cuban alliance with,
122–127, 131–134
Czechoslovakia *v.*, 171
democratic reform of, 354
downplaying, 293–296,
299
Foxtrot mission, 125,
126–127, 132–133
Incidents at Sea
Agreement, 349–354
intelligence-gathering by,
114–115, 188–191
KGB activity of, 318–319,
326, 340, 341–344,
346–347, 375
Mediterranean presence of,
192–193
military threat of, 29, 56
missiles, 95–96, 110–111,
166, 171–172
national security strategy,
117
Navy, 39, 42, 113–116,
134–135, 348
news reports about, 190,
193
Northern Fleet, 84, 87, 95

nuclear competition of,
119–120
Pearl Harbor actions by,
172
Pentagon's assessment of,
124
Scorpion help from,
359–360
Scorpion tracking by,
186–188, 201–208,
304–316
secret information of,
172–178
Six-Day War port access,
134, 138, 191–192
submarines, 63, 119–120,
134–135, 140–142,
192–193
tactical breakthroughs,
135–140, 189–190
Trost's visit to, 354–356
U-boat control, 87
U.S. intervention of,
117–118
Walker's meeting with,
341–342
Spain
Cadiz, 308–309
Rota, 15, 22, 41, 183–188
Sparks, Howard, 263–264
Special Intelligence, 252–254,
302–304
Special Intelligence
Communications
(Spintcomm), 303–304
Special Naval Control
Program missions, 84,
88, 91
Special Operations
Department,
Directorate's, 89
Speed evaluations, 67, 78–80,
101, 140–142
Spintcomm. *See* Special
Intelligence
Communications
"Spooks," 83, 92, 93, 95
Sprint and drift tactic, 283
Spying. *See* Espionage;
Reconnaissance missions
Stalin, Josef, 113–116
Steam generators, 68,
151–152

Stermer, George, 309–310,
311–312
Stone, David B., 147
Structural Analysis Group,
368
Studemann, William O.,
344–345
Sturgeon, USS, 144
Sturgeon-class submarines, 29,
56, 64
Submarine Force Museum,
373
Submarine Safety Program.
See SubSafe
Submariners, attitude of,
99–100
Submarines. *See also* Design;
*specific classes of
Submarines*
British, 63, 169
construction, 56, 60,
61–62
Electric Boat Co., 56, 60,
61, 63
French, 169–170
German U-boat, 58,
62–63, 73
history, 61
Israeli, 169
Soviet, 63, 119–120,
134–135, 140–142,
192–193
test depth, 47, 80
World War II, 106
SubMiss (submarine missing
alert), 8–18
canceled, 82
communications, 7–9, 11,
18, 263–264
news reports, 9–12, 17,
213
theories, 18
SubSafe (Submarine Safety
Program), 32, 157–159
Atlantic Submarine Force
assessment, 149,
161–162
Suez Canal crisis, 118
Sullivan, Paul E., 156, 158
Summers, Charles and Hila,
186
Summers, Richard, 197, 206
letters from, 186,
196–197, 203

Sunbird, USS, 22
Supreme Allied Commander
Atlantic. *See* SACLANT
Sweeney, John D., Jr., 23,
202–203
Sweeney, John, Sr., 202
Sweet, John Charles, 148
Swordfish, USS, 177–178, 195
Syria
political struggles of, 118,
191–192
Soviet ports of, 134
Szilárd, Leó, 58

Tactics
Crazy Ivan, 135–136, 283,
314
electric rabbit, 141–142,
145, 199–200
fishplay, 82
intelligence-gathering,
88–90
sonar bypassing, 135–140
Soviet Union, 135–140,
189–190
sprint and drift, 283
TAG. *See* Technical Advisory
Group
Tallahatchie County, USS, 32,
201, 202, 357
Tang-class submarines, 63, 73
Taranto, Italy, 185, 188,
193–197
Tautog, USS, 97
Technical Advisory Group
(TAG)
focused operations search
by, 217–220, 233–234
search miscommunication
with, 226–229, 234
Technology
battery, 62, 64
construction, 61
encryption, 181, 337–340
German U-boat, 62–63
internet, 286–287
mapping, 244
nuclear propulsion, 56–64
SASS, 244
sonar, 92–93, 105–106,
128–129, 244,
268–270, 282
U.S. Navy's development
in, 28–29, 56–62

World War II, 28–29, 62–63, 105–106
Tennant, David L., 154
Teodolit, 314
Terceira Island
  Compass Island on, 220
  Mizar on, 236, 242
  Petrel's stop at, 277
Test depth, 47, 80, 155
Testimonies
  Bernard's, 33
  Clarke's, Jared, 32
  Garrison's, 299
  Greene's, Wallace A., 31, 182–183, 292–293, 298
  Parrish's, 32, 252
  revealing, 291–292
  Schade's, 31, 38, 247, 249–252, 254–255, 291
  Smith's, D., 296–297
  Walker's, J., 328–330, 338–342
Tet Offensive, 335, 336
Tew, Lewis M., 277
Thames River, inaugural launch into, 54–56
Theories
  battery explosion, 46–47
  Court of Inquiry, 36, 47, 49–50, 225, 366
  Craven's, 50–51, 223–225, 233, 366–367
  Crazy Ivan, 283, 314
  foul play, 170
  Holmes's, 366, 367
  hull implosion, 233, 368
  Moorer's, 367
  Offley's, 297, 315–316
  probability of, 232–233
  Schade's, 47, 225, 226, 366
  SubMiss, 18
  torpedo explosion, 35, 39–40, 47, 49, 50–51, 223–225, 366–367
  trash disposal, 47
Thimble Shoal Channel, 19, 21
Thompson Saville, Lynn, 198
Thor missiles, 123
Thresher, USS, 25, 32, 359
  design, 155–156
  devastation of, 155
  memorials, 372–373
  sinking, 156
  wreckage, 217, 219, 351
Thresher-class submarines, 56, 64
Thule, Greenland, 169
Time, 327–328
Tomahawk missiles, 174
Tonkin, Gulf of, 322
Top Secret/Code Word orders, 90
Torpedoes
  compartment layout, 70–71, 72
  design, 62, 70–71, 72, 105, 223–224
  explosion theory, 35, 39–40, 47, 49, 50–51, 223–225, 366–367
  room on *Skipjacks,* 72
Totem, HMS, 169
Training exercises, 81–82, 141–142, 145, 292
Trash disposal theory, 47
Traylor, James T., 236, 239
Trieste II, 46, 365, 368
Tringa, USS, 183
Trost, Carlisle A. H., 354–356, 371–372
Tse-tung, Mao, 170
Tullibee, USS, 56, 94
Tunisia, Soviet ports of, 134
Tunny, USS, 160
Tusk, USS, 87
Twenty Thousand Leagues Under the Sea (Verne), 59
"Two-ocean war," 103–104. *See also* World War II

U–2 spy planes, 87, 125, 360
U–20, 100
U–39, 103
U–85, 106
U–151, 102–103
U–701, 104
U-boats
  about, 58, 62–63, 73
  Soviet control of, 87
  World War I campaign, 100–103
  World War II campaign, 103–107
Underwood, Joseph D., 5, 149, 182, 209–210
United Arab Public, 118
U.S. Atlantic Fleet, 88, 90
U.S. Navy. *See also specific naval organizations*
  British attack on, 332
  chain of command, 88
  corporate mentality of, 29
  Experimental Diving Unit, 20
  Incidents at Sea Agreement, 349–354, 356
  K–129 response of, 172–173
  North Korean attack on, 332
  Soviet spies in, 317–327
  Soviet task force, 39, 42
  strength, 114–115
  Task Unit 42.2.1, 21
  technology, 28–29, 56–62
  WWI U-boat campaign against, 100–103

Verde, Cape, 15, 313–314
Verdun, Battle of, 102
Victor-class submarines, 98, 134–135, 141
Vietnam War, 168–169, 361
  1968 happenings in, 211, 335–336
  post-, 27–29
Vindeggen, 102–103
Violetti, Robert
  in August Bay, 198
  background on, 205
  letters from, 186, 188, 194, 198–201, 204–206, 207–208
  in Naples, 200
  Soviet confrontation experience of, 207–208
Violetti, Salvatore and Luella, 4, 205
Virginia Beach School Board, 211
Virginia Capes day cruises, 82
Virginia-class submarines, 64
The Virginian-Pilot, 24, 27, 50, 211–212
Vladivostok, Russia, 168, 175
von Hendendorf, Graf, 102
von Nostitz, Heinrich, 102–103

Voss, Ronald J., 149
Vukasin, John P., 328, 340

Waccamaw, USS, 22, 26
Wahoo, USS, 106–107, 206
Walker, Arthur
    arrest of, 320
    background on, 323,
        342–343, 374–375
    trial of, 326
Walker, John Anthony, Jr.
    arrest of, 318–320, 322
    background on, 319,
        321–323, 326, 332, 374
    damage-assessment of, 331,
        342–345
    interviews about, 324–325,
        330–332, 343–344
    Soviet meeting, 341–343,
        346–347
    testimony of, 328–330,
        338–342
    trial of, 326–327
Walker, Michael L.
    arrest of, 320
    background on, 323, 375
    trial of, 327
Walker-*Pueblo* connection,
    340–341, 343, 347
Walker-*Pueblo-Scorpion*
    connection, 343–344,
    346–347, 358–359
Walter, Hellmuth, 62–63
Warfare, submarine

Cold War, 86–100
    Pearl Harbor, 99, 103–107
    World War I, 100–103
    World War II, 103–107,
        248–249
Warner, John, 350
Washington Post, 341
Wehrmacht, 113
Weinbeck, Arliss, 206
Weinbeck, Leo
    background on, 206–207
    letters from, 186, 206
Wells, James M., 147,
    149–150, 151–152
Western Electric, 128
Westinghouse, 60, 64
Wettern, Desmond, 81
Whiskey-class submarines, 63,
    115–116, 130
White House, 84, 90
White Sea, 95
White, Steven A., 11, 21
Whitworth, Jerry
    arrest of, 325–326
    background on, 374–375
    trial of, 327, 328–330,
        338, 344–345
"Widowmaker," 120. *See also*
    K–19
Wilkinson, Eugene P., 119
William H. Standley, USS, 21,
    276
William M. Wood, USS, 4, 13
Williams, Joe, 249

Williams, Ronald, 4
Willis, Robert A., 148
Winterwind, Operation, 173
Wiretappping undersea, 89
Woodrow Wilson, USS, 188
World War I, 88, 100–103
World War II, 29, 59
    cryptography, 337
    report declassification, 37
    Schade's efforts during,
        248–249
    submarine design, 106
    submarine warfare,
        103–107, 248–249
    technology, 28–29, 62–63,
        105–106
Wreckage
    K–129, 173–178, 355
    Scorpion, 33–34, 40, 46,
        228, 231, 239,
        271–277, 368
    Thresher, 217, 219, 351
Wright, Dee Ann, 246
WTAR Norfolk news, 9–11

Yankee-class submarines, 98,
    110, 135
Yeltsin, Boris, 374, 375
Yoachum, Robert, 211–212
Yokosuka, Japan, 177, 333
Yurchenko, Vitaly, 345

Zulu-class submarines, 115